ASCENT

CENTER FOR TECHNICAL KNOWLEDGE

AutoCAD® Civil 3D® 2018
Fundamentals

Student Guide
Imperial - 1st Edition

AUTODESK.
Authorized Publisher

ASCENT - Center for Technical Knowledge®
AutoCAD® Civil 3D® 2018
Fundamentals
Imperial - 1st Edition

Prepared and produced by:

ASCENT Center for Technical Knowledge
630 Peter Jefferson Parkway, Suite 175
Charlottesville, VA 22911

866-527-2368
www.ASCENTed.com

Lead Contributor: Michelle Rasmussen

ASCENT - Center for Technical Knowledge is a division of Rand Worldwide, Inc., providing custom developed knowledge products and services for leading engineering software applications. ASCENT is focused on specializing in the creation of education programs that incorporate the best of classroom learning and technology-based training offerings.

We welcome any comments you may have regarding this student guide, or any of our products. To contact us please email: feedback@ASCENTed.com.

The following are registered trademarks or trademarks of Autodesk, Inc., and/or its subsidiaries and/or affiliates in the USA and other countries: 123D, 3ds Max, Alias, ATC, AutoCAD LT, AutoCAD, Autodesk, the Autodesk logo, Autodesk 123D, Autodesk Homestyler, Autodesk Inventor, Autodesk MapGuide, Autodesk Streamline, AutoLISP, AutoSketch, AutoSnap, AutoTrack, Backburner, Backdraft, Beast, BIM 360, Burn, Buzzsaw, CADmep, CAiCE, CAMduct, Civil 3D, Combustion, Communication Specification, Configurator 360, Constructware, Content Explorer, Creative Bridge, Dancing Baby (image), DesignCenter, DesignKids, DesignStudio, Discreet, DWF, DWG, DWG (design/logo), DWG Extreme, DWG TrueConvert, DWG TrueView, DWGX, DXF, Ecotect, Ember, ESTmep, FABmep, Face Robot, FBX, Fempro, Fire, Flame, Flare, Flint, ForceEffect, FormIt 360, Freewheel, Fusion 360, Glue, Green Building Studio, Heidi, Homestyler, HumanIK, i-drop, ImageModeler, Incinerator, Inferno, InfraWorks, Instructables, Instructables (stylized robot design/logo), Inventor, Inventor HSM, Inventor LT, Lustre, Maya, Maya LT, MIMI, Mockup 360, Moldflow Plastics Advisers, Moldflow Plastics Insight, Moldflow, Moondust, MotionBuilder, Movimento, MPA (design/logo), MPA, MPI (design/logo), MPX (design/logo), MPX, Mudbox, Navisworks, ObjectARX, ObjectDBX, Opticore, P9, Pier 9, Pixlr, Pixlr-o-matic, Productstream, Publisher 360, RasterDWG, RealDWG, ReCap, ReCap 360, Remote, Revit LT, Revit, RiverCAD, Robot, Scaleform, Showcase, Showcase 360, SketchBook, Smoke, Socialcam, Softimage, Spark & Design, Spark Logo, Sparks, SteeringWheels, Stitcher, Stone, StormNET, TinkerBox, Tinkercad, Tinkerplay, ToolClip, Topobase, Toxik, TrustedDWG, T-Splines, ViewCube, Visual LISP, Visual, VRED, Wire, Wiretap, WiretapCentral, XSI.

NASTRAN is a registered trademark of the National Aeronautics Space Administration.

All other brand names, product names, or trademarks belong to their respective holders.

General Disclaimer:

Notwithstanding any language to the contrary, nothing contained herein constitutes nor is intended to constitute an offer, inducement, promise, or contract of any kind. The data contained herein is for informational purposes only and is not represented to be error free. ASCENT, its agents and employees, expressly disclaim any liability for any damages, losses or other expenses arising in connection with the use of its materials or in connection with any failure of performance, error, omission even if ASCENT, or its representatives, are advised of the possibility of such damages, losses or other expenses. No consequential damages can be sought against ASCENT or Rand Worldwide, Inc. for the use of these materials by any third parties or for any direct or indirect result of that use.

The information contained herein is intended to be of general interest to you and is provided "as is", and it does not address the circumstances of any particular individual or entity. Nothing herein constitutes professional advice, nor does it constitute a comprehensive or complete statement of the issues discussed thereto. ASCENT does not warrant that the document or information will be error free or will meet any particular criteria of performance or quality. In particular (but without limitation) information may be rendered inaccurate by changes made to the subject of the materials (i.e. applicable software). Rand Worldwide, Inc. specifically disclaims any warranty, either expressed or implied, including the warranty of fitness for a particular purpose.

AS-C3D1801-FND1IM-SG   //   IS-C3D1801-FND1IM-SG

Contents

Preface xi

In this Guide xiii

Practice Files xvii

Chapter 1: The AutoCAD Civil 3D Interface 1-1

   1.1 **Product Overview**.. 1-2

   1.2 **AutoCAD Civil 3D Workspaces** 1-3
       Start Tab 1-4

   1.3 **AutoCAD Civil 3D User Interface** 1-7

  **Practice 1a Overview of AutoCAD Civil 3D and
  its User Interface** 1-12

   1.4 **AutoCAD Civil 3D Toolspace** 1-15
       Prospector Tab.. 1-16
       Settings Tab 1-18
       Survey Tab 1-19
       Toolbox Tab 1-19

   1.5 **AutoCAD Civil 3D Panorama**.. 1-21

  Practice 1b AutoCAD Civil 3D Toolspace 1-23

   1.6 **AutoCAD Civil 3D Templates, Settings, and Styles** 1-30
       Drawing Settings in Detail 1-30
       Styles 1-41
       Templates 1-48

  Practice 1c AutoCAD Civil 3D Styles... 1-52

  Chapter Review Questions.. 1-58

  Command Summary 1-60

Chapter 2: Project Management **2-1**

2.1 AutoCAD Civil 3D Projects **2-2**
Single-Design Drawing Projects 2-2
Multiple Drawings Sharing Data using Shortcuts 2-2
Multiple Drawings Sharing Data with Autodesk Vault 2-3

2.2 Sharing Data **2-4**

2.3 Using Data Shortcuts for Project Management **2-5**
Update Notification 2-6
Removing and Promoting Shortcuts 2-7
eTransmit Data References 2-7
Data Shortcut Workflow 2-8
Workflow Details 2-8
Advantages of Data Shortcuts 2-9
Limitations of Data Shortcuts 2-9

Practice 2a Starting a Project **2-10**

Practice 2b Manage File Sizes with Data Shortcuts **2-14**

**Practice 2c Share Projects with Team Members
Outside the Office Network** **2-24**

Chapter Review Questions **2-27**

Command Summary **2-28**

Chapter 3: Parcels **3-1**

3.1 Lines and Curves **3-2**

Practice 3a Beginning a Subdivision Project **3-5**

3.2 Introduction to Parcels **3-8**
ROW Parcel 3-9
Parcel Style Display Order 3-10
Parcel Properties 3-11
Parcel Labels and Styles 3-12
Create Parcels from Objects 3-13
Creating Right-of-Way Parcels 3-13

Practice 3b Create Parcels From Objects **3-14**

3.3 Creating and Editing Parcels by Layout Overview **3-20**

3.4 Creating and Editing Parcels **3-23**
Freehand 3-25
Slide Line 3-25
Swing Line 3-25
Free Form Create 3-25
Frontage 3-25

Practice 3c Creating and Editing Parcels 3-26

3.5   Renumbering Parcels 3-30

Practice 3d Rename/Renumber Parcels... 3-31

3.6   Parcel Reports... 3-36

3.7   Parcel Labels 3-37

3.8   Parcel Tables 3-40

Practice 3e Reporting On and Annotating the Parcel Layout........... 3-42

Chapter Review Questions.. 3-48

Command Summary 3-51

Chapter 4: Survey 4-1

4.1   Survey Workflow Overview... 4-2
       Workflow 4-2

4.2   Survey Figures 4-3
       Figure Styles 4-3
       Figure Prefix Database 4-4

Practice 4a Creating Figure Prefixes 4-5

4.3   Points Overview 4-6
       Point Label Style 4-11

Practice 4b Point Marker Styles 4-18

4.4   Point Settings 4-25

4.5   Creating Points.. 4-27

Practice 4c Creating AutoCAD Civil 3D Points............................... 4-28

4.6   Description Key Sets 4-30

Practice 4d Creating a Description Key Set.................................... 4-33

4.7   Importing Survey Data.. 4-38
       Import Points Only.. 4-38
       Duplicate Point Numbers 4-40
       Survey Toolspace 4-41
       Import Points and Figures Using the Survey Database 4-42

Practice 4e Importing Survey Data... 4-46

4.8   Point Groups 4-49
       Defining Point Groups 4-49

Practice 4f Creating Point Groups... 4-55

4.9   Reviewing and Editing Points.. 4-58

Practice 4g Manipulating Points 4-60

4.10 Point Reports.. **4-62**

Practice 4h Point Reports.. **4-64**

Chapter Review Questions... **4-65**

Command Summary **4-67**

Chapter 5: Surfaces... **5-1**

5.1   Surface Process **5-2**

5.2   Surface Properties **5-7**

5.3   Contour Data **5-10**
    Weeding Factors.. 5-11
    Supplementing Factors 5-11
    Contour Issues 5-12
    Minimizing Flat Triangle Strategies 5-13

5.4   Other Surface Data... **5-14**
    DEM Files.. 5-14
    Drawing Objects.. 5-14
    Point Files 5-14
    Point Groups 5-15
    Point Survey Queries 5-15
    Figure Survey Queries 5-15

Practice 5a Creating an Existing Ground Surface **5-16**

5.5   Breaklines and Boundaries... **5-23**
    Breaklines 5-24

Practice 5b Add Additional Data to an Existing Ground Surface **5-29**

5.6   Surface Editing.. **5-37**
    Line Edits 5-38
    Point Edits 5-39
    Simplify Surface 5-39
    Smooth Contours 5-40
    Smooth Surface 5-41
    Copy Surface 5-42
    Surface Paste.. 5-42
    Raise/Lower Surface 5-43
    Adjusting Surfaces Through Surface Properties 5-43

5.7   Surface Analysis Tools.. **5-44**
    Viewing a Surface in 3D.. 5-44
    Quick Profile 5-45

Practice 5c Surface Edits **5-46**

5.8   Surface Labels... **5-57**
    Contour Labels.. 5-58
    Spot and Slope Labels 5-58

5.9 Surface Volume Calculations..5-59
    Volumes Dashboard...5-59
    Bounded Volumes..5-59
    Volume Reports 5-60
    Grid Volume or TIN Volume Surface....................................5-60
    3D Solid Surface from TIN Surface......................................5-61

5.10 Surface Analysis Display 5-63
    Analysis Settings..5-65
    Analysis Data Display 5-66

Practice 5d Surface Labeling and Analysis 5-67

5.11 Point Cloud Surface Extraction 5-74
    Attach Point Cloud 5-74
    Surfaces from Point Clouds 5-79

Practice 5e (Optional) Create a Point Cloud Surface.....................5-84

Chapter Review Questions...5-86

Command Summary 5-89

Chapter 6: Alignments 6-1

6.1 Roadway Design Overview 6-2

6.2 AutoCAD Civil 3D Sites 6-3

6.3 Introduction to Alignments 6-4
    Criteria-Based Design 6-5
    Alignment Types 6-6
    Alignment Segment Types 6-6

Practice 6a Creating Alignments from Objects 6-9

6.4 Alignments Layout Tools 6-14
    Alignment Editing 6-15

Practice 6b Creating and Modifying Alignments............................6-16

6.5 Alignment Properties...6-21
    Station Control Tab 6-21
    Design Criteria Tab 6-21

6.6 Labels and Tables 6-23
    Alignment Point Labels 6-23
    Independent Alignment Labels...6-25
    Alignment Table Styles 6-26

Practice 6c Alignment Properties and Labels 6-27

Chapter Review Questions...6-33

Command Summary 6-34

Chapter 7: Profiles 7-1

  7.1 Profiles Overview 7-2

      Repositioning and Deleting Profile Views 7-3

  7.2 Create a Profile View Style 7-4

  7.3 Create Profiles from Surface 7-10

  7.4 Create Profile View Wizard 7-12

  Practice 7a Working with Profiles Part I 7-16

  7.5 Finished Ground Profiles 7-20

  7.6 Create and Edit Profiles 7-21

      Transparent Commands 7-22

      Assigning Profile Band Elevations 7-23

      Profile Segment Types 7-24

      Profile Labels 7-24

  Practice 7b Working with Profiles Part II 7-25

  Practice 7c Working with Profiles Additional Practice 7-33

  Chapter Review Questions 7-35

  Command Summary 7-36

Chapter 8: Corridors 8-1

  8.1 Assembly Overview 8-2

      Assemblies 8-2

      Subassemblies 8-3

  8.2 Modifying Assemblies 8-6

      Attaching Subassemblies 8-6

      Detaching Subassemblies 8-8

      Copying Assemblies 8-8

      Mirroring Subassemblies 8-9

      Select Similar Subassemblies 8-9

      Sharing Assemblies 8-10

      Getting More Information on Subassemblies 8-10

  Practice 8a Creating Assemblies 8-11

  Practice 8b Creating Assemblies Additional Practice 8-17

  8.3 Creating a Corridor 8-21

      Target Mapping 8-23

      Corridor Frequency 8-24

  8.4 Corridor Properties 8-25

      Information Tab 8-25

      Parameters Tab 8-25

      Codes 8-26

      Feature Lines 8-27

      Slope Patterns 8-27

Practice 8c Working with Corridors - Part I 8-28

8.5   Designing Intersections 8-34
     General Tab 8-34
     Geometry Details Tab 8-35
     Corridor Regions Tab 8-36

Practice 8d Working with Corridors - Part II 8-37

8.6   Corridor Surfaces... 8-44
     Overhang Correction 8-44
     Surface Boundaries.. 8-45

8.7   Corridor Section Review and Edit 8-46

Practice 8e Working with Corridors - Part III 8-48

8.8   Corridor Visualization 8-50
     Line of Sight Analysis... 8-51

Practice 8f Working with Corridors - Part IV..................................... 8-54

Chapter Review Questions.. 8-58

Command Summary 8-60

Chapter 9: Grading 9-1

9.1   Grading Overview 9-2

9.2   Feature Lines.. 9-4
     Feature Line Contextual Tab... 9-4
     Elevation Editor 9-4

Practice 9a Working with Feature Lines 9-6

9.3   Grading Tools.. 9-11
     Grading Creation Tools Toolbar 9-11

Practice 9b Create Grading Groups 9-12

9.4   Modifying AutoCAD Civil 3D Grading 9-18
     Grading Styles.. 9-18
     Feature Line Labels 9-18
     Grading Criteria.. 9-18
     Grading Criteria Set 9-19
     Grading Volumes 9-20

Practice 9c Modify Grading and Calculate Volumes........................ 9-21

Chapter Review Questions.. 9-24

Command Summary 9-25

Chapter 10: Pipe Networks 10-1

10.1 Pipes Overview.. 10-2

10.2 Pipes Configuration 10-3

Practice 10a Configuring Pipe Networks 10-14

10.3 Creating Networks from Objects 10-19

Practice 10b Creating Pipe Networks by Objects 10-20

10.4 The Network Layout Toolbar....................................... 10-22

Practice 10c Creating Pipe Networks by Layout........................ 10-24

10.5 Network Editing.. 10-30
    Pipe (and Structure) Properties.................................. 10-30
    Swap Part... 10-31
    Connect/ Disconnect From Part................................... 10-31

Practice 10d Editing Pipe Networks 10-32

10.6 Annotating Pipe Networks 10-37
    Pipe Networks in Sections 10-38
    Pipe Network Reports and Tables 10-39

Practice 10e Annotating Pipe Networks................................ 10-40

10.7 Pressure Pipe Networks 10-45

Practice 10f Create a Pressure Pipe Network........................... 10-48

Chapter Review Questions... 10-55

Command Summary 10-56

Chapter 11: Quantity Take Off/Sections 11-1

11.1 Sample Line Groups 11-2
    Modifying Sample Line Groups 11-5

Practice 11a Creating Sections - Part I.............................. 11-6

11.2 Section Volume Calculations..................................... 11-10
    Earthwork Volumes 11-10
    Mass Haul 11-11
    Material Volumes 11-11
    Quantity Takeoff Criteria 11-12
    Define Materials 11-12

Practice 11b Quantity Take Off - Part I............................. 11-13

11.3 Pay Items 11-21

Practice 11c Quantity Take Off - Part II
- Integrated Quantity Takeoff 11-22

11.4 Section Views 11-29
    Section View Wizard 11-29

Practice 11d Creating Sections Part II.............................. 11-32

Chapter Review Questions... 11-36

Command Summary 11-37

Chapter 12: Plan Production 12-1

12.1 Plan Production Tools 12-2
   Overview 12-2
   More Information 12-3

12.2 Plan Production Objects 12-4
   View Frames 12-5
   View Frame Groups 12-5
   Match Lines 12-5

12.3 Plan Production Object Edits 12-6
   Name... 12-6
   Description 12-6
   Object style 12-6
   View Frame Geometry Properties Edits................................ 12-7
   Match Line Geometry Properties Edits 12-8

Practice 12a Plan Production Tools I 12-9

12.4 Creating Sheets 12-16

Practice 12b Plan Production Tools II 12-17

12.5 Sheet Sets... 12-21
   Structuring Sheet Sets 12-22
   Editing Sheet Sets... 12-22
   Sheet Set Manager Properties 12-23

Practice 12c Plan Production Tools III 12-26

Chapter Review Questions.. 12-35

Command Summary 12-37

Appendix A: Additional Information A-1

A.1 Opening a Survey Database.. A-2

A.2 Design Data A-3
   Parcel Size A-3
   Pipe Size Conversion.. A-3
   Road Design Criteria A-4
   Traffic Circle Design Criteria A-15
   Intersection Design A-16

Appendix B: AutoCAD Civil 3D Certification Exam Objectives...............B-1

Index Index-1

Preface

The *AutoCAD® Civil 3D® 2018: Fundamentals* student guide is designed for Civil Engineers and Surveyors who want to take advantage of the AutoCAD® Civil 3D® software's interactive, dynamic design functionality. The AutoCAD Civil 3D software permits the rapid development of alternatives through its model-based design tools. You will learn techniques enabling you to organize project data, work with points, create and analyze surfaces, model road corridors, create parcel layouts, perform grading and volume calculation tasks, and layout pipe networks.

Topics Covered

- Learn the AutoCAD Civil 3D user interface

- Create and edit parcels and print parcel reports

- Create points and point groups and work with survey figures

- Create, edit, view, and analyze surfaces

- Create and edit alignments

- Create data shortcuts

- Create sites, profiles, and cross-sections

- Create assemblies, corridors, and intersections

- Create grading solutions

- Create gravity fed and pressure pipe networks

- Perform quantity takeoff and volume calculations

- Use plan production tools to create plan and profile sheets

---

Note on Software Setup

This student guide assumes a standard installation of the software using the default preferences during installation. Lectures and practices use the standard software templates and default options for the Content Libraries.

Students and Educators can Access Free Autodesk Software and Resources

Autodesk challenges you to get started with free educational licenses for professional software and creativity apps used by millions of architects, engineers, designers, and hobbyists today. Bring Autodesk software into your classroom, studio, or workshop to learn, teach, and explore real-world design challenges the way professionals do.

Get started today - register at the Autodesk Education Community and download one of the many Autodesk software applications available.

Visit www.autodesk.com/joinedu/

Note: Free products are subject to the terms and conditions of the end-user license and services agreement that accompanies the software. The software is for personal use for education purposes and is not intended for classroom or lab use.

Lead Contributor: Michelle Rasmussen

Specializing in the civil engineering industry, Michelle authors training guides and provides instruction, support, and implementation on all Autodesk infrastructure solutions, in addition to general AutoCAD.

Michelle began her career in the Air Force working in the Civil Engineering unit as a surveyor, designer, and construction manager. She has also worked for municipalities and consulting engineering firms as an engineering/GIS technician. Michelle holds a Bachelor's of Science degree from the University of Utah along with a Master's of Business Administration from Kaplan University.

Michelle is an Autodesk Certified Instructor (ACI) as well as an Autodesk Certified Evaluator, teaching and evaluating other Autodesk Instructors for the ACI program. In addition, she holds the Autodesk Certified Professional certification for Civil 3D and is trained in Instructional Design.

As a skilled communicator, Michelle effectively leads classes, webcasts and consults with clients to achieve their business objectives.

Michelle Rasmussen has been the Lead Contributor for *AutoCAD Civil 3D: Fundamentals* since 2007.

In this Guide

The following images highlight some of the features that can be found in this Student Guide.

Practice Files

To download the practice files for this student guide, use the following steps:

1. Type the URL shown below into the address bar of your Internet browser. The URL must be typed **exactly as shown**. If you are using an ASCENT ebook, you can click on the link to download the file.

Address bar

`http://www.ASCENTed.com/getfile?id=xxxxxxxx`

File Edit View Favorites Tools Help

2. Press <Enter> to download the .ZIP file that contains the Practice Files.

3. Once the download is complete, unzip the file to a local folder. The unzipped file contains an .EXE file.

4. Double-click on the .EXE file and follow the instructions to automatically install the Practice Files on the C:\ drive of your computer.

Do not change the location in which the Practice Files folder is installed. Doing so can cause errors when completing the practices in this student guide.

`http://www.ASCENTed.com/getfile?id=xxxxxxxx`

Stay Informed!
Interested in receiving information about upcoming promotional offers, educational events, invitations to complimentary webcasts, and discounts? If so, please visit: www.ASCENTed.com/updates/

Help us improve our product by completing the following survey:
www.ASCENTed.com/feedback
You can also contact us at: feedback@ASCENTed.com

FTP link for practice files

Practice Files

The Practice Files page tells you how to download and install the practice files that are provided with this student guide.

Chapter 1

Getting Started

In this chapter you learn how to start the AutoCAD® software, become familiar with the basic layout of the AutoCAD screen, how to access commands, use your pointing device, and understand the AutoCAD Cartesian workspace. You also learn how to open an existing drawing, view a drawing by zooming and panning, and save your work in the AutoCAD software.

Learning Objectives in this Chapter

- Launch the AutoCAD software and complete a basic initial setup of the drawing environment.
- Identify the basic layout and features of AutoCAD interface including the Ribbon, Drawing Window, and Application Menu.
- Locate commands and launch them using the Ribbon, shortcut menus, Application Menu, and Quick Access Toolbar.
- Locate points in the AutoCAD Cartesian workspace.
- Open and close existing drawings and navigate to file locations.
- Move around a drawing using the mouse, the **Zoom** and **Pan** commands, and the Navigation Bar.
- Save drawings in various formats and set the automatic save options using the **Save** commands.

Learning Objectives for the chapter

Chapters

Each chapter begins with a brief introduction and a list of the chapter's Learning Objectives.

Side notes

Side notes are hints or additional information for the current topic.

Instructional Content

Each chapter is split into a series of sections of instructional content on specific topics. These lectures include the descriptions, step-by-step procedures, figures, hints, and information you need to achieve the chapter's Learning Objectives.

Practice Objectives

Practices

Practices enable you to use the software to perform a hands-on review of a topic.

Some practices require you to use prepared practice files, which can be downloaded from the link found on the Practice Files page.

Chapter Review Questions

Chapter review questions, located at the end of each chapter, enable you to review the key concepts and learning objectives of the chapter.

Command Summary

The following is a list of the commands that are used in this chapter, including details on how to access the command using the software's Ribbon, toolbars, or keyboard commands.

Button	Command	Location
	Close	• Drawing Window • Application Menu • Command Prompt: close
	Close Current Drawing	• Application Menu
	Close All Drawings	• Application Menu
NA	Dynamic Input	• Status Bar: expand Customization
Exit Autodesk AutoCAD	Exit AutoCAD	• Application Menu
	Open	• Quick Access Toolbar • Application Menu • Command Prompt: open, <Ctrl>+<O>
	Open Documents	• Application Menu
Options	Options	• Application Menu • Shortcut Menu: Options
	Pan	• Navigation Bar • Shortcut Menu: Pan • Command Prompt: pan or P
	Recent Documents	• Application Menu
	Save	• Quick Access Toolbar • Application Menu • Command Prompt: qsave, <Ctrl>+<S>
	Save As	• Quick Access Toolbar • Application Menu • Command Prompt: save
	Zoom Realtime	• Navigation Bar: Zoom Realtime • Shortcut Menu: Zoom

Command Summary

The Command Summary is located at the end of each chapter. It contains a list of the software commands that are used throughout the chapter, and provides information on where the command is found in the software.

Appendix

A

Certification Exam Objectives

The following table will help you to locate the exam objectives within the chapters of the *AutoCAD/AutoCAD LT® 2015 Essentials* and *AutoCAD/AutoCAD LT® 2015 Beyond the Basics* training guides to help you prepare for the AutoCAD 2015 Certified Professional (Pro.) and User exams.

User	Pro.	Exam Objective	Training Guide	Chapter & Section(s)
		Apply Basic Drawing Skills		
✓	✓	Create, open, and publish files	• Essentials	• 1.1, 1.2, 1.5 • 7.1 • 16.1, 16.2
✓	✓	Draw circles, arcs, and polygons	• Essentials	• 2.5 • 8.1, 8.4
✓	✓	Draw lines and rectangles	• Essentials	• 2.1, 2.3, 2.4
✓	✓	Fillet and chamfer lines	• Essentials	• 11.3
✓	✓	Select objects	• Essentials • Beyond the Basics	• 5.1 • 9.1 • 1.3
✓	✓	Use coordinate systems	• Essentials • Beyond the Basics	• 1.4 • 2.1

Autodesk Certification Exam Appendix

This appendix includes a list of the topics and objectives for the Autodesk Certification exams, and the chapter and section in which the relevant content can be found.

Icons in this Student Guide

The following icons are used to help you quickly and easily find helpful information.

New in 2018	Indicates items that are new in the AutoCAD Civil 3D 2018 software.
Enhanced in 2018	Indicates items that have been enhanced in the AutoCAD Civil 3D 2018 software.

Practice Files

To download the practice files for this student guide, use the following steps:

1. Type the URL shown below into the address bar of your Internet browser. The URL must be typed **exactly as shown**. If you are using an ASCENT ebook, you can click on the link to download the file.

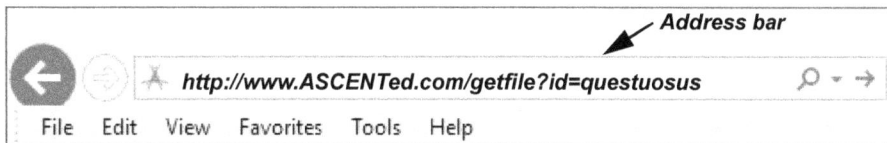

Address bar

http://www.ASCENTed.com/getfile?id=questuosus

File   Edit   View   Favorites   Tools   Help

2. Press <Enter> to download the .ZIP file that contains the Practice Files.

3. Once the download is complete, unzip the file to a local folder. The unzipped file contains an .EXE file.

4. Double-click on the .EXE file and follow the instructions to automatically install the Practice Files on the C:\ drive of your computer.

    Do not change the location in which the Practice Files folder is installed. Doing so can cause errors when completing the practices in this student guide.

http://www.ASCENTed.com/getfile?id=questuosus

Stay Informed!

Interested in receiving information about upcoming promotional offers, educational events, invitations to complimentary webcasts, and discounts? If so, please visit:

www.ASCENTed.com/updates/

Help us improve our product by completing the following survey:

www.ASCENTed.com/feedback

You can also contact us at: *feedback@ASCENTed.com*

The AutoCAD Civil 3D Interface

In this chapter you learn about the AutoCAD® Civil 3D® software interface and terminology. You learn how to navigate the available workspaces, the Toolspace, and how to work in a dynamic model environment. You also learn how to use styles across multiple models, to ensure that your drawings adhere to specific standards.

Learning Objectives in this Chapter

- Switch between the AutoCAD Civil 3D tools, 2D drafting and annotation tools, 3D modeling tools, and planning and analysis tools by changing the workspace.
- Locate the basic features and commands of the AutoCAD Civil 3D software interface which include the Ribbon, Drawing Window, Command Line, Toolspace, etc.
- Access commands by right-clicking on an object or collection of objects in the Prospector and Settings tabs in the Toolspace.
- Access predefined reports and create custom reports to be able to share useful engineering data about AEC objects in a drawing.
- Create and assign object and label styles to correctly display AutoCAD Civil 3D objects for printing and other purposes.

1.1 Product Overview

The AutoCAD Civil 3D software supports a wide range of Survey and Civil Engineering tasks. It creates intelligent relationships between objects so that design changes can be updated dynamically.

- The AutoCAD Civil 3D software uses dynamic objects for points, alignments, profiles, terrain models, pipe networks, etc. Objects can update when data changes. For example, if an alignment changes, its associated profiles and sections update automatically. Commands can be safely undone in the software without the graphics becoming out-of-date with survey and design data.

- These objects are style-based and dynamic, which streamlines object creation and editing.

- AutoCAD Civil 3D objects (surfaces, alignments, etc.) are often stored directly inside drawing files. The only time they are not is when working with the Autodesk Data Management System (Vault), data shortcuts, or a survey database.

- The AutoCAD Civil 3D software, unlike the AutoCAD® Land Desktop software, supports a multiple document interface. This means that more than one drawing file can be open in the same session of the AutoCAD Civil 3D software at the same time. Users of AutoCAD Land Desktop software who are going to use the AutoCAD Civil 3D software, should be aware that, by default, opening a second drawing does not automatically close any currently open drawings.

- The AutoCAD Civil 3D software can be launched by selecting its icon on the desktop or by accessing the command through the Start menu. Depending on the installed version of the software, the icon indicates Imperial or Metric. Once launched, the software initiates with the standard AutoCAD Civil 3D profile. You can also customize the shortcut to have the software launch with a project based setting. This is accomplished using a custom profile.

1.2 AutoCAD Civil 3D Workspaces

When the AutoCAD Civil 3D software is launched for the first time, a *Let's Get Started* window displays, as shown in Figure 1–1. This window is used to verify your AutoCAD Civil 3D license. There are three options for communicating your license information:

- Sign In: Use your Autodesk Subscription account information to verify your purchase.

- Enter a Serial Number: Manually type in your software serial number and software key.

- Use a Network License: Point the software to your network license server to find the software license.

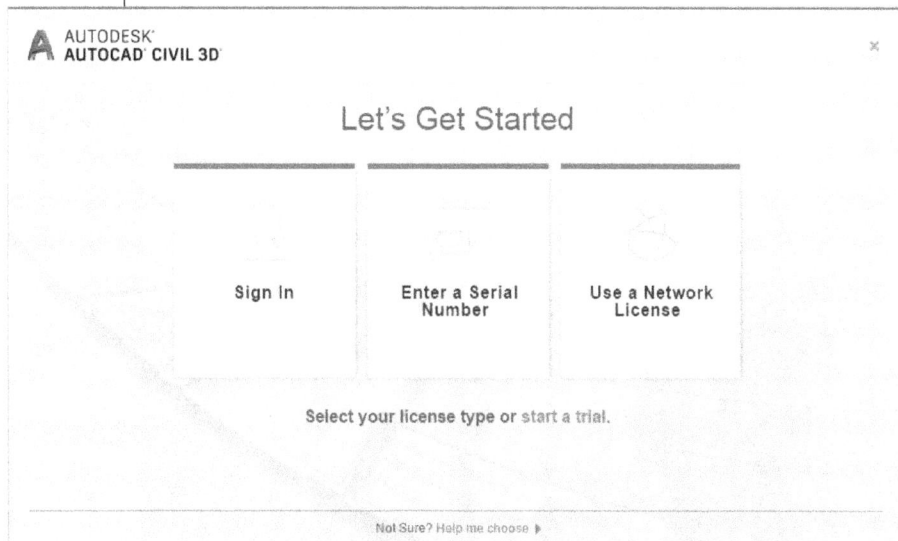

AUTODESK
AUTOCAD CIVIL 3D

Let's Get Started

Sign In   Enter a Serial   Use a Network
                 Number   License

Select your license type or start a trial.

Not Sure? Help me choose ▶

Figure 1–1

Start Tab

By default, the *Start* tab is continually available even when a drawing file is open. It enables you to complete several actions, as shown in Figure 1–2:

- Create new drawings from template files (1)

- Open existing files (2)

- Open a sheet set (3)

- Download online templates (4)

- Open example drawings (5)

- Review and open recent documents (6)

- Review notifications from Autodesk (7)

- Sign in to the Autodesk 360 service (8)

- Send feedback to Autodesk about the AutoCAD Civil 3D software (9)

The *Start* tab is persistent even when other drawings are open. This makes it easier and faster to open or start new drawings.

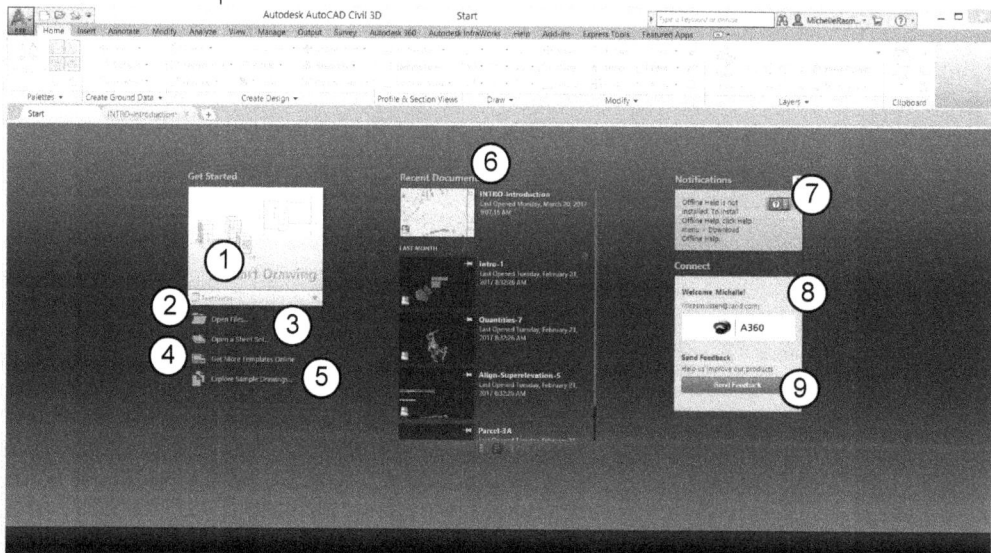

Figure 1–2

It is recommended that you stay in the Civil 3D workspace most of the time. As a review, AutoCAD® Workspaces are saved groupings of menus, toolbars, and palettes, which can be customized as required for specific tasks. You can modify the default Workspaces supplied with the AutoCAD Civil 3D software or create your own. In this material, you work with the Civil 3D workspace, which includes a complete list of AutoCAD Civil 3D-specific Ribbons, drop-down menus, and tools.

Workspaces can be changed using the Workspaces switching icon in the lower right corner of the Status Bar, as shown in Figure 1–3. They can also be modified using the **CUI** command.

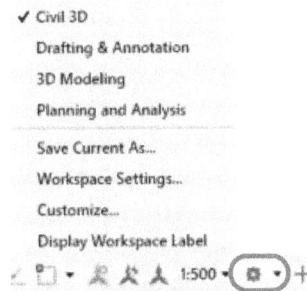

Figure 1–3

Each of the ribbons from the workspaces are shown in order in Figure 1–4 and include the following:

- **Civil 3D workspace:** Contains tools used to create AEC objects, such as surfaces, alignments, profiles, corridors, grading objects, etc.

- **Drafting & Annotation workspace:** Contains tools that are commonly used in the standard AutoCAD software, such as those in the *Home* tab>Draw and Modify panels.

- **3D Modeling workspace:** Contains standard AutoCAD 3D modeling tools for designing 3D solids, mesh surfaces, etc.

- **Planning and Analysis workspace:** Contains tools found in the AutoCAD® Map 3D® software that help you to attach and analyze GIS data for more efficient planning of projects before starting your design.

Civil 3D workspace

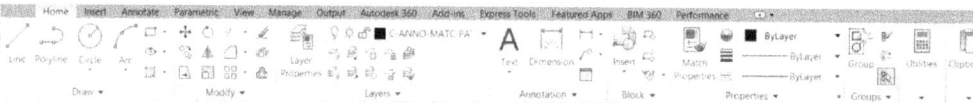
Drafting & Annotation workspace

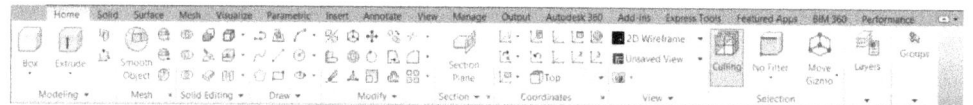
3D Modeling workspace

Planning and Analysis workspace

Figure 1–4

1.3 AutoCAD Civil 3D User Interface

The AutoCAD Civil 3D software user interface is shown in Figure 1–5.

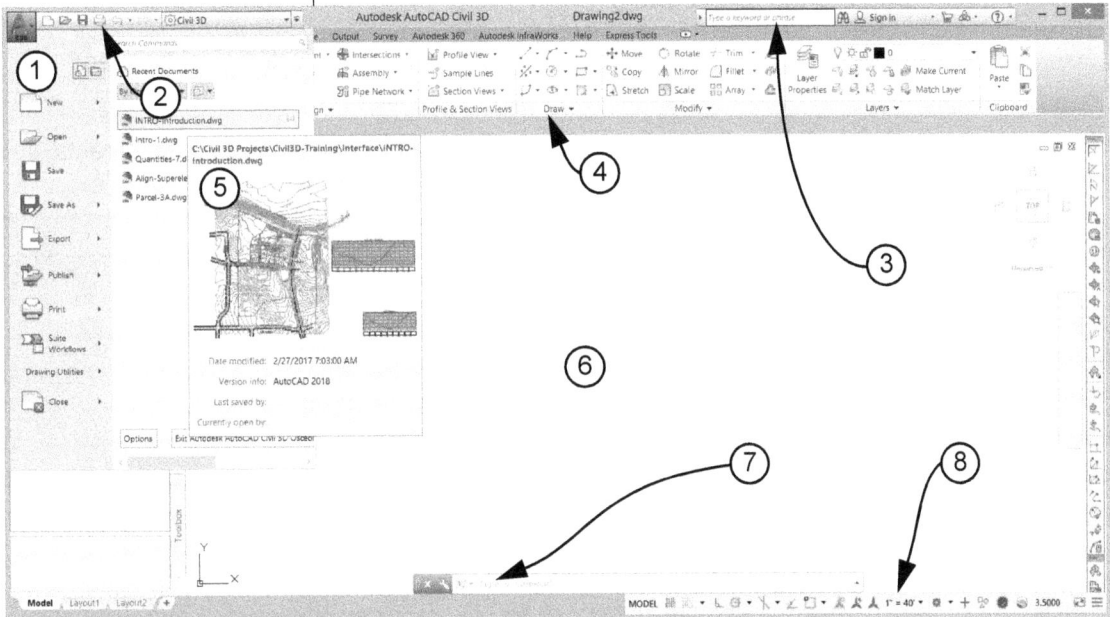

Figure 1–5

1. Application Menu	5. Tooltips
2. Quick Access Toolbar	6. Drawing Window
3. InfoCenter	7. Command Line
4. Ribbon	8. Status Bar

1. Application Menu

The *Application Menu* provides access to commands, settings, and documents, as shown in Figure 1–6. With the Application Menu you can:

- Browse the menus available in the AutoCAD Civil 3D software.

- Perform a search of menus, menu actions, tooltips, and command prompt text strings.

- Browse for recent documents, currently open documents, and commands you have recently executed.

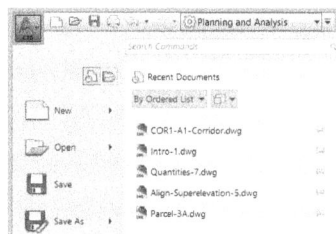

Figure 1–6

2. Quick Access Toolbar

The *Quick Access Toolbar* provides access to commonly used commands, such as **Open**, **Save**, **Print**, etc. You can add an unlimited number of tools to the Quick Access Toolbar by clicking the down arrow on the right, as shown in Figure 1–7.

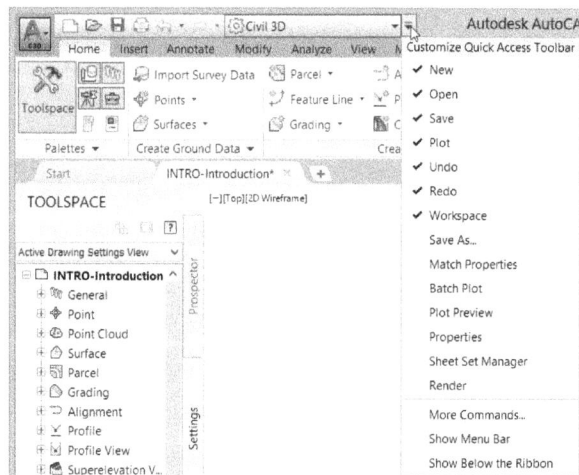

Figure 1–7

Enhanced *in 2018*

3. InfoCenter

The *InfoCenter* enables you to quickly search for help. You can specify which Help documents to search, and collapse or expand the search field (as shown in Figure 1–8) to save screen space. You can also sign in to the A360 service, where you can share files with other design team members using the cloud.

provides the ability to connect to the Autodesk App Store to find additional efficiency enhancing applications.

Figure 1–8

4. Ribbon

The *ribbon* provides a single, compact location for *commands* that are relevant to the current task. It contains tools in a series of *tabs* and *panels* to reduce clutter in the application and maximize drawing space. Selecting a tab displays a series of panels. The panels contain a variety of tools, which are grouped by function, as shown in Figure 1–9.

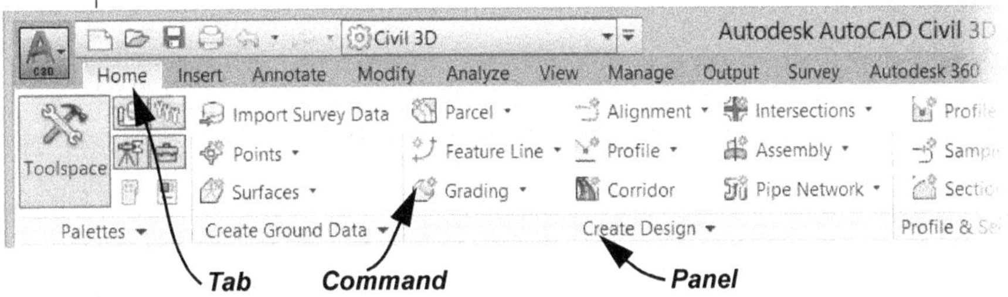

Figure 1–9

Clicking the drop-down arrow expands the panel to display additional tools, as shown in Figure 1–10. Clicking an arrow pointing to the bottom right opens the tool's dialog box, which contains additional options.

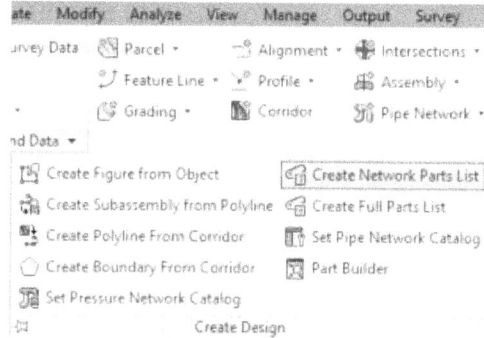

Figure 1–10

You can minimize the ribbon by clicking the arrow successively, as shown in Figure 1–11.

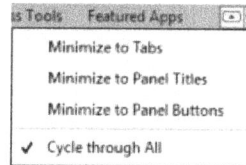

Figure 1–11

There are two classifications of Ribbons: static and contextual.

- **Static Ribbons:** Display the most commonly used tabs, panels, and commands.

- **Contextual Ribbons:** Display the tabs, panels, and commands that are only applicable to the selected object. An example of a contextual ribbon is shown in Figure 1–12.

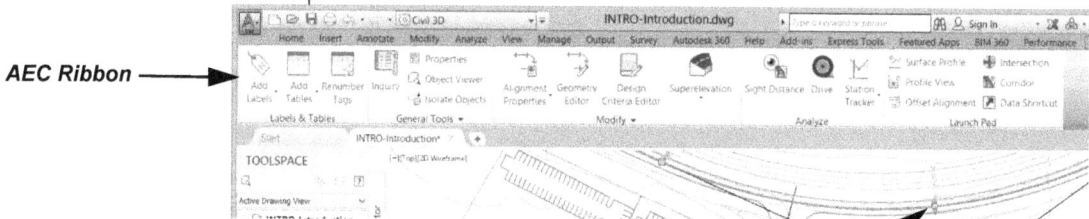

AEC Ribbon →

Selected AEC Object ↗

Figure 1–12

5. Tooltips

Tooltips display the item's name, a short description, and sometimes a graphic. They provide information about tools, commands, and drawing objects, as shown in Figure 1–13.

Tooltips can be turned off and a display delay can be set in the Options dialog box> Display tab.

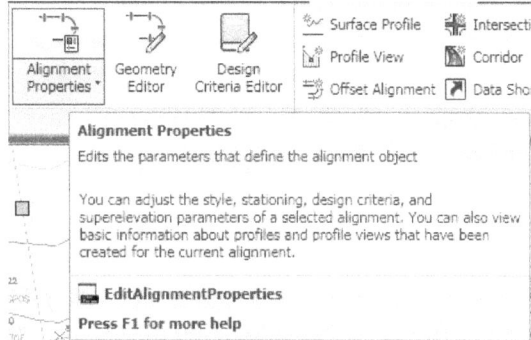

Figure 1–13

6. Drawing Window

The *Drawing Window* is the area of the screen where the drawing displays.

7. Command Line

The *Command Line* is a text window that is located at the bottom of the screen and displays command prompts and a history of commands, as shown in Figure 1–14.

To toggle the Command Line display on or off, press <Ctrl>+<9>.

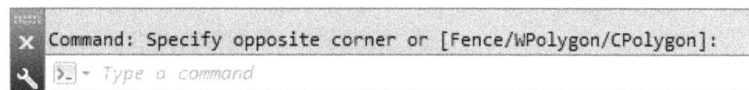

Command: Specify opposite corner or [Fence/WPolygon/CPolygon]:

Type a command

Figure 1–14

8. Status Bar

The *Status Bar* enables you to change many of AutoCAD's drafting settings, such as Snap, Grid, and Object Snap, as shown in Figure 1–15.

Figure 1–15

Practice 1a

Estimated time for completion: 5 minutes

Overview of AutoCAD Civil 3D and its User Interface

Practice Objective

- Locate the basic features and commands of the AutoCAD Civil 3D software interface which includes the Ribbon, Toolspace, Drawing Window, Command Line, etc.

In this practice you will become familiar with AutoCAD Civil 3D's capabilities and learn about its interface.

Task 1 - Set up the practice.

In this task, you will add a folder shortcut in the pane on the left side of the dialog box. This enables you to quickly access the practice files folder in the Open dialog box.

1. If required, start the AutoCAD Civil 3D 2018 Imperial application.

2. In the *Start* tab, click [image] (Open), or expand

   [image] (Application Menu) and select **Open**. In the Select File dialog box, browse to the *C:\Civil 3DProjects\Civil3D-Training* folder.

3. Expand the Tools drop-down list and select **Add Current Folder to Places**, as shown in Figure 1–16.

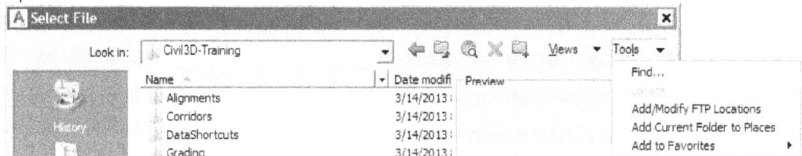

Figure 1–16

4. Double-click on the *Interface* folder to display its contents. Select **INTRO-Introduction.dwg** and then select **Open**.

*If prompted to save the changes to your Places List, click **Yes**.*

5. In the Status Bar, confirm that **Civil 3D** is the active Workspace. The Workspace icon is located in the Status Bar (at the bottom right of the interface) and in the Quick Access Toolbar (at the top left of the interface), as shown in Figure 1–17.

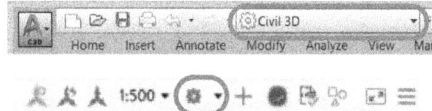

Figure 1–17

6. Select the *Home* tab and ensure that the Layers panel displays. If it is not, right-click anywhere on the ribbon and select **Layers**, as shown in Figure 1–18.

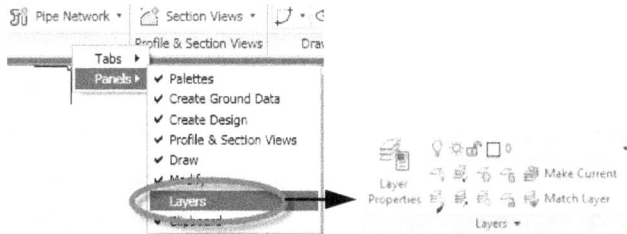

Figure 1–18

By default, the Toolspace is docked to the left side of your drawing window.

7. Locate the AutoCAD Civil 3D Toolspace (as shown in Figure 1–19). If you cannot find it, click ⚒ (Toolspace) in the *Home* tab>Palettes panel.

Figure 1–19

8. Save the drawing as **Example 1.dwg**. To do this, expand (Application Menu) and select **Save As**. In the *File Name* field, type **Example 1** and click **Save**.

Task 2 - Review AutoCAD Civil 3D's Dynamic Object Model.

*Alternatively, select the View tab>Views panel, expand the Named Views drop-down list, and select **Aln-Profile**.*

1. In the top-left corner of the drawing window, select **Top**, expand Custom Model Views and select **Aln-Profile**, as shown in Figure 1–20. This will zoom into a preset view of the alignment and the surface profile to the right.

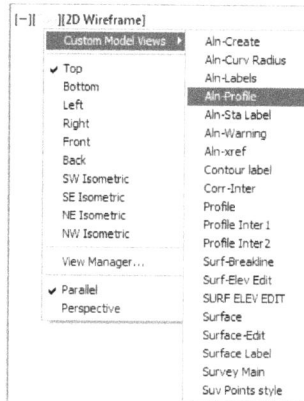

Figure 1–20

If the alignment labels display, they also update.

2. Select the **Jeffries Ranch Rd** alignment to activate its grips, as shown in Figure 1–21. (If you have difficulty selecting the alignment, you might need to set the draw order so that it is on top of all of the other objects.) Select the eastern grip and reposition it. The alignment and profile both update.

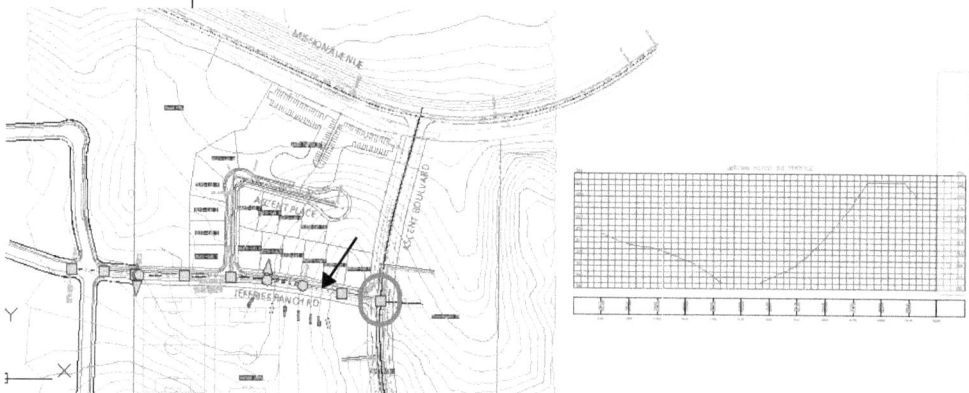

Figure 1–21

3. Hover the cursor near the alignment in its new position. The station, offset, and surface elevation information display through tooltips.

4. Close the drawing without saving.

1.4 AutoCAD Civil 3D Toolspace

The AutoCAD Civil 3D software uses a Toolspace to manage objects, settings, and styles. Each tab uses a hierarchical tree interface to manage objects, settings, and styles. Branches in these hierarchical trees are referred to in the AutoCAD Civil 3D software as *collections*. The Toolspace is an interactive data management tool.

Toolspace operates similar to an AutoCAD tool palette in that it can be resized, set to dock or float, and when floating can be set to auto-hide. The Toolspace is shown floating on the left in Figure 1–22 and docked on the right in Figure 1–22.

Right-clicking on a collection or on an individual object provides many commonly used commands in the shortcut menus.

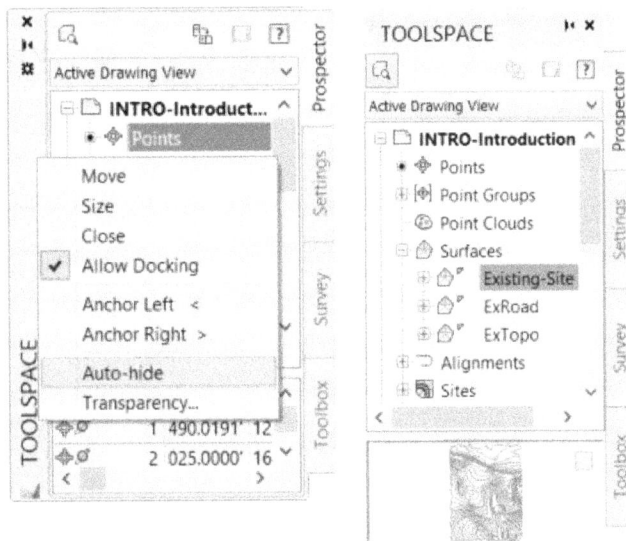

Figure 1–22

- The Toolspace can be closed by selecting the **X** in the upper left or right corner.

- Once closed, it can be opened by clicking (Toolspace) in the *Home* tab>Palettes panel.

Prospector Tab

The Toolspace, *Prospector* tab, lists the AutoCAD Civil 3D objects that are present in open drawings and other important information. Its hierarchical structure dynamically manages and displays objects and their data. As objects are created or deleted, they are removed from the *Prospector* tab. A drop-down list at the top contains the following options:

- **Active Drawing View:** Displays only the AutoCAD Civil 3D objects that are present in the active drawing. If you switch to another drawing, the tree updates to reflect the currently active drawing.

- **Master View:** Displays a list of all open drawings and their objects, project information, and a list of drawing templates. The name of the active drawing is highlighted.

The Toolspace, *Prospector* tab is shown in Figure 1–23.

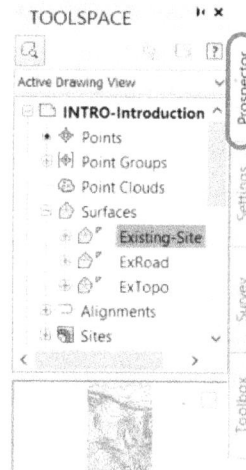

Figure 1–23

- To toggle the display of the Toolspace, *Prospector* tab on or off, click

  (Prospector) in the *Home* tab>Palettes panel.

- Each object type (Points, Point Groups, Alignments, Surfaces, etc.) is allotted a collection, and objects present in a drawing are listed below the respective collection.

- The bottom of the Toolspace, *Prospector* tab displays a list view of items in the highlighted collection or a preview of an object that has been selected in the Toolspace, *Prospector* tab.

- The icon at the top of the Toolspace, *Prospector* tab controls how items in the Prospector tree display. Icons next to objects provide additional information about the object. A list of common icons is as follows:

	Toggles the Toolspace item preview on or off.
	Opens (or closes) the Panorama window. This window only opens if vistas are available to be displayed in the Panorama.
	Opens the AutoCAD Civil 3D Help system.
	Indicates that the object is currently locked for editing.
	Indicates that the object is referenced by another object. In the Toolspace, *Settings* tab, this also indicates that a style is in use in the current drawing.
	Indicates that the object is being referenced from another drawing file (such as through a shortcut or Vault reference).
	Indicates that the object is out of date and needs to be rebuilt, or is violating specified design constraints.
	Indicates that a vault project object (such as a point or surface) has been modified since it was included in the current drawing.
	Indicates that you have modified a vault project object in your current drawing and that those modifications have yet to be updated to the project.

Settings Tab

The Toolspace, *Settings* tab is used to configure how the AutoCAD Civil 3D software operates and the way AutoCAD Civil 3D objects are displayed and printed, as shown in Figure 1–24.

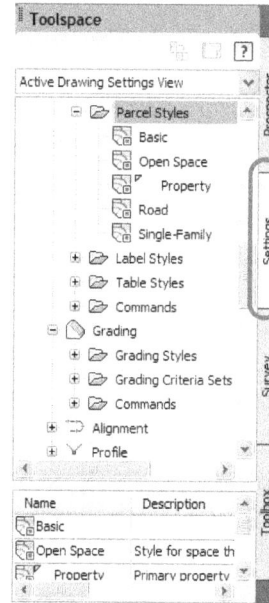

Figure 1–24

Different settings are accessed by right-clicking on the name of a drawing file or on one of the collections located inside the tab.

The collections (such as the *Parcel* collection shown in Figure 1–24) can contain object styles, label styles, command settings, and related controls.

Changes to settings affect all lower items in the tree. For example, assigning an overall text height in the drawing's Edit Label Style Defaults dialog box applies that height to all other settings and styles in the drawing. Applying the same setting in the *Surface* collection's Edit Label Style Defaults only applies the text height to the surface label styles. (Lower items in the tree and styles can be set to override these changes individually as required.)

• All drawing settings originate from the template used to create an AutoCAD Civil 3D drawing.

• To toggle the display of the Toolspace, *Settings* tab on or off, click ▦ (Settings) in the *Home* tab>Palettes panel.

Survey Tab

The Toolspace, *Survey* tab is used to manage survey observations data, as shown in Figure 1–25. Selecting this tab enables you to create a survey database, a survey network, points, and figures, and import and edit survey observation data.

To toggle the Toolspace, Survey tab display on or off, click

🔭 *(Survey) in the Home tab>Palettes panel.*

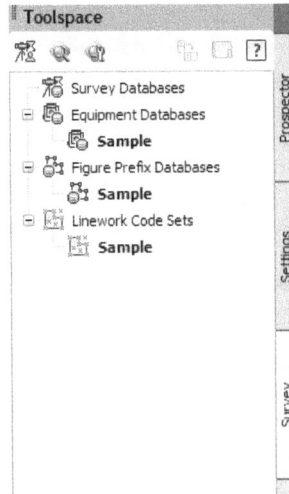

Figure 1–25

Toolbox Tab

The Toolspace, *Toolbox* tab is used to access the Reports Manager and to add custom tools to the AutoCAD Civil 3D interface, as shown in Figure 1–26.

The Toolspace, Toolbox tab can be toggled on and off by clicking

💼 *(Toolbox) in the Home tab>Palettes panel.*

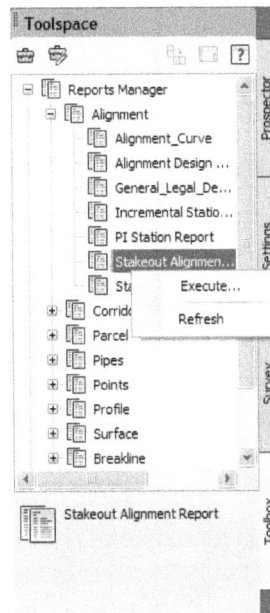

Figure 1–26

The Reports Manager, the only set of tools that displays in the toolbox by default, enables you to generate a large variety of survey and design reports. For example, to launch a Stakeout Alignment Report, right-click on it in the *Alignments* collection and select **Execute**.

The icons in the upper left area of the Toolspace, *Toolbox* tab enable you to:

	Open the Edit Report Settings dialog box, in which you can assign settings for all report types. These settings include items, such as the name to display in the report.
	Open the Toolbox Editor, in which you can add custom reports and other tools.

Once a report has been executed, it can be saved in multiple formats, including .HTML, .DOC, .XLS, .TXT, and .PDF. To save it in a format other than the default .HTML, expand Files of type and select the type of file required, as shown in Figure 1–27.

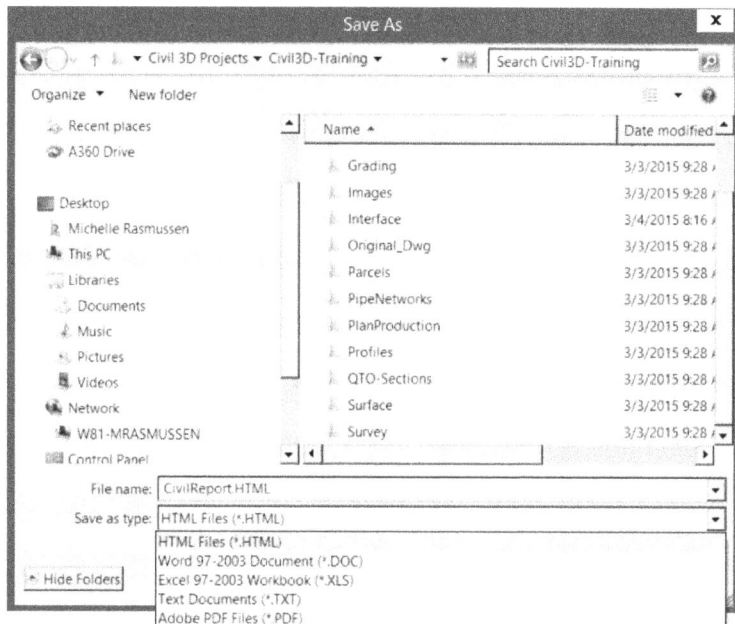

Figure 1–27

1.5 AutoCAD Civil 3D Panorama

The AutoCAD Civil 3D software includes a multi-purpose grid data viewer called the *Panorama window*. It is similar to an AutoCAD tool palette in that it can be docked or floating, and set to auto-hide. Each tab in the Panorama is called a *Vista*. The Panorama can be opened from the AutoCAD Civil 3D Toolspace by clicking ▦ (Panorama), and can be closed by selecting the **X** in the upper left or right corner of the window. You can only display the Panorama after launching a command that uses it, such as **Edit Points** (right-click on a Point Group in the Toolspace, *Prospector* tab in the Toolspace to access this option). The Panorama can display many different kinds of data, such as point properties, alignment, and profile data, as shown in Figure 1–28.

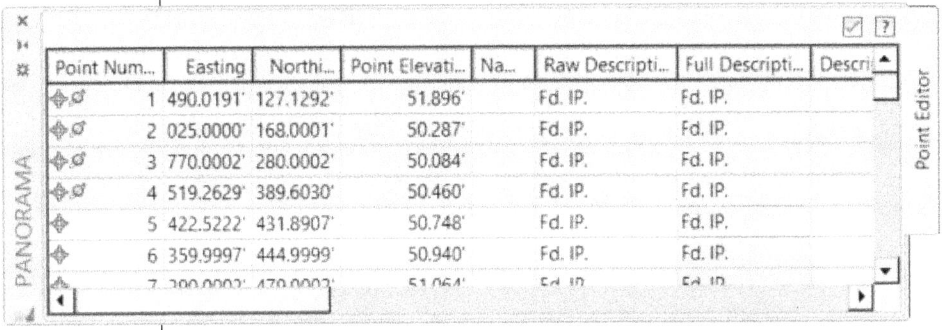

	Point Num...	Easting	Northi...	Point Elevati...	Na...	Raw Descripti...	Full Descripti...	Descri
◈⊘	1	490.0191'	127.1292'	51.896'		Fd. IP.	Fd. IP.	
◈⊘	2	025.0000'	168.0001'	50.287'		Fd. IP.	Fd. IP.	
◈⊘	3	770.0002'	280.0002'	50.084'		Fd. IP.	Fd. IP.	
◈⊘	4	519.2629'	389.6030'	50.460'		Fd. IP.	Fd. IP.	
◈	5	422.5222'	431.8907'	50.748'		Fd. IP.	Fd. IP.	
◈	6	359.9997'	444.9999'	50.940'		Fd. IP.	Fd. IP.	
	7	300.0002'	470.0002'	51.064'		Fd. IP.	Fd. IP.	

Figure 1–28

The Panorama can also display a special Vista called the *Event Viewer*, as shown in Figure 1–29. The *Event Viewer* opens prompting you about the status of the performed action. If every thing was successful, it displays a white circle containing a blue **i**, indicating that it is for informational purposes only. When there are items of interest or an item needs attention, a yellow triangle containing a black **!** (exclamation point) displays.

When the AutoCAD Civil 3D software encounters a processing error, such as when surface breaklines cross or a road model passes over the edge of the existing ground surface, a red circle containing a white **x** displays. When working through a large number of events, you can use **Action>Clear All Events** to clear all of the old entries in the Panorama.

*If a Panorama contains multiple Vistas, selecting a green checkmark only closes the current Vista. To close (hide) the Panorama, select the **X** in the top right or left corner.*

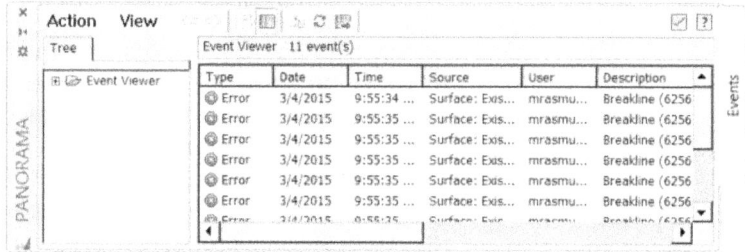

Figure 1–29

Practice 1b

AutoCAD Civil 3D Toolspace

Practice Objective

- Access commands and change the drawing using the AutoCAD Civil 3D Toolspace.

Estimated time for completion: 10 minutes

In this practice you will explore the tabs in the AutoCAD Civil 3D Toolspace.

Task 1 - Review the Toolspace, Prospector tab.

1. Open **INTRO-Introduction.dwg** from the *C:\Civil 3D Projects\Civil3D-Training\Interface* folder.

2. Ensure that the AutoCAD Civil 3D Toolspace displays.

If the Toolspace is not displayed, click

✎ *(Toolspace) in the Home tab>Palettes panel.*

3. Select the Toolspace, *Prospector* tab to make it active. (The tabs are listed vertically along the right side of the Toolspace.)

4. Select the **+** signs to open the collections and the **-** signs to close them. Items displayed in the Toolspace, *Prospector* tab are the design data (also known as AEC objects) currently in the drawing file (such as points, alignments, and surfaces).

5. Collections, such as *Points*, do not have a **+** or **-** sign because they are not intended to be expanded in the tree view of the Toolspace, *Prospector* tab. Select the **Points** collection and the list view displays in the Preview area, describing the AutoCAD Civil 3D points that are currently in the drawing file.

6. Under the *Surface* collection, look for the surface called **ExTopo**. Expand its branch and the *Definition* area inside it. Highlight the items below (breaklines, boundaries, etc.) and note the components displayed in the list view.

7. With Existing Ground's breaklines highlighted in the list view, right-click on *Ridge* and note the commands available in the shortcut menu, as shown on the left in Figure 1–30. Select **Zoom to**.

Similar shortcut menus are available for nearly all of the objects displayed in the Toolspace, Prospector tab.

8. Expand the Point Groups and select the **Boundary Pin Survey** point group. In the Preview area at the bottom, press <Shift> to select both point numbers **2** and **3**, as shown on the right in Figure 1–30. Right-click and select **Zoom To**. Although the points are not displayed, the software knows where they reside in the drawing.

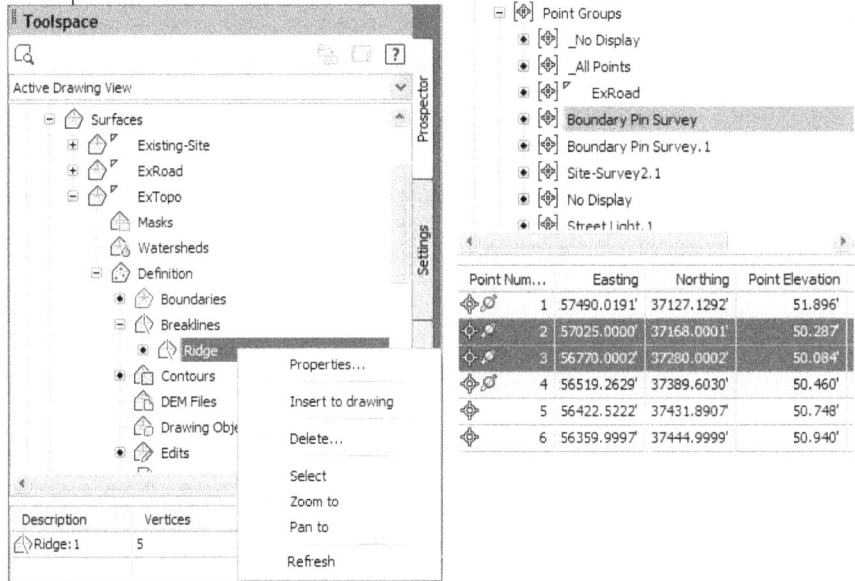

Figure 1–30

Task 2 - Review the Toolspace, Settings tab.

---

1. Select the Toolspace, *Settings* tab, as shown in Figure 1–31.

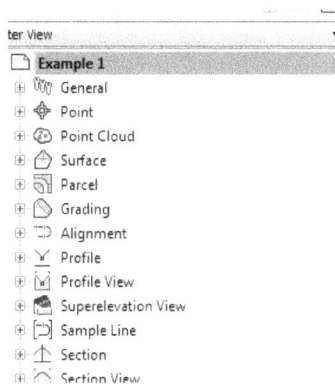

Figure 1–31

2. In the Toolspace, *Settings* tab, right-click on the drawing's name (**INTRO-Introduction.dwg**, at the top), and select **Edit Drawing Settings**.

3. In the Drawing Settings dialog box, select the *Units and Zone* tab, as shown in Figure 1–32.

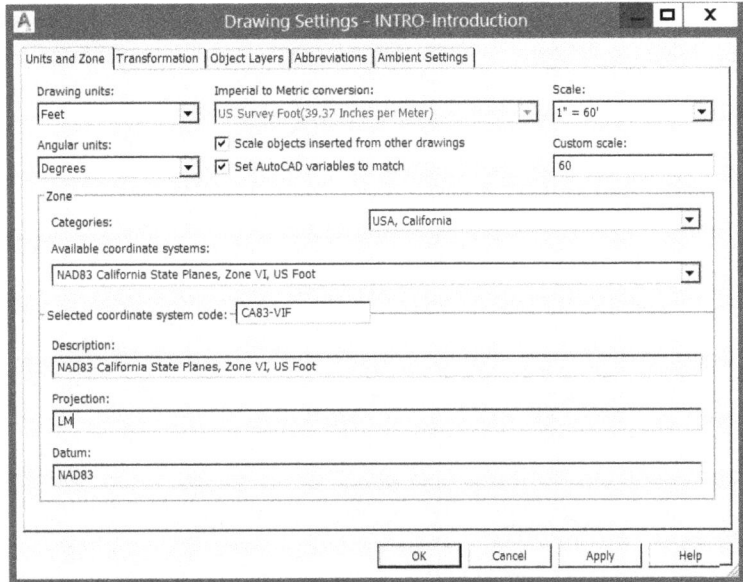

Figure 1–32

4. Expand the Scale drop-down list in the upper right corner and select **1"=40'**.

5. Note the coordinate systems that are available in the *Zone* area, such as CA83-VIF, NAD83 California State Planes, Zone VI, and US Foot.

6. Click **OK** to close the dialog box.

Because AutoCAD Civil 3D labels are annotative, the label annotation size has changed to match the new Drawing Scale.

7. You can also change the Model Space display scale using the **Annotation** icon in the Status Bar. Change it to read **1"=80'**. Note that as you change the scale, all of the labels also change in size, as shown in Figure 1–33.

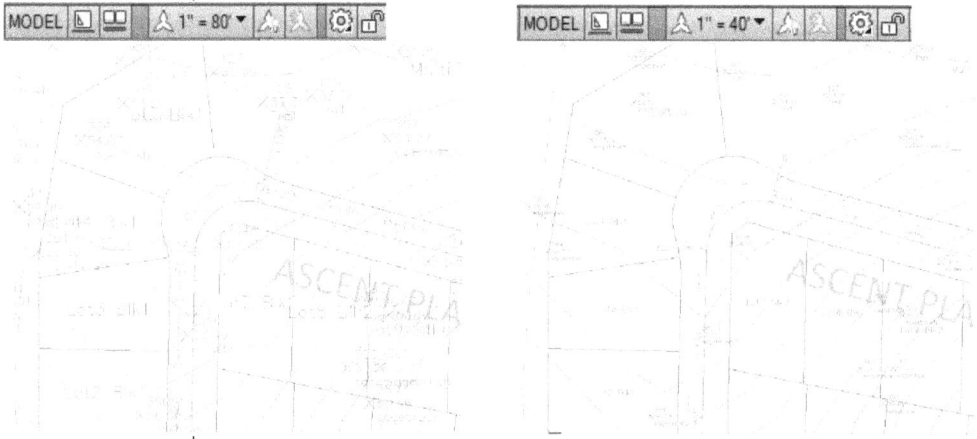

Figure 1–33

8. You can change the display of the contours by changing the style of the surface. In the drawing, select the surface object so that the contextual tab displays in the ribbon, as shown in Figure 1–34.

Figure 1–34

*Alternatively, you can right-click and select **Surface Properties***

9. In the Modify panel, click (Surface Properties).

10. In the *Information* tab, select the drop-down arrow for the surface style, as shown in Figure 1–35. Select any of the predefined styles and click **Apply** to apply the selected style to the surface to preview the results before they display in the dialog box.

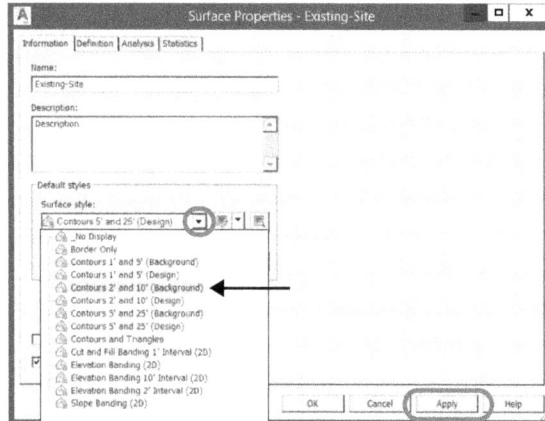

Figure 1–35

11. Click **OK** to exit the Surface Properties dialog box.

12. Save the drawing.

Task 3 - Review AutoCAD Civil 3D's Reports Manager.

1. In the Toolspace, *Toolbox* tab, expand Reports Manager>Alignment, then right-click on **PI Station Report**, and select **Execute,** as shown in Figure 1–36.

*As a shortcut, you can double-click to launch the **Report** without having to select the **Execute** command.*

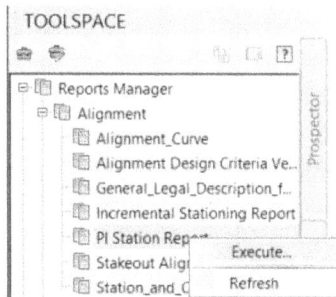

Figure 1–36

2. Accept all of the defaults and click **Create Report**. The report displays, as shown in Figure 1–37.

Alignment PI Station Report

Client:
Client
Client Company
Address 1
Date: 3/4/2015 11:01:41 AM

Prepared by:
Preparer
Your Company Name
123 Main Street

Alignment Name: Ascent Pl
Description:
Station Range: Start: 0+00.00, End: 6+98.38

PI Station	Northing	Easting	Distance	Direction
0+00.00	2,036,643.0632'	6,256,521.2052'		
			353.170'	N1° 18' 05"E
3+53.17	2,036,996.1421'	6,256,529.2258'		
			381.930'	S75° 03' 44"E
6+98.38	2,036,897.6924'	6,256,898.2491'		

Figure 1–37

3. Review the report and close the Internet Browser.

4. In the Create Reports dialog box, click **Done**.

5. In the Toolspace, *Toolbox* tab, expand the *Surface* collection. Select **Surface Report**, right-click, and select **Execute**, as shown in Figure 1–38.

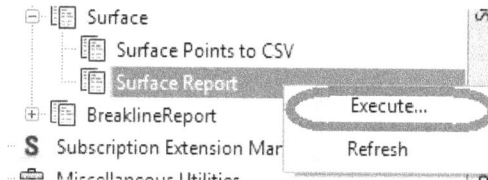

Figure 1–38

6. Accept all of the defaults and click **OK**. Type a filename for the saved report or accept the default. Expand the Files of type drop-down list, select **.XLS** and select **Save**. The report displays in Microsoft Excel, as shown in Figure 1–39. Review and close the report.

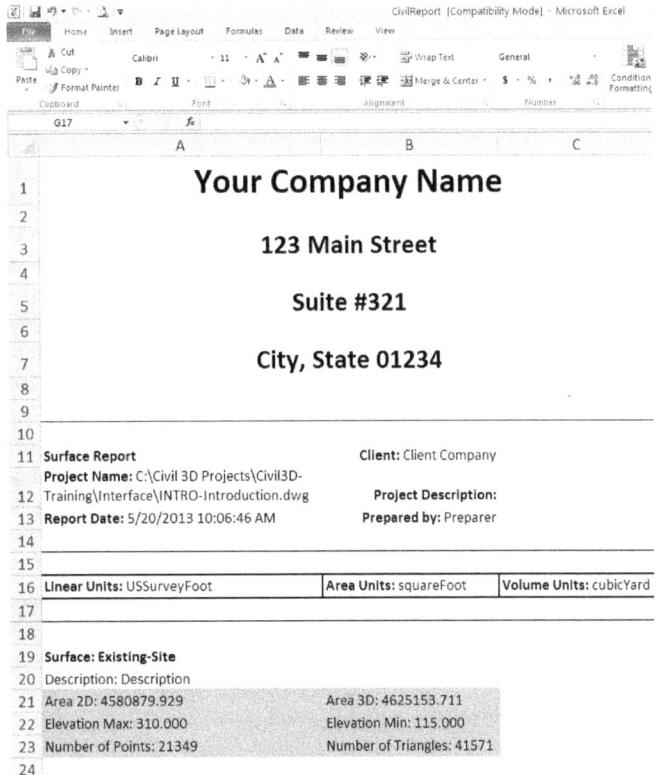

Figure 1–39

1.6 AutoCAD Civil 3D Templates, Settings, and Styles

A drawing template (.DWT extension) contains all blocks, Paper Space title sheets, settings, and layers for a new drawing. As with the AutoCAD software, a template (.DWT) file in the AutoCAD Civil 3D software is the source file from which new drawings acquire their settings, units, layers, blocks, text styles, etc., and therefore, enforces standardization. With the AutoCAD Civil 3D software, in addition to the AutoCAD components noted, the drawing template is also the source for specific AutoCAD Civil 3D styles and settings. As you learn, AutoCAD Civil 3D styles and settings (Feature and Command) have a profound impact on the appearance of objects, labels, and tables. These styles and settings also act as the primary mechanism that controls the behavior and default actions. Selecting the correct template for your intended design and standards needs is a significant component of fully using the benefits that the AutoCAD Civil 3D software offers. Therefore, it is highly recommended that all styles and setting be set up in the template file before you use the AutoCAD Civil 3D software in a project.

To use the AutoCAD Civil 3D software efficiently and effectively, you need to configure styles and settings to control the object display. All of these styles and settings affect the final delivered product and enable you to deliver a product with consistent quality.

To create a template file, use the **Save As** command and in the Save As dialog box, change the *File of Type* to **DWT**.

Drawing Settings in Detail

The values in Drawing Settings influence every aspect of the drafting environment. Each tab has values affecting a specific drawing area. For example, layer naming properties, coordinate systems, default precisions, input and output conventions, abbreviations for alignment, volume units, etc. After implementing the AutoCAD Civil 3D software, you only need to access the first two tabs.

To access Drawing Settings, in the Toolspace, *Settings* tab, select and right-click on the drawing name (at the top), and select **Edit Drawing Settings**.

Units and Zone

In the Drawing Settings dialog box, the *Units and Zone* tab (as shown in Figure 1–40), sets the Model Space plotting scale and coordinate zone for the drawing. The scale can be a custom value or selected from a drop-down list. A zone is selected from a drop-down list of worldwide categories and coordinate systems.

A drawing which has been assigned a coordinate system enables points to report their grid coordinates and/or their longitude and latitude. Conversely, when assigning a coordinate system, grid coordinates and Longitude and Latitude data can create points in a drawing.

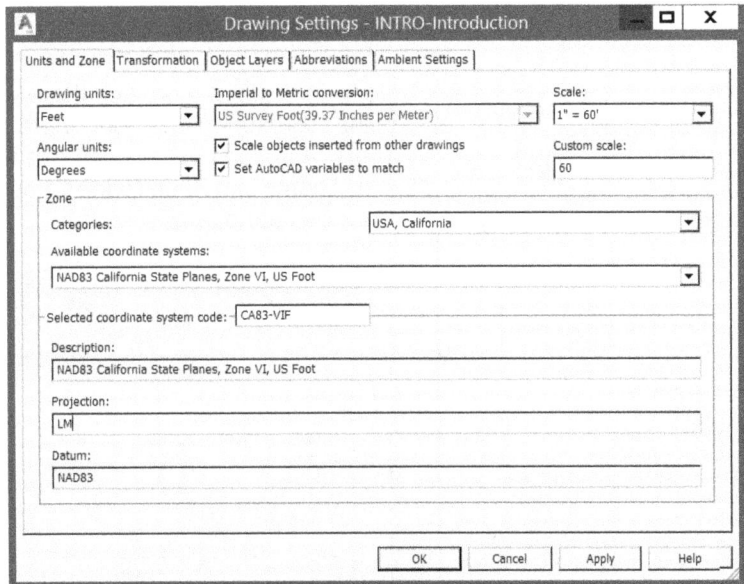

Figure 1–40

When plotting from the *Model* tab, the drawing scale in the upper right corner is the scale at which you would prefer the drawing to be printed. When in the *Model* tab, changing this scale automatically updates all AutoCAD Civil 3D annotations that are scale-dependent. (AutoCAD Civil 3D annotations are automatically resized for correct plotting in each viewport that displays them based on that viewport's scale.)

Changing the drawing scale does not automatically change the **ltscale** variable, since it assumes that you most often prefer to leave it at **ltscale = 1**. If this is not the case, you need to assign this variable manually. Refer to the AutoCAD User Guide if you need more information on variables, such as **ltscale**.

You can also set the drawing scale by assigning a different annotation scale in the Status Bar, as shown in Figure 1–41. In layouts you can change either the VP Scale or Annotation Scale and have both update.

Figure 1–41

Transformation

During the life of a project, there can be reasons to change local point coordinates to a coordinate system. The values in the *Transformation* tab (as shown in Figure 1–42), transform local coordinates to a State Plane Coordinate system, UTM system, or other defined planar system.

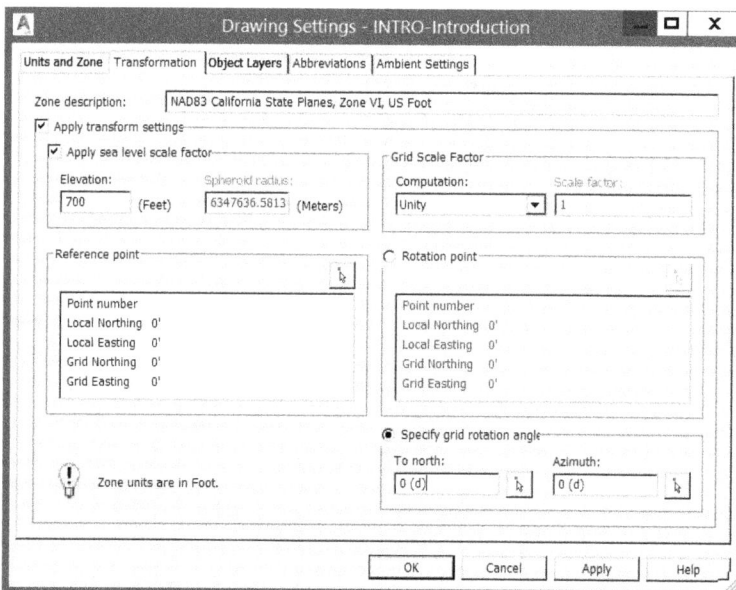

Figure 1–42

Object Layers

The *Object Layers* tab (shown in Figure 1–43), assigns layer names to AutoCAD Civil 3D objects. A modifier, which can be a prefix or a suffix, is associated with each layer's name. The value of the modifier can be anything that is typed into its *Value* field. Traditionally, the value is an * (asterisk) with a separator (a dash or underscore). The AutoCAD Civil 3D software replaces the asterisk with the name of the object of the same type. For example, the base surface layer name is **C-TOPO** with a suffix modifier of -* (a dash followed by an asterisk). When a surface named **Existing** is created, it is placed on the layer **C-TOPO-EXISTING**, and when a surface named **Base** is created it is placed on the layer **C-TOPO-BASE**.

The last column of the *Object Layers* tab enables you to lock the values. When a value is locked at this level, the AutoCAD Civil 3D software does not permit it to be changed by any lower style or setting.

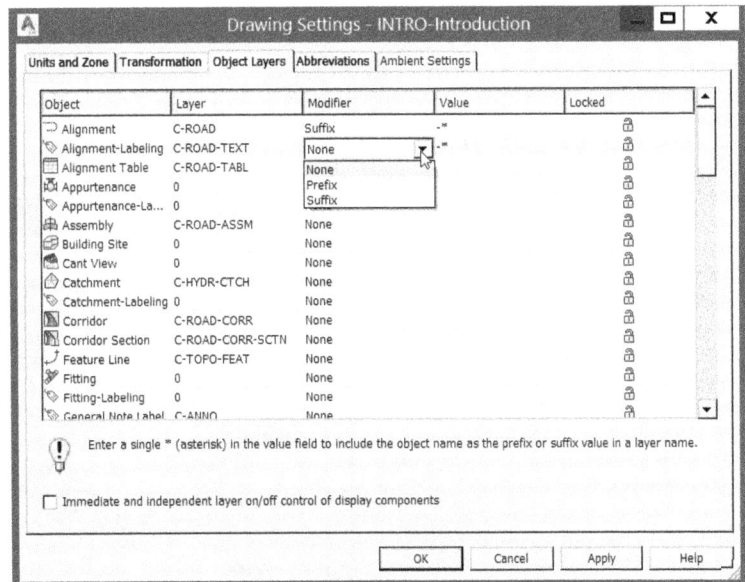

Figure 1–43

To change the listed object layers, double-click on a layer name. In the Layer Selection dialog box (shown in Figure 1–44), select the layer from the list. If the layer does not exist, click **New** in the Layer Selection dialog box. This opens a second dialog box, in which you can define a new layer for the object type.

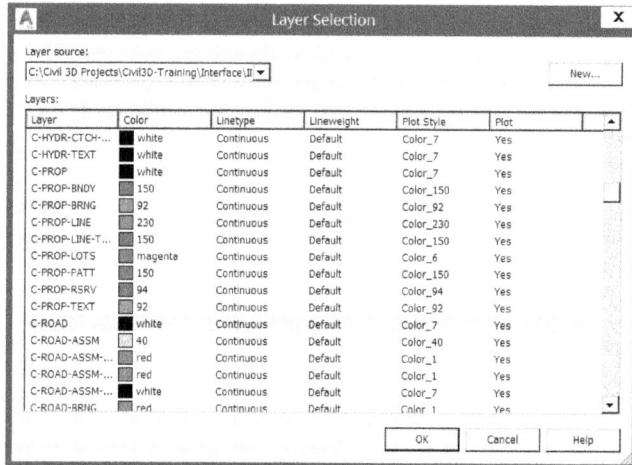

Figure 1–44

Abbreviations

The *Abbreviations* tab (shown in Figure 1–45), sets standard values for reports referencing alignment or profile data. Some entries in this panel have text format strings that define how the values associated with the abbreviation display in a label.

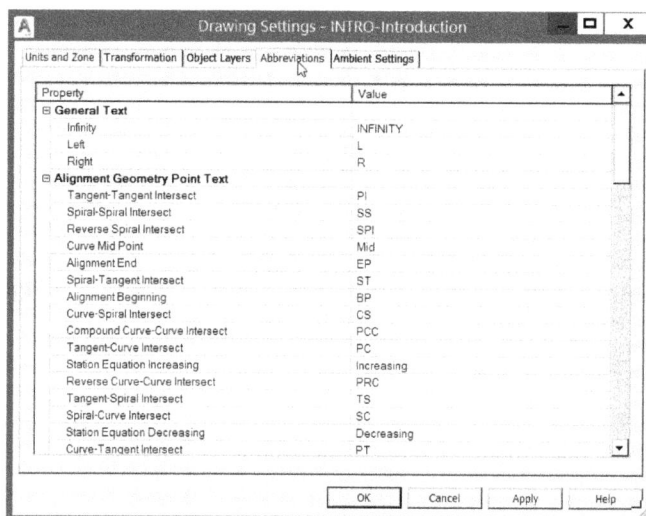

Figure 1–45

Ambient Settings

In the *Ambient Settings* tab (shown in Figure 1–46), the values influence prompting and reports. For example, the *Direction* area affects the prompting for direction input: **Decimal Degrees**, **Degrees Minutes and Seconds** (with or without spaces), or **Decimal Degrees Minutes and Seconds**. Any value set at this level affects everything (labels and commands) in the drawing.

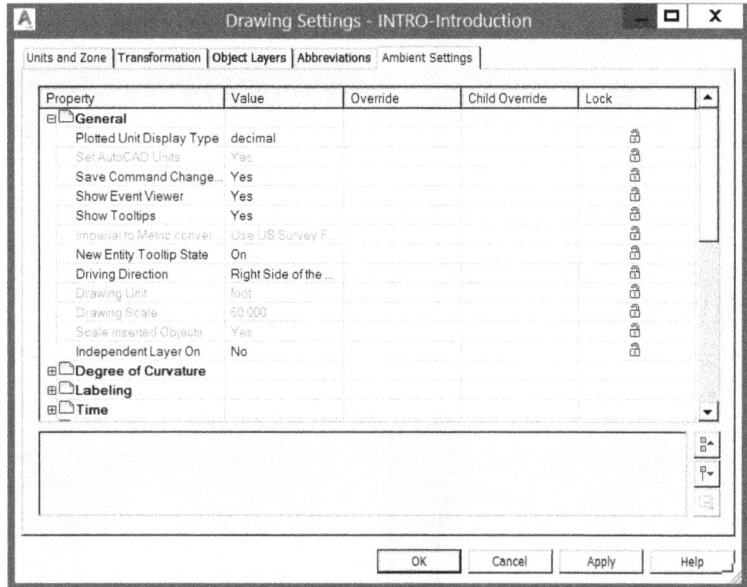

Figure 1–46

Edit Label Style Defaults

The values assigned in the Edit Label Style Defaults dialog box (shown in Figure 1–47), control text style, plan orientation, and the basic behavior of label styles. Similar to Feature Settings, this dialog box is available at the drawing level and at the individual objects level. Editing Label Style defaults at the drawing level affects all label styles in the drawing. Editing them at the object level (such as surfaces) only affects that object's labels.

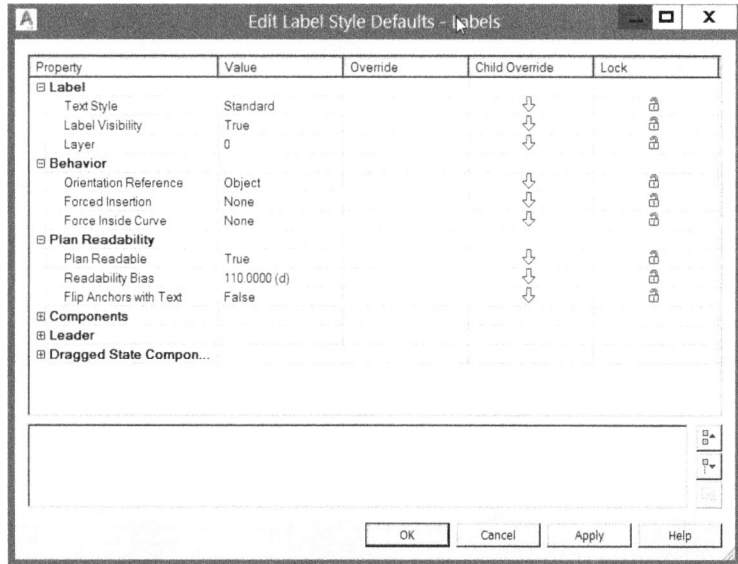

Figure 1–47

In the *Label, Behavior,* and *Plan Readability* areas, the values affect the overall visibility of labels, their default text style, label orientation, and the rotation angle that affects plan readability.

The values in the *Components, Leader,* and *Dragged State Components* areas affect the default text height for the label, colors for the text, leader, surrounding box, and type of leader. There are also several settings defining what happens to a label when you drag it from its original position.

Edit Autodesk LandXML Settings

The LandXML Settings dialog box (shown in Figure 1–48), provides settings that control how Autodesk LandXML data is imported and exported from the AutoCAD Civil 3D software. Autodesk LandXML is a universal format for storing Surveying and Civil Engineering data that enables you to transfer points, terrain models, alignments, etc., between different software platforms. For more information, see *www.landxml.org* and the AutoCAD Civil 3D Help system. The dialog box can be opened by right-clicking on Drawing Name in the Toolspace, *Settings* tab and selecting **Edit LandXMLSettings**.

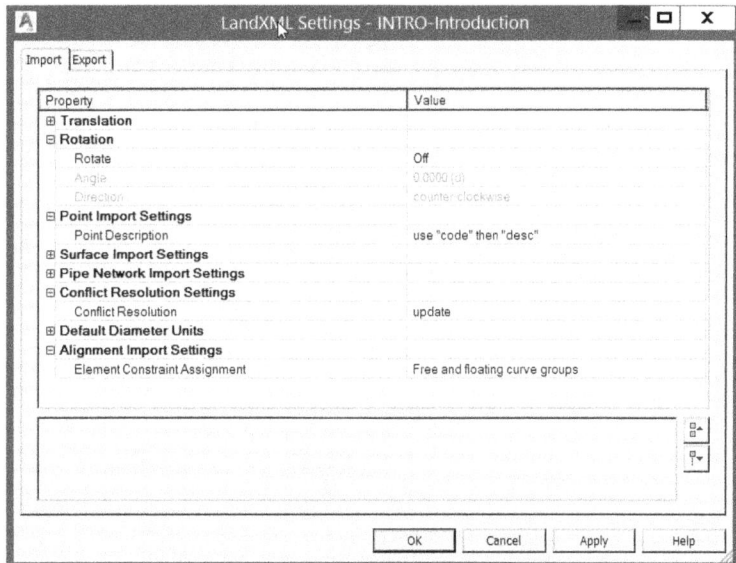

Figure 1–48

Feature Settings

In the Toolspace, *Settings* tab, each object type collection has an Edit Feature Settings dialog box, as shown for Surface in Figure 1–49. Its main function is to assign default naming values, initial Object and Label styles, and overriding the default values found in Edit Drawing Settings for that object type. You can access the feature settings by right-clicking on the object tree in the Toolspace, *Settings* tab and selecting **Edit Feature Settings**.

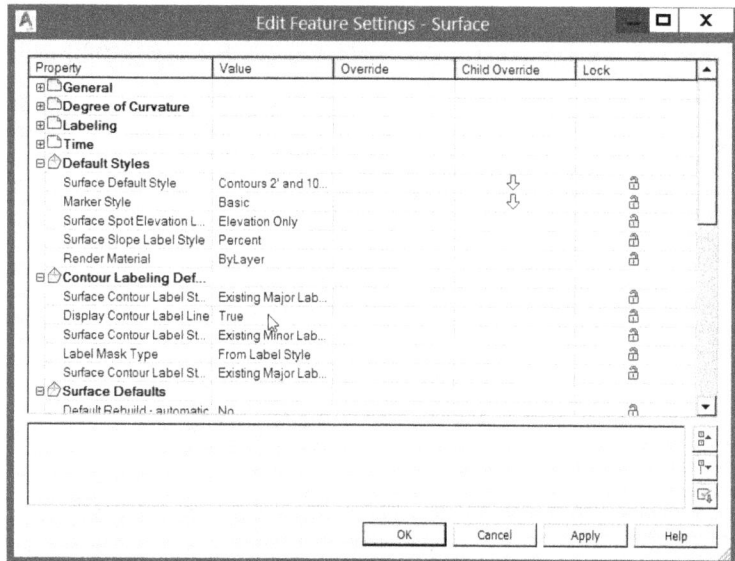

Figure 1–49

Command Settings

Similar to feature settings, in the Edit Command Settings dialog box (shown in Figure 1–50), you can set the default object and label styles used when creating objects with a specific command. Each object type contains a unique set of commands. Typical values in these dialog boxes include the name format (surface 1, parcel 1, etc.), design criteria (minimum area, frontage, length of vertical curve, and minimum horizontal curve), etc. To open the dialog box, expand a collection in the Toolspace, *Settings* tab until the commands display. Right-click on the command to which you want to assign default settings and select **Edit Command Settings**.

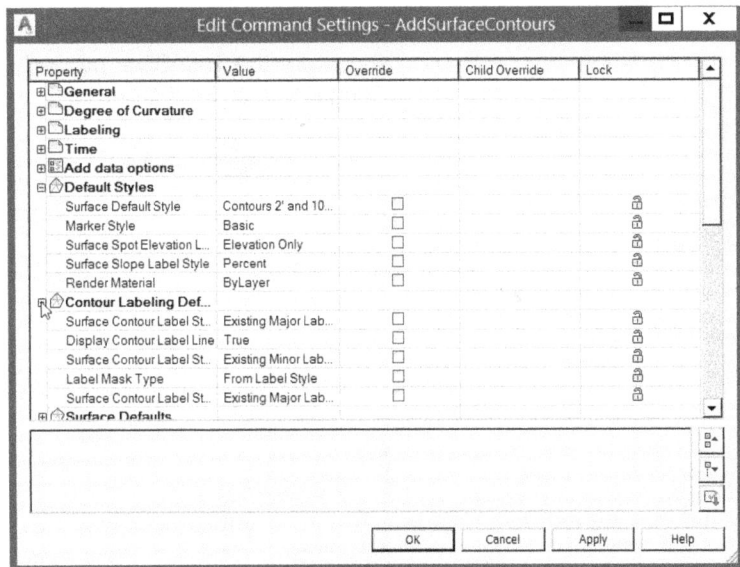

Figure 1–50

Hint: Style and Setting Overrides

In the Edit Label Style Defaults, Feature Settings and similar dialog boxes, a downward pointing arrow in the Child Override column indicates that a setting or style lower in the settings tree has a different value than the one displayed. Selecting the arrow (which creates a red **x** over the icon) and clicking **OK** removes the variant settings and makes all lower settings and styles match those assigned in the dialog box. This can be a quick way of standardizing multiple settings dialog boxes and styles at the same time.

For example, in the Surface Label Style defaults window (shown in Figure 1–51), some surface label styles are assigned a layer other than 0 and a visibility of false, because an arrow is present in the *Child Override* column. Since an arrow is not shown for the Text Style property, all surface label styles are using a text style of **Standard**.

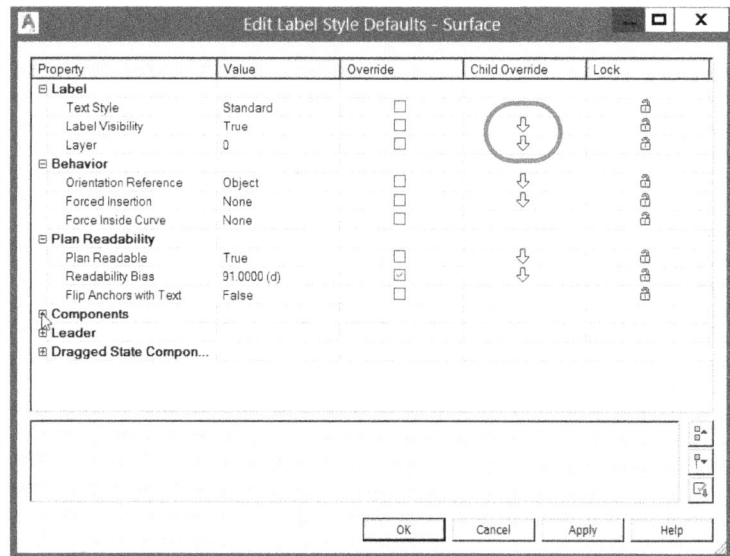

Figure 1–51

The *Override* column indicates whether a value in this window is overriding a higher settings dialog box. Clicking the **Lock** icon prevents you from changing that value in a lower setting's dialog box or style

Styles

Styles are preconfigured groups of settings specific to an individual object type or label that make the objects print the way you want them to print. For example, in the list of surface styles shown in Figure 1–52, each surface style is configured differently to display different features, such as contours at different intervals and on the correct layers. The display of a terrain model could be changed by swapping one surface style for another. Styles enable an organization to standardize the look of their graphics by providing preconfigured groupings of display settings.

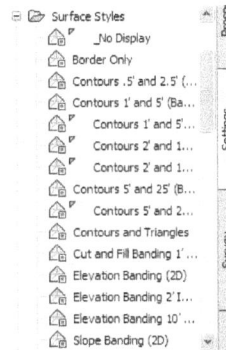

Figure 1–52

The two categories of styles you work with most often are Object Styles and Label Styles. Some objects have table styles as well. Object styles control how AutoCAD Civil 3D objects (points, surfaces, alignments, etc.) display, what combination of components the object displays, which layers they display on, and many other settings. Label Styles are similar except that they control the text and other annotations associated with the objects.

For example, an alignment object style specifies many settings including the layers on which to draw tangents and curve segments (which might be different) and which symbols to add at certain points as required (such as a triangle at the PI point). Alignment label styles include major and minor station labels, the display of station equations, design speeds, and similar annotation. By separating object and label styles, you can mix and match the right combination for a specific object.

Styles are the lowest items in the Toolspace, *Settings* tree and are typically dependent on other settings above them. If a style is given a unique setting, different from feature settings or label style defaults (such as a different text height), then that style is considered to have an override.

Styles in Depth

Styles are central to the AutoCAD Civil 3D software. Their flexibility enables an Office or Company to create a unique *look* for their drawings. By changing the assigned style, you can change the composition of a profile view as shown in Figure 1–53.

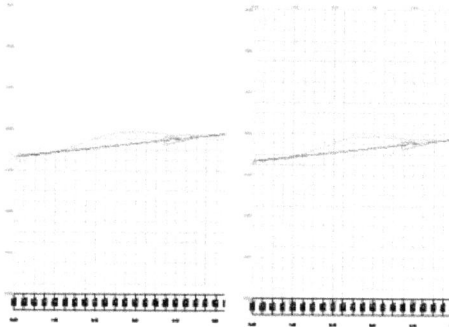

Figure 1–53

In the Toolspace, *Settings* tab, an object type branch identifies each style type and lists its styles below each heading. An example is shown in Figure 1–54.

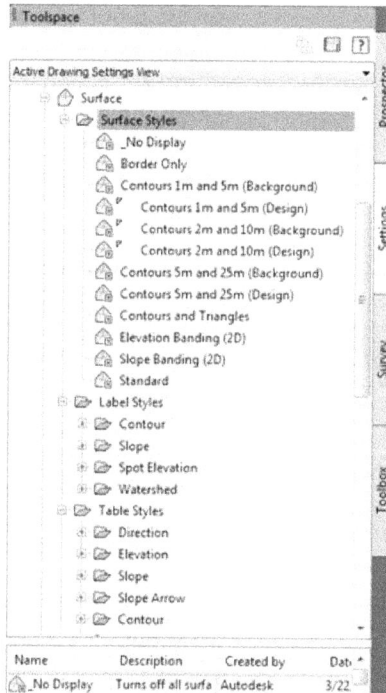

Figure 1–54

Object Styles

Object Styles stylize an object's data for display. To edit a style, in the Toolspace, *Settings* tab, right-click on the style and select **Edit**. Most of the work for all object styles is done in the *Display* tab. For certain objects, other tabs might need to be modified.

For example, in the Surface Style dialog box, the *Display* tab enables you to toggle on or off triangles, borders, contours, and other items as well as define the layer, color, linetype, etc. that are assigned to them, as shown in Figure 1–55. The *Contours* tab sets the contour interval, smoothing, and other settings, as shown in Figure 1–56.

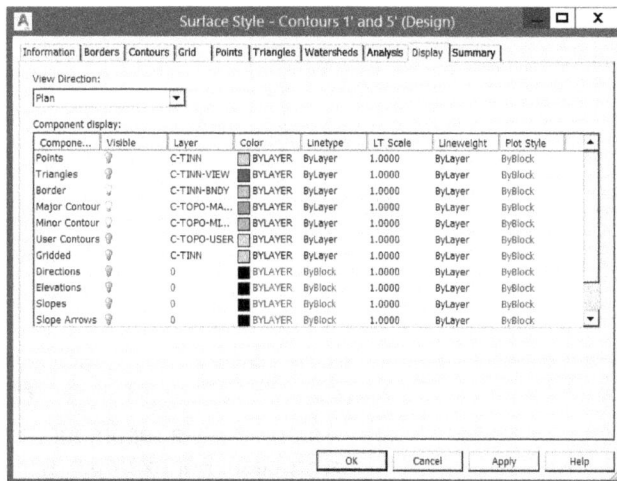

Figure 1–55

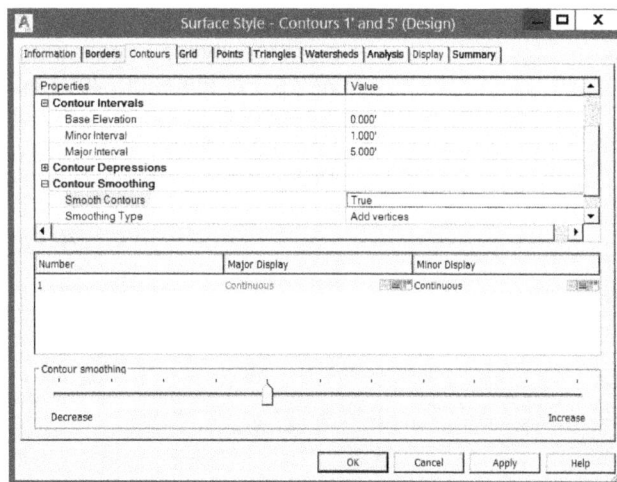

Figure 1–56

From the default AutoCAD Civil 3D template, the respective Parcel Style dialog box for Open Space, Road, or Single Family, (as shown in Figure 1–57), define how each displays their segments and hatching by assigning different layers for the components. The other tabs are rarely used for the Parcel styles.

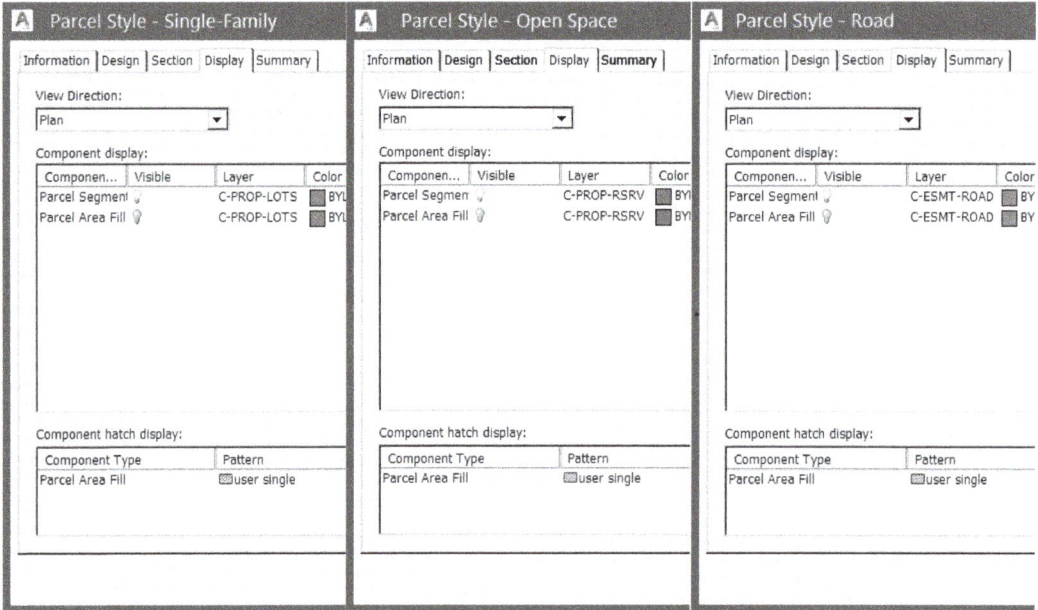

Figure 1–57

An object style represents a specific task, view, type, or stage in a process. For example, a surface style for developing a surface, reviewing surface properties, or documenting surface elevations as contours for a submission. For Parcels, styles represent a type such as open space, commercial, easement, single family, etc. One style can cause an object to look different in various views. For instance, you might want to display both the point and the label in the plan view but only the point marker in a model (3D view). As shown in Figure 1–58, there are four view directions to consider when creating an object style.

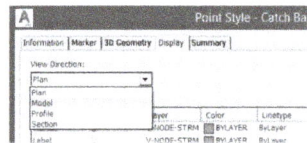

Figure 1–58

Label Styles

Label styles produce annotation of critical values from existing conditions or a design solution. A label annotates a contour's elevations, a parcel's number and area, an horizontal geometry point's station on an alignment, etc.

A label style can have text, vectors, AutoCAD blocks, and reference text. The content of a label depends on the selected object's components or properties. For instance, a Line label can annotate bearing, distance, and coordinates, and use a direction arrow. A Parcel Area label can contain a parcel's area, perimeter, address, and other pertinent values. A surface label can include a spot elevation and reference for an alignment's station and offset.

- To access the values of a label style, in the Toolspace, *Settings* tab, select the style, right-click on its name, and select **Edit**.

- A style's initial values come from Edit Label Style Defaults and the style's definition.

- All labels use the same interface.

- The object properties available for each label vary by object type.

Each label style uses the same tabbed dialog box. The Information tab describes the style and who defined and last modified its contents. The values of the *General* tab affect all occurrences of the label in a drawing. For example, if Visibility is set to False, all labels of this style are hidden in the drawing. Other settings affect the label's text style, initial orientation, and reaction to a rotated view.

The *Layout* tab lists all of a label's components. A label component can be text, line, block, or tick. The Component name drop-down list (shown in Figure 1–59), contains all of the defined components for the style. When selecting a component name in the drop-down list, the panel displays information about the component's anchoring, justification, format, and border.

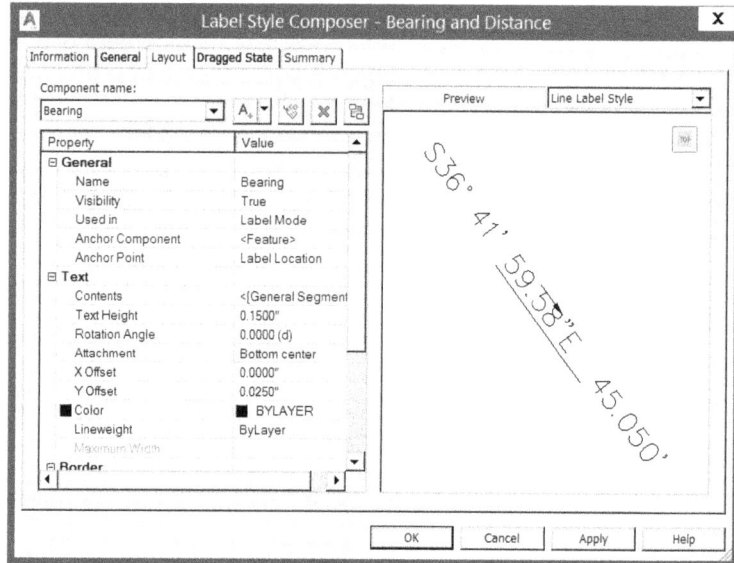

Figure 1–59

When defining a new text component, you assign it an object property by clicking ⋯ (Browse) for Contents. This opens the Text Component Editor dialog box, as shown in Figure 1–60. The Properties drop-down list displays the available object properties. The number and types of properties varies by object type. For example, a parcel area label has more and different properties than a line label does. Once a property has been selected, units, precision, and other settings can be set to display the property correctly in the label. Click ⇨ next to Properties to place the property in the label layout area to the right.

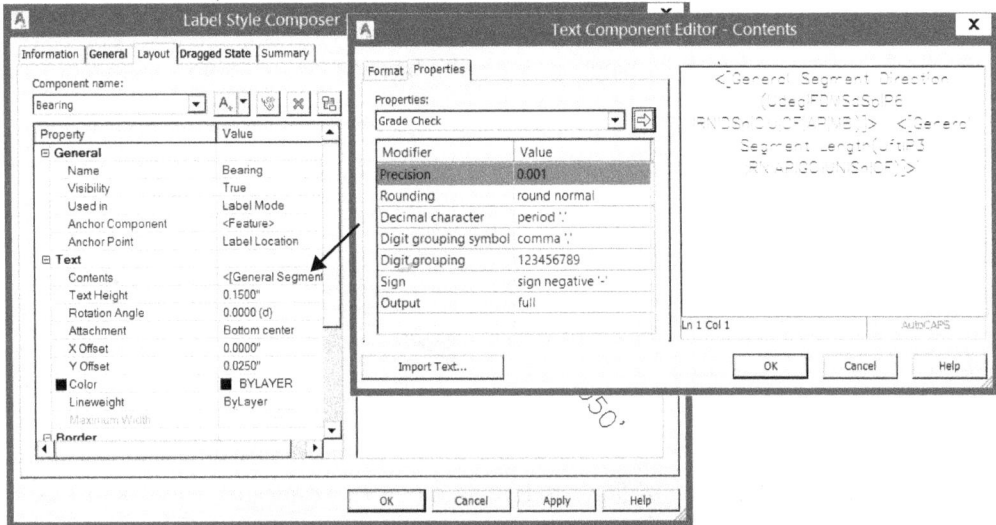

Figure 1–60

The values in the *Dragged State* tab define a label's behavior when it is dragged to a new location in the drawing.

The key to having the label display correctly when it is not in the dragged state, is to line up the Anchor Point of the component with the **Attachment** option for the text. Each has nine options from which to select. The options are shown in Figure 1–61.

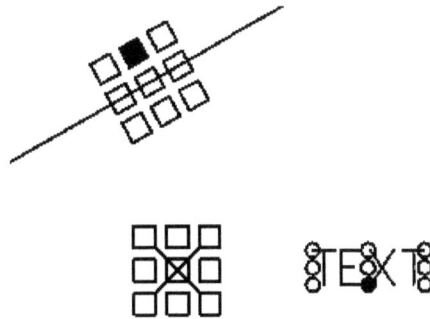

Figure 1–61

Lining up the square hatched Anchor Point with the circular hatched attachment option results in the text centered above the object similar to the bearing distance label shown in Figure 1–62.

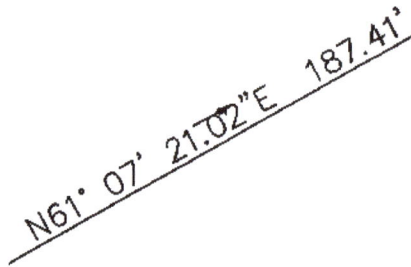

Figure 1–62

Templates

A drawing template (.DWT extension) contains all blocks, Paper Space title sheets, settings, layers, AutoCAD Civil 3D styles, and content-specific settings for a new drawing.

Creating Template Files

To use the AutoCAD Civil 3D software efficiently and effectively, you need to configure styles and settings to control the object display. All of these styles and settings affect the final delivered product and enable you to deliver a product with consistent CAD standards. Once all of the styles required for a set of drawings have been created, saving the file as a template enables you to use the same styles over and over in various projects. To create a template file, use the **Save As** command and in the Save As dialog box, change the *File of Type* to **DWT**. After giving it a name, the Template Options dialog box opens as shown in Figure 1–63. It enables you to enter a description, set the measurement units, and save new layers as reconciled or unreconciled.

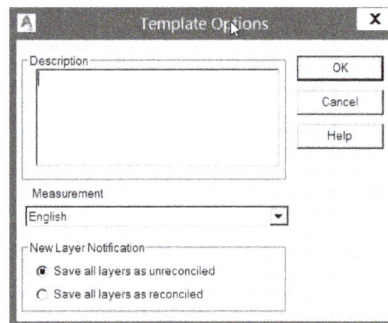

Figure 1–63

Once an AutoCAD Civil 3D style has been created, it can be transferred between drawings and templates by selecting the style and dragging it to the required file. When dragging a style to a drawing, any associated style layers also transfer.

There are three methods of managing styles in a drawing: **Import**, **Purge**, and **Reference**. These commands are located in the *Manage* tab>Styles panel, as shown in Figure 1–64.

Figure 1–64

Import

The **Import** styles command enables you to import the styles from a source drawing into the current drawing. The Import Civil 3D Styles dialog box opens, as shown in Figure 1–65. It lists the styles that are available for import and also displays the style differences between the source and the current drawing. Each style collection lists three subcategories: styles to be added, styles to be deleted, and styles to be updated. When you use the **Import** command, the styles in the design file are overwritten. However, if the styles change in the DWG or DWT source file that you imported, the styles in the design file do not automatically update.

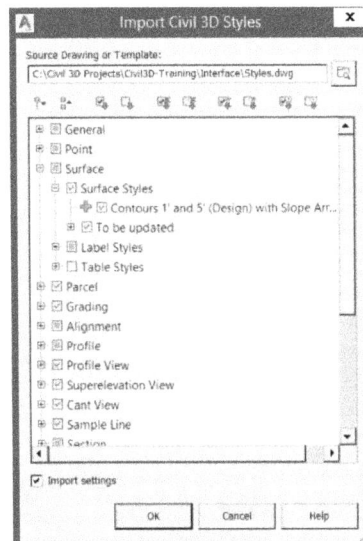

Figure 1–65

Purge

The **Purge** styles command enables you to purge all of the selected unused styles in a drawing. However, you might need to run this command more than once as there might be some styles that are used as parents to other styles. The purging information displays in the Style Purge Confirmation dialog box, as shown in Figure 1–66. The Command Line prompts you when there are no unused styles in the drawing.

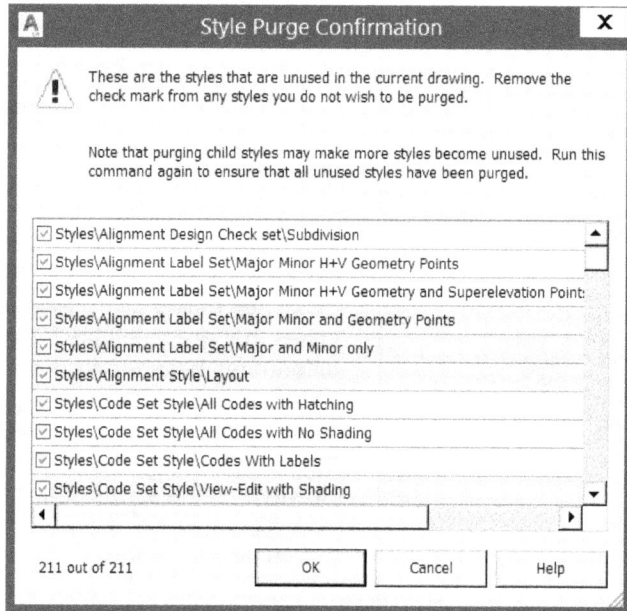

Figure 1–66

Reference

The **Reference** styles command enables you to attach one or more DWG or DWT files to your design file. Styles that are in the attached files override styles with the same name in the design drawing. If the styles in the attached DWG or DWT file change, the styles in the design file also change. Using the **Reference** styles command enables you to maintain a consistent style across multiple drawings, and can be used to implement and maintain a company-wide CAD standard. Figure 1–67 shows the Attach Referenced Template dialog box.

* When multiple style templates are attached, you can set the priority using the arrows on the right of the Attach Referenced Template dialog box.

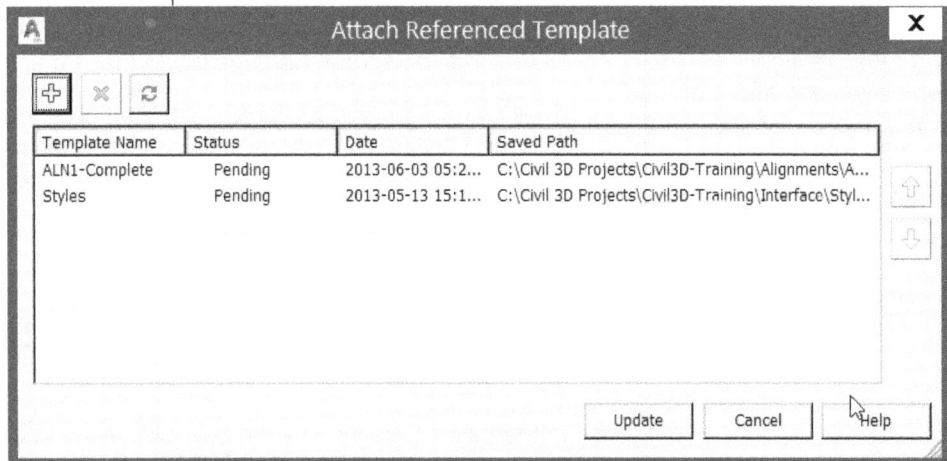

Figure 1–67

Practice 1c

AutoCAD Civil 3D Styles

Practice Objectives

- Create an object and label style to be used in the drawing.
- Import object and label styles to be used in the drawing and purge any styles not being used.

Estimated time for completion: 10 minutes

In this practice you will create AutoCAD Civil 3D styles, import styles, and purge styles for both objects and labels.

Task 1 - Create an object style.

1. Continue working in the drawing from the last practice. If you closed it, open **INTRO-Introduction.dwg** from the *C:\Civil 3D Projects\Civil3D-Training\Interface* folder.

2. Select the Toolspace, *Settings* tab to make it active.

The tabs are listed vertically along the right side of the Toolspace.

3. Click the **+** sign next to Parcel, and then click the **+** sign next to Parcel Styles. Five parcel styles are already in the drawing, but a new one needs to be created to designate blocks.

4. Right-click on Parcel Styles and select **New**. In the *Information* tab, type **Blocks** in the *Name* field.

5. In the *Display* tab, highlight both the Parcel Segment and Parcel Area Fill (press <Shift> to select both), click **0** under the *Layer* column.

6. In the Layer Selection dialog box, click **New** to create a new layer. Name the layer **C-PROP-BLOCK** and set its *color* to **blue**, as shown in Figure 1–68.

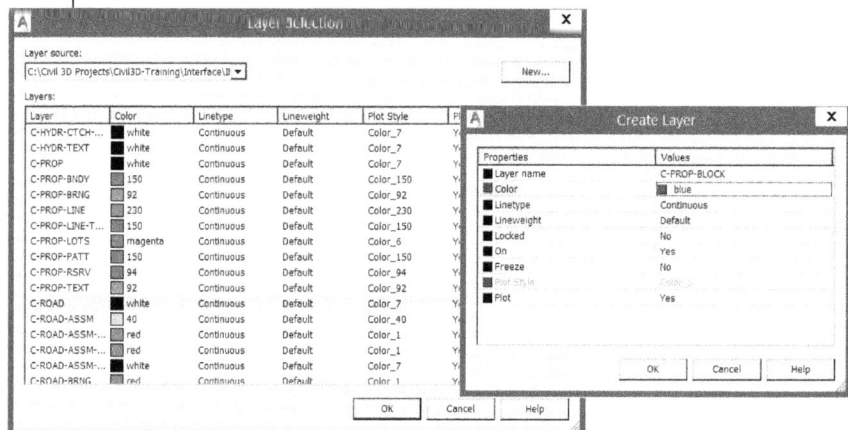

Figure 1–68

7. Click **OK** to exit the Create Layer dialog box.

8. In the Layer Selection dialog box, select the new **C-PROP-BLOCK** layer and click **OK** to exit the Layer Selection dialog box.

9. Verify that the light bulb is on for the Parcel Segment visibility and off for the Parcel Area Fill visibility, as shown in Figure 1–69.

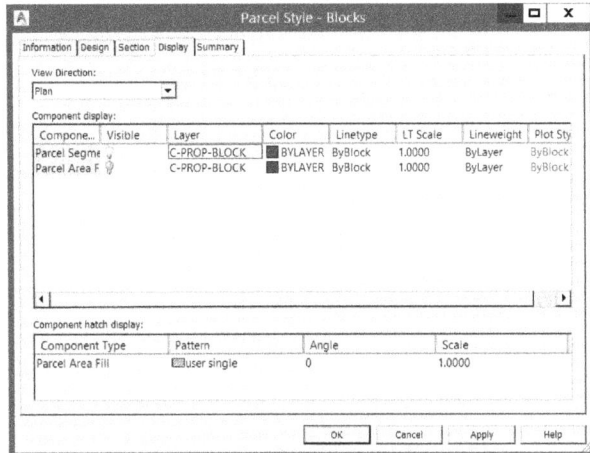

Figure 1–69

10. Click **OK** to exit the Parcel Style dialog box.

11. Save the drawing.

Task 2 - Work with a label style.

---

1. Verify that the Toolspace, *Settings* tab is still active.

2. View the label style default. In the *View* tab>Views panel, expand the Named Views drop-down list and select **Contour label**. It will zoom to a preset view of the contour labels, as shown in Figure 1–70.

Figure 1–70

Note that the labels are not rotated to the correct drafting standards. The contour label style being used is rotating the text so that it remains plan readable (so they do not display upside down). The highlighted labels are rotated more than 90 degrees from horizontal. This is caused by the *Readability Bias* setting being larger than 90 degrees. This setting controls the viewing angle at which the contour text should be flipped.

3. If required, you can change the setting in this specific contour label style only. To assign this new value to all of the surface label styles, in the Toolspace, *Settings* tab, right-click on the *Surface* collection and select **Edit Label Style Defaults**.

4. Under the Plan Readability property, set the *Readability Bias* to **110°**, as shown in Figure 1–71, and click **OK**.

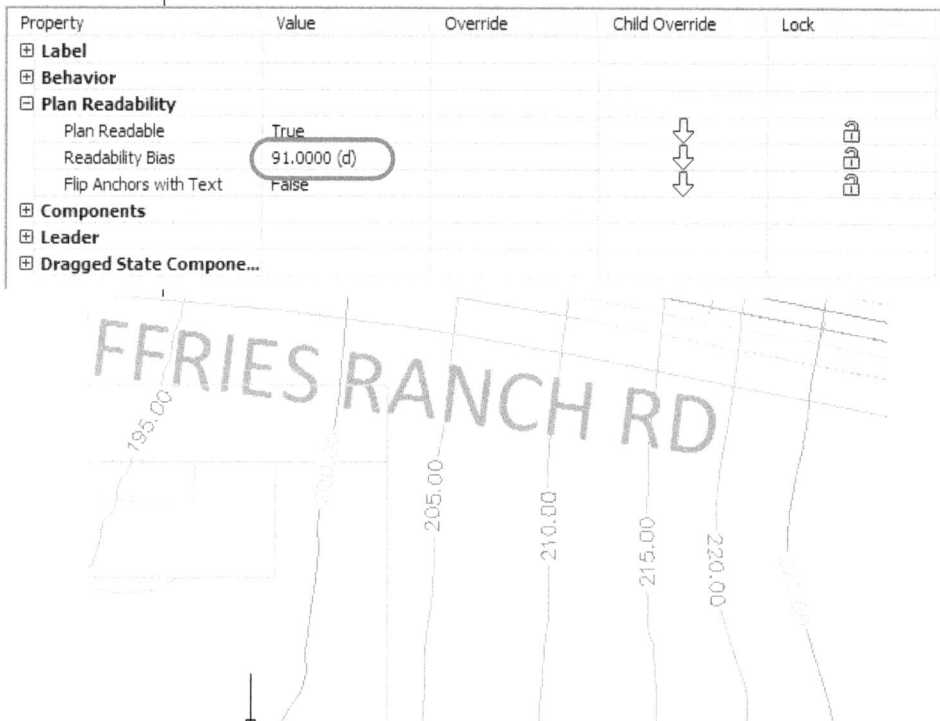

Figure 1–71

5. In the Toolspace, *Settings* tab, click **+** next to Surface, and then click **+** next to Label Styles and Contour. Right-click on Existing Major Labels and select **Edit**.

6. In the *Layout* tab, click ⬚ (Browse) next to Contents to open the Text Component Editor. Delete all of the information in the content area to the right.

7. In the Properties drop-down list, select **Surface Elevation**, change the *Precision* to **1**, and click ⬚ to place it in the content area, as shown in Figure 1–72.

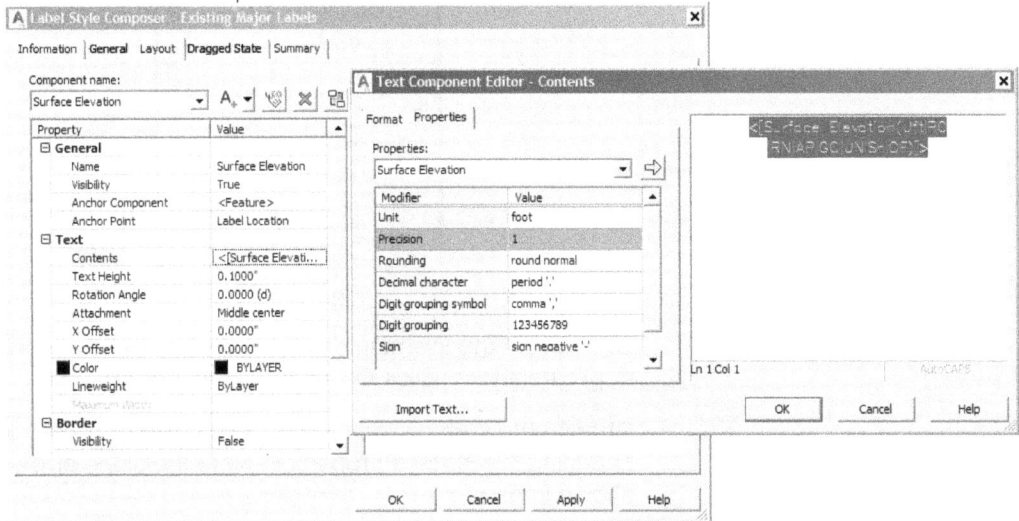

Figure 1–72

8. Click **OK** to exit the Text Component Editor dialog box. Click **OK** again to exit the Label Style Composer dialog box.

9. Repeat Steps 5 to 8 to change the **Existing Minor Labels** style in the same way.

10. Save the drawing.

Task 3 - Import and purge styles.

1. In the *Manage* tab>Styles panel, click ⬚ (Import).

2. Select and open the **Styles.dwg** file from the *C:\Civil 3D Projects\Civil3D-Training\Interface* folder.

3. Expand *Surface Styles* and verify that **Contours 1' and 5' (Design) with Slope Arrows** is selected, as shown in Figure 1–73.

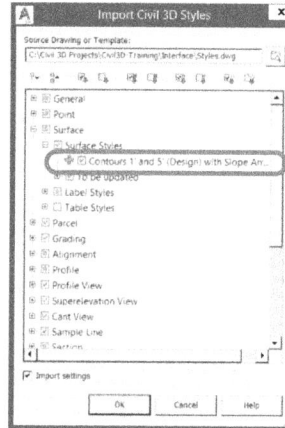

Figure 1–73

4. Click **OK** in the Warning dialog box regarding overwriting duplicate styles. Click **OK** in the Message dialog box.

5. Change the surface style to the newly imported style by changing the surface properties. Note the slope arrows shown in Figure 1–74.

Figure 1–74

6. In the *Manage* tab>Styles panel, click (Purge).

7. Clear any styles that you do not want to purge and click **OK**.

8. Save the drawing.

Task 4 - Attach a styles template.

---

1. In the *Manage* tab>Styles panel, click 🔒 (Reference).

2. In the Attach Referenced Template dialog box, click
   ➕ (Attach New Template).

3. In the *C:\Civil 3D Projects\Civil3D-Training\Interface* folder,
   select the **Styles.dwg** file and then click **Open**.

4. In the Attach Referenced Template dialog box, shown in
   Figure 1–75, click **Update**.

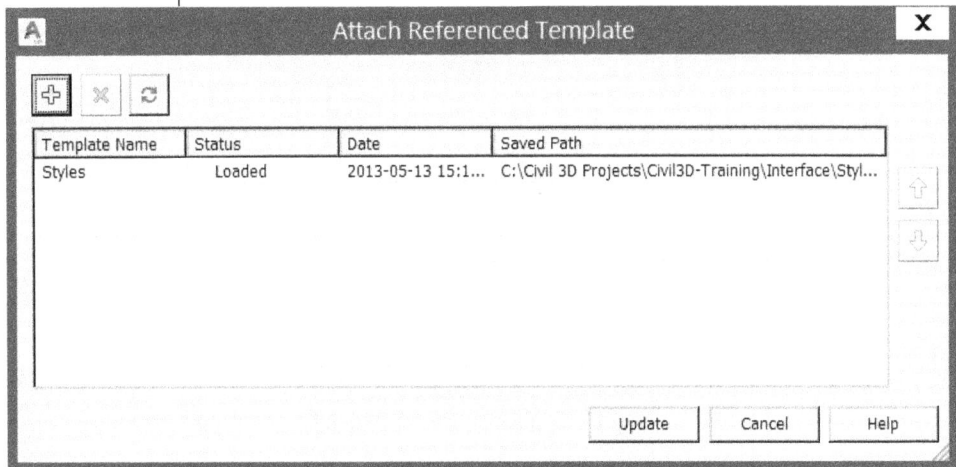

Template Name	Status	Date	Saved Path
Styles	Loaded	2013-05-13 15:1...	C:\Civil 3D Projects\Civil3D-Training\Interface\Styl...

Figure 1–75

5. Save and close the drawing.

Chapter Review Questions

1. Which Workspace should you be in if you want to create an AEC object (surfaces, alignments, profiles, etc)?

    a. 2D Drafting and Annotation

    b. 3D Modeling

    c. Civil 3D

    d. Planning and Analysis

2. What does the Toolspace, *Prospector* tab do?

    a. Sets the layers for AEC objects.

    b. Lists the AEC objects and provides access to their information.

    c. Sets the workspace in which you want to work.

    d. Enables you to connect to GIS data from a number of sources.

3. What does the Toolspace, *Settings* tab do?

    a. Sets the layers and display styles for AEC objects.

    b. Creates templates from which new drawings are based.

    c. Creates new drawings with references to data.

    d. Generates Sheets for printing purposes.

4. How do you open the Edit Drawing Settings dialog box?

    a. Type **CUI** in the Command Line to open the Customize User Interface dialog box.

    b. **Application menu>Drawing Utilities**.

    c. In the Toolspace, *Prospector* tab, right-click on the drawing name.

    d. In the Toolspace, *Settings* tab, right-click on the drawing name.

5. What is the main function of the Panorama window?

    a. Setting up styles for AEC objects.

    b. Reviewing and editing tabular AEC object data.

    c. Pan inside the drawing.

    d. Look at the AEC objects in 3D views.

6. How do you force the styles in a design file to update every time the CAD Manager makes a change to the styles in the company CAD Standards template file?

   a. In the *Manage* tab>Styles panel, click (Reference)

   b. In the *Manage* tab>Styles panel, click (Purge)

   c. In the *Manage* tab>Styles panel, click (Import).

   d. You have to create a new style manually because there is no way to force an update to styles in an existing drawing.

Command Summary

Button	Command	Location
	Close	• **Drawing Window** • **Application Menu** • **Command Prompt:** close
	Close Current Drawing	• **Application Menu**
	Import Styles	• **Ribbon:** *Manage* tab>Styles panel • **Command Prompt:** importstylesandsettings
	Manager Reference Styles	• **Ribbon:** *Manage* tab>Styles panel • **Command Prompt:** AttachReferenceTemplate
	Open	• **Quick Access Toolbar** • **Application Menu** • **Command Prompt:** open, <Ctrl>+<O>
	Prospector	• **Ribbon:** *Home* tab>Palettes panel • **Command Prompt:** prospector
	Settings	• **Ribbon:** *Home* tab>Palettes panel • **Command Prompt:** settings
	Style Purge	• **Ribbon:** *Manage* tab>Styles panel • **Command Prompt:** purgestyles
	Surface Properties	• **Contextual Ribbon:** *Surface* tab> Modify panel • **Command Prompt:** editsurfaceproperties
	Survey	• **Ribbon:** *Home* tab>Palettes panel • **Command Prompt:** survey
	Toolbox	• **Ribbon:** *Home* tab>Palettes panel • **Command Prompt:** toolbox
	Toolspace	• **Ribbon:** *Home* tab>Palettes panel • **Command Prompt:** toolspace

Chapter

2

Project Management

In this chapter you learn about the various project structures that can be used inside of an AutoCAD® Civil 3D® project. Then you create a new project and learn how to move between different projects. Using data shortcuts, you practice creating references to AEC objects to share design data, which ensures that you always have the most up-to-date design data in the current model.

Learning Objectives in this Chapter

- List the three different ways in which AutoCAD Civil 3D project drawings can be organized.
- List the ways in which teams can collaborate with each other and share design information in the AutoCAD Civil 3D software.
- Share design information with other members of the design team using data shortcuts.

2.1 AutoCAD Civil 3D Projects

There are multiple ways of organizing AutoCAD Civil 3D project drawings. Three of the most common approaches are as follows:

Single-Design Drawing Projects

Since AutoCAD Civil 3D surfaces, alignments, and other AEC objects can be entirely drawing-based, you can have a single drawing file act as the repository for all design data. Realistically, this might only be feasible with the smallest projects and/or those worked on by only one person. The only external data would be survey databases, and possibly drawings containing plotting layouts that XREF the single design drawing.

Multiple Drawings Sharing Data using Shortcuts

This approach permits multiple survey and design drawings that share data. For example, a surface could exist in one drawing and an alignment in another. A third could contain a surface profile based on the alignment and terrain model, and all could be kept in sync with each other using Data Shortcuts. This approach is usually preferable to the single-drawing approach, because it permits more than one user to work on the project at the same time (in the different design drawings) and keeps the drawings at a more manageable size. Using data shortcuts is essential in larger projects to ensure that the regeneration time for drawings is at an acceptable speed. This approach does not create any external project data other than survey databases and XML data files that are used to share data between drawings.

Once an object has been referenced into the drawing and the drawing has been saved, the object is saved in the drawing. Therefore, it only needs access to the source drawing for validation and synchronization purposes if the source object changes. This makes it easy to share drawings with others because it ensures that the referenced objects display even if the source drawings are not available.

Shortcuts tend to be efficient for projects with a small number of drawings and project team members. Since the XML data files that connect drawings must be managed manually, keeping a large number of drawings and/or people in sync with shortcuts can be cumbersome. It is highly recommended that you establish procedures to ensure that data is not unintentionally deleted or changed. You will also want to document these procedures very carefully.

Multiple Drawings Sharing Data with Autodesk Vault

The Autodesk® Vault software is a data and document management system (ADMS). It is used in conjunction with other Autodesk® applications in different industries. When working with the Autodesk Vault software, all project drawings, survey databases, and references are managed and stored inside an SQL-managed database. Autodesk Vault consists of user-level access permissions, drawing check-in/out, project templates, automated backups, data versioning, etc. These benefits are offset by the additional time required to manage and administer the database, and in some cases purchasing additional hardware and software. If you work on large projects with multiple design drawings or have many team members (more than 10), you might find that the Autodesk® Vault is the best way to keep those projects organized.

2.2 Sharing Data

In the AutoCAD Civil 3D workflow, you can use two methods of project collaboration to share AutoCAD Civil 3D design data: Data Shortcuts and Vault references.

Autodesk Vault and Data Shortcuts can be used to share design data between drawing files in the same project, such as alignment definitions, profiles, corridors, surfaces, pipe networks, pressure networks, and View Frame Groups. They do not permit the sharing of profile views, assemblies, sample line groups, or other AutoCAD Civil 3D objects. Drawing sets using shortcuts typically use XREFs and reference other line work and annotations between drawings. Whether using Vault Shortcuts or Data Shortcuts, the process is similar.

The example in Figure 2–1 shows the sharing of data in a project collaboration environment. The data is divided into three distinctive levels. Using either Data Shortcuts or Autodesk Vault, these levels can be accessed and contributed to, on a local or remote server or across a WAN.

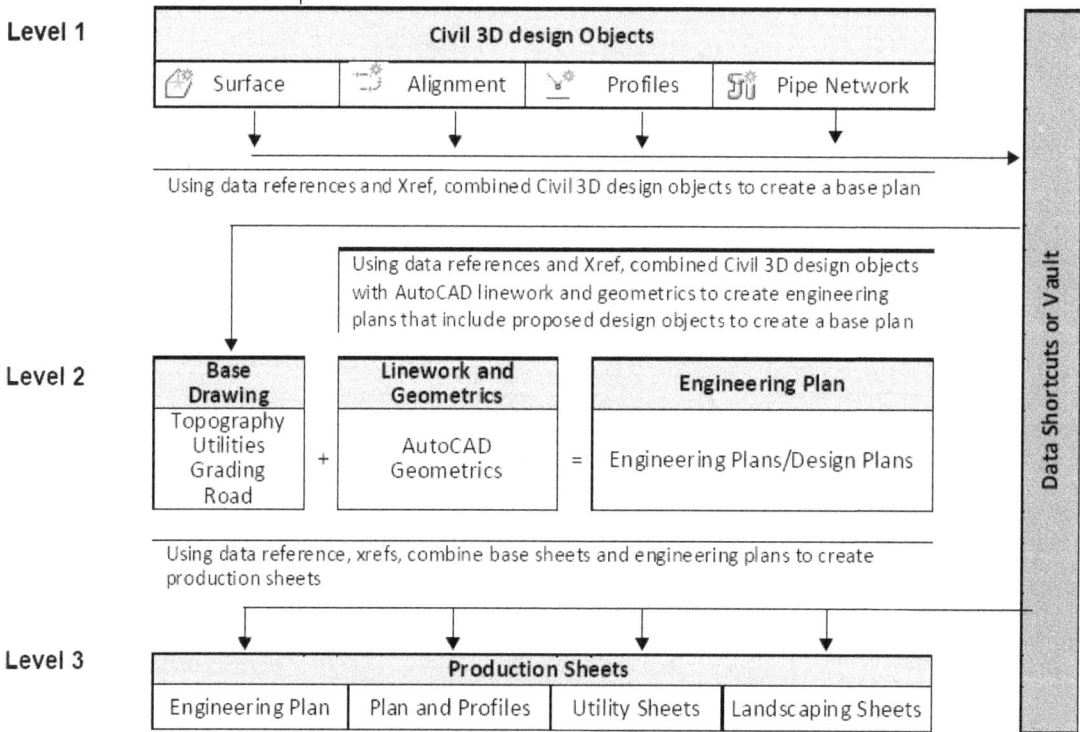

Level 1

Civil 3D design Objects			
Surface	Alignment	Profiles	Pipe Network

Using data references and Xref, combined Civil 3D design objects to create a base plan

Using data references and Xref, combined Civil 3D design objects with AutoCAD linework and geometrics to create engineering plans that include proposed design objects to create a base plan

Level 2

Base Drawing		Linework and Geometrics		Engineering Plan
Topography Utilities Grading Road	+	AutoCAD Geometrics	=	Engineering Plans/Design Plans

Using data reference, xrefs, combine base sheets and engineering plans to create production sheets

Level 3

Production Sheets			
Engineering Plan	Plan and Profiles	Utility Sheets	Landscaping Sheets

Data Shortcuts or Vault

Figure 2–1

2.3 Using Data Shortcuts for Project Management

Data Shortcuts can be used to share design data between drawing files through the use of XML files. Using Data Shortcuts is similar to using the Autodesk Vault software, but does not provide the protection of your data or the tracking of versions the way the Autodesk Vault software does.

Data Shortcuts are managed using the Toolspace, *Prospector* tab, under the *Data Shortcuts* collection or in the *Manage* tab>Data Shortcuts panel, as shown in Figure 2–2. The shortcuts are stored in XML files in one or more working folders that you create. They can use the same folder structure as the Autodesk Vault software. This method simplifies the transition to using the Autodesk Vault software at a future time.

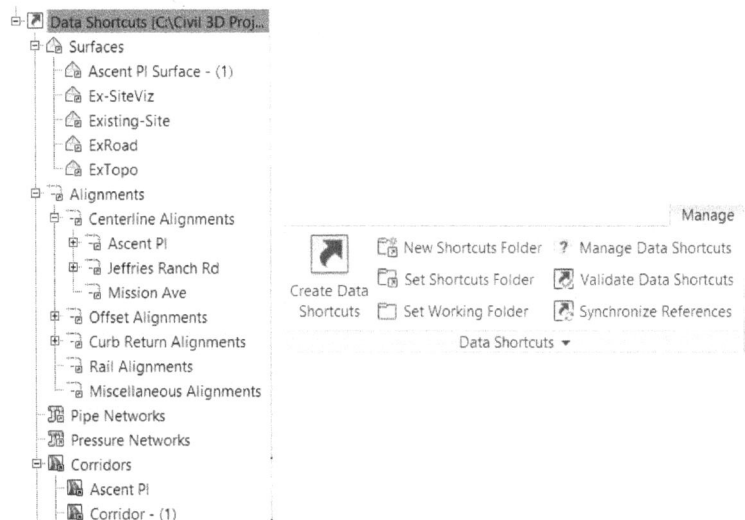

Figure 2–2

Whether using the Autodesk Vault software or Data Shortcuts, the intelligent AutoCAD Civil 3D object design data can be consumed and used on different levels. However, this referenced data only can be edited in the drawing that contains the original object. As referenced data can be assigned a different style than those in the source drawing, you can separate the design phase (where drawing presentation is not critical) from the drafting phase (where drawing presentation is paramount). Therefore, after the styles have been applied at the drafting phase, any changes to the design have minimal visual impact on the completed drawings.

Changing the name of a drawing file that provides Data Shortcuts or the shortcut XML file itself invalidates the shortcut. Although the Data Shortcuts Editor outside the AutoCAD Civil 3D software permits re-pathing if a source drawing moves, shortcuts might not resolve if the source drawing location has changed.

Update Notification

If the shortcut objects are modified and the source drawing is saved, any drawings that reference those objects are updated when opened. If the drawings consuming the data referenced in the shortcuts were open at the time of the edit, a message displays to warn you of the changes, as shown in Figure 2–3.

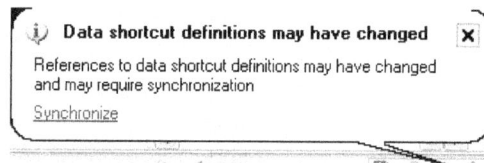

Figure 2–3

The following modifier icons help you to determine the state of many AutoCAD Civil 3D objects.

	The object is referenced by another object. In the Toolspace, Settings tab this also indicates that a style is in use in the current drawing.
	The object is being referenced from another drawing file (such as through a shortcut or Autodesk Vault reference).
	The object is out of date and needs to be rebuilt, or is violating specified design constraints.
	A Vault project object (such as a point or surface) has been modified since it was included in the current drawing.
	You have modified a Vault project object in your current drawing and those modifications have not yet been updated to the project.

Figure 2–4 shows how the modifier icons are used with an AutoCAD Civil 3D object as it displays in the Toolspace, *Prospector* tab.

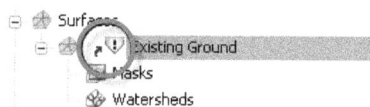

Figure 2–4

To update the shortcut data, select **Synchronize** in the balloon message or right-click on the object in the Toolspace, *Prospector* tab and select **Synchronize**.

Removing and Promoting Shortcuts

Shortcut data can be removed from the Shortcut tree in the Toolspace, *Prospector* tab by right-clicking on it and selecting **Remove**, but this does not remove the data from the drawing. To do so, right-click on the object in the Toolspace, *Prospector* tab and select **Delete**. This removes the shortcut data from the current list, so that the item is not included if a Data Shortcut XML file is exported from the current drawing.

You can also promote shortcuts, which converts the referenced shortcut into a local copy without any further connection to the original. You can promote objects by right-clicking on them in the Toolspace, *Prospector* tab and selecting **Promote**.

eTransmit Data References

Projects that use Data Shortcuts can be packaged and sent to reviewers, clients, and other consultants using the AutoCAD **eTransmit** command. With the **eTransmit** command, all of the related dependent files (such as XML files, XREFs, and text fonts) are automatically included in the package. This reduces the possibility of errors and ensures that the recipient can use the files you send them. A report file can be included in the package explaining what must be done with drawing-dependent files (e.g., XML, XREFs) so that they are usable with the included files. The Create Transmittal dialog box is shown in Figure 2–5.

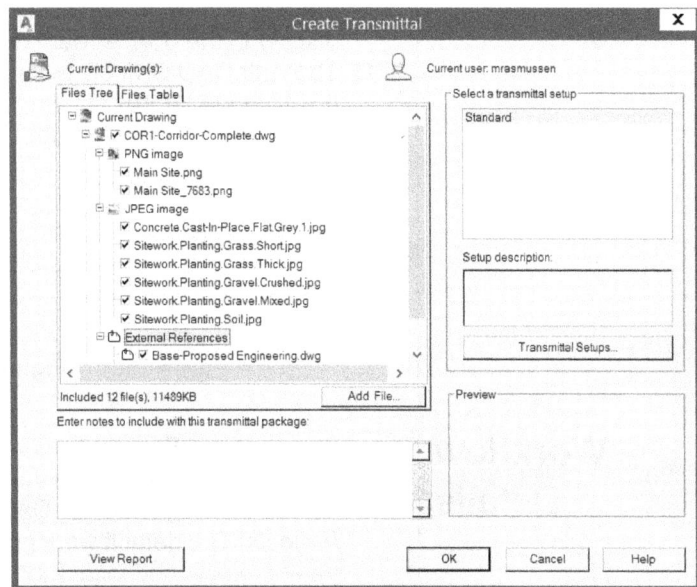

Figure 2–5

Data Shortcut Workflow

1. In the Toolspace, *Prospector* tab, right-click on Data Shortcuts and select **Set the Working Folder…**
2. In the Toolspace, *Prospector* tab, right-click on Data Shortcuts and select **New Data Shortcuts Folder…** to create a new project folder for all of your drawings.
3. Create or import the data that you want to share in the source drawing and save it in the current working folder under the correct project folder.
4. In the Toolspace, *Prospector* tab, right-click on Data Shortcuts and select **Associate Project to Current Drawing**.
5. In the Toolspace, *Prospector* tab, right-click on Data Shortcuts and select **Create Data Shortcuts**.
6. Select all of the items that you want to share, such as surfaces, alignments, or profiles, and click **OK**.
7. Save the source drawing (and close as required).
8. Open, create, and save the drawing to receive the shortcut data. Expand the *Data Shortcuts* collection and the relevant object trees (*Surfaces*, *Alignments*, *Pipe Networks*, or *View Frame Groups*).
9. Highlight an item to be referenced, right-click and select **Create Reference…** Repeat for all of the objects as required. You are prompted for the styles and other settings that are required to display the object in the current drawing.
10. You might also want to add an XREF to the source drawing if there is additional AutoCAD® line work that you want to display in the downstream drawing.
11. The AutoCAD Civil 3D tools for Data Shortcuts are located in the *Manage* tab (as shown in Figure 2–6), and in the Toolspace, *Prospector* tab.

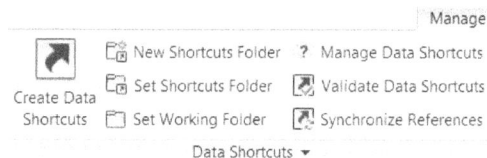

Figure 2–6

Workflow Details

- **Set Working Folder:** Sets a new working folder as the location in which to store the Data Shortcut project. The default working folder for Data Shortcut projects is *C:\Civil 3D Projects*. The default working folder is also used for Autodesk Vault projects and local (non-Vault) Survey projects. If you work with the Autodesk Vault software, local Survey, and Data Shortcut projects, you should have separate working folders for each project type for ease of management.

- **New Shortcuts Folder:** Creates a new folder for storing a set of related project drawings and Data Shortcuts.

- **Create Data Shortcuts:** Creates Data Shortcuts from the active drawing.

Data Shortcuts are stored in the *Shortcuts* folder for the active project and used to create data references to source objects in other drawings. Each Data Shortcut is stored in a separate XML file.

Advantages of Data Shortcuts

- Data Shortcuts provide a simple mechanism for sharing object data, without the added system administration needs of the Autodesk Vault software.

- Data Shortcuts offer access to an object's intelligent data while ensuring that this referenced data can only be changed in the source drawing.

- Referenced objects can have styles and labels that differ from the source drawing.

- When you open a drawing containing revised referenced data, the referenced objects are updated automatically.

- During a drawing session, if the referenced data has been revised, you are notified in the Communication Center and in the Toolspace, *Prospector* tab.

Limitations of Data Shortcuts

- Data Shortcuts cannot provide data versioning.

- Data Shortcuts do not provide security or data integrity controls.

- Unlike the Autodesk Vault software, Data Shortcuts do not provide a secure mechanism for sharing point data or survey data.

- Maintaining links between references and their source objects requires fairly stable names. However, most broken references can easily be repaired using the tools in the AutoCAD Civil 3D software.

Practice 2a

Starting a Project

Practice Objective

- Create a new data shortcut project with the correct working folder for the project being worked on.

Estimated time for completion: 15 minutes

In this practice you will walk through the steps of creating project-based Data Shortcuts folders.

Task 1 - Set the *Working* folder.

In this task, you will set up a new working folder as the location in which to store Data Shortcut projects. The default working folder for Data Shortcut projects is *C:\Civil 3D Projects*.

1. Open **DS-A1-Shortcuts.dwg** from the *C:\Civil 3D Projects\Civil3D-Training\DataShortcuts* folder.

2. In the *Manage* tab>Data Shortcuts panel, click 🗀 (Set Working Folder), as shown in Figure 2–7.

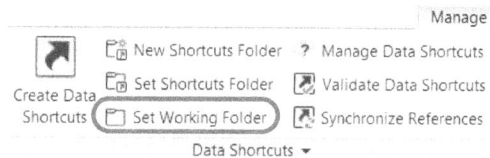

Figure 2–7

3. In the Browse For Folder dialog box, select the *Civil 3D Projects* folder and click **Make New Folder**, as shown on the left in Figure 2–8. Type **Learning Data Shortcuts** as the folder name and click **OK**, as shown on the right in Figure 2–8.

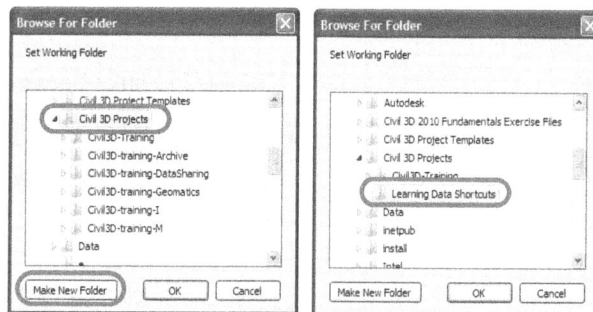

Figure 2–8

Task 2 - Create new *Shortcuts* folders.

In this task, you will create a new folder for storing a set of related project drawings and Data Shortcuts. A second project folder is created to help you understand how to change the project in which you are working.

1. Continue working with the drawing from the previous task.

2. In the *Manage* tab>Data Shortcuts panel, click ⬚ (New Shortcuts Folder), as shown in Figure 2–9.

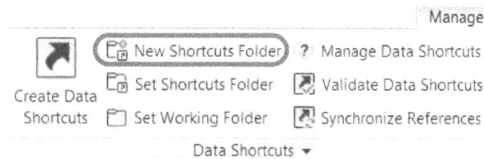

Figure 2–9

3. In the New Data Shortcut Folder dialog box, type **Ascent Phase 1** for the name and select the **Use project template** option. The template is found in the default folder *C:\Civil 3D Templates*, as shown in Figure 2–10. The AutoCAD Civil 3D software will replicate this template folder structure in the Data Shortcuts project folder. Click **OK** to close the dialog box.

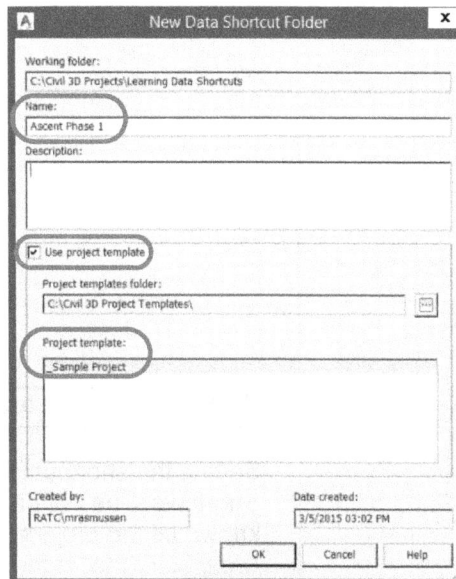

Figure 2–10

4. In the Toolspace, *Prospector* tab, a Data Shortcut folder should be displayed in *C:\Civil 3D Projects\Learning Data Shortcuts\Ascent Phase 1*. In Windows Explorer, verify that the *Civil 3D* folder structure was created for this project, as shown on the right in Figure 2–11.

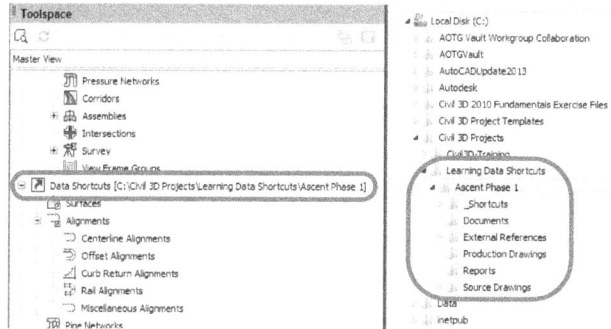

Figure 2–11

5. Create another new shortcuts folder. In the *Manage* tab>Data Shortcuts panel, click [icon] (New Shortcuts Folder).

6. In the New Data Shortcut Folder dialog box, type **Ascent Phase 2** for the name and select the **Use project template** option. Click **OK** to close the dialog box.

   You now have two projects in the working folder: *Ascent Phase 1* and *Ascent Phase 2*, as shown in Figure 2–12.

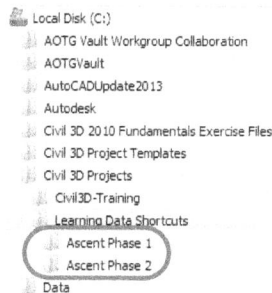

Figure 2–12

Task 3 - Set up *Shortcuts* folder.

Setting the shortcut folder specifies the project path for Data Shortcuts. The path to the current *Data Shortcuts* folder (also known as the project folder) is specified in the Toolspace, *Prospector* tab, in the *Data Shortcuts* collection. The project folder typically contains both Data Shortcuts and source objects for data references.

1. Continue working with the drawing from the previous task.

2. In the *Manage* tab>Data Shortcuts panel, click ⬚ (Set Shortcuts Folder).

3. The current *Data Shortcut* folder is indicated by a green circle with a checkmark. Select **Ascent Phase 1** to make it current and click **OK**, as shown in Figure 2–13.

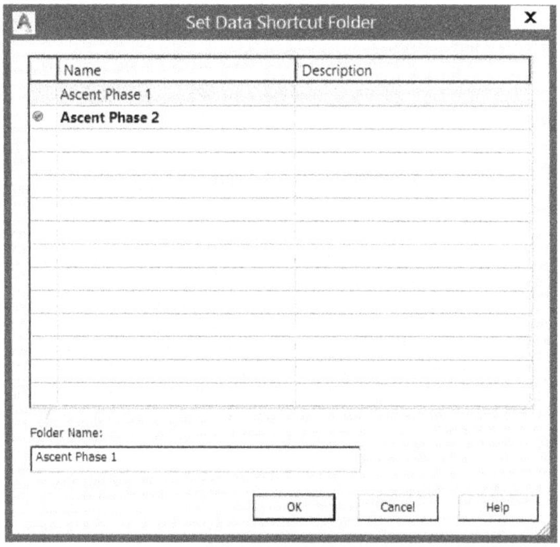

Figure 2–13

4. In the Toolspace, *Prospector* tab, right-click on Data Shortcuts and select **Associate Project to Current Drawing**, as shown in Figure 2–14.

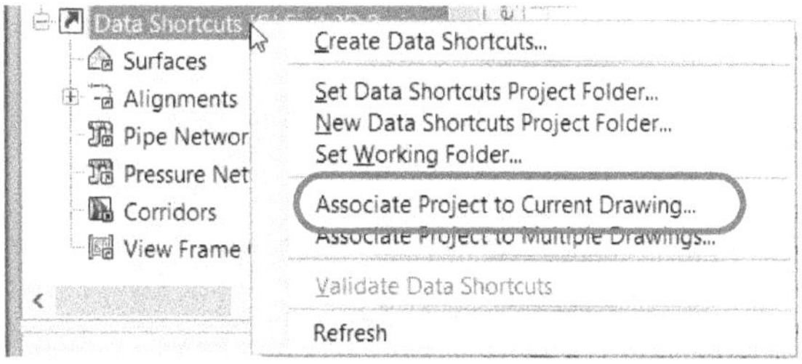

Figure 2–14

5. Verify that **Ascent Phase 1** is the selected project. Click **OK**.

Practice 2b

Manage File Sizes with Data Shortcuts

Practice Objective

- Create Data Shortcuts from objects in a drawing to share with other team members.

Estimated time for completion: 20 minutes

In this practice you will walk through the steps of creating project-based *Data Shortcuts* folders. It simulates a situation in which some design work has been done and you now need to share elements of the design with team members.

Task 1 - Create Data Shortcuts.

1. Continue working with the drawing from the previous practice or open **DS-A1-Shortcuts.dwg**.

2. In the Toolspace, *Prospector* tab, verify that the Data Shortcuts points to the correct folder, as shown in Figure 2–15.

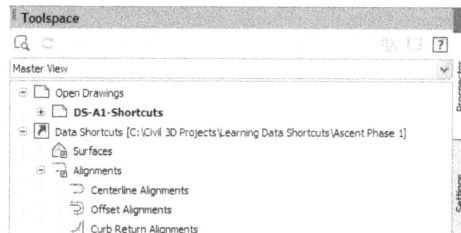

Figure 2–15

3. In the *Manage* tab>Data Shortcuts panel, click (Create Data Shortcuts).

4. If you receive a message that the drawing has not yet been saved, click **OK**. Save the drawing and start the **Create Data Shortcuts** command again.

5. In the Create Data Shortcuts dialog box, a list of all of the available objects for use in shortcuts displays. Select **Surfaces, Alignments, and Corridors** (as shown in Figure 2–16), and then click **OK**.

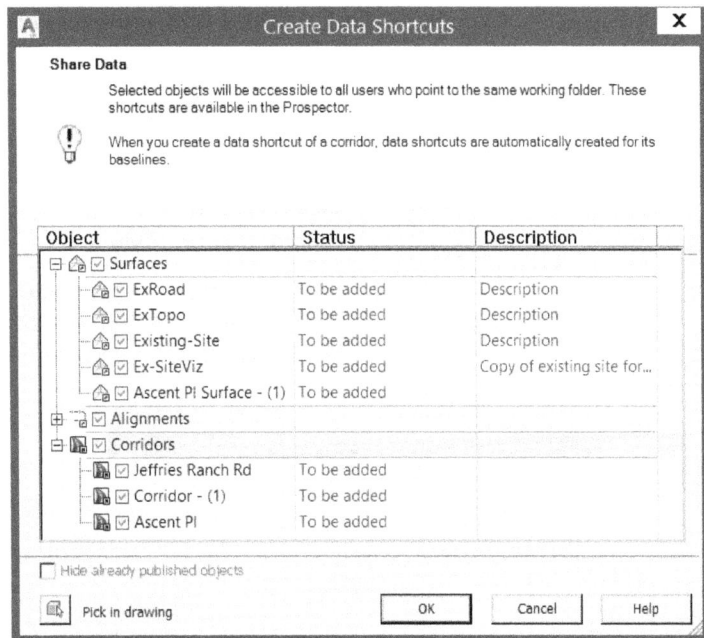

Figure 2–16

6. You have now created shortcuts for the surfaces, alignments, and corridors. This means that if the shortcuts and drawings are in a shared network folder, anyone on the network has access to these AutoCAD Civil 3D objects.

   Note that in the Toolspace, *Prospector* tab, under the *Data Shortcuts* and *Surfaces* collections, you can now access all of the surfaces. In the list view, the source filename and source path display, as shown in Figure 2–17.

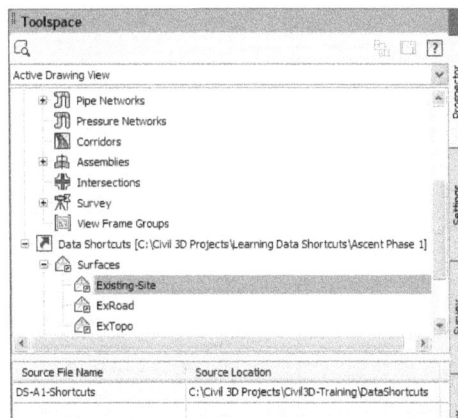

Figure 2–17

7. Save the drawing, but do not close it.

Task 2 - Data-reference Data Shortcuts.

1. Start a new drawing from **_AutoCAD Civil 3D (Imperial) NCS.dwt**. Save the file as **Reference File.dwg**.

2. In the Toolspace, *Prospector* tab, ensure that *Data Shortcuts* point to the *C:\Civil 3D Projects\Learning Data Shortcuts\ Ascent Phase 1* folder.

3. In the Toolspace, *Prospector* tab, right-click on **Data Shortcuts** and select **Associate Project to Current Drawing**, as shown in Figure 2–18.

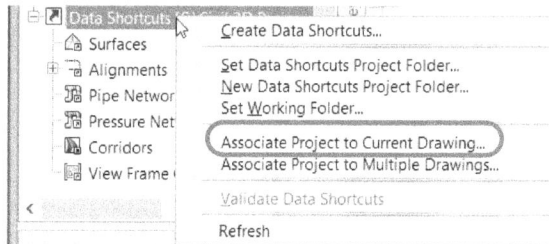

Figure 2–18

4. In the Toolspace, *Prospector* tab, under the *Data Shortcuts* collection, expand the *Surfaces* collection (if not already expanded) and expand the *Alignments>Centerline Alignments* collection, as shown in Figure 2–19.

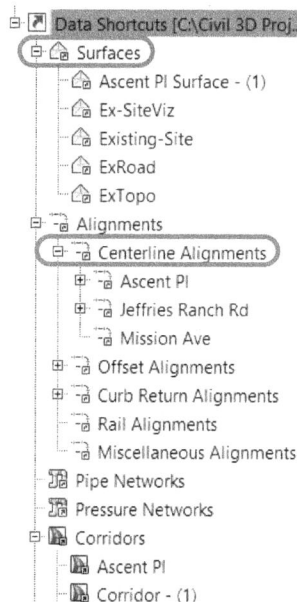

Figure 2–19

5. Under the *Surfaces* collection, select the surface **Existing-Site**, right-click, and select **Create Reference**, as shown in Figure 2–20.

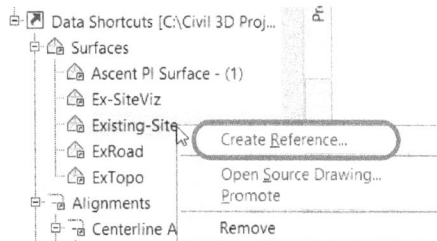

Figure 2–20

6. In the Create Surface Reference dialog box, do the following:

- Type **ExSurface** for the *Name*.
- Type **Data referenced surface** for the *Description*.
- Select **Contours 5' and 25' (Background)** for the *Style*, as shown in Figure 2–21.
- Click **OK** to close the dialog box.
- Type **ZE** and press <Enter> to display the surface reference.

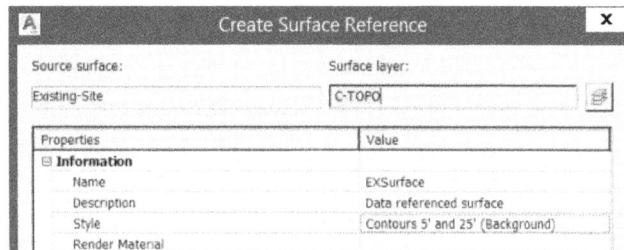

Figure 2–21

7. You will now create a data reference to the alignment. In the *Alignments* collection, right-click on **Ascent PI** and select **Create Reference**.

8. In the Create Alignment Reference dialog box, accept the default for the *Name*. Type **Data referenced alignment** for the *Description*. Set the *Alignment style* to **Layout** and set the *Alignment label set* to **Major and Minor only**. Click **OK** when done, as shown in Figure 2–22.

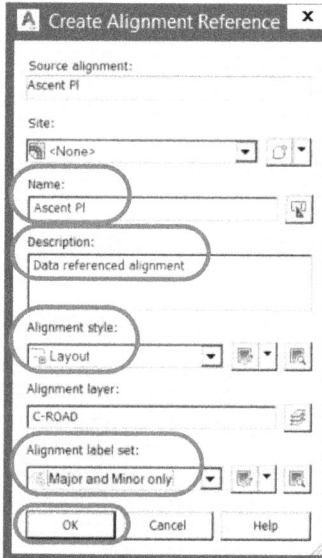

Figure 2–22

9. Zoom in to the end of the Ascent PI alignment, as shown in Figure 2–23.

Figure 2–23

10. Create a data reference to the corridor: in the *Corridors* collection, right-click on **Ascent PI** and select **Create Reference**. Accept all of the defaults and then click **OK**.

11. In Model Space, select the **Ascent PI** referenced alignment.

Note that there are no grips and you cannot graphically redefine this alignment. However, you can add labels using the contextual tab.

12. In the contextual tab>Labels & Tables panel, expand Add Labels and select **Station/Offset - Fixed Point**, as shown in Figure 2–24.

Figure 2–24

13. When prompted to select a point, select the end point of Ascent PI, as shown on the left in Figure 2–25. Select the label and move its location so that it is easier to read, as shown on the right. Note that the station is 6+98.72.

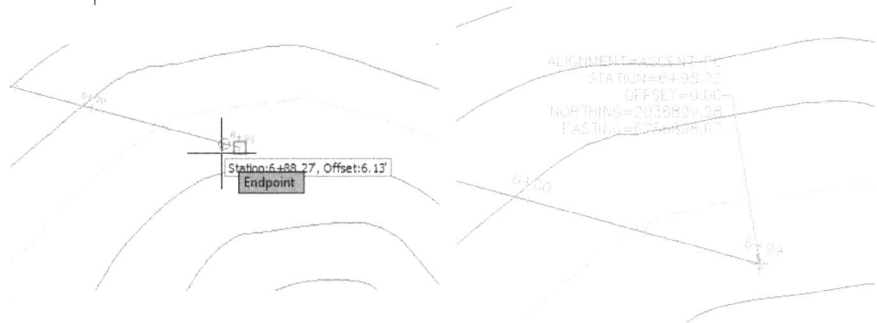

Figure 2–25

14. In the Toolspace, *Prospector* tab, expand the *Surfaces* and *ExSurface* collections, as shown on the left in Figure 2–26. Note that it does not contain the definition elements that might otherwise be displayed in a surface that is not data-referenced, as shown on the right. Therefore, you cannot edit or make design changes to a referenced surface.

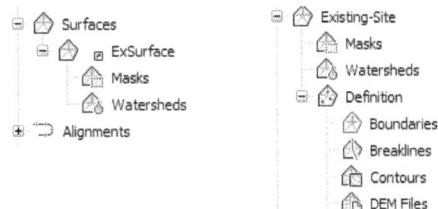

Figure 2–26

15. Save the drawing but do not close it.

Task 3 - Revise original referenced object.

1. In the Toolspace, *Prospector* tab, ensure that *Data Shortcuts* point to the *C:\Civil 3D Projects\Learning Data Shortcuts\Ascent Phase 1* folder.

2. Ensure that the **Master View** is enabled in Toolspace so that all of the drawings that are loaded display. Select **DS-A1-Shortcuts**, right-click and select **Switch to**, as shown in Figure 2–27. **DS-A1-Shortcuts.dwg** is now the current drawing. However, if you had closed the drawing, you need to open **DS-A1-Shortcuts.dwg**.

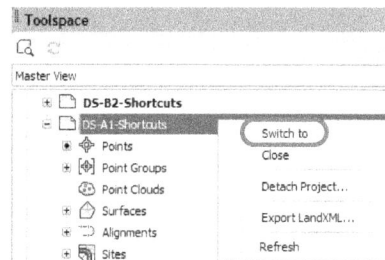

Figure 2–27

3. Zoom into the end of Ascent Pl to get a better view of the cul-de-sac.

4. You will now change the length of this alignment. In Model Space, select the alignment, select the grip that signifies the end of the alignment, and move it to the intersection where it crosses the cul-de-sac bulb, as shown in Figure 2–28.

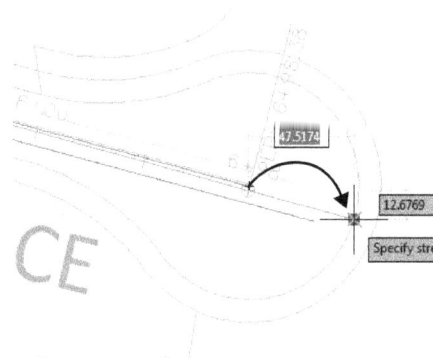

Figure 2–28

5. In the contextual tab>Modify panel, select **Alignment Properties**, as shown in Figure 2–29.

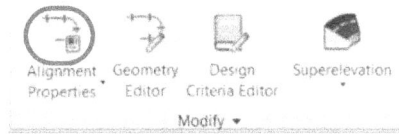

Figure 2–29

6. In the *Station Control* tab in the Alignment Properties - Ascent PI dialog box, set the reference point Station to **100**, as shown in Figure 2–30. A warning displays prompting you that changing the station will affect objects and data that have already been created. Click **OK** to dismiss the warning. Click **OK** to close the Alignment Properties dialog box.

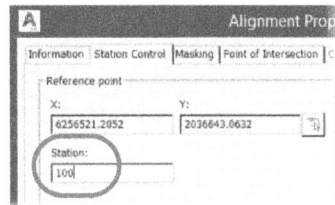

Figure 2–30

7. Save the drawing. This will cause the Data Shortcut to update.

*If you closed the drawing in Step 8, open the drawing **Reference File.dwg**.*

8. If you are continuing with the drawing from the previous task, ensure that the Master view is enabled in the Toolspace so that you can see all of the drawings that are loaded. Select **Reference File**, right-click, and select **Switch to**. **Reference File.dwg** is now the current drawing.

9. In the Status Bar, you should see (Data Shortcut Reference), as shown on the left in Figure 2–31. To synchronize your current drawing, right-click on see (Data Shortcut Reference) and select **Synchronize**, as shown on the right in Figure 2–31.

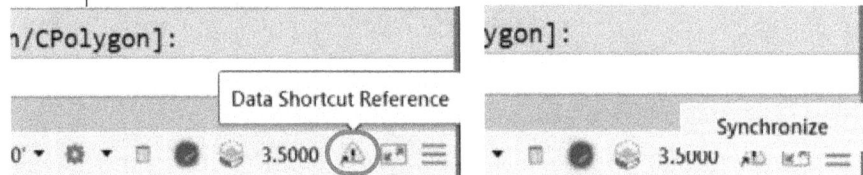

Figure 2–31

10. Alternatively, in the Toolspace, *Prospector* tab, select the alignment **Ascent PI** in the *Alignments* collection. Right-click and select **Synchronize**, as shown in Figure 2–32.

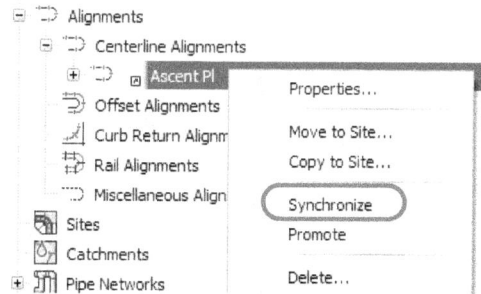

Figure 2–32

11. Note that the alignment has updated geographic information, as shown in Figure 2–33. The end of the alignment has been extended to intersect the cul-de-sac bulb, and the station label is updated to reflect the change to the original alignment design.

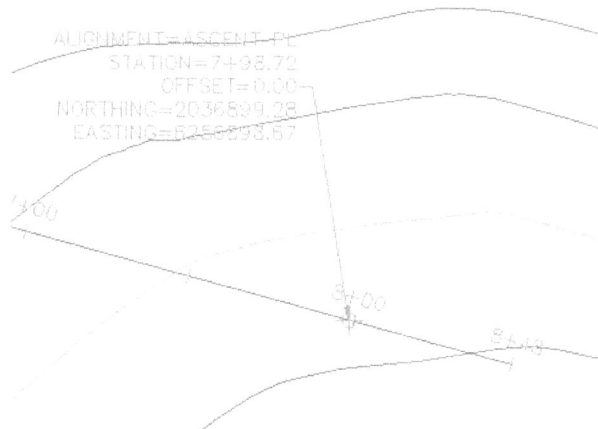

Figure 2–33

12. Save the drawing.

Practice 2c

Share Projects with Team Members Outside the Office Network

Practice Objective

- Create a transmittal package to send to other design professionals on the project team, which includes all of the referenced object drawings, XREFs, and other required files.

Estimated time for completion: 5 minutes

1. Continue working with the previously opened drawing **DS-B2-Shortcuts.dwg**.

2. Expand ![A C3D] (Application Menu), expand Publish, and select **eTransmit**, as shown in Figure 2–34. If a Warning dialog box opens stating that the current drawing is not saved, click **Yes** to save it.

Figure 2–34

3. In the eTransmit dialog box, click **Transmittal Setups**, as shown in Figure 2–35.

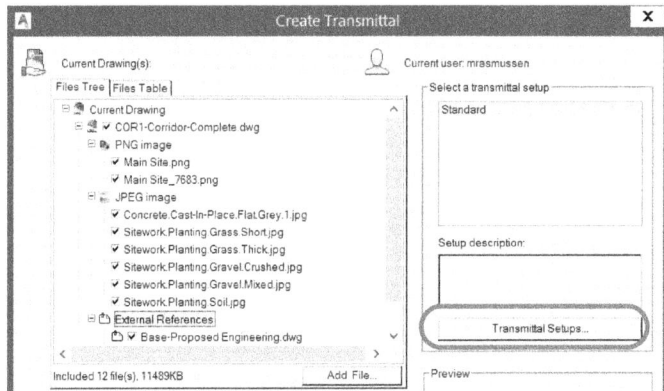

Figure 2–35

4. In the Transmittal Setups dialog box, select the **Standard** setup and click **Modify.**

5. In the Modify Transmittal Setup dialog box, accept the default for *Transmittal file folder.* Expand the Transmittal filename drop-down list and select **Prompt for a filename**. Select the **Keep files and folders as is** option. In the *Include options* area, select all of the options, as shown in Figure 2–36. Accept the remaining defaults and click **OK** to close the dialog box.

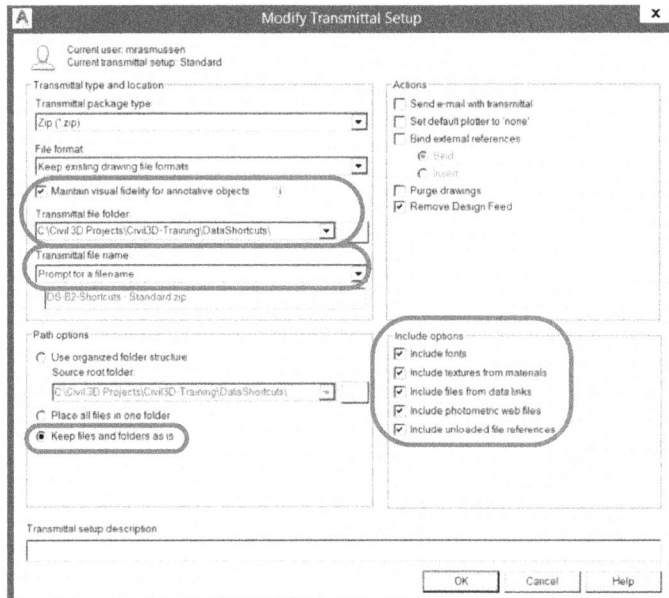

Figure 2–36

6. Close the Transmittal Setups dialog box.

7. Click **OK** to close the Create Transmittal dialog box and create the transmittal.

8. When prompted for the filename for the transmittal file, accept the default and save it. The AutoCAD Civil 3D software will create a compressed file of all of the relevant data.

Chapter Review Questions

1. In the AutoCAD Civil 3D workflow, what are the two main methods of project collaboration (or the sharing of intelligent AutoCAD Civil 3D design data)?

   a. Windows Explorer and X-refs.

   b. Data shortcuts and Vault references.

   c. X-refs and Data shortcuts.

   d. Vault references and X-refs.

2. Why would you want to use Vault references over Data Shortcuts?

   a. Added security and version control.

   b. Permit more people to have access.

   c. It works more like Land Desktop.

   d. It works better with multiple offices.

3. When sharing data in a project collaboration environment, what is the recommended number of levels into which the data should be broken?

   a. 1 level

   b. 2 levels

   c. 3 levels

   d. 4 levels

4. How can you edit an object referenced through Data Shortcuts?

   a. Open the source drawing.

   b. With grips.

   c. Using the Panorama view.

   d. You cannot.

5. What is the file format that Data Shortcuts use to share design data between drawing files?

   a. .SHP

   b. .DWT

   c. .DWG

   d. .XML

Command Summary

Button	Command	Location
	Create Data Shortcuts	**Ribbon:** *Manage* tab>Data Shortcuts panel **Command Prompt:** CreateDataShortcuts
	New Shortcuts Folder	**Ribbon:** *Manage* tab>Data Shortcuts panel **Command Prompt:** NewShortcutsFolder
	Set Shortcuts Folder	**Ribbon:** *Manage* tab>Data Shortcuts panel **Command Prompt:** SetShortcutsFolder
	Set Working Folder	**Ribbon:** *Manage* tab>Data Shortcuts panel **Command Prompt:** SetWorkingFolder

Parcels

In this chapter you learn how to create parcels from a legal description using the AutoCAD® Civil 3D® **Lines** and **Curves** commands, and the transparent commands. Then you learn how to create a subdivision plan using specific design criteria. Labels and tables are added to the plan to correctly communicate the design to contractors and other stakeholders.

Learning Objectives in this Chapter

- Draw Parcels from a legal description.
- Create parcels from objects in the drawing or in an external reference file.
- Change the properties and display order of parcels to ensure that the correct linetype and color display.
- Subdivide parcels into smaller lots using various tools.
- Change the parcel numbers so that they are numbered in order.
- Change area, line, and curve labels into tags and display in a table for better readability of the drawing.
- Create predefined reports to share useful engineering data about the parcels created in the drawing.
- Add annotation to parcels to communicate line bearing, distances, and areas for each lot.

3.1 Lines and Curves

Often, the first thing that has to be drawn up is the legal description of the property being subdivided. Designers need to enter into the computer, in the form of lines and curves, what they are given in a text description. The AutoCAD Civil 3D software makes this task easy with the many options under the **Lines** and **Curves** commands in the *Home* tab>Draw panel. Expanding the lines or curves commands displays several new options that are not found in the AutoCAD® software, as shown in Figure 3–1.

Figure 3–1

A second option is to use transparent commands. These are similar to Object Snaps because they can only be accessed while in another command. Once the required command has been started, you can click the **Transparent** tool or type an apostrophe letter combination in the Command Line for the required **Transparent** command. The benefit to using these to draw parcels over the **Lines** and **Curves** options (shown in Figure 3–1) is that a **Polyline** command can be used to create one entity rather than many individual lines that would need to be joined later.

Transparent Commands

Icon	Command Line	Description
	'AD	**Angle Distance:** Specifies a point location at an angle and distance from a known point and direction.
	'BD	**Bearing Distance:** Specifies a point location at a bearing and distance from a known point (or the last point occupied).
	'ZD	**Azimuth Distance:** Specifies a point location at an azimuth and distance from a known point (or the last point occupied).
	'DD	**Deflection Distance:** Specifies a point location at an angle and distance from a known point and previous direction.
	'NE	**Northing Easting:** Specifies a point location using northing and easting coordinates.
	'GN	**Grid Northing Grid Easting:** Specifies a point location using a grid northing and grid easting. (Note: You must have the drawing zone, coordinate system, and transformations set for grids.)
	'LL	**Latitude Longitude:** Specifies a point location using latitude and longitude. (Note: You must have the drawing zone, coordinate system, and transformations set.)
	'PN	**Point Number:** Specifies a point location using a point number found in the drawing or active project.
	'PA	**Point Name:** Specifies a point location using a point name found in the drawing or active project.
	'PO	**Point Object:** Specifies a point location by picking any part of an existing COGO point in the drawing.
	'ZTP	**Zoom to Point:** Zooms to a point in the drawing or active project by specifying the point number or name.
	'SS	**Side Shot:** Specifies a point location at an angle and distance from a known point and direction (uses the last two entered points to set the reference line).

	'SO	**Station Offset:** Specifies a point location at a station and an offset from an alignment in the current drawing.
	.g	**Point Object Filter:** Specifies a point location by picking any part of an existing COGO point in the drawing.
	'STAE	**Profile Station from Plan:** Specifies a profile view point location by specifying an alignment station in plan and an elevation.
	'SSE	**Profile Station and Elevation from Plan:** Specifies a profile view point location by specifying a surface, an alignment station, and a point in plan view.
	'SPE	**Profile Station and Elevation from COGO Point:** Specifies a profile view point location by specifying a COGO point and an alignment station in plan view.
	'PSE	**Profile Station Elevation:** Specifies a profile view point location by specifying a station and an elevation.
	'PGS	**Profile Grade Station:** Specifies a profile view point location using grade and station values from a known point.
	'PGE	**Profile Grade Elevation:** Specifies a profile view point location using grade and elevation values from a known point.
	'PGL	**Profile Grade Length:** Specifies a profile view point location using grade and length values from a known point (or the last point occupied).
	'MR	**Match Radius:** Specifies a radius equal to that of an existing object.
	'ML	**Match Length:** Specifies a length equal to that of an existing object.
	'CCALC	**Curve Calculator:** Calculates curve parameters based on input.

Practice 3a

Estimated time for completion: 20 minutes

Beginning a Subdivision Project

Practice Objective

- Draw a parcel from a legal description.

In this practice you will use the legal description below to draw a parcel. Later you will create a parcel from the linework.

From the **POINT OF BEGINNING**; thence, S 00° 26' 42.2" W for a distance of 922.4138 feet to a point on a line. Thence, S 00° 24' 20.8" W for a distance of 508.3493 feet to a point on a line. Thence, S 66° 03' 35.8" W for a distance of 92.1845 feet to the beginning of a curve.

Said curve turning to the right through 42° 35' 49.2", having a radius of 627.1788 feet, and whose long chord bears S 87° 21' 30.4" W for a distance of 455.6165 feet to the beginning of another curve.

Said curve turning to the left through an angle of 19° 13' 40.4", having a radius of 154.4828 feet, and whose long chord bears N 80° 57' 25.2" W for a distance of 51.6000 feet.

Thence, S 89° 25' 44.6" W for a distance of 724.9442 feet to a point on a line. Thence, N 00° 11' 09.9" E for a distance of 1904.2647 feet to a point on a line. Thence, S 61° 50' 15.3" E for a distance of 135.9034 feet to a point on a line. Thence, S 64° 05' 35.8" E for a distance of 77.8201 feet to a point on a line. Thence, S 78° 09' 29.2" E for a distance of 63.8821 feet to a point on a line. Thence, S 66° 23' 19.5" E for a distance of 379.2248 feet to a point on a line. Thence, S 66° 17' 17.4" E for a distance of 278.5122 feet to a point on a line. Thence S 84° 58' 37.7" E a distance of 466.8116 feet to the **POINT OF BEGINNING.**

Task 1 - Draw a parcel from a legal description.

1. Open **PCL1-A1-Parcels.dwg** from the *C:\Civil 3D Projects\ Civil3D-Training\Parcels* folder.

2. Start the **Line** command. For the starting point, type **6257490.0191,2037127.1292**.

---

*The legal description at
the beginning of this
practice was used to
find the bearings and
distances to type.*

3. In the Transparent Command toolbar, click (Bearing Distance).

4. For the first line, type the following:
    *   *Quadrant:* **3** (for the southwest quadrant)
    *   *Bearing:* **0.26422**
    *   *Distance:* **922.4138**

    Stay in the **Line** command with the **Bearing Distance Transparent** command running for the next few lines.

5. For the next two line segments, use the following values:

Quadrant	Bearing	Distance
3	0.24208	508.3493
3	66.03358	92.1845

6. Press <Esc> twice to end the command.

7. In the *Home* tab>Draw panel, click (Create Curve from End of Object). Select the last line that was drawn using the **Bearing Distance** command.

8. From the command options, select **Radius**. Set the radius to **627.1788**.

9. From the command options, select **Chord**. Set the chord length to **455.6165**.

10. In the *Home* tab>Draw panel, click (Create Reverse or Compound Curve). Select the last curve drawn.

11. From the command options, select **Reverse**. Set the radius to **154.4828**.

12. From the command options, select **Chord**. Set the chord length to **51.6**.

13. Start the **Line** command. For the starting point, pick the endpoint of the last arc drawn.

14. In the Transparent Command toolbar, click (Bearing Distance).

15. For the remaining line segments:, use the following values:

Quadrant	Bearing	Distance
3	89.25446	724.9442
1	0.11099	1904.2647
2	61.50153	135.9034
2	64.05358	77.8201
2	78.09292	63.8821
2	66.23195	379.2248
2	66.17174	278.5122

16. Press <Esc> once to exit the **Bearing Distance** command. Hold <Ctrl> as you right-click and select **Endpoint**, select the starting point of the parcel to close on the point of beginning.

17. Start the **Polyline Edit** command by typing **PE**. In the model, select one of the lines or curves you just created and press <Enter> to turn it into a polyline.

This prevents closure errors from occuring later.

18. Select the **Join** option and then select all of the lines and curves you just created. Press <Enter> to create one closed polyline. Press <Esc> to end the command.

19. Save the drawing.

3.2 Introduction to Parcels

A Site under development (as shown in Figure 3–2), is the starting point for defining smaller parcels. The development's zoning agreement or covenants determine the size, setback, and other criteria for the new parcels. If a parcel is residential, there might be restrictions affecting minimum parcel areas, setbacks, and where to locate a house. If it is a commercial property, there might be restrictions or specific mandates for access, traffic control, parking spaces, etc. The **Parcel Layout** commands are used for subdividing larger parcels.

Figure 3–2

Sites, parcels, and alignments are closely related. Each can exist by itself and you do not need to have any alignments associated with the parcels. However, you often start with a site boundary and then divide the site into smaller parcels by placing alignments within its boundary.

- Parcels are listed in the Toolspace, *Prospector* tab in the Sites branch, as shown in Figure 3–3.

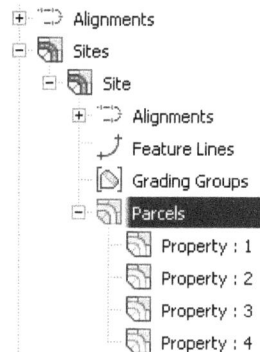

Figure 3–3

- When adding alignments to a site, the Parcels list is updated in the Toolspace, *Prospector* tab.

- As in all other AutoCAD Civil 3D objects, Parcel object layers are controlled in the *Object Layers* tab of the Drawing Settings dialog box, as shown in Figure 3–4.

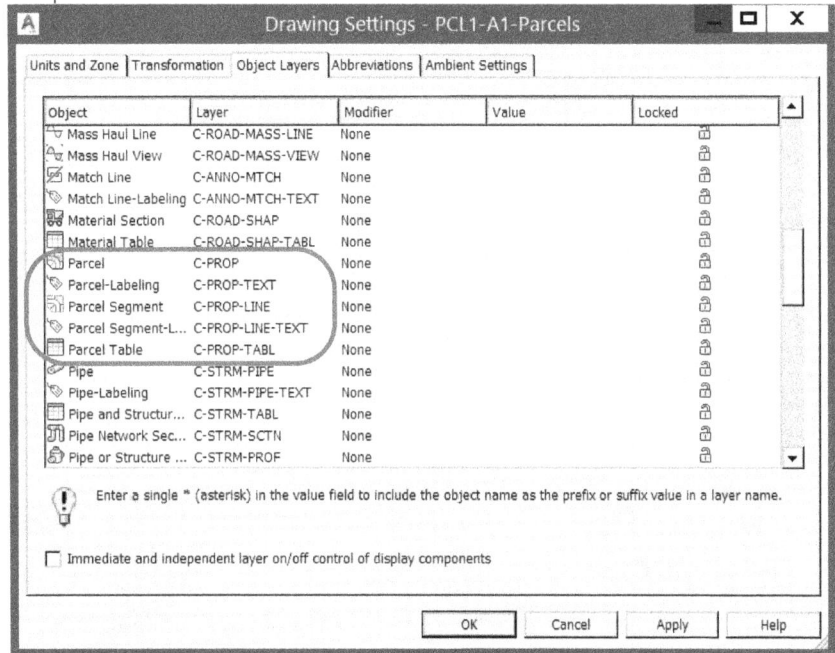

Figure 3–4

ROW Parcel

The right-of-way (ROW) parcel is related to the alignment and parcels. This special parcel represents land that is owned, maintained, and used for the community by a regulatory body (usually the local municipality or Department of Transportation). Typically, the ROW contains road, sidewalks, and utilities. The contents of the ROW depend on the covenants or agreements made before the site is developed. For example, in some cases the sidewalks and utilities might be located in an easement outside the road ROW.

- The AutoCAD Civil 3D software contains a **ROW** command, which creates a parcel using offsets from an alignment.

- A ROW parcel can represent the front yard definition of several potential parcels.

- While normal parcels automatically adjust to changes to an alignment, ROW parcels are static as shown in Figure 3–5. Therefore, you should only create ROW parcels after determining a final location for an alignment.

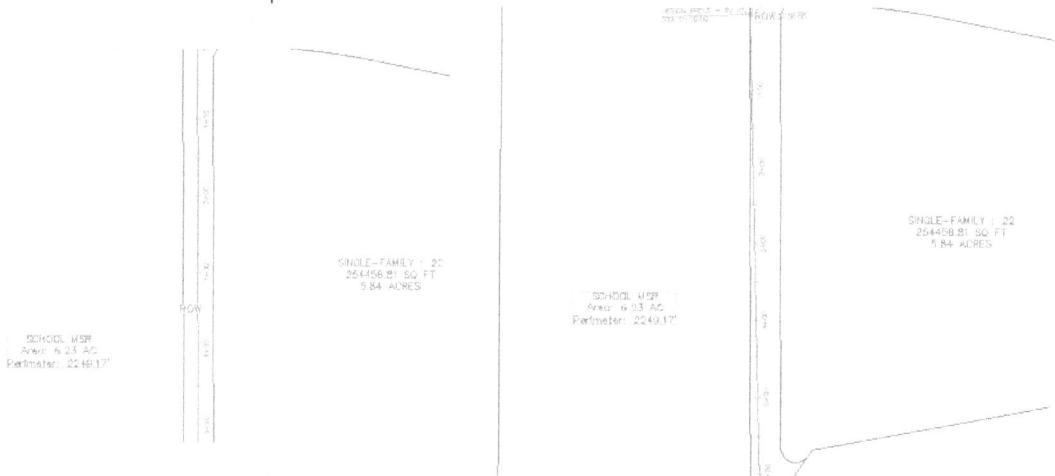

Figure 3–5

Parcel Style Display Order

Parcel segment display is controlled by parcel styles, and parcel lines can abut parcels with different styles. To open the Site Parcel Properties dialog box, select the *Parcels* collection (under *Sites*), right-click and select **Properties**, as shown in Figure 3–6.

Figure 3–6

You can select which parcel style should take precedence in the *Parcel style display order* area of the Site Parcel Properties dialog box, as shown in Figure 3–7. Placing the style for the overall parent tract (the Site Parcel Style) at the top of the list causes the outside parcel lines to display differently than those inside.

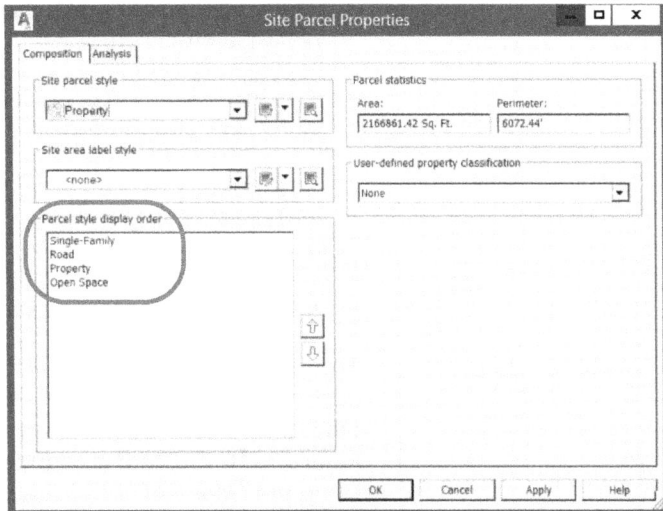

Figure 3–7

Parcel Properties

The properties of a parcel include its name, style, and an *Analysis* tab containing the parcel's area, perimeter, and point-of-beginning (POB). The Parcel Property's *Composition* tab displays the label style, area, and perimeter, as shown in Figure 3–8.

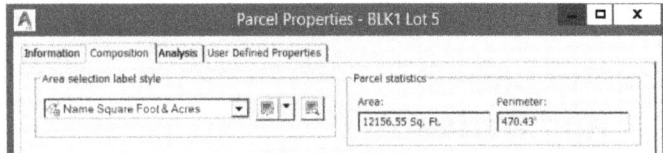

Figure 3–8

The *Analysis* tab contains a parcel boundary Inverse or Mapcheck analysis. In the upper right area of the tab, you can change the POB location and the analysis direction, as shown in Figure 3–9.

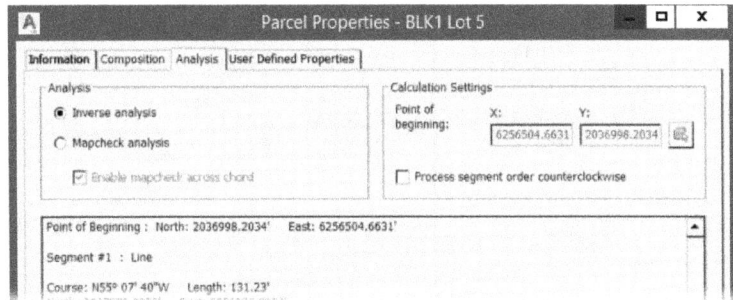

Figure 3–9

- The Mapcheck analysis precision is the same as the drawing distance precision.

- The Inverse report precision is set to the precision of the AutoCAD Civil 3D software (10 to 12 decimal places).

- The default direction of a Mapcheck or Inverse analysis is clockwise. You can change the direction to counter-clockwise if required.

- A POB can be any vertex on the parcel's perimeter.

The *User Defined Properties* tab contains site-specific details, such as the *Parcel Number, Parcel Address, Parcel Tax ID*, and other properties you might want to define, as shown in Figure 3–10. Custom properties can be assigned to a drawing by using the *User Defined Property Classifications* area in the Toolspace, *Settings* tab, under the *Parcels* collection.

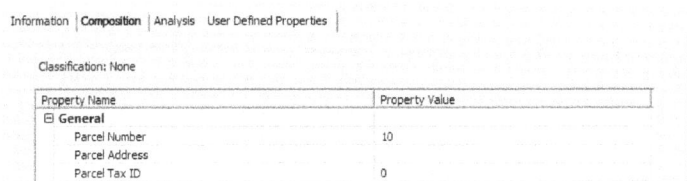

Figure 3–10

Parcel Labels and Styles

There are two types of parcel annotation: an area label for the parcel itself and the segments defining the parcel.

A parcel area label usually consists of a parcel's number or name, area, and perimeter, as shown in Figure 3–11. Most offices define their own parcel label styles. A parcel label style can include several additional parcel properties, address, PIN, Site name, etc. In the AutoCAD Civil 3D software, you select a parcel by selecting a parcel area label, not the parcel segments.

Figure 3–11

Create Parcels from Objects

The AutoCAD Civil 3D software can create parcels from AutoCAD objects, such as closed polylines and closed sequences of lines and arcs. Avoid gaps, multiple polyline vertices at the same location, and polylines that double-back over themselves, which might lead to errors in parcel layouts.

These objects can be selected in the current drawing or from an XREF. Note that AutoCAD Civil 3D parcel lines in an XREF cannot be selected (only lines, arcs, and polylines can be selected). Additionally, AutoCAD Civil 3D parcels created from AutoCAD objects do not maintain a relationship to the objects after creation.

Creating Right-of-Way Parcels

Once a site contains property that has been defined as a parcel and alignments have been generated, you are ready to start creating subdivision plans. One command that can speed up the process is **Parcels>Create ROW**. It automatically creates Right-of-Way parcels based on alignment setbacks.

ROW parcels do not automatically update when alignments change. Therefore, you might want to create ROWs after you are certain where you want the alignments to be for this alternative.

Hint: Multiple Alternatives in the Same Drawing

Sites enable you to organize alignments, parcels, and related data into separate containers, so that parcel lines from one site alternative do not clean up with parcel lines in others. However, sites do not offer layer or other kind of visibility control. Therefore, if you intend to have multiple parcel layout alternatives in the same drawing, you should consider placing parcel area labels and parcel segments on different layers.

Practice 3b

Create Parcels From Objects

Practice Objective

- Create parcels from objects in the drawing or external reference file.

Estimated time for completion: 15 minutes

Task 1 - Create a Site parcel from objects.

1. Continue working with the drawing from the previous practice or open **PCL1-B1-Parcels.dwg**.

2. In the *Home* tab>Create Design panel, expand **Parcel** and select **Create Parcels from Objects**, as shown in Figure 3–12.

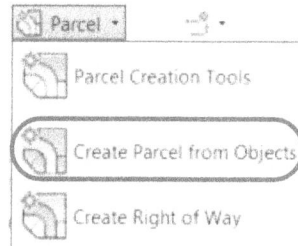

Figure 3–12

3. In the model, select the polyline that represent the property boundary and press <Enter>.

4. In the Create Parcels dialog box, set the following parameters, as shown in Figure 3–13, and then click **OK**.

- *Site:* **Site 1**
- *Parcel style:* **Property**
- *Area Label style:* **Name Area & Perimeter**
- Select **Automatically add segment labels**.
- *Parcel line segment label style:* **(Span) Bearing and Distance with Crows Feet**.
- Select **Erase existing entities**.

One parcel will be created with the parameters entered.

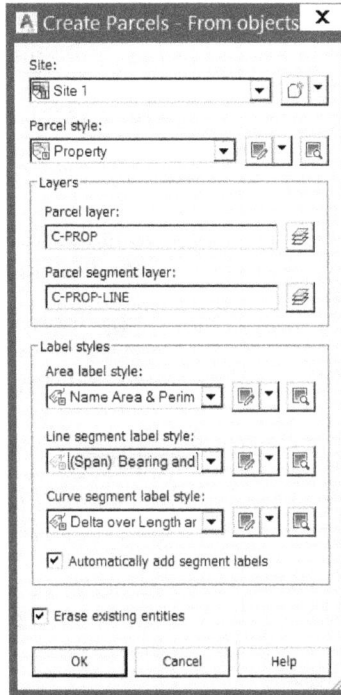

Figure 3–13

5. In the Toolspace, *Prospector* tab, expand the current drawing and select the **Sites>Site1>Parcels** node, as shown in Figure 3–14.

Note: If the + is not displayed next to Parcels, press <F5> to refresh the Toolspace, Prospector tab view.

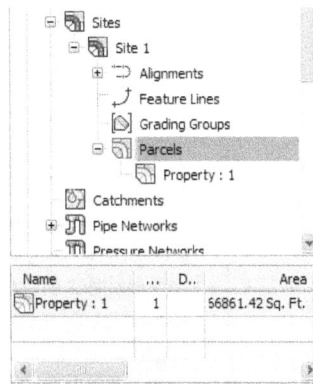

Figure 3–14

Task 2 - Create a new site and parcel from referenced objects.

You have received a drawing from the Land planning department that displays the street layout and different parcels. Using this plan, you will create parcels from XREF objects.

1. Continue working with the drawing from the previous task or open the file **PCL1-B2-Parcels.dwg**.

2. In the Toolspace, *Prospector* tab, right-click on the *Sites* collection and select **New**. Type **C3D Training** as the name and click **OK** to close the dialog box.

3. You now need to move the **Property:1** parcel from *Site 1* to the **C3D Training** site. Expand the *Site1* collection, expand the *Parcels* collection, right-click on the **Property:1** parcel and select **Move to Site**, as shown on the left in Figure 3–15.

4. In the Move to Site dialog box, select **C3D Training**, as shown on the right in Figure 3–15. Click **OK** to close the dialog box.

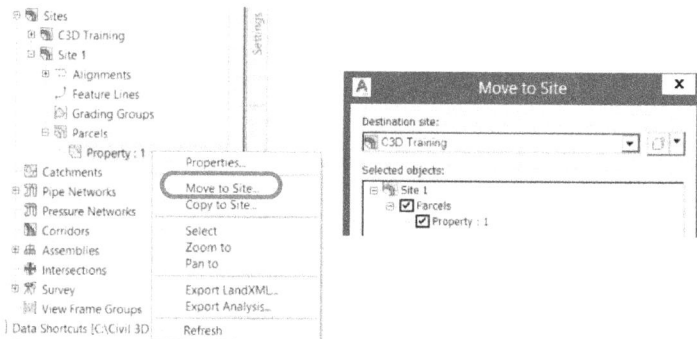

Figure 3–15

Note: To save time, the x-referenced drawing **Base-original Property**, has already been referenced. The zone and units for the project drawings were set. This enables you to geo reference the drawings using **Locate using Geographic data**, as shown in Figure 3–16.

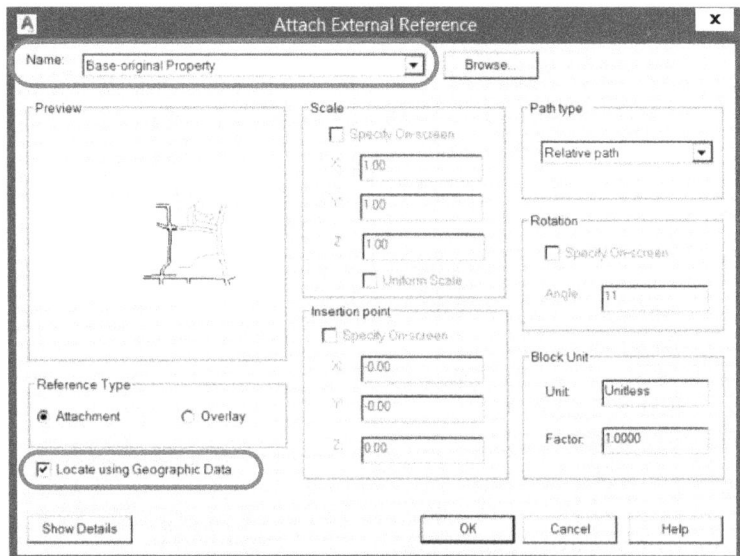

Figure 3–16

5. Thaw the layer **Base-originalProperty|A-Property-Future**.

6. In the *Home* tab>Create Design panel, expand **Parcel** and select **Create Parcels from Objects**. Select XREF from the command options.

7. Draw a rectangle around the linework to select it. Press <Enter> to end the **XREF selection** command.

8. In the Create Parcels - From Objects dialog box, verify that the Site name is **C3D Training** and accept the remaining defaults, as shown on the right in Figure 3–17. Click **OK** to close the dialog box.

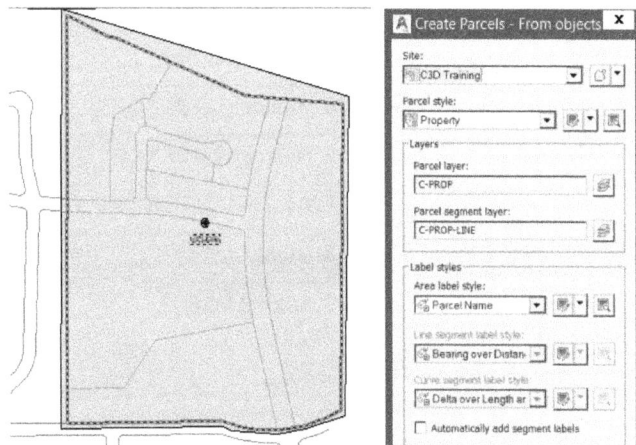

Figure 3–17

9. The project site has nine parcels. Select each parcel label and click (Parcel Properties) on the contextual *Parcels* tab>Modify panel.

10. In the Parcel Properties dialog box, in the *Information* tab, clear the **Use name template in parcel style** option, then rename the parcels according to Figure 3–18 and the table in Step 11.

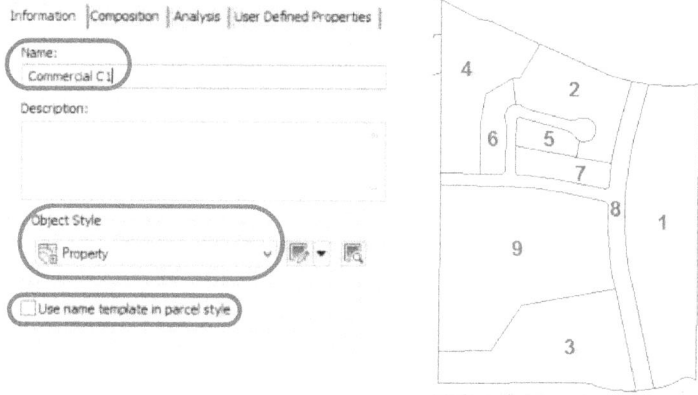

Note that your default parcel numbers might be different because the parcels are randomly numbered.

Figure 3–18

11. Using Figure 3–18 as a reference, set the parcel styles as follows:

Property Name	Style
1. Commercial C1	Property
2. Multi Family MF	Property
3. Municipal Reserve MR	Property
4. Pond PUL	Open Space
5. Residential BLK2 R1	Property
6. Residential BLK1 R1	Property
7. Residential BLK3 R1	Property
8. Right Of Way	Road
9. School MSR	Property

12. In the Toolspace, *Prospector* tab, expand *Sites*, expand the **C3D Training** site, right-click on *Parcels*, and select **Properties**, as shown in Figure 3–19.

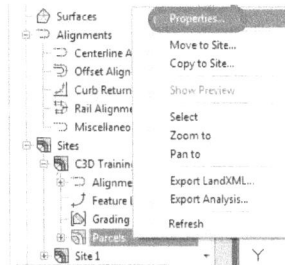

Figure 3–19

If the drawing does not look different after completing Step 13, you might need to adjust the draw order so that the XREF drawing is behind the existing drawing linework.

13. In the Site Parcel Properties dialog box, select **Property** in the *Parcel style display order* area, as shown in Figure 3–20.

Click ⬆ to move it up in the list.

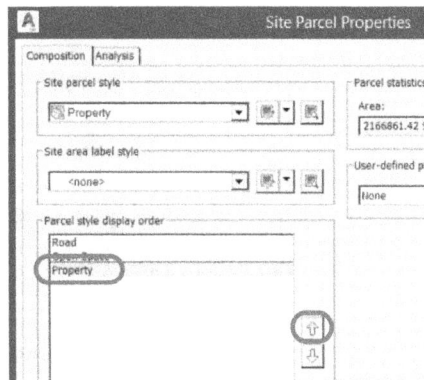

Figure 3–20

14. Click **OK**.

15. Save the drawing.

3.3 Creating and Editing Parcels by Layout Overview

In addition to creating parcels from polylines, arcs, and lines, the AutoCAD Civil 3D software can also intelligently create (and adjust) parcels using commands in the Parcel Layout Tools toolbar. To open the Parcel Layout Tools toolbar, expand Parcel in the Create Design panel, and select **Parcel Creation Tools**, as shown in Figure 3–21.

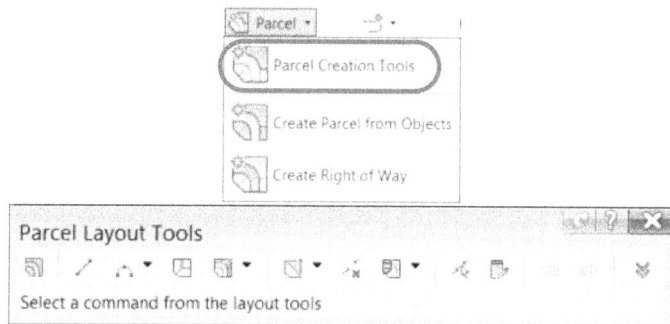

Figure 3–21

- ▧ (Create Parcel) assigns parcel creation settings, such as parcel type, labeling styles, and other parameters.

- The ⟋ **Line** and ⌒ ▾ **Curve** commands can be used to create individual line and curve parcel segments. Segments created with these tools are considered *fixed*.

- ⊞ (Draw Tangent - Tangent with No Curves) enables you to create a series of connected parcel line segments.

- The Parcel Sizing flyout (shown in Figure 3–22), contains a list of commands for creating and editing parcels. The methods used to create parcels include defining the last parcel segment by slide direction, slide angle, swing line, or freehand drawing of a parcel boundary. The most frequently used method is **Slide Line**.

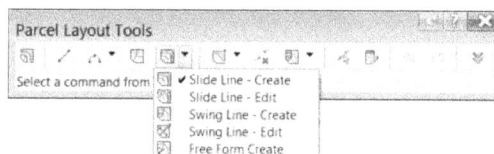

Figure 3–22

- The commands at the center of the toolbar (shown in Figure 3–23), enable you to further edit parcel segments. These commands include inserting or deleting PIs (points of intersection), deleting parcel segments, or creating or dissolving parcel unions.

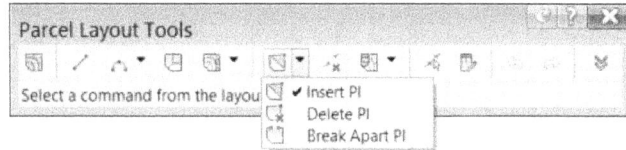

Figure 3–23

- (Pick Sub-Entity) enables you to select a parcel line and display its details in the Parcel Layout Parameters dialog box.

- (Sub-entity Editor) opens and closes the Parcel Layout Parameters dialog box.

- The next two commands enable you to **Undo** and **Redo** parcel edits. These can be used while the Parcel Layout Tools have been opened.

- The drop-down arrow (⤸) expands the toolbar to display the Parcel Creation parameters, as shown in Figure 3–24 (also accessible through the Command Settings of *CreateParcelByLayout* in the Toolspace, *Settings* tab).

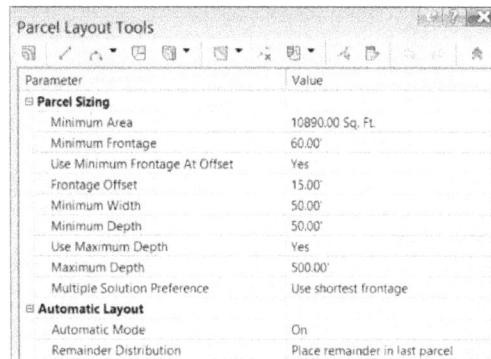

Figure 3–24

- The *Parcel Sizing* area sets the minimum area for parcels to be laid out. *Minimum Frontage* sets the minimum width of a parcel at the ROW or at a setback from the ROW.

- *Use Minimum Frontage At Offset* specifies whether or not to use frontage offset criteria.

- *Frontage Offset* sets the default value for the frontage offset from the ROW.

- *Minimum Width* sets the default minimum width at the frontage offset.

- *Minimum Depth* sets the minimum depth of new or existing parcels at the mid-point and is perpendicular to the frontage of the parcel.

- *Use Maximum Depth* specifies whether or not to use maximum depth criteria.

- *Maximum Depth* sets the maximum depth for new parcels or when editing parcels.

- *Multiple Solution Preference* specifies whether or not to use the shortest frontage or the smallest area when multiple solutions are encountered.

- *Automatic Layout* affects how parcel auto-sizing subdivides a parcel block.

3.4 Creating and Editing Parcels

The **Create Parcel by Layout** tools can help you to quickly create a subdivision plan. Although these tools can make your job easier and are faster than manual drafting, they are only effective in creating the last side of new parcels. Therefore, you might need to create additional (or adjust) parcel lines manually to guide the AutoCAD Civil 3D software to the best solution. For example, the area shown in Figure 3–25, requires you to create minimum 10,225 sq ft (0.23 acres) parcels.

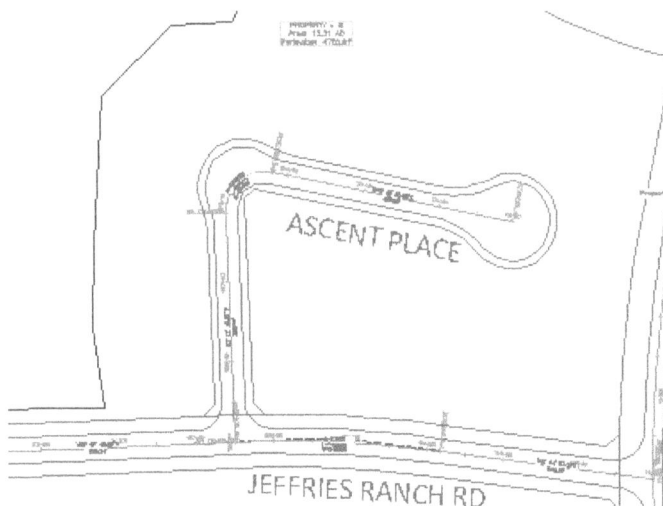

Figure 3–25

The back parcel lines (those along the west and south of the Cul-De-Sac area, and between Jeffries Ranch Rd and Ascent Place) were drawn manually and saved in a separate drawing file. Once inserted, they are used to guide the creation of the parcels next to Ascent Place. If you ask the AutoCAD Civil 3D software to automatically subdivide this area, the result is a total of 15 residential lot parcels, as shown in Figure 3–26.

Figure 3–26

The various creation and editing techniques available in the Create Parcel by Layout toolbar are as follows:

- Freehand

- Slide Line

- Swing Line

- Free Form Create

- Frontage

Freehand	The **Line** and **Curve** commands and ⊞ (Draw Tangent - Tangent with No Curves) enable you to create lot lines without having to specify an area. In contrast, the following commands all create parcels based on a specified area.
Slide Line	The **Slide Line - Create** command enables you to subdivide a larger parcel by creating new parcel lines that hold a specific angle relative to the Right-of-Way, such as 90° or a specific bearing or azimuth. The **Slide Line - Edit** command enables you to modify a parcel to a specified area while holding the same angle from the ROW or a specific bearing or azimuth. The commands are shown in Figure 3–27.

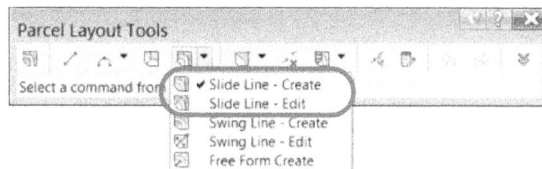

Figure 3–27

Swing Line	The **Swing Line - Create** command enables you to create a new parcel by creating a parcel segment that connects to a specified point, such as a property corner. The **Swing Line - Edit** command enables you to resize a parcel while specifying a lot corner. These commands are shown in Figure 3–28.

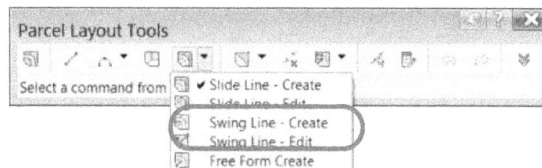

Figure 3–28

Free Form Create	The **Free Form Create** command enables you to create a new lot by specifying an area, attachment point and angle, or two attachment points.
Frontage	When using these routines, you are prompted to select a parcel interior point and trace its frontage geometry. This is a critical step. As you trace the frontage, the command creates a jig (heavy highlight) that recognizes the changing geometry of the frontage line work.

Practice 3c

Creating and Editing Parcels

Practice Objective

Estimated time for completion: 15 minutes

- Create and edit parcels to maximize the number of lots you can create with the required area and frontage.

You have three parcels zoned as single-family residential: Block 1 (1.31ac), Block2 (0.94ac), and Block3 (1.47ac). Your client, the land developer, requires you to maximize the number of lots in these three parcels, while noting the minimum area and frontages as required by the Land Use bylaws.

Task 1 - Create parcels by slide angle.

1. Continue working with the drawing from the previous practice or open **PCL1-C1-Parcels.dwg** from the *C:\Civil 3D Projects\ Civil3D-Training\Parcels* folder.

2. Select the preset view **Parcel-Create**.

3. In the *Home* tab>Create Design panel, expand **Parcel** and select **Parcel Creation Tools**. The Parcel Layout Tools toolbar displays as shown in Figure 3–29.

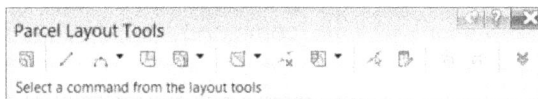

Figure 3–29

4. Click ☒ to expand the *Parcel Creation Tools* and enter the values shown in Figure 3–30. When finished, click ☒ to collapse the expanded toolbar.

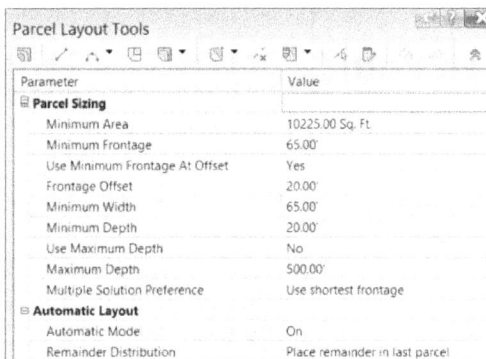

Figure 3–30

5. In the Parcel Layout Tools toolbar, expand ▾ and select **Slide Line - Create**, as shown in Figure 3–31.

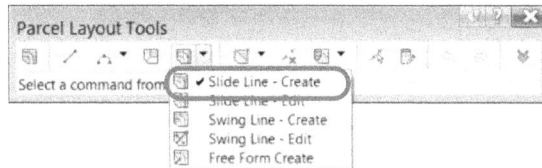

Figure 3–31

6. In the Create Parcels - Layout dialog box, set the following parameters, as shown in Figure 3–32:

- *Site:* **C3D Training**
- *Parcel style:* **Single-Family**
- *Area label style:* **Name Square Foot & Acres**

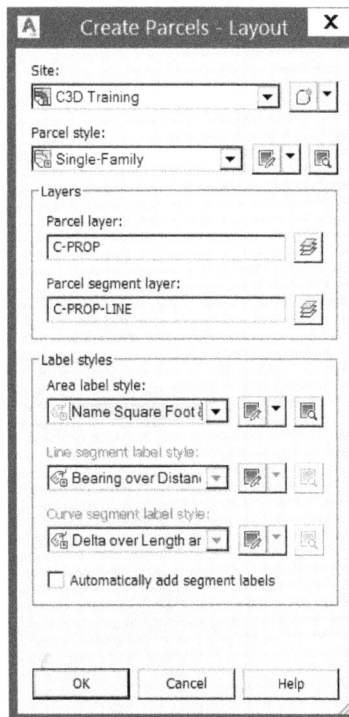

Figure 3–32

7. Click **OK** to accept the changes and close the dialog box.

8. When prompted to select the parcel to be subdivided, select the area label for parcel **RESIDENTIAL BLK1 R1**, as shown in Figure 3–33.

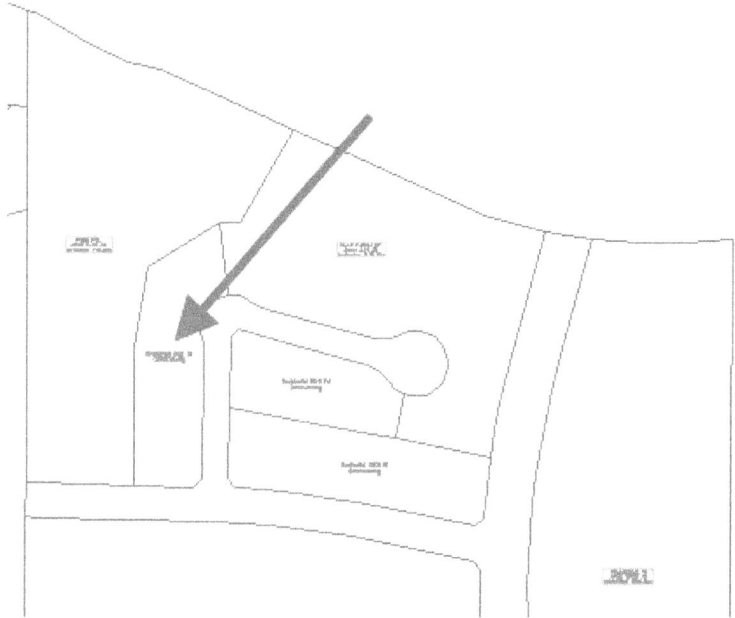

Figure 3–33

9. When you are prompted for the *starting point on frontage*, select the south end of the corner cut. Press <Ctrl>, right-click, and select **endpoint**. Then select the corner cut, **Pt 1**, shown in Figure 3–34.

10. When prompted for the *end point of the frontage*, set the end point of the property line to the north, **Pt 2**, as shown in Figure 3–34. Use the same process as the previous step to set the end point.

11. When prompted for the *angle of the property line* that will be used to define each lot, select a point east of the parcel near **Pt 3**, as shown in Figure 3–34. For the second point, press <Ctrl>, right-click, and select **Perpendicular**. Then select the line at Pt 4.

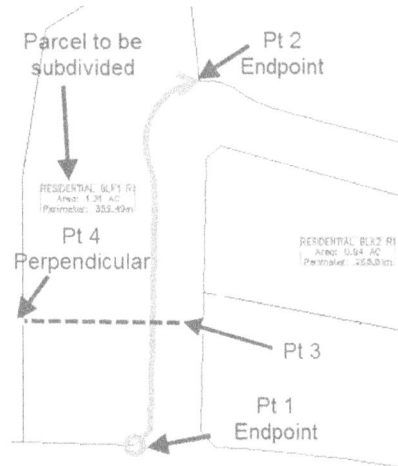

Figure 3–34

12. When prompted to *Accept results*, press <Enter>.

13. When prompted to select another parcel to subdivide, press <Esc> to end the command.

14. Save the drawing.

3.5 Renumbering Parcels

Creating parcels using the methods that have already been taught results in inconsistent parcel numbering. AutoCAD Civil 3D parcels can be renumbered individually using Parcel Properties, or in groups using **Modify>Parcel>Renumber/ Rename**.

This command enables you to specify a starting parcel number and the increment you want to have between parcels. (It also enables you to rename your parcels based on a different name template.) When renumbering, the command prompts you to identify parcels in the order in which you want to have them numbered. The Renumber/Rename Parcels dialog box is shown in Figure 3–35.

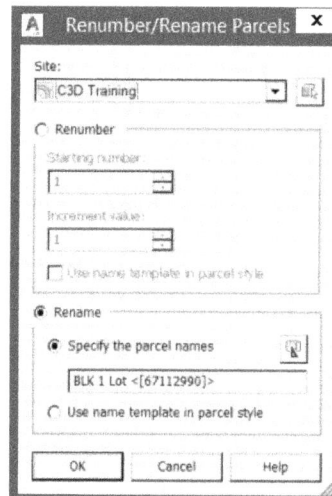

Figure 3–35

Practice 3d

Estimated time for completion: 15 minutes

Rename/Renumber Parcels

Practice Objective

- Renumber the lots created so that they are in sequential order.

Task 1 - Rename and renumber parcels.

1. Continue working with the drawing from the previous practice or open **PCL1-D1-Parcels.dwg**.

2. Select the preset view **Parcel-Create**.

3. Before renaming the newly created parcels, you need to change the label style of the original parcel.

    - Select the parcel label **RESIDENTIAL BLK1 R1**.

    - Right-click, and select **Edit Area Selection Label Style**, as shown in Figure 3–36.

    - Select **Name Square Foot & Acres** as the style and click **OK** to apply the changes and close the dialog box.

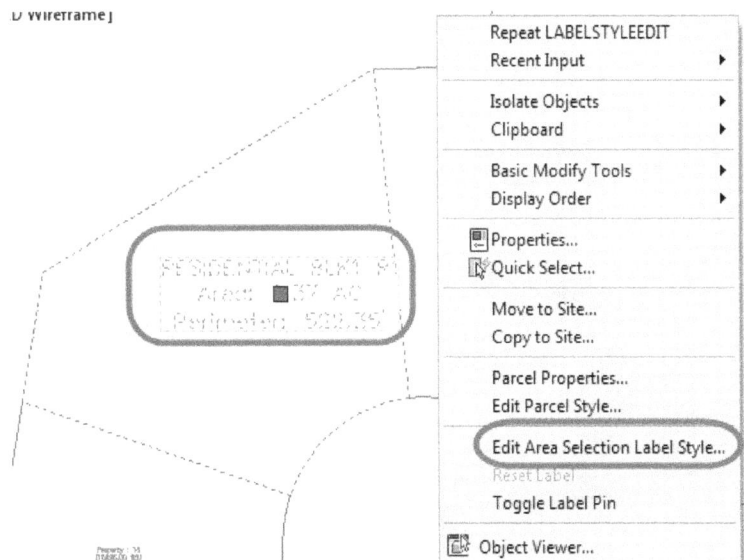

Figure 3–36

4. Rename and renumber the lots so that you have the same numbering system. In the *Modify* tab>Design panel, select **Parcel**. The *Parcel* contextual tab displays.

5. In the *Parcel* tab>Modify panel, click 🔲 (Renumber/Rename), as shown in Figure 3–37.

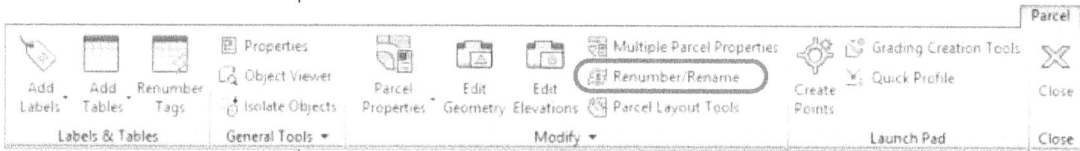

Figure 3–37

6. In the Renumber/Rename Parcel dialog box, set the following options, as shown in Figure 3–38:

   • Select **Rename**.

   • Select **Specify the parcel names**.

   • Click 🔲 (Click to edit name template).

Figure 3–38

7. In the Name Template dialog box, set the following options, as shown in Figure 3–39:

   • Type **BLK1 Lot** followed by a space in the *Name* field.

   • Expand the Property Fields drop-down list.

   • Select **Next Counter** and click **Insert**.

   • Click **OK** to apply the changes and close the dialog box.

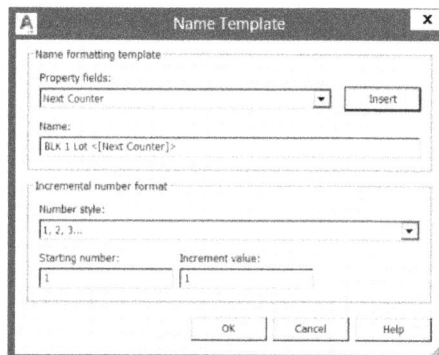

Figure 3–39

8. In the Renumber/Rename Parcel dialog box, click **OK** to accept the changes and close the dialog box.

9. When prompted for the points, select the two points shown in Figure 3–40. Press <Enter> to complete the selection and then press <Enter> again to exit the command.

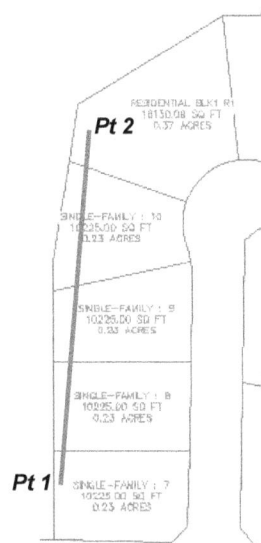

Figure 3–40

10. Save the drawing.

Task 2 - Edit parcels using Swing Line - Edit.

In this task, you adjust the last three lots of the parcel suddivision so that they are more marketable.

1. Continue working with the drawing from the previous task or open the file **PCL1-D2-Parcels.dwg**.

2. You first need to adjust the Lot line between Parcel 3 and Parcel 4. In the *Home* tab>Create Design panel, select **Parcel**. In the expanded list, select **Parcel Creation Tools**.

3. Expand the Parcel Layout Tools toolbar and ensure the *Minimum Area* is set to **10225**. Select **Swing Line - Edit**, as shown in Figure 3–41.

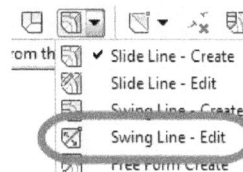

Figure 3–41

4. In the Create Parcel - Layout dialog box, set the following parameters:

   • *Site:* **C3D Training**
   • *Parcel Style:* **Single-Family**
   • *Area Label style:* **Name Square Foot & Acres**

5. You do not want to label segments, so do not enable this option. Click **OK** when done.

6. When prompted, complete the following, as shown in Figure 3–42:

   • To select the parcel line to adjust, select the parcel line between Lot 3 and Lot 4.
   • For the parcel to adjust, select **Lot 3**.
   • For the *start frontage*, select the bottom right corner of **Lot 3, pt1**.
   • For the *end of the frontage*, select the top right corner of **Lot 4, pt2**.
   • For the *swing point*, select the end point of **pt3**.
   • To accept the results, select **Yes**.

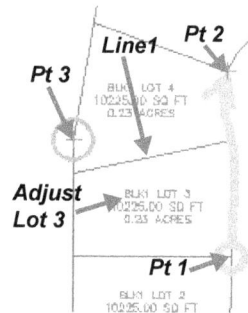

Figure 3–42

7. You have the required results for Lot 3. However, Lot 4 is 10225.00 sq ft and Lot 5 is 16130.09 sq ft. You want to create even-sized lots, each being approximately 13,177.5 sq ft. Display the Parcel Layout Tools toolbar if it is not open.

8. You should still be in the **Swing Line - Edit** command. (If not, repeat Steps 2 to 3 of this task.)

9. In the Parcel Layout Tools toolbar, click ⧨ to expand it. Change the minimum area to **13,177.5 sq ft**. Collapse the toolbar if required, by clicking ⧩ .

10. When prompted, complete the following, as shown in Figure 3–43

   - To select the parcel line to adjust, select the parcel line between Lot 4 and Lot 5 (Line 1).
   - For the parcel to adjust, select **Lot 4**.
   - For the *start frontage*, select the bottom right corner of **Lot 4, pt1**.
   - For the *end of the frontage*, select the top right corner of **Lot 5, pt2**.
   - For the *swing point*, select the end point of **pt3**.

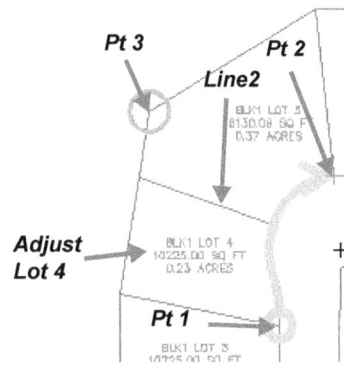

Figure 3–43

11. To accept the results, select **Yes**.

12. Press <Esc> or click **X** in the Parcel Layout Tools dialog box to close it.

13. If time permits, repeat the steps above to subdivide the Parcels Block 2 and Block 3. If you do not complete the subdivisions for Parcels Block 2 and Block 3, you will need to open **PCL-C1-Parcels** in the next practice.

14. Save the drawing.

3.6 Parcel Reports

The AutoCAD Civil 3D software contains several types of parcel reports. Parcel Inverse and Mapcheck data is available in the *Analysis* tab in the Parcel Properties dialog box, as shown in Figure 3–44. The report can be generated clockwise or counter-clockwise, and the point of beginning can be specified.

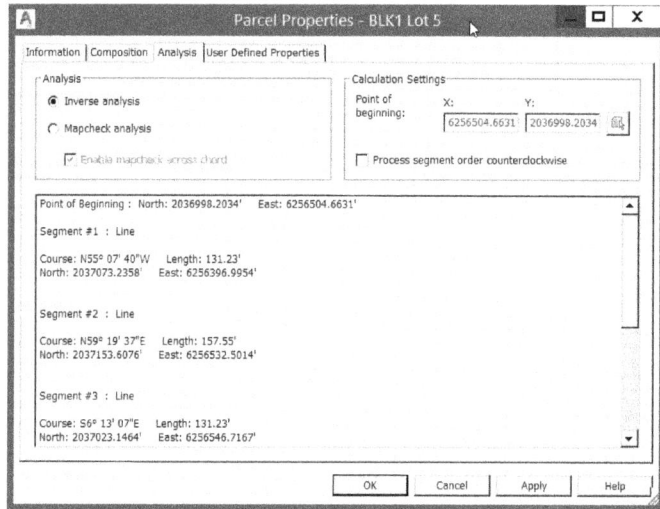

Figure 3–44

This dialog box does not enable output. If you want to generate a printable report, use the AutoCAD Civil 3D Toolbox. It includes several stock Parcel-related reports (such as Surveyor Certificates, Inverse and Mapcheck reports, Metes and Bounds), as shown in Figure 3–45.

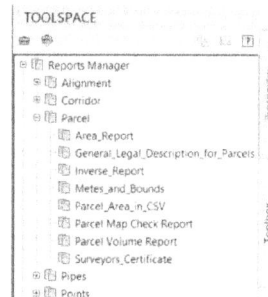

Figure 3–45

Once a report is run, it can be opened in a web browser, word processor, or spreadsheet application. Report settings (such as the Preparer's name) can be assigned by selecting **Report Settings** in the Toolspace.

3.7 Parcel Labels

Parcel area labels are a means of graphically selecting a parcel, such as when creating Right-of-Ways. In the Parcel creation and editing examples, the parcel segment labels were created for you automatically. This section explores the functionality of these labels in more depth.

The Add Labels dialog box (**Annotate>Add Labels>Parcel> Add Parcel Labels...**) can be used to assign the required label styles and place labels in the drawing. It can set the line, curve, and spiral styles and toggle between single and multiple segment labeling, and to access the Tag Numbering Table. The dialog box is shown in Figure 3–46.

Figure 3–46

- Parcel labels, as with all AutoCAD Civil 3D labels, are capable of rotating and resizing to match changes in the viewport scale and rotation.

- A segment label has two definitions: composed and dragged state. A dragged state can be quite different from the original label definition.

- The AutoCAD Civil 3D software can label segments while sizing parcels.

- Labeling can be read clockwise or counter-clockwise around the parcel.

- Labels can be added through an external reference file using the same commands that label objects in their source drawing. This makes it easier to have multiple plans that need different label styles.

- The **Replace Multiple Labels** option is useful when you want to replace a number of parcel segment labels with another style. However, if you are labeling through an external reference file, labels created in the source drawing cannot be modified.

Parcel Area labels are controlled using Parcel Area Label Styles, which control the display of custom information (such as the parcel number, area, perimeter, address, etc.). For example, you can create more than one parcel area label if you need to show different parcel information on different sheets, as shown in Figure 3–47.

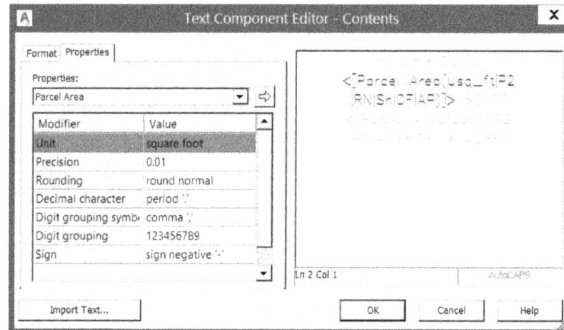

Figure 3–47

Parcel Segment labels annotate the line and curve segments of a parcel, as shown in Figure 3–48. You can label all of the segments of a parcel with one click or only label selected parcel segments.

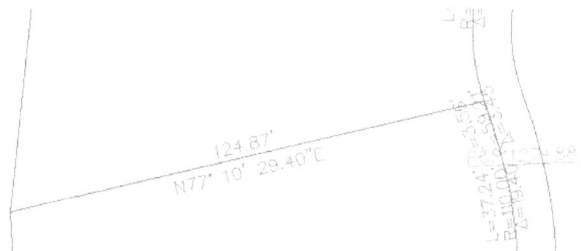

Figure 3–48

All labels have two definitions: one for the original location, and another when it is moved from its original location. A dragged label can remain as originally defined or can be changed to stacked text.

3.8 Parcel Tables

Parcel tables are an alternative to labeling individual parcel areas and segments. An example is shown in Figure 3–49.

Parcel Line and Curve Table			
Line #/Curve #	Length	Bearing/Delta	Radius
L76	112.01	N4° 08' 12.22"W	
L77	395.08	N85° 33' 05.19"E	
L78	471.49	N85° 33' 05.19"E	
L79	210.99	N4° 17' 33.13"W	
L80	211.55	N4° 17' 33.13"W	
L81	115.43	S25° 31' 05.98"W	

Figure 3–49

When creating a table, the AutoCAD Civil 3D software changes the parcel segment labels to an alpha-numeric combination, called a *tag*. A tag with an **L** stands for line and a **C** stands for curve. A segment's tag has a corresponding entry in the table.

- A table can only represent a selected set of label styles.

- The **Add Existing** option (shown in Figure 3–50) creates a table from existing objects. New objects are not added to the table. The **Add Existing and New** option creates a table with existing and new objects.

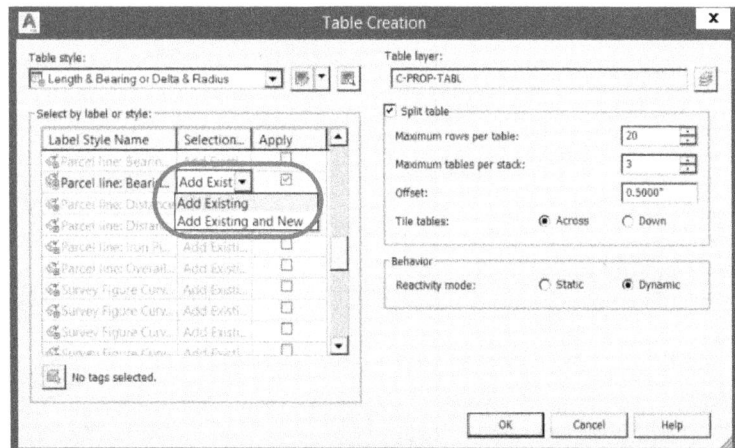

Figure 3–50

- A table can have a dynamic link between a segment's tag and table entry. If the segment changes, the table entry updates.

- The AutoCAD Civil 3D software switches a label to a tag by changing the *Display* mode from **Label** to **Tag**, as shown in Figure 3–51.

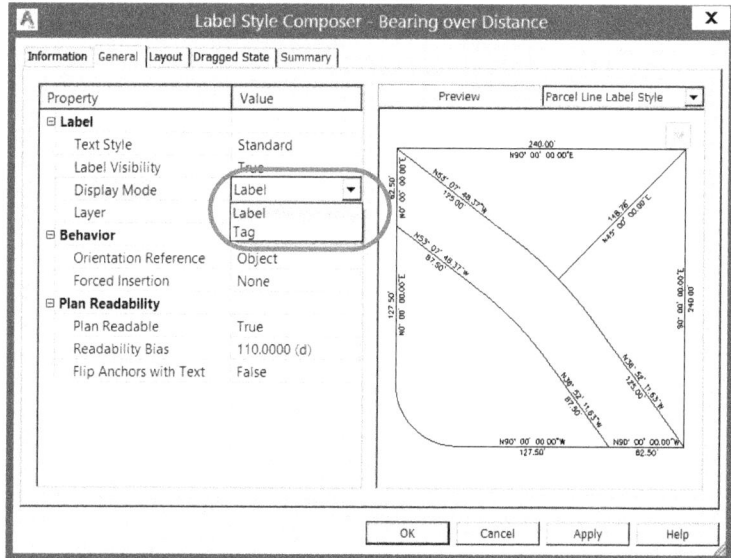

Figure 3–51

Practice 3e

Reporting On and Annotating the Parcel Layout

Practice Objectives

Estimated time for completion: 20 minutes

- Add labels, tags, and tables to the drawing to display useful parcel information.
- Create predefined reports to share useful parcel information in a textual format.

Task 1 - Add Parcel labels.

1. Continue working with the drawing from the previous practice or open **PCL1-E1-Parcels.dwg** from the *C:\Civil 3D Projects\ Civil3D-Training-I\Parcels* folder.

2. In the *Annotate* tab>Labels & Tables panel, click 📎 (Add Labels), as shown in Figure 3–52.

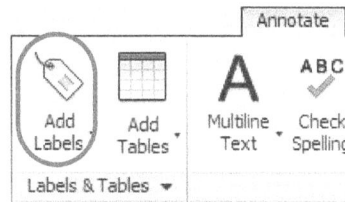

Figure 3–52

3. In the Add Labels dialog box, set the following parameters, as shown in Figure 3–53:
   - *Feature:* **Parcel**
   - *Label type:* **Multiple Segment**
   - *Line label style:* **Bearing over Distance**
   - *Curve label style:* **Delta over Length and Radius**

   Once the parameters are set, click **Add**.

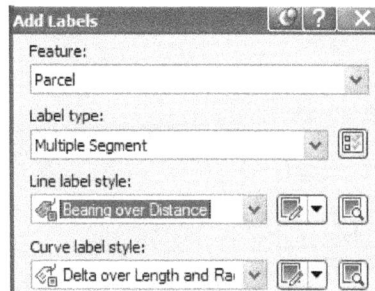

Figure 3–53

4. When prompted to select the Parcels that you want to annotate, select the single-family parcel labels in Model Space.

5. When prompted for the label direction, select **CLockwise**.

6. Continue selecting single-family parcels and labeling them clockwise until all of the single-family parcels are labeled.

7. Press <Enter> when finished labeling the parcels.

8. Select **X** in the Add Labels dialog box, or click **Close** to close the dialog box.

Parcels can also be labeled in an XREF file.

9. Save the drawing.

Task 2 - Create Line and Curve Segment Tables.

The labels are overlapping in a number of locations, making the drawing difficult to read. In this task, you try two methods to fix this. In the first method, you drag the label to a location in which there is no conflict. In the second method, you add a label tag and an associated table.

1. Continue working with the drawing from the previous task or open **PCL1-E2-Parcels.dwg**.

2. Select the preset view **Parcel-Tag1**.

3. Select the label **11.70'**, select the square grip, and drag to place the label in a location in which there is no conflict. Do the same for the label **21.48'**, as shown in Figure 3–54.

Figure 3–54

4. You will now add tags and a table. In the *Annotate* tab>
   Label & Tables panel, expand ⬚ (Add Tables) and select
   Parcel>Add segment, as shown in Figure 3–55.

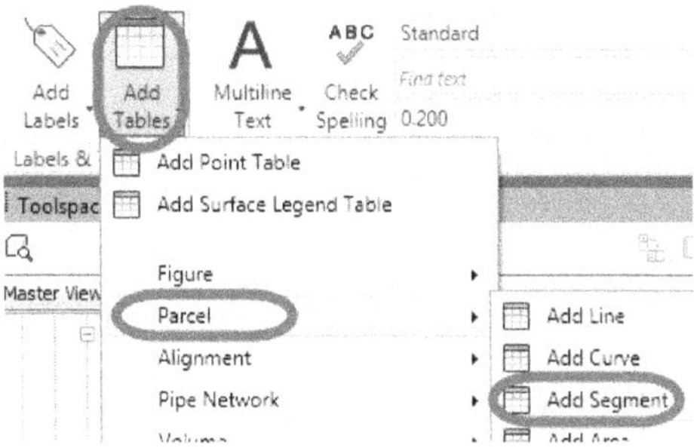

Figure 3–55

5. In the Table Creation dialog box, click ⬚ (Pick on screen)
   and select the labels shown in Figure 3–56. Press <Enter>
   when done.

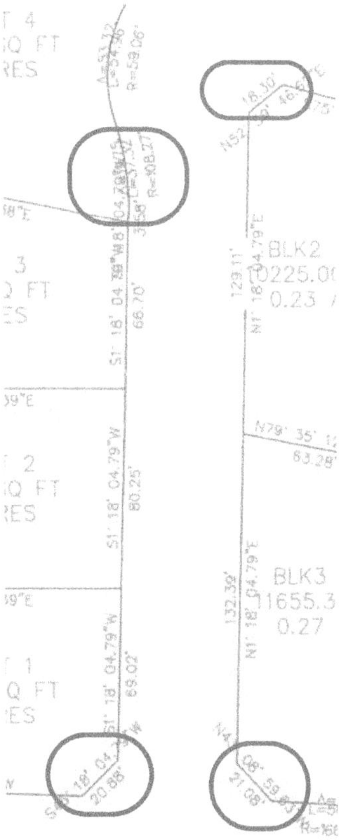

Figure 3–56

6. When prompted to convert labels to tags or to not add labels, select **Convert all selected label styles to tag mode**.

7. Click **OK** to close the Table Creation dialog box.

8. When prompted for a location for the table, select a location in an open space, as shown in Figure 3–57.

Parcel Line and Curve Table			
Line #/Curve #	Length	Bearing/Delta	Radius
C1	37.32	19.75	108.27
L1	20.88	S46° 18′ 04.79″W	
L2	21.08	N43° 08′ 59.63″W	
L3	3.58	S1° 18′ 04.79″W	
L4	18.30	N52° 59′ 46.62″E	

Figure 3–57

9. Save the drawing.

Task 3 - Create a Parcel Area Table.

1. Continue working with the drawing from the previous task or open **PCL1-E3-Parcels.dwg**.

2. In the *Annotate* tab>Label & Tables panel, expand ⬜ (Add Tables) and select **Parcel>Add Area**.

3. In the Table Creation dialog box, in the *Select by label* or *style* area, select the style name **Name Square Foot & Acres**, as shown in Figure 3–58. All parcels with this style will be selected. Click **OK** to close the dialog box.

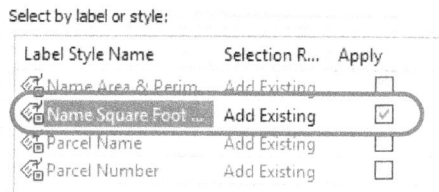

Select by label or style:

Label Style Name	Selection R...	Apply
Name Area & Perim	Add Existing	☐
Name Square Foot ...	Add Existing	☑
Parcel Name	Add Existing	☐
Parcel Number	Add Existing	☐

Figure 3–58

4. Select a location to insert the table into the drawing, as shown in Figure 3–59.

Figure 3–59

5. Save the drawing.

Task 4 - Create a Parcel Report.

1. Continue working with the drawing from the previous task or open **PCL1-E4-Parcels.dwg**.

2. If the Toolspace, *Toolbox* tab is not displayed, go to the *Home* tab>Palettes panel, and click (Toolbox), as shown in Figure 3–60.

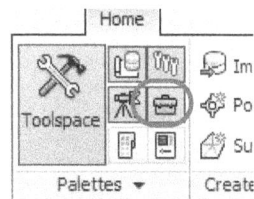

Figure 3–60

3. In the Toolspace, *Toolbox* tab, expand the *Reports Manager* and *Parcel* collections. Right-click on *Surveyor's Certificate* and select **Execute**.

4. In the Export to LandXML dialog box, click (Pick from drawing), located at the bottom left of the dialog box.

5. When prompted to select a parcel, select one of the single-family lots that you created earlier and press <Enter>.

6. In the Export to XML Report dialog box, note that only the Lots you selected now display a checkmark. Click **OK** to close the dialog box.

7. In the Save As dialog box, type the required filename for the report and click **Save** to close the dialog box.

8. Review the report (as shown in Figure 3–61), and close the web browser.

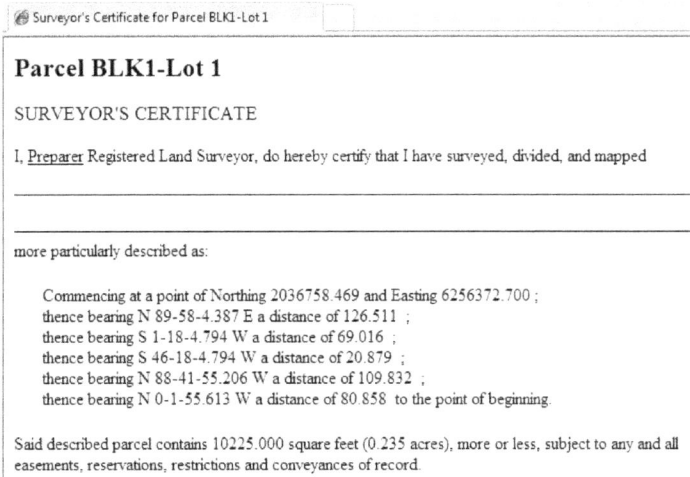

Surveyor's Certificate for Parcel BLK1-Lot 1

Parcel BLK1-Lot 1

SURVEYOR'S CERTIFICATE

I, Preparer Registered Land Surveyor, do hereby certify that I have surveyed, divided, and mapped

more particularly described as:

Commencing at a point of Northing 2036758.469 and Easting 6256372.700 ;
thence bearing N 89-58-4.387 E a distance of 126.511 ;
thence bearing S 1-18-4.794 W a distance of 69.016 ;
thence bearing S 46-18-4.794 W a distance of 20.879 ;
thence bearing N 88-41-55.206 W a distance of 109.832 ;
thence bearing N 0-1-55.613 W a distance of 80.858 to the point of beginning.

Said described parcel contains 10225.000 square feet (0.235 acres), more or less, subject to any and all easements, reservations, restrictions and conveyances of record.

Figure 3–61

9. Save the drawing.

Chapter Review Questions

1. Where are parcels listed?

   a. Under the *Survey* collection, in the Toolspace, *Prospector* tab.

   b. In a site under the *Sites* collection, in the Toolspace, *Prospector* tab.

   c. Under the *Figures* collection, inside the Survey Database.

   d. In the Layers panel, in the *Home* tab.

2. What does a parcel style assign in the *Display* tab?

   a. Layer to which parcel segments are assigned.

   b. How big the parcel can be.

   c. The label text that describes the line segments.

   d. The label text that describes the area and name of the parcel.

3. What is the default direction of a Mapcheck or Inverse report?

   a. Clockwise

   b. Counter-clockwise

   c. Always starts going north.

   d. Always starts going south.

4. How do you adjust parcel display order?

   a. Select the parcel segments, right-click and select **Draw Order**.

   b. Move the parcel up or down in the parcel preview list in the Toolspace, *Prospector* tab.

   c. Select the parcel area label, right-click and select **Draw Order**.

   d. Under Sites, right-click on *Parcels* and select **Properties**.

5. How do you draw a parcel boundary from a legal description in the most efficient way possible?

   a. Calculate the Cartesian coordinate angle for each bearing or azimuth within the legal description and type (distance)<(angle) for each line or curve.

   b. Calculate the cartesian coordinate angle for each bearing or azimuth within the legal description, place the cursor in that direction, and type the distance.

   c. Use the extended **Lines** and **Curves** options in the *Home* tab>Draw panel or **Transparent** commands in the **Line** or **Polyline** command.

   d. There is no fast way to do this.

6. How do you create or subdivide parcels interactively?

   a. Draw parcel segments at each location in which you want a parcel line.

   b. **Create** and **Edit** tools in the Parcel Layout toolbar.

   c. Select the parcel, right-click and select **Subdivide**.

   d. Used the AutoCAD **Measure** or **Divide** commands to help place lot lines and even intervals.

7. Which **Parcel Create** command enables you to hold a specified angle relative to the Right-Of-Way?

   a. Slide line-create

   b. Swing line-create

   c. Free Form create

   d. Use the **Add fixed line** command.

8. What are the types of AutoCAD Civil 3D Parcel labels that can be set up in the *Setting* tab? (Select all that apply.)

   a. Parcel Line

   b. Parcel Area

   c. Parcel Curve

   d. Parcel Perimeter

9. What does the Add Labels dialog box do?

   a. Creates label styles.

   b. Add or change labels interactively after parcel creation.

   c. Add or change labels during parcel creation.

   d. Creates static text describing what you want to label.

10. What are parcel tables an alternative to? (Select all that apply.)

    a. Drawing the parcels.

    b. Creating tags.

    c. Labeling parcel areas in an already crowded drawing.

    d. Labeling parcel segments in an already crowded drawing.

Command Summary

Button	Command	Location
	Add Labels	• **Ribbon:** *Annotate* tab>Labels & Tables panel
	Add Tables	• **Ribbon:** *Annotate* tab>Labels & Tables panel
	Bearing Distance	• **Toolbar:** Transparent Commands • **Command Prompt:** 'bd
	Create Curve from End of Object	• **Ribbon:** *Home* tab>Draw panel • **Command Prompt:** CurveFromEndOfObject
	Create Parcel From Objects	• **Ribbon:** *Home* tab>Create Design panel • **Command Prompt:** ParcelFromObjects
	Create Reverse or Compound Curve	• **Ribbon:** *Home* tab>Draw panel • **Command Prompt:** ReverseOrCompound
	Parcel Creation Tools	• **Ribbon:** *Home* tab>Create Design panel • **Command Prompt:** CreateParcelByLayout
	Rename Renumber	• **Contextual Ribbon:** *Parcels*>Modify • **Command Prompt:** EditParcelNumbers
	Slide-Line Create	• **Toolbar:** Parcel Layout Tools
	Swing-Line Edit	• **Toolbar:** Parcel Layout Tools

Survey

This chapter focuses on automated Field to Finish tools that aid in drafting an accurate and efficient Existing Condition Plan. These tools create a correct existing topography, property lines, right-of-way, and center line locations.

Learning Objectives in this Chapter

- List the steps used to create linework from coordinate files, in a typical survey workflow.
- Create a figure database for stylizing linework automatically.
- Create point marker and label styles to annotate points.
- Set the appropriate point creation settings and the next available point number.
- Create points manually using the Create Points toolbar.
- Assign point symbols, labels, layers, etc., automatically when importing points by setting up Description Key Sets.
- Import points from ASCII files created from the field survey.
- Group points together using common properties, such as name, elevation, description, etc.
- Review and edit points using the Panorama window to ensure accuracy.
- Share information about points used for error checking or stake out points using predefined reports.

4.1 Survey Workflow Overview

Workflow

To create linework from coordinate files, use the following survey workflow:

1. Data needs to be entered into the data collector. The correct language, methodology, and basic rules regarding data entry into the data collector begin with an understanding of Figure Commands and Field Codes (raw descriptions).

2. Data can be transferred from the data collector to the computer using an ASCII file. An ASCII file can be opened in Notepad and data can be separated or delineated by spaces or commas. The most popular transferred format is Point Number, Northing, Easting, Elevation, Description. This material focuses on the different types of Descriptions that can be entered into a data collector so that the user obtains the required automated symbology and linework.

3. If using a field book file (a type of ASCII file), data needs to be converted from the raw coordinate file to a field book (*.FBK) using Survey Link or other methods of the AutoCAD® Civil 3D® software. Autodesk has collaborated with major survey equipment vendors to develop API and drivers that interface their specific survey equipment (Trimble Link, TDS Survey Link, Leica X-Change, TOPCON Link, etc.) with the AutoCAD Civil 3D software.

   If following the **Linework Code Set** command format, you do not need to convert the coordinate file to a field book. Import the file with linework processing toggled on.

4. The AutoCAD Civil 3D software needs to have all of the necessary Styles, Settings, and Figure Prefixes to create, sort, and place points and linework on the required layers.

4.2 Survey Figures

Survey figures consist of linework generated by coding and placed in a file that is imported into the Survey Database. A figure represents linear features (edge-of-pavement, toe-of-slopes, etc.)

A figure has many functions, which include:

- Acting as linework in a drawing.

- Acting as breaklines for a surface definition.

- Acting as parcel lines.

- Acting as a pipe run.

- Acting as targets for *Width* or *Offset Targets* in a Corridor.

- Acting as targets for *Slope* or *Elevation Targets* in a Corridor (e.g., limits of construction for a road rehab project might be to the face of walk, which exists in the drawing as a Survey Figure, hence a target).

The Figure Prefix database should be set up before importing any survey data to obtain the required entities in a drawing. As point and label styles and the Description Key Set need to exist before importing points, figure styles and entries in the Figure Prefix database need to exist before importing survey data.

Figure Styles

Figure styles (found in the Toolspace, *Settings* tab, under Survey>Figures>Figure Styles) affect how the survey linework displays in a drawing. They should be part of your template file. These styles are not critical. However, to make figures work more efficiently, you should define the layers they use in the drawing.

- Figure styles are tied to the Figure Prefix database. The Figure Prefix database assigns a figure style to a figure that is imported into a drawing.

- A figure style includes the layers for its linework and markers.

- A marker is a symbol placed on the figure's segment midpoints and end points. They call attention to the figure's geometry. Although a figure style includes marker definitions, they do not need to display.

- In the Figure Style dialog box, the *Information* tab assigns a name to a style. The *Profile*, and *Section* tabs define how the marker displays in various views.

- The *Display* tab defines which figure's components display and which layers they use for plan, model, profile, and section views, as shown in Figure 4–1.

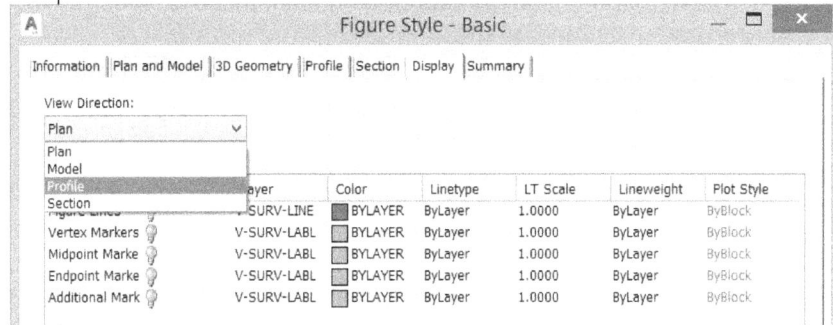

Figure 4–1

Figure Prefix Database

The Figure Prefix database (found in the Toolspace, *Survey* tab) assigns the figure a style, a layer, and defines whether the figure is a surface breakline or lot line (parcel segment). If you did not define any figure styles, you should at least assign a layer to correctly place the figure in the drawing. Toggling on the *Breakline* property, as shown in Figure 4–2, enables you select all of the tagged survey figures and assign them to a surface without having to insert or select from a drawing. Toggling on the *Lot Line* property creates a parcel segment from the figure in the drawing and, if there is a closed polygon, assigns a parcel label and an entry in the survey site.

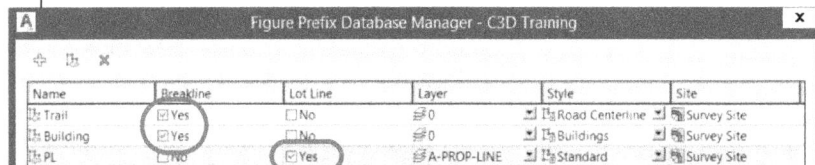

Figure 4–2

If the *Name* is **PL** (as shown in Figure 4–2), any figure starting with PL uses these settings. This is similar to using a Description Key Set, except that the entry in the Figure Prefix database does not need an asterisk (*). The entry Name matches PL1 through PL100. When inserting survey figures in the drawing, Survey checks the Figure Prefix database for style or layer values.

Practice 4a

Creating Figure Prefixes

Practice Objective

- Create a figure database for automatically stylizing linework on importing field book or ASCII files.

Estimated time for completion: 5 minutes

1. Open **SUV1-A1-Survey.dwg**, from the *C:\Civil 3D Projects\ Civil3D-Training\Survey* folder.

2. You might have to change the draw order of the image to be able to view other objects. In Model Space, select the image, right-click, and select **Display Order>Send to Back**.

3. In the Toolspace, select the *Survey* tab. Right-click on *Figure Prefix Databases*, and select **New...**. Type **C3D Training** for the name.

4. Right-click on the newly created C3D Training Figure Prefix database, and select **Make Current**.

5. Right-click on the C3D Training Figure Prefix database again, and select **Manage Figure Prefix Database...**.

6. Click ⊕ to create a new Figure definition. Set the following options, as shown in Figure 4–3:
   - Change the *Name* to **Trail**.
   - Select *Breakline*.
   - Set *Style* to **Road Centerline**.

   Any figure starting with **Trail** will now be selectable for a surface breakline and will use the style **Road Centerline**. As noted earlier, unlike the Description Key Set, an asterisk (*) is not necessary to match Trail1, Trail2, etc.

The AutoCAD Civil 3D software creates a default Figure.

Name	Breakline	Lot Line	Layer	Style	Site
Trail	☑ Yes	☐ No	0	Road Centerline	Survey Site

Figure 4–3

7. Click ⊕ to create a new Figure definition.
   - Change the name to **Building**
   - Set the *Breakline* to **No**
   - Set the *Style* to **Buildings**.

8. Click **OK** to exit the dialog box.

9. Save the drawing.

4.3 Points Overview

Points are often most heavily used at the beginning and end of a project. Surveyors collect data about existing site conditions (elevations, utilities, ownership, etc.) and set out the points for those who are going to build the design. Their world is coordinates, which are represented by points. Each point has a unique number (or name) and a label containing additional information (usually the elevation at the coordinate and a short coded description).

There are no national standards for point descriptions in the Surveying industry. Each company or survey crew needs to work out its own conventions. There are no standards for symbols either. Each firm can have its own set of symbols. The symbols used in a submission set can be specified by the firm contracting the services.

AutoCAD Civil 3D cogo points are a single object with two elements: a point style and a point label style. A cogo point definition is shown in Figure 4–4.

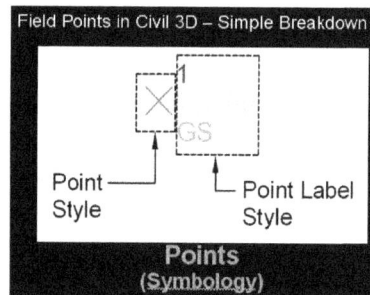

Figure 4–4

The following is important cogo point information:

- A point style (no matter what it displays), an AutoCAD node, a custom marker, or a block is selectable with an AutoCAD **Node** object snap.

A point label is not limited to the point's number, elevation, and description. A point label can contain lines, blocks, and other point properties. For example, point labels might only display an elevation or description. This text can be manually overridden (as shown in Figure 4–5) or it can consist of intelligent variables that represent point characteristics (such as its convergence angle).

In U.S. state plane coordinate systems, the convergence angle is the difference between a geodetic azimuth and the projection of that azimuth onto a grid (grid azimuth) of a given point.

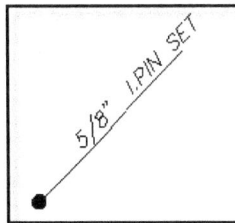

Figure 4–5

Point Marker Styles

A surveyor interacts with points daily. To easily use AutoCAD Civil 3D points, you need to have a basic understanding of them and their related styles.

The AutoCAD Civil 3D software provides metric and imperial template files that contain several point styles: AutoCAD Civil 3D Imperial (NCS) and AutoCAD Civil 3D Metric (NCS). These two templates use the National CAD standards for their layers and provide examples of styles that you can use in a project. To customize these styles, you need to modify and expand the list of point styles. When installing the AutoCAD Civil 3D software, the first thing you should do is set one of these two templates as your default template. Alternatively, you can develop your styles and use your template.

A point style defines a point's display, its 3D elevation, and its coordinate marker size. In the example shown in Figure 4–6, the point style is an X for a ground shot.

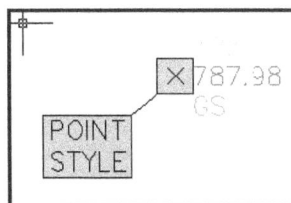

Figure 4–6

The Point Style dialog box has five tabs: *Information*, *Marker*, *3D Geometry*, *Display*, and *Summary*.

The *Information* tab sets the point style's name and description, as shown in Figure 4–7.

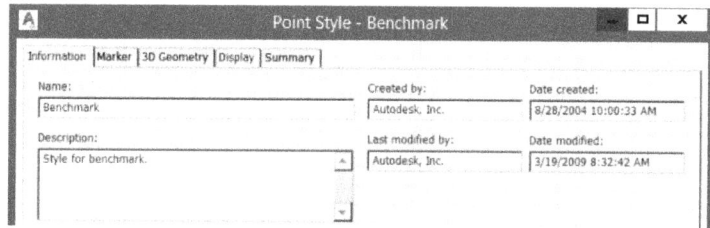

Figure 4–7

The *Marker* tab supports three marker definition methods, as shown in Figure 4–8.

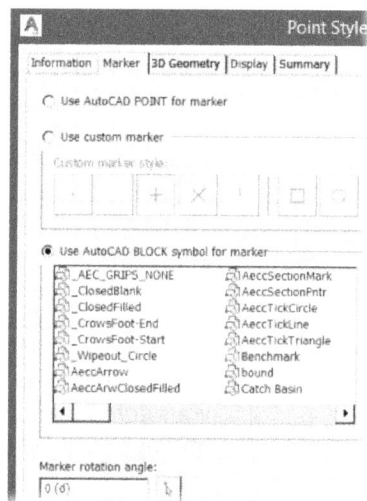

Figure 4–8

- **Use AutoCAD POINT [node] for marker:** All points in the drawing follow AutoCAD's **PDMODE** and **PDSIZE** system variables. You do not have independent control over points using this option.

- **Use custom marker:** This option creates markers similar to an AutoCAD point (node). However, the marker is under the AutoCAD Civil 3D software's control, and each point style can display a different combination of marker styles. When using this option, select the components of the style from the list of Custom marker style shapes. A custom marker can have shapes from the left and right sides. The first comes from one of the five icons on the style's left side, and you can optionally add none, one, or both shapes from the right.

- **Use AutoCAD BLOCK symbol for marker:** This option defines the marker using a block (symbol). The blocks listed represent definitions in the drawing. When the cursor is in this area and you right-click, you can browse to a location containing drawings that you want to include as point markers.

Options for scaling the marker display in the marker panel's top right corner. The most common option is **Use drawing scale** (as shown in Figure 4–9), which takes the marker size (0.100) and multiplies it by the current drawing's annotation scale, resulting in the final marker size. When the annotation scale changes, the AutoCAD Civil 3D software automatically resizes the markers and their labels to be the appropriate size for the scale.

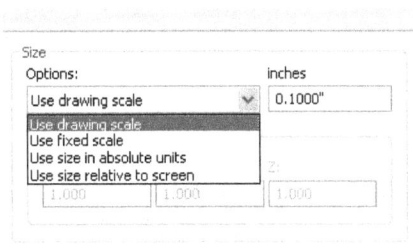

Figure 4–9

The other options are described as follows:

Use fixed scale	Specifies user-defined X, Y, and Z scale values.
Use size in absolute units	Specifies a user-defined size.
Use size relative to screen	Specifies a user-defined percentage of the screen.

The *3D Geometry* tab affects the point's elevation. The default option is **Use Point Elevation** (as shown in Figure 4–10), which displays the point at its actual elevation value.

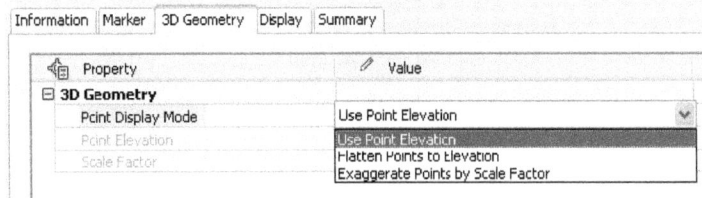

Figure 4–10

The other options are described as follows:

Flatten Points to Elevation	Specifies the elevation to which the point is projected (flattened). The Point Elevation cell highlights if this option is selected and is 0 elevation by default. When using an AutoCAD object snap to select a marker using this option, the resulting entity's elevation is the default elevation of 0. If selecting by point number or point object, the resulting entity is the point's actual elevation.
Exaggerate Points by Scale Factor	Exaggerates the point's elevation by a specified scale factor. When selecting this option, the Scale Factor cell highlights.

The *Display* tab assigns the marker and label layers, and sets their visibility and properties. Setting the property to **ByLayer** uses the layer's properties. Alternatively, you can override the original layer properties by setting a specific color, linetype, or lineweight.

A style's view direction value affects how the point and label components display in the plan, model, profile, and section views, as shown in Figure 4–11.

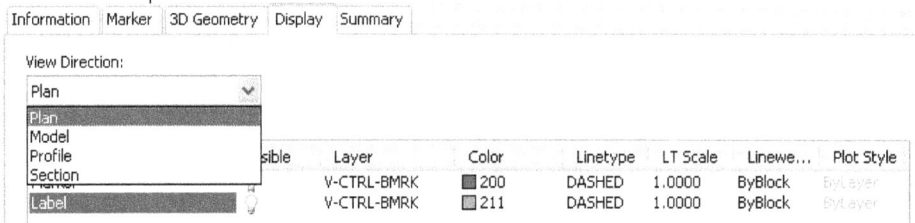

Figure 4–11

The *Summary* tab is a report of all of the style's settings. Controlling a leader arrow from a label in the dragged state, points to the boundary of the marker (yes) or the center of the marker (no). It is also changed under **Marker>Leader** and stops at marker. You can also edit style variables in this tab.

Point Label Style

The AutoCAD Civil 3D point label style annotates point properties beyond the typical point number, elevation and description. A typical point label style is shown in Figure 4–12.

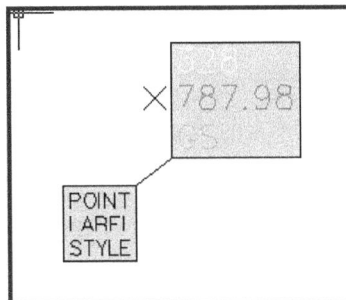

Figure 4–12

All AutoCAD Civil 3D label style dialog boxes are the same. The basic behaviors for a label are in the settings in the Edit Label Style Defaults dialog box. The values in this dialog box define the label layer, text style, orientation, plan readability, size, dragged state behaviors, etc.

In the Toolspace, *Settings* tab, the drawing name and object collections control these values for the entire drawing (at the drawing name level) or for the selected collection (*Surface*, *Alignment*, *Point*, etc.) To open the Edit Label Style Defaults dialog box, select the drawing name or a heading, right-click, and select **Edit Label Style Defaults...**, as shown in Figure 4–13.

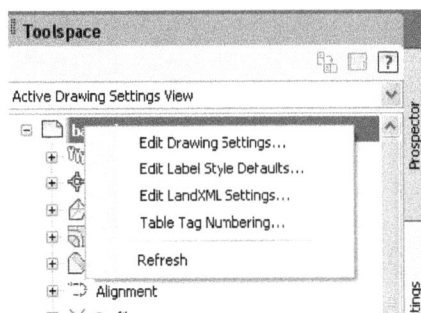

Figure 4–13

The Label Style Composer dialog box contains five tabs, each defining specific label behaviors: *Information*, *General*, *Layout*, *Dragged State*, and *Summary*.

The *Information* tab names the style, as shown in Figure 4–14.

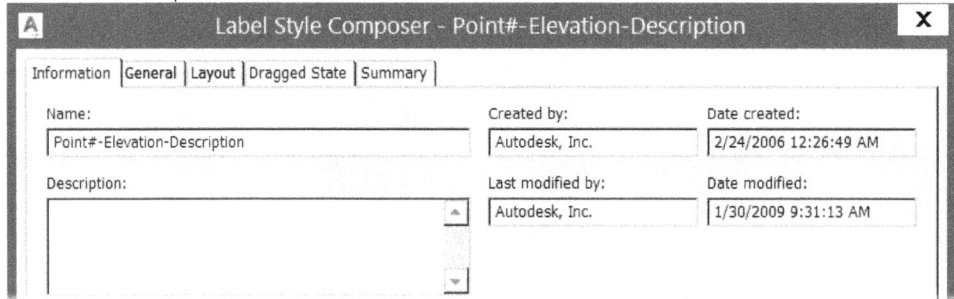

Figure 4–14

The *General* tab contains three properties: *Label* (text style and layer), *Behavior* (orientation), and *Plan Readability* (amount of view rotation before flipping text to read from the bottom or the right side of the sheet), as shown in Figure 4–15.

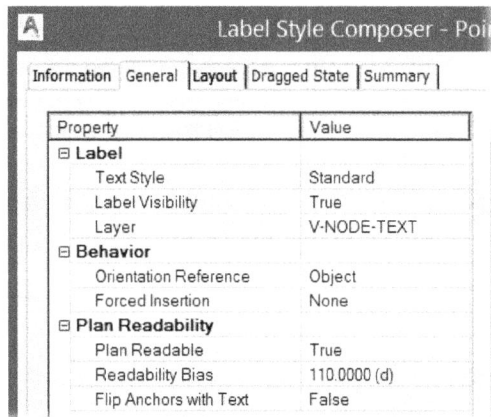

Figure 4–15

The *Label* property sets the *Text Style*, *Label Visibility*, *Layer*. Select the *Value* cell next to the *Text Style* and *Layer* to open browsers and change their values. Selecting the *Label Visibility* cell displays a drop-down list containing the options **true** and **false**.

The *Behavior* property sets two variables that control the label's location. The *Orientation Reference* variable contains the three label orientation options.

Object	Rotates labels relative to the object's zero direction. The object's zero direction is based on its start to end vector. If the vector changes at the label's anchor point, the orientation updates automatically. This is the default setting.
View	Forces labels to realign relative to a screen-view orientation in both model and layout views. This method assumes that the zero angle is horizontal, regardless of the UCS or Dview twist. If the view changes, the label orientation updates as well.
World Coordinate System	Labels read left to right using the WCS X-axis. Changing the view or current UCS does not affect label rotation. The label always references the world coordinate system.

Under the *Behavior* property, the **Forced Insertion** variable has three optional values that specify the label's position relative to an object. This setting only applies when the *Orientation Reference* is set to **Object** and the objects are lines, arcs, or spline segments.

None	Maintains label position as composed relative to the object.
Top	Adjusts label position to be above an object.
Bottom	Adjusts label position to be below an object.

- Note: If you select **Top** or **Bottom**, the value of *Plan Readable* should set to **True**.

The *Plan Readability* property has three variables that affect how text flips when rotating a drawing view.

Under the *Plan Readability* property, the *Plan Readable* variable has two options.

True	Enables text to rotate to maintain left to right readability from the bottom or right side of the drawing.
False	Does not permit text to flip. The resulting text might be upside down or read from right to left.

The *Readability Bias* variable is the amount of rotation required to flip a label to become left to right readable. The angle is measured counter-clockwise from the WCS 0 (zero) direction.

The *Flip Anchors with Text* variable has two options:

True	If the text flips, the text anchor point also flips.
False	The label flips, but maintains the original anchor point. The behavior is similar to mirroring the original text.

The *Layout* tab defines the label contents, as shown in Figure 4–16. A label component is an object property that it labels. Point properties include northing, easting, raw description, etc. A label might have one component with several properties or several components each containing an object property.

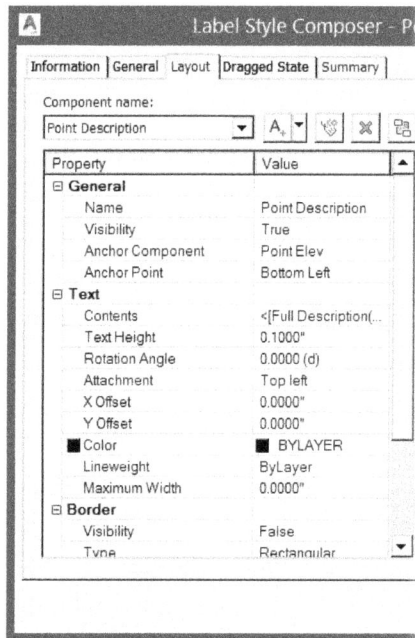

Figure 4–16

A point style label component can be text, lines, or blocks. Other object type label styles can include additional components, such as reference text, tics, directional arrows, etc. To add a component, expand the drop-down list (as shown in Figure 4–17) and select the component type.

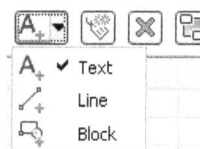

Figure 4–17

The remaining icons in the *Layout* tab are described as follows:

	Copies the current component and its properties.
	Deletes the current component.
	Changes the display order of a label's components. For example, use this icon to change the draw order of the label's components (such as text above a mask).

Depending on the label component type, it might have any combination of three areas: *General*, *Text*, and *Border*. *General* defines how the label attaches to the object or other label components, its visibility, and its anchor point.

If the label component is text, the *Text* property values affect how it displays its object property. To set or modify a label's text value, select the cell next to *Contents* to display ⋯ (shown in Figure 4–18). Click ⋯ to open the Text Component Editor dialog box.

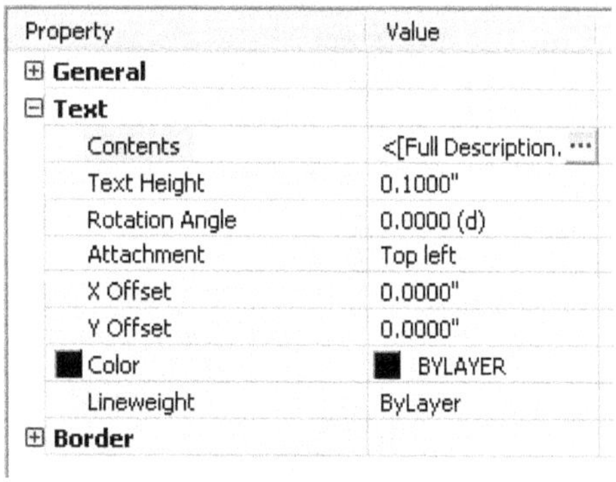

Property	Value
⊞ **General**	
⊟ **Text**	
Contents	<[Full Description. ⋯
Text Height	0.1000"
Rotation Angle	0.0000 (d)
Attachment	Top left
X Offset	0.0000"
Y Offset	0.0000"
◼ Color	◼ BYLAYER
Lineweight	ByLayer
⊞ **Border**	

Figure 4–18

The Text Component Editor dialog box (shown in Figure 4–19), defines the properties that the label annotates. When creating a label component, double-click on the text in the right pane to highlight it. In the left pane, select the property that you want to add, set the property's format values, and then click ⇨ to add the new property to the label component.

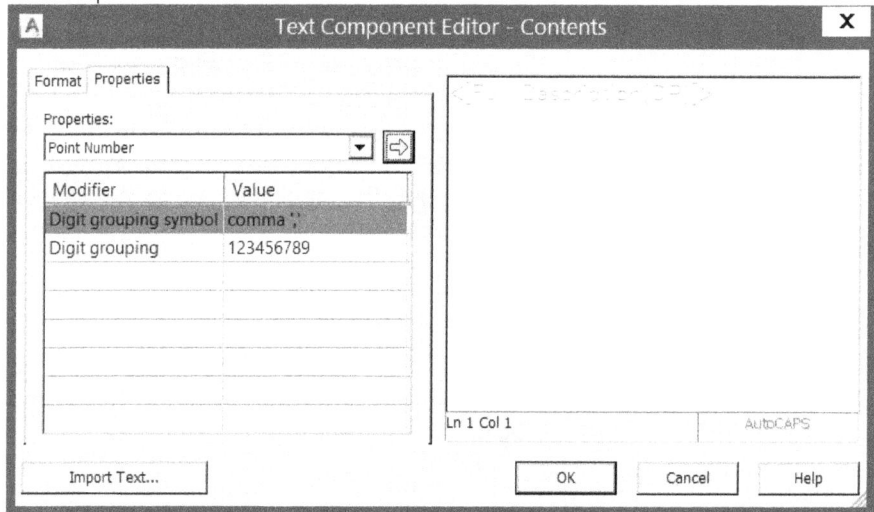

Figure 4–19

It is important to maintain the process order and to remember that the text on the right in brackets needs to be highlighted before you can revise its format values on the left.

The *Dragged State* tab has two properties: *Leader* and *Dragged State Components*. This tab defines how a label behaves when you are dragging a label from its original insertion point.

The *Leader* property defines whether a leader displays and what properties it displays. You can use the label's layer properties in the *General* tab (**ByLayer**) or override them by specifying a color, as shown in Figure 4–20.

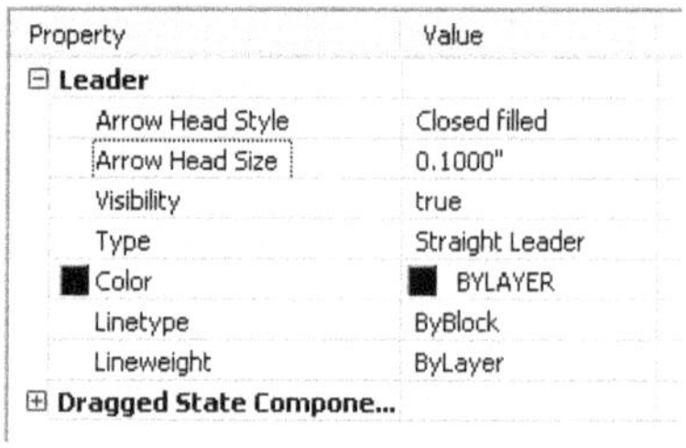

Figure 4–20

The *Dragged State Components* property defines the label component's display after it has been dragged from its original position. Select the cell next to *Display* to view the two display options, as shown in Figure 4–21.

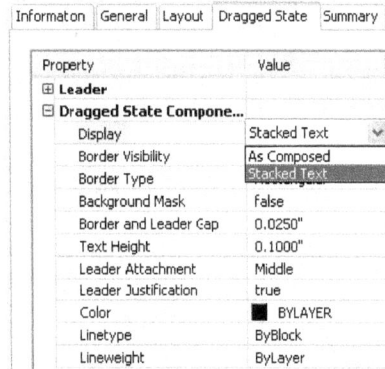

Figure 4–21

As Composed	The label maintains its original definition and orientation from the settings in the Layout panel. When you select **As Composed**, all of the other values become unavailable for editing.
Stacked Text	The label text becomes left justified and label components are stacked in the order listed in Layout's Component Name list. When you select **Stacked Text**, all of the blocks, lines, ticks, and direction arrows are removed.

The *Summary* tab lists the label component, general, and dragged state values for the label style. The label components are listed numerically in the order in which they were defined and report all of the current values.

Practice 4b

Point Marker Styles

Practice Objective

- Create a point marker and label style to ensure that the correct symbol is assigned to specific points.

Estimated time for completion: 35 minutes

In this practice you will create a new point style and apply it to an existing group of points.

Task 1 - Add a Block Symbol.

1. Continue working on the drawing from the previous practice or open **SUV1-B1-Survey-.dwg** from the *C:\Civil 3D Projects\Civil3D-Training\Survey* folder.

The aerial images used in this chapter was attached using the AutoCAD® Map 3D FDO connection.

2. To toggle off the aerial images: In the *Home* tab>Palettes panel, click ⬒ (Map Task Pane) and when prompted, select **ON**.

3. In the Task pane>*Display Manager* tab, clear the **MainSite Imperial** option, as shown in Figure 4–22. Close the map Task pane.

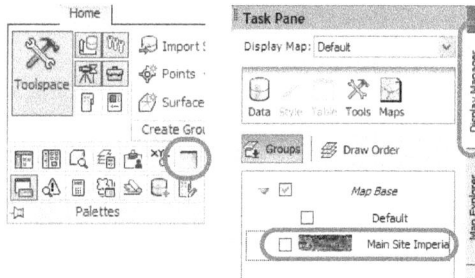

Figure 4–22

4. In the Toolspace, *Settings* tab, expand the *Point* collection until *Point Styles* displays. Expand the *Point Styles* collection.

Review the Point Styles list and note that there is no light pole style.

5. In the *Point Styles* list, select the **Guy pole** style, right-click, and select **Copy…**.

6. In the *Information* tab, change the point style's name to **Light Pole.**

7. Select the *Marker* tab. Select the **Use AutoCAD BLOCK symbol for marker** option. In the block list, scroll across as required and select the AutoCAD block **ST-Light**, as shown in Figure 4–23.

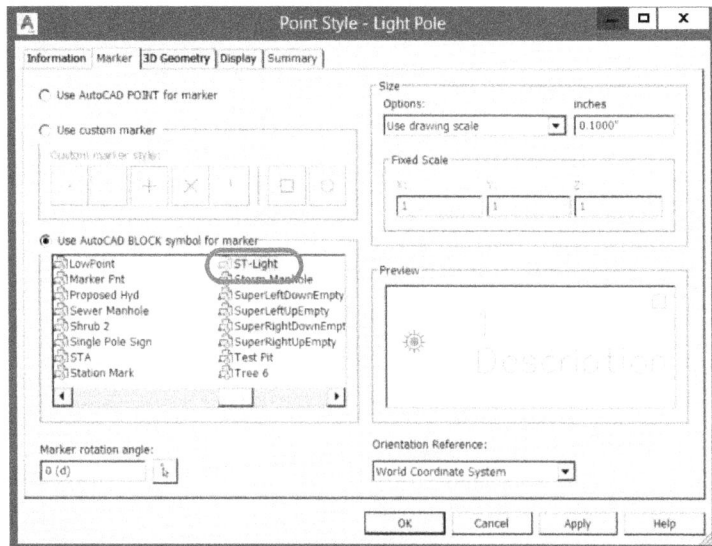

Figure 4–23

8. Select the *Display* tab and note that the layer settings are from the Guy Pole point style.

9. You can reassign the marker and/or label layer by selecting the layer name. Select the layer name to display the drawing layer list.

10. Click **New** in the top right corner of the Layer Selection dialog box. The Create Layer dialog box opens (as shown in Figure 4–24), enabling you to create new layers without having to use the Layer Manager.

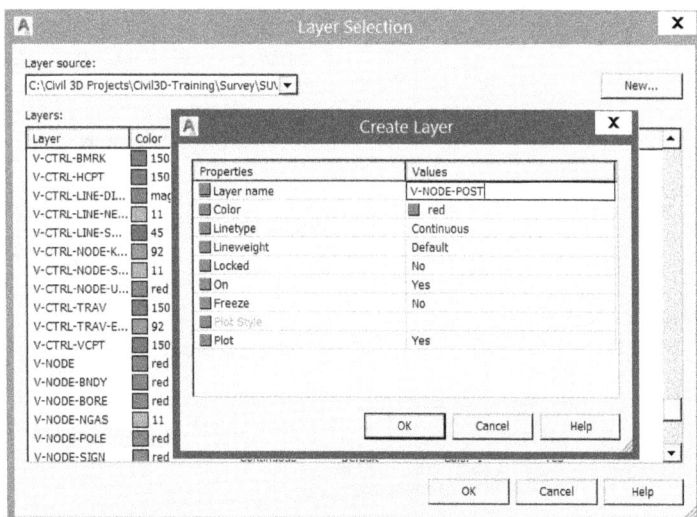

Figure 4–24

11. Type **V-NODE-POST** for the name, as shown in Figure 4–24. Click **OK** to exit the Create Layer dialog box. Click **OK** to exit the Layer Selection dialog box.

12. Click **OK** to create the point style.

13. Review the *Point Styles* list and note that Light Pole is now a point style, as shown in Figure 4–25.

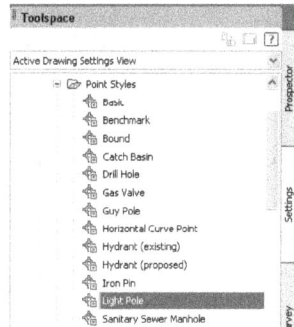

Figure 4–25

14. Save the drawing.

Task 2 - Create a Point Label Style's Components.

---

1. Continue working with the drawing from the previous task, or open **SUV1-B2-Survey.dwg**.

2. In the Toolspace, *Settings* tab, expand the *Point* collection until the *Point Label Styles* list displays.

3. From the list of point label styles, select **Point#-Elevation-Description**, right-click, and select **Copy**.

4. In the *Information* tab, change the name to **Point#-Description-N-E**.

5. Select the *Layout* tab and do the following (shown in Figure 4–26):

   - Select **Point Number** in the *Component name* drop-down list.
   - Set the *Anchor Component* to **<Feature>**.
   - Set the *Anchor Point* to **Top Right**.
   - Set the *Attachment* to **Bottom left**.

These settings attach the bottom left of the label to the top right of the point object.

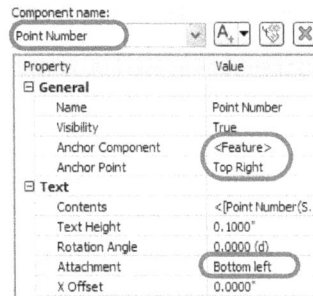

Figure 4–26

Since the elevation label is not required, you can delete it.

6. Select **Point Elev** in the Component name drop-down list and click ⊠, as shown in Figure 4–27. At the *Do you want to delete it?* prompt, click **Yes**.

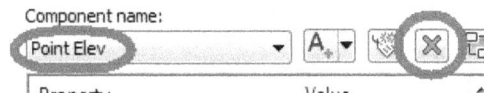

Figure 4–27

7. Select **Point Description** in the Component name drop-down list and do the following (shown in Figure 4–28):

   • Set the *Anchor Component* to **Point Number**.
   • Set the *Anchor Point* to **Bottom Left**.
   • Set the *Attachment* to **Top Left**.

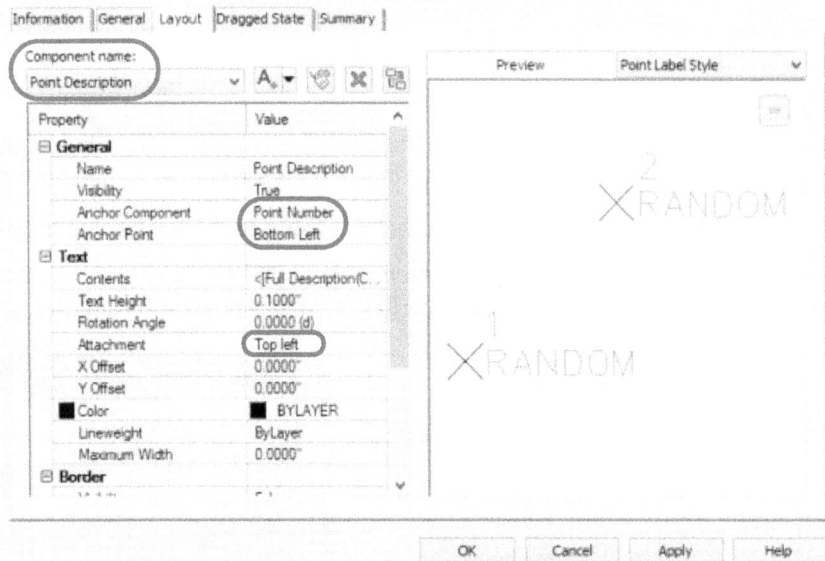

Figure 4–28

You will now add a new text component to display the Northing and Easting.

8. Expand the **Create Text Component** flyout (shown in Figure 4–29) and select **Text** to create a text component.

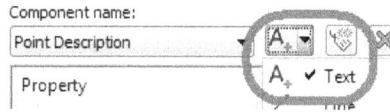

Figure 4–29

9. Change the default *Name* **text.1** to **Coordinates**, and then do the following:

- Set the *Anchor Component* to **Point Description**.
- Set the *Anchor Point* to **Bottom Left**.
- Set the *Attachment* to **Top Left**.

You will now change the contents from the default label set by the AutoCAD Civil 3D software to display the coordinates.

10. Click ⋯ in the *Contents* cell, next to *Label Text*, as shown in Figure 4–30.

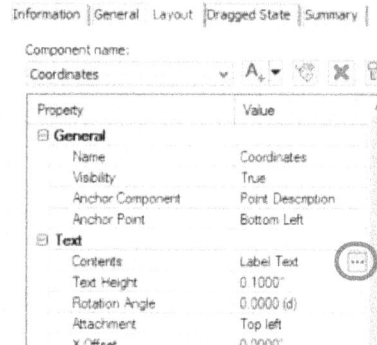

Figure 4–30

11. In the Text Component Editor dialog box, double-click on the text in the right side panel to highlight it and type **N**.

12. Select **Northing** in the Properties drop-down list. Change the *Precision* to **0.001** and click 🔁, as shown in Figure 4–31, to add the code to display the northing.

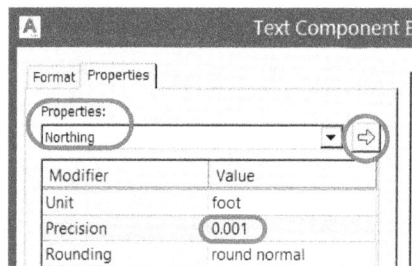

Figure 4–31

In the easting, the value will be displayed to the 4th decimal, P4. Change it so that it matches the northing.

13. Click at the end of the code. Press **<Enter>** to insert a new line followed by the letter **E**. Then select **Easting** in the Properties drop-down list and add it to post the code in the right side panel. The following should be displayed:

N<[Northing(Uft|P3|RN|AP|GC|UN|Sn|OF)]>

E<[Easting(Uft|P4|RN|AP|GC|UN|Sn|OF)]>

14. Select all of the code for the easting. Change the *Precision* to **0.001** and click ⇨ to revise the easting code.

15. Select the *Format* tab and verify that *Justification* is set to **Left**. Click **OK** to accept the changes in the Text Component Editor dialog box, and click **OK** again to accept the changes in the Label Style Composer.

16. Save the drawing.

Task 3 - Apply Style Components.

---

1. Continue working with the drawing from the previous task or open **SUV1-B3-Survey.dwg**.

2. In the Toolspace, select the Toolspace, *Prospector* tab and expand the *Point Groups* collection until the *Street Light* point group displays. Select the **Street Light** group, right-click, and select **Properties**.

3. In the *Information* tab, expand the Point Style drop-down list and select **Light Pole**. Then expand the Point label style drop-down list and select **Point#-Description-N-E**, as shown in Figure 4–32.

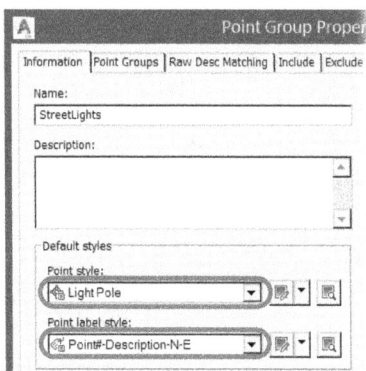

Figure 4–32

4. Click **OK** to accept the changes and close the dialog box.

If the symbol and label do not change, in the Toolspace, Prospector tab, right-click on the Street Light point group and select **Update**.

5. The symbols for the Light pole points have now been changed. Additionally, both the point symbols and point labels are annotative. In the Status Bar, expand the Annotation Scale drop-down list and change the scale of the drawing from *1"=40'* to **1"=30'** as shown in Figure 4–33. The size of the labels and point symbols change.

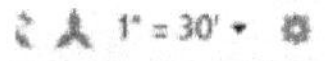

Figure 4–33

6. Save the drawing.

4.4 Point Settings

When creating new points, you must determine the next point number, and which elevations and descriptions to assign and how to assign them. To set the current point number, default elevations, descriptions, and other similar settings, you can use the expanded Create Points toolbar. Click ⤼ in the Create Points toolbar to display the *Points Creation* and *Point Identity* categories (shown in Figure 4–34), which contain the most commonly used values.

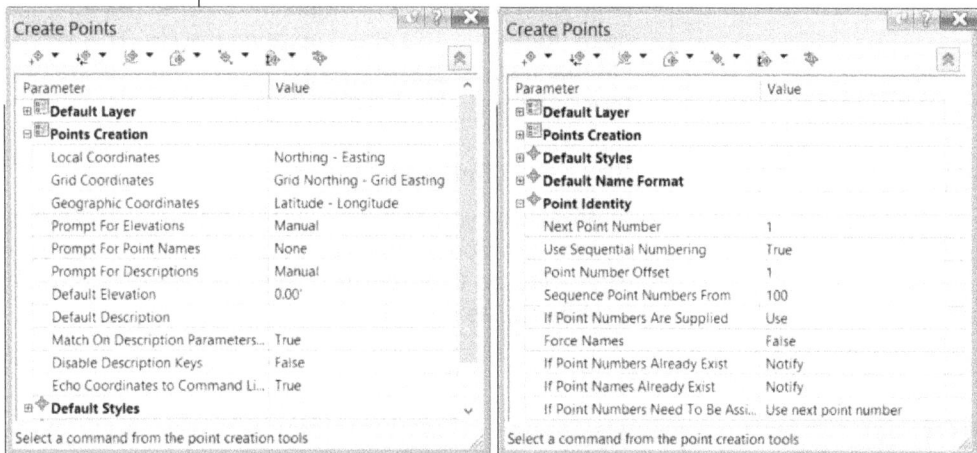

Figure 4–34

Points Creation Values

The *Points Creation* area affects prompting for elevations and/or descriptions. The two properties in this area are *Prompt For Elevations* and *Prompt For Descriptions*. These properties can be set as follows:

None	Does not prompt for an elevation or description.
Manual	Prompts for an elevation or description.
Automatic	Uses the **Default Elevation** or **Default Description** value when creating a point.
Automatic -Object	Creates points along an alignment whose description consists of the **Alignment name** and **Station**. This description is not dynamic and does not update if the alignment changes or the point is moved.

Point Identity Values

The *Point Identity* area sets the default method of handling duplicate point numbers. If there are duplicate point numbers, there are three ways to resolve the duplication:

1. Overwrite the existing point data.
2. Ignore the new point.
3. Assign it a new number.

This area's most critical property is *Next Point Number*. It is set to the first available number in the point list. If a file of imported point data uses point numbers 1-131 and 152-264, the current point number is 132 after importing the file. This value should be set manually to the next required point number before creating new points with the Create Points toolbar.

Hint: Point Settings

Alternatively, you can select the Toolspace, *Settings* tab and expand the *Commands* collection under the *Point* collection. Right-click on **CreatePoints**, and select **Edit Command Settings...**, as shown in Figure 4–35.

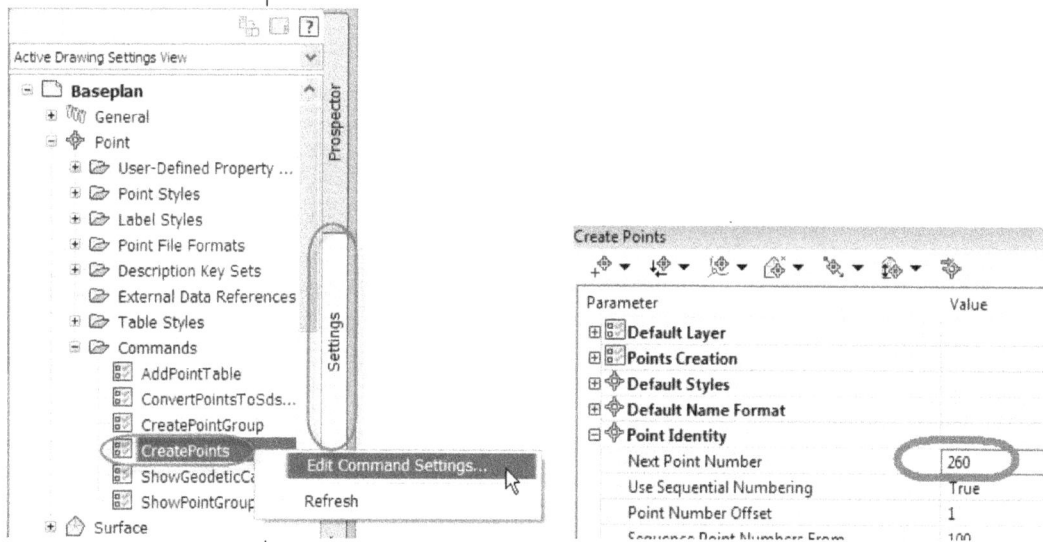

Figure 4–35

4.5 Creating Points

You can create points using the commands in the Create Points toolbar. These commands include:

- **Miscellaneous - Manual:** Creates a new point at specified coordinates.

- **Alignments - Station/Offset:** Creates a point at an alignment's specific station and offset. These points and their descriptions do not update if the alignment is modified or the point is moved. If you prefer a dynamic station and offset labels, consider using an Alignment label instead.

- **Alignments - Measure Alignment:** Creates point objects at a set interval, which is useful for construction staking. Again, these points do not update if the alignment changes.

- **Surface - Random Points:** Creates points whose elevation is from a specified surface. These points do update, but you must manually force the update. If you prefer a dynamic spot label, consider a Surface label instead.

Each icon in the Create Points toolbar has a drop-down list. If you expand it, you can select a command from the list to run, as shown in Figure 4–36.

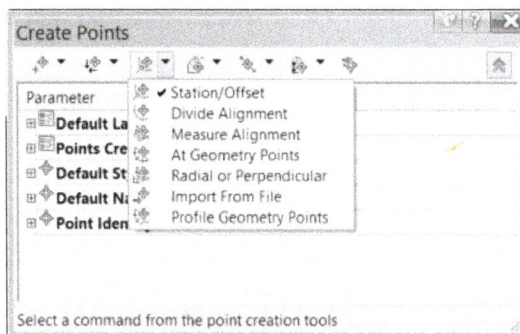

Figure 4–36

Practice 4c

Creating AutoCAD Civil 3D Points

Practice Objective

- Create a point manually then zoom to it using transparent commands.

Estimated time for completion: 10 minutes

In this practice, a fire hydrant was located by GPS. You will add a point object to locate it manually.

1. Continue working with the drawing from the previous practice, or open **SUV1-C1-Survey.dwg**.

2. In the *Home* tab>Create Ground Data panel, select **Points> Point Creation Tools** to display the Create Points toolbar.

   Expand the toolbar by clicking ⩔, as shown in Figure 4–37.

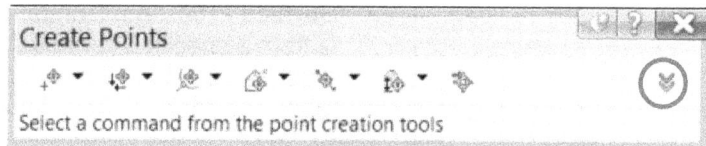

Figure 4–37

3. In the *Point Identity* area in the dialog box, set the *Next Point Number* to **260** and collapse the toolbar, by clicking ⩘.

4. Select the **Manual** option in the miscellaneous group in the toolbar as shown in Figure 4–38.

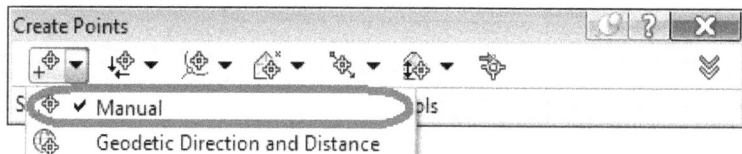

Figure 4–38

5. When prompted for a location, type **6256069.30,2036634.25** and press <Enter>.

The period is a placeholder for the elevation field. Typing zero is not correct because 0 is a valid elevation.

- When prompted for a description, type **HYD** and press <Enter>.

- When prompted for an elevation, press <Enter> to accept the default value of **<.>** (period), because it is unknown.

- Press <Enter> again to finish the command and select **X** in the Create Points dialog box to close it.

- In the Transparent Command toolbar, click ⟡ (Zoom to Point), and type **260**.

6. Save the drawing.

4.6 Description Key Sets

Description Keys categorize points by their field descriptions (raw description). If a point matches a Description Key entry, the point is assigned a point and label style, and a full description (a translation of the raw description). Description Key Sets can also scale and rotate points.

The Description Key's first five columns are the most used entries, as shown in Figure 4–39.

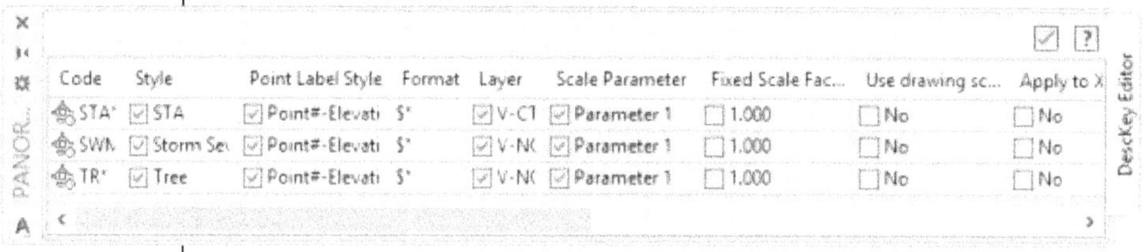

Code	Style	Point Label Style	Format	Layer	Scale Parameter	Fixed Scale Fac...	Use drawing sc...	Apply to X
☑ STA*	☑ STA	☑ Point#-Elevati	S*	☑ V-C1	☑ Parameter 1	☐ 1.000	☐ No	☐ No
☑ SWM	☑ Storm Se	☑ Point#-Elevati	S*	☑ V-NC	☑ Parameter 1	☐ 1.000	☐ No	☐ No
☑ TR*	☑ Tree	☑ Point#-Elevati	S*	☑ V-NC	☑ Parameter 1	☐ 1.000	☐ No	☐ No

Figure 4–39

- To create a new Description Key row, select an existing code, right-click, and select **New**. To edit a code, double-click in the cell.

Code, Point, and Label Style

Description code is a significant part of data collection. Code assigned to a raw description triggers action by the Description Key Set. Each entry in the set represents all of the possible descriptions that a field crew would use while surveying a job. When a raw description matches a code entry, the Key Set assigns all of the row's values to the matching point, including point style, label style, translates the raw description, and possibly assigns a layer. Codes are case-sensitive and must match the field collector's entered raw description.

A code might contain wild cards to match raw descriptions that contain numbering or additional material beyond the point's description. For example, MH* would match MH1, MH2, etc. and UP* would match UP 2245 14.4Kv Verizon. Common wild keys are described as follows:

# (pound)	Matches any single numeric digit. (T# matches T1 through T9.)
@ (at)	Matches any alphabetic character. (1@ matches 1A through 1Z.)
. (period)	Matches any non-alphanumeric character. (T. matches T- or T+.)
* (asterisk)	Matches any string of characters. (T* matches TREE, TR-Aspen, Topo, or Trench.)
? (question mark)	Matches any single character. (?BC matches TBC or 3BC.)

Matching a Key Set entry for the code assigns a Point Style at the point's coordinates. If the *Point Style* is set to **Default**, the *Settings* tab's Point feature *Point Style* is used (set in the Edit Feature Settings dialog box), as shown in Figure 4–40.

Matching a Key Set entry for the code assigns a point label style to annotate important point values. This is usually a number, elevation, and description. If the *Point Style* is set to **Default**, the *Settings* tab's Point feature *Point Label Style* is used (set in the Edit Feature Settings dialog box), as shown in Figure 4–40.

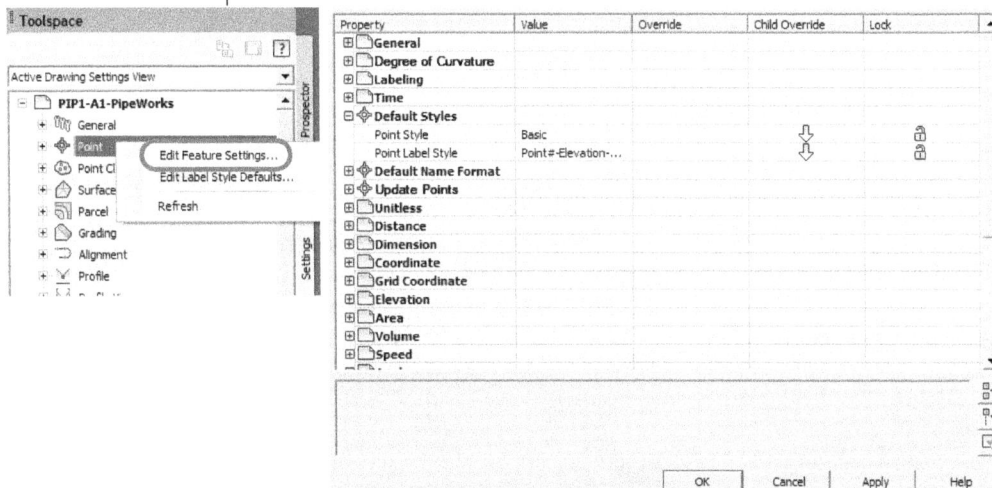

Figure 4–40

Format

The *Format* column translates the raw description (what the surveyor typed) into a full description (what you want it to read). When including spaces in a raw description, the AutoCAD Civil 3D software assigns parameter numbers to each description element. Parameters are represented by a $ sign followed by a number. For example, the description *PINE 6* has two elements: PINE and 6, with PINE as parameter 0 ($0) and 6 as parameter 1 ($1). When the *Format* column contains $*, it indicates that the software should use the raw description as the full description. The *Format* column can reorder the parameters and add characters to create a full description. For example, the raw description *PINE 6* can be translated to 6" PINE by entering **$1" $0**.

A complex raw description is as follows:

TREE D MAPLE 3

For the raw description to match the Description Key Set entry, the entry **TREE** must have an asterisk (*) after TREE (as shown in Figure 4–41). The raw description elements and their parameters are TREE ($0), D ($1), Maple ($2), and 3 ($3). The *Format* column entry of **$3" $2 $0** creates a full description of **3" MAPLE TREE**.

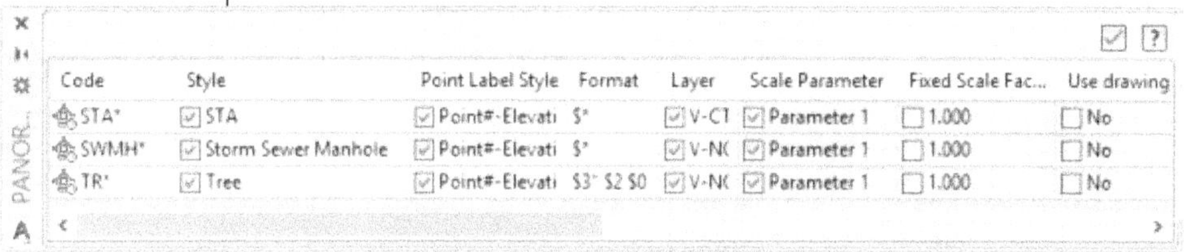

Figure 4–41

If a point does not match any Description Key Set entry, it receives the default styles assigned by the _All Points group.

The *Layer* column assigns a layer to the matching point. If the Point Style already has a marker and label layer, this entry should be toggled off. The Description Key Set also contains the *Scale* and *Rotate Parameter* columns. In the example in Figure 4–41, the 3 for the trunk diameter can also be a tree symbol scaling factor when applied to the symbol's X-Y.

Practice 4d

Creating a Description Key Set

Practice Objective

- Assign point symbols, labels, layers, etc., on importing by setting up Description Key Sets.

In this practice you will learn to create a new Description Key Set entry and apply it to an existing point. In addition you will update the Description Key Set to use parameters.

Estimated time for completion: 25 minutes

Task 1 - Create a new Description Key Set entry.

1. Continue working with the drawing from the previous practice, or open **SUV1-D1-Survey.dwg**.

2. In the Toolspace, *Settings* tab, expand the *Point* collection until the *Description Key Set* collection and its list display.

3. Select **Civil 3D**, right-click, and select **Edit Keys…**

4. Right-click in any *Code* cell and select **New…**, as shown in Figure 4–42.

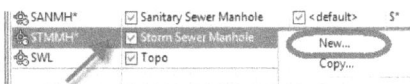

Figure 4–42

5. Double-click in the *Code* cell in the newly created row and type **HYD**, as shown in Figure 4–43.

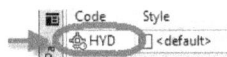

Figure 4–43

6. In the *Style* cell, toggle on the Point Style and select the **Style** cell to open the Point Style dialog box, as shown in Figure 4–44. Select **Hydrant (existing)** in the drop-down list and click **OK** to assign the style to the code.

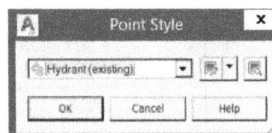

Figure 4–44

7. Leave **<default>** selected as the *Point Label Style* and **$*** as the *Format*. This means the label will be the same as the one entered by the surveyor.

8. Leave the check box toggled off in the *Layer* column.

You do not have a scale parameter and will not be using a fixed scale.

9. Select the **Yes** option in the *Use drawing scale* column, and clear the check box for the **Scale Parameter**, as shown in Figure 4–45.

Code	Style	Point Label ...	F...	Layer	Scale Param...	Fixed ...	Use dra
HYD	☑ Hydrant (existing)	☑ <default>	$*	☐	☐ Parameter 1	☐ 1.000	☑ Yes

Figure 4–45

10. Close the DescKey Editor vista by clicking ☑ in the top right corner of the palette, as shown in Figure 4–46.

Figure 4–46

Task 2 - Apply the new Description Key Set to an existing point.

---

1. Continue working with the drawing from the previous task or open **SUV1-D2-Survey.dwg**.

2. In the Transparent Command toolbar, click ⊕ (Zoom to Point), and then type **260**.

3. In the Toolspace, *Prospector* tab, select the **_All Points** group, right-click, and select **Apply Description Keys**, as shown in Figure 4–47.

The point updates to display the Hydrant symbol and its new description

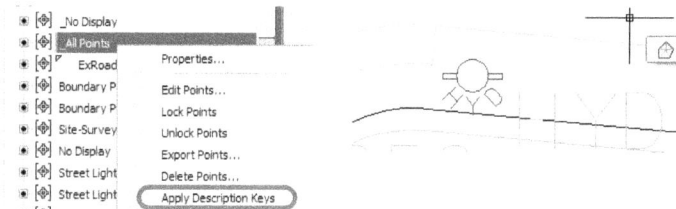

Figure 4–47

4. Save the drawing.

Task 3 - Update the Description Key Set to use parameters.

In this task you will use the Parameters feature to control the display properties of symbols in your drawings. The most common parameter is the **Scale** parameter. With this parameter, a surveyor will enter the size of a tree as part of the description and the description key file will insert a symbol scaled to the value provided by the surveyor. In this case, you want the pumpers on the hydrant to display correctly (i.e., running parallel to the road).

1. Continue working with the drawing from the previous task or open **SUV1-D3-Survey.dwg**

2. In the Toolspace, *Settings* tab, expand *Point>Description Key Sets*. Select **Civil 3D**, right-click, and select **Edit Keys...**, as shown in Figure 4–48.

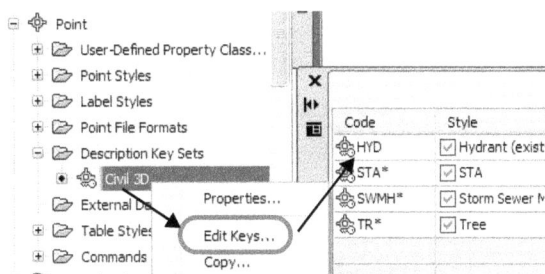

Figure 4–48

In this example, -5 is Parameter1, which you will enter in Step 6.

3. In the HYD row, *Code* column, type **HYD***. The asterisk symbolizes a wildcard, (i.e., any character after the letters HYD).

4. In the HYD row, select the check box in the *Marker Rotate* column, select the cell, and then select **Parameter1** in the drop-down list. The selected parameter is shown in Figure 4–49.

Figure 4–49

The -5 indicates the required rotation.

5. Click ☑ in the top right corner of the dialog box to close the Panorama view.

6. In Model Space, select the Hydrant point object, right-click, and select **Edit Points**.

7. Set the *Raw Description* from HYD to **HYD -5**.

8. Select the row, right-click, and select **Apply Description Keys**, as shown in Figure 4–50.

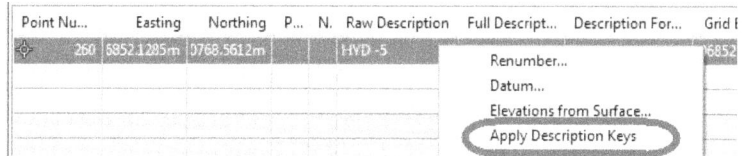

Figure 4–50

9. Click ☑ in the top right corner of the dialog box to close the Panorama view.

   The hydrant has now been rotated to display the hydrant pumpers following the rotation of the road, as shown in Figure 4–51.

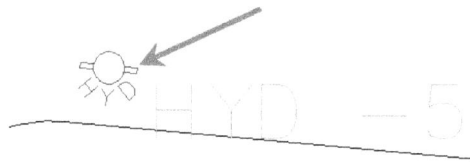

Figure 4–51

10. The label also displays the rotation angle text -5, which you do not want. In the Toolspace, *Settings* tab, expand the *Point* and *Description Key Sets* collections. Select **Civil 3D**, right-click, and select **Edit Keys…**

11. In the HYD row, change the *Format* from $* to **Hydrant**, as shown in Figure 4–52.

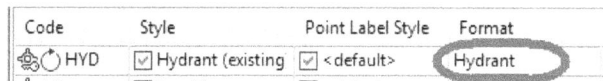

Figure 4–52

12. Click ☑ in the top right corner of the dialog box to close the Panorama view.

13. In Model Space, select the Hydrant point object, right-click, and select **Apply Description Keys**. The changes are now applied, as shown in Figure 4–53.

Figure 4–53

14. Save the drawing.

4.7 Importing Survey Data

The AutoCAD Civil 3D software has methods to import point data from ASCII text files, AutoCAD Land Desktop point databases, and Autodesk LandXML files, as well as methods to convert AutoCAD Land Desktop points to AutoCAD Civil 3D points. The Toolspace, *Survey* tab also inserts points from a survey to a drawing.

Import Points Only

Alternatively, you can click ✦ (Import Points) in the Create Points toolbar.

There are two methods of launching the import point feature, one is by using the *Insert* tab and the other is using the **Points** creation tool in the Toolspace, *Prospector* tab.

How To: Use the *Insert* tab method

1. In the *Insert* tab, click ✦ (Points from File).This opens the Import Points dialog box.
2. In the Import Points dialog box, set the file format, select the files to import, set any advanced options, and click **OK** to import the points.

How To: Use the Point Creation tools method

1. Open the Create Points dialog box by expanding Points in the *Home* tab, expanding the drop-down list and selecting a **Create Points** option, as shown on the left in Figure 4–54. Alternatively, in the Toolspace, *Prospector* tab, select **Points**, right-click and select **Create...**, as shown on the right.

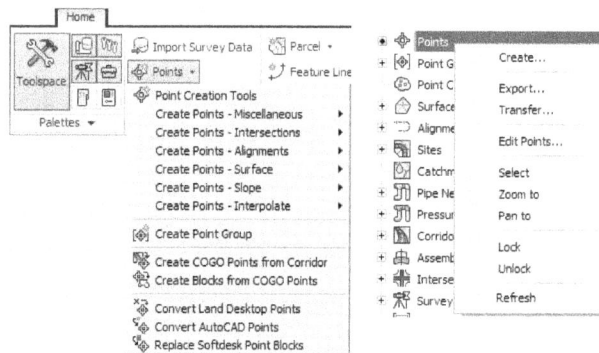

Figure 4–54

All commands in the Points drop-down list can also be accessed in the Create Points toolbar, as shown in Figure 4–55.

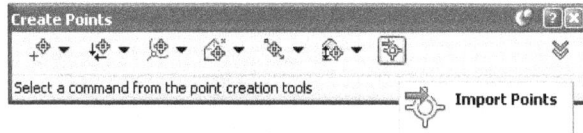

Figure 4–55

2. Click ⊕ (Import Points) to open the Import Points dialog box.
3. In the Import Points dialog box, under the *Specify point file format* area, select the required format.
4. After setting the format, click ⊕ on the right to open the Select Source File dialog box.
5. In the Select Source File dialog box, browse to the import point file, select it, and select **Open**. You can assign the imported points to a new or existing point group by selecting the **Add Points to Point Group** option and selecting the point group in the drop-down list. Select any **Advanced options** as required. The Import Points dialog box is shown in Figure 4–56.

You can select multiple files if they have the same file format.

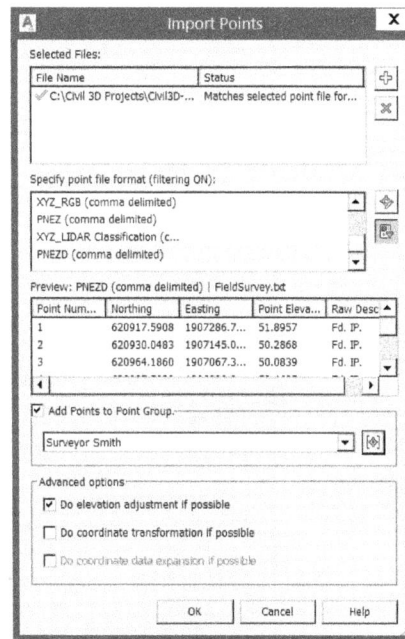

Figure 4–56

To import points directly from an AutoCAD Land Desktop point database, select the External Project Point Database format and browse for the project's COGO subfolder. Then locate and select the **Points.mdb** file.

If a drawing contains all or a subset of all points, you only need to convert the points into AutoCAD Civil 3D cogo points.

Duplicate Point Numbers

If an imported file creates duplicate point numbers, the AutoCAD Civil 3D software overwrites, merges, or reassigns them during the import process. When encountering duplicate point numbers, the AutoCAD Civil 3D software can assign the next available number, add an offset value (add 5000 to each point number that conflicts), overwrite points (replaces the current point values with the file's values), or merge points (add the file's values to an existing point's values). If using the offset method, the new point numbers are kept unique in the drawing. If using the next available number method, the new points blend into the original points and are difficult to identify.

The offset method is preferred when resolving duplicate point numbers. When importing points that will potentially duplicate point numbers, the Create Points toolbar's *Point Identity* settings, as shown in Figure 4–57, is the default when handling duplicate point numbers.

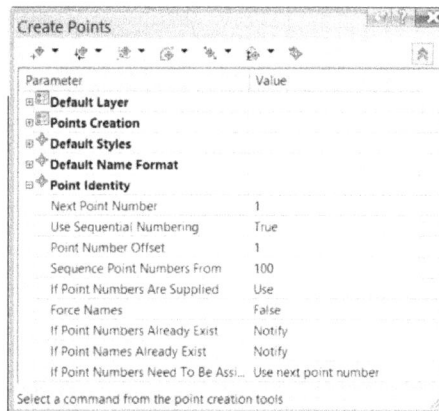

Figure 4–57

In the *Point Identity* settings, set the duplicate point resolution method for the *If Point Numbers Already Exist* variable. The four methods are **Renumber**, **Merge**, **Overwrite**, and **Notify**, as shown in Figure 4–58. The import process never overwrites point data unless you specify that it should do so.

If Point Numbers Are Supplied	Use
Force Names	false
If Point Numbers Already Exist	Notify
If Point Names Already Exist	Renumber
If Point Numbers Need To Be Assi...	Merge
	Overwrite
	Notify

Figure 4–58

When encountering a duplicate point, the Duplicate Point Number dialog box opens. After you define a resolution, it can be assigned to the current duplicate point or to all encountered duplicate points.

Survey Toolspace

The Toolspace, *Survey* tab displays a panel through which all surveys are processed. Survey uses graphics to display field book imports, figure and network previews, and points. If you toggle off these graphics, you can process a survey without a drawing being open. If you want to display these graphics, you need to have a drawing open. Survey prompts you to open a drawing if you do not have one open.

The Toolspace, *Survey* tab contains Survey settings, Equipment defaults, Figure Prefixes, and Linework Code Sets. Survey's settings can be on a local or network folder. It is preferred to use a network folder in larger offices because all users can then standardize the file values.

How To: Display the Toolspace, *Survey* Tab

If your Toolspace does not display the *Survey* tab, click

(Survey) in the *Home* tab>Palettes panel, as shown in Figure 4–59.

Figure 4–59

Import Points and Figures Using the Survey Database

After collecting and coding the data, and then downloading and converting it, the next step in Survey is to import the survey data, review it, and place the survey points and figures into a drawing. A working folder defines where the local Survey Database is located. The preferred location is a network folder, in which you place the local Survey Databases. The Survey User Settings dialog box sets the defaults for all new Survey Databases. You should set these before starting Survey. The Survey Working Folder is the location for all of the Survey Databases and can be local or on the network. The default working folder is *C:\Civil 3D Projects*.

How To: Set the Working Folder for the Survey Database

1. In the Toolspace, *Survey* tab, select **Survey Databases**.
2. Right-click and select **Set working folder...**, as shown in Figure 4–60.

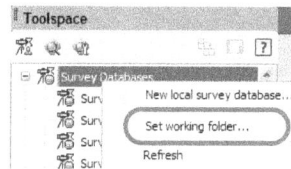

Figure 4–60

Survey Database

A Survey Database is a subfolder in the working folder. The Survey Working Folder contains the Survey's settings and observation database. This database contains the Survey's Networks, Figures, and Survey Points.

To import a field book, you use the Survey's *Import Events* collection. *Import Events* provides access to an Import wizard, which guides you through the steps of importing a file. To open the Import wizard, select **Import Events** in the Survey, right-click, and select **Import survey data...**

Survey Database Folders cannot be deleted in AutoCAD Civil 3D Survey. If you want to delete the working folder, this process must be done manually, external to the AutoCAD Civil 3D software.

The Specify Database page is shown in Figure 4–61. It sets the survey, creates a new survey, and edits the Survey's settings.

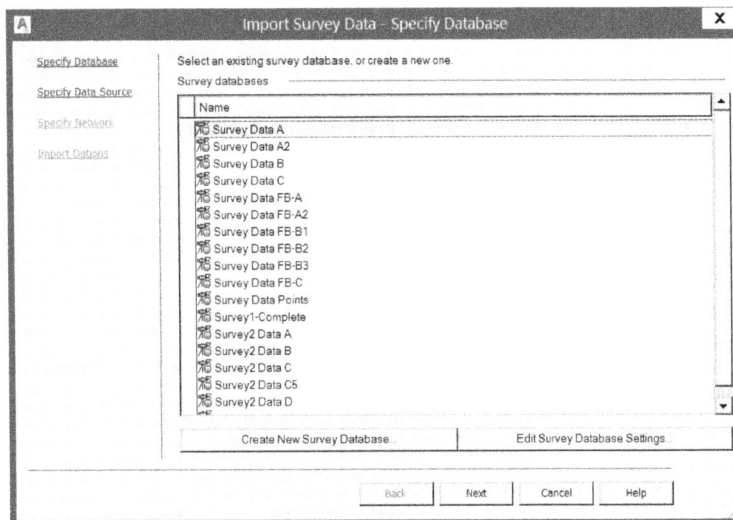

Figure 4–61

Click **Next**. The *Specify Data Source* page (shown in Figure 4–62), defines the file import type, the file's path, and its format (if it is a coordinate file).

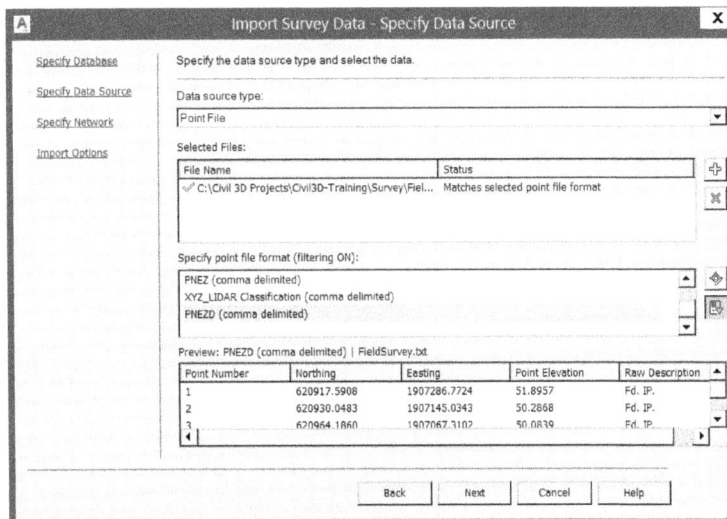

Figure 4–62

Click **Next**. The *Specify Network* page (shown in Figure 4–63), enables you to change the network or create a new survey network.

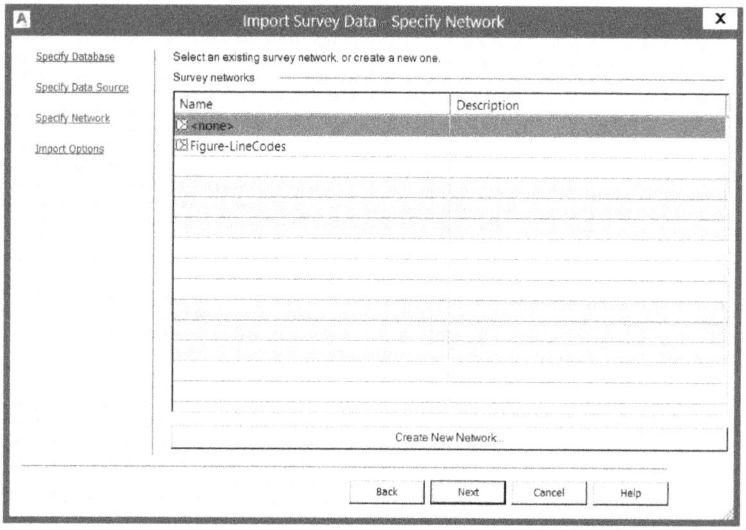

Figure 4–63

Click **Next**. The *Import Options* page (shown in Figure 4–64), sets the values for the import. These settings affect what the import does and which support files it uses.

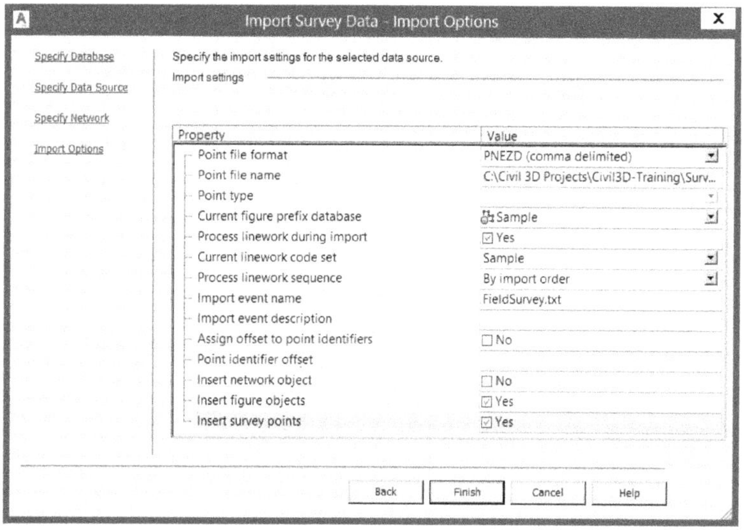

Figure 4–64

If the field book has figure coding from a conversion, you do not need to toggle on the *Process linework during import* property. This is for ASCII files other than field books that have **Linework Code Set** commands included in the point's description.

Inserting figures requires entries to be in the Figure Prefix database and figure styles to be in the drawing. This is required to point the figure and linework to the correct layers in the drawing and to specify whether the figure is also a breakline in a surface.

When inserting points, it is necessary to have a Description Key Set defined to assign points, point label styles, and layers, and to translate raw descriptions to full descriptions.

Open a Survey Database for Editing

Only one Survey Database can be edited at a time. When opened for editing, this prepares the survey for reading and writing.

There are options to set the path or location for the Survey Database project files, and for all of the settings. When you create a new Survey Database, a Windows folder is created with the same name. If you close a drawing with a survey open, the Survey Database closes automatically. You must start a new drawing and then open the required Survey Database. You can only have one Survey Database open at a time.

How To: Open a Survey Database

1. In the Toolspace, *Survey* tab, expand the *Survey Database* collection.
2. Select the survey database that you want to open, right-click, and select **Open for edit** or **Open for read-only**, depending your requirements, as shown in Figure 4–65.

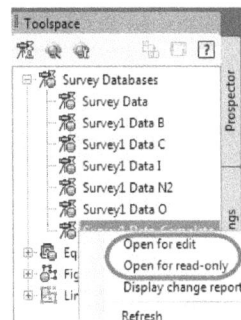

Figure 4–65

Practice 4e

Importing Survey Data

Practice Objective

- Import points from and export points to ASCII files created from the field survey.

In this practice you will import an ASCII file created in the field.

Estimated time for completion: 10 minutes

Task 1 - Import an ASCII file.

1. Continue working with the drawing from the previous practice or open **SUV1-E1-Survey.dwg** from the *C:\Civil 3D Projects\ Civil3D-Training\Survey* folder.

2. In the *Home* tab>Create Ground Data panel, click ⬙ (Import Survey Data).

3. On the Specify Database page, click **Create New Survey Database...**, as shown in Figure 4–66.

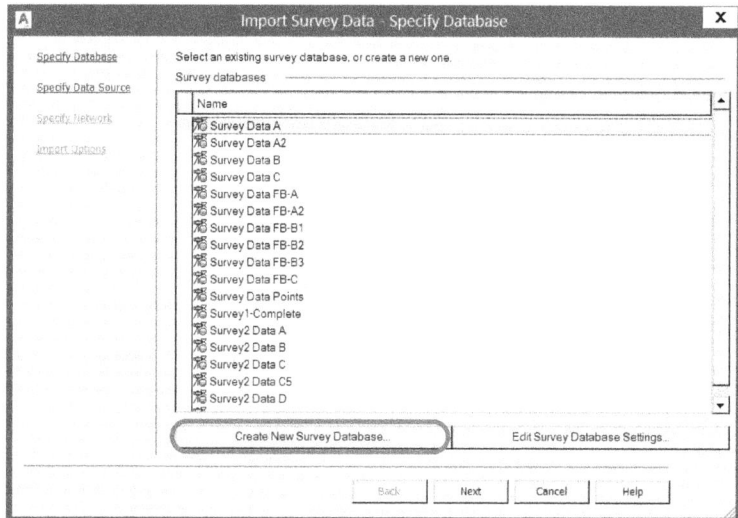

Figure 4–66

4. Type **Training** for the name and click **OK**.

5. Click **Edit Survey Database Settings...** as shown in Figure 4–67.

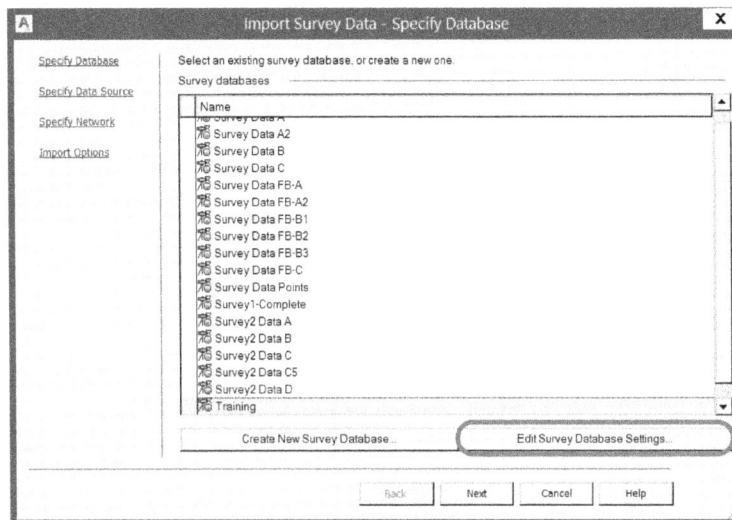

Figure 4–67

6. Under *Units* in the Survey Database Settings dialog box, for the *Coordinate Zone*, click the **Browse** icon. In the Select Coordinate Zone dialog box, select **NAD83 California State Planes, Zone VI, US Foot** (as shown in Figure 4–68). Click **OK** twice and then click **Next**.

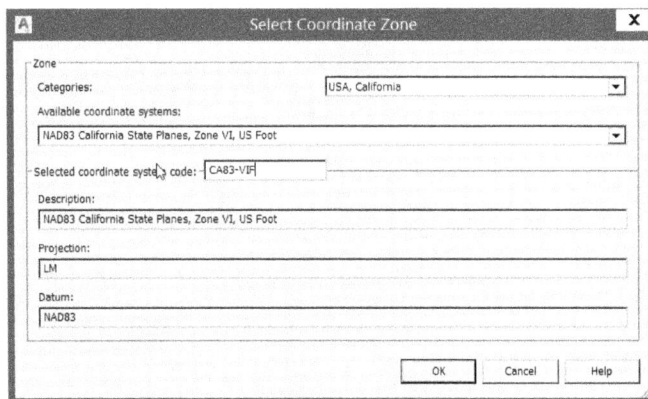

Figure 4–68

7. On the Specify Data Sources page, expand the Data source type drop-down list and select **Point File**, as shown in Figure 4–69. Click ⊞ (Add file) and browse to *C:\Civil 3D Projects\Civil3D-Training\Survey*. Select **Field Survey.txt** and open it. Finally, for the file format, select **PNEZD (comma delimited)**. Click **Next**.

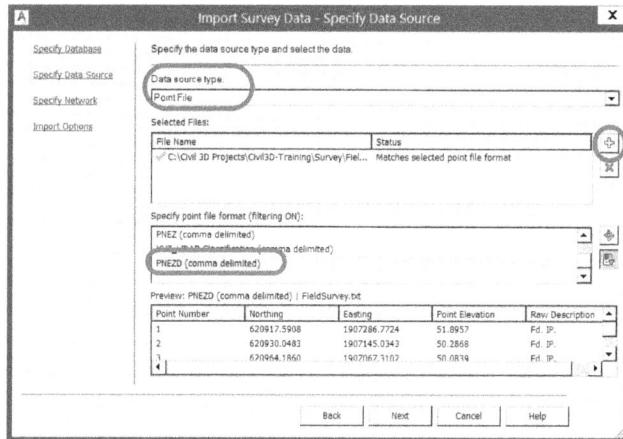

Figure 4–69

8. On the Survey Network page, click **Next**.

9. On the Import Options page, select **Process linework during import**, **Insert figure objects**, and **Insert survey points**, as shown in Figure 4–70. Click **Finish**.

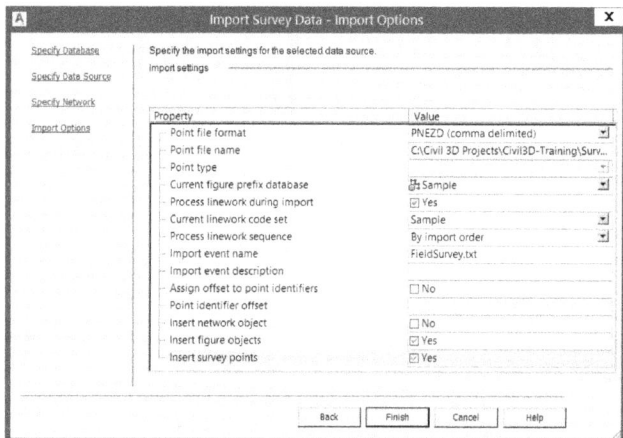

Figure 4–70

10. Save the drawing.

4.8 Point Groups

Point groups organize points that share common descriptions and characteristics (such as existing storm, gas lines, building corners, etc.). Point groups also enable points to display different point or label styles. For example, a Landscape Architect needs to display different symbols for each tree species, while an Engineer only needs to display a generic tree symbol. The Description Key Set enables you to assign the tree species symbols for the Landscape Architect, and a point group enables generic tree symbols to override the symbols for the Engineer. Another function of a point group is to hide all of the points.

In the AutoCAD Civil 3D software, point groups can be defined in the template along with a Description Key Set. When you create a new drawing from this template and import points, they are assigned their symbols and can be sorted into point groups.

All points in a drawing belong to the **_All Points** point group. Consider this point group as the point database. It cannot be deleted and initially is not in a drawing until you add points. All new point groups include all drawing points or a subset of drawing points (referenced points from the **_All Points** point group).

Defining Point Groups

To create a new point group, select the Toolspace, *Prospector* tab, right-click on the *Point Groups* collection and select **New...** Alternatively, in the *Home* tab, expand *Points* and select **Create Point Group**.

When you select **New...** or **Create Point Group**, the Point Group Properties dialog box opens. It has nine tabs, each affecting the point group's definition.

The *Point Groups*, *Raw Desc Matching*, *Include*, and *Query Builder* tabs add points to the point group. The *Exclude* tab removes points from a point group.

The *Information* tab defines the point group's name. The *Point style* and *Point label style* should remain at their defaults, unless you want to use either style to override the assigned styles of the points in the point group. The points in the point group display their originally assigned styles until you toggle on the override. A point group can be locked by toggling on the **Object locked** option to prevent any changes to the group. The Point Group Properties dialog box is shown in Figure 4–71.

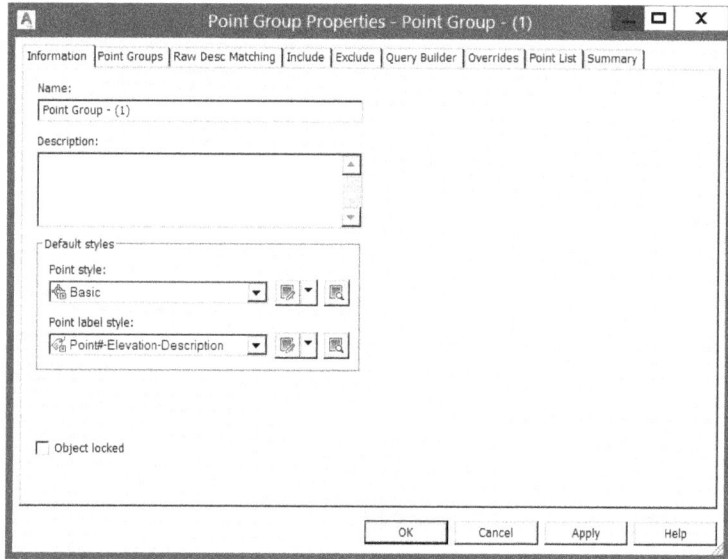

Figure 4–71

The *Point Groups* tab lists the drawing's groups. A point group can be created from other point groups. When you select a point group name, the group and its points become members of the new point group. For example, the point group **Trees** is created from the point groups *Maple*, *Walnut*, *Oak*, etc.

The *Raw Desc Matching* tab lists codes from the Description Key Code set. When you toggle on the code, any point matching the code becomes part of the point group.

If you cannot select a point with the previous two methods, the *Include* tab enables you to include points by specifically entering in the selection criteria. The criteria include the point number (point number list or by selection), elevation, name, raw description, full description, and all points.

- **With numbers matching:** Selects points by a point number range or list. When creating a list, sequential point numbers are hyphenated (1-20) and individual numbers are in a comma delimited list. A point list can include sequential and individual points (1-20, 14, 44, 50-60). Select **Selection Set in Drawing** to select the points in the drawing and list their point numbers at the top of the *Include* tab.

- **With elevations matching:** Enables you to select points by entering a specific elevation or by specifying a minimum and/or maximum elevation. For example, valid entries include >100,<400, and >100. The first entry only includes points whose elevation is above 100, but less than 400. The second entry only includes points whose elevation is greater than 100. A point without an elevation cannot be selected using this method. An elevation range, defined by separating the start and end numbers with a hyphen, includes points whose elevation falls in the range (1-100). This can be combined with greater or less than symbols.

- **With names matching:** Selects points based on matching their point names. Enter one or more point names separated by commas.

- **With raw/full descriptions matching:** Selects points based on matching an entered raw or full description. Enter one or more descriptions separated by commas. You can use the same wildcards as the Description Key Set. Generally, this method uses the asterisk (*) as the wildcard after the description (e.g., PINE*, CTV*, CL*, etc.).

- **Include all points:** Assigns all points in the drawing to the point group. When this option is toggled on, all other **Include** options are disabled.

The *Exclude* tab has the same options as the *Include* tab, except for the **Include All Points** option.

The *Query Builder* tab creates one or more expressions to select points. Each query is a row selecting points. As with all SQL queries, you combine expressions using the operators AND, OR, and NOT. You can also use parentheses to group expressions.

The *Overrides* tab overrides the points in the point group's raw description, elevation, point style, and/or point label style. For example, you can override specific tree species symbols with a generic tree symbol, override a label style when displaying this group, or override the point and label style with none (to hide all points).

The point group display order affects points and their overrides. To change how the point groups display, modify the Point Group display order.

The *Point List* tab displays the point group's points. This tab enables you to review points that are currently in the point group.

The *Summary* tab displays the point group's settings. You can print this tab as a report by cutting and pasting it into a document.

Updating Out-of-Date Point Groups

After defining point groups and adding points to a drawing, the group becomes out of date before assigning the points to the group. This enables you to verify that the point(s) should become part of the group. To review why a group is out of date, select the group, right-click, and select **Show Changes...** If the changes are correct, select **Update** to add the points to the group. If you know that all of the groups displaying as out of date should be updated, right-click on the *Point Groups* collection and select **Update**. At this level, the command updates all of the point groups.

Overriding Point Group Properties

When working with points, you might want them to display different labels, not be displayed, or display different symbols. Each required change is a function of a point group override. A point group that contains all of the points and overrides their symbols and labels with none does not display any points. This is similar to freezing all of the layers involved with points. A point group that changes the symbols that a group displays overrides the label styles assigned to the point in the point group. To display a different symbol, the point group overrides the assigned point styles. To set the style and override the assigned styles, toggle on the point group in the *Overrides* tab and set the styles in the *Override* column of the point group, as shown in Figure 4–72.

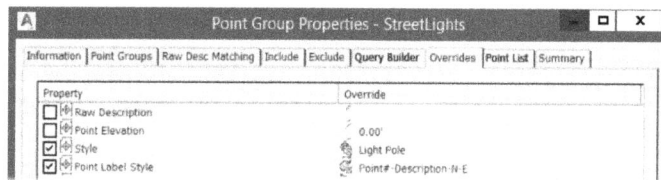

Figure 4–72

Point Groups Display Properties

When creating a point group, it is placed at the top of the point group list. The point group list is more than a list of point groups; it is also the AutoCAD Civil 3D's point draw order. The AutoCAD Civil 3D software draws the point groups starting from the bottom of the list to the top. If **_All Points** is the first drawn point group and the remaining point groups are subsets of all points, the individual point group does not display, but all of the points display.

To display point groups that are a subset of all points, you must create a point group whose purpose is to hide all points. This popular point group is commonly called *No Display*. With this group, any point group drawn after it displays its members without *seeing* the other points.

The AutoCAD Civil 3D software draws point groups from the bottom to the top of the list. To manipulate the display order, right-click on the *Point Groups* collection in the Toolspace, *Prospector* tab and select **Properties**. The Point Groups dialog box opens, enabling you to modify the point group display order using the arrows on the right, as shown in Figure 4–73.

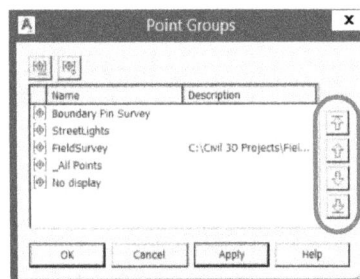

Figure 4–73

These arrows enable you to select the required point group and move it up or down in the list (or all of the way to the top or bottom of the list with one click, ⬆/⬇) in the hierarchy for display purposes. The Point Groups dialog box has two additional icons at the top. The first icon displays the difference between point groups and the second icon updates them all.

If you use Description Key Sets, a point displays the assigned point and label style when it is part of any point group. The only time the point displays another style is when you override the style (in the Point Group Properties dialog box, in the *Overrides* tab).

With the Description Key Set and display order shown in Figure 4–74, the points display their originally assigned point label styles.

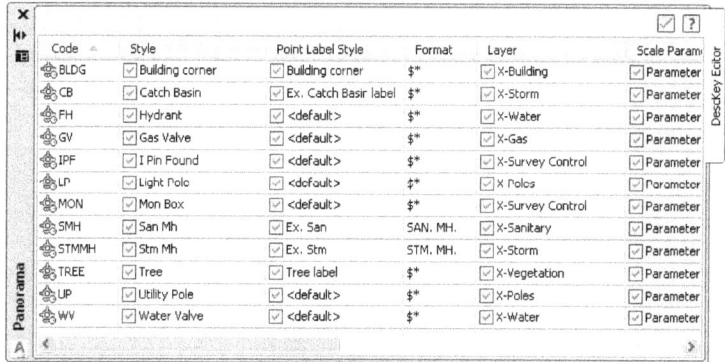

Code	Style	Point Label Style	Format	Layer	Scale Param
BLDG	☑ Building corner	☑ Building corner	$*	☑ X-Building	☑ Parameter
CB	☑ Catch Basin	☑ Ex. Catch Basin label	$*	☑ X-Storm	☑ Parameter
FH	☑ Hydrant	☑ <default>	$*	☑ X-Water	☑ Parameter
GV	☑ Gas Valve	☑ <default>	$*	☑ X-Gas	☑ Parameter
IPF	☑ I Pin Found	☑ <default>	$*	☑ X-Survey Control	☑ Parameter
LP	☑ Light Pole	☑ <default>	$*	☑ X-Poles	☑ Parameter
MON	☑ Mon Box	☑ <default>	$*	☑ X-Survey Control	☑ Parameter
SMH	☑ San Mh	☑ Ex. San	SAN. MH.	☑ X-Sanitary	☑ Parameter
STMMH	☑ Stm Mh	☑ Ex. Stm	STM. MH.	☑ X-Storm	☑ Parameter
TREE	☑ Tree	☐ Tree label	$*	☑ X-Vegetation	☑ Parameter
UP	☑ Utility Pole	☑ <default>	$*	☑ X-Poles	☑ Parameter
WV	☑ Water Valve	☑ <default>	$*	☑ X-Water	☑ Parameter

Figure 4–74

The *No Display* point group includes all of the points, but overrides the originally assigned point style and point label styles with **<none>**. When *No Display* is moved to the list's top, no points display. The Point Groups dialog box is shown in Figure 4–75.

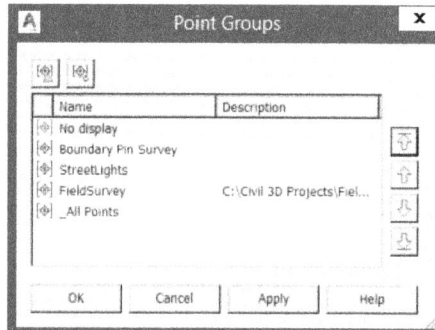

Figure 4–75

Practice 4f

Creating Point Groups

Practice Objective

- Draw Parcels from a legal description using lines and curves or polylines and transparent commands.

In this practice you will create point groups.

Estimated time for completion: 10 minutes

Task 1 - Create Point Groups (Boundary Pin Survey).

1. Continue working with the drawing from the previous practice or open **SUV1-F1-Survey.dwg**.

2. In the Toolspace, *Prospector* tab, select **Point Groups**, right-click, and select **New...**, as shown in Figure 4–76.

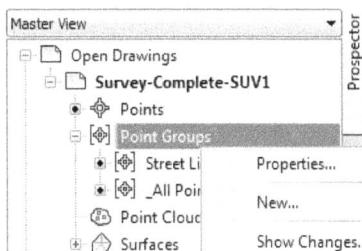

Figure 4–76

3. In the Point Group Properties dialog box, in the *Information* tab, type **Boundary Pin Survey** in the *Name* field, set the *Point style* to **Iron Pin**, and set the *Point label style* to **Elevation and Description**, as shown in Figure 4–77.

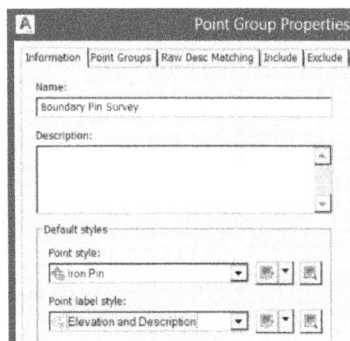

Figure 4–77

4. Select the *Include* tab. Select the **With raw description matching** option. Type ***IP.** (verify that a period follows IP) in the field to select all of the points that have the last three characters *IP.* (iron pin). You can confirm this in the *Point List* tab, as shown in Figure 4–78.

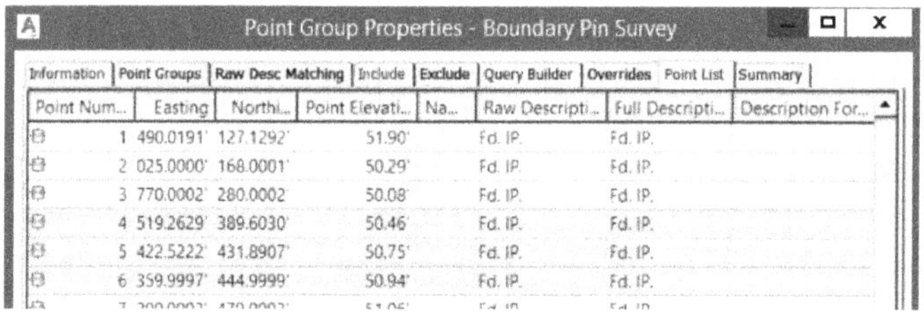

Figure 4–78

5. Click **OK** to close the dialog box and apply the changes.

Task 2 - Create point groups (No display).

Continue working with the drawing from the previous task. In this task you will use the point group to control the points display. Not only will you be able to display the same point differently, but you will also be able to control the visibility of the points. This eliminates needing to use the Layer command to thaw and freeze layers.

1. As in Task 1, select **Point Groups**, right-click, and select **New...** to create a new point group. In the *Information* tab, type **No display** for the *Name*.

2. Select **<none>** for both the *Point style* and the *Point label style*, as shown in Figure 4–79.

Figure 4–79

3. Select the *Overrides* tab and select **Style** and **Point Label Style**, as shown in Figure 4–80.

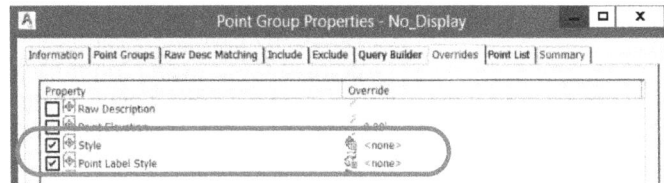

Figure 4–80

4. Select the *Include* tab, select **Include all points** to set it to **True**. Select the *Point List* tab to confirm that all of the points have been included.

5. Click **OK** to create the point group. Note that the points have disappeared.

6. To control the hierarchy and the display of the point group style, select the Toolspace, *Prospector* tab, select **Point Groups**, right-click, and select **Properties**.

7. In the Point Groups dialog box, select the **Boundary Pin Survey** point group and move it to the top of the list by clicking ⬆. Click **OK** to apply the changes. Only the points in the Boundary Pin point group display. If the property pins are not displayed you might need to **regen** the drawing (type **RE**, and press <Enter).

8. Experiment with moving point groups up and down the list to control the display of points.

9. Save the drawing.

4.9 Reviewing and Editing Points

Reviewing and editing point data occurs throughout the AutoCAD Civil 3D environment. It is as simple as selecting a point in the drawing, right-clicking, and selecting **Edit Points…**. You can also edit points using the shortcut menu in the *Points* heading in the Toolspace, *Prospector* tab. Alternatively, you can select a point entry in the Toolspace, *Prospector's* preview area.

Repositioning Point Labels

Each point label style has **Dragged State** parameters. These parameters affect the label's behavior when moving the label from its original label position. Depending on the **Dragged State** parameters, a label can change completely (Stacked text) or display as it was originally defined (As composed). An example of a label is shown in Figure 4–81.

When selecting a point, it displays multiple grips. Click the move grip when you want to relocate the label.

Figure 4–81

A point displays three grips when selected. Use the **Rectangle** label grip to Move, Rotate, and Toggle sub item grips and Reset the label. Use the Diamond point object grip to Move and Rotate both the label and marker, Rotate just the marker, reset marker rotation, and Reset all. The third grip is a plus symbol that enables you to add vertices to the leader, as shown in Figure 4–82.

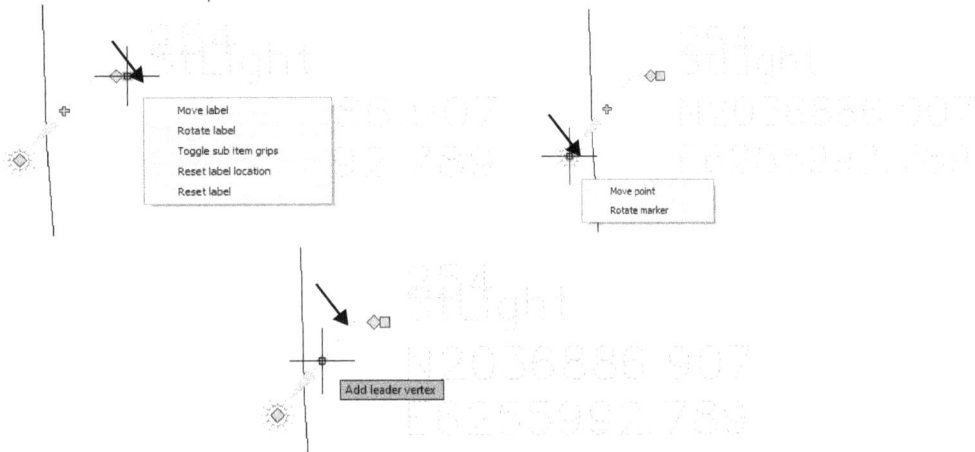

Figure 4–82

- Each label component can be modified and the change is only for that point.

- Point objects can be set to automatically rotate to match the current view using style settings. If this is not preferred, they can have a rotation assigned directly through the AutoCAD Properties dialog box.

- You can reset a label to its original position by selecting the point, right-clicking, and selecting **Reset Label**.

Practice 4g

Manipulating Points

Practice Objective

- Modify the label position for points to ensure that the plan is readable.

Estimated time for completion: 5 minutes

Task 1 - Modify the position of the labels.

1. Continue working with the drawing from the previous practice or open **SUV1-G1-Survey.dwg**.

2. In the Toolspace, *Prospector* tab, right-click on Point Group and select **Properties**. Select the **No display point group** and press <Down Arrow> to move it to the bottom of the list. Click **OK**.

This positions the point at the center of the screen.

3. In the preview point list, scroll down until the point number **260** displays. Select it, right-click, and select **Zoom to**.

4. In a typical drafting workflow, points can overlap, making them illegible. Since the Point Style's text height is a function of the drawing scale, changing the *Annotation Scale* changes the text size. In the Status Bar, set the *Annotation Scale* to **1"=40'**, as shown in Figure 4–83, to change the point size in the drawing.

Figure 4–83

5. Select point 260 to display its grips. Select the Drag Label grip, as shown in Figure 4–84, to relocate the label.

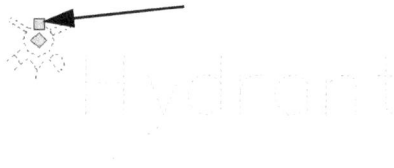

Figure 4–84

6. With the label still displaying grips, hover on the Rectangle grip and select **Reset Label**.

7. With the label still displaying grips, hover over the Square label grip to display the options for moving, rotating, and additional sub item grips, as shown in Figure 4–85. Select **Rotate label** and rotate the label.

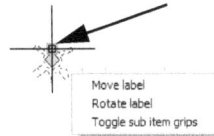

Move label
Rotate label
Toggle sub item grips

Figure 4–85

8. With the label still displaying grips, hover over the diamond point grip to display the options to move, rotate label and marker, and Rotate marker, as shown in Figure 4–86. Select **Rotate marker** and rotate the marker.

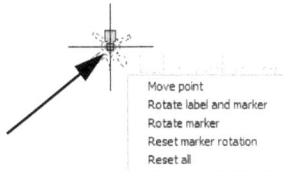

Move point
Rotate label and marker
Rotate marker
Reset marker rotation
Reset all

Figure 4–86

9. Save the drawing.

4.10 Point Reports

The surveyor needs to produce point reports. These can include a record list for the project, a checklist to find errors, reference for field crews, stakeout, etc. Incorporating survey data with an AutoCAD Civil 3D engineering project is unique in that it relies on connection and communication with third party survey equipment and software. Autodesk has collaborated with the major survey equipment vendors (TDS Survey Link, TOPCON Link, Trimble Link, Carlson Connect, and Leica X-Change) and they have developed applications that interface their equipment with the AutoCAD Civil 3D software.

AutoCAD Civil 3D points can be exported and then uploaded to the survey equipment without relying on manually created lists. However, a documented point list might be required. There are several ways to create reports about points.

Point Reports - Reports Manager

The AutoCAD Civil 3D Reports Manager produces several point reports. To create reports from the Reports Manager, the Toolspace, *Toolbox* tab must be available. To display the Toolspace, *Toolbox* tab, go to the *Home* tab>Palettes panel, and select **Toolbox**. Then select the Toolspace, *Toolbox* tab and expand the *Reports Manager* collection to display a list of object type reports, as shown in Figure 4–87.

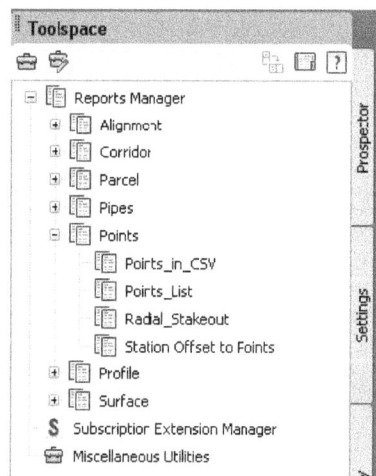

Figure 4–87

Points are easily organized into a convenient, legible list that displays the point number, northing, easting, elevation, and full description (as shown in Figure 4–88). Another point report lists the points' station and offset values relative to an alignment. Another report calculates distances and angles from an occupied and a backsight. You can transfer points to Microsoft Excel spreadsheets using a CSV report.

To create these reports, select the report's name, right-click, and select **Execute...**

Number	Northing	Easting	Elevation	Description
1	632055.919	2208068.041	900.655	MON
2	631396.467	2207989.483	900.171	MON
3	630834.659	2207979.534	898.369	MON
4	631382.131	2207989.229	900.174	MON

Figure 4–88

Point Editor Reports

Another report method is to use the Point Editor vista. In the Toolspace, *Prospector* tab, select **Points**, right-click, and select **Edit...** to display the Point Editor vista, as shown in Figure 4–89.

Figure 4–89

In the vista, you can select individual points using <Ctrl> or select blocks of points using <Shift>. When done selecting points, right-click and select **Copy to clipboard**. You can then paste the copied points into Microsoft Excel, Notepad, or any application that accepts the points, as shown in Figure 4–90.

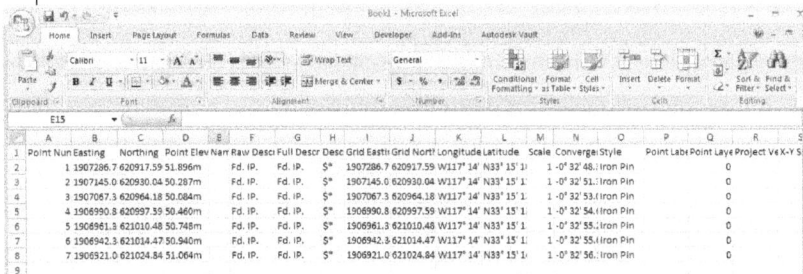

Figure 4–90

Practice 4h

Estimated time for completion: 5 minutes

Point Reports

Practice Objective

- Share information about points used for error checking or staking out points using predefined reports.

Task 1 - Create Point Reports.

1. Continue working with the drawing from the previous practice or open **SUV1-H1-Survey.dwg**.

2. If the Toolspace, *Toolbox* tab is not displayed in the

   Toolspace, select the *Home* tab and click (Toolbox), as shown in Figure 4–91 to display the Toolspace, *Toolbox* tab.

Figure 4–91

3. Select the Toolspace, *Toolbox* tab and expand the *Reports Manager* collection to display the list of object type reports. Expand the *Points* collection, as shown in Figure 4–92.

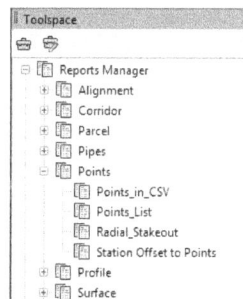

Figure 4–92

4. Select **Point List**, right-click, and select **Execute**.

5. In the Export to LandXML dialog box, click **OK** to generate the report. In the Save As dialog box, type a filename or accept the default **CivilReport.html**, and save the file. If the file exists, you will be prompted to replace it.

6. The point list displays in Internet Explorer. Review the report and when done, close it.

Chapter Review Questions

1. If you need linework, which method should you use to import survey data?

   a. Import survey data using the Survey Database.

   b. Import survey data using the **Import Points** command.

   c. Import survey data using the Map Explorer.

   d. Create points using the Toolspace, *Prospector* tab.

2. If you need to analyze the field data using the analysis tools available in the Survey Database, you must use a field book file rather than a text file.

   a. True

   b. False

3. Which of these is not a function of a survey figure in the AutoCAD Civil 3D software?

   a. Automate linework creation from survey data.

   b. Make creating view frames easier.

   c. Make creating breaklines for a surface easier.

   d. Make creating parcel boundaries from survey data easier.

4. Which of these is NOT an option to define a survey figure?

   a. Import survey data using the Survey Database.

   b. In the Toolspace, *Survey* tab, right-click on Figures and select **Create figure from objects**.

   c. In the Toolspace, *Survey* tab, right-click on Figures and select **Create figure interactively**.

   d. In the Point Creation Tools toolbar, select the option to process linework to ensure that figures are created as you create points.

5. Which tab in the Point Label Style Composer dialog box controls the appearance of a point label when the point label grip is selected in the drawing and moved away from the point itself?

   a. *General* tab

   b. *Layout* tab

   c. *Dragged State* tab

   d. *Summary* tab

6. How do you control the next point number to be used in a drawing?

   a. The **Point Identity** parameters located in the expanded area in the Create Points toolbar.

   b. Under Label Styles in the Toolspace, *Settings* tab.

   c. In the Toolspace, *Survey* tab, right-click on Survey Points.

   d. In the Toolspace, *Prospector* tab, right-click on Survey Points.

7. Can the **_All Points** point group be deleted?

   a. Yes

   b. No

8. Can a point group be made out of point groups?

   a. Yes

   b. No

Command Summary

Button	Command	Location
	Create Points	• **Ribbon:** *Home* tab>Create Ground Data panel
	Import Points from File	• **Ribbon:** *Insert* tab>Import panel • **Toolbar:** Create Points • **Command Prompt:** ImportPoints
	Import Survey Data	• **Ribbon:** *Home* tab>Create Ground Data panel • **Command Prompt:** ImportSurveyData
	Survey	• **Ribbon:** *Home* tab>Palettes panel
	Survey User Settings	• **Toolspace:** *Survey* tab
	Zoom To Points	• **Toolbar:** Transparent Commands • **Command Prompt:** 'ZTP

Surfaces

In this chapter you learn how to create a surface from survey data. Then you refine the surface using breaklines, boundaries, and making other edits. Finally, you analyze the surface and annotate it to communicate the existing conditions.

Learning Objectives in this Chapter

- List the steps required to build a surface in the AutoCAD® Civil® 3D software.
- Adjust and edit a surface using surface properties and various commands.
- Add existing contour data to a surface to take advantage of data created by someone else.
- Add drawing objects to a surface to improve the accuracy of a TIN model.
- Add breaklines and boundaries to a surface to improve its accuracy.
- Analyze a surface using a quick profile or the object viewer.
- Label contour elevations, slope values, spot elevations, and watershed delineations to communicate surface information.
- Calculate the volume of cut and fill or adjusted cut and fill between two surfaces.
- Analyze a surface to determine the buildable area for the project conditions.
- Create AutoCAD Civil 3D surfaces from point cloud data files.

5.1 Surface Process

The surface building process can be divided into the following steps:

1. Assemble the data.
2. Assign the data to a surface.
3. Evaluate the resulting surface.
4. Add breaklines, assign more data, modify the data, or edit the surface as required.

1. Assemble data.

The first step in surface building is to acquire the initial surface data. This can be points, contours, 3D polylines, feature lines, AutoCAD® objects, ASCII coordinate files, or boundaries. Each data type provides specific information about a surface.

2. Assign data to a surface.

Acquired data is assigned to a surface. Once assigned, the AutoCAD Civil 3D software immediately processes this data and a surface object is created.

Surfaces are listed individually in the *Surfaces* collection in the Toolspace, *Prospector* tab. Each surface contains content information, as shown in Figure 5–1. The surface content includes *Masks, Watersheds,* and *Definition* elements. The *Definition* contains a list of all of the surface data that has been applied, including boundaries, breaklines, and points. The Toolspace, *Prospector* tab displays data for each type of surface data in the list view when one of these types is selected.

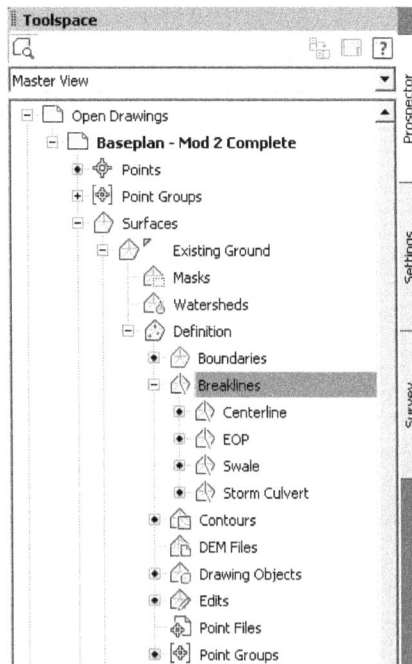

Figure 5–1

The AutoCAD Civil 3D software processes the initial data into one of two types of surfaces. The first type, the **Triangulated Irregular Network** (TIN) surface, is the most common. With triangulated surfaces, surface points are connected to adjacent points by straight lines, resulting in a triangular mesh. Surfaces generated from contour lines have surface points created at their vertices, modified by weeding and supplementing factors. An example of this type of surface is shown in Figure 5–2.

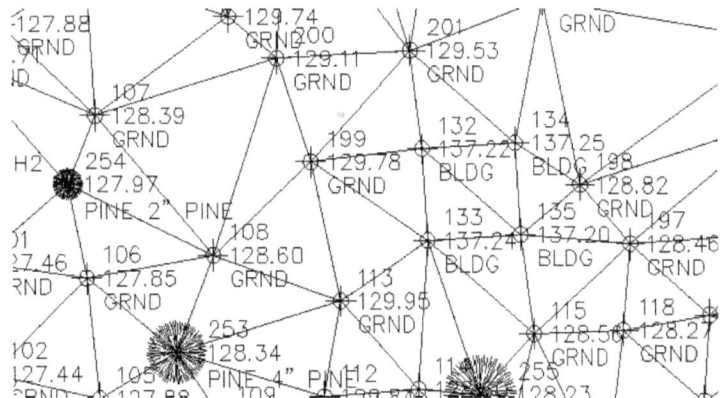

Figure 5–2

The second type of surface is a *Grid* surface. This surface interpolates and assigns an elevation from the surface data to each grid intersection. Most of the elevations at grid intersections are interpolated. **Digital Elevation Models** (DEMs) are a type of grid surface used in GIS applications. An example of this type of surface is shown in Figure 5–3.

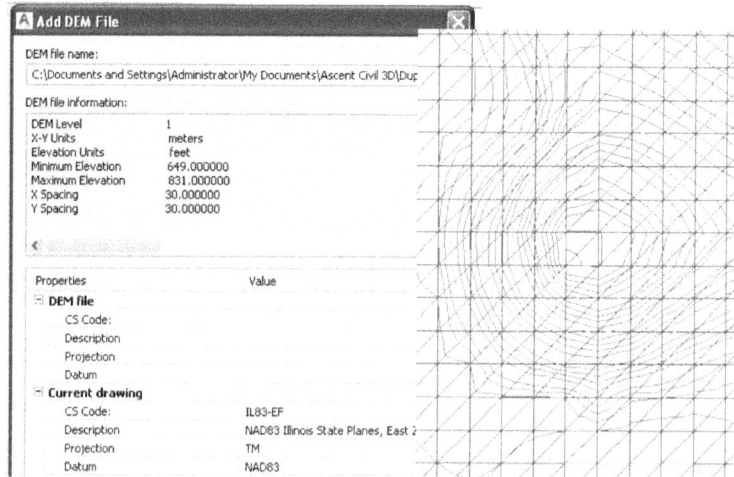

Figure 5–3

3. Evaluate the resulting surface.

Surfaces, especially ones created from points, typically need some attention to represent them as accurately as possible. For any four adjacent surface points, there are two possible triangulations, as shown in Figure 5–4.

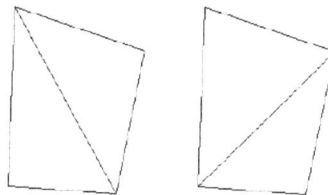

Figure 5–4

The differences can be difficult to envision when viewing the triangles from above, but these two configurations provide entirely different geometries. For example, note the surface shown in Figure 5–5.

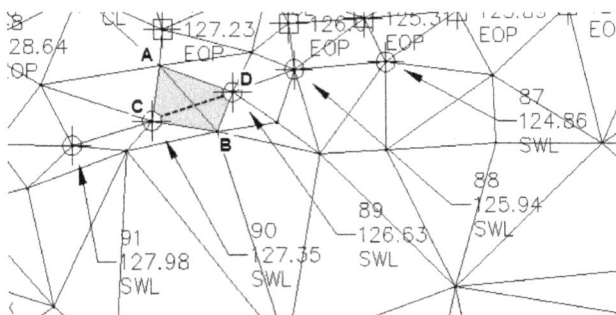

Figure 5–5

The triangulated points A, B, C, and D have a TIN line running from A to B. This configuration ignores the fact that C and D are both part of a continuous swale (SWL), indicated by the dashed line. In a 3D view, this configuration would resemble the example shown on the left in Figure 5–6. The correct triangulation has the triangle line *following* the linear feature rather than *crossing* it, as shown on the right.

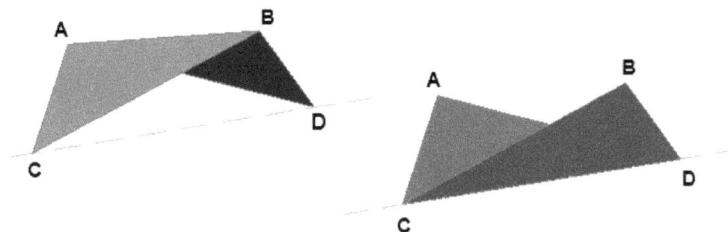

Figure 5–6

When creating surfaces, representing linear features correctly is extremely important. Examples of linear features include road center lines, edges-of-pavement, road shoulders, swales, berms, tops and bottoms of banks, and headwalls. Adding breaklines that follow linear features ensures that a terrain model is triangulated correctly along the features, rather than across them.

Other types of issues to watch out for include bad elevations (blown shots), elevations at 0 where there should be no chance of such elevation values, and points that were surveyed above or below the ground (e.g., the tops of fire hydrants). Unwanted triangles along the edges of the surface might connect points that should not be connected, which could also present problems.

In addition to the casual inspection of the triangles, surfaces can be evaluated by creating contour lines, reviewing the surface in 3D, and using the **Quick Section** command.

4. Add breaklines, assign more data, modify the data, or edit the surface as required.

After you have evaluated the surface, you can add the necessary breaklines or edit the surface directly to make adjustments. If the triangulation errors are isolated, editing the surface directly might be faster than creating and applying breaklines. For example, the triangulation issue above could be addressed by *swapping* the edge that crossed the swale center line. To do so, right-click on Edits under a Surface's definition in the Toolspace, *Prospector* tab and select **Swap Edge**, as shown in Figure 5–7.

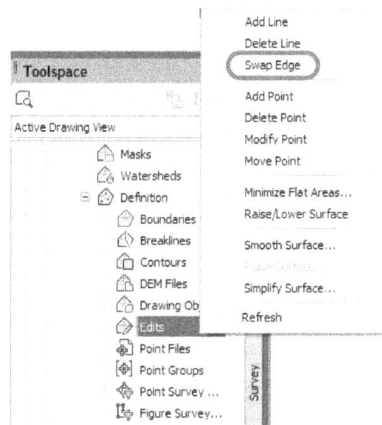

Figure 5–7

Other options enable you to add, move, modify, or remove points from the surface (but not change or erase the point object on which they were based), as well as add or remove triangle lines directly. **Minimize Flat Areas** is a group of algorithms that can be used to minimize the number of flat areas created by contour data. **Raise/Lower Surface** enables you to raise and lower the entire surface by a set amount, and a **Smooth Surface** enables you to smooth surfaces using the **Natural Neighbor** or **Kriging** method. (Contour smoothing is handled through surface styles. These techniques smooth the actual surface geometry.)

5.2 Surface Properties

The *Definition* tab in the Surface Properties dialog box displays the permitted **Build**, **Data**, and **Edit** operations for a surface. The *Operation Type* column is a record of the surface data addition and edits. Using the checkboxes, you can toggle off individual actions in the history and display the resulting changes to the surface. The entries can be toggled on or off no matter where they display in the history. This helps to isolate possible errors or review features (such as surface slopes) that are greatly affected by the addition of a headwall or retaining wall.

You can change the order of items in the list of operations. Operations higher in the list are applied to the surface before items further down in the list. Open this dialog box by right-clicking on the surface name in the Toolspace, *Prospector* tab (or by selecting the surface in the drawing and right-clicking) and selecting **Surface Properties…**.The dialog box is shown in Figure 5–8.

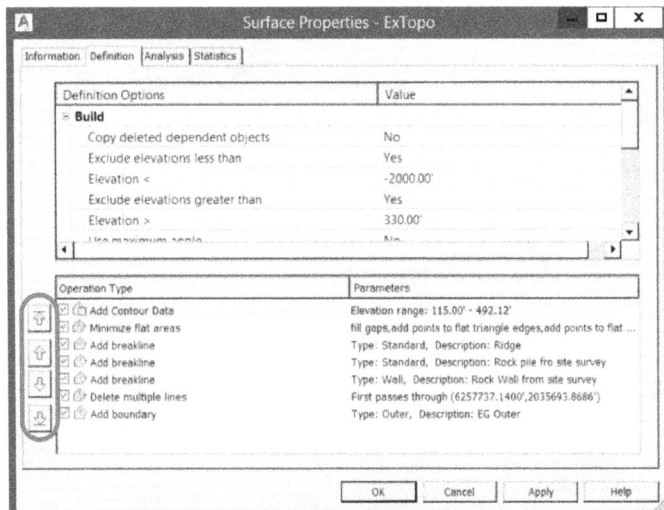

Figure 5–8

The *Information* tab enables you to rename the surface, edit the description, apply a surface object style, and render material, which controls how the surface displays in a rendered view.

The *Statistics* tab displays the current surface slope, elevation, and triangulation. It contains three areas:

- **General:** Provides an overall view of the surface. The **Minimum**, **Maximum**, and **Mean** elevations are the important entries in this area and provide the first hint of bad or incorrect data.

- **Extended:** Reports the **2D** and **3D** surface areas and **Minimum**, **Maximum**, and **Mean** slope values.

- **TIN:** Reviews the number of triangles, minimum and maximum triangle areas, and leg lengths in the surface.

The areas of triangles, along with the minimum and maximum triangle side lengths are indicators of data consistency. Generally, the longest triangles form around the perimeter of the surface. Limiting the length of triangle edges removes these types of triangles from the surface. You can delete these lines rather than try to set an optimum length, or you can create a boundary to prevent these types of triangles from being created.

When surfaces are created, they are assigned properties based on the *Build Options* area in the Edit Command Settings dialog box, as shown on the right in Figure 5–9. To open this dialog box, right-click on the **Create Surface** command and select **Edit Command Settings**, as shown on the left in Figure 5–9.

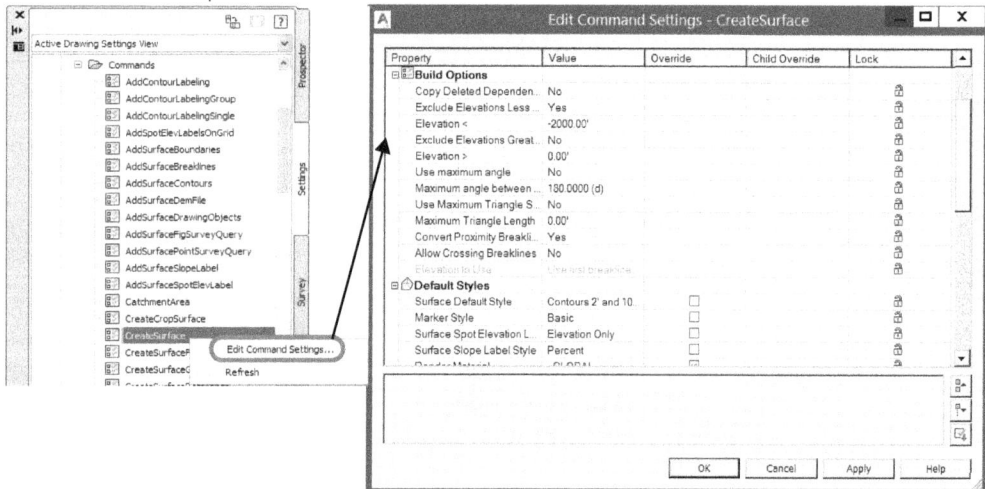

Figure 5–9

Surface Rebuilding

Some surface edits and point modifications can render a surface out of date. At that point, the surface is flagged as being out of date in the Toolspace, *Prospector* tab, as indicated by the **Drawing Item Modifier** icon shown in Figure 5–10.

Figure 5–10

When this occurs, you can right-click on the surface in the Toolspace, *Prospector* tab and select **Rebuild**. This updates the surface to reflect the recent changes. Alternatively, you can right-click on the surface in the Toolspace, *Prospector* tab and select **Rebuild-Automatic**, which updates the surface automatically without input from you. However, toggling this option on increases the strain on the computer resources and graphics capabilities so it is recommended that you leave it toggled off.

5.3 Contour Data

Contour data is available from many sources. Large sites are often surveyed using aerial photogrammetry, which provides contour polylines and spot elevations. Contour data can also be obtained from other AutoCAD Civil Engineering applications, such as AutoCAD Land Desktop.

In the AutoCAD Civil 3D software, polylines with elevation are useful as custom contour objects. Whether using polylines or AutoCAD Land Desktop contour objects, the AutoCAD Civil 3D software builds a surface by triangulating between contours. The end of each triangle side connects to a vertex of two different contours.

When processing contours for surface data, the AutoCAD Civil 3D software inspects the contour vertices for two conditions: too many data points representing similar data (e.g., 10 vertices on 15 units of contour length in an almost straight line), and not enough data points over the length of a contour.

You can set the values for these conditions in the Add Contour Data dialog box (as shown in Figure 5–11) when you add contour data.

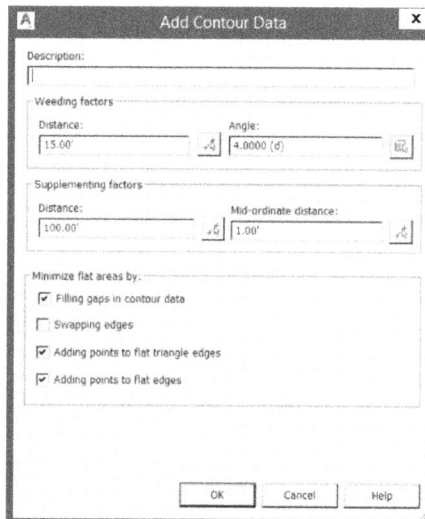

Figure 5–11

Weeding Factors

The *weeding* process removes redundant vertices from contours. The first step in the weeding process is to inspect three adjacent contour vertices, whose overall distance is shorter than a user-specified distance (e.g., three vertices in less than 15 units of contour). When encountering this situation, the weeding process prompts you about the change in direction between the three vertices. For example, does the direction from vertex 1 to vertex 2 change more than four degrees when going from vertex 2 to vertex 3? If not, the vertices are almost in a straight line and are too close. The AutoCAD Civil 3D software considers vertex 2 to be redundant and removes it from the surface data. This process repeats for the next three vertices. If the distance is under 15 units and the change of direction is less than four degrees, the next vertex 2 is removed from the data.

If a contour has three vertices in less than 15 units, and turns more than four degrees, vertex 2 is kept because the change in direction is significant. If there are more than 15 units between the three vertices, the AutoCAD Civil 3D software moves on to the next group.

An important feature of weeding is not what it removes from the data, but what is left over. If not enough data remains, the numbers for the weeding factors should be set to lower values.

Supplementing Factors

When the AutoCAD Civil 3D software inspects contour data, it uses supplementing factors to add vertices to the surface data. The first supplementing factor is the distance between contour vertices. When the distance between vertices is over 100 units, The AutoCAD Civil 3D software adds a vertex to the data along the course of the contour. The second supplementing factor is a mid-ordinate distance for the curve segments of a contour. If curves are distributed throughout the contour data, a setting of 0.1 is a good starting point.

- All weeding and supplementing factors are user-specified.

- Weeding and supplementing does not modify the contours or polylines in a drawing, only their data.

- There is no *correct* setting for weeding and supplementing. Varying the values creates more or less surface data.

Contour Issues

You should be aware of two issues when working with contour data: bays and peninsulas within the contours and the lack of high and low point elevations. These two issues affect triangulation and the quality of a surface.

Bays and peninsulas within contours represent gullies or isolated high points on a surface. As long as there is data to work with, the AutoCAD Civil 3D software builds a surface by triangulating between contours of different elevations. When the software cannot triangulate between different contours, the triangulation switches to connecting vertices on the same contour.

The **Minimize Flat Faces** command helps mitigate this situation by forcing the triangulation to target different contours, as shown in Figure 5–12. However, this method, similar to the edge swap method, does not correct every problem on a contour surface.

• To launch the **Minimize Flat Faces** command, in the Toolspace, *Prospector* tab, right-click on the *Edits* heading in the *Definition* collection of a surface and select the command.

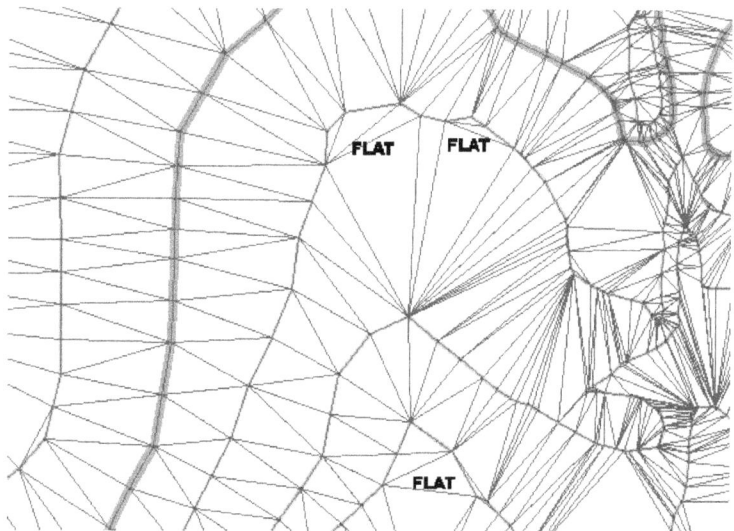

Figure 5–12

The second issue with contour data regards the loss of high and low points. Contours represent an elevation interval (120, 122, 123, etc.). However, the top of a hill could be 123.04 or 136.92 and the only contours present are for the elevations of 123 or 136. Spot elevations are required in the surface data to help correctly resolve the high and low spots of a surface.

• Flat spots and the loss of high and low points affect the calculation of volumes for earthworks, as shown in Figure 5–13.

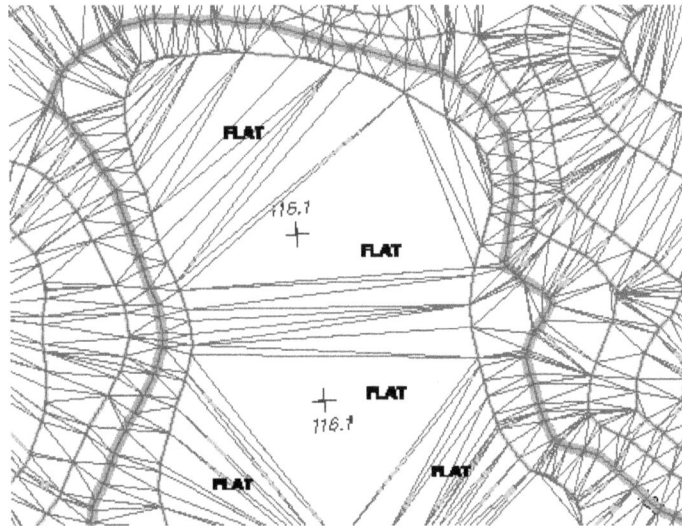

Figure 5–13

Minimizing Flat Triangle Strategies

By default, the Add Contour Data dialog box suggests using the **Minimize flat areas by:** options shown in Figure 5–14.

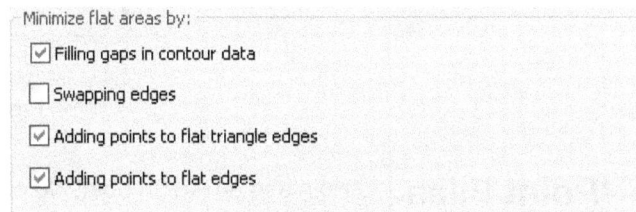

Figure 5–14

Together, these three methods attempt to detect and resolve peninsulas, bays, and other issues by adding additional points and filling in gaps based on surface trends. Generally, these provide the most expected results. The **Swapping edges** option is provided as a way of emulating how other terrain modeling software (such as AutoCAD Land Desktop) traditionally approached minimizing flat areas.

5.4 Other Surface Data

DEM Files

Digital Elevation Models (DEMs) are grid-based terrain models primarily used by GIS applications to represent large areas. Since they are large-scale and grid-based, they are generally only used in the AutoCAD Civil 3D software for preliminary design and other approximate tasks.

Drawing Objects

AutoCAD points, text, blocks, and other objects can be used as surface data. Individual AutoCAD Civil 3D point objects can also be selected using the **Drawing Objects** option. Selected objects need to have a valid elevation value.

- All data added as drawing objects is considered point data.

- You can add 3D lines and polyfaces using this method, but each end point is treated as if it were a point object. Linework is not treated as contours or breaklines. The Add Points From Drawing Objects dialog box is shown in Figure 5–15.

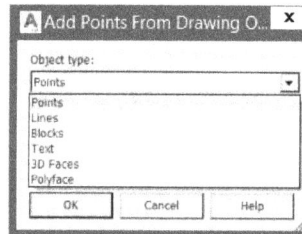

Figure 5–15

Point Files

Points in an ASCII point file can be used as surface data.

- You can use any import/export file format.

- This is an excellent way to create a large surface from a massive number of points, as it bypasses creating point objects, thereby reducing drawing overhead.

Point Groups

Using previously defined points groups in a surface definition enables you to isolate only the points on the ground to ensure that the tops of walls and invert elevations do not distort the surface.

Point Survey Queries

Select points in a survey database can be used as surface data by creating a survey query. The point data is used, but point objects are not created.

- Dynamic references to the points provide a more seamless update if changes to the database or query are made.

- This is an excellent way to create a large surface from a massive number of points, as it bypasses creating point objects, thereby reducing drawing overhead.

- Points from a survey query display under point groups in the surface definition.

Figure Survey Queries

Select figures in a survey database can be used as surface data. The figures are used as breaklines, but 3D polylines are not created in the drawing.

- Dynamic references to the figures provide a more seamless update if changes to the database or query are made.

- This is an excellent way to create a large surface from a massive number of figures, as it bypasses creating 3D polylines and turning them into breaklines, thereby reducing drawing overhead.

- Figures from a survey query display under breaklines in the surface definition.

Practice 5a

Creating an Existing Ground Surface

Practice Objective

*   Add contour data and point data to a surface that already exists in the drawing.

Estimated time for completion: 15 minutes

In this practice you will define the surface with surface data. You will use this model to create existing ground contours and for reference during the design. You will begin the model with the provided contours and the previously created **Existing Ground** point group.

Task 1 - Create a surface and set properties.

1. Open **SUF1-A1-Surface.dwg**.

2. In the Toolspace, *Prospector* tab, select **Surfaces**, right-click, and select **Create Surface**.

3. For the *Type*, select **TIN surface**. For the *Name*, type **ExTopo** and for the *Style*, select **Contours 2' and 10' (Background)**, as shown in Figure 5–16.

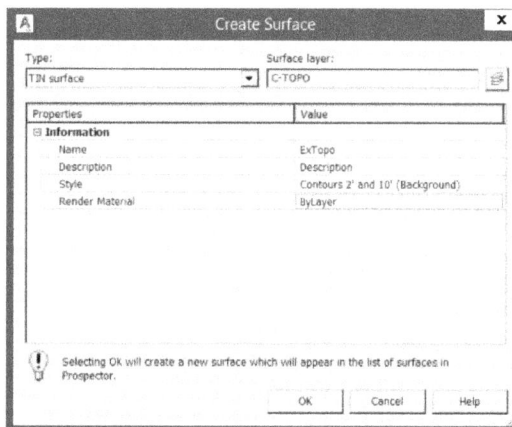

Figure 5–16

4. Click **OK** to accept the changes and close the dialog box.

5. Save the drawing.

Task 2 - Define a surface with contour data.

1. Continue working with the drawing from the previous practice or open **SUF1-A2-Surface.dwg**.

2. In the *Insert* tab>Block panel, click ⬚ (Insert Block) and select **More Options**.

3. From the *C:\Civil 3D Projects\Civil3D-Training\Surface* folder, insert **Site-Contours.dwg** using the following parameters:
   - *Insertion point*: **0,0,0**,
   - *Scale*: **1**
   - *Rotation*: **0**
   - Ensure that **Uniform Scale** and **Explode** are selected, as shown in Figure 5–17.

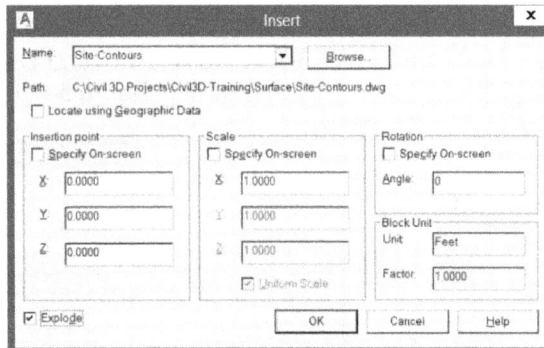

Figure 5–17

4. In the *Home* tab>Layers panel, click ⬚ (Isolate). Do the following before isolating the layers:
   - Type **S** for **Settings**.
   - Select **Off** and then select **Off** again to ensure that **layiso** does not lock the layer by changing the settings to toggle off isolated layers.

If this setting is not changed, the C-TOPO layer will lock and the AutoCAD Civil 3D software will not create the surface.

5. Select one major and one minor contour from the **Site-Contours.dwg** to isolate the layers **A-TOPO-MAJR** and **A-TOPO-MINR**.

6. Expand the *Surfaces* collection in the Toolspace, *Prospector* tab.

7. Expand the *ExTopo* surfaces collection and the *Definition* collection.

8. Select the **Contours** data element, right-click, and select **Add...**, as shown in Figure 5–18.

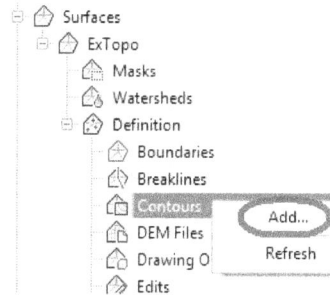

Figure 5–18

9. In the Add Contour Data dialog box, accept the defaults, as shown in Figure 5–19, and click **OK**.

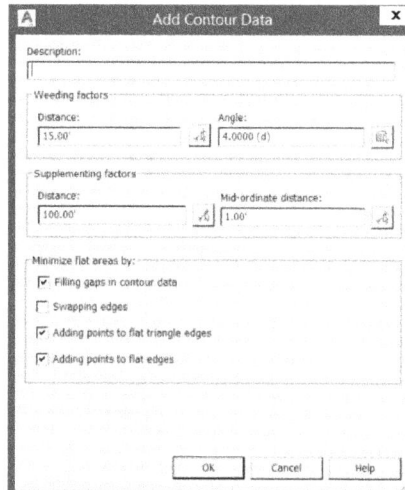

Figure 5–19

10. When prompted to select contours, use the AutoCAD window or crossing selection method to select all of the AutoCAD contour objects on the screen, as shown in Figure 5–20. Press <Enter> to end the command.

Figure 5–20

11. The AutoCAD Civil 3D software has created a surface. However, only the original two isolated contour layers display, the surface is not displayed. You need to restore the previous layer state. To do so, click ⧉ (Unisolate) in the *Home* tab>Layer panel as shown in Figure 5–21.

Figure 5–21

After freezing the original contours, if the contours for the new surface are not displayed, verify that the C-TOPO layer is not frozen.

12. Freeze the layers **A-TOPO-MAJR** and **A-TOPO-MINR** by clicking ⧉ (Layer Freeze) and selecting the contours you selected when adding contours to the surface. This will clean up the drawing while ensuring that you do not accidentally modify the surface by changing any of the original contour polylines.

13. If you select the green surface boundary or any contour line, the *Tin Surface: ExTopo* contextual tab displays, as shown in Figure 5–22.

Figure 5–22

14. Save the drawing.

Task 3 - Define surface with point data.

In examining the **ExTopo** surface more closely, note that although the internal site contours correctly reflect the surveyed point elevations, the original contours are out of date or have missing information in the area of the existing road, **Mission Avenue** (the road running east to west at the top of the site). However, you have a detailed survey of the road. Using this data, you will generate a surface.

1. Continue working with the drawing from the previous task or open **SUF1-A3-Surface.dwg**.

If the points still display in the model, you might have to right-click on Point Groups and select ***Update***.

2. Although the point group that you use in this practice has been created, you should change the display order of the point groups to display them clearly. To do so, in the Toolspace, *Prospector* tab, right-click on *Point Groups* and select **Properties**. Move the **_No Display** point group to the top and then move the **ExRoad** point group above it.

3. In the Toolspace, *Prospector* tab, select the **Surfaces** collection, right-click, and select **Create Surface**.

4. In the Create Surface dialog box, select **TIN surface** for the surface type, type **ExRoad** for the surface name, and select **Contours 2' and 10' (Background)** for the style.

5. Click **OK** to accept the changes and close the dialog box.

6. Expand the *Surfaces* collection in the Toolspace, *Prospector* tab and expand the *ExRoad* collection.

7. Expand the *Definition* collection, select *Point Groups*, right-click, and select **Add...**, as shown in Figure 5–23.

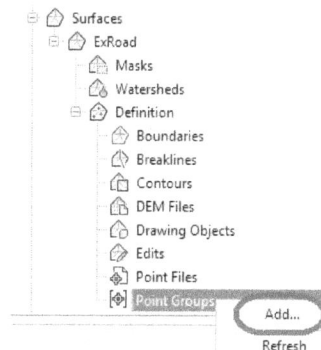

Figure 5–23

8. In the Point Groups dialog box, select the **ExRoad** points group, as shown in Figure 5–24. Click **OK** to accept the changes and close the dialog box.

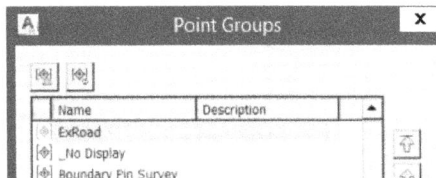

Figure 5–24

9. Save the drawing.

Task 4 - Create a surface contour style.

1. Continue working with the drawing from the previous task or open **SUF1-A4-Surface.dwg**.

2. Since there is very little grade change along the road, the frequency of the contours is small, making the surface difficult to see. Expand the *Surfaces* collection, right-click **ExRoad** and select **Surface Properties**.

3. In the Surface Properties dialog box, in the *Information* tab, expand [icon] to the right of the *Surface style* field and select **Copy Current Selection**, as shown in Figure 5–25.

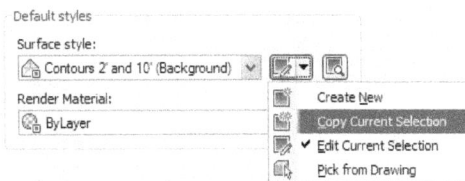

Figure 5–25

4. In the *Information* tab, type **Contours 0.5' and 2.5' (Background)** for the style name, as shown in Figure 5–26.

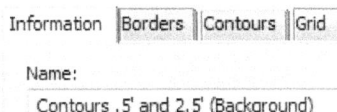

Figure 5–26

5. In the *Contours* tab, expand the *Contour Intervals* collection and type **0.5'** for the *Minor Interval* and **2.5'** for the *Major Interval*, as shown in Figure 5–27.

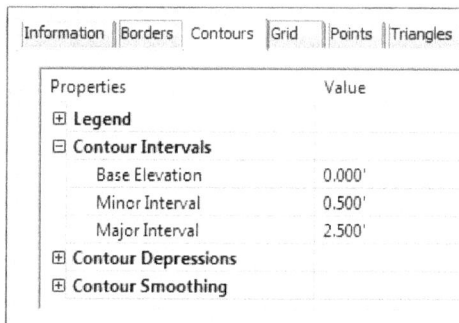

Information	Borders	Contours	Grid	Points	Triangles

Properties	Value
⊞ **Legend**	
⊟ **Contour Intervals**	
Base Elevation	0.000'
Minor Interval	0.500'
Major Interval	2.500'
⊞ **Contour Depressions**	
⊞ **Contour Smoothing**	

Figure 5–27

6. Click **OK** to accept and close the Edit Style dialog box, and click **OK** to close the Surface Properties dialog box.

7. Zoom into the existing road at the north end of the site and note the detail contours identifying the crown of the road.

8. Save the drawing.

5.5 Breaklines and Boundaries

A surface can include data from boundaries, breaklines, contours, Digital Elevation Model files (DEMs), drawing objects (AutoCAD points, individual AutoCAD Civil 3D points, lines, 3D faces, etc.), manual edits, and point files. The *Boundaries* collection displays above the *Breaklines* collection under the surface's *Definition* (in the Toolspace, *Prospector* tab), as shown in Figure 5–28. However, you should generally add boundaries after adding breaklines to a surface. If you use the Data Clip boundary type, any data that you add to the surface (point file, DEM file, or breakline) is only added to the area within the boundary. In that case, breaklines can be added to the surface after a Data Clip boundary type. Surface edit operations are not affected by the Data Clip boundary.

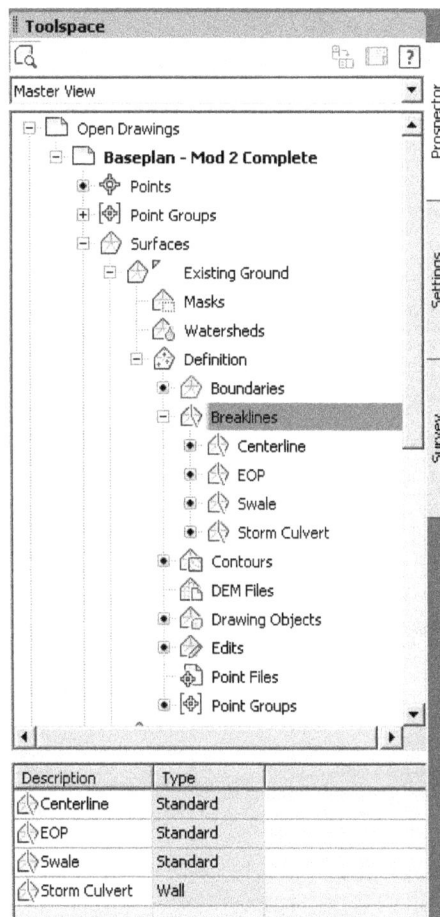

Figure 5–28

Breaklines

Breaklines affect surface triangulation and are important in point-based surfaces. They ensure that terrain models are triangulated correctly along linear features, as shown in Figure 5–29.

Surface before breaklines have been applied along the center line of a road.

Surface after breaklines have been applied along the center line of a road.

Figure 5–29

- When adding a breakline to a surface, the AutoCAD Civil 3D software creates an entry under the *Breakline>Definition* collections, based on a description that you supply.

- When you define multiple breaklines at the same time, the AutoCAD Civil 3D software creates a single entry under the *Breaklines* collection. However, they are listed separately in the Toolspace, *Prospector* tab's List View.

- Breaklines can be defined as one of four types: **Standard**, **Proximity**, **Wall**, and **Non-Destructive**.

Standard Breaklines

A standard breakline is one that has valid elevations assigned at each vertex.

- Standard breaklines can be defined from 3D lines, 3D polylines, survey figures, or grading feature lines.

- The number of points generated along a breakline can be reduced by specifying a *Weeding* factor or increased by specifying a *Supplementing* factor, similar to weeding and supplementing factors for contour data.

- Curves in standard breaklines are approximated through the use of a mid-ordinate distance, similar to the way curved boundaries are resolved.

- For AutoCAD Land Desktop users, tasks that you might have applied to 3D polylines in AutoCAD Land Desktop should use grading feature lines in the AutoCAD Civil 3D software. This is because grading feature lines are more efficient in many ways, including their support of 3D curves.

- When drafting 3D lines, polylines, or feature lines, you can use AutoCAD Civil 3D's transparent commands. For example, using the **Point Object** (**'PO'**) transparent command to select a point as a vertex of a 3D polyline prompts the AutoCAD Civil 3D software to assign the point's elevation to the vertex of the polyline.

- Standard breaklines can also be defined from ASCII breakline data files (.FLT file extension).

Proximity Breaklines

Proximity breaklines do not need to have elevations at their vertices. A polyline at elevation 0 could be used as a proximity breakline. When a proximity breakline is defined, the AutoCAD Civil 3D software automatically assigns vertex elevations from the nearest TIN data point, such as a nearby point object or contour line vertex.

- The AutoCAD Civil 3D software can define proximity breaklines from 2D polylines or grading feature Lines.

- The AutoCAD Civil 3D software does not support curves in proximity breaklines. Arc segments are treated as if they were straight line segments.

- One of the default options in the surface *Build* area enables the conversion of all proximity (2D) breaklines into standard (3D) breaklines. After conversion, the breakline is listed as a standard breakline and has the same elevations as the point objects that are at each vertex.

Wall Breaklines

- A wall breakline can be used to represent both the top and bottom of a wall, curb, or other sheer face.

- Wall breaklines are defined by 3D lines, 3D polylines, or feature lines. When defining them from linework, the object itself is meant to define either the top or bottom of the wall.

- The other end of the wall (top or bottom) is defined interactively by entering the absolute elevations or height differences from the defining line.

- If a Wall breakline starts as a 2D polyline or feature line, it can contain curve segments.

- The number of points generated along a breakline can be reduced by specifying a *Weeding* factor or increased by specifying a *Supplementing* factor.

Survey Figures as Breaklines

Figures created by surveyors can be used as breaklines if a connection exists between the drawing and the survey database.

How To: Add Survey Figures as Breaklines

1. Open the survey database for editing.
2. In the Toolspace, *Survey* tab, expand the *Survey Data* collection and select **Figures**. The list of figures in the grid view displays at the bottom of the Toolspace.
3. Select the figures, right-click, and select **Create breaklines…**, as shown in Figure 5–30.

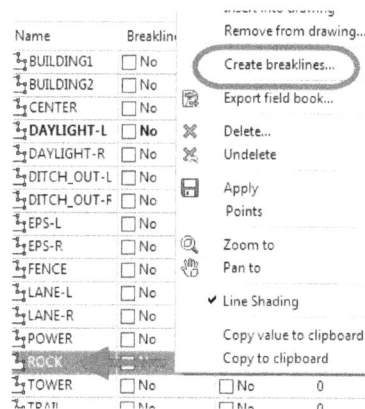

Figure 5–30

4. In the Create Breaklines dialog box, select the surface on which to place the breaklines, and then in the *Breakline* column, select **Yes** on to create the breaklines, as shown in Figure 5–31. Click **OK** to close the dialog box.

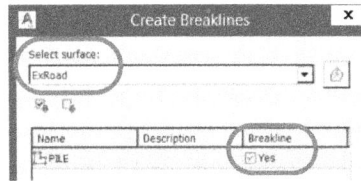

Figure 5–31

Boundaries

Boundaries provide interior or exterior limits to the surface triangulation. Boundaries are typically created from 2D closed polylines. There are four types of boundaries: **Outer**, **Hide**, **Show**, and **Data Clip**. An outer boundary should be one of the last items added to a surface, because adding data outside an existing boundary extends the surface past the boundary.

*   An **Outer** boundary hides or excludes data outside its edge.

*   A **Hide** boundary hides an interior portion of a surface to delineate features (such as water bodies and building footprints).

*   A **Show** boundary displays a portion of a surface within a Hide boundary (e.g., to display an island in a pond).

*   A **Data Clip** boundary acts as a filter on all data, including points, DEMs, and breaklines added to the surface after the creation of the Data Clip boundary. If a data clip boundary is used, any data added after it, that falls outside the data clip boundary, is ignored.

A boundary can contain arc segments. To better represent surface elevations around an arc, the AutoCAD Civil 3D software uses a mid-ordinate value to calculate where the triangles interact with the boundary. The mid-ordinate value is the distance between the midpoint of the cord and the arc. The smaller the mid-ordinate value, the closer the surface data is to the original arc. An example is shown in Figure 5–32.

Figure 5–32

A boundary can limit a surface to the data within it. When you want to extend the triangulation exactly to a boundary line, select the **Non-destructive breakline** option in the Create Boundary dialog box. A non-destructive breakline fractures triangles at their intersection with the boundary. The resulting triangles preserve the original elevations of the surface at the boundary intersection as close as possible.

The example in Figure 5–33 shows the following:

1. The surface with a polyline is used as an outer boundary.
2. The boundary is applied without the **Non-destructive breakline** option. This is typically used when the boundary polyline is approximate and not meant to represent a hard edge.
3. The boundary is applied with the **Non-destructive breakline** option. Non-destructive breaklines are often used to create a specific termination limit for the surface (such as at a parcel boundary).

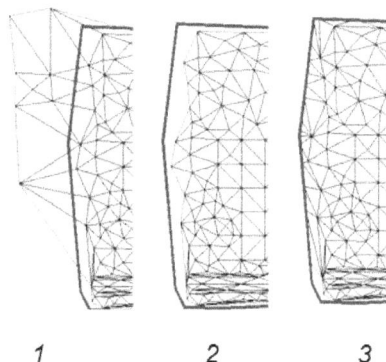

1   2   3

Figure 5–33

Practice 5b

Add Additional Data to an Existing Ground Surface

Practice Objective

*   Improve the accuracy of a surface by adding various breaklines, such as standard breaklines, wall breaklines, and breaklines from survey figures.

Estimated time for completion: 20 minutes

Task 1 - Add surface breaklines.

TIN lines are generally created using the shortest distance between points. To further define a surface, you might need to supplement it with breaklines of ridges, ditches, walls, etc., that accurately define the surface. These breaklines prevent the software from triangulating directly between points that are bisected by a breakline. The breakline becomes part of the triangulation between the two adjacent points.

1. Continue working with the drawing from the previous practice or open **SUF1-B1-Surface.dwg**.

2. Select any part of the **ExTopo** surface in Model Space.

The contextual tab displays.

3. In the contextual *Surface* tab>Modify panel, select Surface Properties as shown in Figure 5–34. The Surface Properties dialog box opens.

Figure 5–34

4. In the *Information* tab, expand the Surface style drop-down list and select **Contours and Triangles**, as shown in Figure 5–35. Click **OK** to close the dialog box.

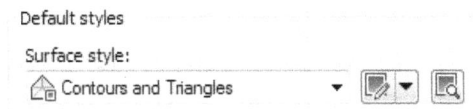

Default styles

Surface style:

Contours and Triangles

Figure 5–35

Now that the triangulations display, you will examine how adding a feature line impacts the surface.

5. In the *View* tab>Views panel, expand the drop-down list and select **Surf-Breakline**. This zooms into the breakline that is located north of the existing road as shown in Figure 5–36.

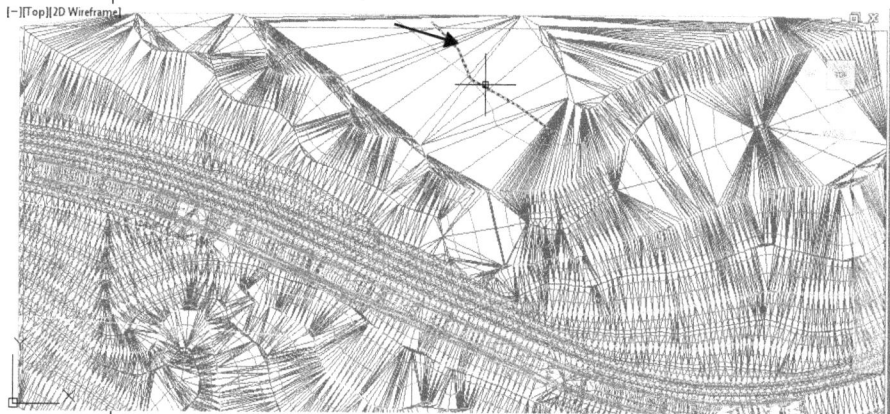

Figure 5–36

The triangulation crosses the breakline.

6. Expand the *Current Drawing* collection in the Toolspace, *Prospector* tab and then expand the *Surfaces>ExTopo> Definition* collections. Select **Breaklines**, right-click, and select **Add**, as shown in Figure 5–37.

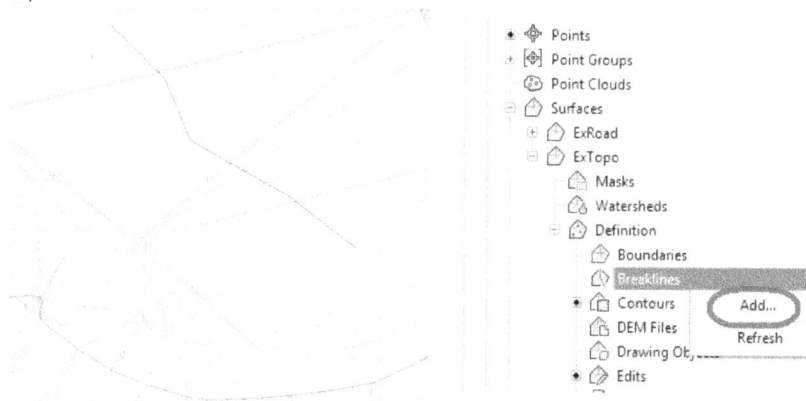

Figure 5–37

7. Type **Ridge** in the *Description* field, as shown in Figure 5–38. Accept all of the defaults and click **OK** to close the dialog box.

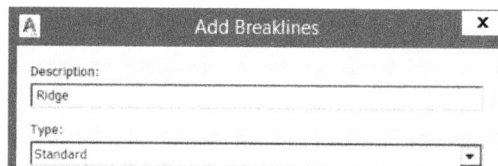

Figure 5–38

8. When prompted to select objects, select the red 3D polyline and press <Enter> to complete the command.

9. The surface should rebuild automatically. Note that the triangulation now takes the breakline into consideration, as shown in Figure 5–39.

*If the **ExTopo** surface is marked as out-of-date*

⚠ *. Select the **ExTopo** surface, right-click, and select **Rebuild Automatic**.*

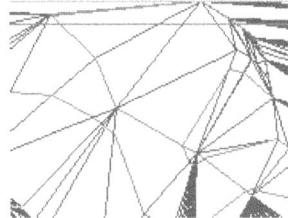

Figure 5–39

10. Save the drawing.

Task 2 - Set up the survey database.

In this practice you will need to incorporate survey data into the surface. To do so, you must first establish a connection to the survey database. If you have not completed the practices in the Survey section you will need to open the survey database **Survey1 Data_Complete** to open the connection.

1. Continue working with the drawing from the previous task or open **SUF1-B2-Surface.dwg** from the C:\Civil 3D Projects\Civil3D-Training\Surface folder.

If the Toolspace, Survey tab, click 🏕 in the Home tab>Palettes panel to toggle it on.

2. In the Toolspace, *Survey* tab, right-click on Survey Databases and select **Set working folder**, as shown in Figure 5–40.

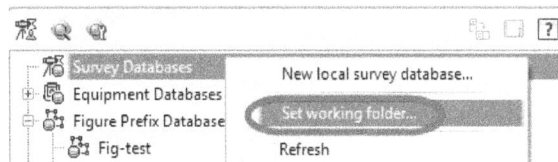

Figure 5–40

3. Select the *Survey Databases* folder in the *C:\Civil 3D Projects\Civil3D-Training\Survey* folder, as shown in Figure 5–41.

Figure 5–41

4. Select the survey database **Survey Data_Complete**, right-click, and select **Open for edit**, as shown in Figure 5–42.

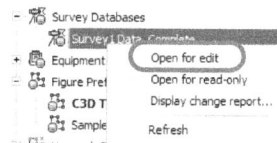

Figure 5–42

Task 3 - Add field book figures as breaklines.

In the task, you will add breaklines to the surface from figures that were created when the field books were imported.

1. Continue working with the drawing from the previous task or open **SUF1-B3-Surface.dwg**.

2. Open the survey database **Survey1 Data_Complete,** if it is not already open.

3. In the Toolspace, *Survey* tab, expand the *Survey1 Data_Complete* collection and select **Figures**. The list of figures in the grid view displays at the bottom of the Toolspace.

4. Select the figure **Pile**, right-click, and select **Create breaklines...**, as shown in Figure 5–43.

Figure 5–43

5. In the Create Breaklines dialog box, select **ExTopo** for the surface, and select the **Yes** option in the *Breakline* column to create breaklines, as shown in Figure 5–44. Click **OK** to close the dialog box.

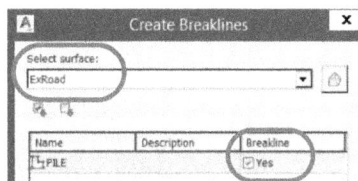

Figure 5–44

6. The AutoCAD Civil 3D software will zoom in to the location of the breakline, and open the Add Breaklines dialog box. Type **Rock pile from site survey** in the *Description* field, and ensure that **Standard** is selected in the Type drop-down list, as shown in Figure 5–45. Click **OK** to close the dialog box.

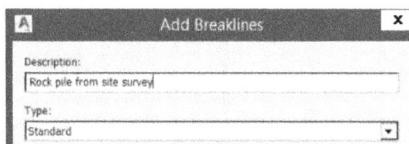

Figure 5–45

The Event Viewer vista in the Panorama opens. You have received a number of errors with crossing breaklines. You can Zoom to the error by selecting **Zoom to** in the far right column. For now you need to clear these errors from the event log file.

7. Click **Action** in the Panorama and select **Clear All Events**, as shown in Figure 5–46.

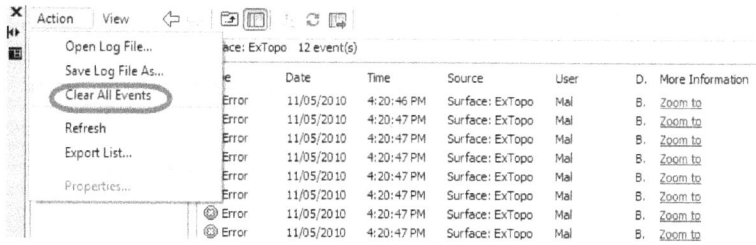

Figure 5–46

8. Close the Panorama by clicking ☑ (checkmark) in the dialog box.

9. In Model Space, select the **ExTopo** surface. The *Tin Surface: ExTopo* contextual tab displays. In the Modify panel, select **Surface Properties** as shown in Figure 5–47.

Figure 5–47

10. The Surface Properties - ExTopo dialog box opens. In the *Definition* tab, expand the *Build* collection and set the value of *Allow crossing breaklines* to **Yes**. Set the value for the *Elevation to use* field to **Use last breakline elevation at intersection**, as shown in Figure 5–48. When you have finished, click **OK**.

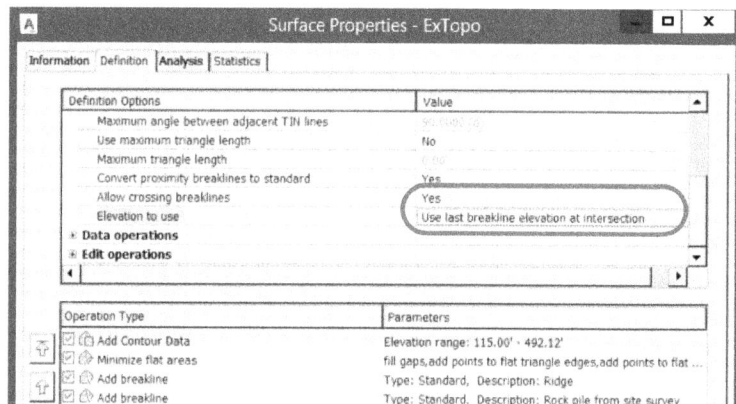

Figure 5–48

11. When prompted to *Rebuild the surface* or *Mark as out of Date*, select **Rebuild the surface**. When you review the surface contours, note that the surface has used the figure as a breakline.

12. Save the drawing.

Task 4 - Add a Wall Breakline.

In the task, you will add a wall breakline to the surface from figures that were created when the field books were imported.

1. Continue working with the drawing from the previous task or open **SUF1-B4-Surface.dwg**.

2. Open the survey database **Survey1 Data_Complete**, if it is not already open.

3. In the Toolspace, *Survey* tab, expand the *Survey Data* collection and select **Figures**. Note the list of figures in the grid view at the bottom of the Toolspace.

4. Select the **Wall** figure, right-click, and select **Create breaklines**.

5. In the Create Breaklines dialog box, select the **ExTopo** surface and select the **Yes** option in the *Breakline* column to create breaklines. Click **OK** to close the dialog box.

6. The AutoCAD Civil 3D software zooms in to the location of the breakline, and opens the Add Breaklines dialog box. Type **Rock wall from site survey** in the *Description* field, and ensure that **Wall** is selected in the Type drop-down list, as shown in Figure 5–49. Click **OK** to close the dialog box.

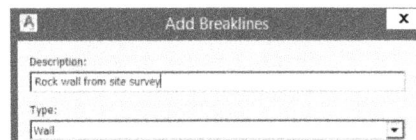

Figure 5–49

7. At the prompt to pick the offset side, select a point to the south of the wall break line, as shown in Figure 5–50.

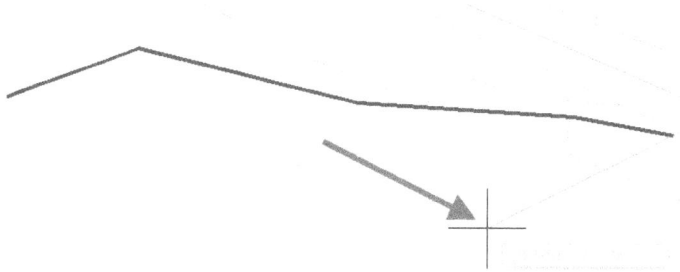

Figure 5–50

8. When prompted to select the option for the wall height, select the default **All** option because the wall has a constant height.

The wall has a constant height of 1.5' from the base.

9. When prompted for the elevation difference or elevation, type **1.5'** and press <Enter>.

10. Save the drawing.

5.6 Surface Editing

There are three ways of adjusting surfaces graphically: using lines, points, and area edit tools (such as **Minimize Flat Areas** and **Smooth Surface**). All of these tools are available by right-clicking on the *Edits* heading in a surface's *Definition* area (Toolspace, *Prospector* tab), as shown in Figure 5–51.

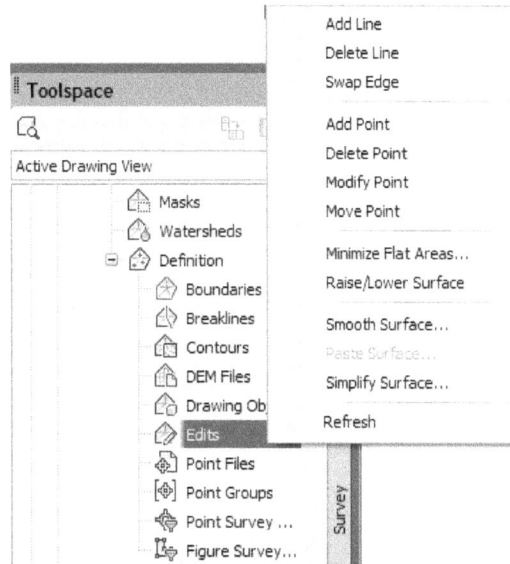

Figure 5–51

- The AutoCAD Civil 3D software considers each graphical surface edit to be additional data that can be removed later.

- Most surface edits apply immediately. If the drawing item modifier icon displays (as shown in Figure 5–52), then an edit has rendered the surface out of date. When this happens, a surface should be rebuilt by right-clicking on the surface name in the Toolspace, *Prospector* tab and selecting **Rebuild**.

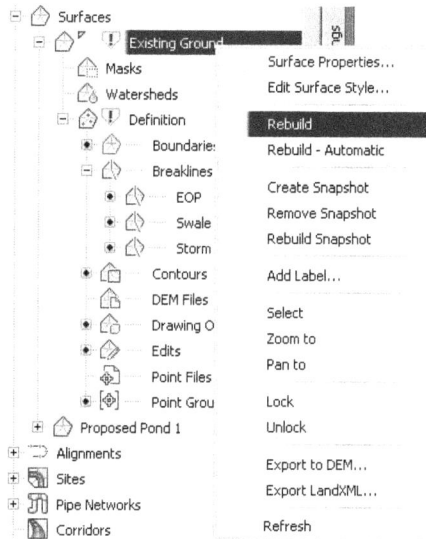

Figure 5–52

- To have a surface automatically rebuild as required, right-click on the surface name in the Toolspace, *Prospector* tab and select **Rebuild-Automatic**. However, toggling this option on increases the use of computer resources and graphics capabilities, so it is recommended that you leave it toggled off.

- To delete an edit from a surface permanently, remove it from the *Edits* list in Toolspace, *Prospector's* preview area or from the *Operations Type* list in the *Definition* tab in the Surface Properties dialog box.

Line Edits

The line editing commands include **Add Line**, **Delete Line**, and **Swap Edge**. The **Add Line** and **Delete Line** commands add or remove triangle lines. The **Delete Line** command is often only applied around the outside edge of a surface to remove unwanted edge triangulation. Deleting lines in the interior of a surface causes both of the triangles next to the removed line to be deleted, leaving a hole in the surface that needs to be repaired by adding another line.

If you are considering deleting a line only to replace it with the opposite diagonal, such as the central line shown in Figure 5–53, using the **Swap Edge** command instead might be more efficient.

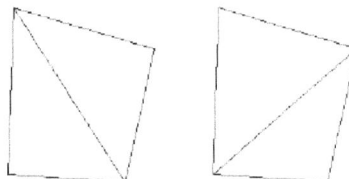

Figure 5–53

Adding an interior line that crosses many existing triangles swaps them where possible to adhere to the geometry represented by the added line. This method can be a good way of swapping multiple edges at the same time.

Point Edits

The Point editing commands can **Add**, **Delete**, **Modify**, or **Move** surface points. They do not affect point objects in the drawing, but rather the surface points created from them. Surface points can be adjusted or deleted as required.

When an AutoCAD Civil 3D point object is adjusted (e.g., moved), the surface containing that point data might not be identified as being out of date nor update automatically. In this situation, you should rebuild the surface.

Simplify Surface

As the collection methods of surface data continue to evolve, yielding significantly larger data sets, the drawing file size increases in proportion to the surface data contained in the drawing. The AutoCAD Civil 3D software has a limit of 2.5 million vertices for a surface. Once it exceeds this limit, the software prompts you to store surface data to an external file with an .mms extension. The resulting external surface files can be quite large. To avoid this, you can simplify your surface using the Simplify Surface wizard. Extra points can be removed from a surface without compromising its accuracy. Points that you might want to remove include points that are in an external point file or database, or redundant points in areas of high data concentration where the value of this extra information is minimal. There are two simplification methods available.

- **Edge Contraction:** This method simplifies the surface by using existing triangle edges. It contracts triangle edges to single points by removing one point. The location of the point to which an edge is contracted is selected so that the change to the surface is minimal.

- **Point Removal:** This method simplifies the surface by removing existing surface points. More points are removed from denser areas of the surface.

When you simplify a surface, you specify which regions of the surface the operation should address. The region options include using the existing surface border, or specifying a window or polygon. The **Pick in Drawing** icon enables you to select the region from the drawing. If a closed line exists in the drawing that you want to use as the region boundary, you can select the **Select objects** option and then use the **Pick in Drawing** icon to select the boundary. Curves in the boundary are approximated by line segments. The line segment generation is governed by a *Mid Ordinate Distance* value that you determine.

Once you have selected the region, the dialog box displays the *Total Points Selected In Region* value. You can refine the surface reduction options by setting a percentage of points to remove, the maximum change in elevation, or the maximum edge contraction error.

Smooth Contours

Although not a true surface edit, AutoCAD Civil 3D surface contours can be smoothed to reduce their jagged appearance using the Surface Object Style settings. There are two approaches to this: the *Add Vertices* method and the *Spline Curve* method. The *Add Vertices* method enables you to select a relative smoothness from the slider bar at the bottom of the Surface Style dialog box, as shown in Figure 5–54.

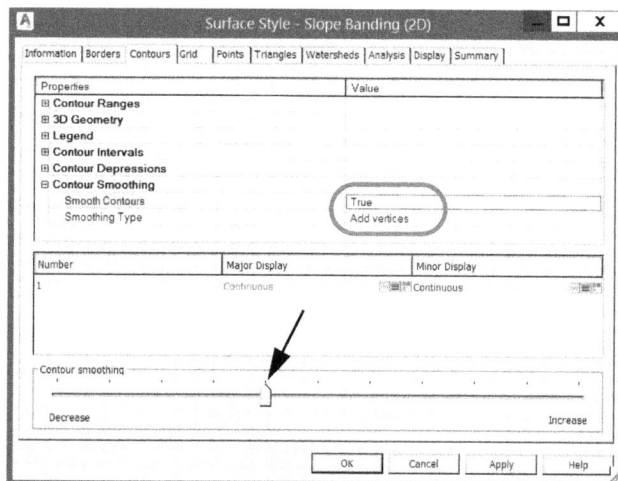

Figure 5–54

The *Spline Curve* method generates very smooth contours, but the contours are more liberally interpolated and might overlap where surface points are close together. This approach is best applied to surfaces with relatively few data points or in areas of low relief, as shown in Figure 5–55.

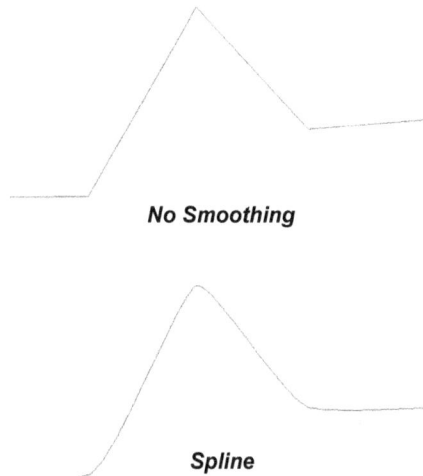

No Smoothing

Spline

Figure 5–55

Smooth Surface

The Smooth Surface edit introduces new, interpolated elevations between surface data. It is used to create a more realistic-looking terrain model, though not necessarily a more accurate one. Generally, surface smoothing works best with point-based surface data.

The AutoCAD Civil 3D software has two smoothing methods: *Natural Neighbor* and *Kriging*.

- *Natural Neighbor* interpolates a grid of additional data points that produce a smoother overall terrain model.

- *Kriging* reads surface trends to add additional data in sparse areas.

Surface smoothing is applied by right-clicking on the *Edits* collection under a surface's *Definition* and selecting **Smooth Surface**. The Smooth Surface dialog box and example of surface smoothing are shown in Figure 5–56.

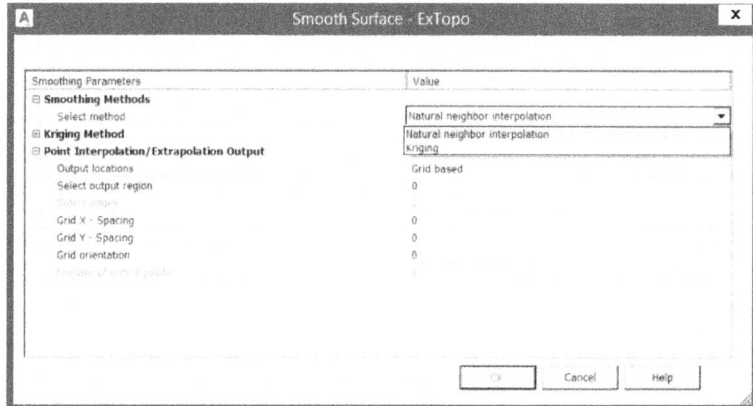

Figure 5–56

Copy Surface

The AutoCAD Civil 3D software does not have a copy surface command, but surface objects can be copied using the AutoCAD **Copy** command (**Modify>Copy**). When copying surface objects, select the same base and then a second point to ensure that the surface is not moved during the copy. After a copy, a duplicate surface is created and displays in the Toolspace, *Prospector* tab. The copy has the same name as the original followed with a number in parenthesis, such as (1). These copied surfaces can be renamed as required. Surface copies are independent of each other and can be edited.

Surface Paste

The **Surface Paste** command enables the AutoCAD Civil 3D software to combine multiple surfaces into a single surface. You might want to paste into a copy of a surface if you want to keep the original unmodified. For example, a finished condition surface is needed that includes a proposed surface (*Proposed*) along with the existing ground (EG) around its periphery. In this situation, you would first create a new surface and name it **Finished Ground**. In the *Surfaces* collection in the Toolspace, *Prospector* tab, right-click on the Finished Ground surface's *Edit* collection and select **Paste** to merge in the **Existing ground (EG)** and **Proposed** surfaces.

Once the command has executed, the surface's **EG** and **Proposed** surfaces are left unchanged, and the **Finished Ground** surface represents a combination of the two. If you did not create the **Finished Ground** surface, but pasted the **Proposed** surface into the **EG** surface, you would not have the original **EG** surface for reference in profiles and other places. If surfaces are pasted in the wrong order, the order can be rearranged using the *Definition* tab in the Surface Properties dialog box.

Surfaces remain dynamically linked after pasting. Therefore, if the **Proposed** surface changes, the **Finished Ground** surface updates to display the change.

Raise/Lower Surface

The **Raise/Lower Surface** command adds or subtracts a specified elevation value. This adjustment is applied to the entire surface. It is useful for modeling soil removal and changing a surface's datum elevation.

Adjusting Surfaces Through Surface Properties

In addition to the graphical edit methods, you can adjust surfaces by changing their surface properties. Surface property adjustments include setting a *Maximum triangle length* or *Exclude elevations* greater or less than certain values. You can also enable or disable the effects of certain surface data (such as breaklines and boundaries) by disabling them in the dialog box.

To locate these options (as shown in Figure 5–57), right-click on a surface in the Toolspace, *Prospector* tab and select **Surface Properties**.

Definition Options	Value
⊟ **Build**	
Copy deleted dependent objects	No
Exclude elevations less than	No
Elevation <	0.000'
Exclude elevations greater than	No
Elevation >	0.000'
Use maximum triangle length	No
Maximum triangle length	0.000'
Convert proximity breaklines to standard	Yes
Allow crossing breaklines	No
Elevation to use	Use average breakline elevation at intersection
⊞ **Data operations**	
⊞ **Edit operations**	

Figure 5–57

5.7 Surface Analysis Tools

Viewing a Surface in 3D

AutoCAD's default view, the overhead or plan view, is not the only way to view a surface. The AutoCAD **3D Orbit** command and the AutoCAD Civil 3D **Object Viewer** tilt the coordinate space to display a 3D surface model. How the surface displays is dependent on the assigned style. You can view a surface in 3D using the Object Viewer or directly in the drawing window using the **3D Orbit** command. Both have similar navigation controls, but the Object Viewer enables you to review your surface in 3D without changing your current view.

Both methods can display a wireframe (3D Wireframe and 3D Hidden), conceptual, or realistic view. By default, a Conceptual display is a cartoon-like rendering without edge lines, while a Realistic display has material styles with edge lines. Both viewing methods use the AutoCAD ViewCube, which uses labels and a compass to indicate the direction from which you are viewing a model.

The Object Viewer method is shown in Figure 5–58.

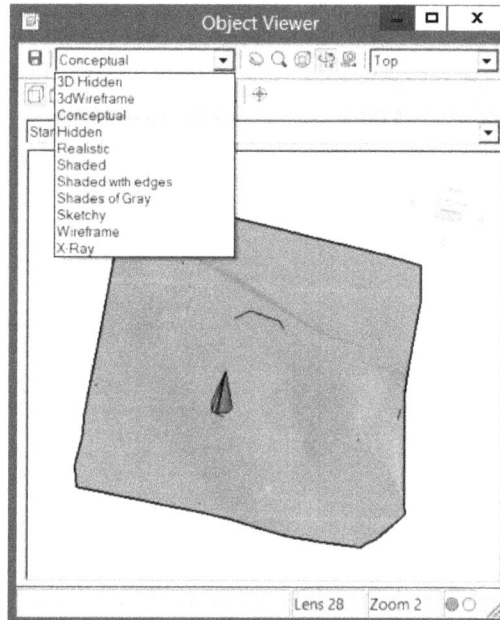

Figure 5–58

Quick Profile

Understanding the affect of breaklines and other data on a surface is critical to generating an accurate surface. The **Analyze>Ground Data>Quick Profile** command enables you to produce an instant surface profile with minimal effort.

A *Quick Profile* is a temporary object, which disappears from the drawing when you save or exit. If you need a more permanent graphic, you should create an alignment and profile.

Quick Profiles can be created along lines, arcs, polylines, lot lines, feature lines, or survey figures, or by selecting points. In addition to the command being located in the *Analyze* tab, you can select one of the previously mentioned objects, right-click, and select **Quick Profile**. Two examples of the Quick Profile are shown in Figure 5–59.

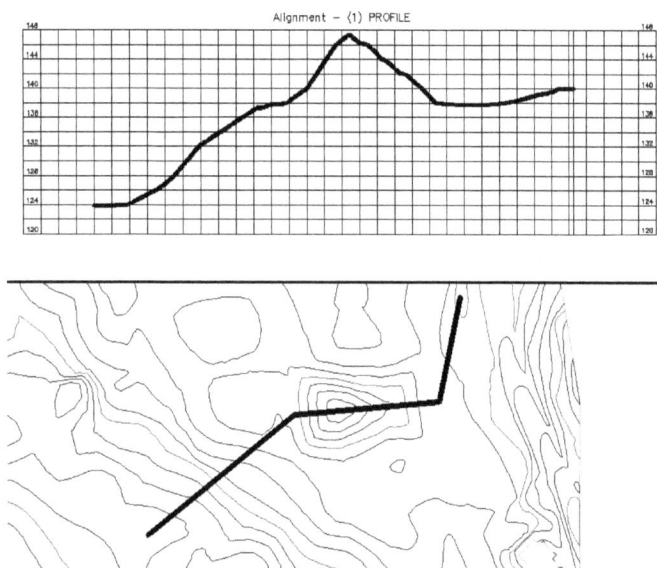

Figure 5–59

Practice 5c

Surface Edits

Practice Objective

- Edit a surface using definition options in the surface properties and commands found in the Toolspace.

Estimated time for completion: 30 minutes

In this practice you will refine a previously created surface. The **ExTopo** surface has some triangulations that are not valid. You will eliminate these TIN lines using three methods: you will set the maximum triangle edge length, delete TIN lines (triangle edges), and add a boundary to the surface. Each of these methods has advantages and disadvantages and should be used appropriately.

Task 1 - Set the maximum triangle length.

1. Continue working with the drawing from the previous practice or open **SUF1-C1-Surface.dwg** from the *C:\Civil 3D Projects\Civil3D-Training\Surface* folder.

*Ensure that the **ExTopo** surface is using the **Contours and Triangles** surface style.*

2. Select the preset view **Surface-Edit**, as shown in Figure 5–60.

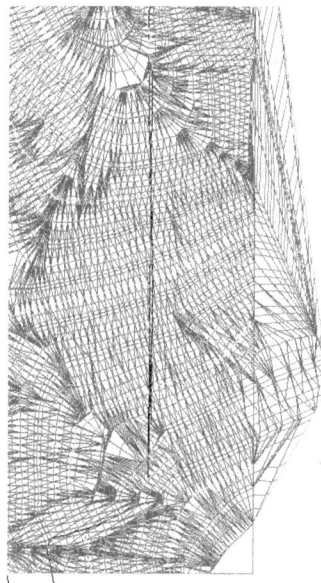

Figure 5–60

3. In Model Space, select the **ExTopo** surface. The *Tin Surface ExTopo* contextual tab will display. In the *Modify* panel, select **Surface Properties**, as shown in Figure 5–61.

Figure 5–61

4. The Surface Properties dialog box opens. Select the *Definition* tab and expand the **Build** options in the *Definition Options* area.

Although there are invalid triangle lengths that are less than that length in this area, entering a smaller number might remove some valid triangles in the site.

5. Set the *Use maximum triangle length* value to **Yes** and the *Maximum triangle length* value to **330'**, as shown in Figure 5–62. Click **OK** to close the dialog box and accept the changes.

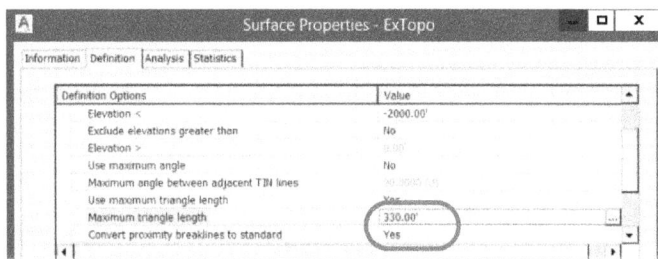

Figure 5–62

All triangles that have edge lengths greater than 330' are removed from the surface.

6. When prompted to *Rebuild the surface* or *Mark the surface as out-of-date*, select **Rebuild the surface**.

7. Save the drawing.

Task 2 - Delete lines.

Although you have eliminated triangle edge lengths greater than 330', you still have some triangles that you will remove using a scalpel (i.e., deleting selected lines).

1. Continue working with the drawing from the previous task or open **SUF1-C2-Surface.dwg**.

Figure 5–63 shows the lines that you will be deleting.

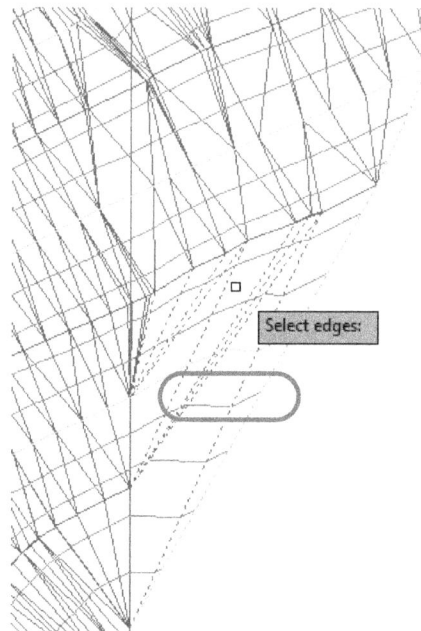

Figure 5–63

2. In Model Space, select the **ExTopo** surface. The *Tin Surface ExTopo* contextual tab will display. In the *Modify* panel, expand the ⬦ (Edit Surface) drop-down list, and select **Delete Line**, as shown in Figure 5–64.

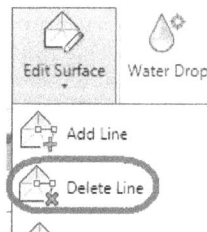

Figure 5–64

3. Select each of the required TIN lines in Model Space, as shown in Figure 5–65. When you have finished, press <Enter> to end the selection and press <Enter> to end the command.

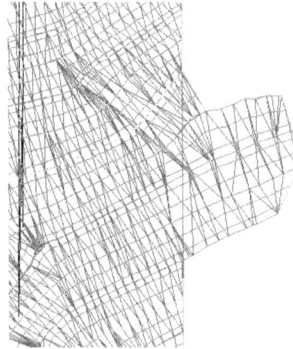

Figure 5–65

4. Save the drawing.

Task 3 - Add a boundary.

The **Delete Line** command can be effective, but might not efficiently clean up the edges of large surfaces. A surface boundary might be useful if you have a well-defined boundary.

1. Continue working with the drawing from the previous task or open **SUF1-C3-Surface.dwg**.

2. If you are not still in the drawing view from the previous task, select the *View* tab>Views panel and select the preset view **Surface-Edit**.

3. In Model Space, select the **ExTopo** surface. The *Tin Surface ExTopo* contextual tab will display. In the *Modify* panel, click

   (Add Data), expand the drop-down list and select **Boundaries**, as shown in Figure 5–66.

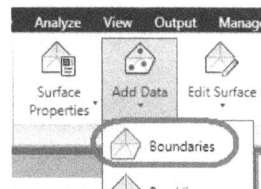

Figure 5–66

4. The Add Boundaries dialog box opens, as shown in
   Figure 5–67. Type **EG Outside** in the *Name* field, and select
   Outer in the Type drop-down list. Do not select the
   Non-destructive breakline option, because you do not want
   to trim to this polyline shape. Instead, the dialog box options
   selected will erase all of the triangle lines that cross or are
   beyond the boundary. Click **OK** to accept the changes and
   close the dialog box.

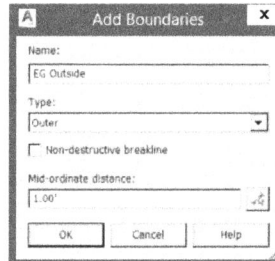

Figure 5–67

*You might have to regen
the screen to display the
boundary.*

5. When prompted to select an object, select the red polyline
   that represents the boundary, as shown in Figure 5–68.

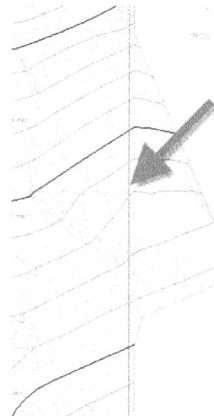

Figure 5–68

6. Examine how this boundary affected the surface. The
   boundary excluded all data that crossed or fell beyond it. This
   boundary is a dynamic part of the **ExTopo** surface.

7. (Optional) Select the boundary line and move the grips. Note
   how the surface expands or contracts to match the change in
   the boundary. Undo the changes.

8. Save the drawing.

Task 4 - Set the elevation range.

In reviewing the drawing, you need to address an error in the site. The original topographical contour file contains an invalid piece of data that has transferred to the surface.

1. Continue working with the drawing from the previous task or open **SUF1-C4-Surface.dwg**.

2. Select the preset view **Surf Elev Edit**.

3. In Model Space, as shown on the left in Figure 5–69, select the **ExTopo** surface, right-click, and select **Object Viewer**.

4. In the Object Viewer, click and drag the view, as shown on the right in Figure 5–69, to rotate the 3D view to identify the issue.

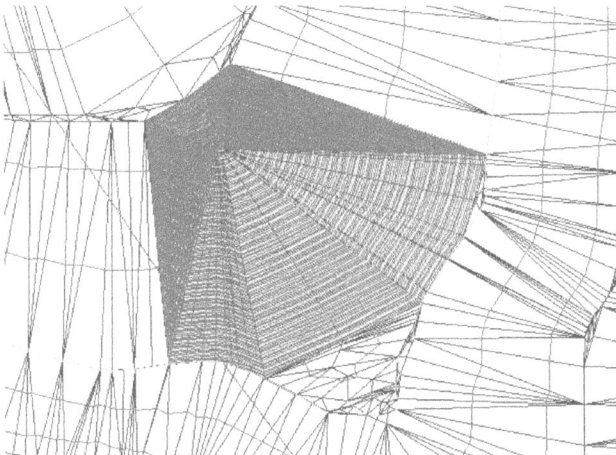

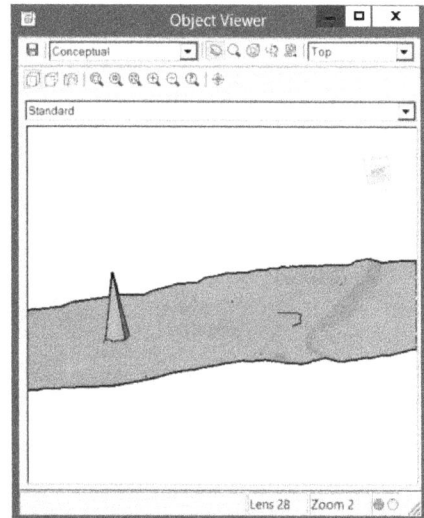

Figure 5–69

5. Close the Object Viewer by selecting **X** in the top right corner of the dialog box.

6. In Model Space, select the **ExTopo** surface. The *Tin Surface ExTopo* contextual tab will display. In the Modify panel, select **Surface Properties**, as shown in Figure 5–70. The Surface Properties dialog box opens.

Figure 5–70

7. Select the *Statistics* tab and expand the value list in the *General* area.

8. When you review the site conditions, note that the site ranges from an elevation of roughly 100' to 330'. However, the statistics indicate that the surface ranges from an elevation of 110' to 500', as shown in Figure 5–71.

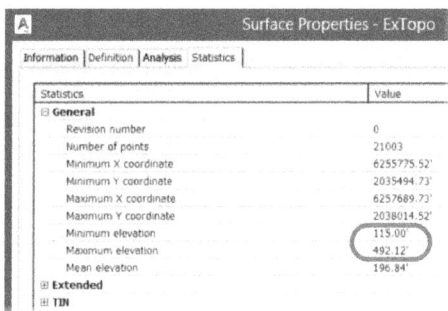

Figure 5–71

9. To correct the surface, select the *Definition* tab. Expand *Build* properties and set the *Exclude elevation less than* value to **Yes**. Set the *Elevation* < value to **100'**, the *Exclude elevation greater than* value to **Yes**, and the *Elevation* > value to **330'**, as shown in Figure 5–72.

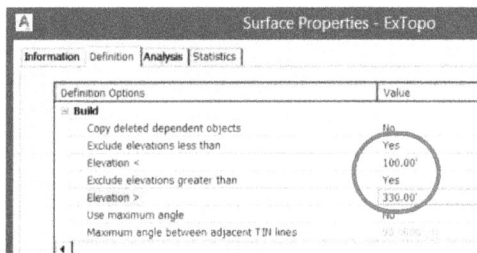

Figure 5–72

10. Click **OK** to accept the changes and close the dialog box.

11. When prompted to *Rebuild the surface* or *Mark the surface as out-of-date*, select **Rebuild the Surface**.

12. Save the drawing.

All points that are above an elevation of 330' are removed and the error is fixed.

Task 5 - Review edits in the Toolspace, *Prospector* tab **and in the Surface Properties dialog box.**

The history of all of the changes made to a surface is saved in the drawing. You can apply and remove these changes selectively to the surface.

1. Continue working with the drawing from the previous task or open **SUF1-C5-Surface.dwg**.

2. Select the preset view **Surface-Edit**.

3. In the Toolspace, *Prospector* tab, expand the *Surfaces* collection and select the **ExTopo** surface. Right-click and select **Surface Properties**. In the Surface Properties dialog box, clear the **Add boundary** *Operation Type* (as shown in Figure 5–73), and click **Apply**.

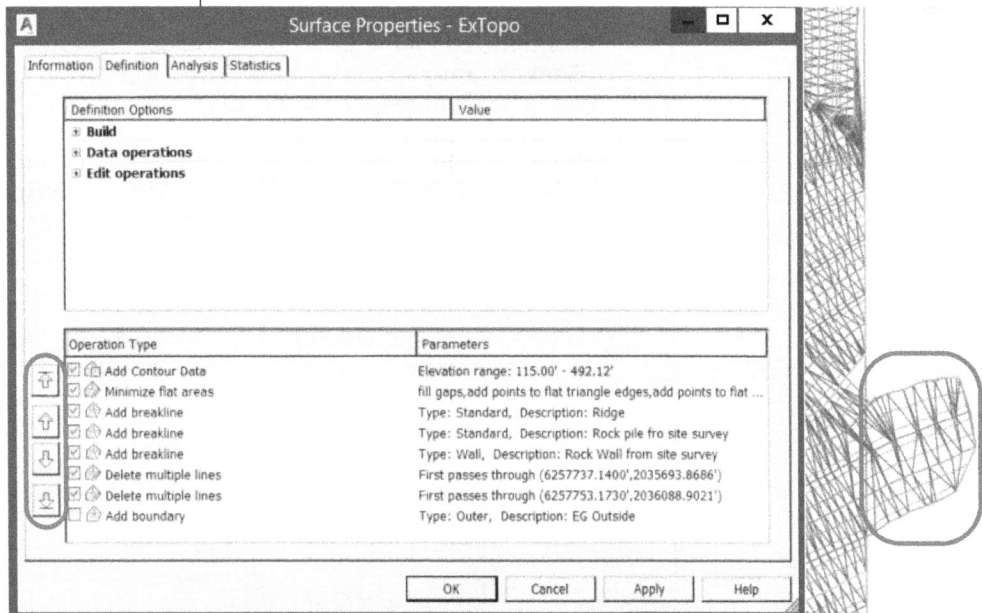

Figure 5–73

4. When prompted, select **Rebuild the Surface** in the Warning dialog box that opens. The boundary is ignored.

5. Re-select the **Add boundary** *Operation Type* and click **Apply**. When prompted, select **Rebuild the Surface** in the Warning dialog box that opens.

6. Save the drawing.

The boundary is once again used in the surface definition.

Task 6 - Create a composite surface.

In the preceding tasks, you created a surface from available contour data. However, the data around the existing road, **Mission Avenue** (the road running east to west at the top of the site), was inaccurate, so you surveyed the road and created a surface. You need to create a composite surface that represents the site condition combined with the road.

1. Continue working with the drawing from the previous task or open **SUF1-C6-Surface.dwg**.

2. Select the preset view **Survey Main**.

3. In the Toolspace, *Prospector* tab, right-click on the *Surfaces* collection and select **Create Surface**.

4. Select **TIN surface** for the surface *Type*. Type **Existing-Site** for the surface name and **Composite surface of ExTopo and ExRoad** for the *Description*. Select **Contours 2' and 10' (Background)** for the surface *Style*. Click **OK** to close the dialog box and create a surface.

5. In the Toolspace, *Prospector* tab, select the *Surfaces* collection. In the preview list area, select the **ExRoad** and **ExTopo** surfaces. Right-click on the *Style* column heading and select **Edit**, as shown in Figure 5–74.

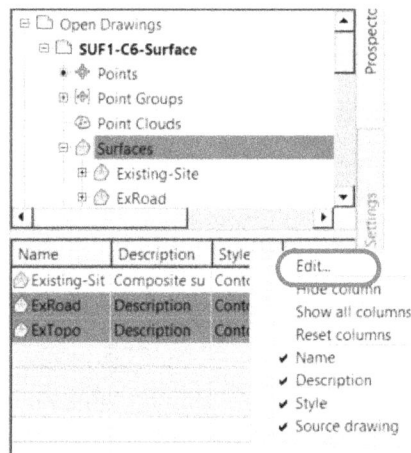

Figure 5–74

6. Set the surface style to **_No Display** and click **OK** to accept the changes and close the dialog box.

7. In the Toolspace, *Prospector* tab, expand the *Surfaces> Existing-Site>Definition* collections for that surface and select **Edits**. Right-click and select **Paste Surface...**, as shown in Figure 5–75.

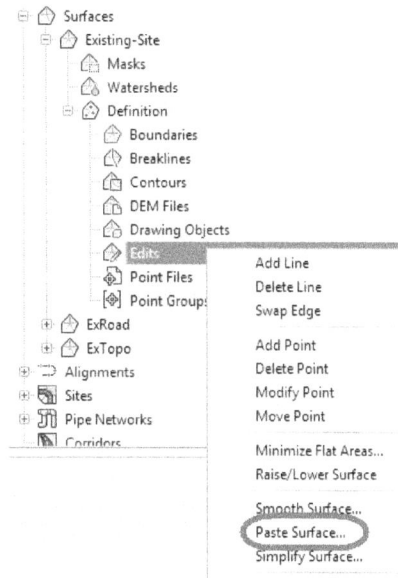

Figure 5–75

To select both surfaces, hold <Ctrl> when selecting the second surface.

8. In the Select Surface to Paste dialog box, select the **Ex Topo** and **Ex Road** surfaces, as shown in Figure 5–76. Once selected, click **OK** to close the dialog box.

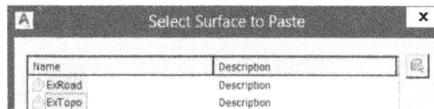

Figure 5–76

Note that the **ExRoad** surface was pasted first, followed by the **ExTopo** surface. In the area of overlap along the road, the **ExTopo** surface data will take precedence. This is not the required result.

9. In Model Space, select the **Existing-Site** surface from the surfaces listed in the *Surfaces* collection in the Toolspace, *Prospector* tab. The contextual tab for the surface object will display. Select **Surface Properties** in the ribbon panel. The Surface Properties - Existing Site dialog box opens. In the *Definition* tab, note the order of the paste operations, as shown in Figure 5–77.

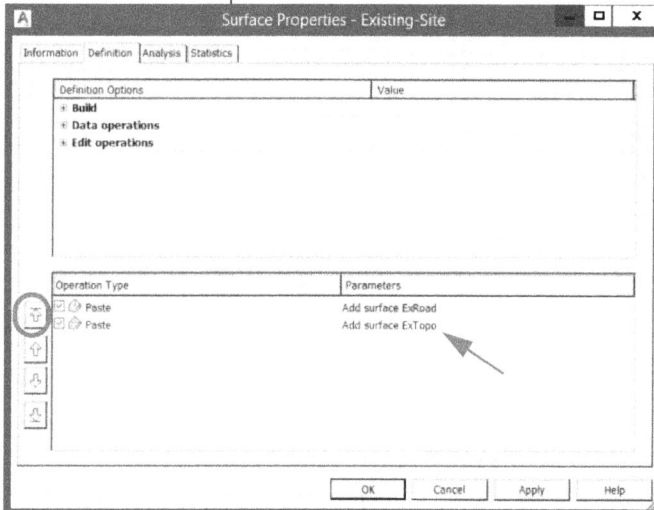

Figure 5–77

10. Select the **Paste** operation with the value **Add surface ExTopo** and move it to the top of the list by clicking [⬆].

11. Click **Apply**. When prompted to *Rebuild the surface* or *Mark the surface as out-of-date*, select **Rebuild the Surface**.

12. Click **OK** to exit the dialog box.

    As a consequence of the AutoCAD Civil 3D software's dynamic abilities, any changes to either the **ExTopo** or **ExRoad** surface will be reflected in the **Existing-Site** surface.

13. Save the drawing.

5.8 Surface Labels

Surface labels can be used to label contour elevations, slope values, spot elevations, and watershed delineations. Label values update if the surface changes.

To create surface labels, in the *Annotate* tab>Labels & Tables panel, expand Add Labels and select **Surface** to access the surface label flyout menu, as shown in Figure 5–78.

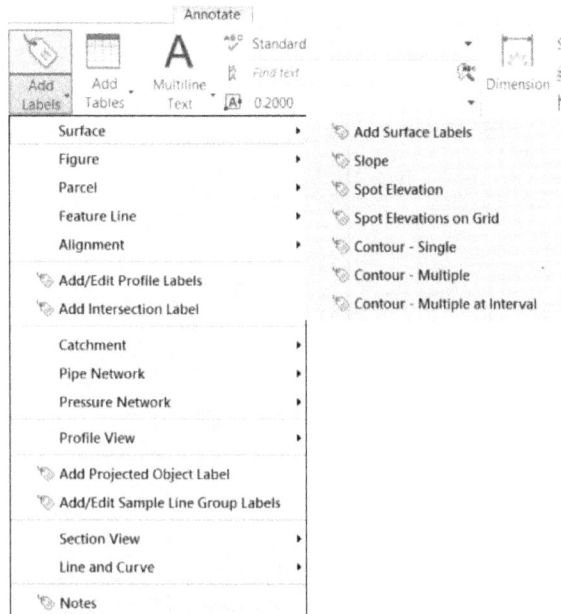

Figure 5–78

You can also click ✎ (Add Labels) to open the Add Labels dialog box, as shown in Figure 5–79. This dialog box enables you to select the feature and label type while being able to control the label style on the fly.

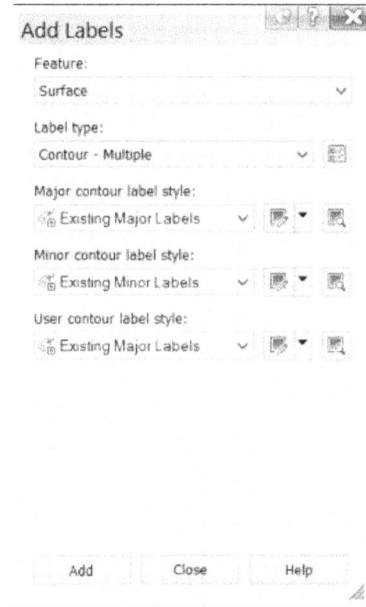

Figure 5–79

Contour Labels

Contour labels can be created individually, as multiples along a linear path, or as multiples along a linear path with repeated labels at a set interval. Multiple contours are aligned along an object called a *Contour Label Line*, which can be repositioned as needed, and in turn updates the position of its labels. These label lines have a selectable property that can make them visible only when an attached label is selected. If they are left visible, they should be placed on a non-plotting layer.

Spot and Slope Labels

Spot elevation and slope labels can be created as needed to annotate a surface. These are dynamic surface labels and not point objects, although they might look similar to points. Slopes can be measured at a single point or interpolated between two points.

5.9 Surface Volume Calculations

You can generate volume calculations in the AutoCAD Civil 3D software in many ways. Surface-to-surface calculations are often used to compare an existing ground surface to a proposed surface to determine cut and fill quantities. In the AutoCAD Civil 3D software, quantities can be adjusted by an expansion (cut) or a compaction (fill) factor. Surfaces representing different soil strata can be compared to each other to determine the volume between the soil layers. There are multiple ways of comparing surfaces to each other in the AutoCAD Civil 3D software.

Volumes Dashboard

In the *Analyze* tab>Volumes and Materials panel, click

🕂 (Volumes Dashboard).

The Volumes Dashboard creates a volume surface based on a graphical subtraction of one surface from the other, as shown in Figure 5–80.

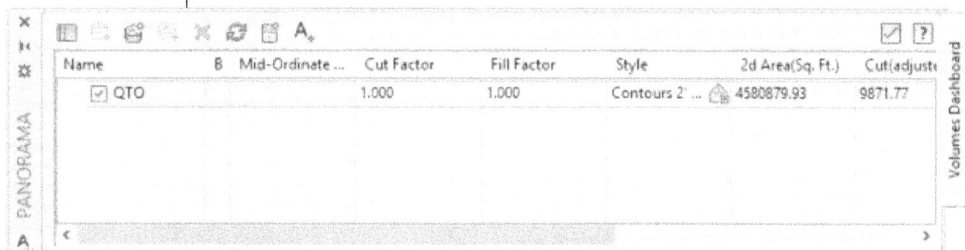

Figure 5–80

The *Net Graph* column color displays in red if the surface difference results in a net cut, and green if it is a net fill. You can have multiple volume entries listed if you are comparing multiple surfaces. If any surfaces change, return to this vista and click

♻ (Recompute Volumes) to update the calculations. Alternatively, you can add another volume entry. Select the same two surfaces and compare before and after volume calculations.

Bounded Volumes

The area to calculate cut and fill can be limited by clicking

📥 (Add Bounded Volume). This limits the calculations to the area defined by a polyline, polygon, or parcel.

Volume Reports

The dashboard's cut/fill summary contents can be placed directly into the drawing by clicking A_+ (Insert Cut/Fill Summary) inside the Volumes Dashboard. In addition, you can create a volume report from the dashboard contents to include in specifications or other project documents by clicking 📝 (Generate Volume Report) inside the Volumes Dashboard.

Grid Volume or TIN Volume Surface

This method enables you to assign the surfaces you want to compare as object properties of a volume surface. The volume between the surfaces is calculated and included in the volume surface object properties. The TIN surface calculation is the same one conducted in the Volumes Dashboard. The Grid surface calculation is based on a grid of points interpolated from both surfaces, rather than all of the surface points of both. Grid surfaces tend to be less accurate, but faster to calculate and easier to prove by manual methods.

A grid of spot elevation labels that list the elevation differences between two surfaces can be generated from either a Grid Volume surface or TIN Volume surface. Once the volume surface is created, you can create the labels. In the *Annotate* tab>Labels & Tables panel, expand Add Labels, expand Surface, and select **Spot Elevations on Grid**, as shown in Figure 5–81.

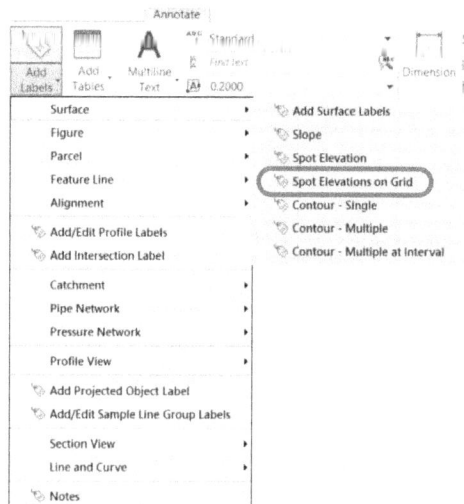

Figure 5–81

3D Solid Surface from TIN Surface

AutoCAD Civil 3D software has the capability to extract a 3D solid surface from any TIN surface. During the extraction process, you can define the vertical properties, the output properties, and which surface to extract.

Vertical Definition

Three options are available for setting the vertical definition of a 3D solid from a TIN surface, as shown in Figure 5–82.

1. The first option creates a solid with a consistent depth across the entire surface. This may be used to quickly calculate the volume of top soil to be removed.
2. The second options creates a solid with a fixed elevation. This option may be used to quickly calculate the water volume of a pond, which will have a consistent water elevation.
3. The last option creates a solid between two surfaces. This could be used to create various solids from soil report point. Doing so provides a solid for each type of material.

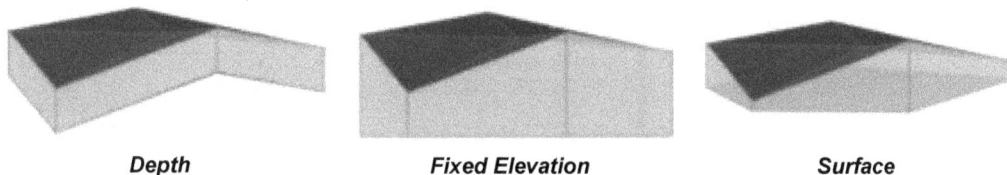

Depth   *Fixed Elevation*   *Surface*

Figure 5–82

Output Properties

Multiple output settings enable you to define where the solid is created during the extraction process. The layer and color for the solid can also be set. Then, you can create the solid in the current drawing or in a new drawing. If you select a new drawing, you can set the file path and name of the new drawing by clicking

 (Browse).

How To: Create a 3D Solid Surface

1. In the model, select a TIN surface.
2. In the contextual *Surface* tab>Surface Tools panel, expand

   (Extract from Surface) and select (Extract Solids from Surface).
3. In the Extract Solid from Surface dialog box, shown in Figure 5–83, set the vertical definition and the required drawing output.

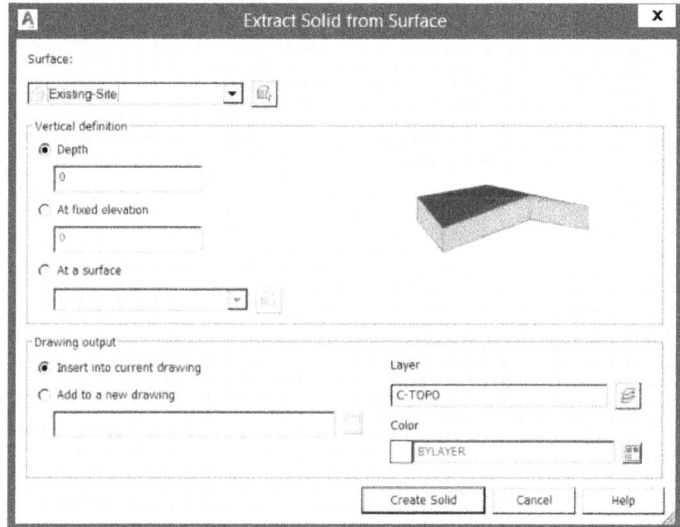

Figure 5–83

4. Click **Create Solid**.

5.10 Surface Analysis Display

The AutoCAD Civil 3D software can calculate and display many different surface analyses, including:

- **Contours:** This analysis can display contours differently based on their elevation ranges.

- **Directions:** This analysis can render surface triangles differently depending on which direction they face.

- **Elevations:** This analysis can render surface triangles differently depending on their elevation ranges.

- **Slopes:** This analysis can render surface triangles differently depending on their slope ranges.

- **Slope Arrows:** This analysis creates a dynamic slope arrow that points downslope for each triangle, colorized by slope range.

- **User-Defined Contours:** This analysis can display user-defined contours differently based on their elevation ranges.

- **Watersheds:** This analysis can calculate watershed areas, and render them according to area type. The AutoCAD Civil 3D watershed analysis usually results in a very large number of individual watersheds. Although a **Catchment Areas** command is available to assist in drawing the catchment areas, it is still up to the engineers to draw their own conclusions on how these should be merged together into catchment areas.

The above analyses are calculated on demand for each surface and their results are stored under the surface's Surface Properties.

In addition, the following separate utilities might be helpful when analyzing surfaces:

- **Check for Contour Problems:** Used to locate problems with the contour data, including crossing or overlapping contours. To access this command, in the *Surface* tab>expanded

  Analyze panel, select [icon] **Check for Contour Problems**, as shown in Figure 5–84.

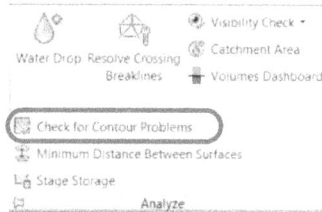

Figure 5–84

- **Resolve Crossing Breaklines:** Identifies and fixes any breaklines that create an invalid condition when two elevations exist at the intersection point of two breaklines. The breaklines can be found in the drawing, in a survey figure, or in the survey database. To access this command, in

  the *Surface* tab>Analyze panel, click [icon] (Resolve Crossing Breaklines).

- **Water Drop:** Draws a 2D or 3D polyline indicating the expected flow path of water across the surface from a given starting point. To access this command, in the *Surface* tab>

  Analyze panel, click [icon] (Water Drop).

- **Catchment Area:** Draws a 2D or 3D polyline indicating the catchment boundary and catchment point marker for a surface drainage area. To access this command, in the

  Surface tab>Analyze panel, click [icon] (Catchment Area). You should use this command in conjunction with the **Water Drop** command to determine an accurate placement of catchment regions and points.

- **Visibility Check>Zone of Visual Influence:** Analyzes the line of sight for 360 degrees around a single point. To access this command, in the *Surface* tab>Analyze panel, click

  (Visibility Check>Zone of Visual influence). This command is good for analyzing if towers, buildings, and other objects can be seen within a certain radius.

- **Minimum Distance Between Surfaces:** Identifies the (X,Y) location where two overlapping surfaces are the closest elevation. To access this command, in the *Surface* tab>

  Analyze panel, click (Minimum Distance Between Surfaces). If there is more than one location with the shortest distance between the two surfaces (because it is flat), then the location might be represented by a series of points, a line, or a closed polyline.

- **Stage Storage:** Calculates volumes of a basin from a surface, using either a surface or polylines to define the basin. To access this command, in the *Surface* tab>Analyze

  panel, click (Stage Storage). Either the *Average End Area* or the *Conic Approximation* method, or both are used to calculate volumes for the stage storage table.

Analysis Settings

You apply a surface analysis using the *Analysis* tab in the Surface Properties dialog box. In this tab, you can select the number of ranges and a legend table to be used. All of the remaining analysis settings are located in the *Surface Object* style, including whether to display in 2D or 3D, the color scheme, elevations, range groupings, etc. If you want to change the number of ranges or the range values, use the settings in this tab at any time.

Analysis Data Display

Overall visibility, layer, linetype, and related controls for analysis elements are managed using the *Display* tab in the Object Style dialog box, as shown in Figure 5–85. The component entries for *Slopes, Slope Arrows, Watersheds*, etc., are displayed. These can be set to display different settings and combinations of elements in 2D and 3D.

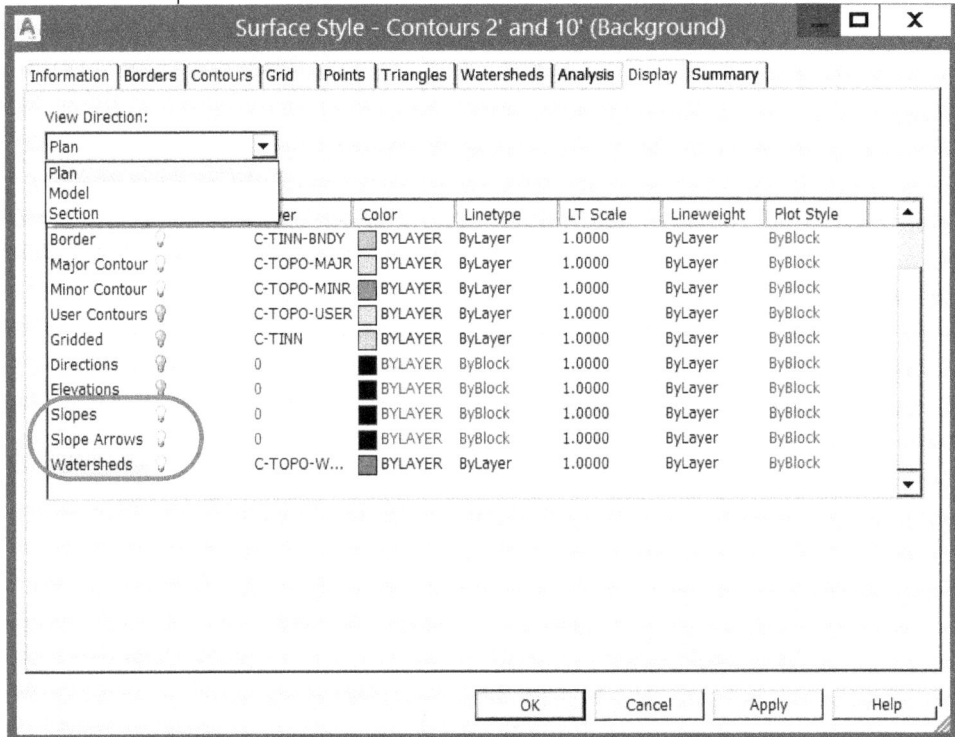

Figure 5–85

Practice 5d

Estimated time for completion: 20 minutes

Surface Labeling and Analysis

Practice Objective

• Communicate information about the surface by labeling and analyzing it.

Task 1 - Add surface labels.

1. Continue working with the drawing from the previous practice or open **SUF1-D1-Surface.dwg** from the *C:\Civil 3D Projects\Civil3D-Training\Surface* folder.

2. Select the preset view **Surface Label**.

3. Select the **Existing-Site** surface in Model Space. In the contextual *Surface* tab>Labels & Tables panel, expand Add Labels and select the **Contour - Multiple**, as shown in Figure 5–86.

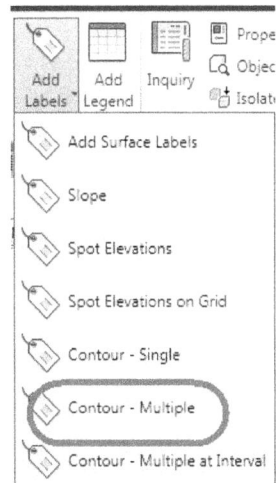

Figure 5–86

4. When prompted to select the first point, specify any point. When prompted for the next point, select a second and third point that creates a line intersecting all of the contours that you want to label, as shown in Figure 5–87. Press <Enter> when done.

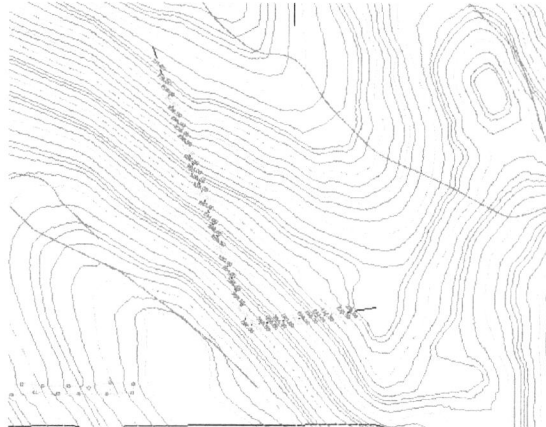

Figure 5–87

5. Move and reorient the contour label line. The labels update.

6. The *Display Contour Label Line* property can be set to only be visible when contour labels are selected. To change the visibility property, select the line in Model Space and select **Properties** in the contextual *Label* tab>General Tools panel. In the Properties dialog box, set the *Display Contour Label Line* property and the *Display Minor Contour Labels* property to **False,** as shown in Figure 5–88.

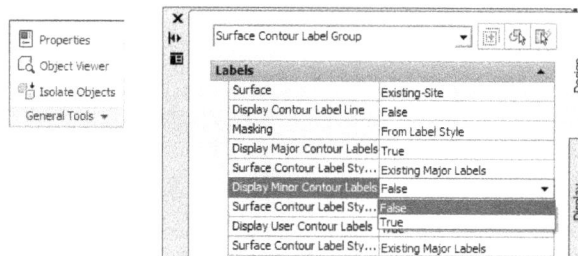

Figure 5–88

7. Close the Properties dialog box and press <Esc> to cancel your selection.

Once the grips disappear, the line is no longer displayed. Select a contour label to have the contour label line temporarily display for editing.

8. To have all of the future contour label lines behave this way in this drawing, select the *Settings* tab in the Toolspace. Select **Surface**, right-click, and select **Edit Feature Settings...**, as shown in Figure 5–89.

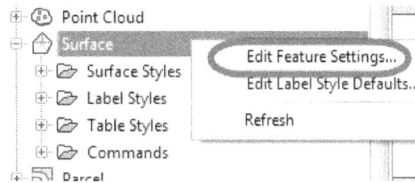

Figure 5–89

9. In the Edit Feature Settings dialog box, expand *Contour Labeling Defaults* and set the *Display Contour Label Line* property to **False** and change *Surface Contour Label Style Minor* to **<none>**, as shown in Figure 5–90. Click **OK** to accept the changes and close the dialog box.

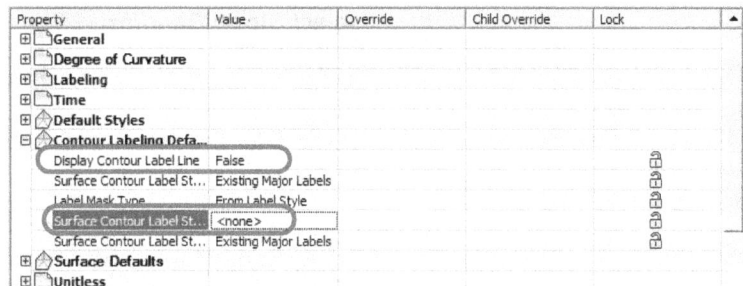

Figure 5–90

10. Select the **Existing-Site** surface again in Model Space. In the contextual *Surface* tab>Labels & Tables panel, expand Add Labels and select **Contour - Multiple**.

11. Select two points that will draw a line across some contours and press <Enter> when done. The contour label line and minor contour labels do not display.

12. Select the **Existing-Site** surface in Model Space. In the contextual *Surface* tab>Labels & Tables panel, expand Add Labels and select **Slope**.

13. To accept the prompt for the default One-point label, press <Enter>, and select a point in Model Space within the surface boundary. The AutoCAD Civil 3D software will place the slope value at that point. When you finish placing the labels, press <Enter> to exit the command.

14. (Optional) Using the process from Steps 10 and 11, experiment with labeling the surface with spot elevations and two point slopes. Note that you will be able to copy a label and place it at a different location. As the labels are dynamic, the values will change to reflect the surface information at the location of the label.

Task 2 - Perform a slope analysis.

1. Continue working with the drawing from the previous task or open **SUF1-D2-Surface.dwg**.

2. Select the preset view **Surface**.

3. Select the **Existing-Site** surface in Model Space. In the contextual *Surface* tab>Modify panel, select **Surface Properties**.

4. In the *Information* tab in the Surface Properties dialog box, select **Slope Banding (2D)** as the surface style.

The AutoCAD Civil 3D software calculates a range of values to fit within the specified number of ranges.

5. In the *Analysis* tab, select **Slopes** for the *Analysis type* and select **5** for the number of ranges to use. Click ⬇ (Run Analysis).

6. Change the range values for Range1 to 0-2%, Range2 to 2-5%, Range3 to 5-10% Range4 to 10-20%, and Range5 to 20-70000%, as shown in Figure 5–91.

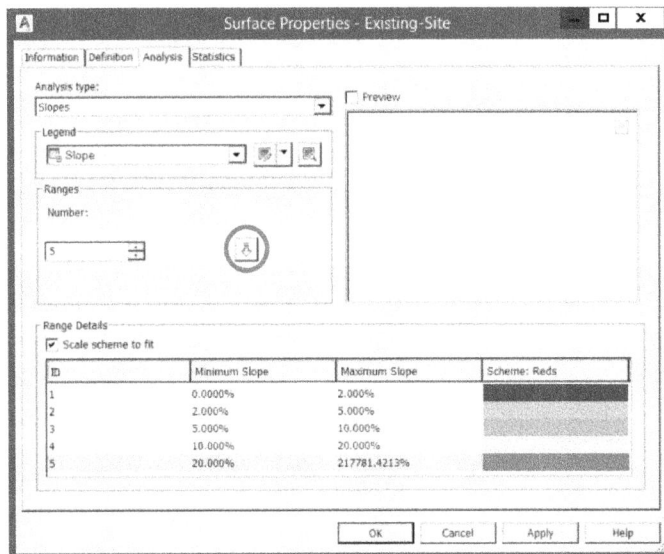

Figure 5–91

7. Change the range of colors for the slope range to match those shown in Figure 5–91. To change the color, click on it to open the Select Color dialog box, as shown in Figure 5–92, and select the required color. Click **OK** to close the dialog box.

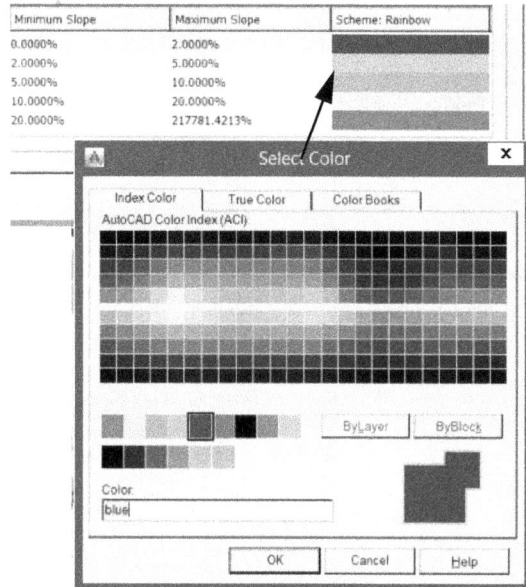

Figure 5–92

8. Click **OK** to close the dialog box and apply the changes. Press <Esc> to exit the surface selection.

9. Review the area that you want to develop. The slope ranges will be an issue.

10. You need to create a slope values table. Select the **Existing-Site** surface in Model Space. In the contextual *Surface* tab>Labels & Tables panel, select **Add Legend**.

11. Select **Slopes** from the command options, and then select **Dynamic** for a dynamic table.

Because this table is dynamic, any changes made to the surface or to the ranges in the analysis will update the table automatically.

12. When prompted for the top corner of the table (top left), select a location in an open area to the right of the surface, as shown in Figure 5–93. Press <Esc> to exit the selection.

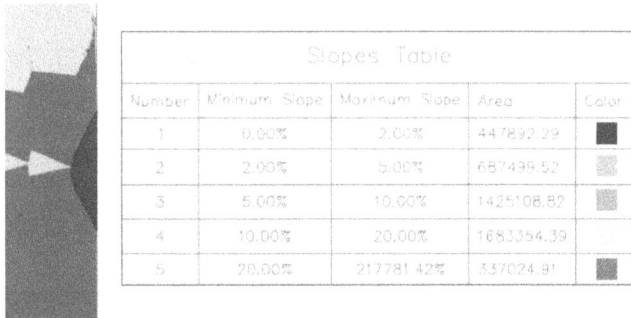

Figure 5–93

13. (Optional) Open the Surface Properties dialog box (Steps 3 to 7) and change the number of slope ranges or the values. The Model Space Legend table will be updated.

14. Save the drawing.

Task 3 - Create a 3D solid.

Continue working with the drawing from the previous task or open **SUF1-D3-Surface.dwg**.

1. Select the **Existing-Site** surface in Model Space. In the contextual *Surface* tab>Surface Tools panel, expand

   (Extract from Surface) and select (Extract Solids from Surface).

2. In the Extract Solid from Surface dialog box, shown in Figure 5–94, set the following:

   • Surface: *Existing-Site*
   • Vertical definition: *At fixed elevation* = **100**
   • Drawing output: *Add to a new drawing* and save it to ...**\Surface\3D-Solid.dwg**.

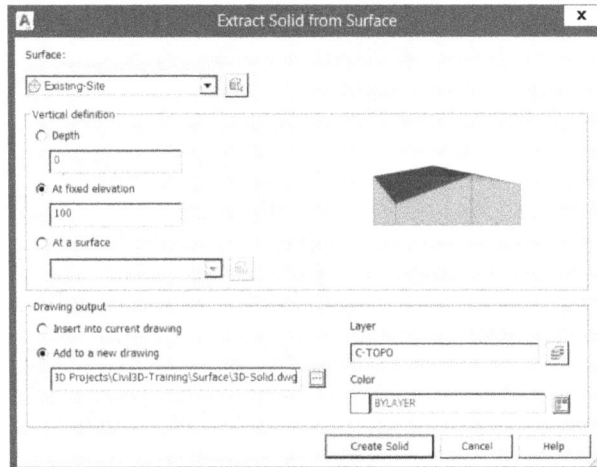

Figure 5–94

3. Click **Create Solid**.

4. Click **OK** when prompted.

5. Open the ...**\Surface\3D-Solid.dwg**, orbit the model, and verify that the bottom of the solid surface is at elevation 100, as shown in Figure 5–95.

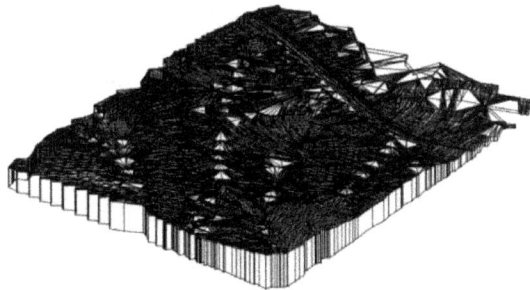

Figure 5–95

6. Close the drawing without saving.

5.11 Point Cloud Surface Extraction

Point Clouds are dense groupings of points created by 3D scanners. The AutoCAD software has been capable of working with point clouds from its previous versions. The accepted point cloud file formats are .RCP and .RCS. They are faster and more efficient than the previous file formats and are created using the Autodesk Recap software.

- As with XREFs, images, and other externally referenced files, you can attach and manage point clouds using the External References Manager.

- Point cloud object snaps have been added to the *3D Object Snap* tab in the Drafting Settings dialog box and the 3D Object Snap options in the Status Bar.

- In a point cloud, you can use the **Object** option in the **UCS** command to align the active UCS to a plane.

- Dynamic UCS now aligns to a point cloud plane according to point density and alignment.

Attach Point Cloud

In the Attach Point Cloud dialog box, you can preview a point cloud and its detailed information (such as its classification and segmentation data) before attaching it, as shown in Figure 5–96. You can also use a geographic location for the attachment location (if the option is available).

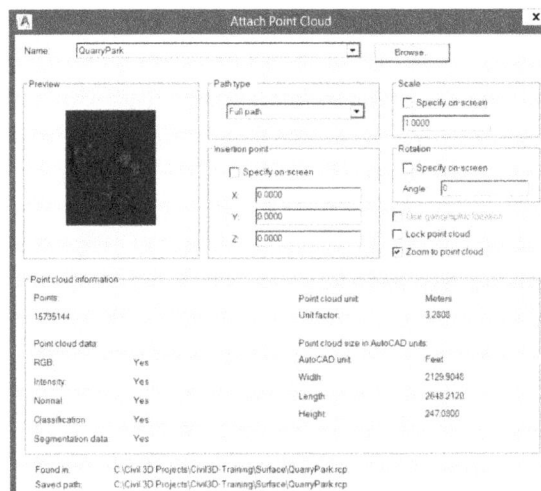

Figure 5–96

How To: Attach a Point Cloud

1. In the *Insert* tab>Point Cloud panel, click ⬤ (Attach).
2. In the Select Point Cloud File dialog box, expand the Files of type drop-down list and select an option, as shown in Figure 5–97. In the *Name* area, select a file and click **Open**.

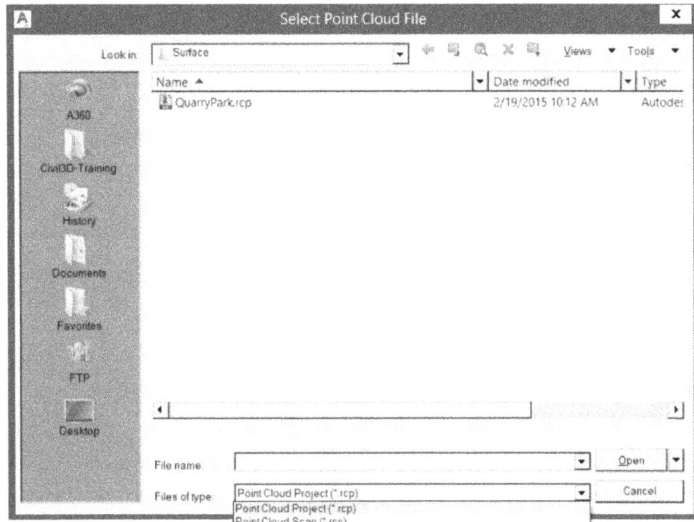

Figure 5–97

- The AutoCAD software can attach Point Cloud Project (RCP) and Scan (RCS) files (which are produced by the Autodesk ReCap software).

- The Autodesk ReCap software enables the creation of a point cloud project file (RCP) that references multiple indexed scan files (RCS). It converts scan file data into a point cloud format that can then be viewed and modified in other products.

3. In the Attach Point Cloud dialog box, click **Show Details** to display the point cloud information

4. In the Path type, Insertion point, Scale, and Rotation areas, set the options that you want to use to attach the point cloud, as shown in Figure 5–98. Click **OK**.

Figure 5–98

5. At the *Specify insertion point* prompt, click in the drawing to locate the point cloud.

Point Cloud Transparency

When point clouds exist in a drawing with other geometry, it can be difficult to see anything behind the point cloud. A tool in the *Point Cloud* contextual tab>Visualization panel enables you to adjusts the transparency of the point cloud, as shown in Figure 5–99. Alternatively, you can adjust the point cloud transparency in the Properties palette, as shown in Figure 5–99.

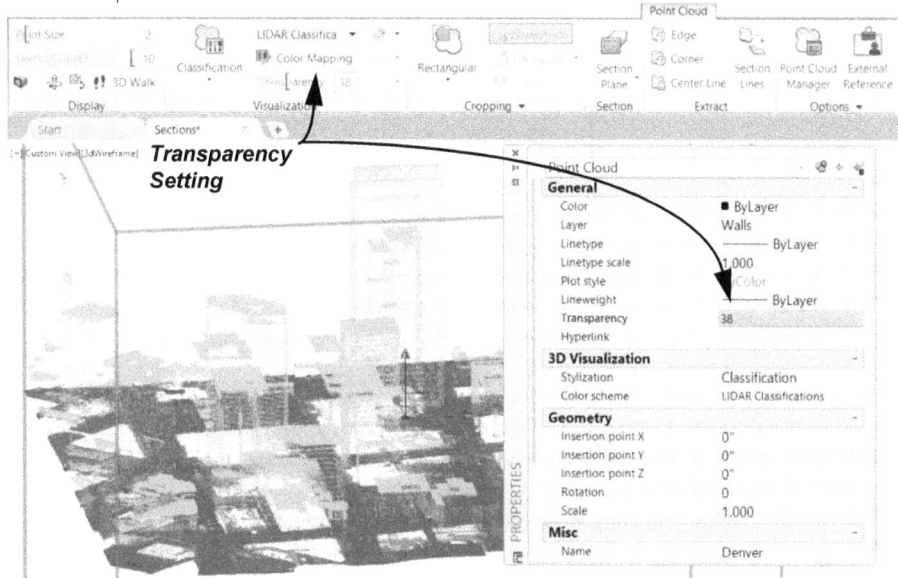

Figure 5–99

Cropping Point Clouds

Displaying the bounding box around the point cloud data enables you to determine its position in 3D space relative to the other objects in the drawing. The cropping tools in the Cropping panel enable you to display only the information that is required for your project, as shown in Figure 5–100. The cropping boundary can be rectangular, circular, or polygonal and is normal to the

screen. You can use ⊞ (Invert) to reverse the displayed points from inside to outside the boundary.

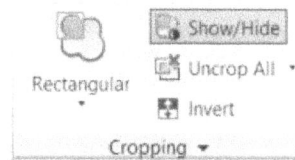

Figure 5–100

A tool in the Cropping panel (displayed by expanding the panel) enables you to save and restore named cropping states. Both the visibility of the scans and regions as they are displayed and the cropping boundary are maintained in named cropping states, as shown in Figure 5–101.

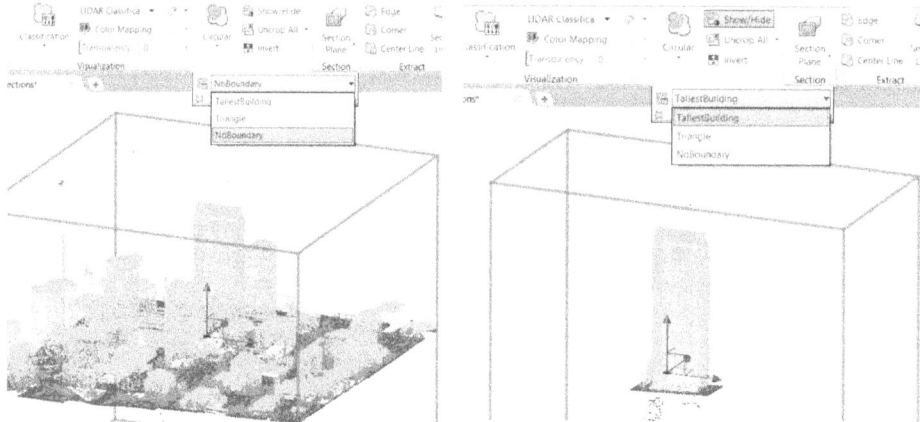

Figure 5–101

Hint: List Crop States

The **POINTCLOUDCROPSTATE** command can be used to **S**ave, **R**estore, and **D**elete crop states, as shown in Figure 5–102. Using the **?** option will list all of the available crop states.

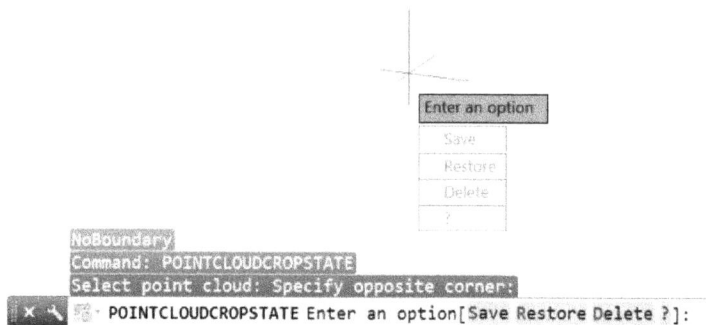

Figure 5–102

How To: Save a Named Crop State

1. Once a point cloud has been attached, select it in the model.
2. In the *Point Cloud* contextual tab>Cropping panel, select an appropriate crop boundary, as shown in Figure 5–103.

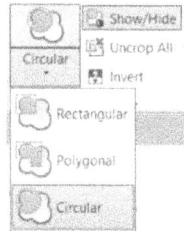

Figure 5–103

3. In the model, pick points to draw the boundary. If a Polygonal boundary was selected, press <Enter> when done.
4. At the cursor, select either **Inside** or **Outside** to indicate which points to keep.
5. Expand the *Point Cloud* contextual tab>Cropping panel, click

    (New Crop State).
6. Enter a name for the new crop state.

Surfaces from Point Clouds

Point clouds can be used to create AutoCAD Civil 3D surfaces. Once a point cloud has been attached to the drawing, it can be used to create a surface. In the *Home* tab>Create Ground Data

panel, expand Surfaces and select (Create Surface from Point Cloud), as shown in Figure 5–104.

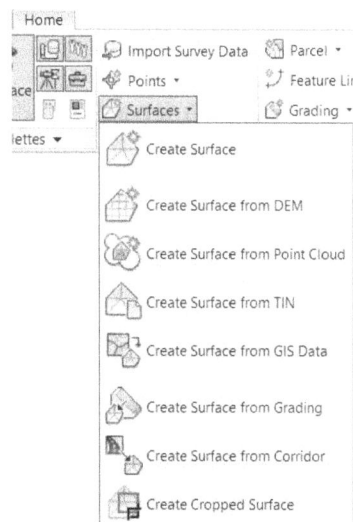

Figure 5–104

(Create Surface from Point Cloud) extracts point data from the point cloud to create a TIN surface. During the surface creation process, you can:

- Name the surface.

- Select a style for the surface.

- Select a render material.

- Select part or all of a point cloud.

- Select a filter method for Non-Ground points.

Point Cloud Selection

If there are one or more point clouds in the model, it is important to communicate to the software which points from the point clouds to use in the surface. The three available options for this are described as follows:

Button	Description
	Add an entire point cloud
	Remove a selection from the list
	Add a selected area of a point cloud

Non-Ground Point Filtering

When point clouds are created, they create points on any and every object visible in the scan area. This means that points can fall at the tops of buildings, trees and other structures. In order to create a surface that represents the ground terrain, the points that are not on the ground must be filtered out. Three filter methods exist when creating a surface from point clouds:

1. Planar average: Predicts the elevation of a surface by finding the average elevation of a plane of points. An example is shown in Figure 5–105.

Figure 5–105

2. Kriging interpolation: Predicts the elevation of a surface by computing a weighted average of the elevations of neighboring points. An example is shown in Figure 5–106. This is usually the most accurate option.

Figure 5–106

3. No filter: Uses the point cloud point elevations for the surface elevations. An example is shown in Figure 5–107.

Figure 5–107

How To: Create a Surface from Point Clouds.

1. In the *Home* tab>Create Ground Data panel, expand

   Surfaces and select 🐞 (Create Surface from Point Cloud).
2. In the model, select the point cloud or select any of the following options in the command line, as shown in Figure 5–108.
   - **Window**
   - **polyGon**
   - **polyLIne**

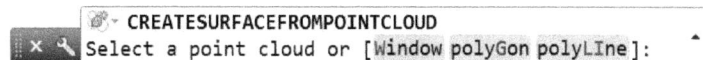

Figure 5–108

3. In the Create TIN Surface from Point Cloud dialog box - General page, type a surface name, set the surface style, and render material, as shown in Figure 5–109. Click **Next>**.

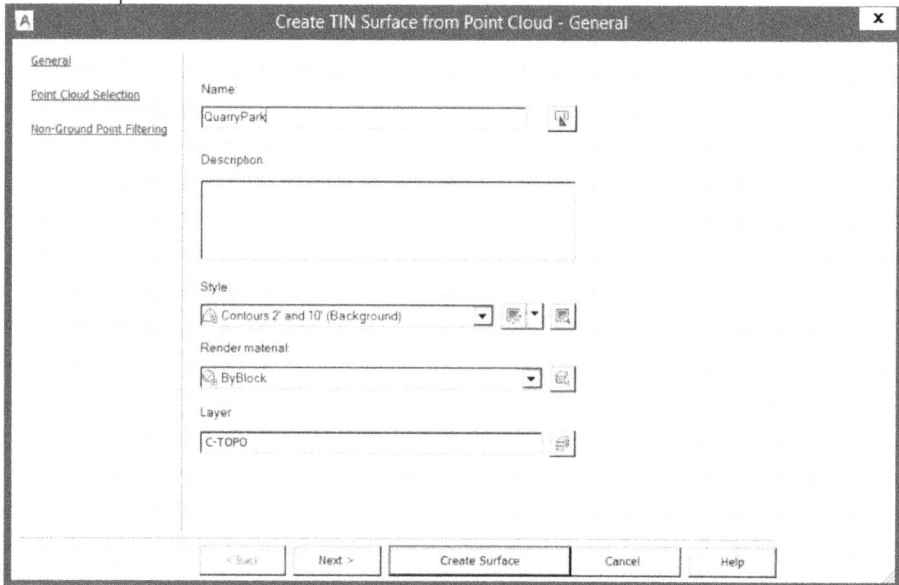

Figure 5–109

4. In the Create TIN Surface from Point Cloud dialog box - Point Cloud Selection page, select the Point clouds or parts of the Point clouds, as shown in Figure 5–110. Click **Next>**.

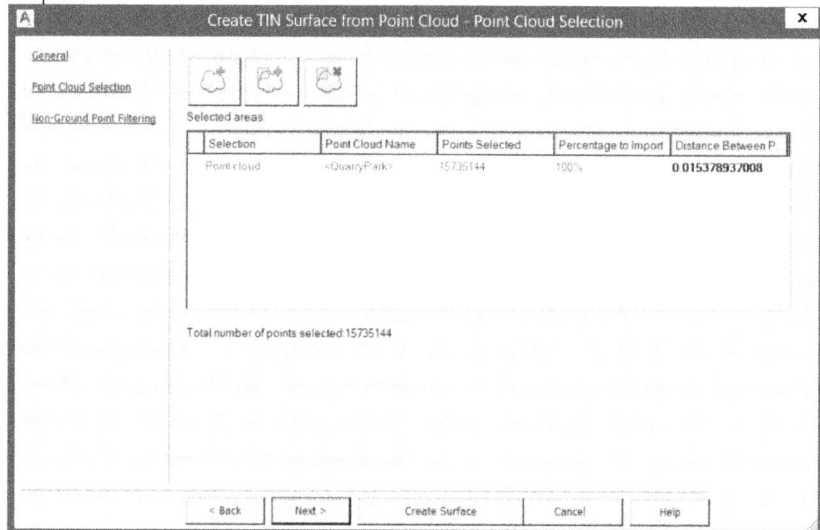

Figure 5–110

5. In the Create TIN Surface from Point Cloud dialog box - Non-Ground Point Filtering page, select a filter method and click **Create Surface**, as shown in Figure 5–111.

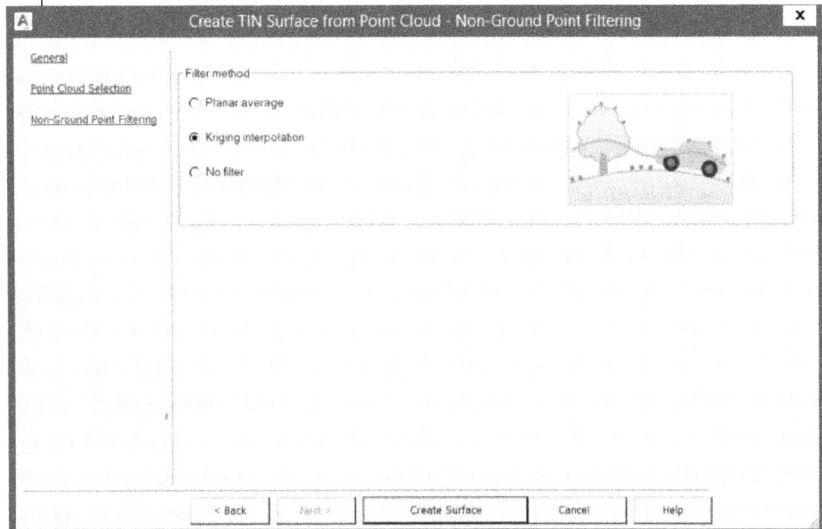

Figure 5–111

6. In the Point Cloud Processing in Background message box, click **Close**.

Practice 5e

(Optional) Create a Point Cloud Surface

Estimated time for completion: 15 minutes

Practice Objective

- Communicate information about a surface by labeling and analyzing it.

In this practice you will attach a Point Cloud to a new drawing file, as shown in Figure 5–112. You will then create a surface from the point cloud.

Figure 5–112

Task 1 - Attach a Point Cloud.

1. Start a new drawing from the **_AutoCAD Civil 3D (Imperial) NCS.dwt**.

2. In the *Insert* tab>Point Cloud panel, click ⬚ (Attach).

3. In the Select Point Cloud File dialog box, navigate to your practice files folder. In the *Name* area, select **Quarry Park.rcs** and click **Open**.

4. Accept the default options in the Attach Point Cloud dialog box, click **OK**, and use an insertion point of **0,0**.

5. Save the file.

Task 2 - Analyze the Point Cloud.

1. Select the point cloud. In the *Home* tab> Create Ground Data panel, expand **Surfaces** and select 🐾 (Create Surface from Point Cloud).

2. In the model, select the point cloud.

3. In the Create TIN Surface from Point Cloud dialog box General page, type **Quarry Park** for the surface name. Leave all other defaults and click **Next>**.

4. In the Create TIN Surface from Point Cloud dialog box Point Cloud Selection page, select Point cloud and then click

   🖼 (Remove a selection from the list).

5. In the same page, click 🖼 (Add a selected area of a point cloud). In the model, draw a window around the area indicated in Figure 5–113, and click **Next>**.

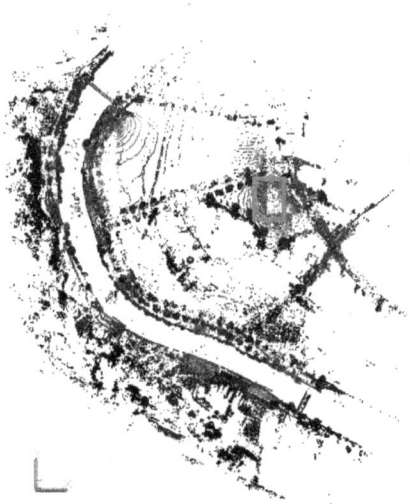

Figure 5–113

6. In the Create TIN Surface from Point Cloud dialog box Non-Ground Point Filtering page, select **Kriging interpolation** and click **Create Surface**.

7. In the Point Cloud Processing in Background message box, click **Close**. It may take a few minutes to process the points.

8. Close the file without saving.

Chapter Review Questions

1. Put the following steps in the order suggested for building a surface.

Step	Answer
a. Add Breaklines, assign more data, modify the data, or edit the surface, as required.	
b. Assign data to a surface.	
c. Accumulate data.	
d. Evaluate the resulting surface.	

2. What controls how an AutoCAD Civil 3D surface displays (whether it displays contours, TIN lines, or an analysis)?

   a. Surface Style

   b. Surface Definition

   c. AutoCAD Layers

   d. Surface Boundary

3. Where would you set the lowest and highest acceptable elevations for a surface?

   a. In the Create Surface dialog box when you are first creating the surface.

   b. In the *Definition* tab in the Surface Properties dialog box.

   c. In the *Analysis* tab in the Surface Properties dialog box.

   d. Under Edits within the surface definition.

4. Select which type of breakline this statement defines: *This type of breakline is a 3D polyline or Feature Line. It does not need a point object at each vertex because each has its own elevation.*

   a. Non-Destructive

   b. Proximity

   c. Wall

   d. Standard

5. A Quick Profile disappears when you save or exit a drawing.

   a. True

   b. False

6. What are the types of edits that can be done to a surface? (Select all that apply.)

   a. Line Edits

   b. Point Edits

   c. Simplify Surface

   d. Grip Edit

7. How do you remove an edit from a surface? (Select all that apply.)

   a. Clear it in the Operations Type list in the Surface Properties in the *Definition* tab.

   b. Remove it from the Edits list in the Prospector's Preview.

   c. Select it and press <Delete>.

   d. Delete it from the Operations Type list of the Surface Properties in the *Definition* tab.

8. Which type of boundary would you use to ensure that any data that you add to a surface is ignored if it falls outside that boundary?

   a. Hide

   b. Show

   c. Data Clip

   d. Outer

9. Which of the following is not a surface label that is available out of the box in the AutoCAD Civil 3D software?

   a. Contour Labels

   b. Spot Elevation Labels

   c. Slope Labels

   d. Cut/Fill Labels

10. How do you calculate the volume between two surfaces in a specific parcel?

   a. Bounded Volumes

   b. Grid Volume Surface

   c. TIN Volume Surface

   d. Show Cut/Fill Labels in a grid pattern

11. Which of the following is not a surface analysis that you can run in the AutoCAD Civil 3D software?

    a. Slope Analysis

    b. Visibility Check

    c. Runoff Coefficient Analysis

    d. Water Drop

12. Which of the following are vertical definition options when creating a solid surface from a TIN surface? (Select all that apply)

    a. Kriging interpolation

    b. Depth

    c. Fixed elevation

    d. Surface

13. Which of the following can be selected when creating a surface from point clouds?

    a. Style for the surface

    b. Render material

    c. Part or all of a point cloud

    d. All of the above.

Command Summary

Button	Command	Location
	Add Data	• **Contextual Ribbon:** *Surface* tab> Modify panel
	Catchment Area	• **Contextual Ribbon:** *Surface* tab> Analyze panel • **Command Prompt:** Catchment Area
	Create Surface	• **Ribbon:** *Home* tab>Create Ground Data panel • **Command Prompt:** CreateSurface
	Create Surface from point clouds	• **Contextual Ribbon:** *Point Cloud* tab> Civil3D panel
	Edit Surface	• **Contextual Ribbon:** *Surface* tab> Modify panel
	Extract Solids from Surface	• **Contextual Ribbon:** *Surface* tab> Surface Tools panel
	Resolve Crossing Breaklines	• **Contextual Ribbon:** *Surface* tab> Analyze panel • **Command Prompt:** BreaklineTool
	Surface Properties	• **Contextual Ribbon:** *Surface* tab> Modify panel • **Command Prompt:** EditSurfaceProperties
	Volumes Dashboard	• **Ribbon:** *Analyze* tab>Volumes and Materials panel • **Contextual Ribbon:** *Surface* tab> Analyze panel • **Command Prompt:** VolumesDashboard
	Water Drop	• **Contextual Ribbon:** *Surface* tab> Analyze panel • **Command Prompt:** CreateSurfaceWaterdrop

Chapter 6

Alignments

Alignments can represent the center line of a road, a curb return, the edge of a travel way, and much more. In this chapter you learn how to create an alignment, move an alignment to another site, and adjust an alignment. Then you create an alignment table and labels to communicate the design information to contractors and other stakeholders.

Learning Objectives in this Chapter

- List the various types of projects that are going to use alignments and profiles in their designs.
- Create a site for alignments, parcels, grading objects, etc. to be located.
- Create an alignment from existing design data.
- Create an alignment from scratch using specific design criteria and the Alignment Layout Tools.
- Control the station numbering and design speeds along the alignment using alignment properties.
- Communicate design information by adding alignment labels and tables.

6.1 Roadway Design Overview

Alignments and Profiles are used in nearly every civil engineering project to help lay out roads, railways, runways, and walking and bike trails (any kind of linear design feature). In these types of applications, alignments are used to represent center lines, lane boundaries, shoulders, right-of-ways, construction baselines, and similar features. In addition, many other kinds of projects can benefit from alignments, such as swales, waterways, utilities, and some types of earthwork (such as levee, dam, and landfill designs).

Roads are typically designed through multiple 2D views: plan (top view), profile (side view), and cross-section (left to right view). The result of this approach is a set of documents showing the alignment as a plan, a profile as part of a profile view, and a series of cross-sections. The AutoCAD® Civil 3D® software uses these views, resulting in a 3D roadway model called a corridor. An example is shown in Figure 6–1.

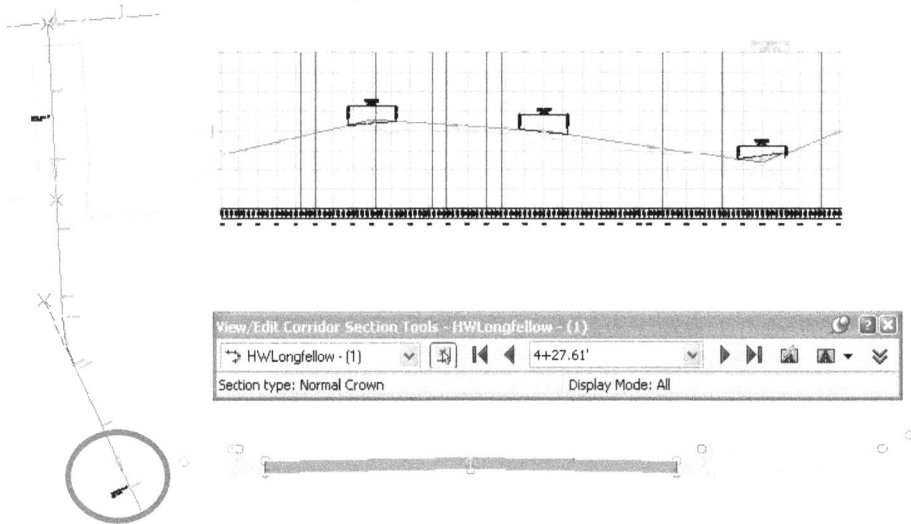

Figure 6–1

6.2 AutoCAD Civil 3D Sites

Alignments, profiles, cross-sections, feature lines, grading groups, and parcels can be organized into containers referred to as *sites* in the AutoCAD Civil 3D software. A site serves as a logical grouping of design data, such as:

- A specific phase of a project.

- A named geographic area in a larger project.

- A design alternative.

Sites are managed using a collection in the Toolspace, *Prospector* tab (as shown in Figure 6–2). A drawing can have any number of sites, or none at all.

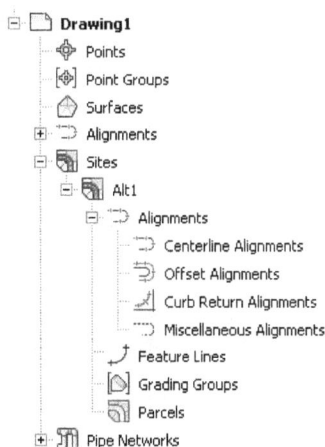

Figure 6–2

Profiles and cross-section data display in the Toolspace, *Prospector* tab below the alignment tree on which they are based. Corridors are stored in their own collection in the Toolspace, *Prospector* tab, separate from the site's collection.

Parcel lines only interact with other parcels and alignments in the same site. This enables multiple parcel and road alternatives to be present in the same drawing at the same time.

Alignments and their profiles and cross-sections might exist in a drawing without being part of a specific site. Those that are not, are located in the separate *Alignment* collection below the *Surfaces* collection in the Toolspace, *Prospector* tab. This enables alignments to exist in the drawing and not interact with any parcels, or to create a parcel if the alignment closes on itself (e.g., the bulb of a cul-de-sac).

6.3 Introduction to Alignments

An AutoCAD Civil 3D alignment is an AEC object that resembles an AutoCAD® polyline. Alignments have rule-based constraints that make them very powerful design tools. Alignments can contain tangents (line segments), circular curves, and spirals.

The appearance and annotation of alignments are controlled by object and label styles. These styles are flexible, have an extensive list of label properties, and control layer assignments for objects and their labels.

AutoCAD Civil 3D alignments can be created in the following ways:

- If previously defined, alignments can be imported from Autodesk LandXML®, directly from an AutoCAD® Land Desktop project, or from an InfraWorks model.

- A polyline can be converted directly to an alignment. Converted polylines follow the direction of the original polyline object.

- An alignment can be created interactively using the Alignment Layout toolbar.

- Individual AutoCAD lines and arcs can be converted to alignments using the Layout toolbar as well.

When creating new alignments, remember that you can use transparent commands to draw line segments by **Angle and Distance**, **Bearing and Distance**, **Azimuth and Distance**, and **Deflection Distance**. These commands are available in the Transparent Commands toolbar, as shown in Figure 6–3. They are extremely helpful when you need to stay within a specific right-of-way and you have the legal description of that right-of-way.

Figure 6–3

Criteria-Based Design

Default or custom standards can be used in the AutoCAD Civil 3D software to evaluate alignment and profile designs. The Design Criteria Editor enables you to view, edit, or create criteria files (such as AASHTO tables). When you create a new alignment, the Create Alignment dialog box opens, as shown in Figure 6–4. You can tell the software what type of alignment you are creating to make intersection design easier later. The dialog box includes a *Design Criteria* tab that enables you to type the starting design speed, use criteria-based design, use a design criteria file, or use a design check set.

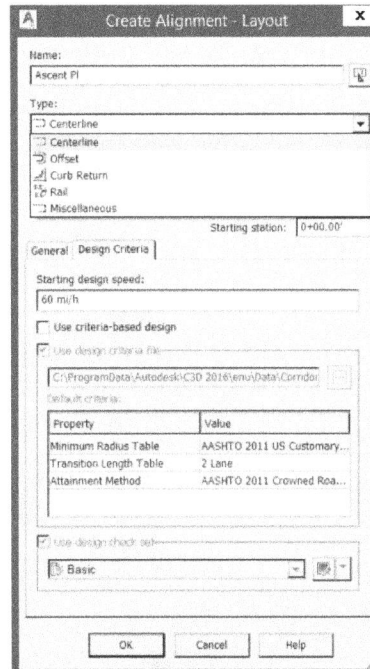

Figure 6–4

When an entity does not meet the criteria in the file it displays with a warning marker. Hover over the marker and note which criteria the entity violates, as shown in Figure 6–5.

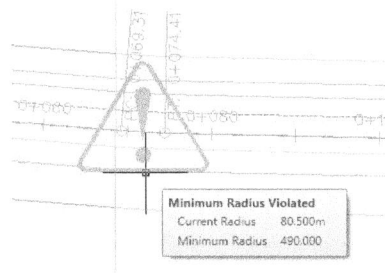

Figure 6–5

A warning marker also displays in the sub-entity and grid view editors when a violation occurs. This marker disappears when the value meets the required criteria.

Alignment Types

There are 5 different types of alignments that can be used in a design.

1. A **Centerline alignment** is the most commonly used type of alignment. You can use it when you know the location and design parameters of the centerline of the road, trail, or other linear feature being designed.

2. An **Offset alignment** is used to create transitions in a corridor design. You can use it when you want to target a transition line, such as a curb return, bus turnout lane, or other deviation from the original widths.

3. A **Curb Return alignment** is used when you want to base the design of the road from the curb location or when you need to connect the edges of two intersecting roadways.

4. A **Rail alignment** is the newest type of alignment. You can use it when you need to calculate curves along chords rather than arcs. It also enables you to set the track width and calculate cants.

5. A **Miscellaneous alignment** is available when the type of alignment you are creating does not fall into any of the other categories.

Alignment Segment Types

Each alignment tangent, circular curve, and spiral falls into one of three categories.

1. A **fixed segment** is one that is defined by specific criteria that only have a limited ability to be dynamically updated. Fixed curves hold their initial constraints (such as length and radius) and do not remain tangent at either end if a neighboring line segment is adjusted. You should avoid fixed curves in alignments that you might want to dynamically update (such as proposed alignments).

Alignments imported from the Autodesk LandXML software (and directly from the AutoCAD Land Desktop software) contain all fixed segments. Alignment segments created from individual lines and arcs are also created as fixed segments. These fixed curves can be deleted and replaced with other types as required.

2. A **floating element** is one that depends entirely on the object before it in the alignment. If a preceding object is moved, stretched, or otherwise adjusted, a floating element (and everything following it) translates accordingly while holding all of the initial constraints (length, radius, pass-through-points, etc.).

   For example, the alignment shown in Figure 6–6 begins with a fixed line followed by a series of floating curves and a floating line that together define a cul-de-sac. Changing the end point of the fixed line causes all of the floating elements to translate while maintaining the original length of the floating line, and the original length, radius, and direction of the following curves. Floating elements only stay tangent at one end to neighboring segments if they are adjusted.

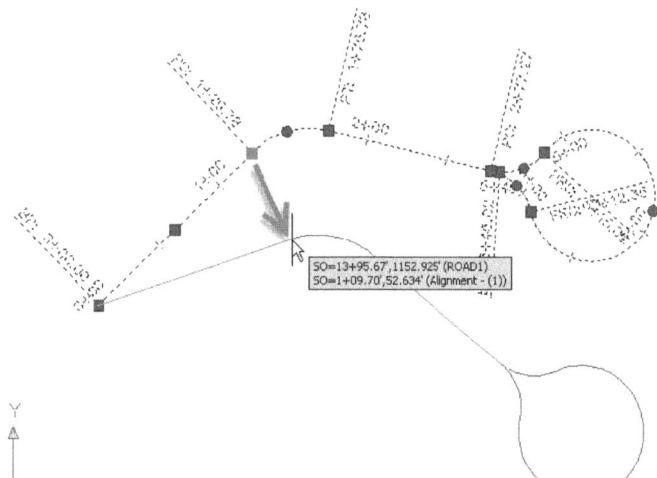

Figure 6–6

3. A **free segment** is one that is adjusted if the geometry of either neighboring segment is changed. Free segments always adjust to remain tangent to adjacent segments at both ends. For example, the free line shown in Figure 6–7 was drawn connected to two fixed arcs. If either of the arcs were assigned a different property (such as a new radius), the line would be completely redrawn to remain tangent to both.

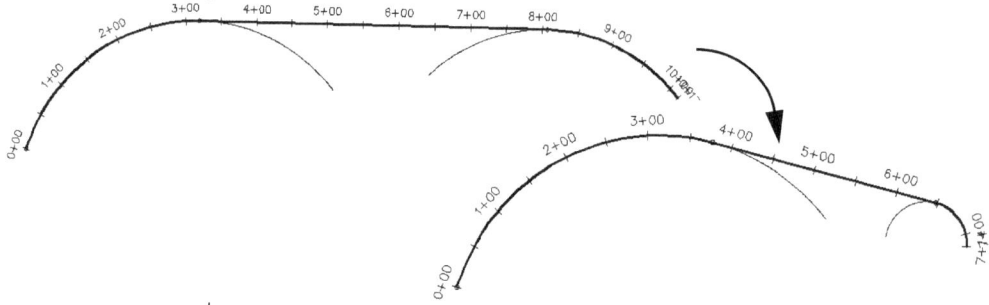

Figure 6–7

- Alignments created by layout and polyline are made of fixed lines and free curves and spirals. These tend to be the most flexible types of alignments.

- Because of their flexibility and ability to remain tangent through changes, free and floating elements are more useful in alignments that are subject to change, such as those for proposed roadway center lines.

Practice 6a

Creating Alignments from Objects

Practice Objective

- Create alignments from objects in the drawing or in an external reference file attached to the drawing.

Estimated time for completion: 15 minutes

In this practice you will create horizontal alignments using two methods. First, you will create an alignment from an existing polyline that defines a road center line alignment. Second, you will create an alignment from a XREF file that defines a proposed center line alignment.

Task 1 - Create Alignment from a Polyline.

1. Open **ALN1-A1-Alignment.dwg** from the *C:\Civil 3D Projects\Civil3D-Training\Alignments* folder.

    In the drawing, the red polyline running east-west represents the existing center line alignment of Mission Avenue, as shown in Figure 6–8.

Figure 6–8

2. In the *Home* tab>Create Design panel, expand Alignment, and select (Create Alignment from Objects), as shown in Figure 6–9. Select the west end of the polyline representing **Mission Ave polyline** (as shown in Figure 6–8) and press <Enter>.

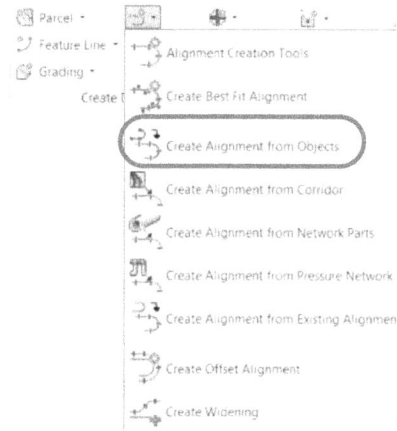

Selecting the west end of the polyline identifies the start direction of the alignment.

Figure 6–9

*If you want to reverse the direction of the alignment, you need to select **Reverse**.*

3. Verify that the alignment direction arrow is pointing East and press <Enter> to accept the alignment direction.

4. In the Create Alignment from Objects dialog box, assign the values shown in Figure 6–10 to define the properties of this alignment:

Note: The difference between having an alignment in a site or not, is that if an alignment is in a site, any parcels in that same site will be divided by the alignment that bisects the parcel.

- *Alignment name:* **Mission Ave**
- *Type:* Leave as **Centerline**
- *Description:* Type a description if required
- *Starting station:* **0**
- *Site* (*General* tab): **None**
- *Alignment Label Set:* **All Labels**
- Clear the **Add curves between tangents** option.
- Accept the remaining default values.

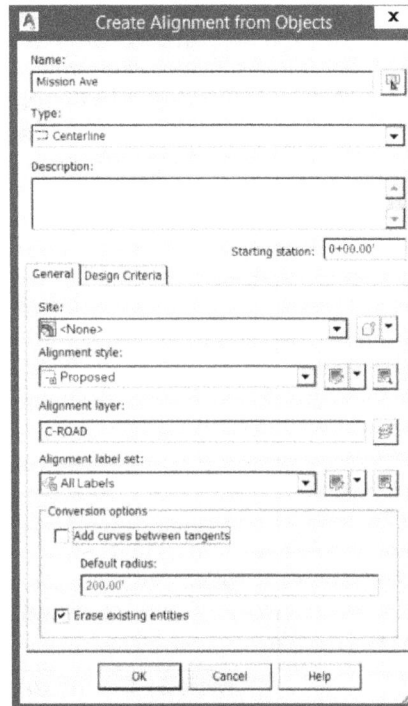

Figure 6–10

5. Select the *Design Criteria* tab shown in Figure 6–11. Ensure that the following are set, then click **OK**:

- Design speed is set to **60mi/h**.
- Both the **Use criteria-based design** and **Use design criteria file** options should be selected.

This means that the AutoCAD Civil 3D software will reference the design criteria file **Autodesk Civil 3D Imperial (2011) Roadway Design Standards.xml**.

An AutoCAD Civil 3D alignment is automatically created complete with labeling.

Figure 6–11

6. Select the preset view **Aln-Warning**. Hover the cursor over the exclamation mark at approximately the station 19+26 on the alignment and note which design check was violated, as shown in Figure 6–12. In this case, the radius is 1033.46, but the minimum radius for a 60mi/hr road based on the AASHTO table must be greater than 1505.

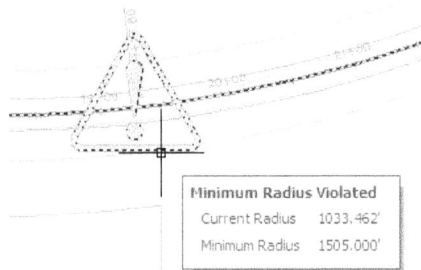

Minimum Radius Violated
Current Radius   1033.462'
Minimum Radius   1505.000'

Figure 6–12

7. Save the drawing.

Task 2 - Create an Alignment by Object (XREF).

1. Continue working with the drawing from the previous task or open **ALN1-A2-Alignment.dwg**.

2. Select the preset view **Aln-xref**.

3. In the *Home* tab>Create Design panel, expand **Alignment**, and select (Create Alignment from Objects). When prompted to select an object, type **Xref** or **X** and press <Enter>. You will then be prompted to select a XREF object.

4. Select the west end of the polyline representing **Jeffries Ranch Rd** center line (the black line), as shown in Figure 6–13, and press <Enter>.

Selecting the west end of the XREF line identifies the start direction of the alignment.

ASCENT PLACE

ASCENT BOULEVARD

JEFFRIES RANCH RD

Figure 6–13

5. Verify that the alignment direction arrow is pointing East and press <Enter> to accept the alignment direction.

6. In the Create Alignment from Objects dialog box, type **Jeffries Ranch Rd** for the alignment name and accept all of the default values.

For this alignment, you will not be using design criteria.

7. In the *Design Criteria* tab, ensure that the **Use criteria-based design** option is cleared, as shown in Figure 6–14.

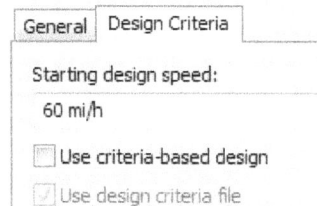

General	Design Criteria

Starting design speed:

60 mi/h

☐ Use criteria-based design

☑ Use design criteria file

Figure 6–14

8. Click **OK** to close the dialog box and create the alignment.

9. Save the drawing.

6.4 Alignments Layout Tools

Alignments are created and edited using the Alignment Layout toolbar, which can be opened from the *Home* tab>Create Design panel. Expand Alignment and select ⌐ (Alignment Creation Tools), as shown at the top of Figure 6–15. The Alignment Layout Tools toolbar displays, as shown at the bottom of Figure 6–15.

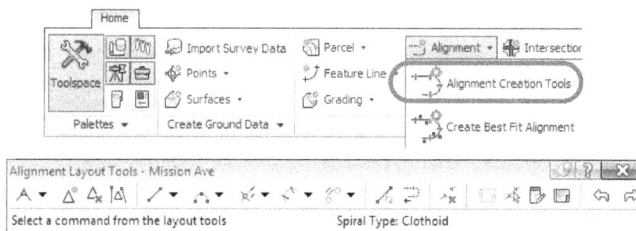

Figure 6–15

To create or add to an alignment interactively by locating new Points of Intersection (PIs), select one of the first two options in the Draw Tangents drop-down list, as shown in Figure 6–16.

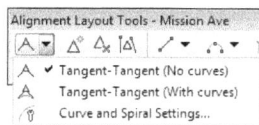

Figure 6–16

These two methods (with or without curves) are similar to drawing an AutoCAD polyline. If the **With Curves** option is selected, default curve information can be assigned in the Curve and Spiral Settings dialog box, as shown in Figure 6–17.

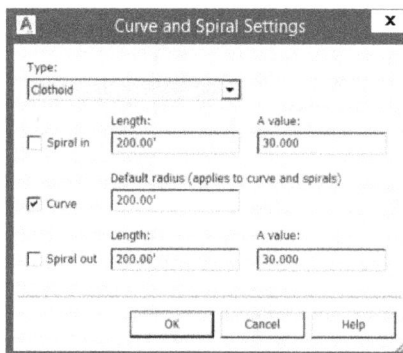

Figure 6–17

The Layout toolbar also includes tools that enable you to:

	Create new Points of Intersection (PIs).
	Delete PIs (and associated curves).
	Break apart PIs.
	Convert AutoCAD lines and arcs to alignment segments.
	Delete a line, circular curve, or spiral segment.
	Edit best-fit data for all entities.
	Select an individual segment for editing in the Sub-Entity Editor.
	Review and adjust alignment properties (length, radius, etc.) in the Alignment Entities Vista.
	Undo a recent alignment edit.
	Redo a recent alignment edit.

Most of the other tools in the Layout toolbar are intended for creating segments with various constraints.

Alignment Editing

In addition to the Edit tools available in the Alignment Layout toolbar, alignments can be edited using the AutoCAD **Modify** commands, such as **Move** and **Stretch**. Alignment entities can also be grip-edited into new positions. You can delete an alignment using the AutoCAD **Erase** command, or by right-clicking on the name of the alignment in the Toolspace, *Prospector* tab and selecting **Delete**. To open the Alignment Layout toolbar, expand Alignments and select **Edit Alignment Geometry**.

Practice 6b

Estimated time for completion: 15 minutes

Creating and Modifying Alignments

Practice Objective

- Create an alignment from scratch using the Alignment Layout tools.

In this practice you will create a free form alignment, based on some design parameters. You will create an alignment for Ascent Place based on existing design data, as shown in Figure 6–18. According to this data, the street right-of-way extends north at a bearing of N1d18'04.79"E and then east at a bearing of S75d18'31.56"E. The north center line leg is 353.17' to the point of intersection and the east leg is 381.93' from the point of intersection. In addition, the center line of Ascent Place intersects Jeffries Ranch road at sta 5+79.13'.

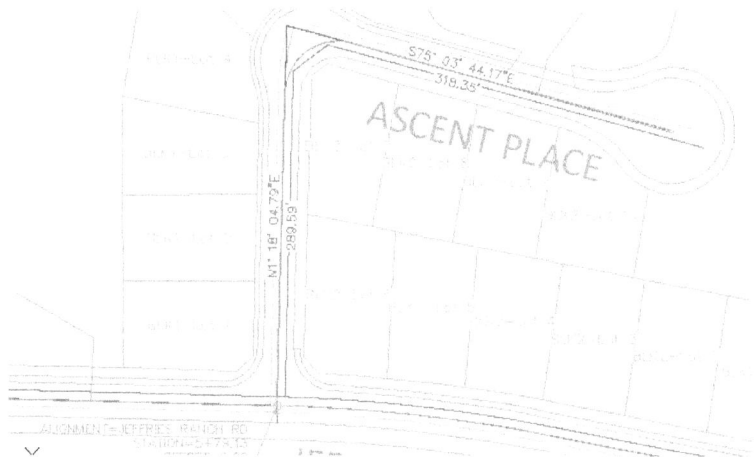

Figure 6–18

Task 1 - Create an Alignment by Layout.

1. Continue working with the drawing from the previous practice or open **ALN1-B1-Alignment.dwg**.

2. Select the preset view **Aln-Create**.

3. Toggle on *Selection* cycling by pressing <Ctrl>+<W>. The alignment object and XREF center line occupy the same location in space (as shown in Figure 6–19), and the selection cycling enables you to select the alignment.

Pressing
<Shift>+<Space> to
cycle through objects
does not work in a
transparent command.

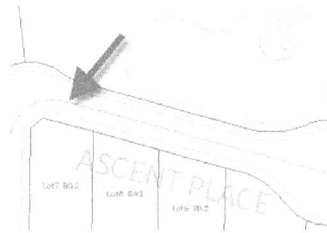

Figure 6–19

4. In the *Home* tab>Create Design panel, expand Alignment, and select ⤳ (Alignment Creation Tools).

5. In the Create Alignment Layout dialog box, type **Ascent PI** for the alignment name and accept all of the default values.

For this alignment, you
will not be using design
criteria.

6. In the *Design Criteria* tab, ensure that the **Use criteria-based design** option is not selected. Click **OK** to close the dialog box and create the alignment.

7. Expand the Tangent tool icon and select ⌒ (Curve and Spiral Settings), as shown in Figure 6–20.

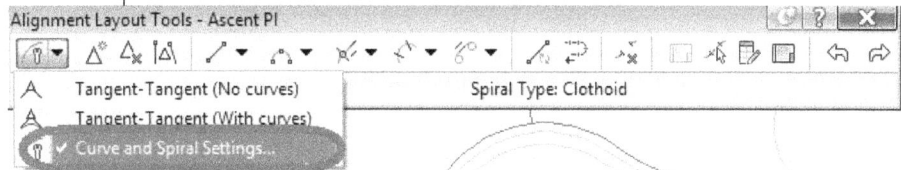

Figure 6–20

8. For the curve settings, ensure that the **curve** option is selected. Set the curve radius to **30.00'**, and click **OK** to close the Curve and Spiral Settings dialog box.

9. Expand the Tangent tool icon and select the

   A (Tangent-Tangent (With curves)) to start creating the horizontal alignment.

You want to start the
alignment at a reference
station to Jeffries Ranch
Rd.

10. When prompted for the start of the alignment, click

    ⊤ (Station Offset) on the Transparent Tools toolbar.

11. When prompted for an alignment, select **Jeffries Ranch Rd**. In the Selection Cycling dialog box, click **Alignment**.

12. When prompted for a station, type **579.13'** and press <Enter>.

13. When prompted for the offset, type **0** and press <Enter>. Press <Esc> to exit the transparent command.

The AutoCAD Civil 3D software has now established the starting location of the alignment by converting the station/offset to a X,Y value.

14. You will specify the next point using the transparent command to enter a bearing and a distance. Click

    (Bearing Distance) on the Transparent Tools toolbar and enter the following:

    - Type **1** and press <Enter> for the NE quadrant.
    - Type **1.180479** and then press <Enter> for the bearing.
    - Type a distance of **353.17'** and press <Enter>.
    - Press <Esc> to exit the transparent command.

15. You will specify the next point using the transparent command to enter a turned angle and a distance. Click

    (Angle Distance) on the Transparent Tools toolbar and do the following:

    - Type **C** and press <Enter>, since you will be entering a counter-clockwise include angle.
    - Type the include angle of **76.3636** and press <Enter>.
    - Type **381.93** and press <Enter> for the distance.

16. Press <Esc> to exit the transparent command and press <Enter> to complete the horizontal alignment.

17. Close the **Alignment** layout tool by clicking **X** in the top right of the dialog box.

18. Save the drawing.

Task 2 - Edit Alignments.

1. Continue working with the drawing from the previous task or open **ALN1-B2-Alignment.dwg**.

2. Set **Aln-Curv Radius** as the active view.

3. Select the alignment **Ascent PI**. In the contextual Alignment tab>Modify panel, click (Geometry Editor).

4. In the alignment Tool Layout toolbar, click (Pick Sub-entity), as shown in Figure 6–21.

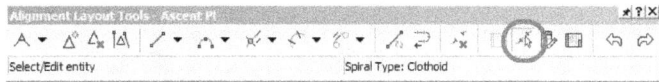

Figure 6–21

5. When prompted to select the sub-entity, select the curve. Change the radius to **50'** and press <Enter>, as shown in Figure 6–22.

Note that the radius dynamically changes in the graphics view.

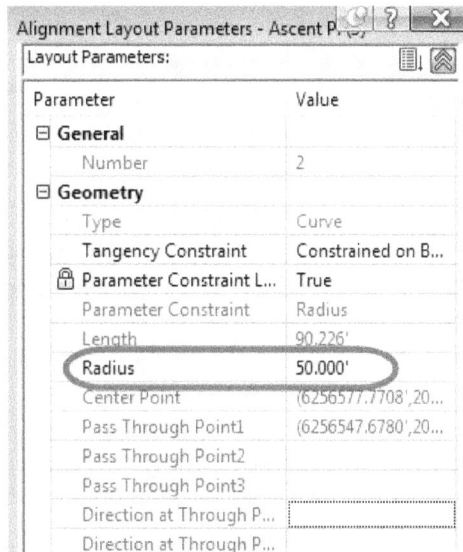

Figure 6–22

6. Select (Delete Sub-entity) in the Alignment Layout toolbar, as shown in Figure 6–23. Select the curve and press <Enter> to exit the command.

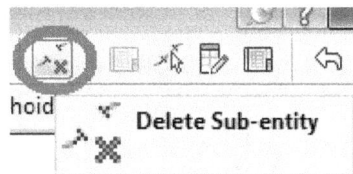

Figure 6–23

7. In the Alignment Layout toolbar, expand the curve drop-down list and select ⛰ (Free Curve Fillet (between two entities, radius)) as shown in Figure 6–24.

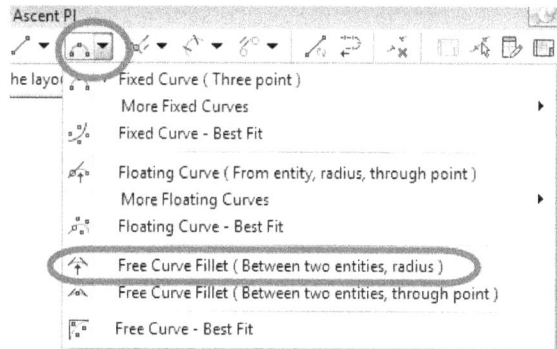

Figure 6–24

8. Select the two tangents and press <Enter> to accept that the angle is **less than 180 deg**. For the radius, type **50'**, press <Enter>, and press <Enter> again to complete the command. The results are shown in Figure 6–25.

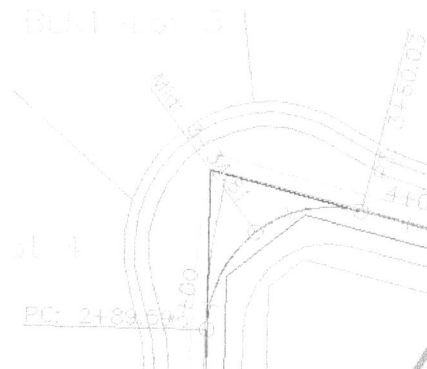

Figure 6–25

9. Close the Alignment Layout toolbar and save the drawing.

10. Save the drawing.

6.5 Alignment Properties

The Alignment Properties dialog box (found by right-clicking on the alignment name in the Toolspace, *Prospector* tab and selecting Properties) controls stationing, station equations, references to the alignment by profiles and profile views, design speeds, superelevation settings, and related controls.

Station Control Tab

The *Station Control* tab sets the beginning station of the alignment. All labeling referencing the alignment dynamically updates its values when any change occurs to the alignment.

The *Station Equation* area of the panel adds and deletes equations from the alignment. A station equation is a point along the alignment where the stationing changes. The equation can represent the meeting of two stationing systems or the change in authority over the center line.

When adding an equation, the AutoCAD Civil 3D software displays a station jig reporting its station at the cursor. You set the station by selecting a point along the center line or entering a specific station value. After identifying the station equation point, set the station ahead value and whether the stationing increases or decreases.

Design Criteria Tab

Each roadway can have multiple design speeds that reflect the conditions, design, and type of roadway surface. Design speeds affect the amount of superelevation and other safety concerns (stopping sight distance, passing sight distance, etc.) surrounding the roadway design.

When working with superelevations and vertical curves, the design speed of the roadway is critical for computing the correct parameters for the road design. When setting design speeds, the AutoCAD Civil 3D software displays a station selection jig and prompts for a station at the Command Line. After setting the station for the speed, you set the speed and enter any comments. You set the station in the drawing and refine its value in the *Design Speeds* tab in the Alignment Properties dialog box.

The option to **Use criteria-based design** is also found here, as shown in Figure 6–26. Select this option, and then decide whether you plan to use a design criteria file or design checks that you have created yourself.

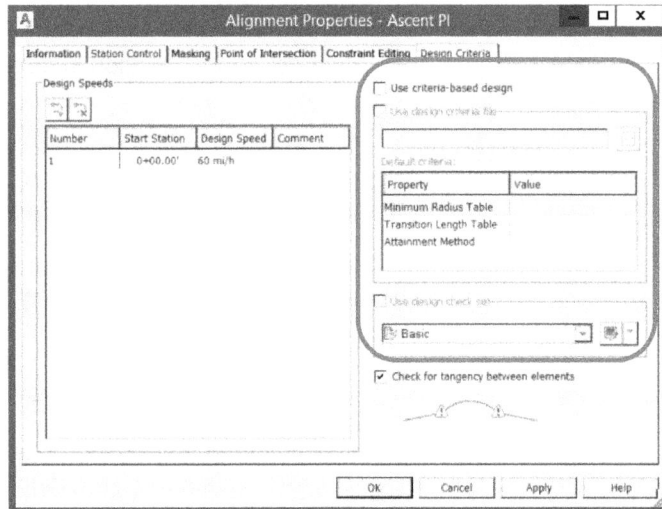

Figure 6–26

6.6 Labels and Tables

Alignment labels fall into two general categories: those controlled as a group using the **Edit Alignment Labels** command (referred to here as *Alignment Point Labels*), and those managed individually (referred to here as *Independent Alignment Labels*). Alignment labels of both types can be selected, repositioned, and erased separate from the alignment object itself.

Alignment Point Labels

Alignment point labels are organized into five categories, each of which is controlled by specific label styles:

*   Major and Minor Stations

*   (Horizontal) Geometry Points, such as Points of Curvature (PCs)

*   Station Equations

*   Design Speeds

*   Profile Geometry Points, such as Points of Vertical Curvature (PVCs)

*   Superelevation Critical Points

The AutoCAD Civil 3D software enables you to organize various alignment point labels into **Alignment Label Sets**, as shown in Figure 6–27, to simplify adding a group of them at the same time.

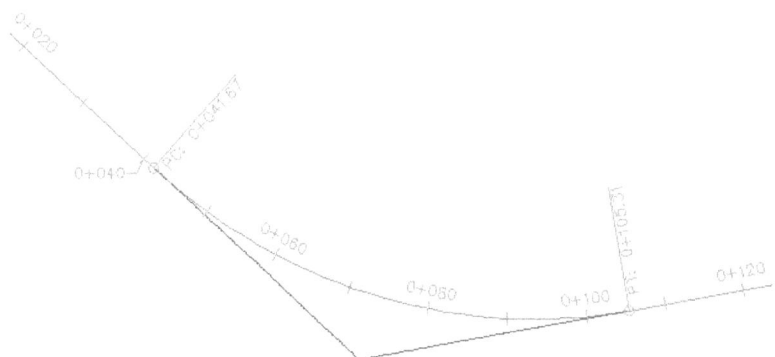

Figure 6–27

Alignment point labels are organized into *label groups*, so that when one is selected, all similar labels on the alignment are also selected, as shown in Figure 6–28. This enables you to change their properties (e.g., using the AutoCAD Properties dialog box), or erase them all at once.

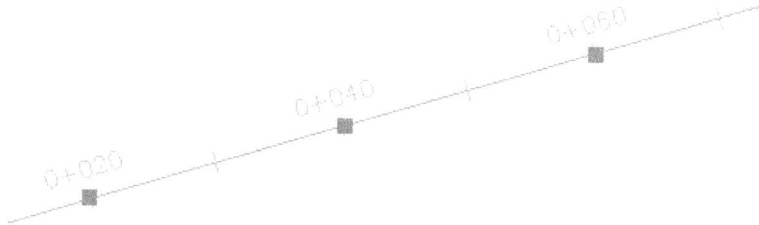

Figure 6–28

If you only want to select one of these labels (e.g., to erase one of them), hold <Ctrl> when selecting.

If you select an alignment and a large number of grips highlight, you have probably selected an alignment station label group, as shown in Figure 6–29. If you want to select the alignment itself (rather than the labels), press <Esc>, zoom in, and try again.

Figure 6–29

Alignment point labels can be added when the alignment is defined and can later be managed by right-clicking on an alignment and selecting **Edit Alignment Labels**.

Independent Alignment Labels

Independent Alignment Labels can be used to add labels to alignment segments, and station and offset labels. They can be added using the Add Labels dialog box, which can be opened from the *Annotate* tab>Add Labels panel. Expand Alignment and select **Add Alignment Labels...**, as shown in Figure 6–30.

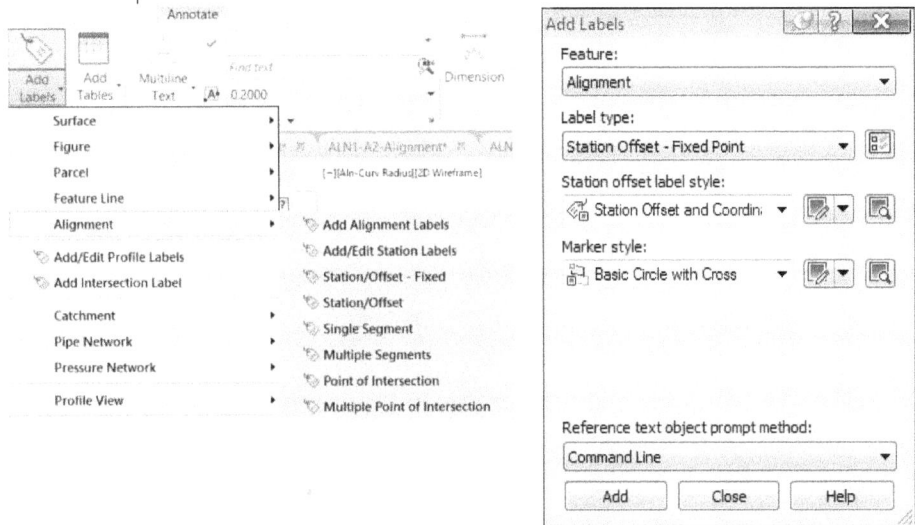

Figure 6–30

These labels include:

- **Station and offset label type:** (Shown in Figure 6–31), which moves with the alignment if it changes to maintain the same station and offset.

- **Station and offset – fixed point label type:** Does not move if the alignment changes, and its station and offset values update to reflect the alignment edit.

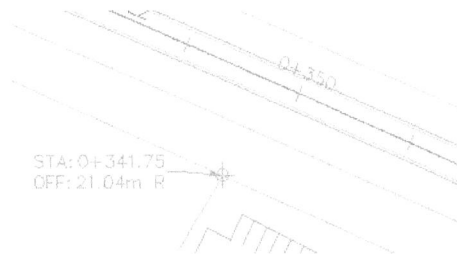

Figure 6–31

- **Single segment label type:** Adds a single line, curve, or spiral label to one alignment segment.

- **Multiple segment label type:** Adds a single line, curve, or spiral label to each alignment segment at the same time, as shown in Figure 6–32.

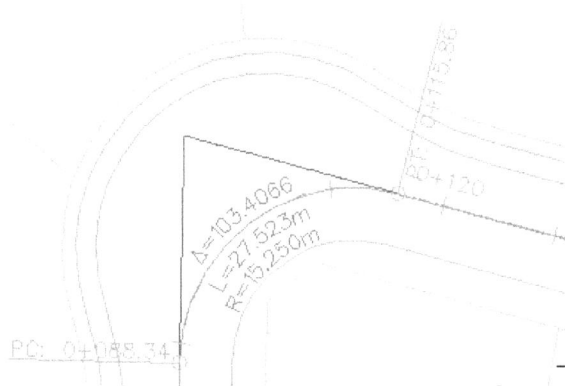

Figure 6–32

- **Point of intersection label type:** Adds a curve (or spiral-curve-spiral group) label at the tangent intersection, and labels the intersection of two tangents (sometimes called an *angle point*).

- **Multiple point of intersection label type:** Adds a curve (or spiral-curve-spiral group) to all of the intersections in the alignment.

Alignment Table Styles

If required, alignment segments can be given *tag* labels (such as **C1** shown in Figure 6–33) and the segment data can be tabulated. For more information, see *Setting Up Label Styles To Be Used as Tags* in the AutoCAD Civil 3D Help.

Mission Ave				
Number	Radius	Length	Line/Chord Direction	A Value
L1		29.91	S81° 52' 26.21"E	
C1	650.00	170.21	S74° 22' 19.17"E	
L2		226.52	S66° 52' 12.12"E	
C2	315.00	321.29	N83° 54' 37.46"E	
L3		33.61	N54° 41' 27.03"E	

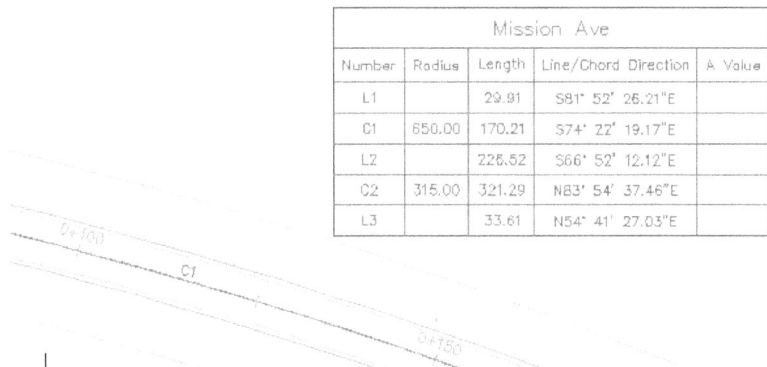

Figure 6–33

Practice 6c

Alignment Properties and Labels

Practice Objective

Estimated time for completion: 15 minutes

- Communicate design information by adding alignment labels and tables.

Task 1 - Edit Alignment Properties.

1. Continue working with the drawing from the previous practice or open **ALN1-C1-Alignment.dwg**.

2. Set **Aln-Warning** as the active view.

   When you created this alignment, you typed 60mi/hr as the speed. Note that, based on the design criteria, the radius is below the minimum. The warning displays in both the Model Space and in the Panorama view, as shown in Figure 6–34.

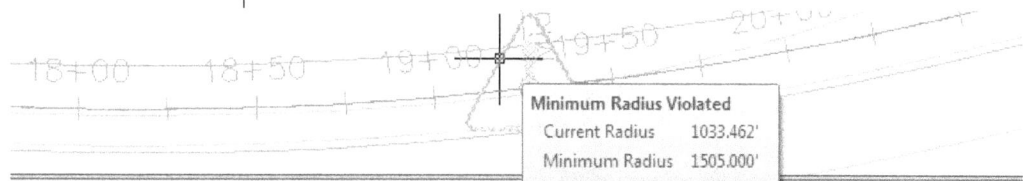

No.	Type	Tangency Constraint	Param...	Parameter C...	Length	Radius	Minimum Ra...	Design Speed
1	Line	Not Constrained (Fixed)	🔒	Two points	98.145'			60 mi/h
2	Curve	Constrained on Both Sides (Free)	🔒	Radius	558.444'	2132.542'	1505.000'	60 mi/h
3	Line	Not Constrained (Fixed)	🔒	Two points	743.165'			60 mi/h
⚠ 4	Curve	**Constrained on Both Sides (F...**	🔒	Radius	1054.085'	⚠1033.462'	1505.000'	60 mi/h
5	Line	Not Constrained (Fixed)	🔒	Two points	110.262'			60 mi/h

Figure 6–34

You need to fix the properties of this alignment to reflect the correct speed.

3. Select the alignment **Mission Ave**. In the contextual

   Alignment tab>Modify panel, select ⬚ (Alignment Properties).

4. In the *Design Criteria* tab, change the *Design Speed* to **50mi/hr** as shown in Figure 6–35, and click **OK** to exit.

Now that you have the correct design speed, the radius is within the minimum requirements.

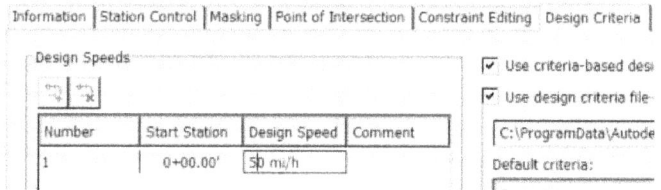

Figure 6–35

5. Press <Esc> to clear the selection and save the drawing.

Task 2 - Add and change alignment labels.

1. Continue working with the drawing from the previous task or open **ALN1-C2-Alignment.dwg**.

2. Currently, the station label intervals are every 100'. Change it to show station labels at every **50'**. Select the alignment **Mission Ave**, right-click, and select **Edit Alignment Labels**, as shown in Figure 6–36.

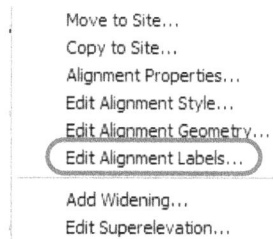

Figure 6–36

3. In the Alignment Labels dialog box, change the *Increment* for the Major labels to **50'** and the Minor labels to **25'**, as shown in Figure 6–37. Click **OK** to close the dialog box and apply the changes.

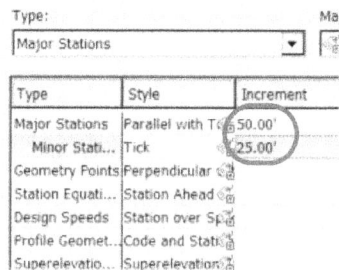

Figure 6–37

4. With the alignment Mission Ave still selected, expand Add Labels and select **Multiple Segment** in the Labels & Tables panel, as shown in Figure 6–38.

Figure 6–38

5. When prompted to select the alignment, select the **Mission Ave** alignment again (as shown in Figure 6–39), and press <Enter> to complete and exit the command.

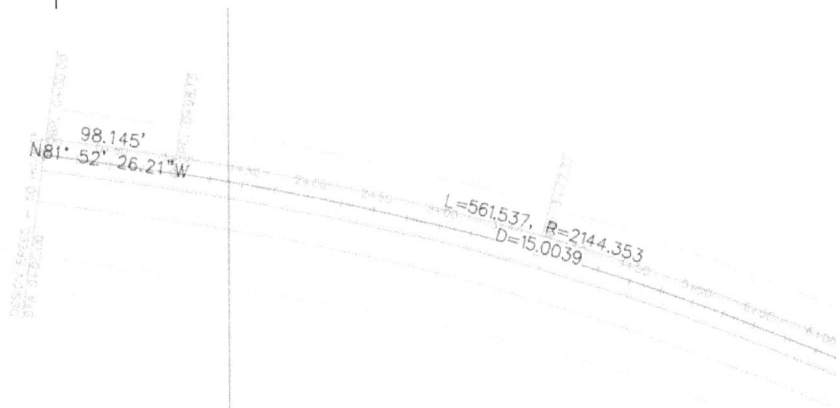

98.145'
N81° 52' 26.21"W

L=561.537, R=2144.353
D=15.0039

Figure 6–39

6. Select **Aln-Label** as the active view.

7. To create a Table listing the segments, select the alignment again, expand Add Tables and select **Add Segments** in the Labels & Tables panel, as shown in Figure 6–40.

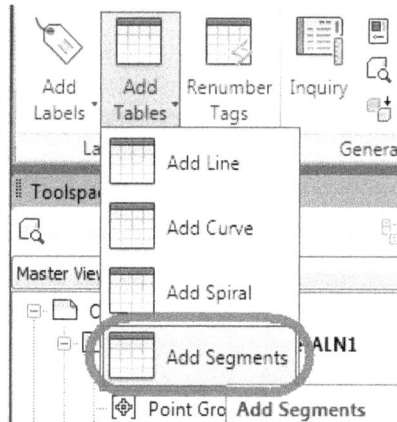

Figure 6–40

8. In the Alignment table creation dialog box, set the options as shown in Figure 6–41 and click **OK** when done.

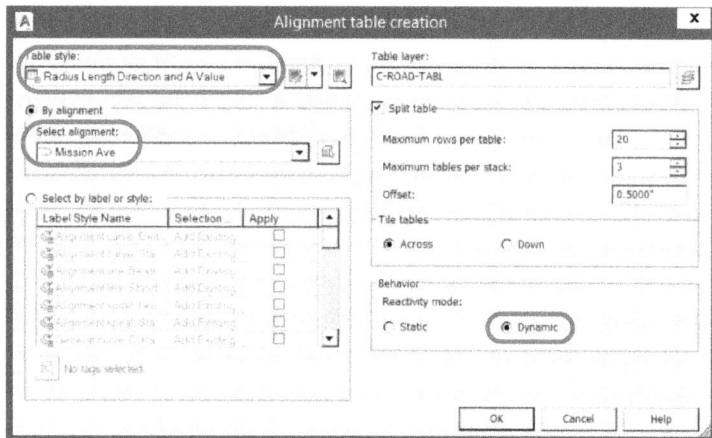

Figure 6–41

9. The AutoCAD Civil 3D software will convert the labels to tags. Select a point in Model Space to set the location of the table, as shown in Figure 6–42.

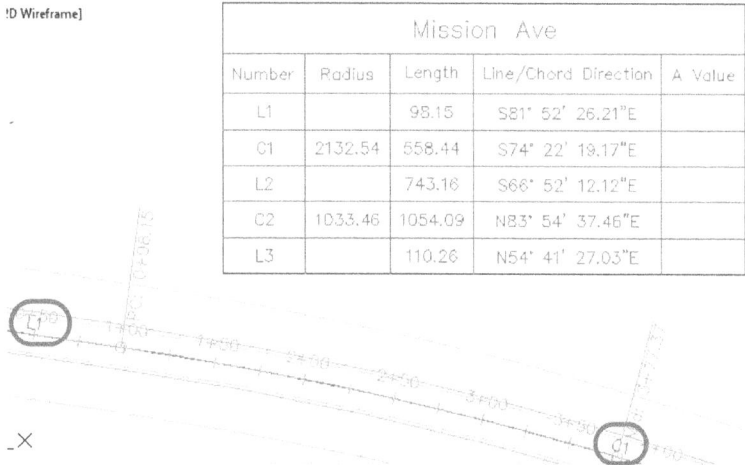

!D Wireframe]

Mission Ave				
Number	Radius	Length	Line/Chord Direction	A Value
L1		98.15	S81° 52' 26.21"E	
C1	2132.54	558.44	S74° 22' 19.17"E	
L2		743.16	S66° 52' 12.12"E	
C2	1033.46	1054.09	N83° 54' 37.46"E	
L3		110.26	N54° 41' 27.03"E	

Figure 6–42

10. Select **Aln-Sta Label** as the active view.

11. Select the **Jeffries Ranch Rd** alignment and in the contextual tab, expand Add Labels and select **Station/Offset - Fixed Point** in the Labels & Tables panel, as shown in Figure 6–43.

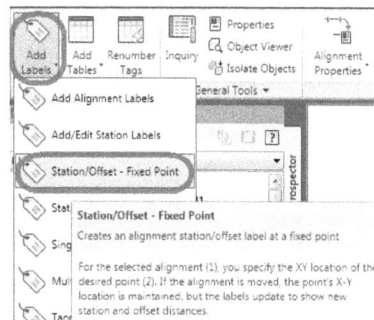

Figure 6–43

12. Select the end point where the Ascent PI alignment intersects with Jeffries Ranch Rd, as shown on Figure 6–44. Because of all of the AutoCAD Civil 3D labels around the intersection, it might be advisable to use either the Apparent or the Endpoint osnap.

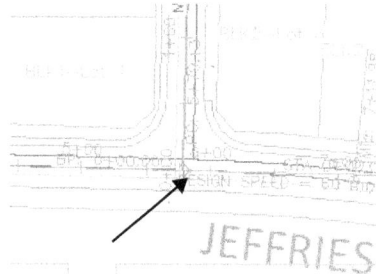

Figure 6–44

13. Press <Enter> to end the command and press <Esc> to clear the selection.

14. Select the label and using the Move grip, move the label to a location to avoid clutter, as shown on the right in Figure 6–45.

Figure 6–45

15. Save the drawing.

Chapter Review Questions

1. When can an alignment subdivide parcels?

   a. When it is a design style.

   b. When the parcels are ROW parcels.

   c. When they are in the same drawing file.

   d. When they are in the same site.

2. How do you open the Alignment Layout toolbar for an existing alignment?

   a. Select the alignment in the drawing.

   b. Right-click on **Alignments** in the Toolspace, *Prospector* tab.

   c. In the *Home* tab>Create Design panel, select **Edit Alignments**.

   d. Select **Alignments** in the Toolspace, *Prospector* tab.

3. How do you select an individual alignment Station label for deletion?

   a. Click on it.

   b. Right-click on it.

   c. Hold <Ctrl> as you select it.

   d. Hold <Shift> as you select it.

4. To change minor stations in the alignment from 50 feet to 25 feet...

   a. Change the settings in the alignment.

   b. Change the minor increment in the label set to 25 feet.

   c. Change the station style.

   d. Change the alignment label style.

5. The Alignment Style controls the color of the major and minor tics.

   a. True

   b. False

Command Summary

Button	Command	Location
	Alignment Creation Tools	• **Ribbon:** *Home* tab>Create Design panel • **Command Prompt:** CreateAlignmentLayout
	Alignment Properties	• **Contextual Ribbon:** *Alignment* tab> Modify panel • **Command Prompt:** editalignmentproperties
	Create Alignment from Objects	• **Ribbon:** *Home* tab>Create Design panel • **Command Prompt:** CreateAlignmentEntities
	Curve & Spiral Settings	• **Toolbar:** Alignment Layout Tools
	Delete Sub-entity	• **Toolbar:** Alignment Layout Tools
	Free Curve Fillet	• **Toolbar:** Alignment Layout Tools
	Geometry Editor	• **Contextual Ribbon:** *Alignment* tab> Modify panel • **Command Prompt:** editalignment
	Pick Sub-entity	• **Toolbar:** Alignment Layout Tools
	Sub-entity Editor	• **Toolbar:** Alignment Layout Tools
	Tangent-Tangent (with Curves)	• **Toolbar:** Alignment Layout Tools

Profiles

Profiles are lengthwise vertical representations of an alignment. In this chapter you learn how to show what the existing ground is doing vertically along an alignment. Then you create a design profile to control the vertical slope and vertical curves for a road design.

Learning Objectives in this Chapter

- List the various items that form a profile view.
- Set the grid spacing and required labels for displaying a profile in a profile view.
- Create a surface profile to indicate what the ground is doing vertically along an alignment.
- Create a profile view to display an alignment vertically with a grid and preset labels included.
- List the various types of vertical curves and why they are used in profiles.
- Create a profile that previews the finished ground by following specific design parameters.

7.1 Profiles Overview

A profile is the second plane of a roadway design. It is a view of the alignment from one side of the center line with elevations along the alignment. An AutoCAD® Civil 3D® profile is a combination of a *profile view* and any number of *profiles* displayed in the view, as shown in Figure 7–1.

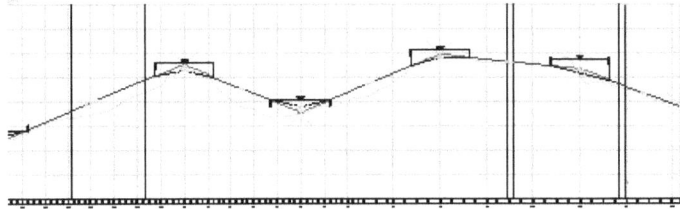

Figure 7–1

- A *profile view* consists of a profile grid and its annotation. The view's vertical lines represent alignment stationing and the horizontal lines represent elevations.

- A *profile* represents a surface or roadway vertical design. A typical road design profile view contains two profiles: the existing ground and a proposed vertical design. The existing ground profile represents elevations along the path of the alignment, usually from a sampled surface. The proposed vertical design defines elevations along the path of the proposed roadway. You can have any number of existing and proposed vertical alignments displayed in the same profile view at the same time.

AutoCAD Civil 3D Profiles are managed by:

- **Profile View Properties:** Control settings specific to individual profiles, such as datum elevation and maximum height.

- **Profile View Styles:** Affect how the grid and its annotations display.

- **Profile Styles:** Control how the profile linework displays.

- **Bands:** Control optional, additional annotation that can be displayed across the top or bottom of a profile view. Bands are grouped into Band Sets to make it easier to apply multiple, related bands at the same time. An example of a profile band is the elevation and station data shown in Figure 7–2.

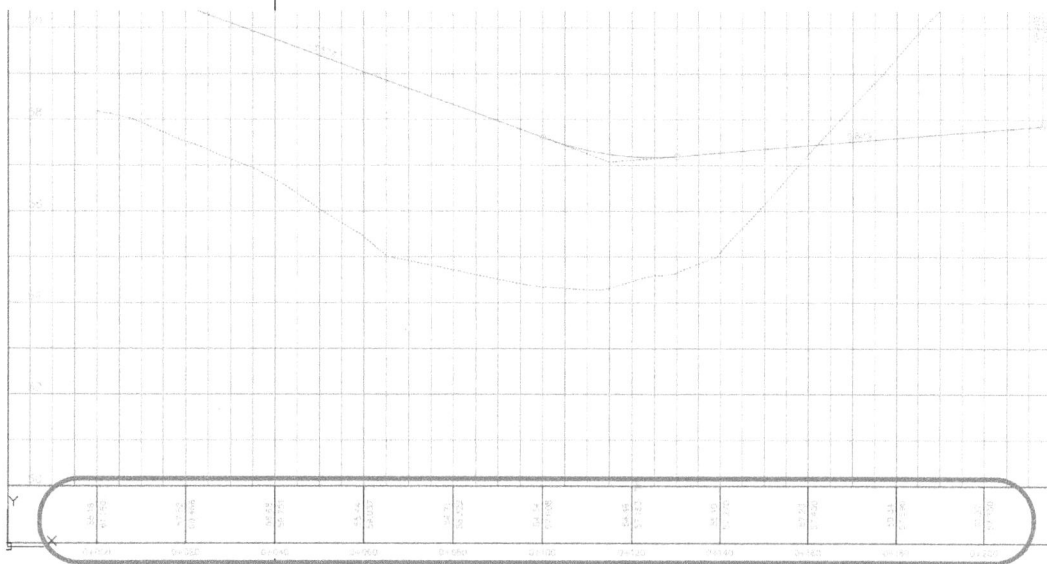

Figure 7–2

Repositioning and Deleting Profile Views

AutoCAD Civil 3D Profile Views are safe to reposition as required with the AutoCAD® **Move** command, and copy with the AutoCAD **Copy** command. They can also be erased with the AutoCAD **Erase** command. Erasing a profile view also erases the design profile grade line that is attached. However, if the profile grade line exists in another profile view, the profile grade line data is saved.

7.2 Create a Profile View Style

Profile view styles control the format of the grid, titles, axis annotations, and other elements used for displaying profiles. To set up a new profile view style, select the Toolspace, *Settings* tab. Expand the *Profile View* collection, right-click on *Profile View Styles*, and select **New**. Typically, this is already set up for you in the drawing template, but you might sometimes need to change some of the settings.

Information Tab

The *Information* tab enables you to enter basic information about the style, such as the name, a description, who it was created by and when, and who it was last modified by and when, as shown in Figure 7–3.

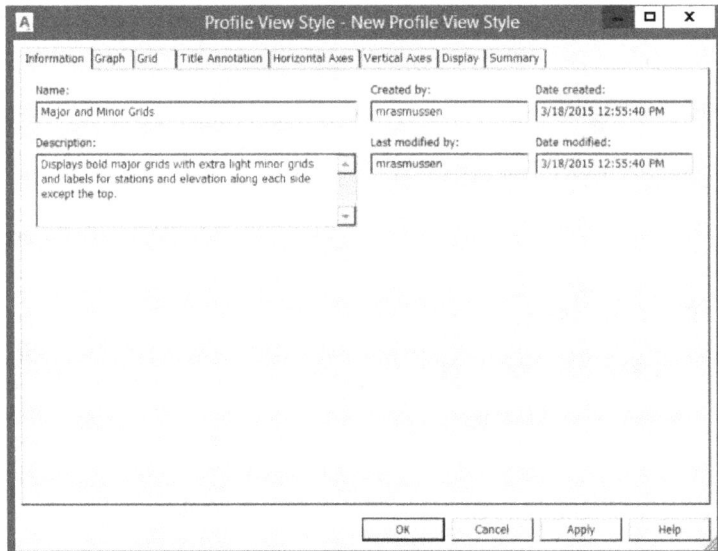

Figure 7–3

Graph Tab

The *Graph* tab enables you to set the vertical exaggeration for greater visibility in the profile view and the profile direction. The vertical scale can be set in two ways:

1. By dividing the current horizontal scale of the drawing by the vertical scale value, which gives you the vertical exaggeration value. This is usually set at a one to ten ratio. Therefore, if the horizontal scale is 1"=50', the *Vertical exaggeration* is set to **5**.
2. You can select the vertical scale from a list, as shown in Figure 7–4.

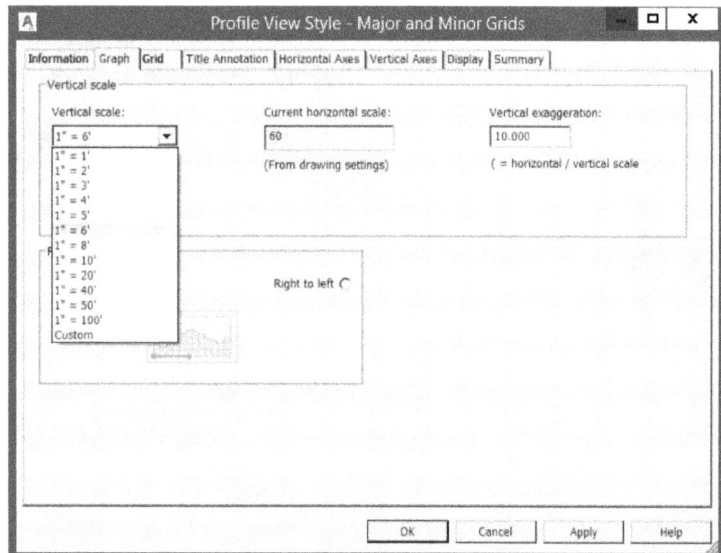

Figure 7–4

3. If required, you can change the flow direction from left to right (the default is right to left).

Grid Tab

The *Grid* tab is used to specify the clipping, padding, and axes offset in the profile view grid.

- The **Clip vertical grid** option enables you to trim the vertical grid lines at either the existing ground or finished ground profiles or the highest profile.

- The **Clip horizontal grid** option does the same for the horizontal grid lines, as shown in Figure 7–5.

- The **Grid padding** enables you to add extra grid boxes at the beginning and end of the profile, and to the top and bottom.

- The **Axis offset** specifies the distance to offset the axis beyond the profile extents.

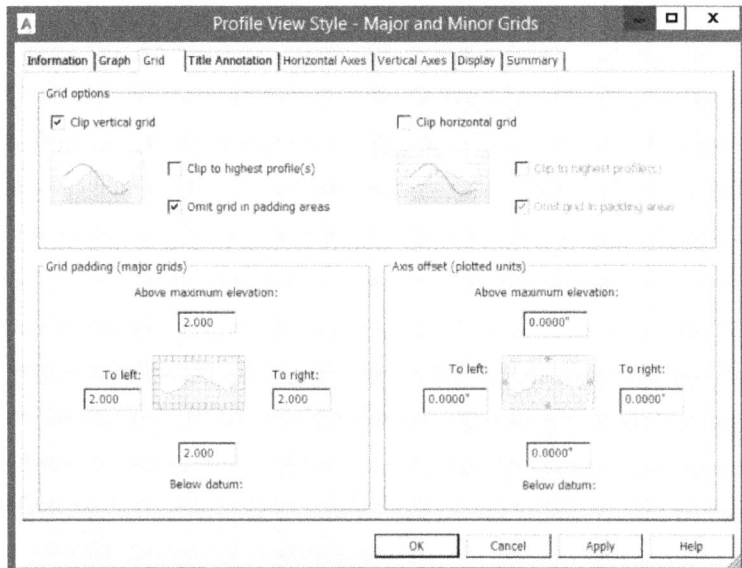

Figure 7–5

Title Annotation Tab

The *Title Annotation* tab enables you to specify the text style, contents, justification, and location of the profile view and axis titles, as shown in Figure 7–6.

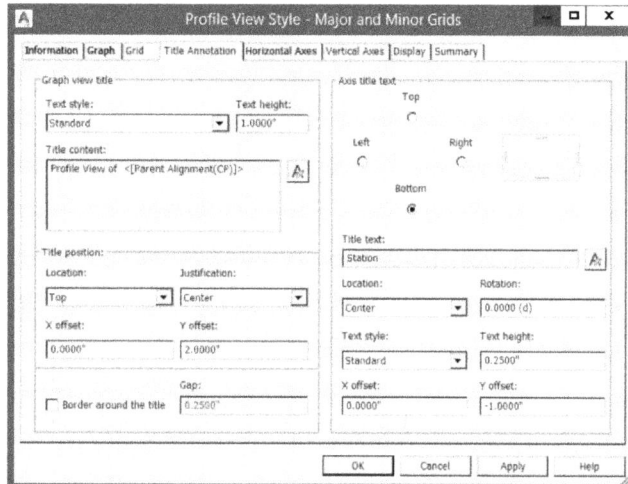

Figure 7–6

Horizontal Axes Tab

The *Horizontal Axes* tab enables you to specify the annotation for the top and bottom axes of the profile view. From here you can set the major and minor intervals for station labels and/or ticks, and the horizontal geometry tick details, as shown in Figure 7–7.

Note: You can have different values for top and bottom.

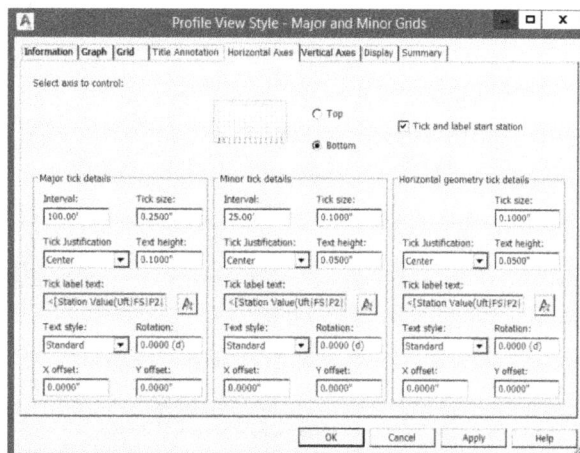

Figure 7–7

Vertical Axes Tab

The *Vertical Axes* tab enables you to specify the elevation label details, such as vertical interval, justification, content, text styles, and tick sizes, as shown in Figure 7–8.

Note: You can have different values for left and right.

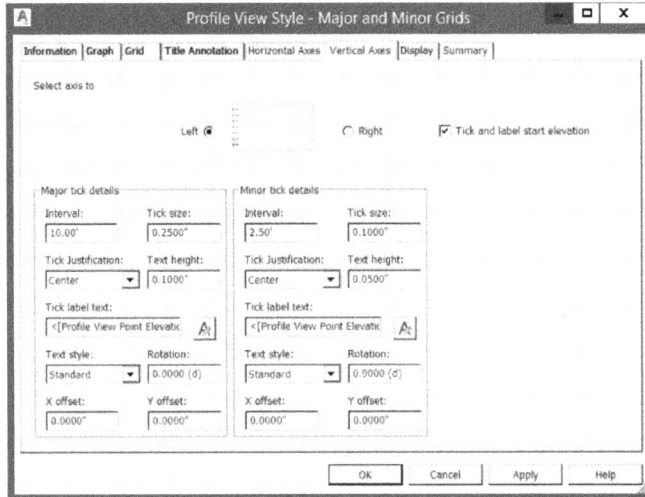

Figure 7–8

Display Tab

The *Display* tab enables you to set which components display and which layer, color, linetype, and other properties they use, as shown in Figure 7–9.

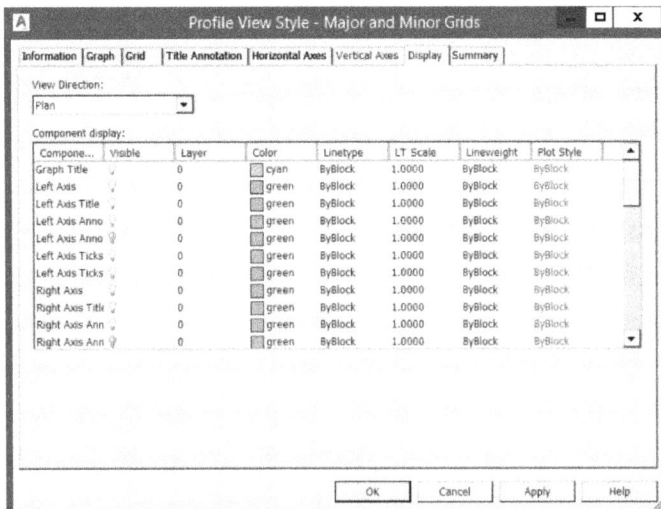

Figure 7–9

Summary Tab

The *Summary* tab enables you to review all of the settings that were selected on the other tabs for a quick reference, as shown in Figure 7–10.

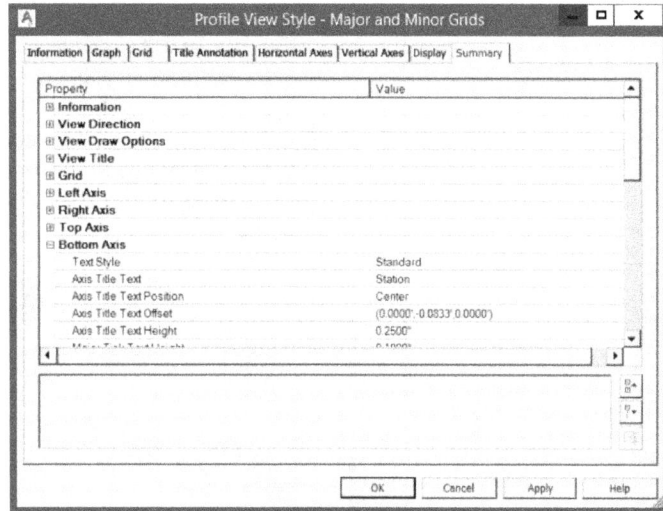

Figure 7–10

7.3 Create Profiles from Surface

Most profile views display at least one profile based on a
surface, such as from an existing ground terrain model. To create
a profile from a surface, use the following steps:

1. In the *Home* tab>Create Design panel, click 〰️ (Profile>
   Create Surface Profile).
2. In the Create Profile from Surface dialog box (shown in
   Figure 7–11), select the required alignment and surface(s).
3. Enter the required station range.
4. Click **Add>>** to sample each surface based on these
   settings.

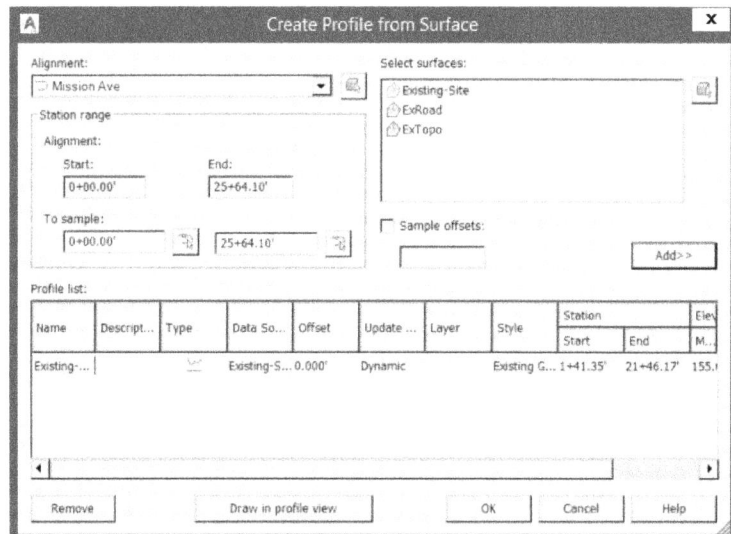

Figure 7–11

This creates a profile along the alignment itself with a zero offset.
If you want to sample at an offset from the alignment, select the
Sample Offsets option. Enter a positive (+) value to sample the
right side and a negative (-) value to sample the left side of the
alignment, and then click **Add>>**. You can sample multiple
offsets by entering values one at a time and clicking **Add>>** after
each or putting a comma between offset values to add them all
at the same time.

There are two ways to exit this dialog box (other than clicking **Cancel**):

- If you do not have a profile view of this alignment in the drawing, click **Draw in profile view**. This opens the Create Profile View dialog box.

- If you already have a profile view of this alignment, click **OK** and any new profiles are added to the existing view. If you clicked **OK** accidentally without having a view in which to display the profile, go to the *Home* tab> Profile and Section

  Views panel, and click (Profile View>Create Profile View).

7.4 Create Profile View Wizard

You can create a profile view at any time using ⌗ (Profile View>Create Profile View). All of the settings selected in the wizard can be reassigned later using Profile View Properties (except for the alignment on which they are based).

The *General* page in the Create Profile View wizard enables you to select the alignment that you want to work with and to assign the profile view a name, description, view style, and layer. The **Show offset profiles by vertically stacking profile views** option (shown in Figure 7–12), enables you to display offset profiles in a different view from the center line profile without overlapping.

*Clicking **Draw in profile view** in the Create Profile from Surface dialog box opens the same wizard.*

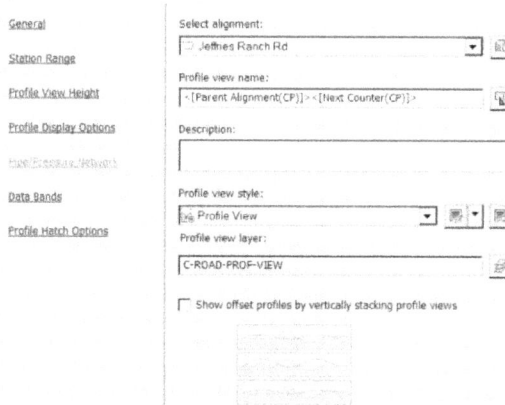

Figure 7–12

The *Station Range* page (shown in Figure 7–13), enables you to select the station range with which you want to work. The **Automatic** option includes the entire alignment's length.

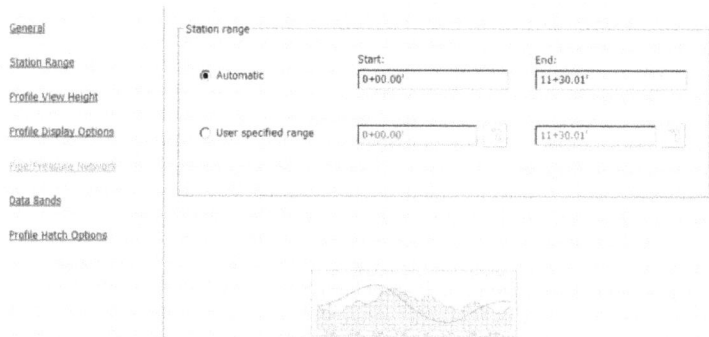

Figure 7–13

The *Profile View Height* page (shown in Figure 7–14), enables you to select the required height of the profile grid.

Figure 7–14

- The **Automatic** option creates a profile view that is sized to avoid having to be split.

- The **User Specified** option enables you to assign specific minimum and maximum heights to the profile view. If a profile in one of these views has an elevation below or above the specified values, the profile view is split to accommodate it. If a profile needs to be split you can assign different styles to control the different portions of the split profile.

Figure 7–15 shows a profile view that has been split.

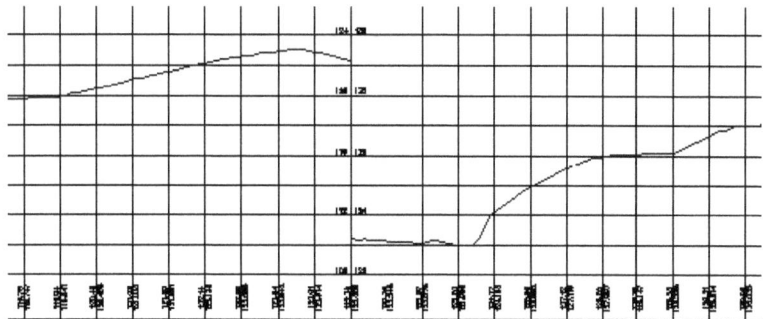

Figure 7–15

The *Stacked Profile* page (shown in Figure 7–16), enables you to set the number of stacked views, the gap between those views, and the styles for each one.

*This page is only available if you selected the **Show offset profiles by vertically stacking profile views** on the General page.*

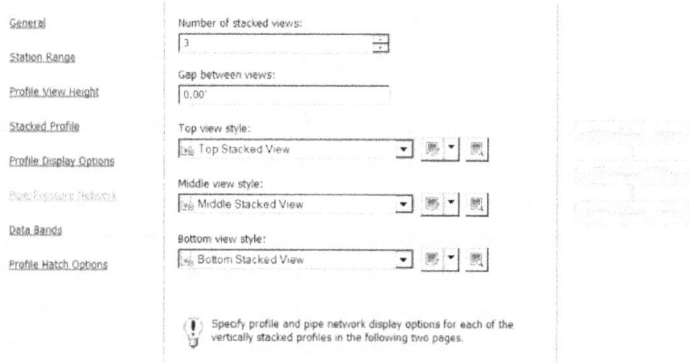

Figure 7–16

The *Profile Display Options* page (shown in Figure 7–17), enables you to apply specific controls to profiles that display in the views.

Some of the most important options include:

- **Draw:** Disabling this option prevents the profile from being displayed in the view.

- **Style:** Sets the profile style to display in the profile.

- **Labels:** Sets the profile label set to display in the profile.

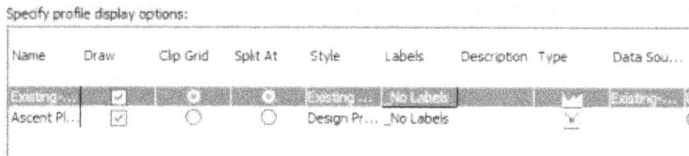

Figure 7–17

The *Data Bands* page (shown in Figure 7–18), enables you to select the bands that you want to include. Bands are additional profile information that can be included along the top or bottom of a profile. Bands are applied in this dialog box by selecting a Band Set.

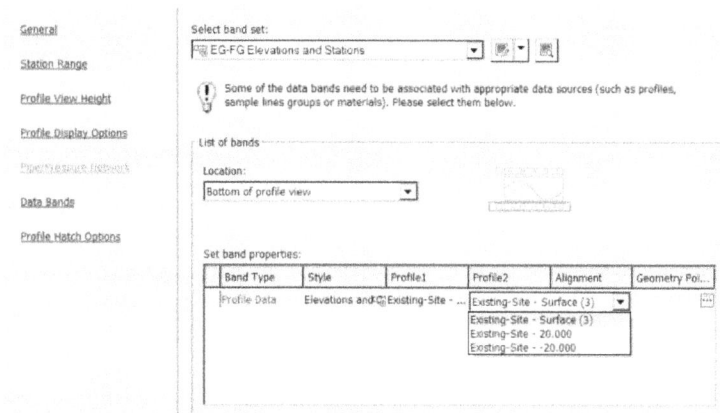

Figure 7–18

The **Profile Hatch** option is shown in Figure 7–19. You can hatch the profile according to the *Cut Area*, *Fill Area*, *Multiple boundaries*, or *From criteria* that you import. If you select one of these options, the software enables you to specify the upper and lower boundaries for the hatch area.

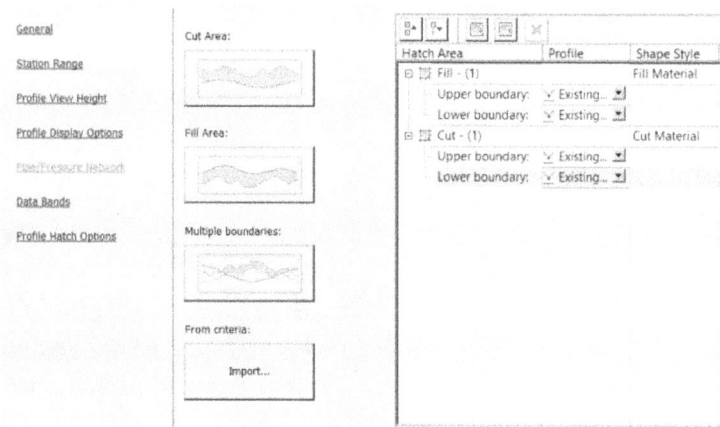

Figure 7–19

When satisfied, click **CreateProfile View** to create the profile view. After the profile view is created these settings can be reviewed and adjusted using **Profile View Properties**. To open this dialog box, select the profile view, right-click and select **Profile View Properties**.

Practice 7a

Working with Profiles Part I

Practice Objective

- List the various types of projects that use alignments and profiles in their designs.

Estimated time for completion: 15 minutes

In the following practices you will create profile views and a profile vertical design. In a production collaboration environment, you can use data references to share data between team members, i.e., surfaces and horizontal alignments.

Based on specific design workflow, the horizontal alignment and design profiles often reside in the same drawing. This is the workflow that you will use. However, you can assume that the horizontal alignments are fixed and that you only need to reference them into the profile drawing. In that case, you can practice using data shortcuts or Vault shortcuts.

Task 1 - Create surface profiles.

1. Open **PRF1-A1-Profile.dwg** from the *C:\Civil 3D Projects\ Civil3D-Training\Profiles* folder.

2. In the *Home* tab>Create Design panel, click [⌇] (Profile> Create Surface Profile), as shown in Figure 7–20.

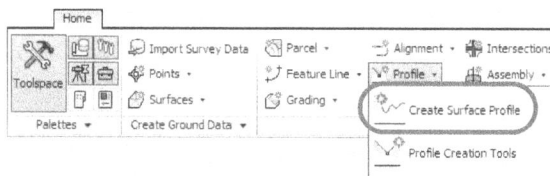

Figure 7–20

3. In the Create Profile from Surface dialog box:
   - Select the **Jeffries Ranch Rd** alignment.
   - Highlight the **Existing-Site** surface and click **Add>>**.
   - Click **Draw in profile view**, as shown in Figure 7–21.

This samples an existing ground profile along the center line, the entire length of Jeffries Ranch Rd.

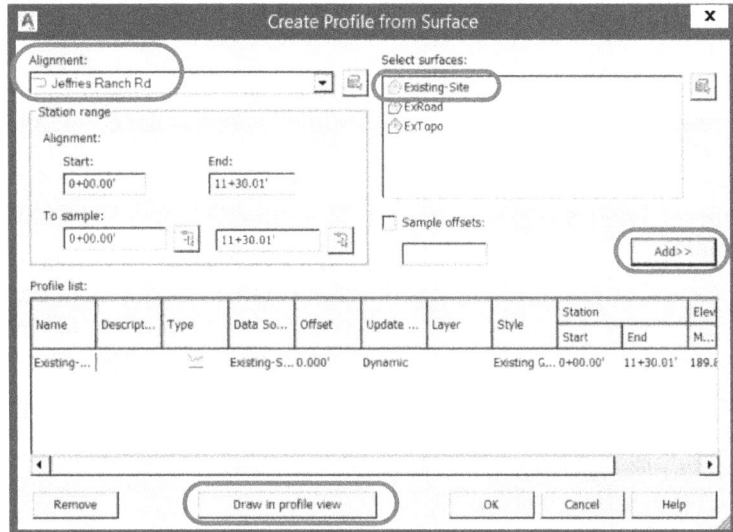

Figure 7–21

*If you clicked **OK** instead, expand Profile View and select **Create Profile View** in the Home tab>Profile & Section Views panel.*

4. In the Create Profile View wizard, set the following options, as shown in Figure 7–22:

   • In the *General* page, confirm **Jeffries Ranch Rd** as the alignment.

   • Set the *Profile view style* to **Profile View**.

   • Click **Next>**.

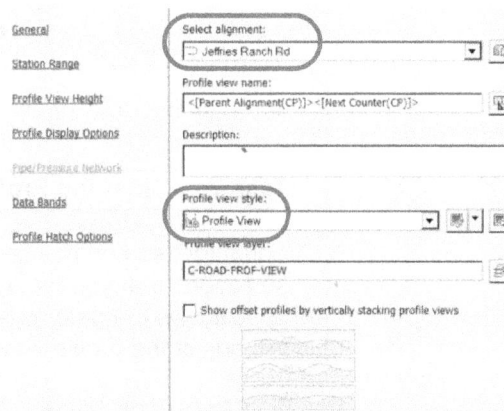

Figure 7–22

5. Accept the defaults in the *Station Range* page and click **Next>**.

6. Accept the defaults in the *Profile View Height* page and click **Next>**.

Note: You will set which profiles to use for profiles 1 and 2 in the data bands after a finish ground profile has been created.

Note: The surface profile displays although the surface contours are not displayed in the plan view. This is because the surface exists in the drawing but is set to a **No Display** *style.*

7. Accept the defaults in the *Profile Display Options* page and click **Next>**.

8. In the *Data Bands* page, accept **EG-FG Elevations and Stations** for the band set, and click **Next>**.

9. In the *Profile Hatch Options* page, accept the default of no hatching and click **Create Profile View**

10. If the event viewer displays, close it by clicking the checkmark in the top right corner. When prompted for a location for the profile, click a point to the right of the plan view to define the lower left corner of the Profile View, as shown in Figure 7–23.

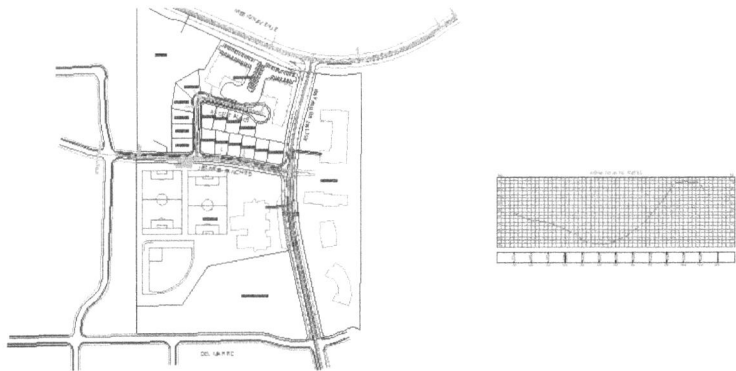

Figure 7–23

11. Repeat Steps 3. to 10. for the alignment **Ascent Pl**.

12. Save the drawing.

Task 2 - Adjust the Profile View.

You might sometimes be required to modify some of the selections that you made in the Create Profile View Wizard, specifically, the datum elevation or grid height. In this task, you will adjust the profile view.

1. Continue working with the drawing from the previous task or open **PRF1-A2-Profile.dwg**.

2. Select the **Ascent PI** profile view, right-click, and select **Profile View Properties**, as shown in Figure 7–24.

*You can also select the Toolspace, Prospector tab and expand Alignments> Centerline Alignments> Ascent PI>Profile Views. Right-click on Ascent PI2 and select **Properties**.*

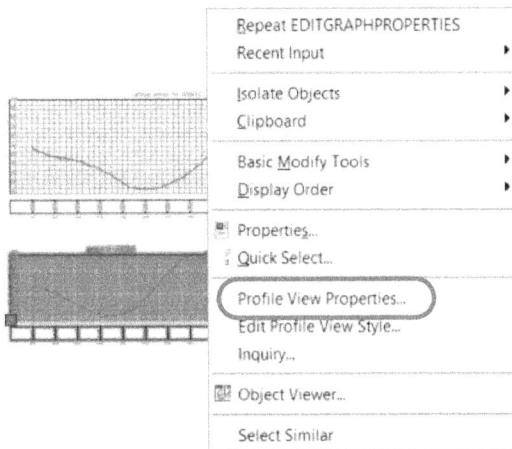

Figure 7–24

3. In the *Elevations* tab, select the **User specified height** option. Type a *Minimum* of **165** and a *Maximum* of **210**, as shown in Figure 7–25. Click **OK**.

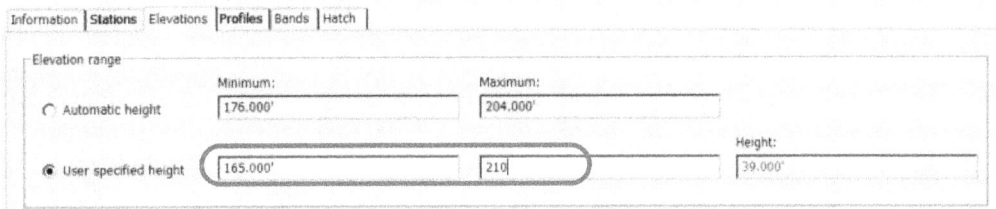

Figure 7–25

4. Save the drawing.

7.5 Finished Ground Profiles

Finished ground profiles (also referred to as proposed profiles or proposed vertical alignments) are often created interactively using the Profile Layout Tools toolbar, as shown in Figure 7–26. This is similar to how alignments are created by layout. The toolbar can be opened by going to the *Home* tab>Create Design panel and expanding Profile and selecting **Profile Creation Tools**.

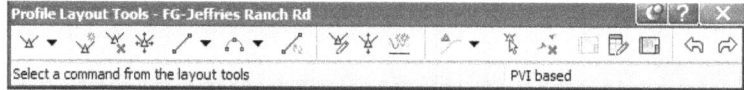

Figure 7–26

* Using these tools, you can add tangents and vertical curves.

* Vertical curves transition a vehicle from one tangent grade to another and occur in two situations: Crest (top of a hill) and Sag (valley).

* There are multiple types of vertical curves to transition between changing the tangent grades of a crest or sag: **Circular**, **Parabolic**, **Asymmetric Parabolic**, and **Best Fit**. Roadways almost always use parabolic (equal length) curves. Asymmetric parabolic curves are usually only used if layout constraints do not permit an equal-length curve. True circular curves are used in some parts of the world for low-speed rail design. Generally, they should *never* be used for roadways (which could lead to vehicle vaulting or bottoming out). Best fit curves follow the most likely path through a series of points.

* In the Toolspace, *Settings* tab, in the Profile heading, the Edit Features Settings set the default curve type, styles, and command settings.

Most vertical designs have regulations affecting the minimum and maximum values for tangent slopes, distances along tangents between vertical curves, and safety design parameters for passing sight and stopping sight distances. Refer to local design manuals for more information on these design constraints.

The points connecting tangents in a finished ground profile are referred to as a *Point of Vertical Intersection* (PVI).

7.6 Create and Edit Profiles

Similar to the Alignments Layout toolbar, the Profile Layout Tools toolbar contains an overall vista (Profile Grid View) and Profile Layout Parameters (segment data viewer). These vistas enable you to review and edit the vertical design. The settings used when creating a finished ground profile can be selected in the Draw Tangents flyout in the toolbar, as shown in Figure 7–27. This toolbar is used to edit any kind of profile, including profiles created from surfaces.

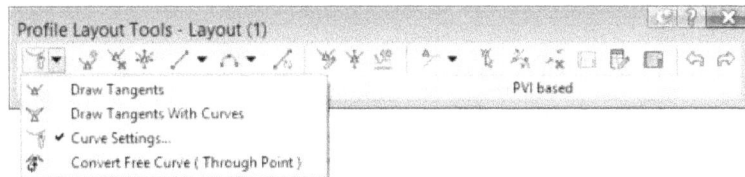

Figure 7–27

Other toolbar commands (shown in Figure 7–28), enable you to **Add**, **Delete**, or **Move** individual tangents, PVIs, or vertical curve segments.

* When editing a profile in the layout parameters or grid view, editable parameters display in black.

* You can graphically edit a design profile using grips. As soon as you select the profile, a contextual tab displays in the ribbon that is specific to that profile.

Figure 7–28

* When graphically editing a vertical alignment, the tangents, PVIs, and vertical curves display grips that represent specific editing functions, as shown in Figure 7–29.

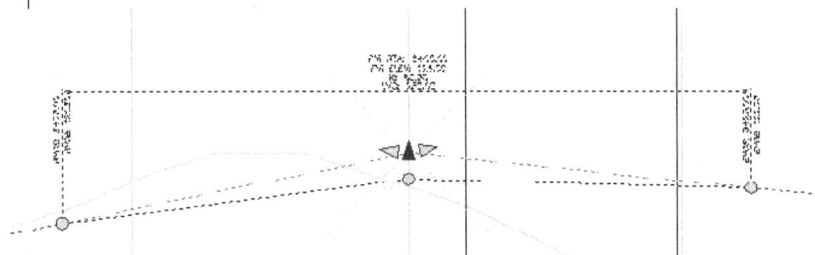

Figure 7–29

- The center triangular grip moves the PVI to a new station and/or elevation.

- The triangles left and right of the center extend the selected tangent, hold its grade, and modify the grade of the opposite tangent to relocate the PVI.

- The middle or end circular grips lengthen or shorten the vertical curve without affecting the location of the PVI.

- When you move the cursor to the original location of the grip, the cursor snaps to that location.

Transparent Commands

The AutoCAD Civil 3D software has several transparent commands that can be extremely helpful when creating or editing a finished ground profile. They are listed as follows in the order in which they are shown in the Transparent Commands toolbar (from left to right), as shown in Figure 7–30:

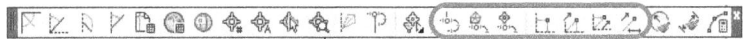

Figure 7–30

- (**Profile Station from Plan**): When creating or adjusting a PVI, this command enables you to pick a point in plan view next to the base alignment. The AutoCAD Civil 3D software then calculates the station value automatically and prompts you for the elevation to use at that station.

- (**Profile Station and (surface) Elevation from Plan**): This command is similar, except that it enables you to determine an elevation from a surface.

- (**Profile Station and Elevation from COGO Point**): This command enables you to determine station and elevation values for a PVI based on the location of a point object.

- (**Profile Station Elevation**): By default, when adding a PVI you are prompted for a drawing's X,Y location. If you would rather enter a station value and elevation, use this command.

- **(Profile Grade Station):** This command enables you to locate a PVI based on a grade and an ending station value.

- **(Profile Grade Elevation):** This command enables you to locate a PVI based on a grade and an ending elevation value.

- **(Profile Grade Length):** This command enables you to locate a PVI based on a grade and tangent length.

Assigning Profile Band Elevations

Profile band elevations are assigned using Profile View Properties, in the *Bands* tab. When you create a profile view, you should review the band settings and verify that each profile band is assigned the correct profile in the *Profile1* and *Profile2* fields, as shown in Figure 7–31. The AutoCAD Civil 3D software does not make any assumptions about which profile to use in either field.

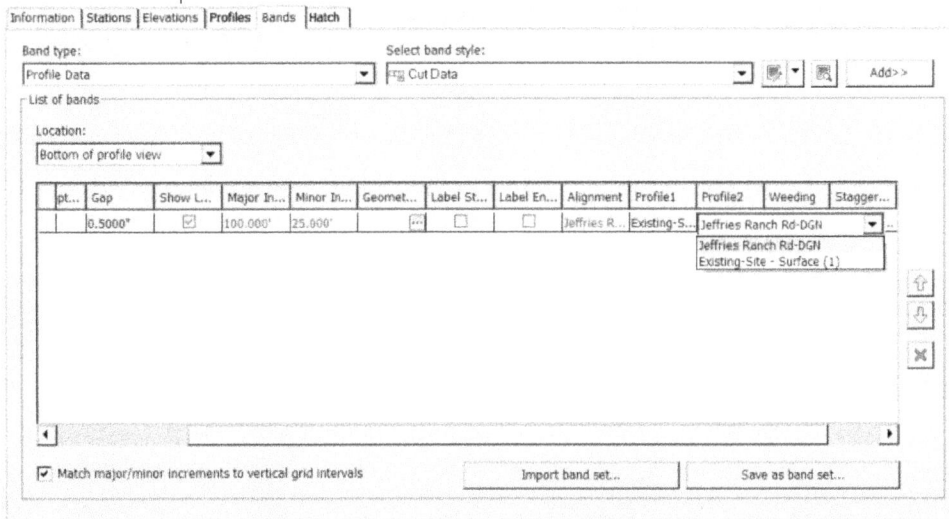

Figure 7–31

Using the styles supplied with the AutoCAD Civil 3D templates, the existing ground surface would be assigned the *Profile1* field, and the finished ground profile would be assigned the *Profile2* field.

Profile Segment Types

Profile segments created by layout (tangent lines, parabolas, and circular curves) can be created as fixed, free, or floating.

Profile Labels

Profiles have dynamic labels that are organized into two categories:

- **Profile labels:** Include labels for Major and Minor Stations, Horizontal Geometry Points, Profile Grade Breaks, Lines, and Crest and Sag curves. These can be selected when the profile is created and managed later by right-clicking on a profile and selecting **Edit Labels**.

- **Profile View labels:** Include a Station & Elevation label type and a Depth label type. These are created by going to the *Annotate* tab>Labels & Tables panel, expanding Add Labels, expanding Profile View, and selecting **Add Profile View Labels**, as shown in Figure 7–32. They can be removed using the AutoCAD **Erase** command.

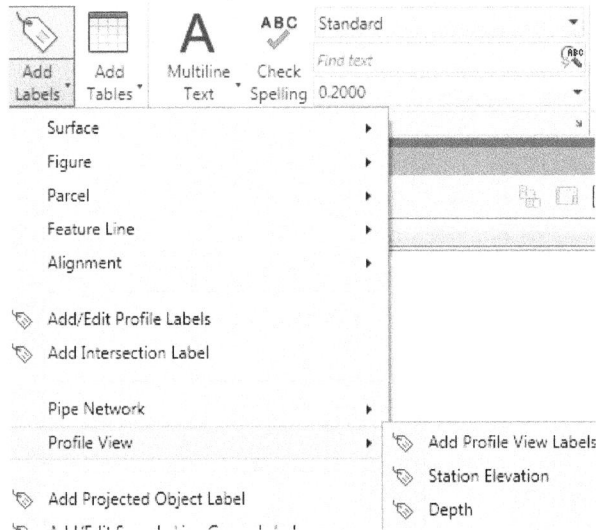

Figure 7–32

Practice 7b

Working with Profiles Part II

Practice Objective

* Create finished ground profiles using specific design parameters.

Estimated time for completion: 20 minutes

Before starting any type of design, you need to obtain all of the constraints. The tie in elevation for Jeffries Ranch Rd at the east end is 200.02'. You also know that based on survey data that the tie in elevations at the west end at station 0+06.17' is 207.78', with an existing grade of approximately 3.79%. The cul-de-sac will be based on the grade of Jeffries Ranch Rd and an adjacent grade at Ascent Blvd. The low point overflow drainage in the Knuckle will be addressed by an overland gutter to the pond. Figure 7–33 roughly shows the type of street drainage that you want to establish.

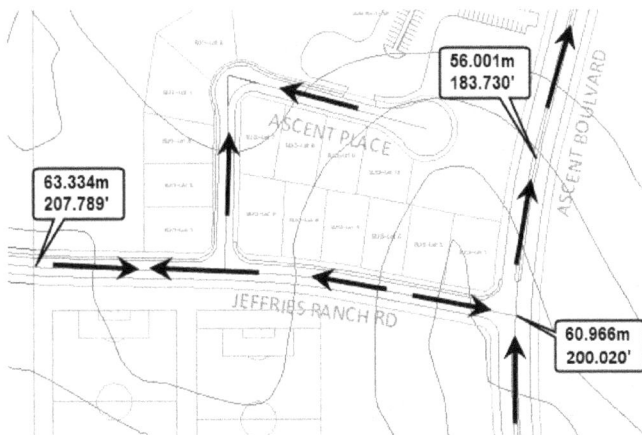

Figure 7–33

Task 1 - Create the Finished Ground Profile.

1. Continue with the previous drawing or open **PRF1-B1-Profile.dwg**.

2. Zoom to the Jeffries Ranch Rd profile view. In the *Home* tab> Create Design panel, expand **Profile** and select **Profile Creation Tools**. When prompted to select a profile view, select the **Jeffries Ranch Rd** profile view.

Alternatively, select the ***Jeffries Ranch Rd*** *profile view, and in the contextual tab>Launch Pad panel, select* ***Profile Creation Tools***

3. In the Create Profile dialog box that opens, for the *Name,* click 🔲 (Edit name template) to the right.

4. In the Name Template dialog box, set the following, as shown in Figure 7–34:

   • In the *Property fields* field, select **Alignment Name** and then click **Insert**.

   • In the *Name* field, after **<[Alignment Name]>**, type -**DGN**.

   • Click **OK** to close the dialog box

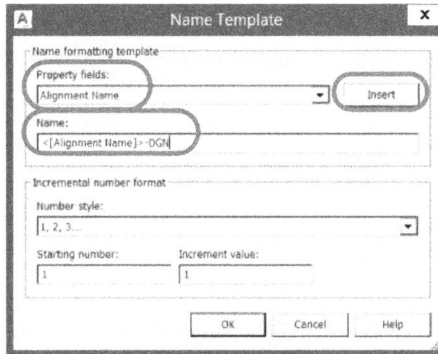

Figure 7–34

5. Set the *Profile style* to **Design Profile** and the *Profile label set* to **Complete Label Set** as shown in Figure 7–35. Click **OK**.

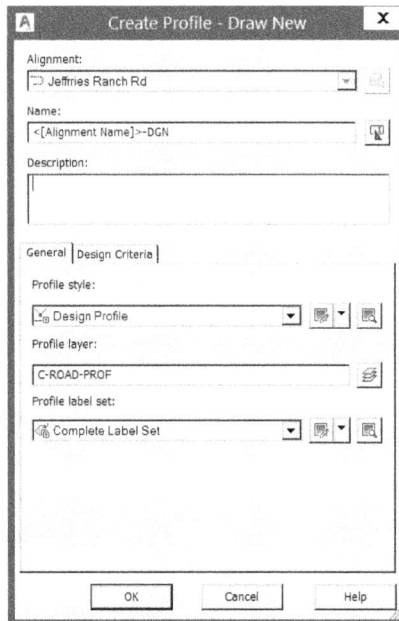

Figure 7–35

6. Expand the drop-down list in the Profile Layout Tools toolbar and select **Draw Tangents**, as shown in Figure 7–36. The AutoCAD Civil 3D software prompts you for a start point, which indicates the location of the road's first PVI.

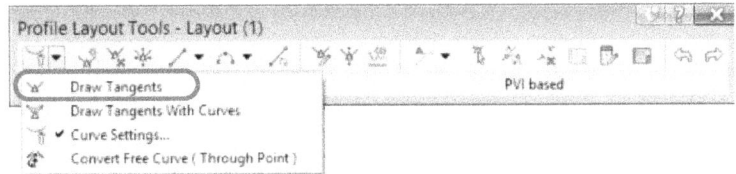

Figure 7–36

7. In the Transparent Commands toolbar, click ⬚⬝ (Profile Station Elevation), and then proceed as follows:

    • Select any part of the Jeffries Ranch Rd profile view.
    • Type a starting station of **6.17'** and press <Enter>.
    • Type a starting elevation of **207.78'**, and press <Enter>.
    • Press <Esc> to exit this transparent command.

*You want to set the next point based on a grade to a given station, so you will use the **Profile Grade Station** transparent command.*

8. Click ⬚⬝ (Profile Grade Station) in the Transparent Commands toolbar to enter a grade followed by a station, as follows:

    • For the grade, type **-3.79** and press <Enter> (to indicate -3.79%).
    • For the station, type **328.08'** and press <Enter>.
    • Press <Esc> to end the transparent command.
    • Press <Esc> again to end the layout command.

The profile is shown in Figure 7–37. Close the Profile Layout Tools, as shown on the top right of Figure 7–37.

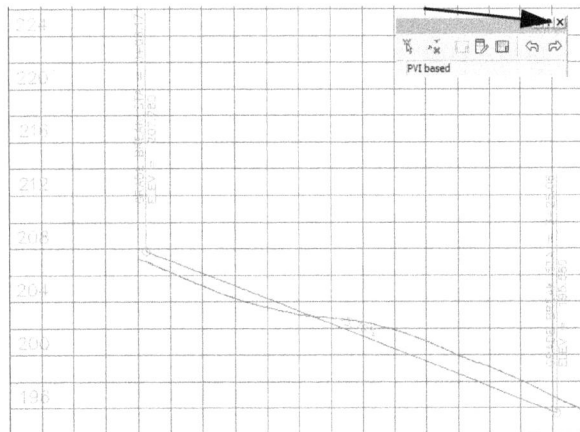

Figure 7–37

9. At any time, you can continue to edit a profile by selecting it, right-clicking, and selecting **Edit Profile Geometry**. In the Jeffries Ranch Rd profile view, select the **DGN** grade line drawn in Step 8. In the contextual tab>Modify Profile panel, click ⌄⊿ (Geometry Editor) to edit it.

10. To continue adding PVIs, return to the Profile Layout Tools toolbar and expand ⊻▾ and select **Draw Tangents**. When prompted for the start point, snap to the end point of the last segment that you drew (i.e., sta=328.08' elev=195.58').

11. In the Transparent Commands toolbar, click ↗↤ (Profile Grade Length), and then proceed as follows:
   - Select the **Jeffries Ranch Rd** profile view.
   - For the grade, type **0.8** and press <Enter>.
   - For the length, type **482.283'** and press <Enter>.
   - Press <Esc> to exit the transparent command.

12. To tie back to the final design point, click ⌐⊥ (Profile Station Elevation) in the Transparent Commands toolbar, and then proceed as follows:
   - Type an end alignment station of **1130.01'** and press <Enter>.
   - Type a tie in elevation of **200.02'** and press <Enter>.
   - Press <Esc> to exit the transparent command.
   - Press <Enter> to exit the **Draw Tangent** command.

13. In the Profile Layout Tools toolbar, click **X** to close it.

Task 2 - Adjust the FG Profile.

---

1. Continue with the previous drawing or open **PRF1-B2-Profile.dwg**.

2. Select the **Jefferies Ranch Rd-DGN1** profile that you drew in the previous task and note the grips that display.

3. In the contextual tab>Modify Profile panel, click ⌄⊿ (Geometry Editor).

The PVIs do not have any vertical curves. You will add them to the design using the **Free Vertical Curve (Parabola)** option, as shown in Figure 7–38. You could have also done this at the initial stage of the design using the **Draw Tangent with Curves** tool rather than the **Draw Tangent** tool.

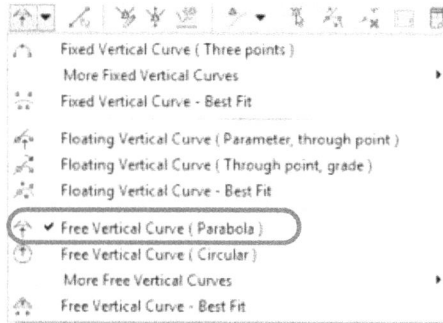

Figure 7–38

4. Click ⬆ (Free Vertical Curve (Parabola)), and when prompted to select the first entity, select the incoming grade (1) and then select the outgoing grade (2), as shown in Figure 7–39. Type **100'** for the length of vertical curve.

5. Do the same for the second vertical curve. Select entities (3) and (4) (as shown in Figure 7–39) and type **100'** for the length of the vertical curve. Press <Enter> to exit the command.

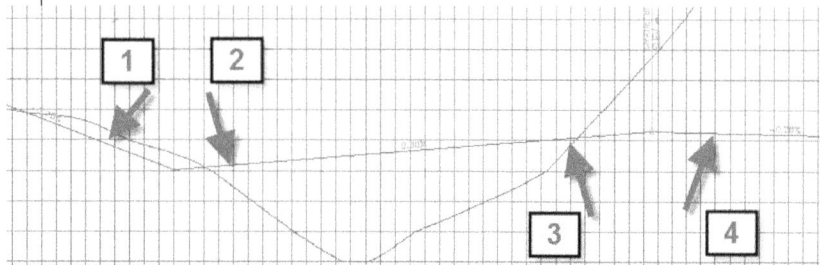

Figure 7–39

6. In the Profile Layout Tools toolbar, click 🖼 (Profile Grid View).

The Profile Entities vista should display in the Panorama.

7. The *Grade In* elevation at the station 11+30.01' is 0.18%. This is less than minimum, so you need to change it to **-0.8%** while maintaining both PVI stations. However, the elevation at station 8+10.37' will be revised. Select the *Grade In* elevation and change *0.18* to **-0.8**, as shown in Figure 7–40.

No.	PVI Station	PVI Elevation	Grade In	Grade Out
1	0+06.17'	207.780'		-3.79%
2	3+28.08'	195.579'	-3.79%	0.80%
3	8+10.37'	199.438'	0.80%	0.18%
4	11+30.01'	200.020'		0.18%

Figure 7–40

8. You will change the *Grade In* elevation at station 8+10.37' to also be **0.80%**. Select the *Grade In* elevation and change *1.45* to **0.8**, as shown in Figure 7–41. This affects the elevation at station 3+28.08.

No.	PVI Station	PVI Elevation	Grade In	Grade Out
1	0+06.17'	207.780'		-3.79%
2	3+28.08'	195.579'	-3.79%	1.45%
3	8+10.37'	202.577'	1.45%	-0.80%
4	11+30.01'	200.020'	-0.80%	

Figure 7–41

At this point, the as built grade from station 0+06.17' is no longer 3.79%. However, from a simple calculation you know that if you move the PVI from station 3+28.08', elevation 198.72' to station **2+60.04'**, elevation **198.16'**, you will be able to preserve the 3.79% grade and the 0.8% minimum grade. There are two methods to accomplish this:

- Edit the station and elevation in the grid view, as shown in Figure 7–42.

No.	PVI Station	PVI Elevation	Grade In	Grade Out
1	0+06.17'	207.780'		-2.81%
2	3+28.08'	198.719'	-2.81%	0.80%
3	8+10.37'	202.577'	0.80%	-0.80%
4	11+30.01'	200.020'	-0.80%	

Figure 7–42

- Alternatively, in Model Space, move the PVI to a station and elevation. For training proposes, perform the more complex process of the two.

The following steps correct the grade.

9. In Model Space, select the **DGN** grade line to display its grips.

10. At the 3+28.08' PVI station, select the center PVI grip. For the new location, click ⛏ (Profile Station and Elevation).
    - When prompted for the profile view, select one of the grid lines of the Jeffries Ranch Rd profile view.
    - Type a station value of **260.04'** and press <Enter>.
    - Type an elevation value of **198.16'** and press <Enter>.

11. The grid view should have the values shown in Figure 7–43. Click the **X** in the Profile Layout Tools toolbar to close both the grid view and toolbar.

No.	PVI Station	PVI Elevation	Grade In	Grade Out
1	0+06.17'	207.780'		-3.79%
2	2+60.04'	198.160'	-3.79%	0.80%
3	8+10.37'	202.577'	0.80%	-0.80%
4	11+30.01'	200.020'	-0.80%	

Figure 7–43

Task 3 - Update profile bands.

The profile views display existing ground elevations in both the existing and proposed slots of the profile bands, as shown in Figure 7–44. In this task, you will change the right label to a finished ground profile label.

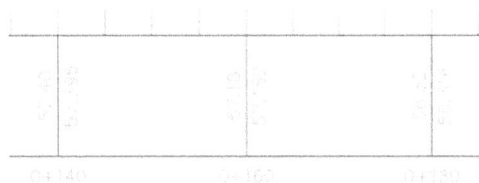

Figure 7–44

1. Continue with the drawing from the previous task or open **PRF1-B3-Profile.dwg**.

2. To update, select the Jeffries Ranch Rd profile view, right-click, and select **Profile View Properties**. In the *Bands* tab, assign Profile2 to reference Jeffries Ranch Rd-DGN, as shown in Figure 7–45. Click **OK**.

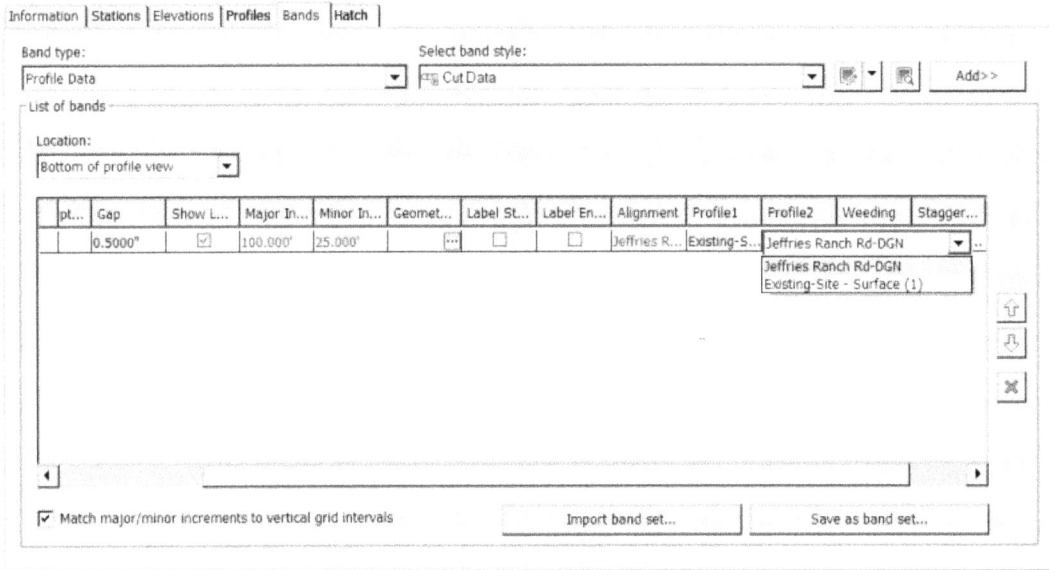

Information | Stations | Elevations | Profiles | Bands | Hatch |

Band type:

Profile Data ▾

List of bands

Location:

Bottom of profile view ▾

pt...	Gap	Show L...	Major In...	Minor In...	Geomet...	Label St...	Label En...	Alignment	Profile1	Profile2	Weeding	Stagger...
	0.5000"	☑	100.000'	25.000'	[...]	☐	☐	Jeffries R...	Existing-S...	Jeffries Ranch Rd-DGN ▾		..

Select band style:

Cut Data ▾ | Add>>

Jeffries Ranch Rd-DGN
Existing-Site - Surface (1)

☑ Match major/minor increments to vertical grid intervals   Import band set...   Save as band set...

Figure 7–45

The profile band displays existing ground elevations on the left and design elevations on the right, as shown in Figure 7–46.

Figure 7–46

3. Save the drawing.

Practice 7c

Working with Profiles Additional Practice

Estimated time for completion: 15 minutes

Practice Objective

- Create finished ground profiles using specific design parameters.

Task 1 - (Optional) Create a second FG Profile.

In this task, you will create a design grade for Ascent Place. To do this, you will use the tie in elevation at Jeffries Ranch Rd of 200.72'. Design requirements include PVI at station 3+77.461' elev 187.237' and a slope of 0.8% to the end station of 6+98.72'.

If you are not able to complete this task on your own, use the following steps.

1. Continue with the drawing from the previous practice or open **PRF1-C1-Profile.dwg**.

2. Zoom into the Ascent Pl profile view. In the *Home* tab>

   Create Design panel, expand **Profile**, and click ⤴ (Profile Creation Tools). When prompted to select a profile view, select the **Ascent Pl** profile view.

3. The Create Profile dialog box opens. Set the following, as shown in Figure 7–47:
   - Set the name as you did in the previous practice, in Steps 2 and 3, or type **Ascent Pl-DGN** for the *Name*.
   - Set the *Profile style* to **Design Profile**.
   - Set the *Profile label set* to **Complete Label Set**.
   - Click **OK**.

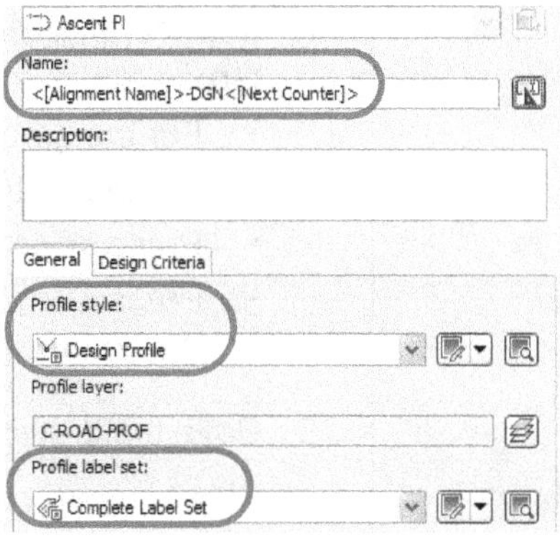

Figure 7–47

4. Expand the drop-down list in the Profile Layout Tools toolbar and select ⍩ (Curve Settings), as shown in Figure 7–48.

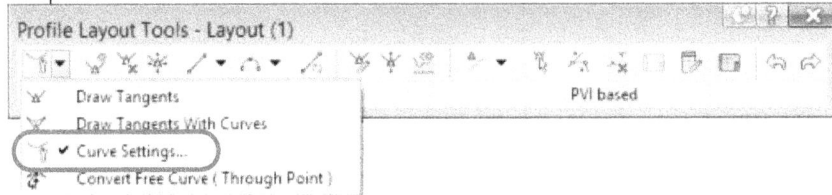

Figure 7–48

5. In the Vertical Curve Settings dialog box, for both the Crest and Sag curves:
   - Set the curve type to **Parabolic**.
   - Select the **Length** option and type **100'** as the length.
   - Click **OK** to close dialog box.

6. Click ⍩ ▾ (Draw Tangent with Curves).

7. The AutoCAD Civil 3D software prompts you for a start point, which indicates the location of the road's first PVI. Proceed as follows:
   - In the Transparent Commands toolbar, click ⊡ (Profile Station Elevation).
   - When prompted for a profile view, select the **Ascent PI** profile view.
   - Type a starting station of **0** and press <Enter>.
   - Type **200.72'** and press <Enter> for the starting elevation.
   - For the next station, type **377.46'** and press <Enter>.
   - Type **187.24'** and press <Enter> for the elevation.
   - Press <Esc> to exit this transparent command.

8. In the Transparent Commands toolbar, click ⊡ (Profile Grade Station).
   - For the grade, type **0.80** and press <Enter>.
   - For the station, type **698.72'** and press <Enter>
   - Press <Esc> to exit the transparent command.
   - Press <Enter> to exit the **Profile Draw** command.
   - Click the **X** to close the Profile Layout Tools toolbar.

9. Save the drawing.

Chapter Review Questions

1. You can safely relocate profile views in the AutoCAD Civil 3D software using the AutoCAD **Move** command.

    a. True

    b. False

2. Which of the following is not a vertical curve option in the AutoCAD Civil 3D software?

    a. Circular

    b. Parabolic

    c. Spiral

    d. Asymmetric Parabolic

3. Which grip do you use to move the PVI to a new station and elevation at the same time?

    a. ⌖ Circular

    b. △ Center Triangle

    c. ◁ Sideways Triangle

    d. ▫ Square

4. What do Profiles 1 and 2 annotate in profile bands?

    a. Profile elevations of two different profiles from the same alignment.

    b. Alignment stations.

    c. Tangent Slopes.

    d. Vertical curve lengths.

5. Which of the following **Transparent** command tools helps you to design a finished ground profile?

    a. ▱

    b. ▱

    c. ▱

    d. ▱

Command Summary

Button	Command	Location
	Create Profile from Surface	• **Ribbon:** *Home* tab>Create Design panel • **Command Prompt:** CreateProfileFromSurface
	Create Profile View	• **Ribbon:** *Home* tab>Create Design panel • **Command Prompt:** CreateProfileView
	Curve Settings	• **Toolbar:** Profile Layout Tools
	Draw Tangents	• **Toolbar:** Profile Layout Tools
	Draw Tangents with Curves	• **Toolbar:** Profile Layout Tools
	Free Vertical Curve (Parameter)	• **Toolbar:** Profile Layout Tools
	Geometry Editor	• **Contextual Ribbon:** *Profile* tab>Modify panel • **Command Prompt:** editprofilelayout
	Profile Creation Tools	• **Ribbon:** *Home* tab>Create Design panel • **Command Prompt:** CreateProfileLayout
	Profile Properties	• **Contextual Ribbon:** *Profile* tab>Modify panel • **Command Prompt:** editprofileproperties

Chapter

8

Corridors

Corridors are 3D representations of a road design. In this chapter you create a typical cross-section of a road (called an assembly) to communicate how the road is laid out perpendicular to the center line. Next, you apply the assembly to an alignment and profile you have designed. Then you create finished ground surfaces to help visualize the final design.

Learning Objectives in this Chapter

- List the various types of assemblies available and their uses.
- Design the typical cross-section of a road by creating an assembly and adding subassemblies to it.
- Create a corridor model using previously created alignments, profiles, and assemblies.
- Modify a corridor by changing parameters and other properties.
- Create a corridor model representing the location where two roads intersect that accounts for lane widening and curb returns.
- Create a finished ground surface from the design corridor.
- Review and edit corridor sections to make changes to a selected station.
- Preview the final design by driving down the road virtually.

8.1 Assembly Overview

Assemblies

An *assembly* defines the attachment point of a roadway cross-section to the horizontal and vertical alignments. This attachment point occurs at the midpoint of the assembly marker (or assembly baseline), as shown in Figure 8–1. The 3D progression of the attachment point along the corridor is also sometimes referred to as the *profile grade line*.

Figure 8–1

Assemblies can be placed anywhere in a drawing (centerline of roads, curb returns, sidewalks, off ramps, railways, etc). Assembly styles only affect the display of the marker itself (i.e., color, layer, etc.).

Assembly Types

The type of road or railway that an assembly represents can be very important, especially if it is used in a corridor that requires superelevation axis of rotation or cant. When a superelevation or cant is calculated for an alignment, it is important to also select an assembly type that matches these design needs. There are six types of assemblies:

- **Undivided Crowned Road:** Enables you to specify the axis about which the corridor is superelevated.

- **Undivided Planar Road:** Enables you to specify the axis about which the corridor is superelevated and the default highside location for planar roads.

- **Divided Crowned Road:** Enables you to specify the axis about which the corridor is superelevated and whether the median maintains its shape or becomes distorted as the corridor superelevates.

- **Divided Planar Road:** Enables you to specify the axis about which the corridor is superelevated and whether the median maintains its shape or becomes distorted as the corridor superelevates.

- **Railway:** Enables you to specify the cant about which the corridor is going to bank.

- **Other:** Used for all other types of corridors that are not listed above.

Subassemblies

Assemblies are assigned *subassemblies*, which represent individual components of the proposed cross-section (such as lane or curb subassemblies). Subassemblies attach to the left or right side of an assembly's attachment point. When building an assembly, you build from the middle out to the left or right edges.

- The library of stock subassemblies supplied with the AutoCAD® Civil 3D® software uses of a wide array of dynamic parameters (e.g., dimensions such as lane width and slope). If these values change, the road model can automatically update. Custom dynamic subassemblies can also be created using the .net programming language.

- You can create static subassemblies (without dynamic parameters) from polylines.

- Each point (vertex) of a subassembly can be assigned a name or *point code* for reference later. A point is a potential location for offset and elevation annotation. It is also a connection point for an adjacent subassembly. For example, points are commonly assigned at edge-of-travelways, back-of-curbs, gutters, etc. Marker styles define the properties for points and their labels.

- Corridors can generate *feature lines* at every location that is assigned a point code. These linear 3D objects can be used as input for surfaces and grading solutions.

- Lines in subassemblies are referred to as *links*. A link can be automatically given a slope or grade label in the cross-sections as required. Links can also be used as surface data. Link styles define the properties of a link and its labels.

- A subassembly *shape* is an area enclosed by links. Shapes are typically assigned material types and can be used to calculate quantities. Shape styles define the display properties of a shape.

- Marker styles, feature line styles, and link and shape styles are all assigned based on a Code Set Style. The Code Set Style assigns the styles to be applied based on the codes assigned to these objects. Code Sets and each of these styles are all configured under the *Multipurpose Styles* collection in the Toolspace, *Settings* tab.

The example in Figure 8–2 shows an assembly containing lane, curb, and daylight subassemblies. This assembly has been assigned to display an offset and elevation marker (point) label at the edge of the lane, a pavement slope (link) label, and shape labels displaying the area of the sub-base.

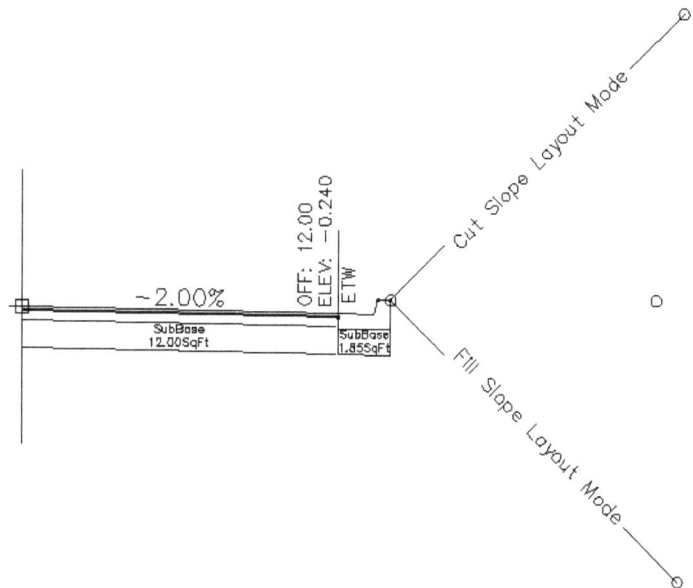

Figure 8–2

- Each subassembly attaches to the assembly connection point or to a point on an adjacent subassembly. OSNAPs are not necessary.

- You should assign each assembly and its subassemblies, a logical, unique name during creation. This is helpful later in the corridor creation process when you are working with very complex corridors that include intersections, transitions, and other components.

- AutoCAD Civil 3D Help contains extensive documentation for each subassembly.

The Toolspace, *Prospector* tab lists each assembly with a further breakdown of each subassembly associated with it, in a tree structure, as shown in Figure 8–3.

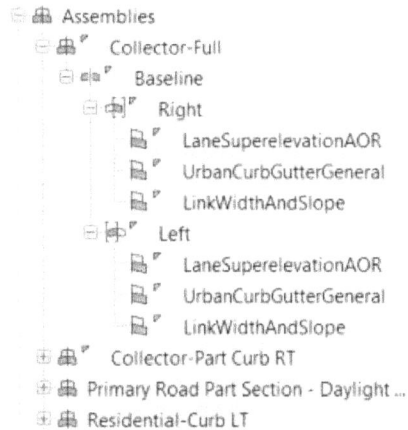

Figure 8–3

To review their interconnections and parameters, select the assembly, right-click, and select **Assembly Properties**. The Assembly Properties dialog box opens as shown in Figure 8–4.

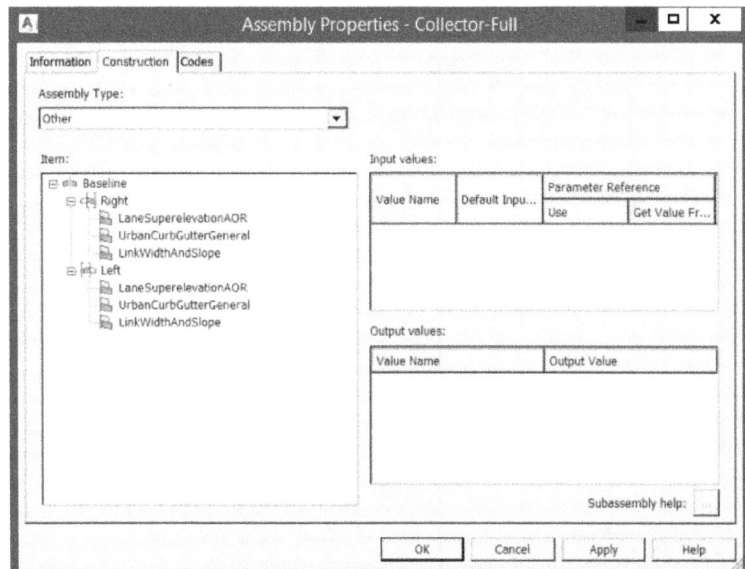

Figure 8–4

8.2 Modifying Assemblies

Attaching Subassemblies

The easiest way to add an AutoCAD Civil 3D subassembly to an assembly is using the Tool Palettes. You can open the Tool Palettes by clicking [icon] in the *Home* tab>Palettes panel, as shown in Figure 8–5, or in the *View* tab>Palettes panel. You can also use <Ctrl>+<3>.

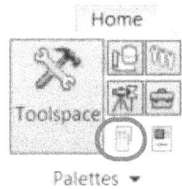

Figure 8–5

The AutoCAD Civil 3D software provides a number of stock subassembly tool palettes, as shown in Figure 8–6. In addition, it is continually updating and adding new subassemblies with every release.

Figure 8–6

The Help file is an invaluable resource for an updated list, and information about the specific attributes and properties of each subassembly, as shown in Figure 8–7.

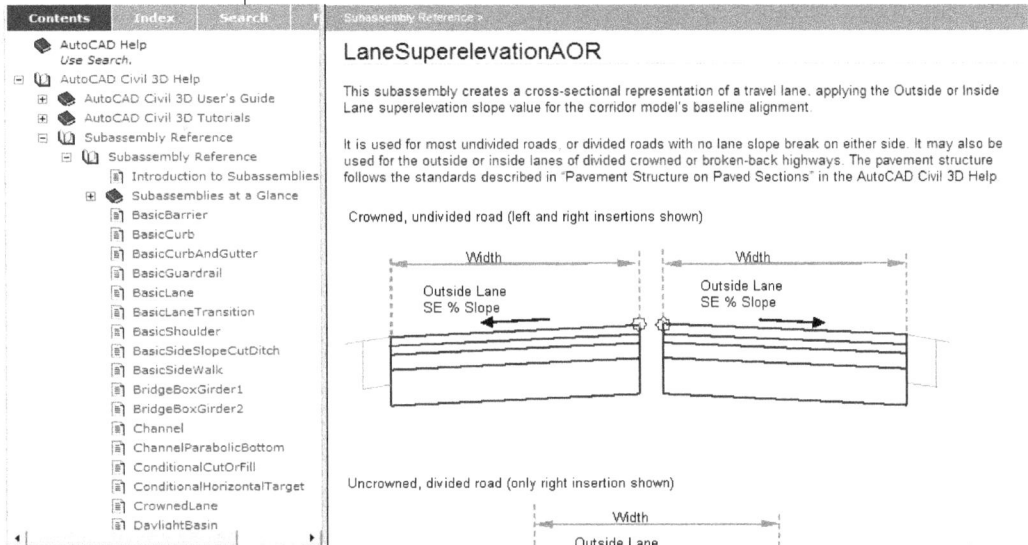

Figure 8–7

Additional subassemblies can be accessed using the Corridor Modeling catalogs. Open the catalog by selecting an assembly or subassembly from the drawing. In the *Assembly/Subassembly* tab>Launch Pad panel, click **Catalog**, as shown in Figure 8–8.

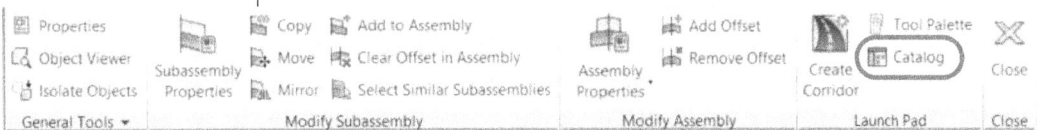

Figure 8–8

You can drag and drop the catalog onto a Tool Palette, if required. When working with the Tool Palettes and Properties palette, you might find it helpful to toggle off the **Allow Docking** option to prevent them from docking on the sides of the screen. Right-click on the palette's title bar to set the option, as shown in Figure 8–9.

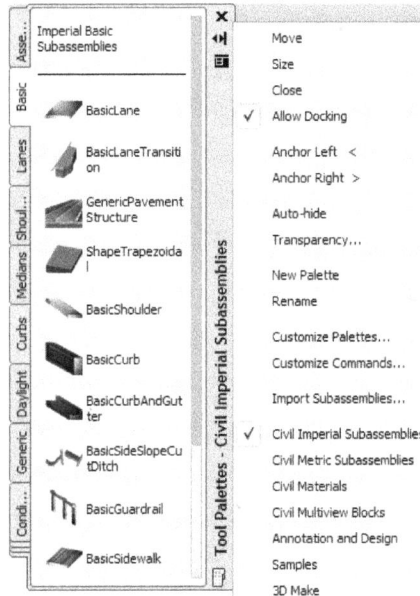

Figure 8–9

Detaching Subassemblies

Individual subassemblies can be deleted directly from an assembly with the AutoCAD® **Erase** command or using Assembly Properties. Assemblies can also be deleted with the **Erase** command.

Copying Assemblies

Assemblies can be copied with the AutoCAD **Copy** command or by clicking (Copy) in the *Assembly* tab>Modify Subassembly panel. Copying an assembly creates an independent assembly without a relationship to the original. Select the assembly by selecting the **Assembly Baseline**.

Mirroring Subassemblies

In the AutoCAD Civil 3D software, subassemblies can be mirrored across the assembly to which it is attached by selecting the subassemblies, right-clicking, and selecting **Mirror** or clicking ⬚ (Mirror) in the *Assembly* tab>Modify Subassembly panel. This enables you to create one side of the roadway and to create a mirrored image for the other side in one step.

> **Hint: AutoCAD Mirror**
>
> The basic AutoCAD Mirror command does not work for this. You need to use the Mirror option from the shortcut menu or in the Modify Subassembly panel.

Select Similar Subassemblies

It is often necessary to create multiple assemblies with the same subassemblies for various purposes. For example, a corridor that includes an intersection might need a full assembly that includes both sides of the road, an assembly that includes just the right side of the road, and another that includes just the left side of the road. It might also include two other assemblies that require the assembly marker to be placed at the edge of pavement rather than the crown, as shown in Figure 8–10.

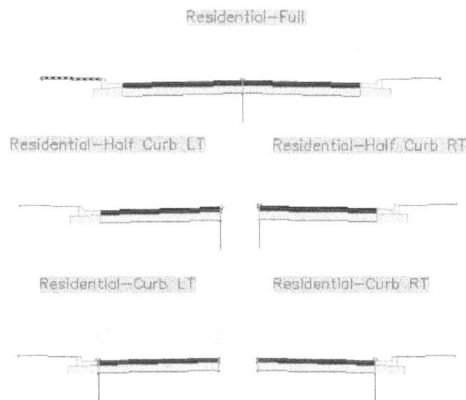

Residential—Full

Residential—Half Curb LT   Residential—Half Curb RT

Residential—Curb LT   Residential—Curb RT

Figure 8–10

However, making changes to all of the assemblies when a design parameter changes can be time consuming. To ensure that all similar subassemblies are modified at the same time when a design change occurs you can select one subassembly, click ⬚ (Select Similar Subassemblies) in the *Assembly* tab> Modify Subassembly panel, and change the parameter in the AutoCAD properties palette.

Sharing Assemblies

Assemblies can be shared with the AutoCAD Civil 3D software in three ways:

- Assemblies can be dragged from the drawing area to a Tool Palette. The Tool Palette can then be shared.

- The Content Browser can be used to add assemblies to a catalog.

- Assemblies can be placed in their own drawing files and shared by dragging the assembly drawing into the destination drawing file. If this method is used, the assembly drawing must only contain the assemblies that you want to share.

Getting More Information on Subassemblies

Many subassemblies have a large number of parameters. If you want to read the documentation on a subassembly, right-click on its tool icon in a Tool Palette and select **Help**. You can also find out more from Subassembly Properties and Assembly Properties using the **Subassembly help** icon, as shown in Figure 8–11.

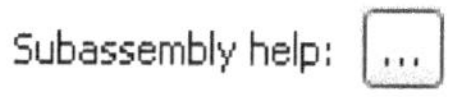

Subassembly help: [...]

Figure 8–11

Practice 8a

Creating Assemblies

Practice Objective

- Create and modify assemblies for use in a corridor model.

Estimated time for completion: 15 minutes

In this practice you will create two assemblies: one for Jeffries Ranch Rd and the second for the existing Ascent Pl that contains daylighting.

Task 1 - Create the Collector Road assembly.

A typical cross-section of Jeffries Ranch Rd is shown in Figure 8–12. (See Appendix A for the design criteria.)

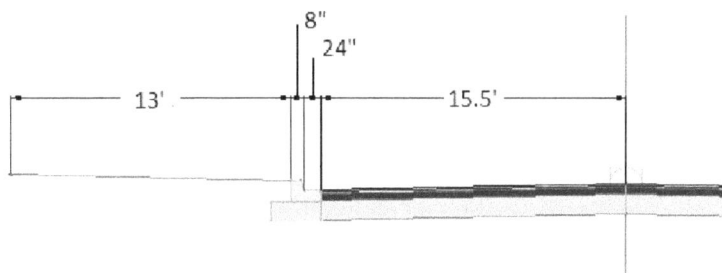

Figure 8–12

1. Continue working with the drawing from the previous task or open **COR1-A1-Corridor.dwg** from the *C:\Civil 3D Projects\ Civil3D-Training\Corridors* folder.

2. In the *Home* tab>Create Design panel, click 🔲 (Create Assembly).

3. In the Create Assembly dialog box, name the new assembly **Collector-Full**. Leave the other settings at their defaults, as shown in Figure 8–13. Click **OK** to close the dialog box.

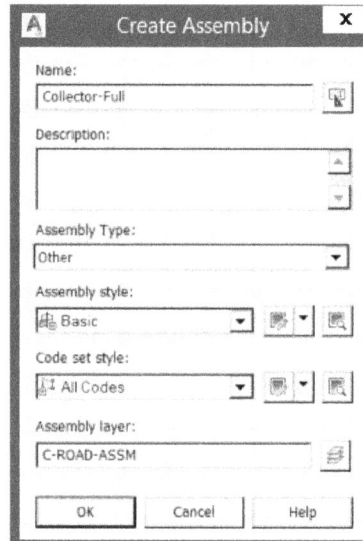

Figure 8–13

4. When prompted, locate the assembly baseline to the left of the profile view Jeffries Ranch Rd in the current drawing, as shown in Figure 8–14.

Once selected, the AutoCAD Civil 3D software will change the view to zoom into the assembly baseline location.

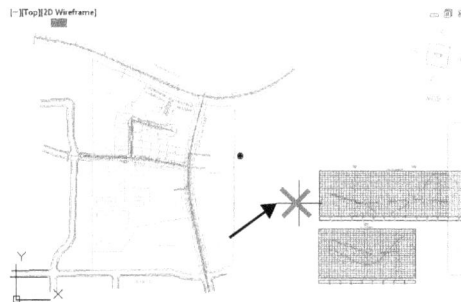

Figure 8–14

5. Open the Tool Palettes by clicking ⬚ (Tool Palettes) in the *Home* tab> Palettes panel.

6. In the Lanes Tool Palette, select the
LaneSuperelevationAOR subassembly to add it to your
assembly. In the Properties palette, set the following, as
shown in Figure 8–15:

- *Side:* **Right**
- *Width*: **15.5'**
- *Slope*: **-2%**
- Select the assembly baseline to attach the subassembly
  to the assembly.

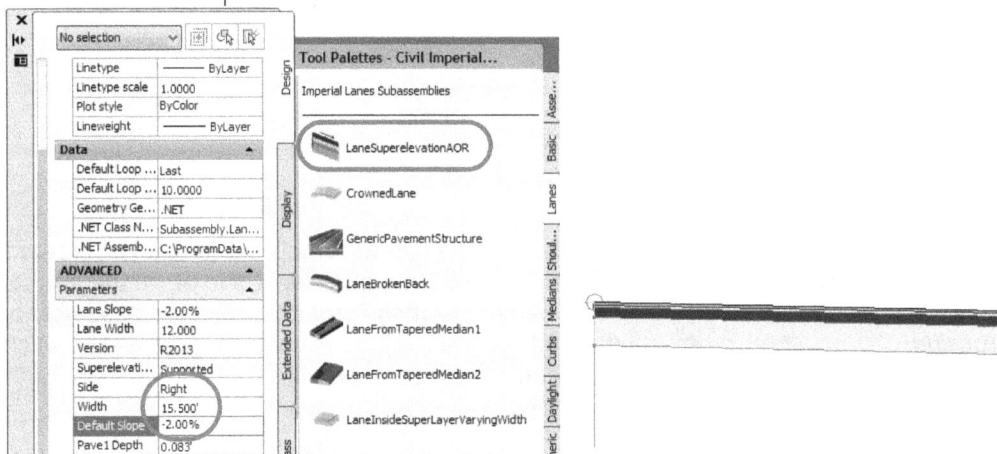

Figure 8–15

7. In the Subassemblies Tool Palette, select the *Curbs* tab and
select the **UrbanCurbGutterGeneral** subassembly. In the
Advanced Properties, set the following:

- *Side*: **Right**
- *Dimension B*: **24"**
- Insert the subassembly by selecting the circle at the end
  of the **LaneInsideSuper** subassembly, as shown in
  Figure 8–16. Press <Esc> to exit the subassembly
  command.

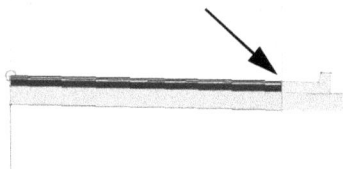

Figure 8–16

8. You will now create a subassembly that links the back of curb to property line. In the Subassemblies Tool Palette, select the *Generic* tab, and select the **LinkWidthAndSlope** subassembly. In the Advanced Properties, set the following:

- *Side parameter:* **Right**
- *Width:* **13'**
- Insert the subassembly by selecting the circle at the end of the **UrbanCurbGutterGeneral** subassembly, as shown in Figure 8–17.
- Press <Esc> to exit the subassembly command.

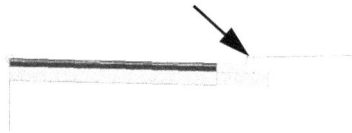

Figure 8–17

Do not select the assembly baseline, and do not use window crossing.

9. Select the three sub-assemblies that you just created on the right side, right-click, and select **Mirror**. At the *select marker point within assembly:* prompt, select the assembly baseline (the red vertical line), as shown in Figure 8–18, which represents the road center line.

Figure 8–18

10. Save the drawing.

Task 2 - Create the Residential Road assembly.

A typical cross-section of Ascent Pl is shown in Figure 8–19. (See Appendix A for design criteria.)

Note that this task is similar to Task 1. You can use this Task as a test of your knowledge in creating a residential road assembly or you can skip this task and open the backup drawing in Task 3.

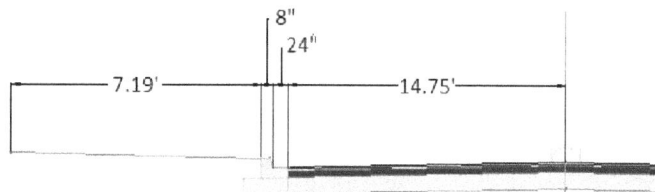

Figure 8–19

1. Continue working with the drawing from the previous task or open **COR1-A2-Corridor.dwg**.

2. In the *Home* tab>Create Design panel, click ⬛ (Create Assembly).

3. In the Create Assembly dialog box, name the new assembly **Residential-Full**. Leave the other settings at their defaults and click **OK**. Click in the drawing to place the new assembly.

4. Follow the same steps in Task 1 to create the residential assembly. For this assembly:

    • Set the pavement LaneSuperelevationAOR *width* to **14.75'**.
    • **UrbanCurbGutterGeneral** subassembly *Dimension B* is set to **24"**.
    • LinkWidthAndSlope *width* to **7.193'**.

Task 3 - Copy and modify an assembly.

Copying an assembly can be helpful if you need another, similar assembly for other design purposes. In the following task, you will create assemblies that are required by the Intersection wizard for the intersection area of Jeffries Ranch Rd and Ascent Place. It would be helpful to understand the names and the configuration of the different assemblies.

1. Continue working with the drawing from the previous task if you completed creating all of the assemblies or open **COR1-A3-Corridor.dwg** from the *C:\Civil 3D Projects\ Civil3D-Training\Corridors* folder.

2. Start the AutoCAD **Copy** command. Copy the **Collector-Full** assembly to a location just below the original, as shown in Figure 8–20.

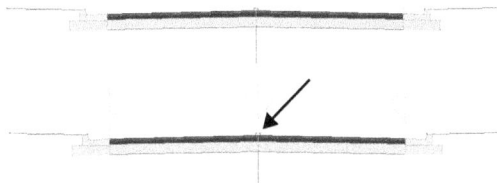

Figure 8–20

3. Select the bottom assembly baseline, right-click, and select **Assembly Properties**.

4. In the *Information* tab, change the *Name* to **Collector - Part Curb RT,** and click **OK**.

5. Start the AutoCAD **Erase** command and erase the left **UrbanCurbGutterGeneral** and the left **LinkWidthAndSlope**, as shown in Figure 8–21.

Figure 8–21

6. Save the drawing.

Practice 8b

Creating Assemblies Additional Practice

Estimated time for completion: 15 minutes

Practice Objective

- Create and modify assemblies for use in an intersection model.

In the previous practice, you created all of the Jeffries Ranch Rd assemblies that were required for the intersection. In this practice, you will create all of the required Ascent Place assemblies.

Task 1 - Create the assemblies required for the intersection.

1. Continue working with the drawing from the previous practice if you completed creating all of the subassemblies or open **COR1-B1-Corridor.dwg** from the *C:\Civil 3D Projects\ Civil3D-Training\Corridors* folder.

2. Start the AutoCAD **Copy** command. Copy the **Residential -Full** assembly to two locations below the original, as shown in Figure 8–22.

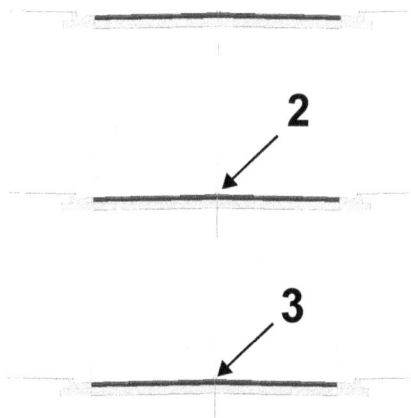

Figure 8–22

3. Select the second assembly baseline, right-click, and select **Assembly Properties**. In the *Information* tab, change the *Name* to **Residential - Half Curb LT,** and click **OK**.

4. Start the AutoCAD **Erase** command and erase the right **LaneSuperelevationAOR**, the right **UrbanCurbGutterGeneral**, and the right **LinkWidthAndSlope**.

5. Select the third assembly baseline, right-click, and select **Assembly Properties**. In the *Information* tab, change the *Name* to **Residential - Half Curb RT**, and click **OK**.

6. Start the AutoCAD **Erase** command and erase the left **LaneSuperelevationAOR**, the left **UrbanCurbGutterGeneral**, and the left **LinkWidthAndSlope**, as shown in Figure 8–23.

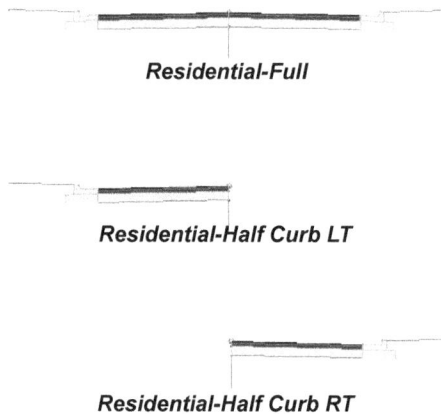

Residential-Full

Residential-Half Curb LT

Residential-Half Curb RT
Figure 8–23

Task 2 - Create a Curb Return assembly.

To include the intersection in the corridor model, you need another assembly to go around the curb returns. This assembly will have the assembly baseline at the edge of pavement or flange of the curb and gutter. It is important to create the assembly with the lane inserted first for the **Intersection** tool to be able to set the correct transitions at the centerline.

1. Continue working with the drawing from the previous task if you completed creating all of the subassemblies or open **COR1-B2-Corridor.dwg**.

Open the Tool Palettes

by clicking 🔲 *in the View tab> Palettes panel, if it is not already open.*

2. In the *Home* tab>Create Design panel, expand **Assembly** and select **Create Assembly**.

3. In the Create Assembly dialog box, name the new assembly **Residential-Curb Return**. Leave the other settings at their defaults, and click **OK**. Click in the drawing to place the new assembly.

4. In the Lanes Tool Palette, select the **LaneSuperelevationAOR** subassembly to add it to your assembly. Confirm that the following are set:
   - *Side:* **Left**
   - *Width*: **14.75'**
   - *Slope*: **+2%**.
   - To add the Left lane subassembly, select the assembly baseline object.

5. In the Curbs tool palette, select the **UrbanCurbGutterGeneral** subassembly to add it to your assembly.

6. Confirm that the following are set:
   - *Side*: **Right**
   - *Dimensions B*: **24"**
   - Select the assembly baseline to add the curb and gutter, as shown in Figure 8–24.

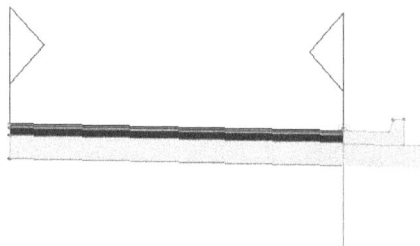

Figure 8–24

You will now create a subassembly that links the back of curb to the property line.

7. In the Subassemblies Tool Palette, select the *Generic* tab, and select the **LinkWidthAndSlope** subassembly. In the Advanced Properties, set the following:
   - *Side*: **Right**
   - *Width*: **7'**
   - Insert the subassembly at the end of the **UrbanCurbGutterGeneral** subassembly, as shown in Figure 8–25.

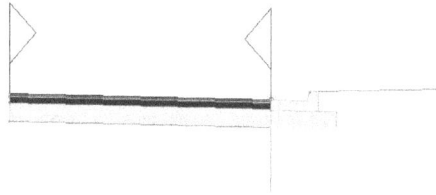

Figure 8–25

8. Press <Esc> to exit the subassembly command and save the drawing.

8.3 Creating a Corridor

A corridor is a 3D model of a proposed design based on
alignments or feature lines, profiles, and assemblies. Corridors
can be used to create terrain models (such as a finished ground
terrain model) and generate section data. Corridors display as
complex drawing objects consisting of individual cross-sections,
feature lines that connect marker points (locations where point
codes are assigned), and other related data, as shown in
Figure 8–26.

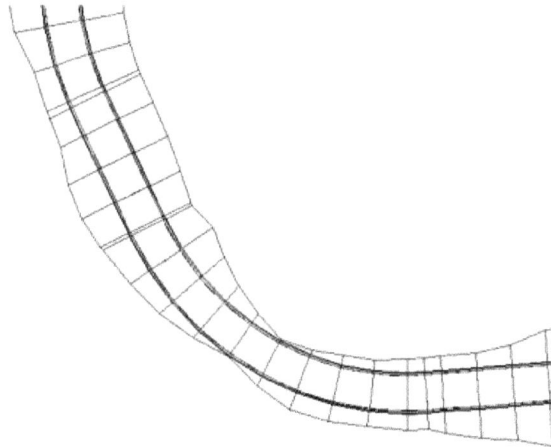

Figure 8–26

Corridors can be used to represent an individual alignment,
profile, feature line and assembly (such as for a single road) or
can contain multiples of each. When modeling intersections, it is
often easiest to have all intersecting roads as part of the same
corridor object. However, it might not be practical to include all of
the proposed roads in a single corridor on large projects. You
can have any number of corridors present in the same drawing
file.

To create a corridor, click 🏗 (Corridor) in the *Home* tab>Create Design panel. A dialog box opens in which you can enter a description, corridor style, layer, alignment or feature line, profile, assembly, and target surface, as shown on the left in Figure 8–27. It also has an option that enables you to set the baseline and region parameters. By selecting this, when you click **OK** a second dialog box opens as shown on the right of Figure 8–27.

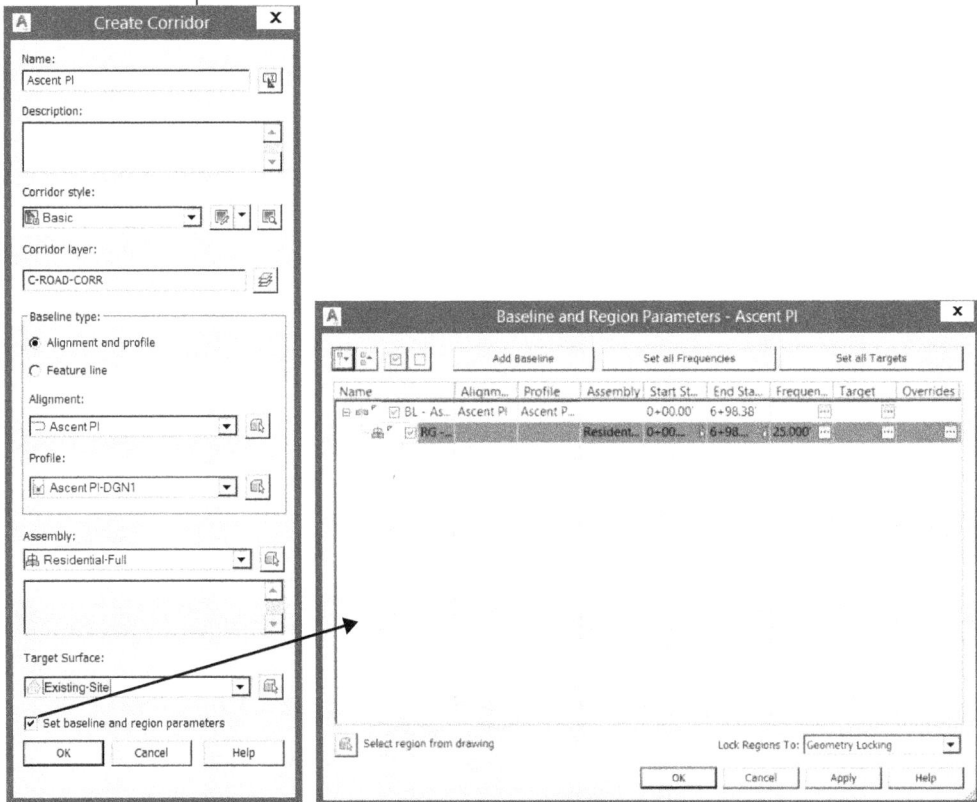

Figure 8–27

Target Mapping

Target Mapping is where you assign a surface to which daylight subassemblies are graded or alignments, feature lines, and polylines that cause lanes and other subassemblies to stretch.

Many stock subassemblies include transitional components, such as the lanes you added to the 2 Lane Road assembly. These lanes can have their outside edge-of-travelway (ETW) controlled by other alignments, feature lines, survey figures, and 3D polylines as required, which can be used to specify widening and contraction of the lanes. These lanes also include profile controls at the ETW points. These types of controls are all assigned using Target Mapping.

In the Target Mapping dialog box (shown in Figure 8–28), the subassembly name and assembly groups are listed. Giving these items logical names is important. Otherwise, it would be difficult to tell them apart in this dialog box.

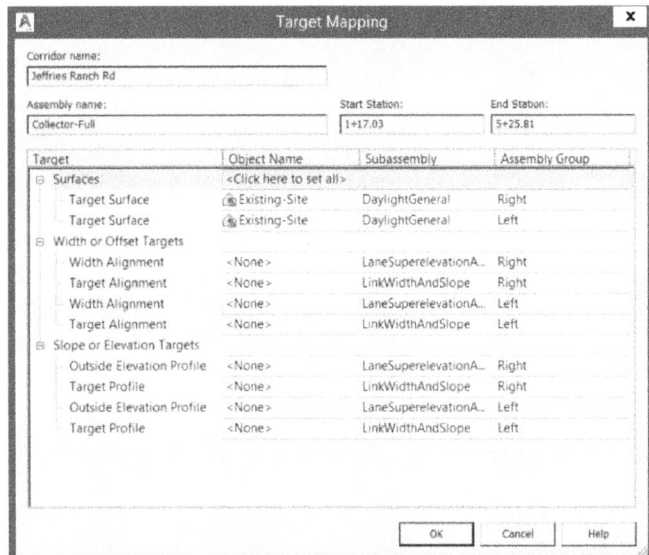

Figure 8–28

Corridor Frequency

The corridor frequency determines how often assemblies are applied to the corridor model, as shown in Figure 8–29. The frequency can be set for tangents separate from curves to provide more control over the model's size and accuracy. The more frequently the assembly is applied to the corridor model, the more accurate the model. A higher frequency also causes the model to require more computer resources, as it increases the size of the model. It is important to set the frequency at a level that balances the level of required accuracy with a reasonably sized corridor model.

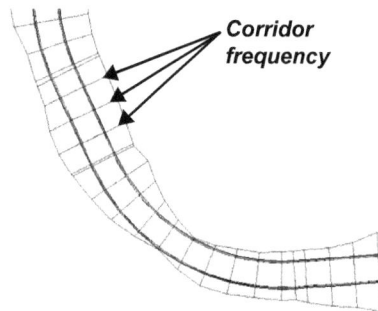

Corridor frequency

Figure 8–29

Frequency locations for curved baselines can be set **By curvature**, or **At an increment**, as shown in Figure 8–30. If the **At an increment** option is selected, assemblies are applied at a specified number of units along the curve. If the **By curvature** option is selected, the radius of the curve determines how frequently the assemblies are applied to the corridor model.

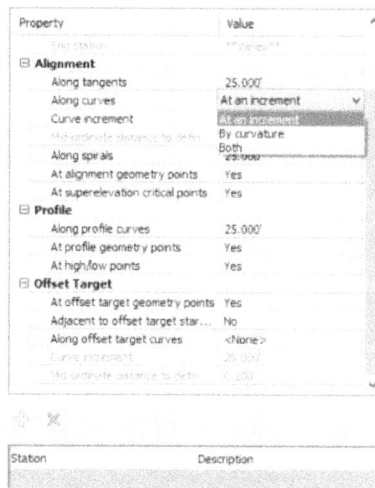

Figure 8–30

8.4 Corridor Properties

Once created, corridors are adjusted in the Corridor Properties dialog box.

Information Tab

The *Information* tab enables you to name the corridor (recommended), add a description, and select a corridor style.

Parameters Tab

The *Parameters* tab enables you to review and adjust corridor parameters, including which alignments, profiles, and assemblies are being used. Each unique road center line is listed here as a *baseline*. In each baseline there is at least one *region*. Each region is an area over which a specific assembly is applied. You can have multiple baselines and multiple regions in the same baseline as required. The *Parameters* tab is shown in Figure 8–31.

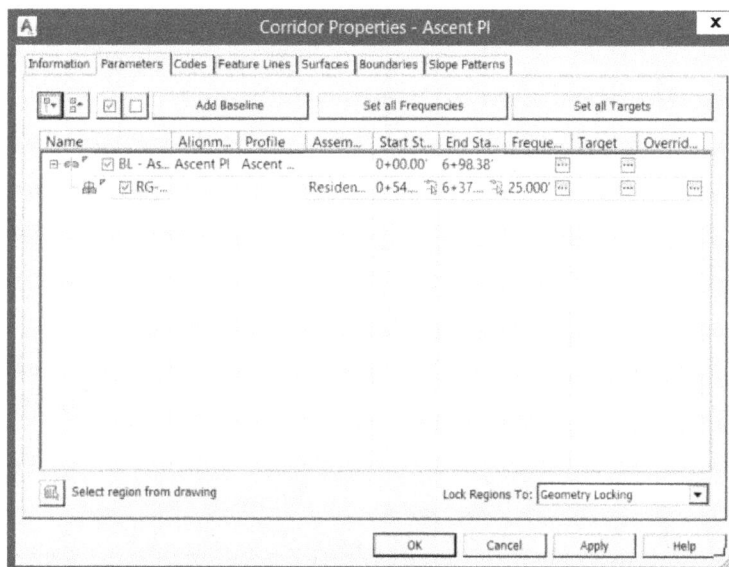

Figure 8–31

Each region has controls that enable you to review the Target Mapping, and the *Frequency* at which corridor sections should be created. If the corridor has had overrides applied using the Corridor Section Editor (select the corridor, *Corridor* tab> Modify panel), then those can be reviewed here as well.

At the top of the dialog box are two important icons: **Set all Frequencies** and **Set all Targets**. These can be used to assign frequencies and targets to all corridor regions. Otherwise, these properties can be adjusted for individual regions using ⬛ (Ellipsis), which is available in the *Frequency* and *Targets* columns.

Codes

The *Codes* tab lists all of the codes that are available in the corridor based on the subassemblies in the assembly, as shown in Figure 8–32. These codes are available for section labels and quantity take-off.

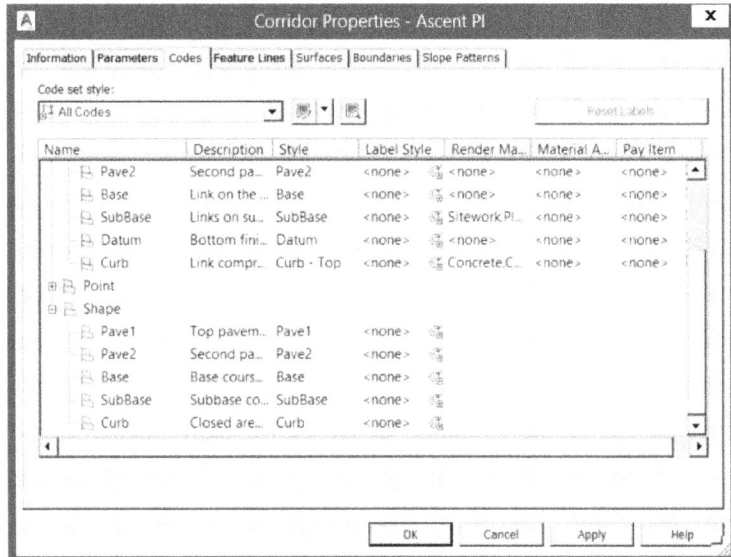

Figure 8–32

Feature Lines

Feature lines are named 3D linework that connect marker points (locations assigned point codes) in your assemblies, as shown in Figure 8–33. From any feature line listed in the *Feature Lines* tab, you can export a polyline or feature line (such as for grading purposes).

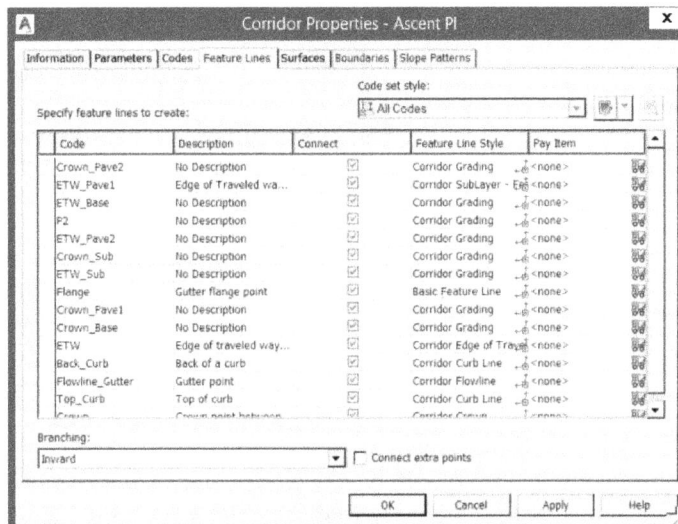

Figure 8–33

Slope Patterns

Slope patterns can be used to indicate whether an area of side slope is a cut or fill. The *Slope Patterns* tab is shown in Figure 8–34.

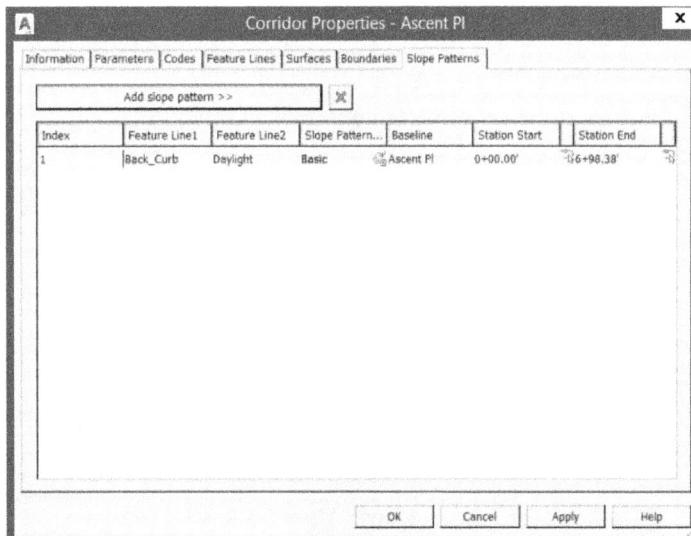

Figure 8–34

Practice 8c

Estimated time for completion: 15 minutes

Working with Corridors - Part I

Practice Objective

- Create a corridor model using previously created alignments, profiles, and assemblies.

Task 1 - Create a corridor with regions.

In this practice, you will use the assemblies to create a corridor for both Jeffries Ranch Rd and Ascent Pl. You will also learn how to split a region.

1. Continue working with the drawing from the previous practice or open **COR1-C1-Corridor.dwg** from the *C:\Civil 3D Projects\Civil3D-Training\Corridors* folder.

2. In the *Home* tab>Create Design panel, click 🖾 (Corridor). Enter the following:

   - Name it **Jeffries Ranch Rd**
   - For the alignment, select **Jeffries Ranch Rd**
   - For the profile, select **Jeffries Ranch Rd-DGN1**
   - For the subassembly, select **Collector-Full**
   - Verify that the **Set baseline and region parameters** option is selected, as shown in Figure 8–35.

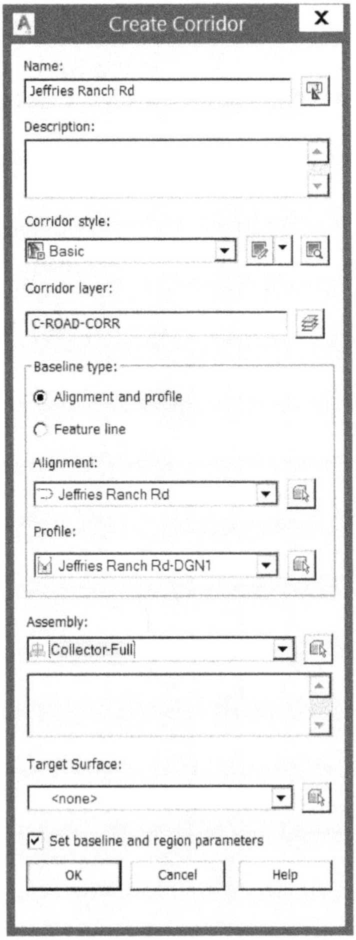

Figure 8–35

3. Click **OK**. The baseline and region parameters dialog box should open.

In this practice, you will create Jeffries Ranch Road and Ascent Pl as two independent corridors. Note that this will also create two separate surfaces. As you will be creating an intersection in the Jeffries Ranch Rd, you need to create two regions: one before the intersection, and one after the intersection.

4. The dialog box identifies the Baseline (BL) as *BL-Jeffries Ranch Rd - (1)*. This baseline currently has one Region (RG). In the Baseline and Region Parameters dialog box, set the following options, as shown in Figure 8–36:

- Change the region name to **RG-Before Intersection**.
- Adjust the start station to **117.03'**.
- Right-click on RG-Before Intersection and select **Split Region**.

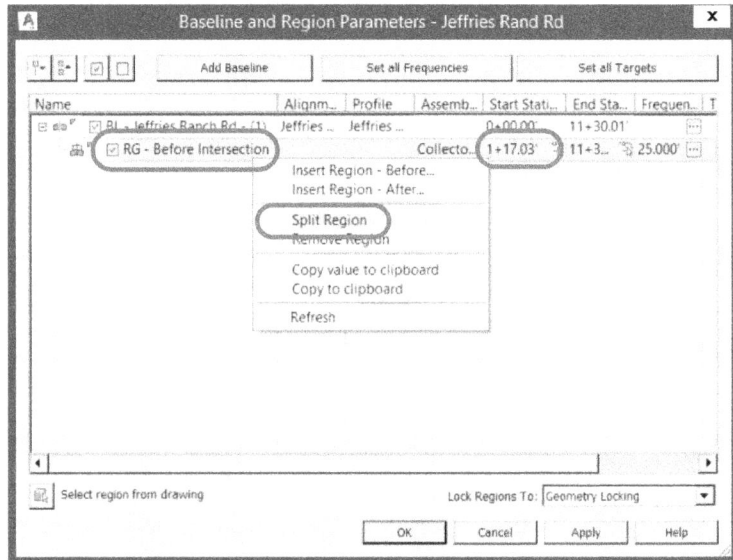

Figure 8–36

5. You now need to enter the start and end stations for the regions. You have already typed **117.03'** for the start station for the **RG-Before Intersection**. Enter the following values, as shown in Figure 8–37.

- RG-Before Intersection End station: **525.81'**
- RG-After Intersection Start station: **630.74'**
- RG-After Intersection End station: **1035.92'**
- Press <Enter> to return to the Baseline and Region dialog box.

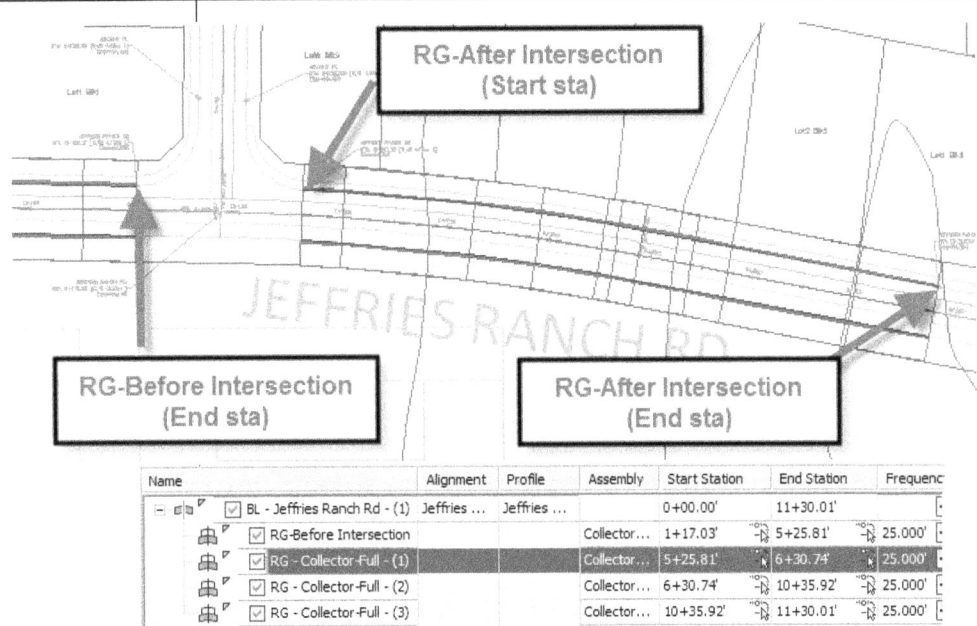

Figure 8–37

6. In the Baseline and Region Parameters dialog box, right-click on RG - Collector-Full - (1) and select **Remove Region**. Do the same for RG - Collector-Full - (3).

7. Click **OK** to apply the changes and close the dialog box. If prompted, rebuild the corridor.

8. Save the drawing.

Task 2 - Create a corridor.

In this task, you will use the assemblies to create a corridor, applying the **Residential-Full** subassembly from station to station.The steps to accomplish this are similar to those in Task 1. If you have time, you can complete this task, otherwise skip this task and open the backup drawing when instructed to do so in the next practice.

1. Continue working with the drawing from the previous task or open **COR1-C2-Corridor.dwg**.

2. In the *Home* tab>Create Design panel, click (Corridor).

3. Name it **Ascent PI**, then enter the following, as shown in Figure 8–38:

- For the alignment, select **Ascent PI** from the list
- For the profile, select **Ascent PI-DGN1** from the list
- For the subassembly, select **Residential-Full**
- Verify that the **Set baseline and region parameters** option is selected.

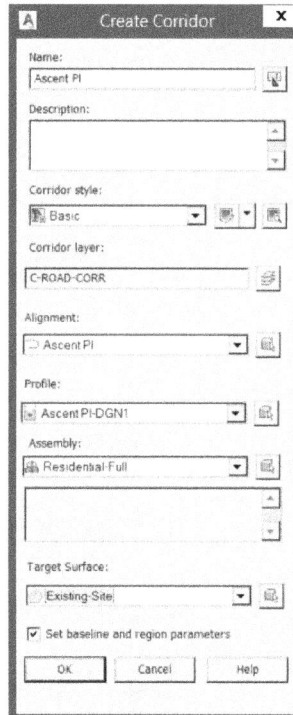

Figure 8–38

4. Click **OK**. The Baseline and Region Parameters dialog box opens.

5. The dialog box identifies the Baseline (BL) as *BL-Ascent Pl*. This baseline currently has one Region, which is assigned the **Residential - Full Assembly**. Set the following options, as shown in Figure 8–39:

   - Rename the region to **RG – Start**.
   - Adjust the *Start Station* to **54.13'**
   - Adjust the *End Station* to **265.48'**.
   - Click **OK** to create the corridor. If prompted, rebuild the corridor.

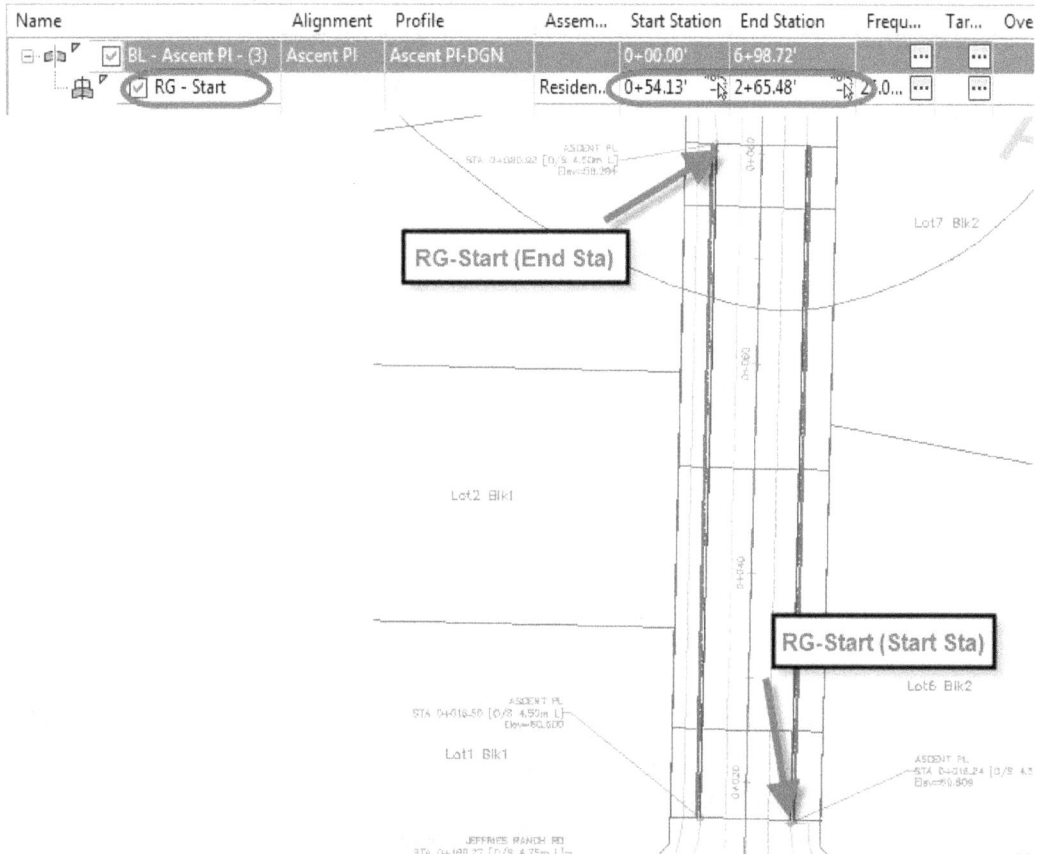

Name	Alignment	Profile	Assem...	Start Station	End Station	Frequ...	Tar...	Ove
⊟ ⊡ ☑ BL - Ascent Pl - (3)	Ascent Pl	Ascent Pl-DGN		0+00.00'	6+98.72'		...	...
☑ RG - Start			Residen..	0+54.13'	2+65.48'	25.0...	...	...

Figure 8–39

6. Save the drawing.

8.5 Designing Intersections

Intersection objects are complex corridor models that automatically create offset and curb return geometry where two intersecting alignments meet. As changes are made to the underlying information (alignments, profiles, assemblies, and surfaces) the intersection geometry is automatically updated. There are four types of Intersection objects, as shown in Figure 8–40. This training guide only covers the standard intersection.

Figure 8–40

To create an intersection, select the *Home* tab>Create Design panel and click (Create Intersection). You are prompted to pick the intersection of two roads. The Create Intersection Wizard then opens.

General Tab

The *General* tab enables you to name the intersection (recommended), add a description, and select intersection marker and label styles.

An important element on this tab is the intersection corridor type. You can keep the primary road crown maintained or have all road crowns maintained, as shown in Figure 8–41. If you only maintain the crown of the primary road, the secondary road's profile is adjusted automatically.

*Note: The intersection corridor type cannot be changed once you click **Create Intersection** and exit the Create Intersection Wizard.*

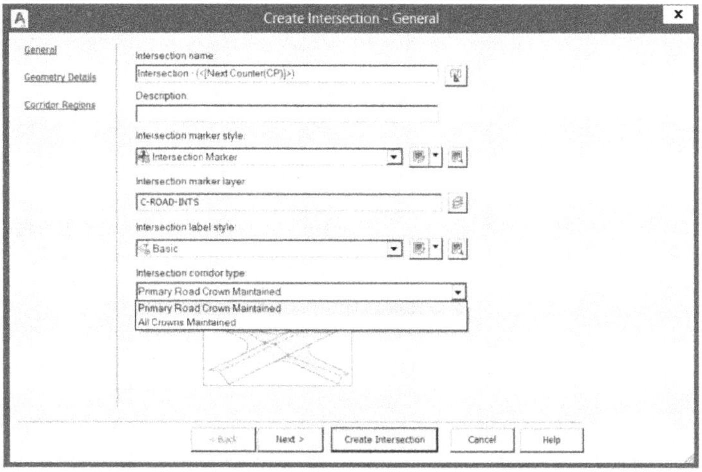

Figure 8–41

Geometry Details Tab

The *Geometry Details* tab enables you to set the road that is going to be the primary road, as shown in Figure 8–42. It is also where you set the **Offset** and **Curb Return** parameters, which include parameters for both alignments and profiles.

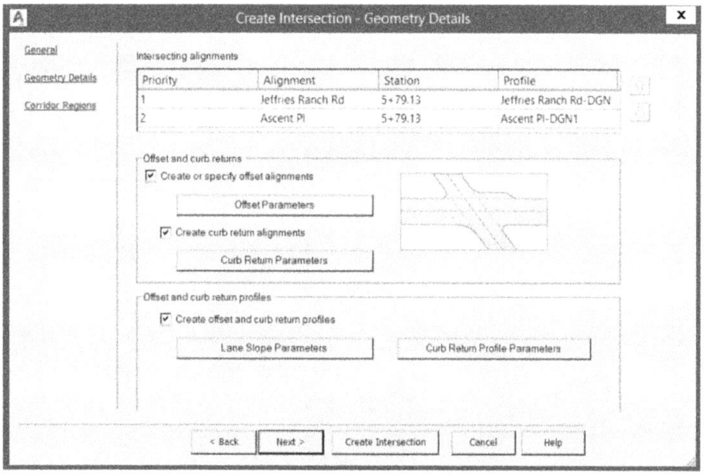

Figure 8–42

Corridor Regions Tab

The *Corridor Regions* tab enables you to create a new corridor or add the intersection corridor to an existing corridor, as shown in Figure 8–43.

This is also where you select the assemblies to use in each of the corridor regions. Some assembly sets ship with the AutoCAD Civil 3D software and can be located by clicking **Browse**. By default, a Metric or Imperial assembly set displays various assemblies that are set in the window.

Click ⊡ for each Corridor Region Section Type and select the appropriate assembly, as required. As you select a region, the wizard highlights that region in the preview at the bottom of the window. If you select any assemblies that use daylight subassemblies, do not forget to set the target surface at the top right.

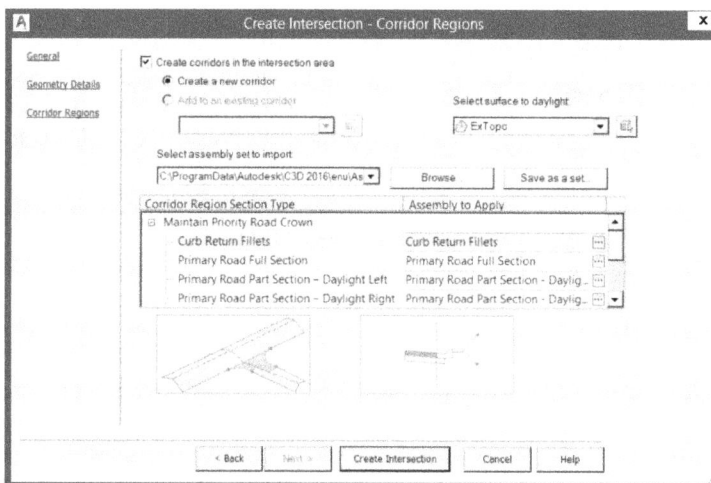

Figure 8–43

Once all of the parameters have been set, you can click **Create Intersection** to create the intersection object.

Practice 8d

Estimated time for completion: 25 minutes

Working with Corridors - Part II

Practice Objective

- Create an intersection object to represent how two roads should meet.

Task 1 - Create an intersection.

In this task, you will create an intersection at Jeffries Ranch Rd and Ascent Pl. This intersection will fill in the gap you left in the Jeffries Ranch Rd corridor by setting regions.

1. Open **COR1-D1-Corridor.dwg** from the *C:\Civil 3D Projects\Civil3D-Training\Corridors* folder.

2. In the *View* tab>Views panel, select the preset view **Corr-Inter**.

3. In the *Home* tab>Create Design panel, click ⊹ (Create Intersection).

4. The AutoCAD Civil 3D software sets an **Intersection** object snap and prompts you to *Select Intersection Point*. Select the intersection of the Jeffries Ranch Rd and Ascent Pl alignments, as shown in Figure 8–44.

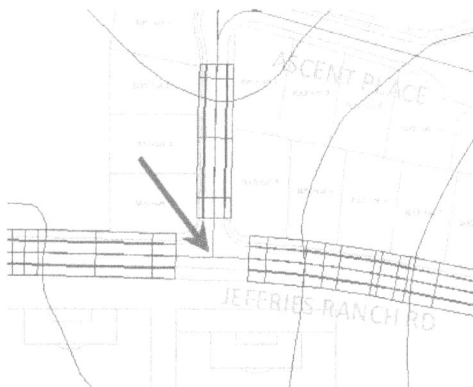

Figure 8–44

Note: If you are having problems selecting the intersection point, press <Esc> to exit the **Intersection** command. In Model Space, select the two alignments **Jeffries Ranch Rd** and **Ascent Pl**, right-click, expand *Display order* and select **Bring to front**. Then create the intersection.

If this were a four-way intersection, you would be prompted to select the Primary road. In this case, the AutoCAD Civil 3D software assumes that Jeffries Ranch Rd is the primary road.

5. Position the Create Intersection wizard so that the intersection is also displayed in the drawing.

6. In the *General* page, set the following options, as shown in Figure 8–45:

   - *Intersection Name:* Type **Intersection–(Jeffries Ranch & Ascent Pl)**.

   - Accept the default *Intersection Marker Style* and *Intersection Label Style* settings.

   - *Intersection Corridor Type:* Select **Primary Road Crown Maintained**.

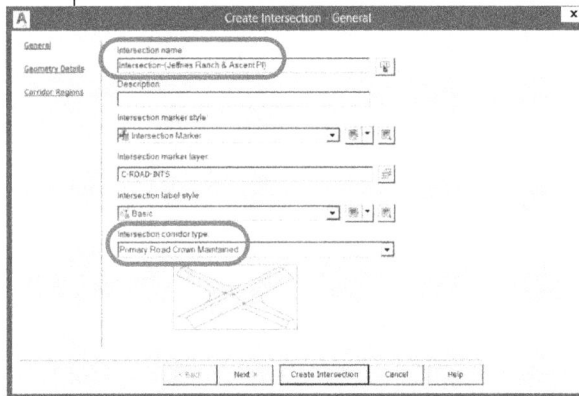

Figure 8–45

7. Click **Next>**.

8. In the *Geometry Details* page, the alignments, intersection stations, and profiles to be used are listed. The profile can be changed here as required. In the *Offset and curb returns* area, select the **Create or specify offset alignments** option and click **Offset Parameters**, as shown in Figure 8–46.

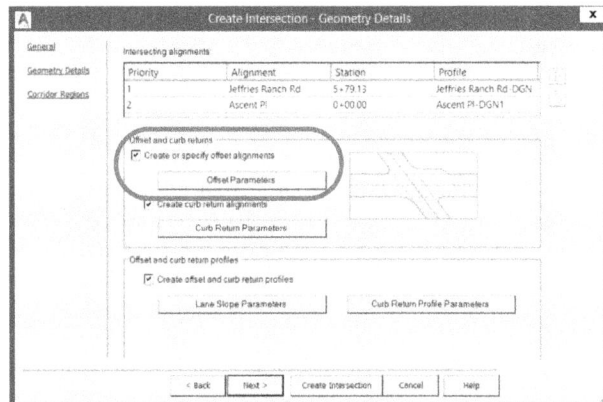

Figure 8–46

In the Intersection Offset Parameters dialog box, note that selecting the **Primary Road** or **Secondary Road** highlights the respective alignment in the drawing.

9. For this project, set the following options:

    • Set the offset parameters for the Primary Road, Jeffries Ranch Rd to **15.5'** for the right and left sides.

Because this is a simple intersection, you do not need to add additional offsets.

    • For the Secondary Road, Ascent Pl, set the offset parameters to **14.75'** for the right and left sides.

Review and click OK.

10. In the *Geometry Details* page, select the **Create curb return alignments** option and click **Curb Return Parameters**.

11. In the Intersection Curb Return Parameters dialog box, note the preview for the **NE-Quadrant** in the drawing. Set the *Curb Return Radius* to **38.55'**, as shown in Figure 8–47, and accept the remaining default values. Note the preview as you make the edits.

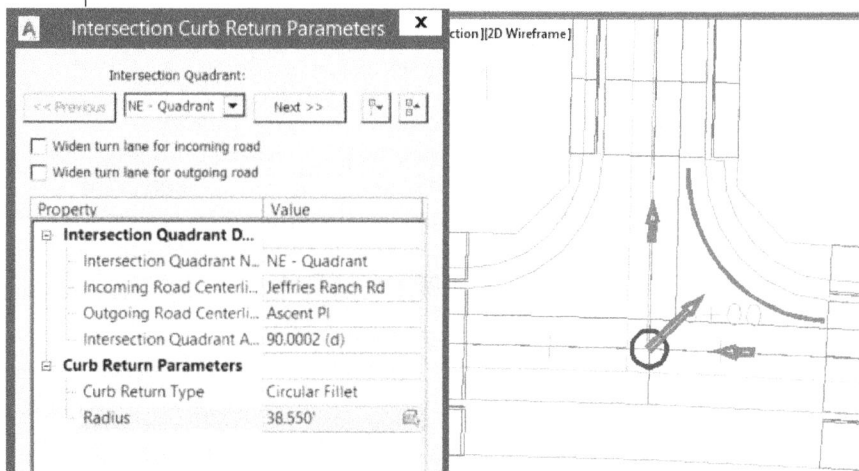

Figure 8–47

12. Click **Next>>** at the top of the dialog box to switch to the **NW-Quadrant**. Note the change in the drawing. Set the *Curb Return Radius* to **38.55'**, as shown in Figure 8–48, and accept the remaining default values. Click **OK** to return to the *Geometry Details* page.

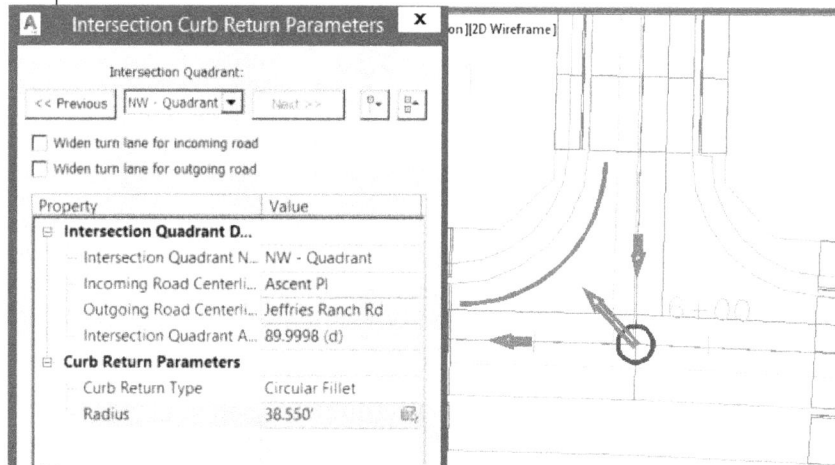

Figure 8–48

13. To automatically create curb return profiles, in the *Offset and curb return profiles* area, select the **Create offset and curb return profiles** option as shown in Figure 8–49. Accept the defaults for the **Lane Slope** and **Curb Return Profile** parameters and click **Next>**.

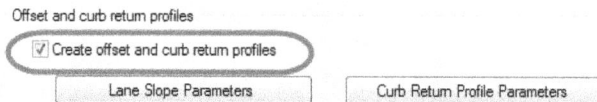

Figure 8–49

14. In the *Corridor Regions* page, you can create a new corridor or add this intersection to an existing corridor. Select the **Create corridors in the intersection area** option and select the **Create a new corridor** option, as shown in Figure 8–50.

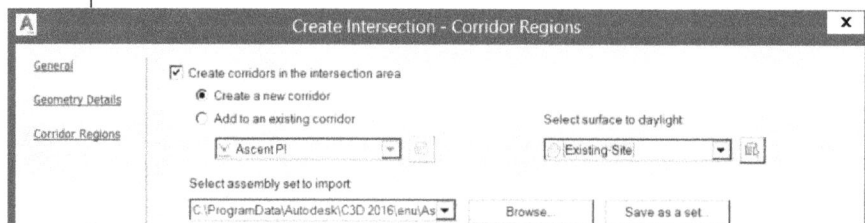

Figure 8–50

15. For the Curb Return Fillets, click on 🔳 and select the **Residential – Curb Return** assembly, as shown in Figure 8–51. Click **OK**.

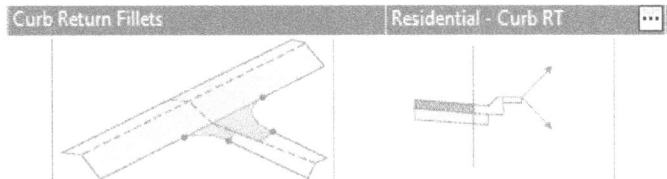

Figure 8–51

16. For the Primary Road Full Section, select the **Collector - Full** assembly, as shown in Figure 8–52.

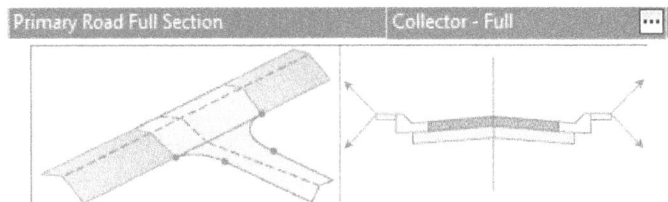

Figure 8–52

17. For the Primary Road Part Section – Daylight Left, accept the default value as shown in Figure 8–53, as this is not applicable to your intersection.

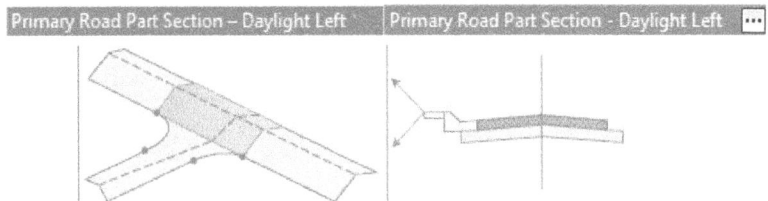

Figure 8–53

18. For the Primary Road Part Section – Daylight Right, select the **Collector – Part Curb RT** assembly, as shown in Figure 8–54.

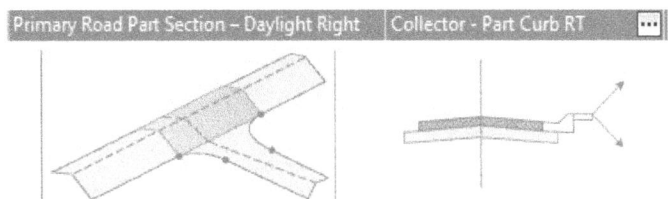

Figure 8–54

19. For the Secondary Road Full Section, select the **Residential – Full** assembly, as shown in Figure 8–55.

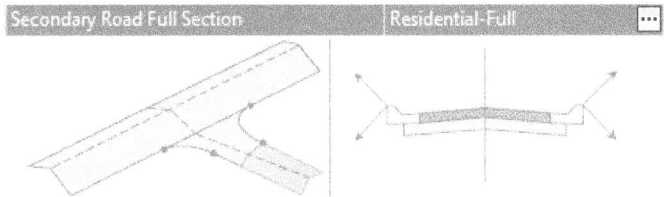

Figure 8–55

20. For the Secondary Road Half Section – Daylight Left, select the **Residential - Half Curb LT** assembly, as shown in Figure 8–56.

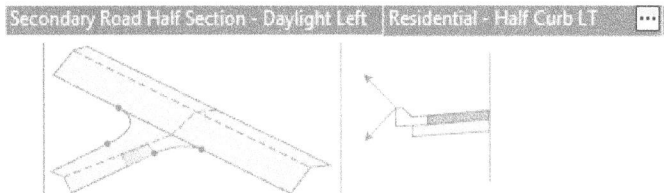

Figure 8–56

21. For the Secondary Road Half Section – Daylight Right, select the **Residential - Half Curb RT** assembly, as shown in Figure 8–57.

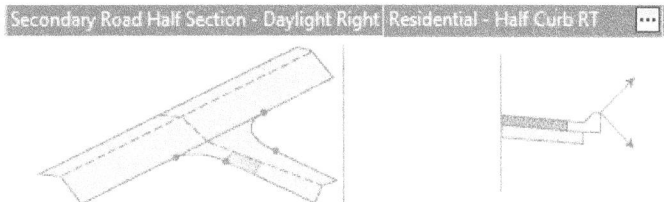

Figure 8–57

22. When finished, click **Create Intersection**. You might need to perform a **REGEN** to display the newly created Intersection Corridor.

23. In the Events Viewer, expand **Action**, and select **Clear All Events**, as shown in Figure 8–58. Click the **X** to close the Events Viewer.

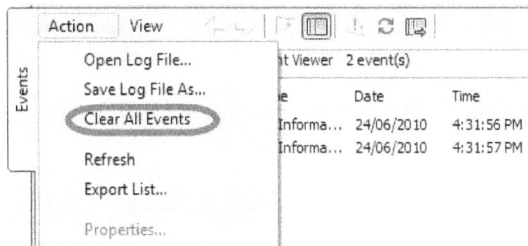

Figure 8–58

24. Save the drawing.

8.6 Corridor Surfaces

The *Surfaces* tab in the Corridor Properties dialog box enables you to build the proposed surfaces based on corridor geometry. You can create these surfaces from corridor links, and/or from feature lines based on marker points (point codes). As the corridor changes, its surfaces automatically update.

The two most common types of corridor surfaces are Top and Datum surfaces.

- **Top surfaces:** Follow the uppermost geometry of the corridor. These are useful for many purposes, such as in the display of finished ground contours and as a way of determining rim elevations of proposed utility structures.

- **Datum surfaces:** Generally follow the bottommost corridor geometry. These can be used in both Surface-to-Surface volume calculations and Section-based Earthworks calculations to determine site cut and fill totals (when compared to existing ground).

- **Corridor surfaces:** As with all AutoCAD Civil 3D surfaces, these cannot contain vertical elements. Include slight offsets so that vertical curbing and similar geometry are not absolutely vertical.

Overhang Correction

In some configurations, AutoCAD Civil 3D assemblies might have top or datum points, or links in locations that might lead to incorrect surfaces, such as the datum surface represented by the heavy line in Figure 8–59.

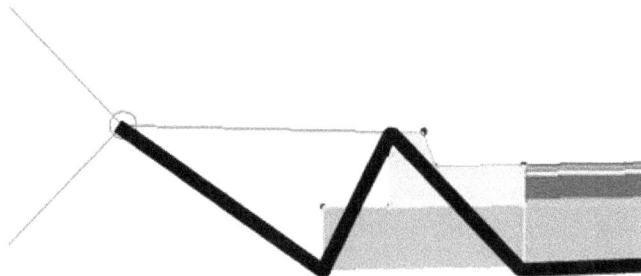

Figure 8–59

In these cases, the **Overhang Correction** option forces these surfaces to follow either the top or bottom of the corridor geometry, as shown in Figure 8–60. This setting is typically only required for datum surfaces.

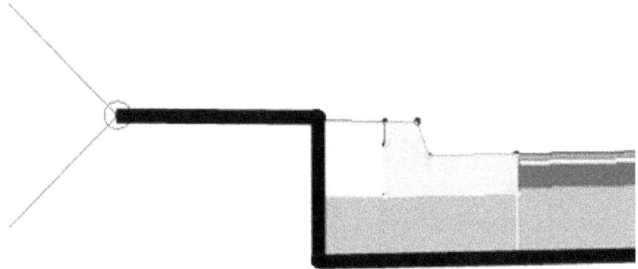

Figure 8–60

Surface Boundaries

Corridor surfaces, as with all AutoCAD Civil 3D surfaces, often benefit from a boundary to remove unwanted interpolation between points. The *Boundaries* tab in the Corridor Surfaces dialog box enables you to add these boundaries in a number of ways: by selecting a closed polyline or by interactively tracing the boundary using a jig.

The best option is often to *automatically* add a boundary that follows the daylight feature lines on both sides. This can be done using the new **Create Boundary from Corridor Extents** command.

8.7 Corridor Section Review and Edit

Creating complex corridors can be greatly simplified using

(Corridor Section Editor). It is accessed through the shortcut menu or contextual ribbon after selecting a corridor, as shown in Figure 8–61.

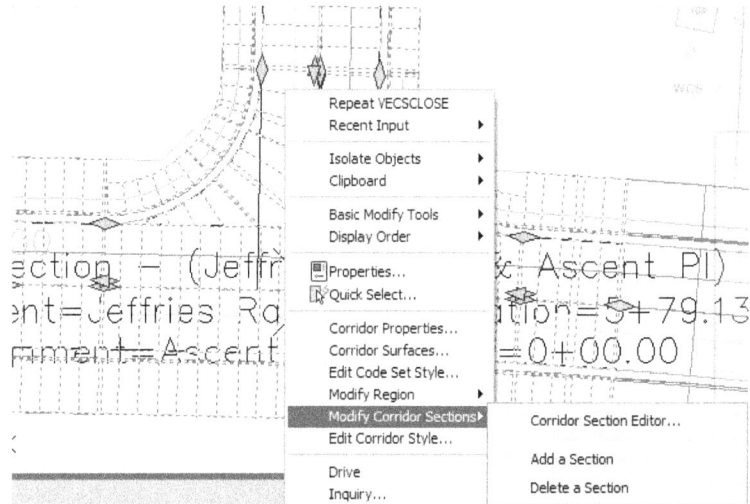

Figure 8–61

This command launches the *Section Editor* contextual tab, which enables you to review and edit sections interactively using the appropriate panels. The **Parameter Editor**, as shown in Figure 8–62, enables you to review and change most subassembly parameters.

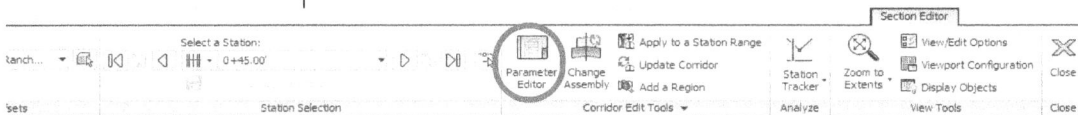

Figure 8–62

The editor enables you to modify those sections that need special attention, such as different daylight slopes. The editor also enables you to add and remove some subassemblies or links directly to and from a section. These parameter changes, additions, and deletions can be done for a single section or for a range of sections. An example is shown in Figure 8–63.

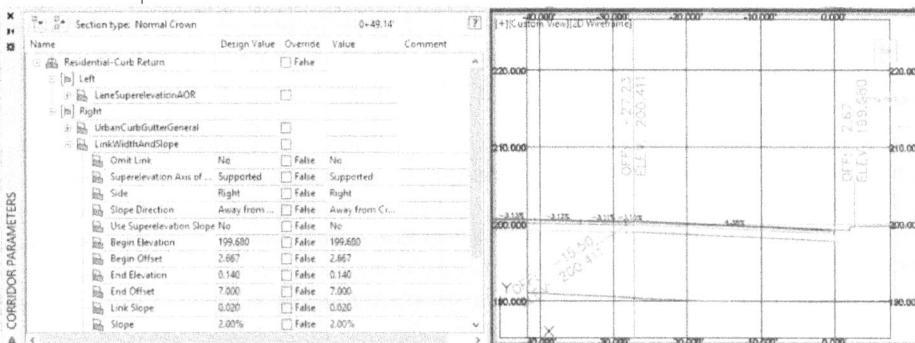

Figure 8–63

To more easily display the modifications in the corridor section, you can work in three different zoom modes in the **View/Edit Corridor Section** command:

- **Zoom To Extents:** Ensures that the full assembly is in view when you navigate to another station after zooming in.

- **Zoom to a Subassembly:** Ensures that a selected subassembly remains at the center of the view when you navigate to another station. The zoom level is also maintained.

- **Zoom to an Offset and Elevation:** Ensures that the current zoom level is maintained when you navigate to another station after a zoom.

Before launching the **Corridor Section Editor** command, you can set up multiple viewports using (Edit Viewport Configuration) for viewing the plan, profile, and section during the **Section Edit** command. Then, while in the **Corridor Section Editor** command, a Station Tracker indicates the current section (with a vertical line), in both the plan view and any associated profile views.

Practice 8e

Working with Corridors - Part III

Practice Objective

- Create a finished ground surface from the design corridor.

Estimated time for completion: 10 minutes

Task 1 - Create corridor surfaces.

1. Continue working with the drawing from the previous practice or open **COR1-E1-Corridor.dwg**.

2. In the AutoCAD Model Space window, select the **Ascent PI corridor** and click 🗀 (Corridor Properties) on the contextual *Corridor* tab > Modify Corridor panel.

3. In the *Surfaces* tab, do the following, as shown in Figure 8–64.

   - Click 🔲 (Create a Corridor Surface).
   - The surface displays in the dialog box with the default name **Ascent PL Surface - (1)**. Rename the surface to **Road 1** by clicking on the surface name.
   - The default surface style **Contours 2' and 10' (Design)** works well for this task, so leave it as the active surface style.
   - In the *Add Data* area, verify that the *Data type* is set to **Links** and the *code* is set to **Top**. Click ⊞ (Add Surface Item)

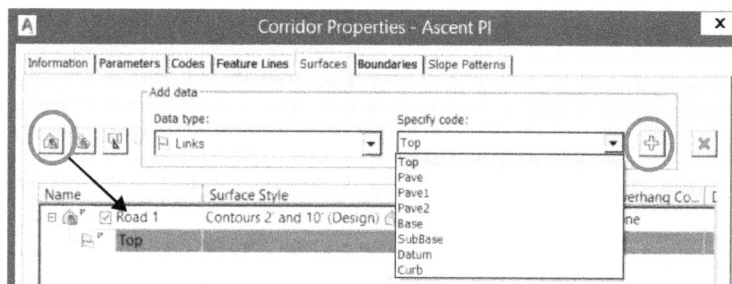

Figure 8–64

4. Select the *Boundaries* tab. Right-click on the corridor surface name and select **Corridor extents as outer boundary**, as shown in Figure 8–65.

This automatically adds a boundary that follows the corridor extents (in most cases, the daylight lines) on both sides.

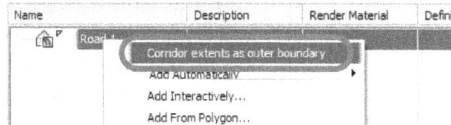

Name		Description	Render Material	Defini
🏠	Road	Corridor extents as outer boundary		
		Add Automatically	▶	
		Add Interactively...		
		Add From Polygon...		

Figure 8–65

5. Click **OK** to close the Corridor Properties dialog box. If prompted, select **Rebuild the Corridor**. The corridor surface has been created and displays using contours.

8.8 Corridor Visualization

Visualizing corridors in a 3D view can be very helpful to ensure that the true design intent has been followed. Displaying the corridor along with the existing ground surface around it also helps to ensure that there are good sight distances as you drive down the corridor. Unfortunately, if there is a large cut area, the existing ground surface might obstruct the corridor from view, as shown on the left of Figure 8–66.

In these cases, it might be necessary to create a hide boundary in the existing ground surface using the outer boundary of the corridor surface. Doing so cuts a hole in the existing ground surface only where the corridor surface resides, as shown on the right of Figure 8–66. In addition, the interior boundary is updated if the corridor changes.

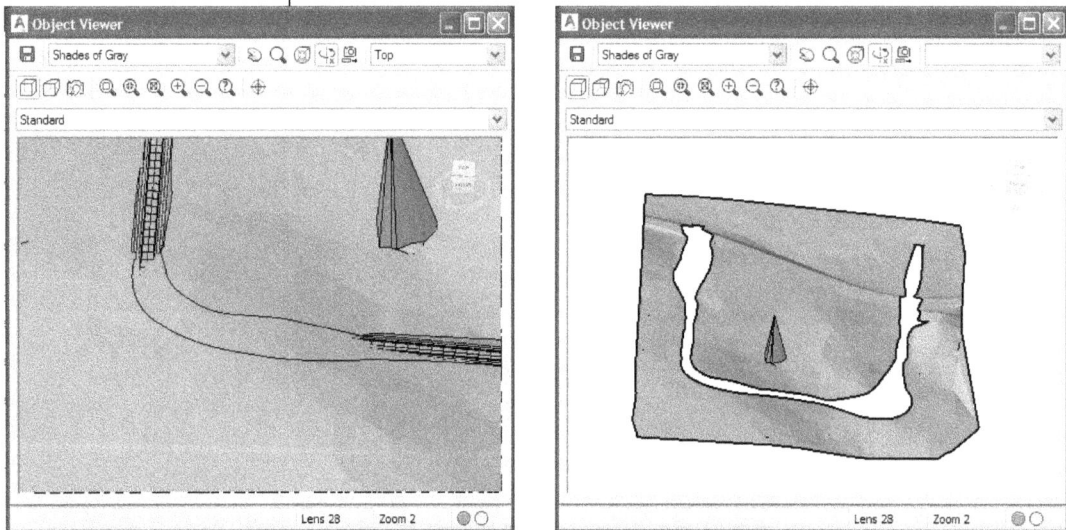

Figure 8–66

To make this work correctly, you need to copy the existing ground surface before adding the corridor surface as a hide boundary. This is because the corridor daylight lines reference the existing ground. If a hide boundary is then created from a surface that is referencing the surface into which it is being placed, a circular reference is created. To avoid this, create a new surface, paste the existing ground surface into it, and then create the hide boundary for the existing ground from the corridor surface. This ensures that the boundary is updated as the corridor changes without creating a circular reference.

Once the circular reference issue has been corrected, you can use ⊙ (Drive) in the *Alignment* tab>Analyze panel. You can then click ▷❙❙ (play/pause) in the *Drive* contextual tab to preview the finished design in relation to the existing ground surface as you drive down the corridor, as shown in Figure 8–67. While in the **Drive** command, you can change the drive path to another linear object if you have a network of road alignments, such as a subdivision, that you want to simulate driving through.

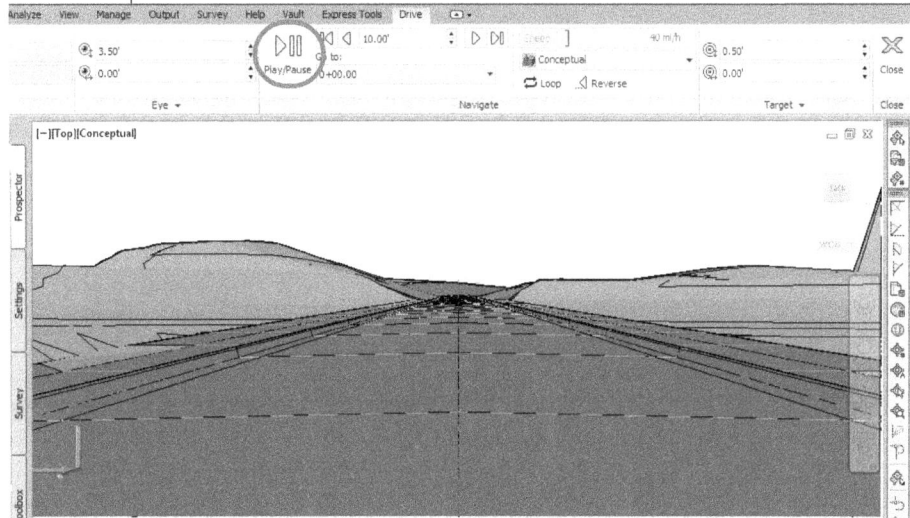

Figure 8–67

Line of Sight Analysis

The sight distances along a roadway can be calculated using the ⊙ (Sight Distance) command found on the contextual *Corridor* tab > Analysis panel. This enables you to ensure that the design meets the minimum sight distances at specified intervals along a corridor. You can set the minimum sight distance.

How To: Check Sight Distance Along a Roadway

1. On the contextual *Corridor* tab > Analyze panel, click ⊙ (Sight Distance).

2. In the Sight Distance Check dialog box, in the *General* tab, select the **Alignment** and **Profile** to analyze. Set the **From station, To station**, **Check interval**, and **Select surface to check against** fields, as shown in Figure 8–68. Click **Next>**.

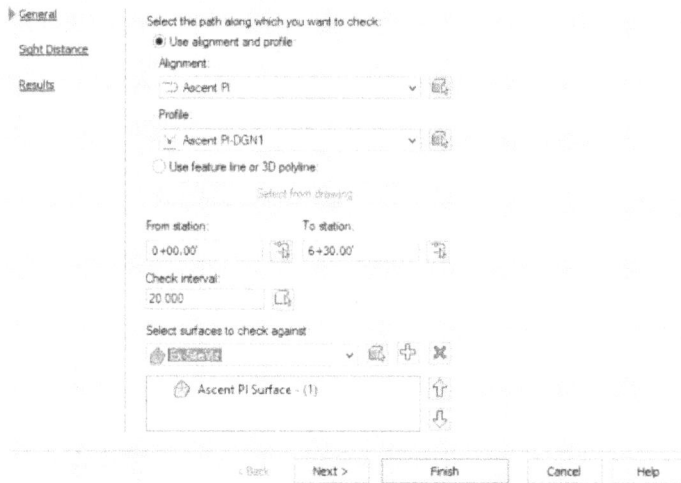

Figure 8–68

3. In the Sight Distance Check dialog box, in the *Sight Distance* tab, set the **Minimum sight distance**, **Eye height**, **Eye Offset**, **Target height**, and **Target offset**, as shown in Figure 8–69. Click **Next>**.

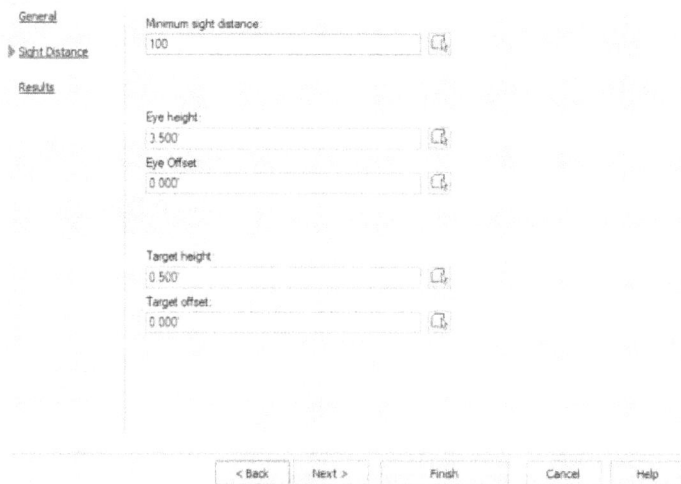

Figure 8–69

4. In the Sight Distance Check dialog box, in the *Results* tab, select the components to display in the model. Set the **Select hatch display for obstructed area** pattern, and select the file format and save location for the report, as shown in Figure 8–70. Click **Finish**.

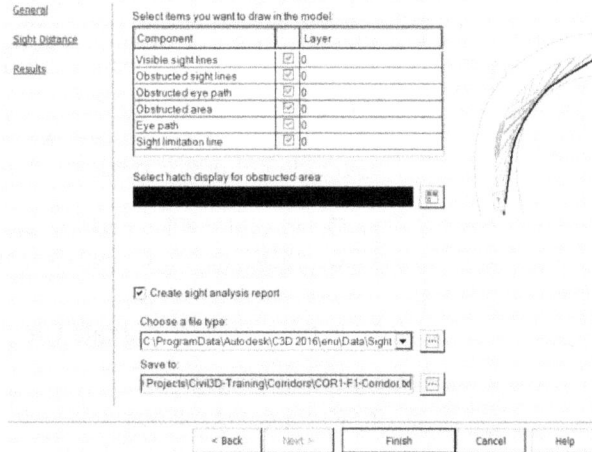

Figure 8–70

Practice 8f

Working with Corridors - Part IV

Practice Objective

Estimated time for completion: 10 minutes

- Display the corridor in 3D along with the existing ground surface to visualize what it is like to drive on the road.

Task 1 - Analyze the site visually using the Drive command.

In this task, you will create a copy of the corridor surface to avoid possible circular references when you use the corridor surface as a hide boundary inside the existing site surface.

1. Open **COR1-F1-Corridor.dwg** from the *C:\Civil 3D Projects\ Civil3D-Training\Corridors* folder.

2. In the *Home* tab>Create Ground Data panel, click ⌂ (Create Surface).

3. Proceed as follows:
   - Type **Ex-SiteViz** for the name.
   - For the description, type **Copy of the Existing Site for visualization purposes**
   - Select **Contours 2' and 10' (Background)** for the style.
   - Select **Sitework.Planting.Grass.Thick** for the render material.
   - Click **OK**.

4. In the Toolspace, *Prospector* tab, expand the definition of the new **Ex-SiteViz** surface. Right-click on Edits and select **Paste Surface**. Select **Exiting-Site** and click **OK**.

5. Right-click on Boundaries and select **Add**.

6. In the Add Boundaries dialog box, name it **AscentPI**, and select **Hide** in the list of boundary types. Verify that **Non-Destructive** is selected and click **OK**.

7. Type **S** for surface and select the **Ascent PI** corridor surface.

8. In the *Modify* tab, select **Alignments**. In the *Alignments* contextual tab, click 🔵 (Drive), and select **Ascent PI**. Press <Enter> to select a profile from the list. Select **Ascent PI-DGN1** and click **OK**.

9. In the *Drive* contextual tab, click ▷▯▯ (Play/Pause).

10. Click **X** to close the contextual *Drive* tab.

Task 2 - Analyze the sight distance.

In this task you will use the **Sight Distance** command to ensure that the design meets the minimum required sight distances.

1. Continue working in the same file from the last task, or open **COR1-F2-Corridor.dwg** from the *C:\Civil 3D Projects\ Civil3D-Training\Corridors* folder.

2. On the *Modify* tab>Design panel, click ▣ (Corridor).

3. On the contextual *Corridor* tab>Analyze panel, click ▣ (Sight Distance).

4. In the Sight Distance Check dialog box, in the *General* tab, (shown in Figure 8–71), proceed as follows:
   - In the *To station* field, type **630**
   - In the *Select surface to check against* field, select **Ex-SiteViz**.
   - Click **Next>**.

Figure 8–71

5. In the Sight Distance Check dialog box, in the *Sight Distance* tab, do the following, as shown in Figure 8–72:

- In the *Minimum sight distance* field, type **100**.
- Click **Next>**.

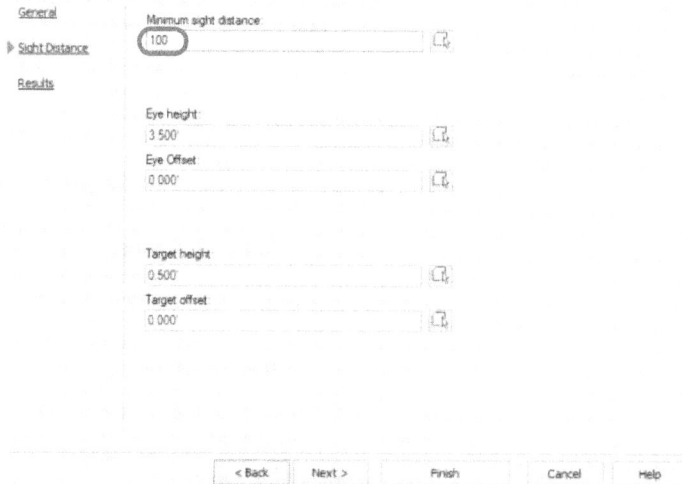

Figure 8–72

6. In the Sight Distance Check dialog box, in the *Results* tab, accept the default values, as shown in Figure 8–73. Click **Finish**.

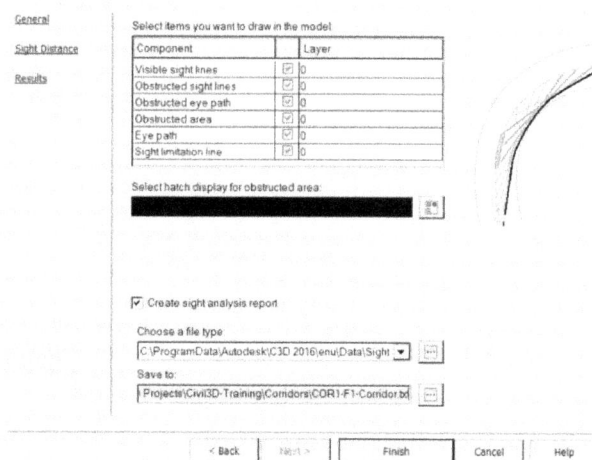

Figure 8–73

7. In the model, note that the obstruction lines go right to the property line of lot 7, as shown in Figure 8–74.

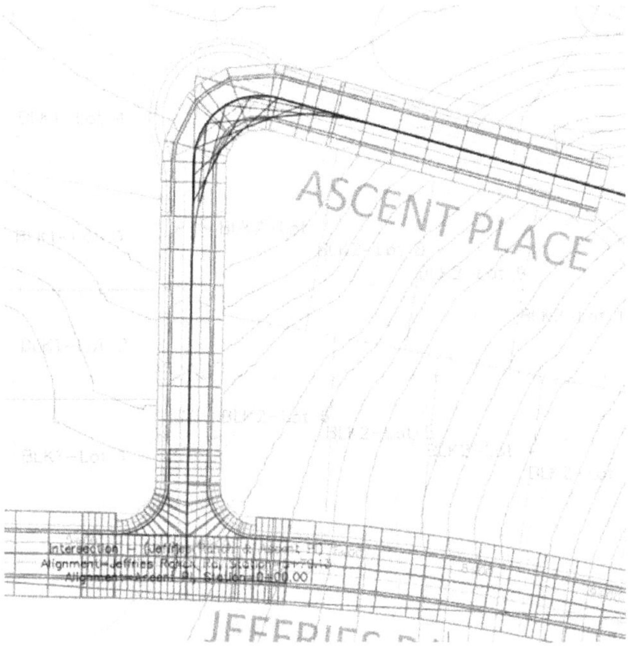

Figure 8–74

Chapter Review Questions

1. Where would you find subassemblies to attach to an assembly?

   a. Tool Palettes

   b. *Home* tab>Create Design panel

   c. *Modify* tab>Design panel

   d. *Insert* tab>Block panel

2. How do you change the width of a lane in the corridor model? (Select all that apply.)

   a. Advanced Properties

   b. Assembly Properties

   c. Subassembly Properties

   d. Corridor Properties

3. Which of the following items must you have before you can create a corridor model? (Select all that apply.)

   a. Assembly

   b. Profile

   c. Survey Database

   d. Alignment or feature line

4. Which tab in the Create Intersection Wizard do you use to set the Curb Return Parameters?

   a. General

   b. Corridor Regions

   c. Geometry Details

5. Where would you go to create a surface representing the finished ground of a corridor model?

   a. Toolspace, *Prospector* tab>*Surfaces* collection.

   b. *Home* tab>Create Ground Data panel.

   c. *Home* tab>Create Design panel.

   d. Corridor Properties

6. What does the Corridor Section Editor enable you to do?

    a. Review and edit each parameter of a subassembly.

    b. Adjust the existing ground grade at a specific station.

    c. Change the assembly being used at a specific station.

    d. Change the grid displayed behind a cross-section.

Command Summary

Button	Command	Location
	Assembly Properties	• **Contextual Ribbon:** *Assembly* tab> Modify Assembly panel • **Command Prompt:** editassemblyproperties
	Copy Subassembly	• **Contextual Ribbon:** *Assembly* tab> Modify Subassembly panel • **Command Prompt:** copysubassemblyto
	Corridor Properties	• **Contextual Ribbon:** *Corridor* tab> Modify Corridor panel • **Command Prompt:** editcorridorproperties
	Corridor Section Editor	• **Contextual Ribbon:** *Corridor* tab> Modify Corridor Sections panel • **Command Prompt:** vieweditcorridorsection
	Create Corridor	• **Ribbon:** *Home* tab>Create Design panel • **Command Prompt:** createcorridor
	Create Intersection	• **Ribbon:** *Home* tab>Create Design panel • **Command Prompt:** createintersection
	Mirror Subassembly	• **Contextual Ribbon:** *Assembly* tab> Modify Subassembly panel • **Command Prompt:** mirrorsubassembly
	Play/Pause Drive	• **Contextual Ribbon:** *Drive* tab> Navigate panel
	Select Similar Subassemblies	• **Contextual Ribbon:** *Assembly* tab> Modify Subassembly panel • **Command Prompt:** selectsimilarSA
	Sight Distance	• **Contextual Ribbon:** *Alignment* tab> Analyze panel • **Contextual Ribbon:** *Corridor* tab> Analyze panel • **Contextual Ribbon:** *Profile* tab> Analyze panel • **Command Prompt:** SightDistanceCheck
	Subassembly Properties	• **Contextual Ribbon:** *Assembly* tab> Modify Subassembly panel • **Command Prompt:** editsubassemblyproperties
	Tool Palettes	• **Ribbon:** *Home* tab>Palettes panel • **Command Prompt:** <Ctrl>+<3>

Grading

Nearly every civil engineering project requires grading the ground to create the correct slope and drainage. In this chapter you use feature lines and grading groups to create a finished ground surface. Then you attempt to balance the cut and fill quantities on the newly created surface.

Learning Objectives in this Chapter

- Create feature lines and grading objects to design the finish ground.
- Display the finish ground correctly by modify grading objects using styles, feature line labels, and grading criteria.

9.1 Grading Overview

AutoCAD® Civil 3D® grading uses objects called *feature lines* and *grading groups*.

- Feature lines are complex, linear 3D objects that define a string of known elevations, such as the perimeter of a proposed pond. Feature lines can be created by converting AutoCAD® lines, arcs, or polylines. Grading feature lines can also be exported from Corridors by selecting the *Modify* tab> Corridor panel and launching the **Feature Lines from Corridor** command.

- Parcel lines double as feature lines, and can be edited directly using the Feature Line Elevation Editor. Parcel lines in the extents of a grading group are also automatically added to the surface, even if they are at elevation 0. (You can avoid this by locating feature lines and parcels in separate sites.)

- The feature lines can be created from an alignment. They can also be dynamically linked to the alignment or corridor model from which they were created.

- The AutoCAD Civil 3D software can calculate the position of one feature line based on another, such as a pond bottom calculated at a specific slope and elevation below the perimeter. Distance, slope, and surface parameters used in solutions are assigned using *grading criteria*.

- *Grading groups* are collections of these solutions that form a contiguous whole, such as the detention pond shown in Figure 9–1.

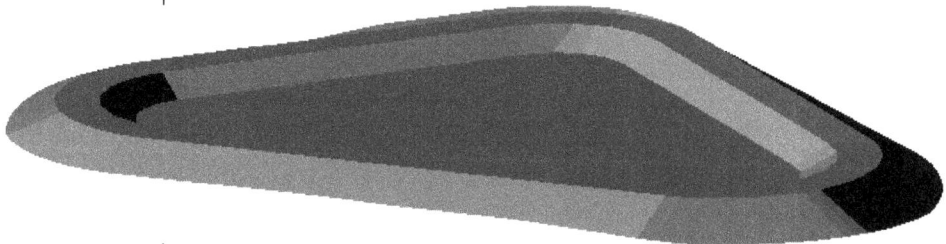

Figure 9–1

- Grading groups can be used to automatically generate AutoCAD Civil 3D surfaces. Tools are also available for calculating grading group volume, and adjusting grading groups to help balance cut and fill.

- Surfaces created from grading groups (as well as corridor surfaces) display in the Toolspace, *Prospector* tab and can be adjusted using normal surface editing tools, such as **Add** or **Delete Surface Point** or **Swap Edge**. These edits are maintained and dynamically reapplied if the grading group is modified.

- Feature lines and grading groups can be organized by site. Any feature lines added in the perimeter of a grading group, within the same site, are automatically added to the grading group.

- Feature lines can also be site-less. This provides more flexibility on how feature lines can be used and how they interact with each other.

- Feature lines can be used to create Corridor models.

9.2 Feature Lines

Feature Line Contextual Tab

The *Feature Line* contextual tab (shown in Figure 9–2), contains commands to edit and modify feature lines. These commands include tools to edit feature line elevations and feature line geometry, such as **Break**, **Trim**, **Extend**, and **Fillet** (which creates a true, 3D curve).

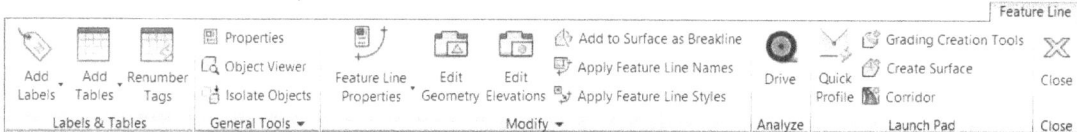

Figure 9–2

The **Create Feature Lines from Objects** command is available in the *Home* tab>Create Design panel, expanded **Feature Line** flyout, as shown in Figure 9–3.

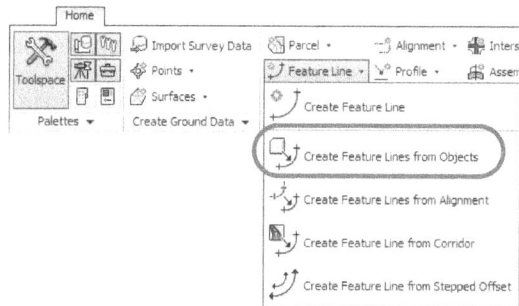

Figure 9–3

Elevation Editor

The Grading Elevation Editor vista (shown in Figure 9–4), enables you to add, modify, or vary the elevations of a feature line. The feature line data is organized into rows, where one row lists the data for a specific vertex.

Station	Elevation	Length	Grade Ahead	Grade Back
0+00.00	191.903'	33.508'	-8.57%	8.57%
0+33.51	189.031'	0.237'	-8.08%	8.08%
0+33.74	189.012'	81.112'	-9.59%	9.59%
1+14.86	181.235'	0.115'	-13.03%	13.03%
1+14.97	181.220'	205.992'	-7.89%	7.89%
3+20.96	164.968'			

Figure 9–4

- **(Select a Feature Line Or Lot Line):** Enables you to change the feature line that you are editing.

- ⌕ **(Zoom to):** Enables you to zoom in to a highlighted vertex.

- ⌇ **(Quick Profile):** Creates a quick profile along the feature line.

- ⌇ **(Raise/Lower):** Raises or lowers all of the feature line vertices by the elevation entered in the edit field on the right.

- ⇧ ⇩ **(Raise/Lower Incrementally):** Raises or lowers the elevations by the elevation increment entered (the default is 1).

- ⌇ **(Set Increment):** Enables you to set the increment value.

- ⌇ **(Flatten Grade or Elevations):** Enables you to flatten selected vertices to a specified grade or single elevation.

- ⌇ **(Insert Elevation Point):** (Green) Adds an elevation control to the feature line. Elevation points provide an elevation control without creating a new vertex. These points are Z-controls without X- or Y-components.

- ⌇ **(Delete Elevation Point):** (Red) Removes elevation points.

- ⌇ **(Elevations from Surface):** Takes the elevations of all of the vertices from the surface if no rows are selected. If a row is selected, it only takes the surface elevation for that vertex.

- ⌇ **(Reverse the direction):** Changes the direction of the feature line by reversing the order of its points.

- ⌇ **(Show Grade breaks only):** Only displays rows for vertices where there is a change to grade.

- ⌇ **(Unselect All Rows):** Clears any selected vertices. With no rows selected, the **Raise/Lower** commands apply to all of the rows.

You can edit the elevations of a feature or parcel line before or after it becomes part of a grading group.

Practice 9a

Estimated time for completion: 15 minutes

*You might need to type **Regen** in the Command Line to regenerate the graphics.*

Working with Feature Lines

Practice Objectives

- Create a feature line from objects.
- Create a feature line using design data.

The first step in grading is to establish existing site conditions. In this practice you will define feature lines for a parking lot and some ball fields.

Task 1 - Create a feature line from objects.

To establish a design control line for the parking lot, you will create a feature line that temporarily extracts elevations from the existing surface. You will then modify the feature line to follow a specific slope. A second feature line will be created using specific design parameters outlining the baseball field to ensure correct drainage.

1. Open **GRD1-A1-Grading.dwg** from the *C:\Civil 3D Projects\Civil3D-Training\Grading* folder.

2. Select the preset view **Grad-ParkingLot**. A red polyline should be displayed that runs north and south through the center of the parking lot.

3. In the *Home* tab>Create Design panel, expand **Feature Line** and select ⬚ (Create Feature Lines from Objects), as shown in Figure 9–5.

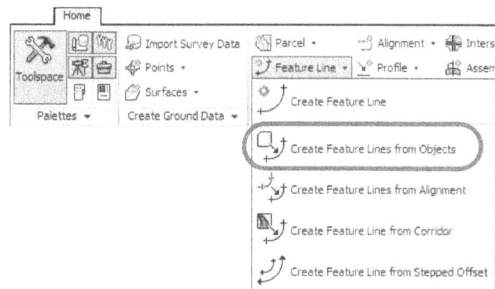

Figure 9–5

4. When prompted to *select the object*, type **X** for (XREF), select the red polyline, and press <Enter>.

5. In the Create Feature Lines dialog box, as shown in Figure 9–6:
   - Create a new site called **Site 1**.
   - In the *Conversion options* area, select **Assign elevations**.
   - Accept all other defaults and click **OK** when done.

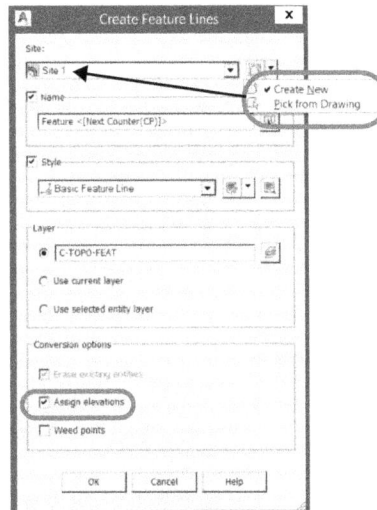

Figure 9–6

6. In the Assign Elevations dialog box, as shown in Figure 9–7:
   - Select **From surface**.
   - Expand the drop-down list and select **Existing-Site**.
   - Clear the **Insert intermediate grade break points** option.
   - Click **OK** to accept the changes and close the dialog box.

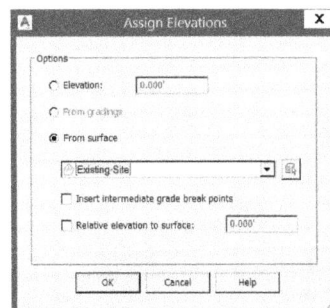

Figure 9–7

A feature line has been created for the center of the parking lot with elevations matching the existing ground surface. Ideally you already have corridors designed for Ascent Pl and Mission Ave so that you can match the designed elevations from them.

7. Select the green feature line that you just created. In the *Feature Line* contextual tab, click 🖼 (Elevation Editor).

If the Edit Elevations panel is not displayed.

Click 🖼 (Edit Elevations) in the Feature Line contextual tab>Modify panel.

8. In the Grading Elevation Editor, place the cursor in the first row, hold <Shift> and pick in the last row to highlight all of the vertices. In the top row, type **-2** in the *Grade Ahead* column to change all of the grades to **-2%**, as shown in Figure 9–8.

Station	Elevation(Actual)	Length	Grade Back	Grade Ahead
0+00.00	191.903'	33.508'		-2.00%
0+33.51	191.233'	0.237'	2.00%	-2.00%
0+33.74	191.228'	81.112'	2.00%	-2.00%
1+14.86	189.606'	0.115'	2.00%	-2.00%
1+14.97	189.603'	205.992'	2.00%	-2.00%
3+20.96	185.484'		2.00%	

Relative to surface:

Figure 9–8

9. Save the drawing.

Task 2 - Create a feature based on design elevations.

In this task you will create a feature line for the baseball field whose elevations have been precalculated to ensure correct drainage. Based on the required drainage for the baseball field, the elevations have been roughly calculated, as shown in Figure 9–9. Use these elevations to create a feature line in the following steps.

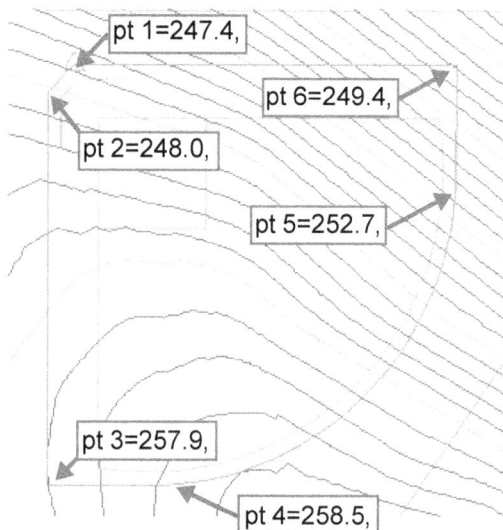

pt 1=247.4,

pt 6=249.4,

pt 2=248.0,

pt 5=252.7,

pt 3=257.9,

pt 4=258.5,

Figure 9–9

1. Continue working with the drawing from the previous task or open **GRD1-A2-Grading.dwg**.

2. Select the preset view **Grad-Baseball**.

3. In the *Home* tab>Create Design panel, expand **Feature Line** and select **Create Feature Line**, as shown in Figure 9–10.

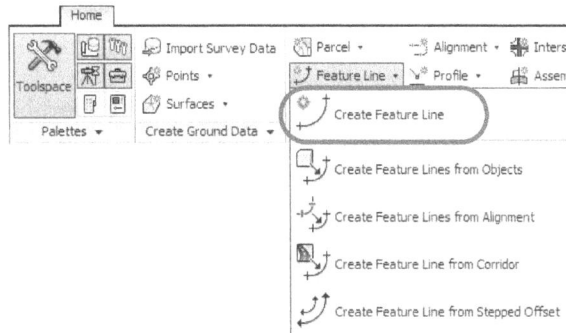

Figure 9–10

4. In the Create Feature Lines dialog box, select **Site 1** and accept all of the other defaults. Click **OK** to close the dialog box and start creating the feature line.

5. When prompted for the feature line points, select the end point **Pt1** (as shown in Figure 9–9). At the *Specify elevation or [surface]:* prompt, type **247.4** and press <Enter>.

6. When prompted for the next point, select end point **Pt2**, as shown in Figure 9–9.

7. You are prompted to *Specify grade or [SLope/Elevation/ Difference/SUrface/Transition] <0.00>:*. If the option is not set to accept elevations, type **E** and press <Enter> to set the default as the elevation.

8. Once the option has been set to accept elevations, you are prompted to *Specify elevation or [Grade/SLope/Difference/ SUrface/Transition]:*. Type **248** and press <Enter>. Continue selecting the end points and entering the elevations for all of points shown in Figure 9–9. After inputting the elevation for point 4, type **A** and press <Enter> to start an arc. After point 5, type **L** and press <Enter> to return to straight lines. When finished entering the elevation for the last point (pt6, **249.4**), type **C** to close the feature line and press <Enter> to exit the command.

9. In Model Space, select the feature line that you just created and in the contextual tab>Modify panel, select **Edit Elevations** to toggle on the Edit Elevations panel, and then select **Elevation Editor**, as shown in Figure 9–11.

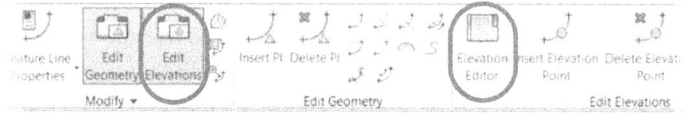

Figure 9–11

10. In the Grading Elevation Editor vista (shown in Figure 9–12), you can change the feature line design.

Station	Elevation	Length	Grade Ahead	Grade Back
0+00.00	247.400'	27.567'	2.18%	-2.18%
0+27.57	248.000'	282.016'	3.51%	-3.51%
3+09.58	257.900'	76.443'	0.78%	-0.78%
3+86.03	258.500'	353.532'	-1.64%	1.64%
7+39.56	252.700'	76.443'	-4.32%	4.32%
8+16.00	249.400'	282.016'	-0.71%	0.71%
10+98.02	247.400'			

Figure 9–12

11. Save the drawing.

9.3 Grading Tools

Grading
Creation Tools
Toolbar

Grading groups are created and edited using the Grading Creation Tools toolbar (as shown in Figure 9–13), which is accessed in the *Grading* tab>Create Grading panel.

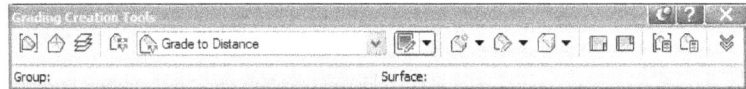

Figure 9–13

Some of the more commonly used tools include:

*   **(Set the Grading Group):** Enables you to consolidate grading objects into a single collection to generate a grading group surface for volume computations.

*   **(Criteria drop-down list):** Enables you to select specific criteria in a given criteria set.

*   **(Create Grading):** Generates a grading solution from the currently selected criteria.

*   **(Edit Grading):** Enables you to change the grading parameters after a solution has been generated.

*   **(Grading Volume Tools):** Opens the Grading Volume Tools toolbar, which provides cut and fill information about the grading group, and adjustment tools.

Practice 9b

Create Grading Groups

Practice Objective

Estimated time for completion: 15 minutes

- Create grading objects to design the finish ground and display the finish ground contours.

Task 1 - Create a grading object that grades to a surface.

The baseball park will have a grade of 4% for 10 feet, and then grade to the existing site surface.

1. Open **GRD1-B1-Grading.dwg** from the *C:\Civil 3D Projects\ Civil3D-Training\Grading* folder.

2. Select the preset view **Grad-Baseball**. The dark green feature line created in the last practice should be displayed.

3. In the *Home* tab>Create Design panel, expand ◌̊ Grading and select **Grading Creation Tools**, as shown in Figure 9–14.

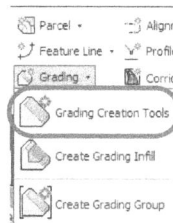

Figure 9–14

4. In the Grading Creation Tools, click ◻ (Set Grading Group), as shown in Figure 9–15.

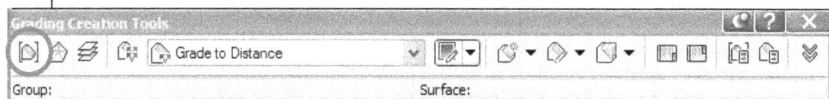

Figure 9–15

5. Select **Site 1** and click **OK**.

6. In the Create Grading Group, type **Baseball Field** as the name. Do not select the **Automatic surface creation** option, as shown in Figure 9–16. Click **OK**.

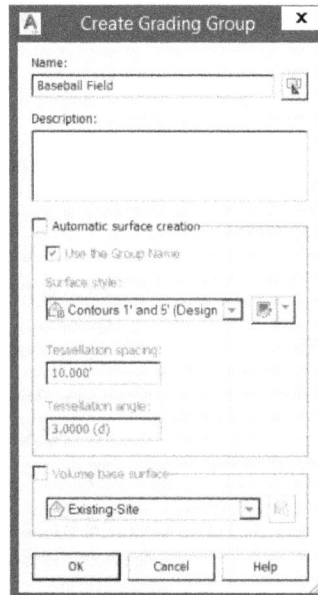

Figure 9–16

7. On the left in the Grading Creation Tools, click ⌂ (Set Target Surface), as shown in Figure 9–17. Select **Existing-Site** and click **OK**.

Figure 9–17

8. In the Grading Creation Tools, set the grading criteria to **Grade to Distance**, as shown in Figure 9–18.

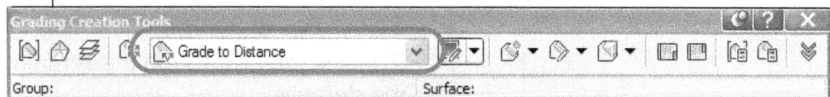

Figure 9–18

9. In the Grading Creation Tools, click ⌖ (Create grading), as shown in Figure 9–19.

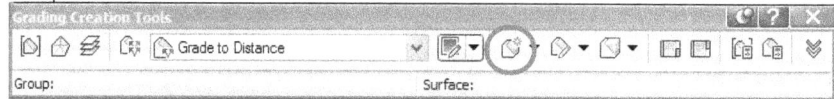

Figure 9–19

10. When prompted:

- To *select the object*, select the dark green feature line outlining the baseball field.
- Pick a point to the outside of the feature line for the side to grade.
- Select **Yes** to apply it to the entire length.
- Type **10** to specify the distance.
- Select **Grade** to specify a format of grade.
- Type **-4** to grade down 4% from the feature line.

11. In the Grading Creation Tools, set the grading criteria to **Grade to Surface**, as shown in Figure 9–20. Click

  ⌖ (Create grading).

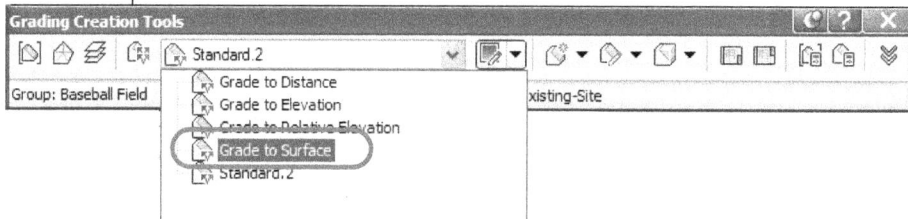

Figure 9–20

12. When prompted:

- To *select the feature*, select the outer-most dark green feature line created with the last grading object.
- Select **Yes** to apply it to the entire length.
- Press <Enter> through the remaining prompts, accepting the defaults.
- Close the Grading Creation toolbar.

13. Save the drawing

Task 2 - Create an infill.

Playing fields are graded for drainage. Grassed surfaces usually have a 1% to 2% minimum slope. The baseball field that you will be working on has a 2% slope across the field with a 4% slope surrounding it before turning into a 2:1 slope out to daylight.

1. Continue working with the drawing from the previous task or open **GRD1-B2-Grading.dwg**.

2. Select one of the grading objects that you created in Task 1. In the contextual *Grading* tab>Modify panel, click

    (Grading Group Properties).

3. In the *Information* tab, select the **Automatic Surface Creation** option. Accept the defaults in the Create Surface dialog box and click **OK**. Select the **Volume Base Surface** option and select **Existing-Site** as the base surface, as shown in Figure 9–21. Click **OK**.

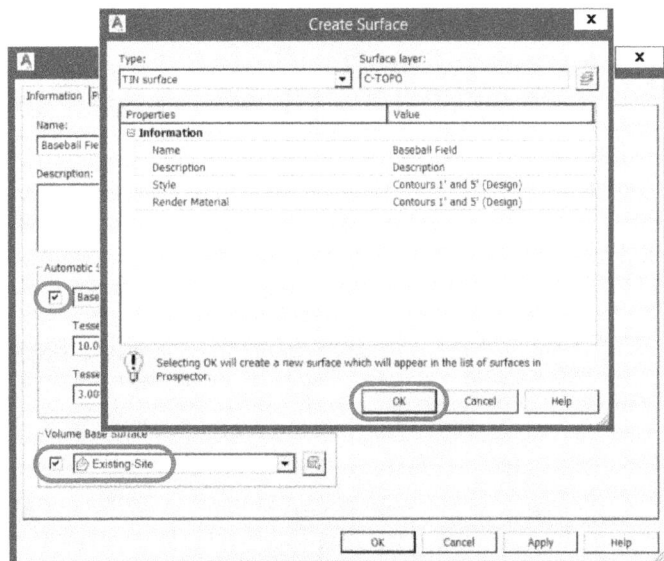

Figure 9–21

4. Select the baseball field surface. In the *Surface* contextual tab, click ⌕ (Object Viewer). Set the view direction to **SW Isometric** and the style to **Shades of Gray**. Note the hole in the surface, as shown in Figure 9–22. Press <Esc> twice to close the object viewer and release the surface.

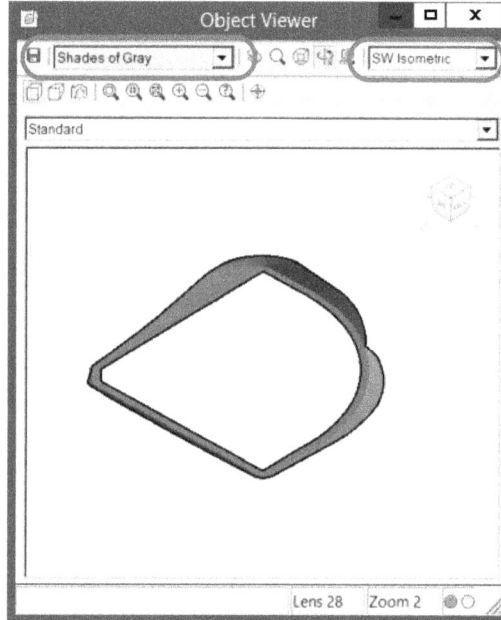

Figure 9–22

*Alternatively, you can expand **Grading**, and click ✑ (Create Infill) in the Home tab>Create Design panel.*

5. Expand **Grading Creation Tools**, and select **Create Infill**, as shown in Figure 9–23.

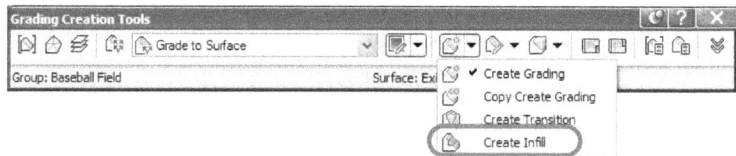

Figure 9–23

6. Pick a point in the middle of the baseball field grading object and press <Enter>. Contours should fill in the middle, as shown in Figure 9–24.

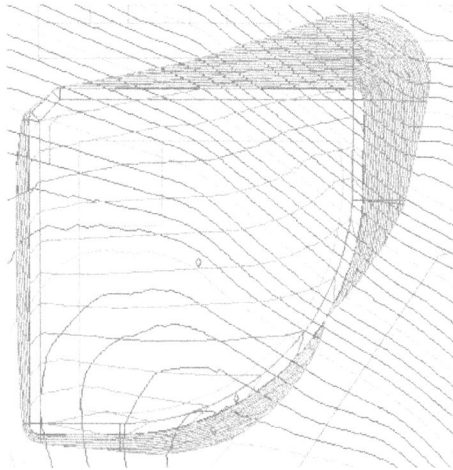

Figure 9–24

7. Save the drawing.

9.4 Modifying AutoCAD Civil 3D Grading

Grading Styles

A grading style defines how the grading solution displays in the drawing window. The components of a grading style include the grading marker (for selecting the grading solution), slope patterns, and solution's layers and their properties.

Feature Line Labels

Feature lines have their own family of labels, which can be accessed in the *Annotate* tab>Add Labels panel, by expanding Feature Line and selecting the **Add Feature Line Labels** command (e.g., a label indicating grade and distance).

Grading Criteria

Grading methods (to a surface, at a specific distance and slope, etc.) are organized inside AutoCAD Civil 3D drawings as grading criteria. Criteria include the grading method, slope projection, and conflict resolution properties.

- The *Grading Method* properties define what you want to grade to. Targets can include *Surface*, *Elevation*, *Relative Elevations*, or *Distance*. If the method uses a distance, you need to specify a default distance. If the method is to a surface, you can specify whether it is only for cut or fill, for both cut and fill, or for a distance. Each setting changes the information that the Grading Method needs to complete its task.

- The *Slope Projection* properties assign the format of the slope (e.g., slope or grade) and the default values when using the command.

- The *Conflict Resolution* properties define how to resolve problem areas, such as internal corners that overlap.

The Grading Criteria dialog box is shown in Figure 9–25.

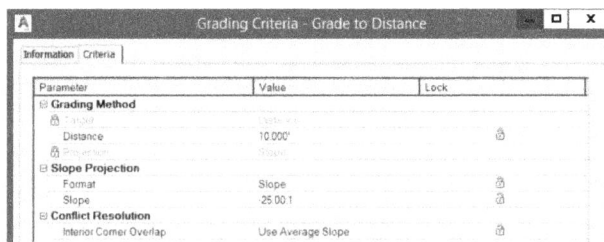

Figure 9–25

Grading Criteria Set

Criteria sets are collections of grading criteria that are useful to group together for a specific task. For example, you can create different sets for residential or commercial site grading, etc. These sets (and the criteria within them) can be found in the Toolspace, *Settings* tab under the *Grading* collection.

In this training guide, you only work with the Basic criteria set provided in the default AutoCAD Civil 3D templates.

Modifying Grading

To modify an existing grading object, select the diamond at the center of the grading object and click 🖉 (Edit Grading) or 🖾 (Grading Editor) in the *Grading* contextual tab>Modify panel. The **Edit Grading** command enables you to make changes to the grading object using the Command Line and similar prompts to when you first created the grading object. The **Grading Editor** opens the Panorama window in which you can modify any part of the grading parameters without needing to go through the full list of options as you would using the **Edit Grading** command. The Grading Editor Panorama is shown in Figure 9–26.

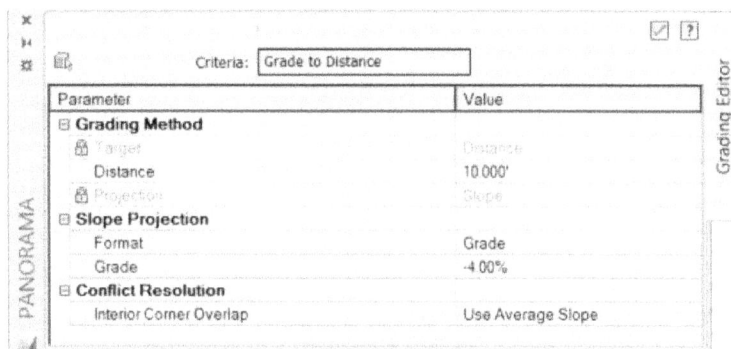

Figure 9–26

Grading Volumes

The Grading Volumes Tools toolbar (shown in Figure 9–27), displays the volume for all or selected grading solutions in a group. One tool raises or lowers all of the members of a grading group by an incremental value. The icon at the far right forces the group or selected grading solution to determine which elevations it needs for balance. Balance is a design that creates as much excavation material as required to fill in depressions in the design area.

- The volumes in the Grading Volume Tools toolbar are dynamically linked to the grading objects.

- Grading volumes change when editing one or all of the grading group objects.

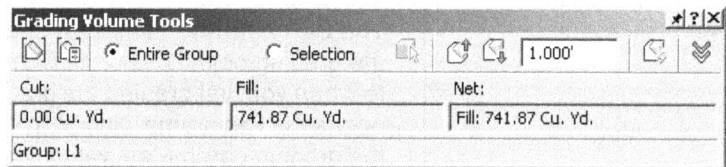

Figure 9–27

Practice 9c

Estimated time for completion: 15 minutes

Modify Grading and Calculate Volumes

Practice Objective

- Modify a grading group using the Grading editor and **Grading Volume** tools.

Task 1 - Modify the grading criteria of a grading object.

For safety reasons, it has been decided to extend the 4% grade encompassing the baseball field from 10' to 15' before starting the steep 2:1 slope going out to daylight. The grade will also change from 4% to 5%. You can accomplish this change using the Grading Editor.

1. Continue working with the drawing from the previous practice or open **GRD1-C1-Grading.dwg** from the *C:\Civil 3D Projects\Civil3D-Training\Grading* folder.

2. Select the preset view **Grad-Baseball**.

3. Select the diamond representing the 4% slope for 10' grading object, as shown in Figure 9–28. In the *Grading* contextual tab>Modify panel, click ⬚ (Grading Editor).

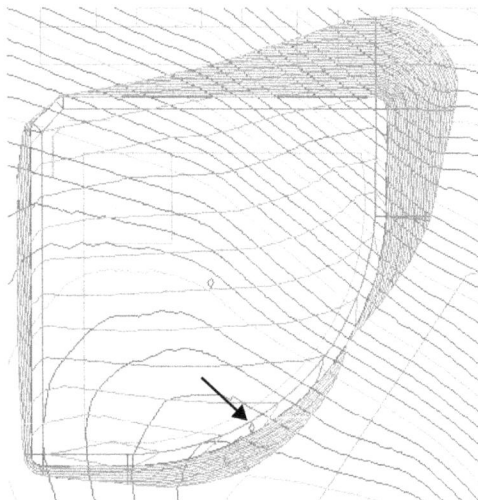

Figure 9–28

Note: Pausing after changing each value ensures that the computer can process the changes, and can help to avoid crashing.

4. In the Grading Editor Panorama, set the *Distance* to **15'** and the *Grade* to **-5%**, as shown in Figure 9–29. Click ☑ to accept the changes.

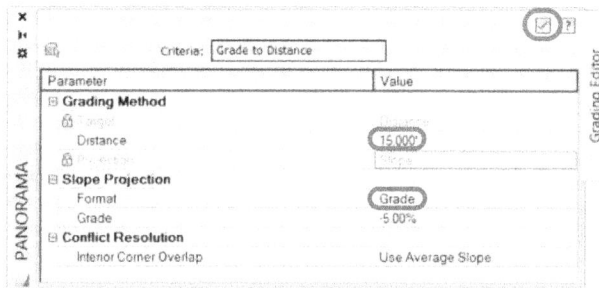

Figure 9–29

5. Save the drawing.

Task 2 - Calculate and balance the volume of a grading group.

In this task you will calculate the volume of the grading group, and then adjust the elevation of the entire group to balance the volume across the grading area.

1. Continue working with the drawing from the previous task or open **GRD1-C2-Grading.dwg**.

2. Select any one of the diamonds representing one of the grading objects in the Baseball Field grading group. In the *Grading* contextual tab>Grading Tools panel, click

   (Grading Volume Tools).

3. Expand the **Grading Volume Tools** by clicking

   (Chevron). Select **Entire Group** to include it in the calculation, as shown in Figure 9–30.

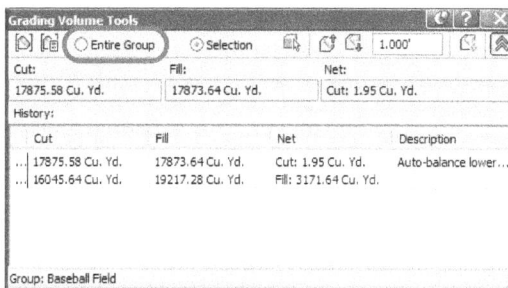

Figure 9–30

4. In the Grading Volume Tools, click ⬚ (Automatically raise/lower to balance).

5. Unfortunately, in a balanced condition, the daylight line to the north cuts into the soccer field. Therefore, you will need to lower the baseball field to correct this. To do so, you will change the elevation change increment to **5'** and click

    ⬚ (Lower selected grade features) as shown in Figure 9–31.

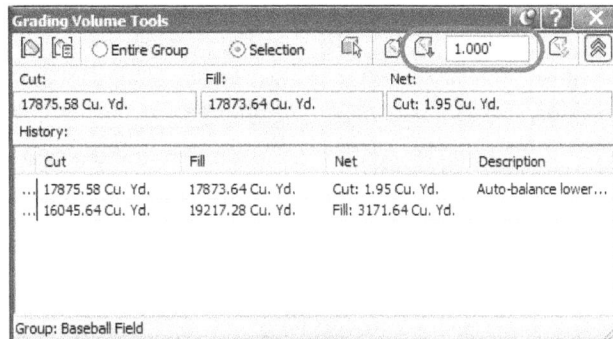

Figure 9–31

6. Continue lowering the grading objects until the display is similar to that shown in Figure 9–32.

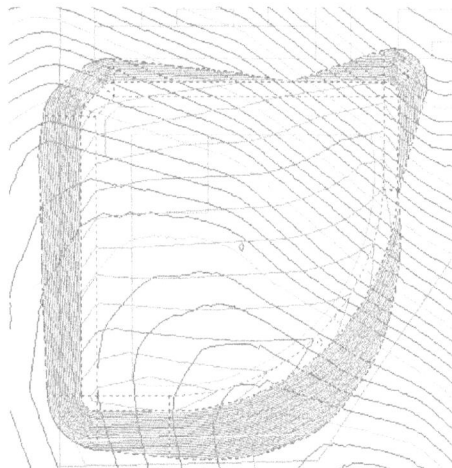

Figure 9–32

7. Save the drawing.

Chapter Review Questions

1. When creating a feature line from objects, which of the following cannot be used to create a feature line?

    a. Lines or arcs

    b. Circles

    c. Polylines or 3D polylines

    d. XREF

2. How do you ensure that you do not create a hole in the middle of your surface when using grading objects to create the finished ground contours?

    a. Grade to the inside.

    b. You cannot prevent holes in grading group surfaces.

    c. Create infill.

    d. Balance the Volumes.

3. What is the best method of editing a grading object without needing to go through each prompt?

    a. Grading Editor

    b. Edit Grading

    c. Delete the grading object and recreate it.

    d. Grip edit the resulting feature lines.

4. The grading object and the feature line have to be in the same site to be able to work together.

    a. True

    b. False

5. In the Grading Elevation Editor, you can edit...

    a. Grading objects

    b. Finish Ground Profiles

    c. Pipe Structures

    d. Feature Lines

Command Summary

Button	Command	Location
	Auto Balance	• **Contextual Toolbar:** Grading Volume Tools
	Create Feature Line	• **Ribbon:** *Home* tab>Create Design panel • **Command Prompt:** drawfeatureline
	Create Feature Line From Objects	• **Ribbon:** *Home* tab>Create Design panel • **Command Prompt:** createfeaturelines
	Edit Elevations	• **Contextual Ribbon:** *Feature Line* tab> Modify panel
	Edit Grading	• **Contextual Ribbon:** *Grading* tab> Modify panel • **Command Prompt:** editgrading
	Elevation Editor	• **Contextual Ribbon:** *Feature Line* tab> Edit Elevations panel • **Command Prompt:** gradingeleveditor
	Grading Creation Tools	• **Ribbon:** *Home* tab>Create Design panel • **Command Prompt:** gradingtools
	Grading Editor	• **Contextual Ribbon:** *Grading* tab> Modify panel • **Command Prompt:** gradingeditor
	Grading Volume Tools	• **Contextual Ribbon:** *Grading* tab> Grading Tools panel • **Command Prompt:** gradingvolumetools
	Lower Grading Features	• **Contextual Toolbar:** Grading Volume Tools
	Raise Grading Features	• **Contextual Toolbar:** Grading Volume Tools

Pipe Networks

In this chapter you learn how to create pipe networks for both gravity-fed pipes and pressurized pipes. You also learn how to create and apply rules to gravity-fed pipes to ensure that they meet design specifications. Then you annotate the pipe networks to communicate the full design intent to contractors and other stakeholders.

Learning Objectives in this Chapter

- List the types of utility networks that can be designed in the AutoCAD Civil 3D software.
- Configure pipe network and pressure pipe network settings.
- Create Pipe Networks from objects in the drawing or external reference file.
- Create and edit pressure or gravity fed pipe networks using various tools.
- Communicate important design information about pipe networks by adding labels to plan and profile views, and creating reports.

10.1 Pipes Overview

The AutoCAD® Civil 3D® software's utility design system is often referred to as AutoCAD Civil 3D Pipes.

- You can create pipe networks in AutoCAD Civil 3D drawings to represent storm sewers, sanitary sewers, pressure pipes, etc. Unlike AutoCAD® Land Desktop®, AutoCAD Civil 3D networks can model multiple, connected trunk lines and laterals as part of the same system.

- In the AutoCAD Civil 3D software, pipes are geared for gravity flow systems (sewers) and pressurized pipes (water). Electrical ducts, and similar types of conduit can also be modeled, but require special attention.

- Pipes are created in plan view interactively or by converting other linework into pipes (including 2D and 3D polylines and feature lines). Pipes can also be imported directly from AutoCAD Land Desktop projects, AutoCAD® Map 3D® software's industry model, and through Autodesk LandXML.

- Pipe networks can be created from customized part lists, styles, and rules that can help lay them out (and display them) appropriately.

- Once created, pipe networks can be displayed in profile and section views. Pipes can be edited in plan or profile, and using layout tools, such as the Grid View Vista (a spreadsheet-like view of pipe network pipes and structures). Changes made in plan, profile, or Grid View automatically update all other displays.

- The AutoCAD Civil 3D software includes an interference check utility to search for possible conflicts between pipe networks.

- The AutoCAD Civil 3D software includes hydrology or hydraulic (H&H) calculators with the Hydraflow Express, the Hydraflow Hydrographs, and the Hydraflow Storm Sewer applications available in the *Analyze* tab. Without these applications, the system is set up to automate the drafting of utility systems, but not to analyze them or suggest pipe sizes.

- Many 3rd party H&H applications also support the Autodesk LandXML transfer of networks configured in the AutoCAD Civil 3D software. Therefore, a conceptual layout might be created in the AutoCAD Civil 3D software, exported to an .STM file for analysis and adjustment, and then reinserted into the AutoCAD Civil 3D software using Autodesk LandXML or the .STM file format.

10.2 Pipes Configuration

The Toolspace, *Settings* tab contains values and styles affecting pipe networks. The *Parts Lists* and *Pipe Rules* are the most important settings. Parts Lists contain typical pipes, fittings, appurtenances, and structures for a type of utility. Pipe Rules trigger error messages if pipes or structures are not created in accordance with predefined design constraints, such as the maximum pipe length or a slope.

Edit Drawing Settings

The Edit Drawing Settings dialog box contains values affecting the pipe layout layers (e.g., pipe networks, fittings, profiles, and section views).

Pipe Network Feature Settings

The Pipe Network Edit Feature Settings dialog box contains values that assign styles, set the pipe network naming convention, set the default pipe and structure rules, and set the default location for pipe and structure labels.

*   To open the Edit Feature Settings dialog box, right-click on Settings in the *Pipe Network* collection, and select **Edit Feature Settings**. The dialog box is shown in Figure 10–1.

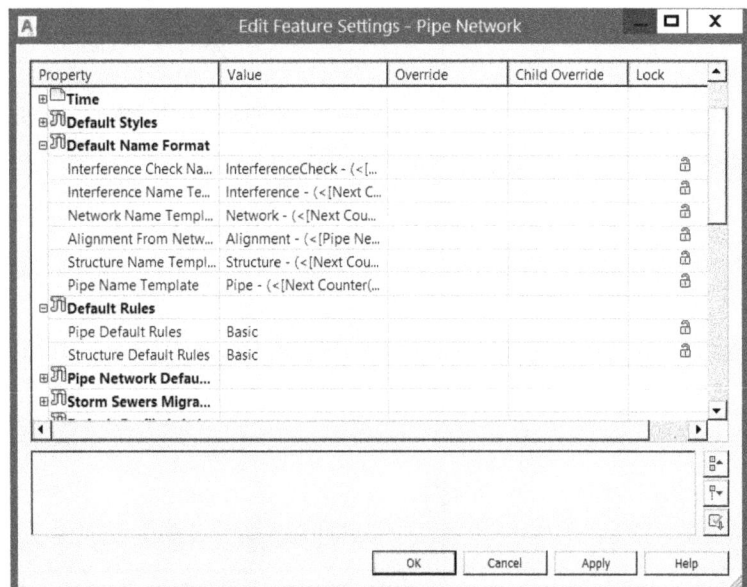

Figure 10–1

Pipe Catalog

The AutoCAD Civil 3D software includes standard catalogs in both Imperial and Metric units. Catalog specifications define the size and shape of the underground structures and pipes for sanitary or storm gravity systems.

- The *US Imperial Pipes* folder contains **US Imperial Pipes.htm**, which displays the components of the Pipe catalog.

- You can view the contents of these libraries by selecting this file and viewing it in Internet Explorer.

- The Pipe catalog includes circular, egg, elliptical, and rectangular shapes. For each pipe shape, the catalog includes inner and outer pipe diameters and wall thicknesses.

Pipe catalog components can be edited by selecting **Modify> Pipe network>Parts List>Part Builder**. The catalog in Internet Explorer is shown in Figure 10–2.

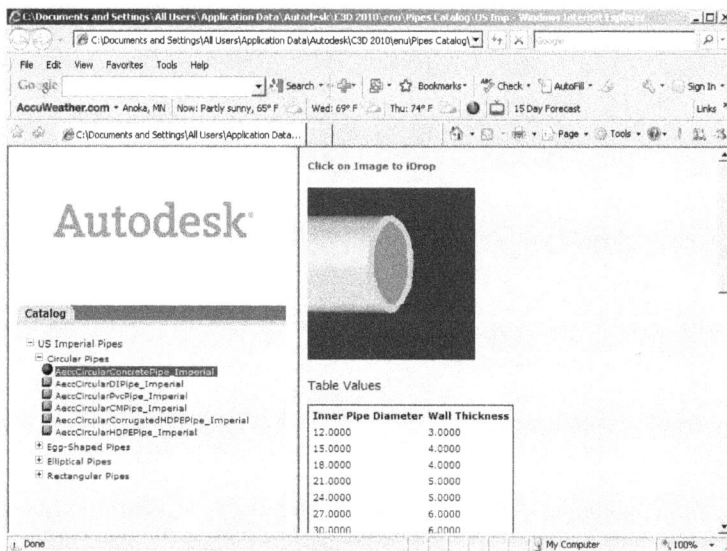

Figure 10–2

Structure Catalog

The Structure catalog includes specifications for inlets, junction structures (circular, rectangular, or eccentric) with or without frames, and simple junction shapes (rectangular or circular).

- The Structure catalog consists of tables and lists that define allowable sizes, thicknesses, and heights.

- The *US Imperial Structure* folder contains **US Imperial Structure.htm**, which is the Structure catalog.

- You can view the files and their contents by selecting a file and viewing it in Internet Explorer, as shown in Figure 10–3.

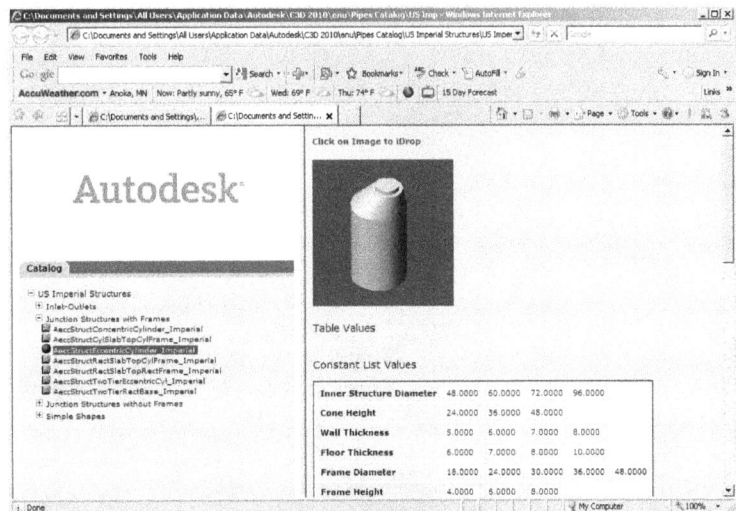

Figure 10–3

Pipe Network Parts Lists

While the catalogs listed above are shared between multiple projects (and multiple users), each AutoCAD Civil 3D drawing can contain any number of Part Lists that are specific to that drawing.

Part Lists are populated with pipes and structures from the catalog and are organized for a specific task (such as Sanitary Sewer and Drain).

- Parts Lists are in the Toolspace, *Settings* tab under the *Pipe Network* collection and *Pressure Network* collection, as shown in Figure 10–4.

- To display a parts list, right-click on its name and select **Edit...**

Pipe Network
    Parts Lists
    Interference Styles
    Commands
Pipe
Structure
Pressure Network
    Parts Lists
    Commands
Pressure Pipe
Fitting
Appurtenance

Figure 10–4

The Pipe Network parts list has typical pipe sizes in the *Pipes* tab and typical structures in the *Structure* tab, as shown in Figure 10–5. If required, you can change a pipe or structure size list, or add a new part type.

Two important settings for each tab are *Rules* and *Render Material*. *Render Material* affects how the pipes and structures display in 3D.

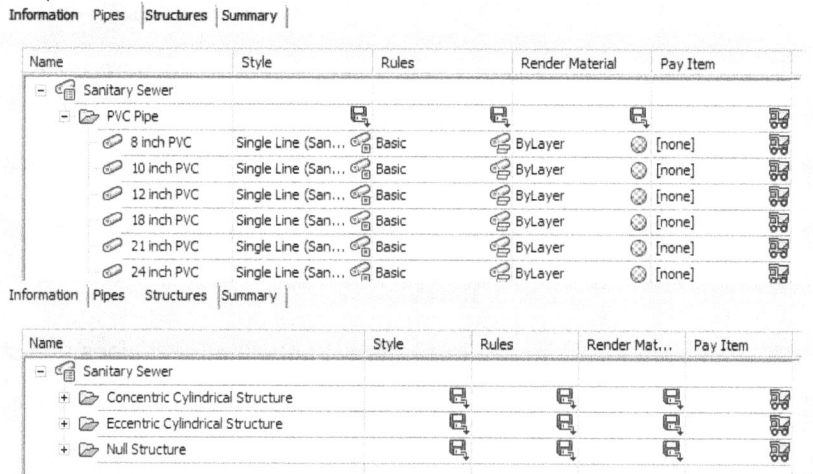

Information Pipes Structures Summary

Name	Style	Rules	Render Material	Pay Item
Sanitary Sewer				
PVC Pipe				
8 inch PVC	Single Line (San... Basic	ByLayer	[none]	
10 inch PVC	Single Line (San... Basic	ByLayer	[none]	
12 inch PVC	Single Line (San... Basic	ByLayer	[none]	
18 inch PVC	Single Line (San... Basic	ByLayer	[none]	
21 inch PVC	Single Line (San... Basic	ByLayer	[none]	
24 inch PVC	Single Line (San... Basic	ByLayer	[none]	

Information Pipes Structures Summary

Name	Style	Rules	Render Mat...	Pay Item
Sanitary Sewer				
Concentric Cylindrical Structure				
Eccentric Cylindrical Structure				
Null Structure				

Figure 10–5

- To add a pipe size or structure size, select the part type heading, right-click, and select **Add a part size**. Then select a new part size from the size list, as shown in Figure 10–6.

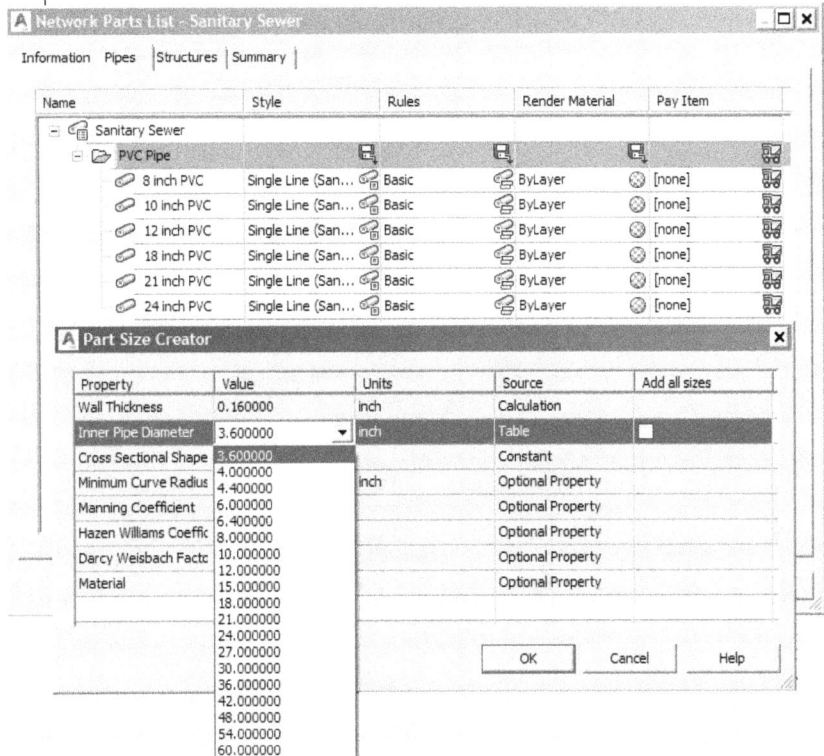

Figure 10–6

- To add a new part family (e.g., concrete pipes for a sanitary system), select the name of the part list, right-click, and select **Add a part family**. Then select a new part family from the list of available parts in the catalog, as shown in Figure 10–7.

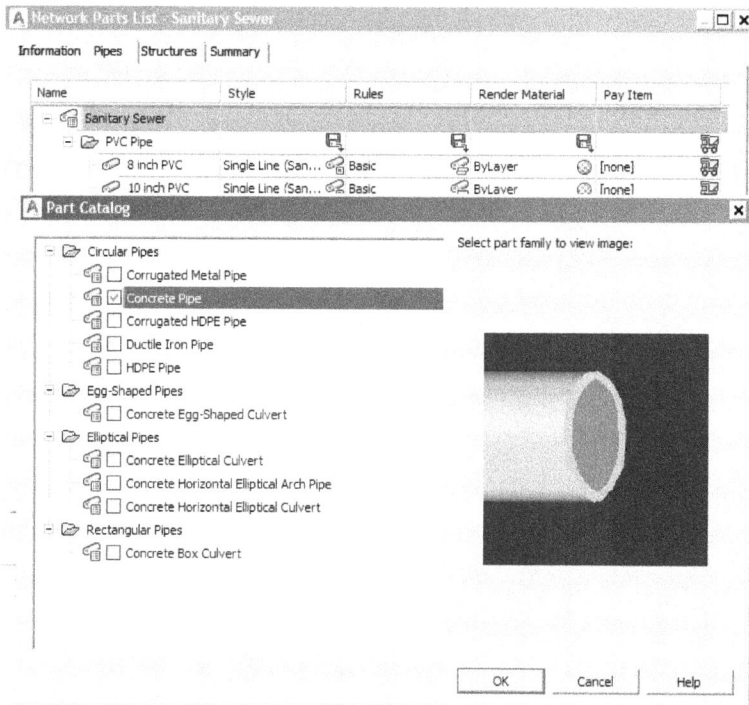

Figure 10–7

The *Pressure Network* parts list has typical pipe sizes in the *Pressure Pipes* tab, typical fitting sizes in the *Fittings* tab, and typical appurtenance sizes in the *Appurtenances* tab, as shown in Figure 10–8. If required, you can change any of the size lists, or add a new part type. An important setting for each tab is *Render Material*. *Render Material* affects how the various parts display in 3D.

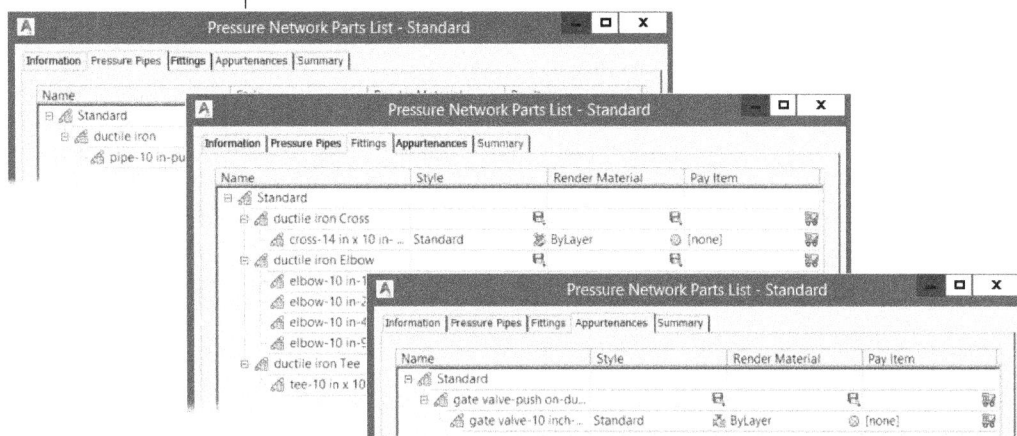

Figure 10–8

Pipe and Structure Styles

The pipe style defines how a pipe displays in plan, profile, and section views. The most critical tab of a Pipe Style is the *Display* tab. By toggling on or off the Component display, a style affects how a network displays in the drawing window (e.g., as a single or double line), its layer name, and color.

A structure style defines how a structure displays in plan and profile views. The plan settings include the plan view symbol and how a structure displays in profile and section views (the outline of the 3D shape).

Pipe styles include the **Clean up Pipe to Pipe Intersections** option for networks, where one pipe connects to another (rather than to a structure). This enables the pipes to seem to fillet together. For this option to work, the pipes must be connected with a *null* structure.

Pipe and Structure Rules

Since pipes and structures often need more than one rule applied to them, individual rules are organized into collections called **rule sets**. Then the rules are prioritized from most important to least important by organizing the order in which they display in the list. You can have different sets for different types of pipe, sizes, and/or systems.

- Pipe rules define minimum/maximum slopes, cover, and maximum pipe segment length.

- Pipe rule sets are located in the Toolspace, *Settings* tab, in the *Pipe Rule Set* collection, as shown in Figure 10–9. To display or edit a rule set, right-click on it and select **Edit**.

Figure 10–9

- Structure rules define the across structure drop's default value, maximum value, and maximum pipe size.

- Structure rule sets are located in the Toolspace, *Settings* tab, under the *Pipe Rule Set* collection.

Pressure Networks do not use rules.

Some pipe and structure rules directly control the layout of new pipes and structures, such as minimum and maximum slope. Some rules are checks that are made after creation, such as maximum pipe length. Rules, such as maximum pipe length, do not prevent you from creating a pipe that is over the maximum length. However, if a pipe is over the maximum length, you are prompted with a warning in the Toolspace, *Prospector* tab and in the Pipe Network Vistas, as shown in Figure 10–10.

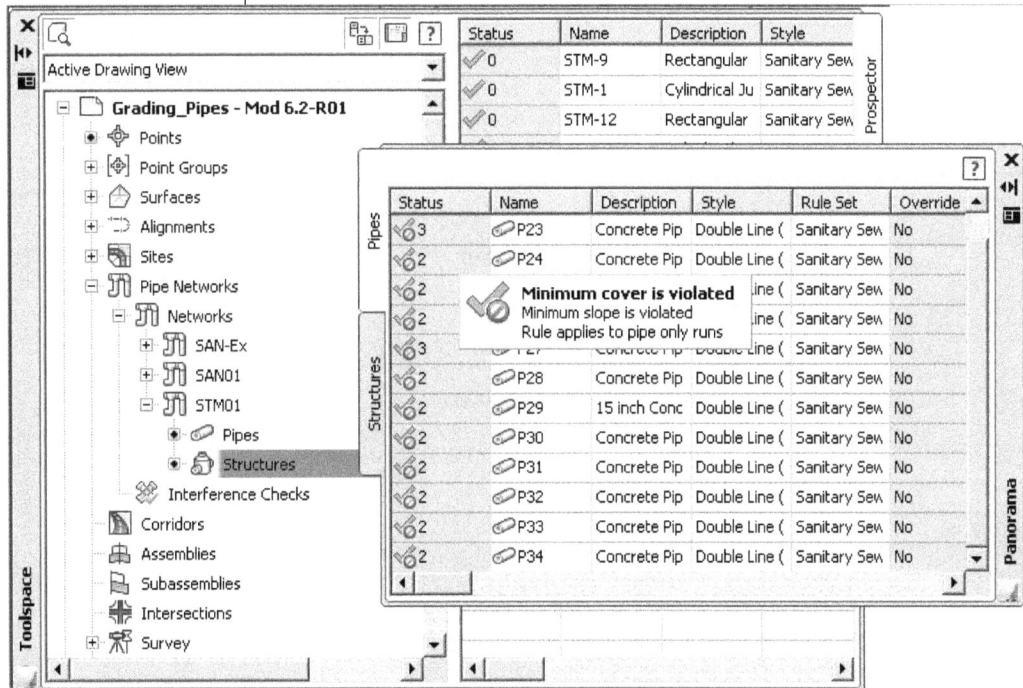

Figure 10–10

Reapplying Pipe Rules

Structure Invert Out elevations are automatically calculated when the structure is first created. Therefore, if new connecting pipes are added to a structure below the lowest invert, the outlet is not automatically lowered until you click ⬚ (Apply Rules) in the *Modify* tab>Pipe Network>Modify panel. An example is shown in Figure 10–11.

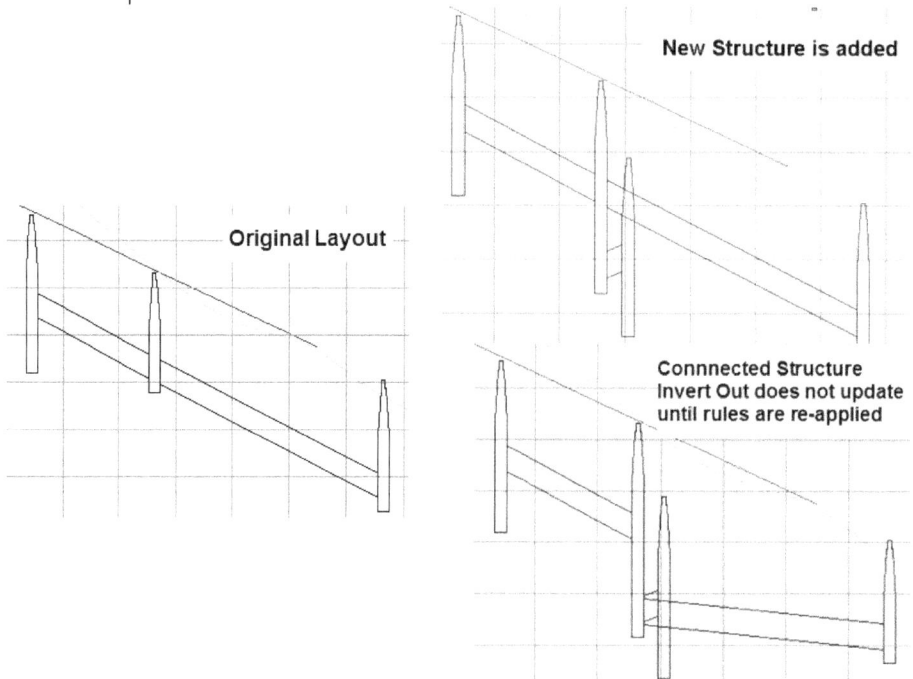

New Structure is added

Original Layout

Connnected Structure Invert Out does not update until rules are re-applied

Figure 10–11

Pipe Layers

Unlike most AutoCAD Civil 3D objects, pipe network layers typically need to be manually reassigned when a pipe network is created. Layers need to be assigned for pipes and structures in plan, profile, and section views. For example, the default AutoCAD Civil 3D templates automatically map to layers appropriate for storm drainage structures when using the Pipe Network Creation Tools and water structures when using the Pressure Pipe Creation Tools. The Pipe Network Layers dialog boxes are shown in Figure 10–12.

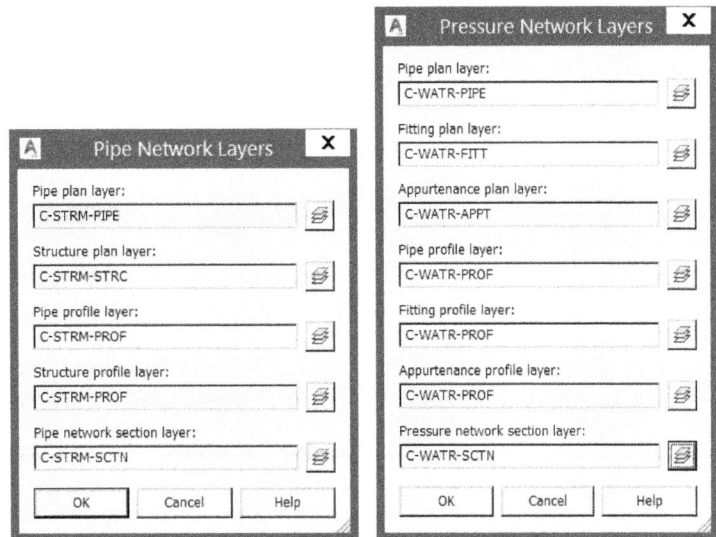

Figure 10–12

If creating a sanitary sewer line, each one needs to be remapped to layers specific to sanitary sewer utilities, such as the examples shown in Figure 10–13.

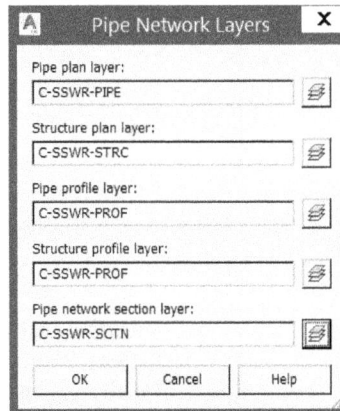

Figure 10–13

Practice 10a

Estimated time for completion: 10 minutes

Configuring Pipe Networks

Practice Objective

• Create feature lines and grading objects to design the finish ground.

Task 1 - Review the Storm Drain Parts List and Rules.

Before creating a network, you should become familiar with the configuration you are about to use.

1. Open **PIP1-A1-PipeWorks.dwg** from the *C:\Civil 3D Projects\Civil3D-Training\PipeNetworks* folder.

2. In the Toolspace, *Settings* tab, expand the *Pipe Network* collection, expand the *Parts Lists* collection, right-click on the *Storm Sewer* part list and select **Edit…**.

3. In the *Pipes* tab, the parts list currently contains a large number of concrete pipes. They are all assigned to use the Basic rule set and a pipe style that displays double lines in plan view, as shown in Figure 10–14.

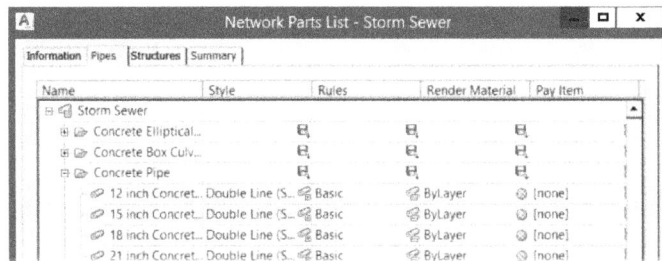

Figure 10–14

4. To add another Pipe type, under **Network Parts List - Storm Sewer**, right-click on **Storm Sewer** and select **Add part family…**, as shown in Figure 10–15.

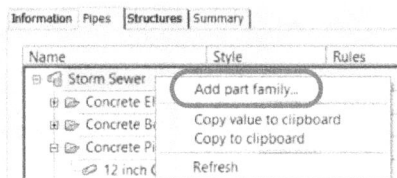

Figure 10–15

5. In the Parts catalog, select **PVC Pipe**, as shown in Figure 10–16. Click **OK** to close the dialog box.

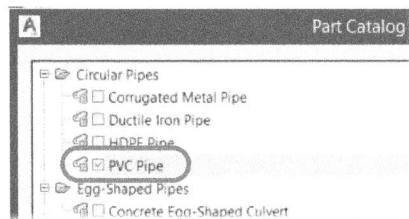

Figure 10–16

6. To add sizes to the part family, select **PVC Pipe**, right-click, and select **Add part size...**, as shown in Figure 10–17.

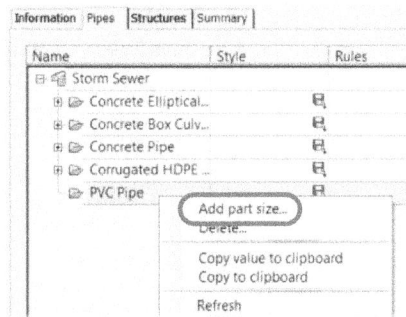

Figure 10–17

To add part sizes, you can select individual sizes in the Value drop-down list or select the checkbox in the Add all sizes column to add all of the available sizes, as shown in Figure 10–18.

7. Select and add the pipe sizes: **8**, **10**, **12**, and **18**. Note that you cannot select all four of these sizes. You will need to add each one separately. Click **OK** to add each one, as shown in Figure 10–18.

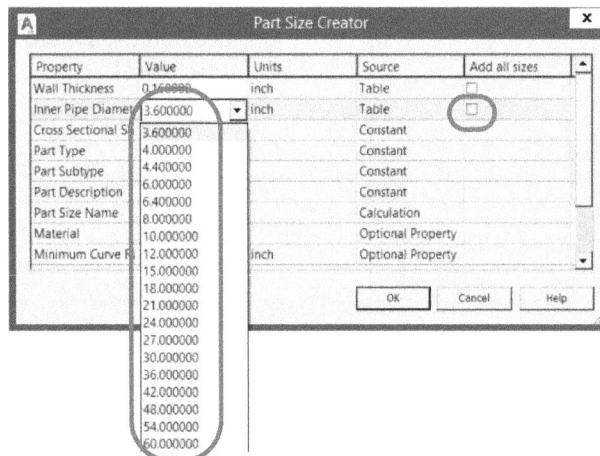

Figure 10–18

When finished, the Network Parts List - Storm Sewer dialog box opens as shown in Figure 10–19.

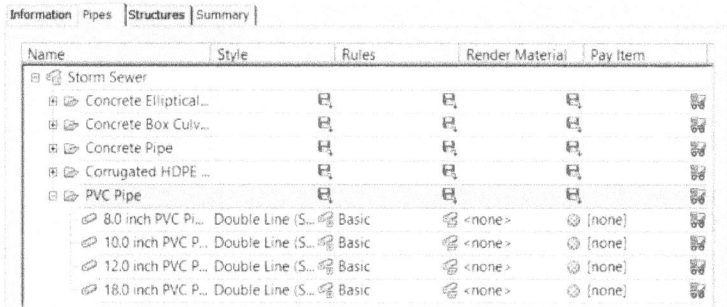

Name	Style	Rules	Render Material	Pay Item
⊟ Storm Sewer				
⊞ Concrete Elliptical...				
⊞ Concrete Box Culv...				
⊞ Concrete Pipe				
⊞ Corrugated HDPE ...				
⊟ PVC Pipe				
8.0 inch PVC Pi... Double Line (S...	Basic	<none>	[none]	
10.0 inch PVC P... Double Line (S...	Basic	<none>	[none]	
12.0 inch PVC P... Double Line (S...	Basic	<none>	[none]	
18.0 inch PVC P... Double Line (S...	Basic	<none>	[none]	

Figure 10–19

8. Select the *Structures* tab. The parts list includes a number of headwalls of different sizes, and catch basins and manholes. Each of these is assigned styles and rules specific to each type, as shown in Figure 10–20.

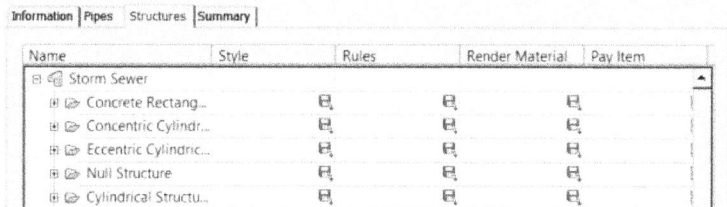

Name	Style	Rules	Render Material	Pay Item
⊟ Storm Sewer				
⊞ Concrete Rectang...				
⊞ Concentric Cylindr...				
⊞ Eccentric Cylindric...				
⊞ Null Structure				
⊞ Cylindrical Structu...				

Figure 10–20

9. Click **OK** to exit.

10. In the Toolspace, *Settings* tab, expand the *Structure* collection, expand the *Structure Rule Set* collection, right-click on the **Basic** rule set and select **Edit...**, as shown in Figure 10–21.

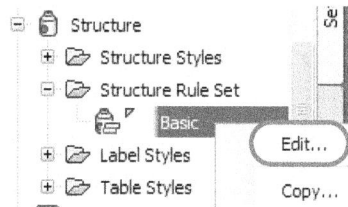

Figure 10–21

Using the arrows at the right side of the Rules tab enables you to prioritize the rules. The rules are processed sequentially from bottom to top. Therefore, place the most important rule at the top of the list.

For this Manhole, in the **Maximum pipe size check** rule you can use a maximum pipe diameter of **4ft**. In the Pipe Drop Across Structure rule, you can have elevations based on **Inverts** and a drop across the manhole of **0.1'** with a **3'** maximum interior drop, as shown in Figure 10–22.

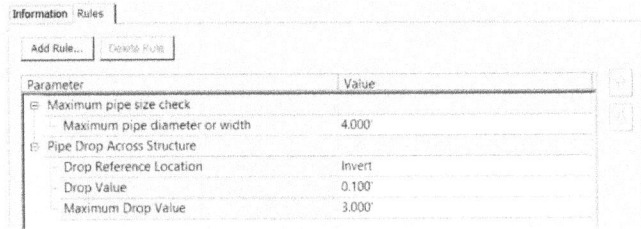

Parameter	Value
⊟ Maximum pipe size check	
Maximum pipe diameter or width	4.000'
⊟ Pipe Drop Across Structure	
Drop Reference Location	Invert
Drop Value	0.100'
Maximum Drop Value	3.000'

Figure 10–22

11. Review and click **OK** to exit without changes.

Task 2 - Review a pressure network parts list.

1. Continue working with the drawing from the previous task or open **PIP1-A2-PipeWorks.dwg**.

2. In the Toolspace, *Settings* tab, expand the *Pressure Network* collection, expand the *Parts Lists* collection, right-click on the Water part list and select **Edit...**, as shown in Figure 10–23.

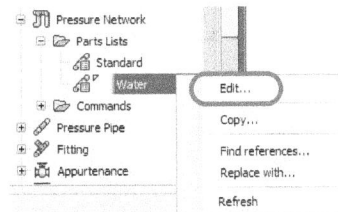

Figure 10–23

3. In the *Pressure Pipes* tab, review the available pipe sizes. To the right of the ductile iron family, select the disk to change all of the styles to **Centerline (Water)**, as shown in Figure 10–24.

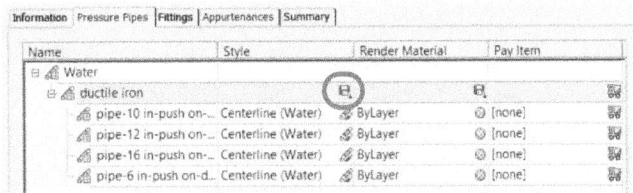

Name	Style	Render Material	Pay Item	
⊟ Water				
⊟ ductile iron				
pipe-10 in-push on-...	Centerline (Water)	ByLayer	[none]	
pipe-12 in-push on-...	Centerline (Water)	ByLayer	[none]	
pipe-16 in-push on-...	Centerline (Water)	ByLayer	[none]	
pipe-6 in-push on-d...	Centerline (Water)	ByLayer	[none]	

Figure 10–24

4. In the *Fittings* tab, review the available fittings. To the right of each family, select the disk to change all of the styles to **Fitting**, as shown in Figure 10–25.

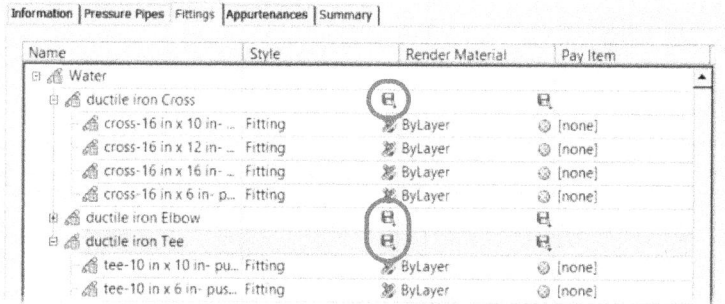

Figure 10–25

5. In the *Appurtenances* tab, review the available valves. To the right of each family, select the disk to set the style to **Valve**, as shown in Figure 10–26.

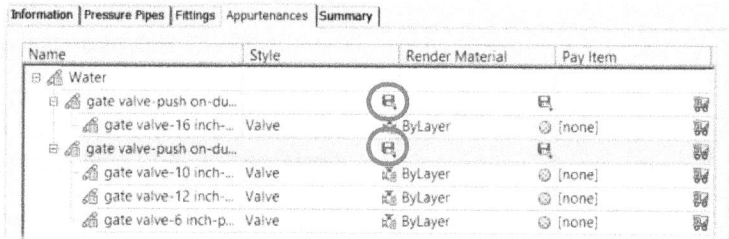

Figure 10–26

6. Click **OK** and save the drawing.

10.3 Creating Networks from Objects

In addition to creating networks by layout, a pipe network can be created from a 2D or 3D object, including a polyline or feature

line. In the *Home* tab>Pipe Network panel, and click 🔲 (Create Pipe Network from Object) to start the creation of a pipe network. Next you are prompted to select the object or type **X** and press <Enter> to select objects from an external reference file. Once selected, a flow arrow displays along the pipe network. The flow is set to the direction in which you drew the original entity but you can reverse the direction by selecting **Reverse**. To leave the flow directions set as is, press <Enter> or select **OK**. A Create Pipe Network dialog box opens enabling you to:

- Name the network

- Set the parts list

- Select the default pipe and structure to use

- Set the surface and alignment to reference

- You can also clean up the drawing as you create the network by selecting the **Erasing existing entity** option, as shown in Figure 10–27.

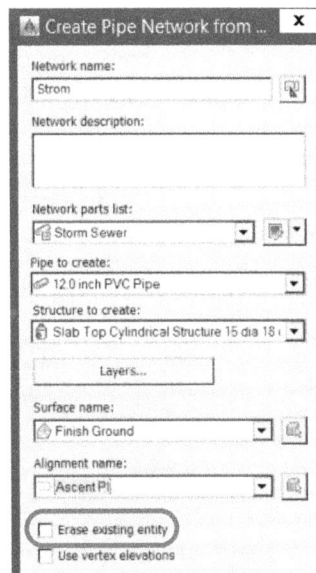

Figure 10–27

Practice 10b

Creating Pipe Networks by Objects

Practice Objective

*   Create a pipe network from objects already in the drawing or external reference file.

Estimated time for completion: 5 minutes

Task 1 - Create a Pipe Network by Object.

In a production environment, the line assignment for utilities is often based on the offsets from the Right-Of-Ways boundary. Based on the tools available in the Network Layout Tools toolbar, it is easier to use the AutoCAD tools to lay out the utility line assignments and then convert it to a pipe network. In this task, you will review the process of converting a line assignment to a pipe network.

1. Continue working with the drawing from the previous practice or open **PIP1-B1-PipeWorks.dwg** from the *C:\Civil 3D Projects\Civil3D-Training\PipeNetworks* folder.

2. Select the preset view **Pipe-Create**. You might need to type **Regen** in the Command Line.

3. In the *Home* tab>Create Design panel, expand **Pipe Network**, and click ⬚ (Create Pipe Network from Object).

4. When prompted to select the object, select XREF in the command option. When prompted to select the XREF object, select the storm line (the red line at the center of the road), as shown in Figure 10–28.

Figure 10–28

5. To ensure that the pipe slopes from the cul-de-sac to the intersection to the south, select **Reverse** to reverse the default flow direction. Press <Enter> to continue.

6. In the Create Pipe Network from Object dialog box set the following, as shown in Figure 10–29.
   - For *Network name*, type **STORM**.
   - In the *Network parts list*, select **Storm Sewer**.
   - For *Pipe to create*, select **12in PVC Pipe**.
   - For *Structure to create*, in the Cylindrical Structure Slab Top Circular Frame structure family, select **Slab Top Cylindrical Structure 15 in dia**.
   - For *Surface name*, select **Finish Ground**.
   - For *Alignment name*, select **Ascent Pl**.
   - Clear the **Use vertex elevations** option.
   - Click **OK** to accept the selection and close the dialog box.

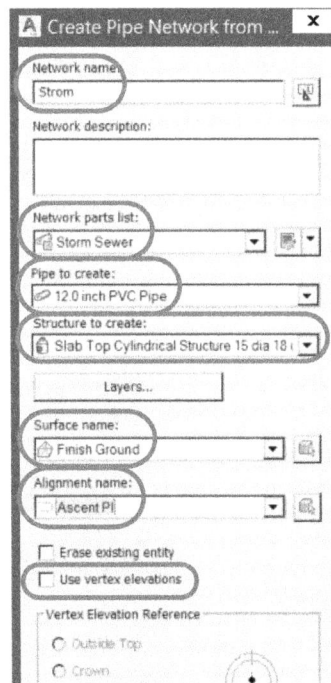

Figure 10–29

The AutoCAD Civil 3D software has created a Pipe network based on the rules and values entered in the Create Pipe Network from Objects dialog box. After you have completed building the network, you will go back and make adjustments to the design inverts, slopes, and part sizes.

7. Save the drawing.

10.4 The Network Layout Toolbar

The Network Layout Tools toolbar contains commands for creating pipe networks by layout (interactively, similar to creating an alignment by layout) and for editing them after creation. This toolbar is opened by selecting *Home* tab>Pipe Network panel, and clicking 🔲 (Pipe Network Creation Tools) or selecting *Modify* tab>Pipe Network panel, and clicking 🔲 (Edit Pipe Network).

> **Hint: Editing Pipes**
>
> If you want to modify or add to a pipe network that you have already defined, use 🔲 (Edit Network) instead of Pipe Network> 🔲 (Create Pipe Network by Layout), as this creates a new network.

The toolbar commands are shown in Figure 10–30.

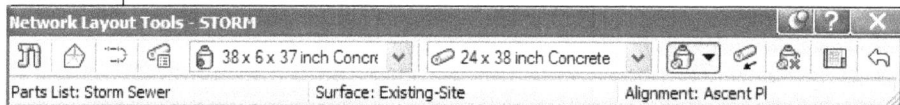

Figure 10–30

- 🔲 **(Pipe Network Properties):** Enables you to review and edit the properties of a pipe network. These include the default labeling, layers, and default parts list to be used.

- 🔲 **(Select Surface):** Enables you to select a surface model to calculate rim elevations and pipe invert elevations. This can be changed while laying out pipes and structures.

- 🔲 **(Select Alignment):** Enables you to specify an alignment to lay out components by station and offset. The selected alignment can be changed while laying out pipes and structures.

- 🔲 **(Parts List):** Enables you to change the current parts list, even in the middle of a layout.

- ⬡ Concentric Structure 1, ▼ | ⬭ 400 mm Concrete Pipe ▼ **(Structure and Pipe drop-down lists):** Enables you to select the next type of structure or pipe to add.

- ▤ ▼ **(Create flyout):** Enables you to select whether you want to lay out pipes only, structures only, or both pipes and structures. When laying out pipes, you graphically select the location of the next structure (or pipe end point if laying out pipes only).

- **(Toggle Upslope/Downslope):** Controls the direction of the next pipe to be laid out in gravity flow networks.

- **(Delete Pipe Network Object):** Enables you to delete a pipe or structure from the network.

- **(Pipe Network Vistas):** Opens a grid view where pipes and structures can be reviewed and have their properties edited. Here you can assign meaningful names to pipes and structures (such as **DMH-1**), which can be included in labels.

- **(Undo):** Enables you to undo the last pipe network edit.

Connecting Pipes and Structures

When creating or editing networks with the Network Layout Tools toolbar, you can connect new pipes to previously created structures (in the same network) by hovering the cursor over that structure until the tooltip image displays, as shown in Figure 10–31. When displayed, click to connect the new pipe to the structure.

Figure 10–31

New pipes and structures can also be used to divide an existing pipe into two pipes. To do so, hover the cursor over the connection point until the tooltip image displays, as shown in Figure 10–32.

Figure 10–32

Practice 10c

Creating Pipe Networks by Layout

Estimated time for completion: 15 minutes

Practice Objective

- Create a gravity fed pipe network by layout.

Task 1 - Create a Pipe Network by Layout.

In this task, you will continue adding to the network using AutoCAD Civil 3D's **Pipe Network** creation tool.

1. Continue working with the drawing from the previous task or open **PIP1-C1-PipeWorks.dwg** from the *C:\Civil 3D Projects\Civil3D-Training\PipeNetworks* folder.

2. Select the preset view **Pipe-Create**.

3. In Model Space, select a part in the STORM network. In the contextual tab>Modify panel, click 🔧 (Edit Pipe Network), as shown in Figure 10–33.

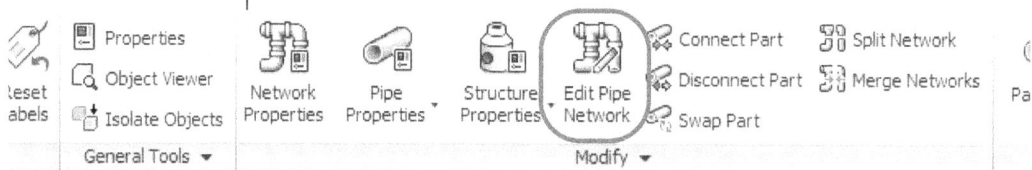

Figure 10–33

4. In the Network Layout Tools - STORM toolbar, shown in Figure 10–34:

   - Click ⤳ (Alignment) and select **Jefferies Ranch Rd**.
   - Select **68 x 6 x 57 inch Concrete Rectangular Headwall** for the manhole structure.
   - Select **12 in PVC Pipe** for the Pipe part.
   - Toggle the slope to **Upslope**.

   - Click 📦 (Draw Pipe and Structure).

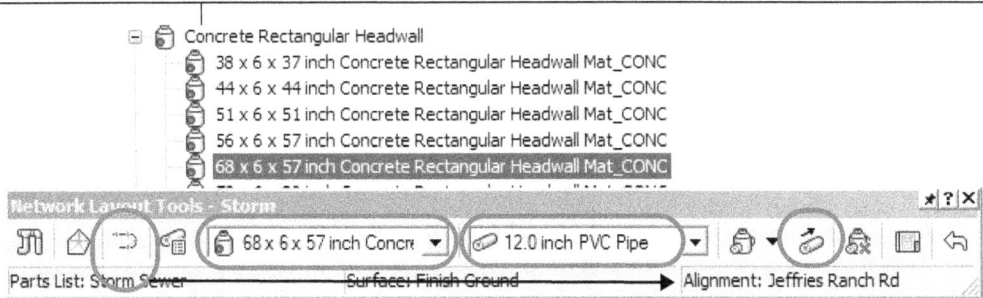

Concrete Rectangular Headwall
  38 x 6 x 37 inch Concrete Rectangular Headwall Mat_CONC
  44 x 6 x 44 inch Concrete Rectangular Headwall Mat_CONC
  51 x 6 x 51 inch Concrete Rectangular Headwall Mat_CONC
  56 x 6 x 57 inch Concrete Rectangular Headwall Mat_CONC
  68 x 6 x 57 inch Concrete Rectangular Headwall Mat_CONC

Network Layout Tools - Storm

68 x 6 x 57 inch Concre ▾   12.0 inch PVC Pipe ▾

Parts List: Storm Sewer   Surface: Finish Ground   Alignment: Jeffries Ranch Rd

Figure 10–34

5. The AutoCAD Civil 3D software prompts you for the locations of the structures. Select end point **pt1** and then select an approximate location near point **pt2** for the next structure location, as shown in Figure 10–35.

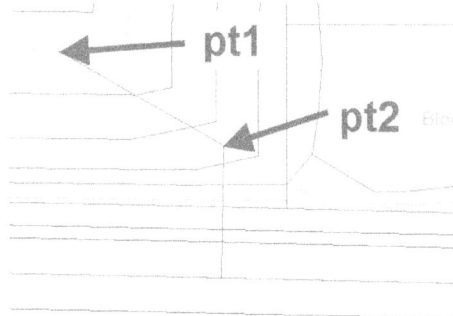

Figure 10–35

6. In the Network Layout Tools - STORM toolbar, select **Slab Top Cylindrical Structure 15 dia 18 dia Frm 4FrHt 4 Slab 3 Wall 4 Floor** for the manhole structure and toggle the slope to **Downslope**, as shown in Figure 10–36.

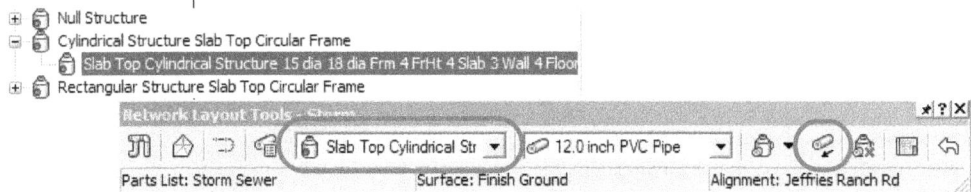

Null Structure
Cylindrical Structure Slab Top Circular Frame
  Slab Top Cylindrical Structure 15 dia 18 dia Frm 4 FrHt 4 Slab 3 Wall 4 Floor
Rectangular Structure Slab Top Circular Frame

Network Layout Tools - Storm

Slab Top Cylindrical Str ▾   12.0 inch PVC Pipe ▾

Parts List: Storm Sewer   Surface: Finish Ground   Alignment: Jeffries Ranch Rd

Figure 10–36

7. In the Command Line, you should be prompted for a structure insertion point. Select **Startpoint** for a new starting point.

You will insert manholes based on Figure 10–37. The first structure, **pt1**, is located at station 11+00 of Jeffries Ranch Rd. The next structure, **pt2**, is located at the beginning of the curve, **pt3** is at the intersection of Jeffries Ranch Rd and Ascent Pl, and **pt4** is at a station of 3+24' along the Jeffries Ranch Rd alignment. Use the information shown in Figure 10–37 as a guide as you complete the following steps.

Figure 10–37

8. The AutoCAD Civil 3D software prompts you for the locations of the structures. Click ⨀ (Station offset), as shown in Figure 10–38.

Figure 10–38

9. When prompted for an alignment, select the **Jeffries Ranch Rd** alignment (select an alignment label if it is difficult to select the alignment centerline). Type **1100'** for the station and type **0** for the offset. Press <Esc> to exit the **Transparent** command while remaining in the **Pipe Layout** command.

10. Use the **end point** osnap to select **pt2** for the next structure, as shown in Figure 10–37.

11. When prompted for the next structure, select **Curve** in the command options to draw a curved pipe. When prompted for the end of curve, select the manhole structure at the intersection of Jeffries Ranch Rd and Ascent Pl, as shown in Figure 10–39.

A symbol should display indicating that you are tying into a manhole.

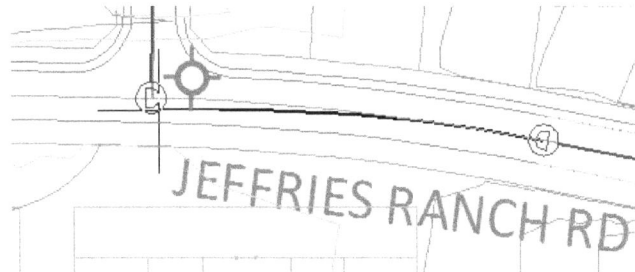

Figure 10–39

You now want to use a different pipe size.

12. In the Network Layout Tools - STORM toolbar, expand the drop-down list and select **18in PVC Pipe**, as shown in Figure 10–40.

Figure 10–40

13. At the prompt for the end of curve, type **L** and press <Enter> to draw a line. When prompted to select the next structure

location, click (Station offset), as shown in Figure 10–41.

Figure 10–41

14. When prompted for an alignment, select the **Jeffries Ranch Rd** alignment (select an alignment label if it is difficult to select the alignment centerline). Type **324'** for the station, and type **0** for the offset. Press <Esc> to exit the command and press <Enter> to exit the prompt for the insertion point of a structure.

You have made a design change and decided to insert a manhole east of the original intended location, as shown in Figure 10–42. This requires you to make further adjustments to the network.

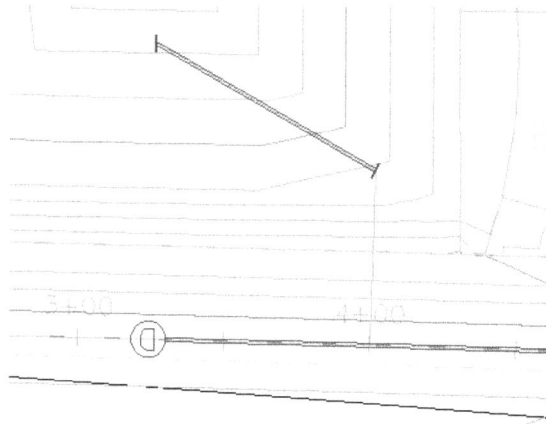

Figure 10–42

15. Close the Network Layout Tools toolbar by clicking the **X**.

16. Save the drawing.

Task 2 - View Pipe network in profile view.

---

1. Continue working with the drawing from the previous task or open **PIP1-C2-PipeWorks.dwg**.

2. Draw a window from left to right around the pipes to select the last three pipes and four structures that you created in the last task, as shown in Figure 10–43.

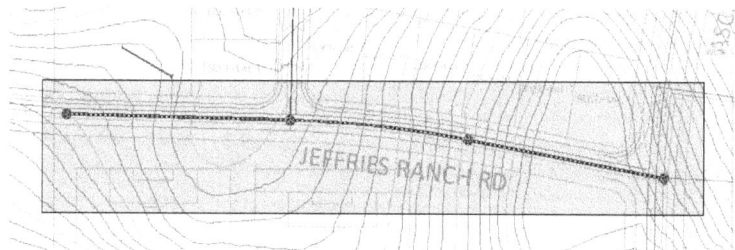

Figure 10–43

3. In the *Pipe Networks* contextual tab>Network Tools panel, click ⬡ (Draw Parts in Profile).

4. When prompted to select the Profile view, select the Jeffries Ranch Road profile view to the right of the site plan. Press <Esc> to release the selected pipe network parts.

5. Because you only selected certain network parts to be added to the profile, you will now review the parts that are relevant to this profile view. Select the Profile view and in the contextual tab>Modify Views panel, click ⬡ (Profile View Properties), as shown in Figure 10–44.

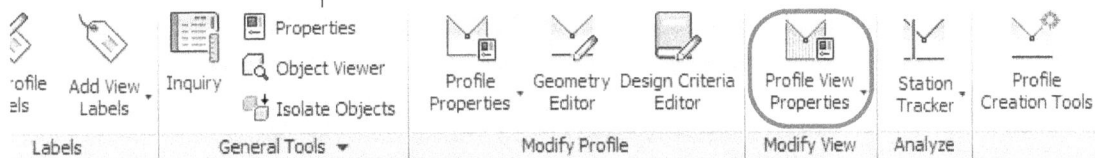

| Labels | | General Tools ▼ | Modify Profile | Modify View | Analyze |

Figure 10–44

6. In the Profile View Properties - Jeffries Ranch Rd dialog box, in the *Pipe Networks* tab, ensure that only the following parts are enabled, as shown in Figure 10–45: **Pipe - 5**, **6,** and **7**, and **Structure - 4**, **7**, **8**, and **9**. Click **OK** to close the dialog box and apply the changes.

Note that your numbers might be slightly different. The key is that not all pipes and structures will be checked.

Figure 10–45

7. Save the drawing.

10.5 Network Editing

You can edit pipe networks by graphically changing the components' locations in plan or profile views, using tabular fields in the Toolspace, *Prospector* tab and Grid View, and using the Object Properties dialog boxes. All of the commands are available in the shortcut menu that displays after you have selected and right-clicked on a part in plan. (Some, but not all, are available in profile.)

Pipe (and Structure) Properties

The Properties dialog box lists the object's name, dimensions, material, rotation angle, sump depth, etc., as shown in Figure 10–46 and Figure 10–47. Those displayed in black can be edited directly, while those displayed in gray are calculated by the software.

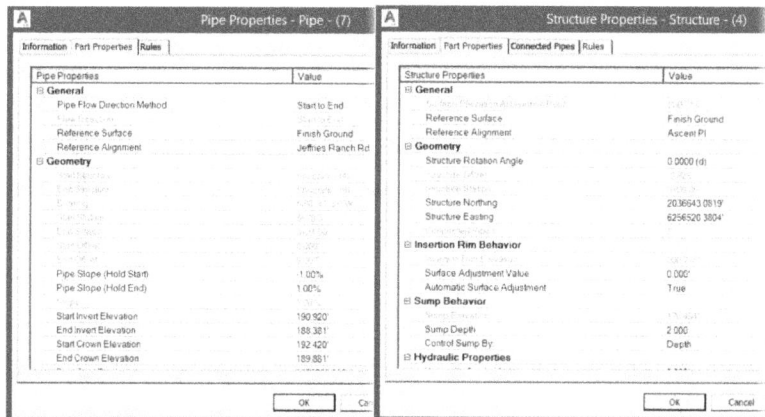

Figure 10–46

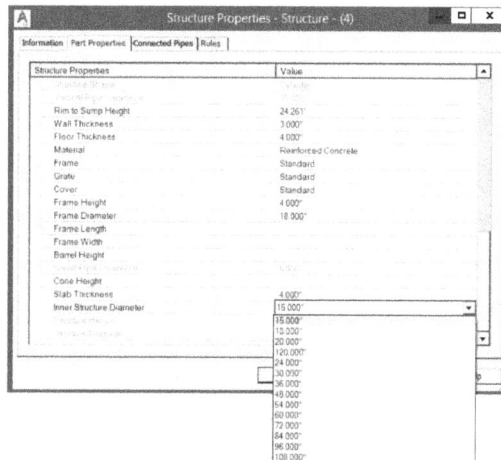

Figure 10–47

Swap Part

The **Swap Part** command exchanges one part for another from the same parts list, but in a different size. When starting the command, the AutoCAD Civil 3D software opens the Swap Part Size dialog box, which contains all of the part sizes from the parts list, as shown in Figure 10–48.

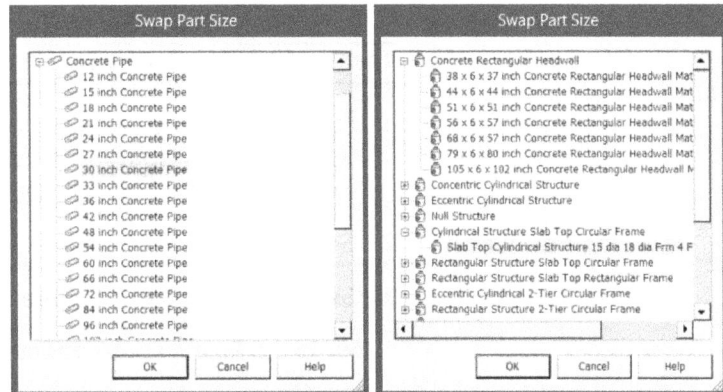

Figure 10–48

Connect/ Disconnect From Part

The **Disconnect From Part** command detaches a selected object from its connected part. Once detached, you can move the selected object and any of its remaining attached items to a new location.

Whether the **Disconnect From Part** or **Connect To Part** command displays in the shortcut menu depends on the state of the selected object. For example, if the object is a structure attached to pipes, the shortcut menu only displays **Disconnect From Part**. If the object is a pipe that is not connected to any other object, the shortcut menu displays **Connect To Part**.

Practice 10d | Editing Pipe Networks

Practice Objective

- Edit the gravity fed pipe networks graphically and using the Network Layout Tools toolbar.

Estimated time for completion: 15 minutes

Task 1 - Modify a pipe network.

1. Continue working with the drawing from the previous task or open **PIP1-D1-PipeWorks.dwg** from one of the *C:\Civil 3D Projects\Civil3D-Training\PipeNetworks* folders.

2. Select the preset view **Pipe-Edit.**

3. Select the headwall structure shown in Figure 10–49.

   - In the *Pipe Networks* contextual tab>Modify panel, click ✑ (Swap Part).
   - Select **12 inch Flared End Section**, and click **OK** to close the dialog box.

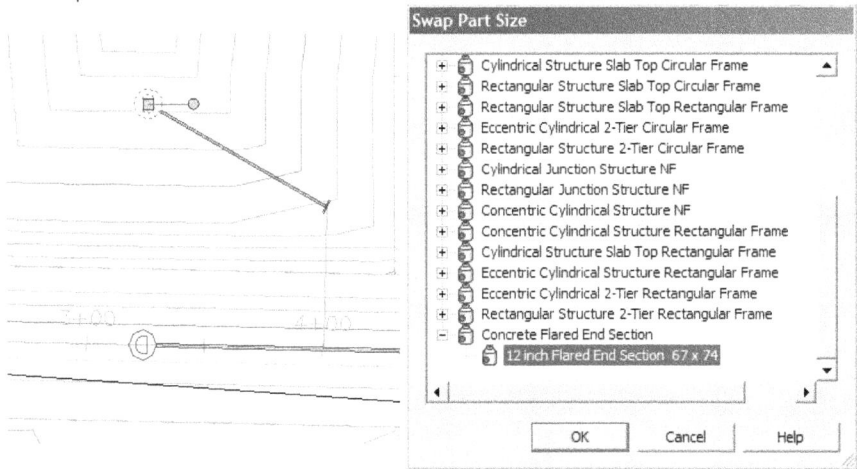

Figure 10–49

4. Keep the same structure selected. In the *Pipe Networks* contextual tab>Modify panel, click 🗄 (Structure Properties). Change the style of this structure to **Flared End Section**, and click **OK** to close the dialog box.

5. Select the same structure again. Note the grips. The square grip enables you to relocate the structure and end of the pipe, while the circular grip enables you to rotate the structure. Select the circular, rotation grip and rotate the structure as shown in Figure 10–50.

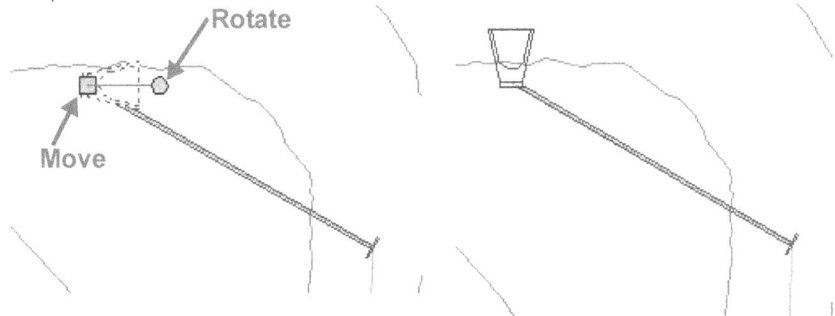

Figure 10–50

6. Press <Esc> to exit the selection.

7. Select the headwall on the opposite end of the pipe. In the

   Pipe Networks contextual tab>Modify panel, click 🗏 (Edit Pipe Network).

8. In the Network Layout Tools toolbar, click 🗑 (Delete Pipe Network Object) and select the south headwall. Press <Esc> to end the **Delete** command.

9. To connect the pipe to the STORM network, select the pipe structure, and select the south east grip to stretch the pipe. Hover the cursor over the manhole on Jeffries Ranch Rd until the connect to structure image displays, as shown in Figure 10–51. Click to accept the connection.

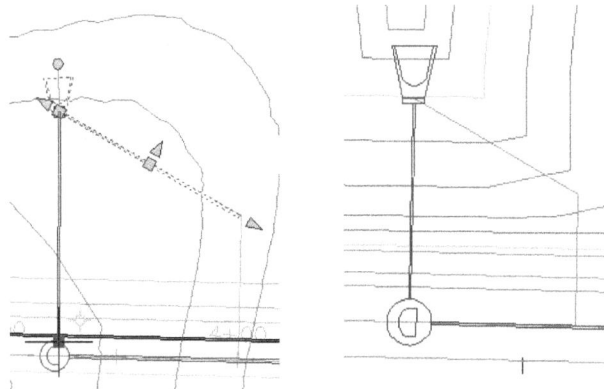

Figure 10–51

10. In Model Space, select the manhole structure that is south of the headwall structure. In the *Pipe Networks* contextual tab> Modify panel, click (Swap Part). In the parts list, select **48x48 Rect 2 Tier Structure 18 x 18 Frm**, as shown in Figure 10–52. Click **OK**. Then press <Esc> to release the part.

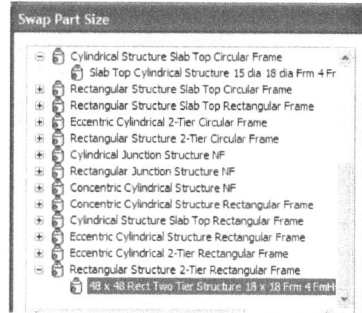

Figure 10–52

11. In Model Space, select the pipe that is connected to the headwall structure**.** In the *Pipe Networks* contextual tab> Modify panel, click (Swap Part). In the parts list, select **24in Concrete Pipe**. Press <Esc>.

Task 2 - Edit network data.

When creating the Pipe network, the AutoCAD Civil 3D software assigned names to each part. In this task, you will rename these parts so that they conform to company standards.

1. Continue working with the drawing from the previous task or open **PIP1-D2-PipeWorks.dwg**.

2. Select the preset view **Pipe-Create**.

3. In the *Modify* tab, select **Pipe Network**.

4. In the *Pipe Networks* tab>Modify panel, expand the drop-down list and select **Rename Parts**, as shown in Figure 10–53.

Figure 10–53

5. At the prompt to select network parts to rename, select the **manhole structure** at the intersection of Jeffries Ranch Rd and Ascent Blvd, and then select the **Flared End Section** that empties into the pond. The software will select all of the pipes and structures between the selected structures. Then select the **manhole structures** at the end of the cul-de-sac. Note that all of the parts between are also selected. Press <Enter> to end the selection.

6. You have selected 11 structures and 9 pipes, as shown in the dialog box in Figure 10–54. Complete the following:

   - For *Structure name template*, type **STM - <[Next Counter(CP)]>**.
   - For *Starting number*, type **1**.
   - For *Pipe name template*, type **Pipe - <[Next Counter(CP)]>**.
   - For *Starting number*, type **1**.
   - In the *Name conflict options* area, select **Rename existing parts**.
   - Click **OK** to accept the changes and close the dialog box.

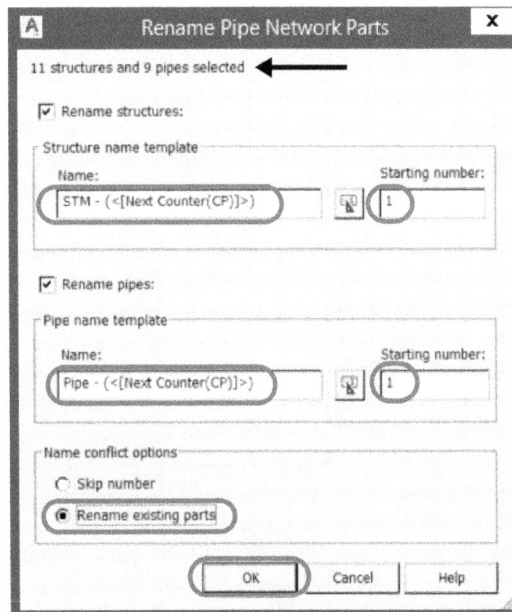

Figure 10–54

7. In the Status Bar, toggle on the **Quick Properties** icon, as shown in Figure 10–55. You will use it to edit the structure name.

Figure 10–55

8. In Model Space, select the **Flared End Section** structure. In the Properties palette, change the *Name* to **Flared End Section**, as shown in Figure 10–56.

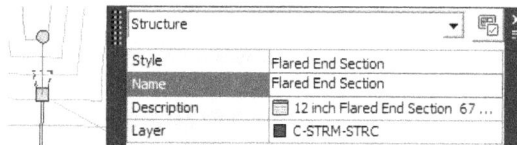

Figure 10–56

9. Save the drawing.

10.6 Annotating Pipe Networks

As with other AutoCAD Civil 3D labels, pipe network plan and profile labels are all style-based. A pipe label style can contain an extensive list of pipe network properties. The labels are scale- and rotation-sensitive and use the same interface for creating or modifying styles.

- The AutoCAD Civil 3D software can label pipes and structures as you draft them or later as required.

- In the *Annotate* tab>Add Labels panel, expand **Pipe Network** and select **Add Pipe Network Labels…** or expand **Add Pressure Network** and select **Add Pressure Network Labels** to label individual objects or an entire network. The Add Labels dialog box is shown in Figure 10–57.

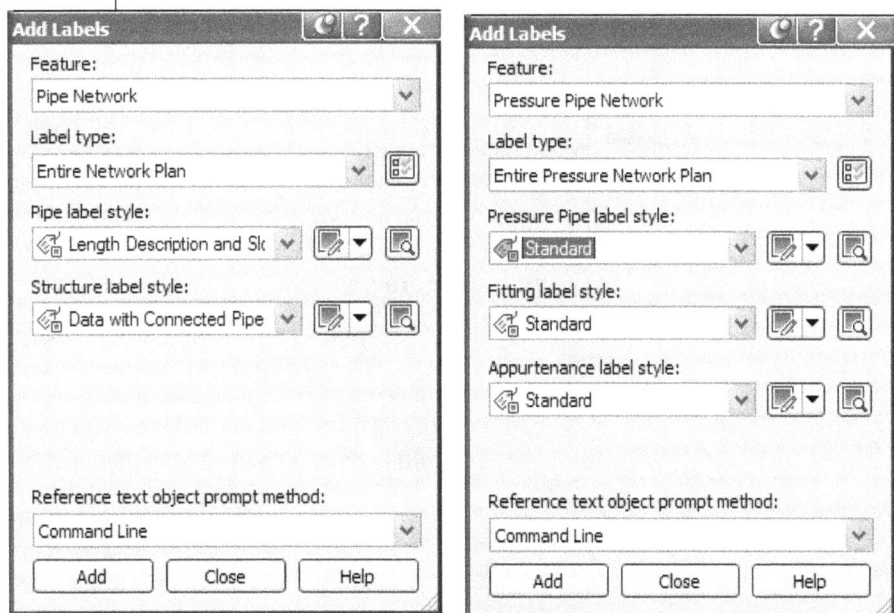

Figure 10–57

Most pipe labels annotate the length and slope of a specific pipe. If you have pipe bends and would rather not label each individual segment as a separate pipe, select the **Spanning** label type. It enables you to select multiple pipes that should be given a single label, which can include overall length, slope, and other properties.

Parts in a network can be renumbered quickly and easily by selecting **Modify>Pipe Network>Modify (panel)>Rename Parts**. Another method is to renumber each one manually using the Pipe Network Vistas view, which can be accessed in the Network Layout Tools toolbar, as shown in Figure 10–58. Labels automatically display the new part label.

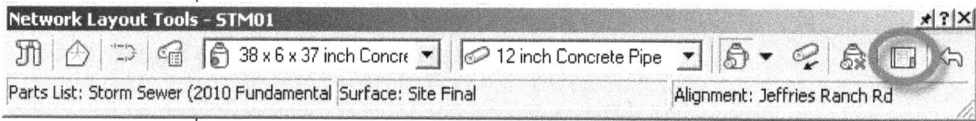

Figure 10–58

Pipe Networks in Sections

To display pipe networks in sections, they need to be included as a data source for the sections' sample line group. If a sample line group has been created before a pipe network, they are not automatically included. To include them, open the sample line group's Properties dialog box, select the *Sections* tab, and click **Sample more sources...**, as shown in Figure 10–59.

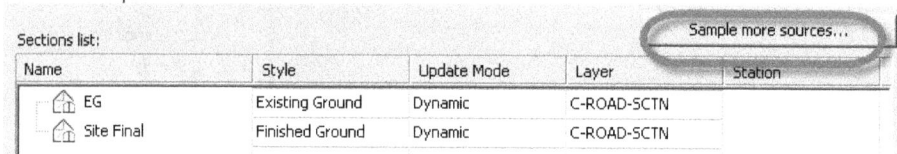

Figure 10–59

Pipe Network Reports and Tables

Pipe reports are available in the Toolspace, *Toolbox* tab (**Home>Palettes> Toolbox**), as shown in Figure 10–60.

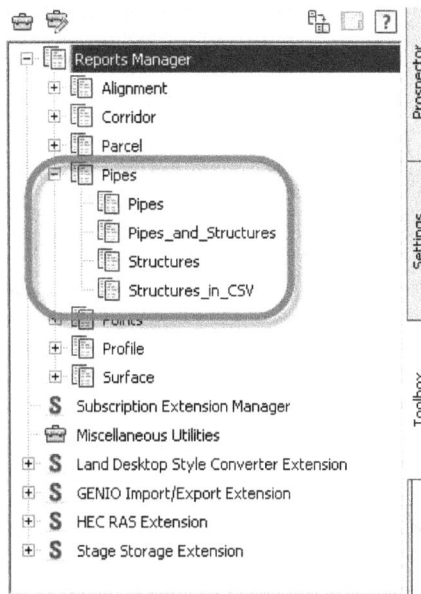

Figure 10–60

Pipe tables can be created inside drawing files using **Annotate> Add Tables>Pipe Network>Add Structure and Annotate> Add Tables>Pipe Network>Add Pipe**.

Practice 10e

Annotating Pipe Networks

Estimated time for completion: 20 minutes

Practice Objective

- Communicate important design information about pipe networks by adding labels to plan and profile views and creating reports.

Task 1 - Annotate pipe networks.

1. Continue working with the drawing from the previous practice or open **PIP1-E1-PipeWorks.dwg**.

2. Select the preset view **Pipe-Create**.

3. In the *Annotate* tab>Labels & Tables panel, select **Add Labels**, as shown in Figure 10–61.

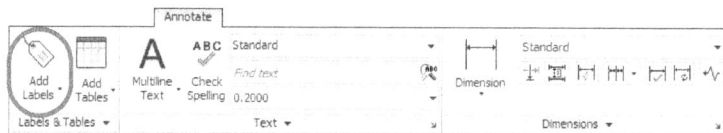

Figure 10–61

4. In the Add Labels dialog box, set the following parameters, as shown in Figure 10–62:

- *Feature:* **Pipe Network**
- *Label type:* **Entire Network Plan**
- *Pipe label style:* **Length Description and Slope**
- *Structure label style:* **Data with connected Pipes** (Storm)

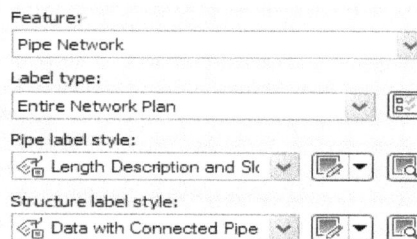

Figure 10–62

5. Click **Add**. When prompted, select any part in the **Storm network**.

6. Click **X** or click **Close** to close the Add labels dialog box.

7. Save the drawing.

Task 2 - Add labels to parts in the profile view.

1. Continue working with the drawing from the previous task or open **PIP1-E2-PipeWorks.dwg**

2. In the *Annotate* tab>Labels & Tables panel, select **Add Labels**.

3. In the Add Labels dialog box, set the following parameters, as shown in Figure 10–63:

   - *Feature:* **Pipe Network**
   - *Label type:* **Entire Network Profile**
   - *Pipe label style:* **Length Description and Slope**
   - *Structure label style:* **Data with Connected Pipe (Storm)**

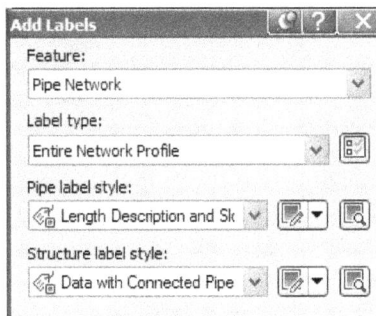

Figure 10–63

4. Click **Add**.

5. When prompted, select any of the network parts in the profile view, and click **X** to close the dialog box.

6. Save the drawing.

Task 3 - Create a Structure table.

1. Continue working with the drawing from the previous task or open **PIP1-E3-PipeWorks.dwg**.

2. In Model Space, select any Storm Pipe network part. In the *Pipe Networks* contextual tab>Labels & Tables panel (shown in Figure 10–64), expand ⬚ (Add Tables) and select **Add Structure**.

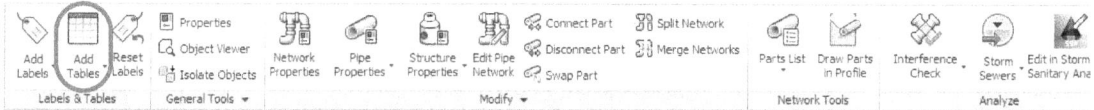

Figure 10–64

3. In the Structure Table Creation dialog box, for *Table style*, select **Structure with Pipes**. Select **Dynamic** and accept all of the other defaults. Click **OK** to close the dialog box, as shown in Figure 10–65.

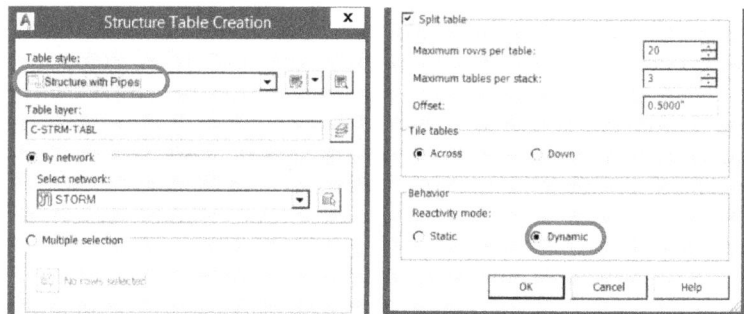

Figure 10–65

4. Zoom to an open space and insert the table, as shown in Figure 10–66.

Figure 10–66

5. Save the drawing.

Task 4 - Generate a Pipe network report.

1. Continue working with the drawing from the previous task or open **PIP1-E4-PipeWorks.dwg**.

2. In the *Home* tab>Palettes panel, click (Toolbox), as shown in Figure 10–67.

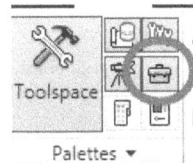

Figure 10–67

3. In the Toolspace, *Toolbox* tab, expand the *Reports Manager* collection, expand the *Pipes* collection, and select **Pipes_and_Structures**, as shown in Figure 10–68. Right-click and select **Execute**.

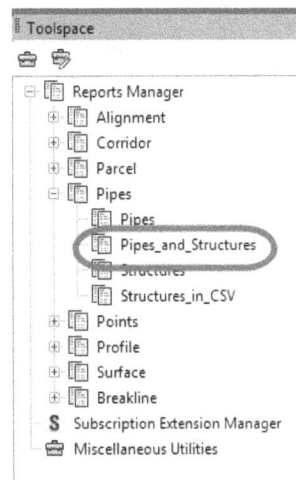

Figure 10–68

4. In the Export to XML Report dialog box, accept the defaults because you only have one network. Click **OK**.

5. Type **Pipes** for the name and ensure that the file format is **HTML**. Click **Save**. If prompted to overwrite the file, select **Yes**. The report displays as shown in Figure 10–69.

Your Company Name

123 Main Street

Suite #321

City, State 01234

Pipes and Structures Report	**Client:** Client Company
Project Name: C:\Civil 3D Projects\Civil3D-Training\PipeNetworks\PIP1-F3-PipeWorks.dwg	**Project Description:**
Report Date: 4/20/2012 4:49:52 PM	**Prepared by:** Preparer

Pipe Network: Storm
Pipes

Name	Shape	Size (in)	Material	US Node	DS Node	US Invert (ft)	DS Invert (ft)	2D Length (ft) center-to-center edge-to-edge	% Slope
Pipe - (9) (Storm)	Circular	D:12.00		STM - (11) (Storm)	STM - (10) (Storm)	185.73	181.98	374.56 359.56	1.00
Pipe - (8) (Storm)	Circular	D:12.00		STM - (10) (Storm)	STM - (9) (Storm)	181.98	181.35	63.03 48.03	1.00
Pipe - (7)	Circular	D:12.00		STM - (9)	STM - (8)	181.35	178.45	269.83	1.00

Figure 10–69

6. Save the drawing.

10.7 Pressure Pipe Networks

Pressure Pipe Networks are available for designing and laying out pressurized systems, such as water networks. There are three types of pressure pipe network objects: Pipes, Fittings, and Appurtenances.

Pressure Pipes can be created from existing objects (lines, arcs, 2D and 3D polylines, splines, feature lines, alignments, and survey figures) or created by layout.

Pressure Pipes

To start the Pressure Pipe Layout command, in the *Home* tab> Create Design panel, expand **Pipe Networks** and click

(Pressure Network Creation Tools). This opens the Create Pressure Pipe Network dialog box, as shown in Figure 10–70. In it, you can type a name and description, set the parts list to use, and the surface and alignment to reference. You can also set label styles for pipes, fittings, and appurtenances so that they receive labels as you layout the pressure network.

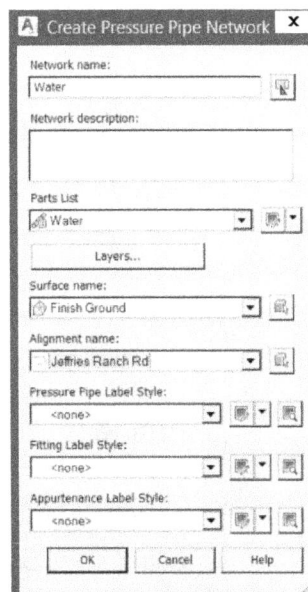

Figure 10–70

Once in the command, the *Pressure Network Plan Layout* contextual tab displays, as shown in Figure 10–71.

Figure 10–71

The reference surface and alignment that were set up during creation display in the Network Settings panel along with the current parts list. The Cover setting is also found in the Network settings panel and specifies the minimum depth the network should be below the selected surface. Ideally, you would select a finished ground surface. In the Layout panel, you can select the pipe material to use. Pressure pipes can be laid out by themselves or with bends. When you lay a pipe out by itself

using (Pipes Only), you can set the deflection angle with a compass glyph at pipe to pipe match locations (vertices), as shown on the left in Figure 10–72. Note that the ticks only permit a slight bend in the pipe when a fitting is not used. Using the

 (Pipes & Bends) in the *Layout* tab automatically places fittings with many more bend options in the compass glyph (up to 90 degree bends), as shown on the right in Figure 10–72.

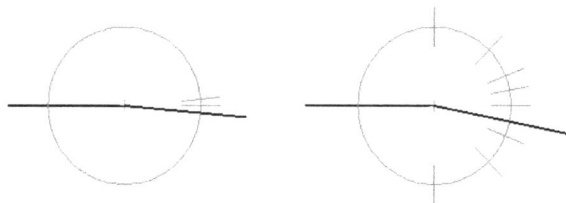

Figure 10–72

Fittings

Fittings enable you to specify the T's and other bends to layout a pressurized utility network. Additional fittings can be added to the AutoCAD Civil 3D software using the parts catalog. To add

additional fittings to a network in the drawing click (Add Fitting) in the *Pressure Network Plan Layout* tab>Insert panel.

Appurtenances

Appurtenances are valves, which can be added in the same manner as fittings. Click ⚙ (Add Appurtenance) in the *Pressure Network Plan Layout* tab>Insert panel.

New 💡
in **2018**

Swap Pressure Parts

Similar to gravity fed pipe networks, pressure pipe networks have the option to exchange one part for another, but in a different type, part family, or size. To start the command, select the part, right-click, and select **Swap Pressure Part.** The Swap Pressure Network Parts dialog box displays as shown in Figure 10–73.

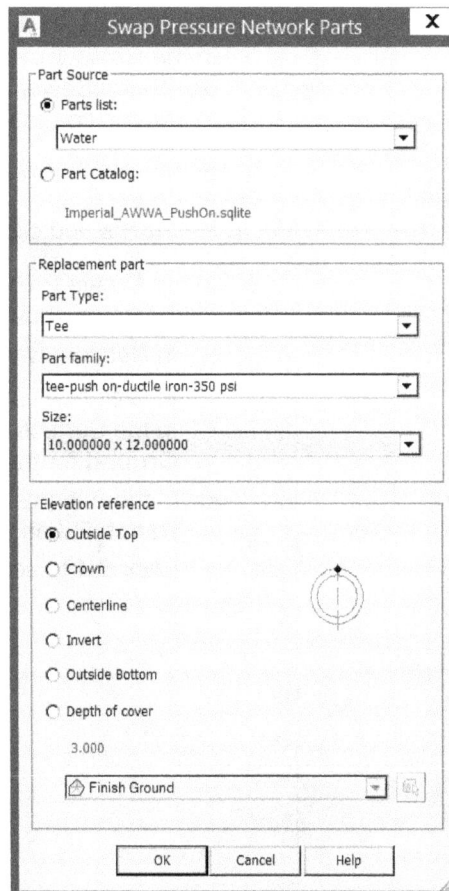

Figure 10–73

Practice 10f

Estimated time for completion: 15 minutes

Create a Pressure Pipe Network

Practice Objective

- Create and edit a pressure pipe network.

Task 1 - Create a Pressure Pipe Network.

In this task, you will create a water network using the **Pressure Pipe Network** commands.

1. Continue working with the drawing from the previous practice or open **PIP1-F1-PipeWorks.dwg** from the *C:\Civil 3D Projects\Civil3D-Training\PipeNetworks* folder.

2. Select the preset view **Pipe-Create**.

3. In the *Home* tab>Layers panel, click (Layer Off). Select any Storm Sewer pipe network label and then press <Enter> to end the command.

4. In the *Home* tab>Create Design panel, expand **Pipe Networks** and click (Pressure Network Creation Tools).

5. In the Create Pressure Pipe Network dialog box, do the following, as shown in Figure 10–74:
    - In *Network Name*, type **Water**.
    - In the Parts List drop-down list, select **Water**.
    - In the Surface name drop-down list, select **Finish Ground** for the reference surface.
    - In the Alignment name drop-down list, select **Jeffries Ranch Rd** as the reference alignment.
    - Click **OK** to accept the selection and close the dialog box.

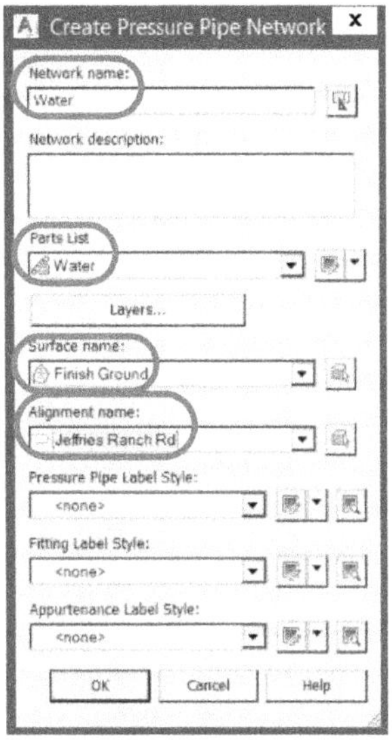

Figure 10–74

6. In the *Pressure Network Plan Layout* contextual tab>
Network Settings panel, verify that the cover is set to **3'**, as
shown in Figure 10–75.

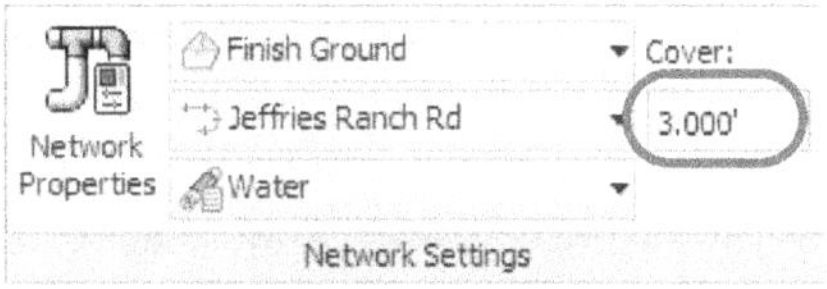

Figure 10–75

7. In the *Pressure Network Plan Layout* contextual tab> Layout

panel, click ✎ (Pipes Only) and set the pipe size and
material to **pipe-12 in-push on-ductile iron**, as shown in
Figure 10–76.

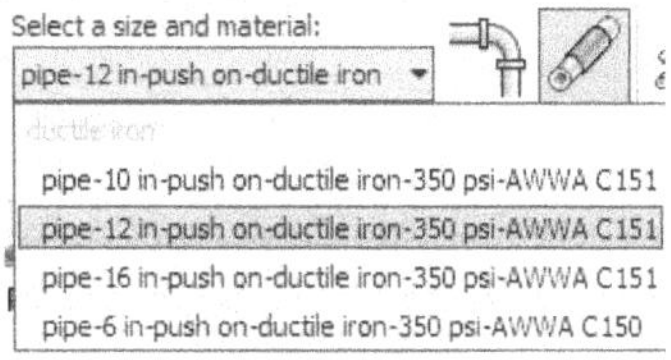

Figure 10–76

8. In the drawing, use the **Endpoint** object snap to help you select the points along the polyline north of the storm sewer, as shown in Figure 10–77.

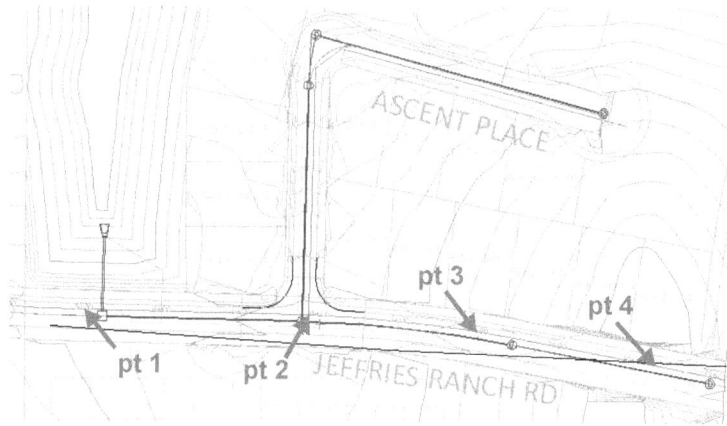

Figure 10–77

9. At the second point the pipe only glyph should be displayed, as shown in Figure 10–78. Rather than accept one of the deflection angles, type **C** and press <Enter> to start a curve.

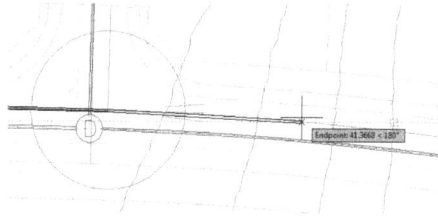

Figure 10–78

10. After the third point, type **S** and press <Enter> to make a straight pipe run. Then, place pt 4.

11. Press <Enter> to end the command and save the drawing.

Task 2 - Place fittings and appurtenances

1. Continue working with the drawing from the previous task or open **PIP1-F2-PipeWorks.dwg**

2. In the *Pressure Network Plan Layout* contextual tab> Layout panel, click (Add Fitting).

3. Select the end point where you placed point 2 in the previous task, as shown in Figure 10–79. Press <Esc> to end the command.

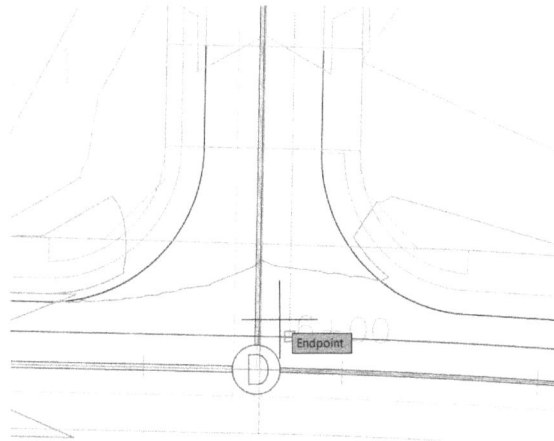

Figure 10–79

4. Note that the fitting is set in the wrong rotation. Select it and pick the circular grip. Rotate it as shown in Figure 10–80. Press <Esc> to release the fitting.

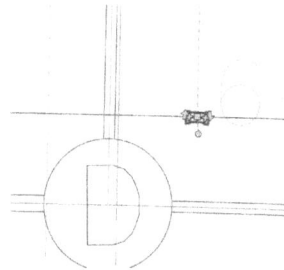

Figure 10–80

After placing the fitting, note that you need to extend the pressure network along Ascent Pl. To do this, first change the fitting so that you can tee off this location.

5. Select the fitting placed in Step 3. Right-click and select **Swap Pressure Parts**.

6. In the Swap Pressure Network Parts dialog box, do the following, as shown in Figure 10–81.

- For the *Part Type*, select **Tee**.
- For the *Part Family*, select **tee-push on-ductile iron-350 psi**.
- For the *Size*, select **10.000000 x 12.0000000**.
- Click **OK**.

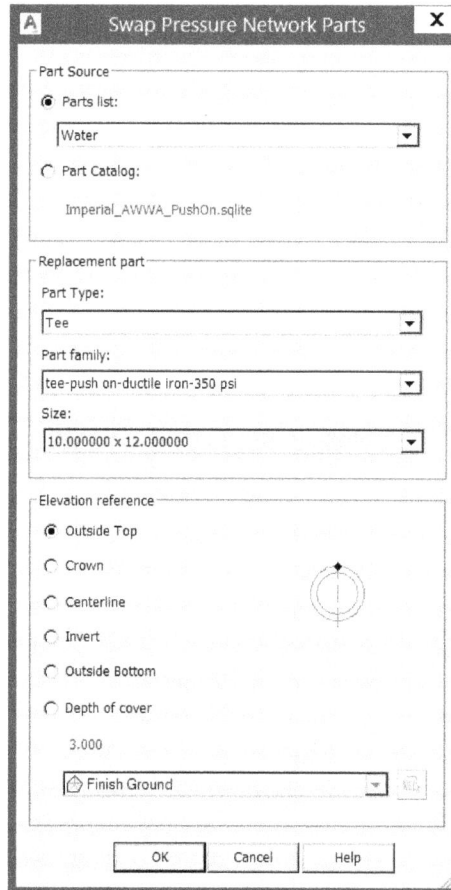

Figure 10–81

7. Select it and pick the circular grip. Rotate it, as shown in Figure 10–82. Press <Esc> to release the fitting.

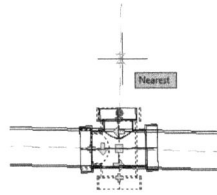

Figure 10–82

8. In the *Pressure Network Plan Layout* contextual tab> Layout panel, click (Pipes & Bends).

9. Set the pipe size and material to **pipe-10 in-push on-ductile iron**. Hover over the tee fitting that you placed until the structure tooltip image displays, as shown in Figure 10–83. Click to accept the connection and start the new pipe.

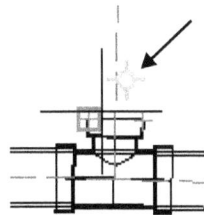

Figure 10–83

10. Use the **Endpoint** object snap to help you select the next point as shown in Figure 10–84.

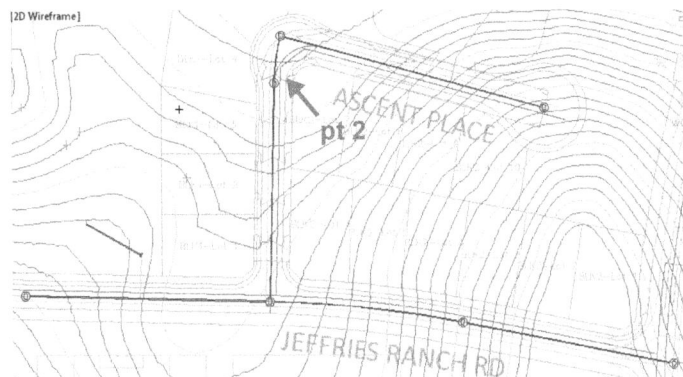

Figure 10–84

11. Note that the bend options available for the next pipe will require you to make a change in the original conceptual design, as shown in Figure 10–85. Hover the cursor over the intended pipe intersection and then move the cursor to the left along the projectory of the original pipe alignment. Click when the preprogrammed bend displays to intersect the intended route. Press <Esc> to end the command.

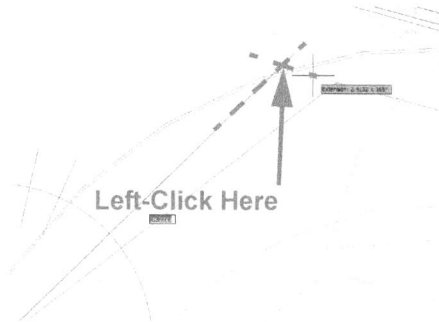

Figure 10–85

12. Save the drawing.

Task 3 - Draw pressure pipes in the profile view.

1. Continue working with the drawing from the previous task or open **PIP1-F3-PipeWorks.dwg**

2. Select the three water pipes running along Jeffries Ranch Rd. In the *Pressure Networks* contextual tab, click

   (Draw Parts in Profile).

3. When prompted, select the **Jeffries Ranch Rd** profile view.

4. Save the drawing.

Chapter Review Questions

1. What does the **Swap Part** command do? (Select all that apply.)

   a. Make a pipe a structure.

   b. Make a structure a pipe.

   c. Change a pipe for another pipe of another size or material.

   d. Change a structure for another structure type or size.

2. What type of structure CANNOT be used in a regular pipe network?

   a. Headwall

   b. Manhole

   c. Gate Valve

   d. Catch Basin

3. Pressure pipe networks can contain all of the following except...

   a. Manhole

   b. Appurtenances

   c. Pipes

   d. Fittings

4. To draw pipes and structures in a profile view you need to...

   a. Manually draw each pipe and structure with the profile creation tools.

   b. Click **Draw Parts in Profile View** on the Network Layout Tools toolbar.

   c. Select the profile view, right-click and select **Draw Parts from Pipe Network**.

   d. Select the pipes and structures in the plan view, click **Draw in Profile View** on the *Pipe Network* contextual tab, and select the profile view in which you want to draw.

5. Pipe Networks can be created from feature lines.

   a. True

   b. False

Command Summary

Button	Command	Location
	Create Pipes From Objects	• **Ribbon:** *Home* tab>Create Design panel>Pipe Network • **Command Prompt:** createnetworkfromobject
	Draw Parts in Profile	• **Contextual Ribbon:** *Pipe Networks* tab>Network Tools panel • **Command Prompt:** addnetworkpartstoprofile
	Draw Pressure Parts in Profile	• **Contextual Ribbon:** *Pressure Networks* tab>Network Tools • **Command Prompt:** addpressurepartstoprof
	Edit Pipe Network	• **Contextual Ribbon:** *Pipe Networks* tab>Modify panel
	Pipe Network Creation Tools	• **Ribbon:** *Home* tab>Create Design panel>Pipe Network • **Command Prompt:** createnetwork
	Pressure Network Creation Tools	• **Ribbon:** *Home* tab>Create Design panel>Pipe Network • **Command Prompt:** createpressurenetwork

Chapter

11

Quantity Take Off/Sections

In this chapter you create sample lines along the roadway to show what the existing ground and finished ground are doing at predetermined stations along the alignment. You use these samples to help calculate cut and fill quantities, and material quantities. You also show the sections by creating section views.

Learning Objectives in this Chapter

- Sample existing and proposed data along an alignment in preparation to create sections and section views.

- Calculate volumes for earthwork and other materials along a corridor model.

- Calculate the cost of design by assigning pay items to specific objects.

- Create section views to display cross-sectional elevations of existing and proposed surface data at predefined intervals along an alignment.

11.1 Sample Line Groups

Sample lines are objects that sample corridor elements for display in cross-sections and are used to form the basis of material lists that are used in corridor volumetric calculations. Sections are organized into groups for ease of selection and for managing common properties. A drawing can have any number of sample line groups for the same alignment.

The **Sample Lines** command is located in the *Home* tab>Profile & Section Views panel, as shown in Figure 11–1.

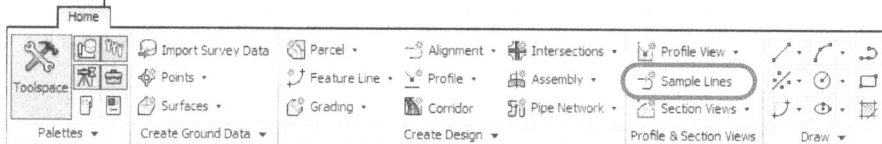

Figure 11–1

Selecting this command opens the Create Sample Line Group dialog box, as shown in Figure 11–2.

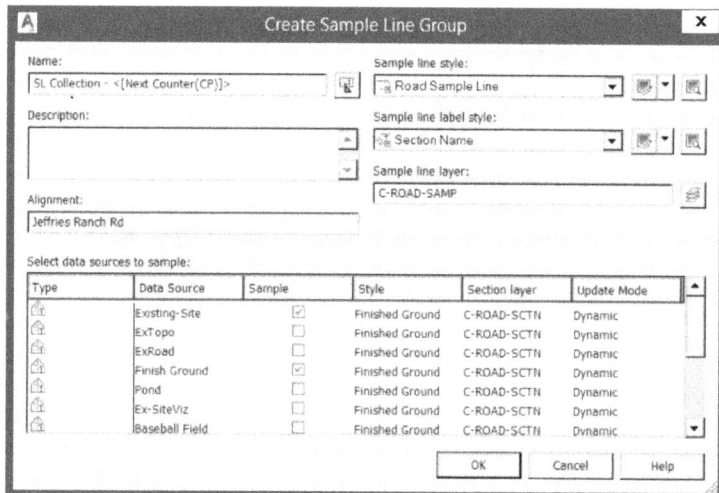

Figure 11–2

The Create Sample Line Group dialog box identifies all of the elements that might be included in the section:

- (corridor geometry)

- (terrain surfaces)

- (corridor surfaces)

- (pipe networks).

The *Select data sources to sample* area displays:

- The object type

- Where the object comes from

- Whether or not to sample the object

- The style to use for the sections

- The preferred layers

- The update mode for the section.

After adjusting the values for the Create Sample Line dialog box and clicking **OK**, the Sample Line Tools toolbar becomes active, as shown in Figure 11–3.

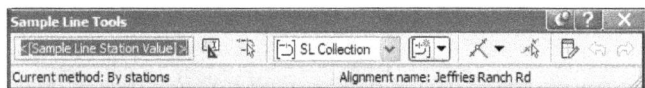

Figure 11–3

The Sample Line Tools toolbar is the control center for creating sample lines. The default method is **At a Station**, as shown in Figure 11–4, which means you are able to select a specific station at which to add a sample line.

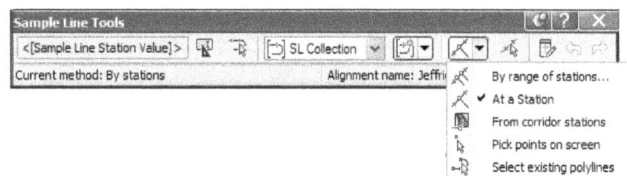

Figure 11–4

Other methods include:

- **By range of stations:** Enables you to specify a range of stations, sampling width, and other options where you want sample lines to be created. Sampling increments can be relative to an absolute station, or relative to a station range set.

- **From corridor stations:** Creates a sample line at all of the predefined corridor sections. This method also opens the Create Sample Line dialog box in which you can define the station range and swath widths for the sections.

- **Pick points on screen:** Enables you to select points in the drawing to define the path of the section. This type of section can have multiple vertices.

- **Select existing polylines:** Includes section lines based on existing polylines in the drawing. The polyline does not have to be perpendicular to the center line and can have multiple segments.

The dialog box that opens for the **By range of stations** option is shown in Figure 11–5.

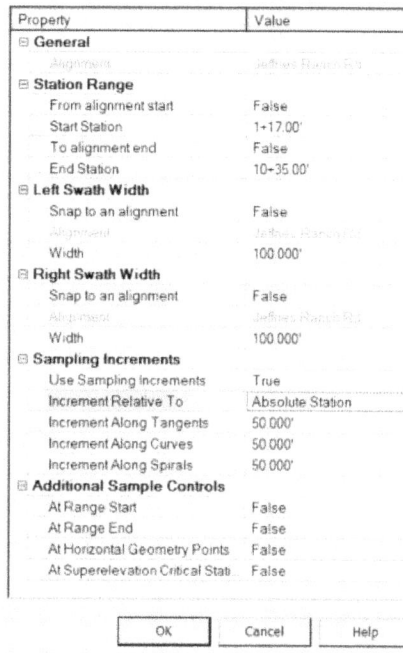

Property	Value
⊟ **General**	
Alignment	Jeffries Ranch Rd
⊟ **Station Range**	
From alignment start	False
Start Station	1+17.00'
To alignment end	False
End Station	10+35.00'
⊟ **Left Swath Width**	
Snap to an alignment	False
Alignment	Jeffries Ranch Rd
Width	100.000'
⊟ **Right Swath Width**	
Snap to an alignment	False
Alignment	Jeffries Ranch Rd
Width	100.000'
⊟ **Sampling Increments**	
Use Sampling Increments	True
Increment Relative To	Absolute Station
Increment Along Tangents	50.000'
Increment Along Curves	50.000'
Increment Along Spirals	50.000'
⊟ **Additional Sample Controls**	
At Range Start	False
At Range End	False
At Horizontal Geometry Points	False
At Superelevation Critical Stati...	False

OK   Cancel   Help

Figure 11–5

After creating the sample line group, the Toolspace, *Prospector* tab lists the individual sample lines under the sample line group's name. Each entry in the list includes all of the sampled elements for a section, as shown in Figure 11–6.

Figure 11–6

Modifying Sample Line Groups

New sample line groups can be added, existing groups can be deleted, swath widths (section sample width) can be adjusted, and new data sources can be added (such as newly created pipe networks) using the commands in the Modify drop-down list in the Sample Line Tools toolbar or the contextual *Sample Line* tab, as shown in Figure 11–7.

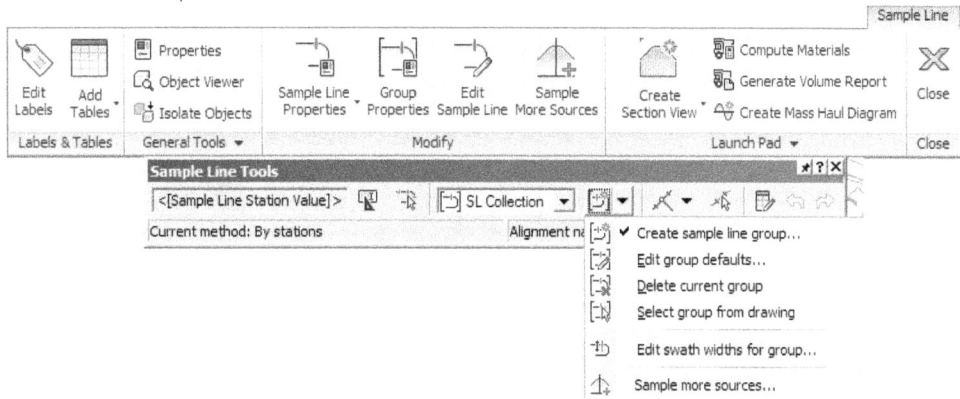

Figure 11–7

Sample line properties (such as display styles) can also be adjusted through the sample line group's properties, in the Toolspace, *Prospector* tab.

Practice 11a

Creating Sections - Part I

Practice Objective

- Create sample lines and review sample line data in preparation for creating cross-section sheets.

Estimated time for completion: 10 minutes

Task 1 - Create sample lines.

1. Open **QTO1-A1-Sections.dwg** from the *C:\Civil 3D Projects\Civil3D-Training\QTO-Sections* folder.

2. If not already set, change the *Annotation Scale* to **1"=30'** in the Status Bar, which is a scale more appropriate for displaying cross-sections.

3. In the *Home* tab>Profile and Section Views panel, click

   (Sample Lines).

4. When prompted to select an alignment, press <Enter> and select **Jeffries Ranch Rd**. Click **OK** to exit the dialog box.

The Create Sample Line Group dialog box opens, listing multiple data sources.

5. Verify that the *Sample* column is cleared of all but the **Existing-Site, Finish Ground**, **Jeffries Ranch Rd**, **Jeffries Ranch Rd surface, Corridor - (1), Corridor - (1) surface,** and **Water** as shown in Figure 11–8. Leave the other settings at their defaults and click **OK**.

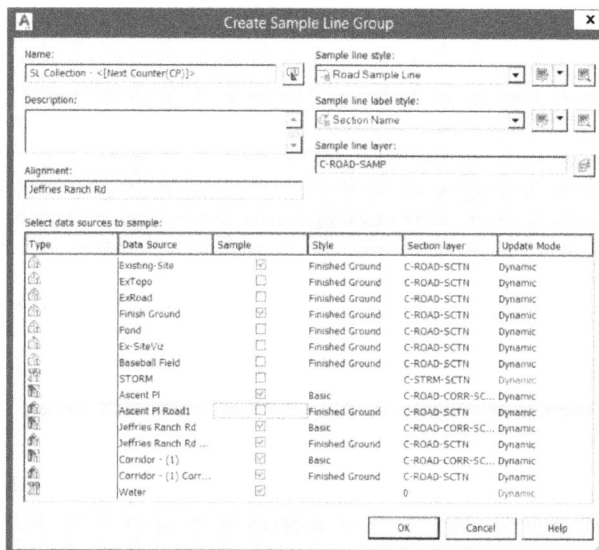

Figure 11–8

6. In the Sample Line Tools toolbar, select to create sample lines **By range of stations...**, as shown in Figure 11–9.

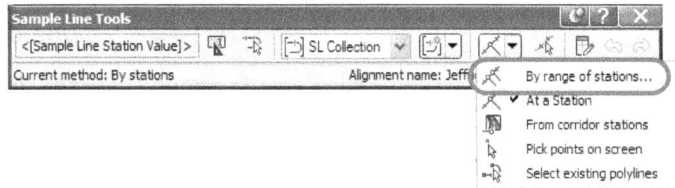

Figure 11–9

7. In the Create Sample Lines dialog box, review the settings, as shown in Figure 11–10.

   - Under *Station Range*, set *From alignment start* and *To alignment end* to **False**.
   - Set the *Start Station* to **117'** and the *End Station* to **1035'**.
   - Set both the Left and Right Swath Width[s] to **100'**.
   - Under *Sampling Increments*, set *Increment Along Tangents* and *Increments Along Curves* to **50'**.

This is because the alignment extends beyond the design ground data.

Property	Value
⊟ **General**	
Alignment	Jeffries Ranch Rd
⊟ **Station Range**	
From alignment start	False
Start Station	1+17.00'
To alignment end	False
End Station	10+35.00'
⊟ **Left Swath Width**	
Snap to an alignment	False
Alignment	Jeffries Ranch Rd
Width	100.000'
⊟ **Right Swath Width**	
Snap to an alignment	False
Alignment	Jeffries Ranch Rd
Width	100.000'
⊟ **Sampling Increments**	
Use Sampling Increments	True
Increment Relative To	Absolute Station
Increment Along Tangents	50.000'
Increment Along Curves	50.000'
Increment Along Spirals	50.000'
⊟ **Additional Sample Controls**	
At Range Start	False
At Range End	False
At Horizontal Geometry Points	False
At Superelevation Critical Stati...	False

Figure 11–10

8. Click **OK** when done.

9. In the Command Line, press <Enter> to close the dialog box.

10. Save the drawing.

Task 2 - Review Sample Line Data.

1. Continue working with the drawing from the previous task or open **QTO1-A2-Sections.dwg**.

2. In the Toolspace, *Prospector* tab, expand the *Alignment* collection, expand the *Centerline Alignments* collection, expand the *Jeffries ranch Rd* collection, expand the *Sample Line Groups* collection, and select **SL Collection**, as shown in Figure 11–11.

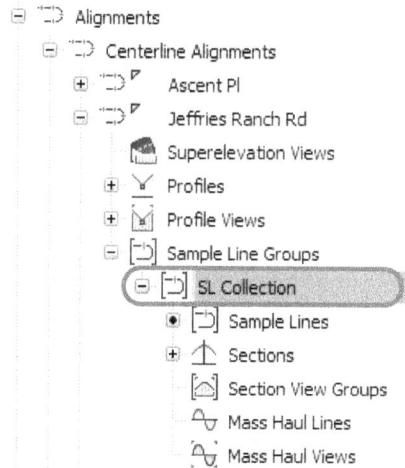

Figure 11–11

3. Right-click and select **Properties**. In the Sample Line Group Properties dialog box, in the *Sections* tab, you can re-assign styles and layers, and add new data sources.

4. Click **Sample more sources...** in the top right corner.

5. Select **Storm** from the list on the left and click **Add**, as shown in Figure 11–12. Click **OK** to exit.

Note that the Pressure Pipes do not display here.

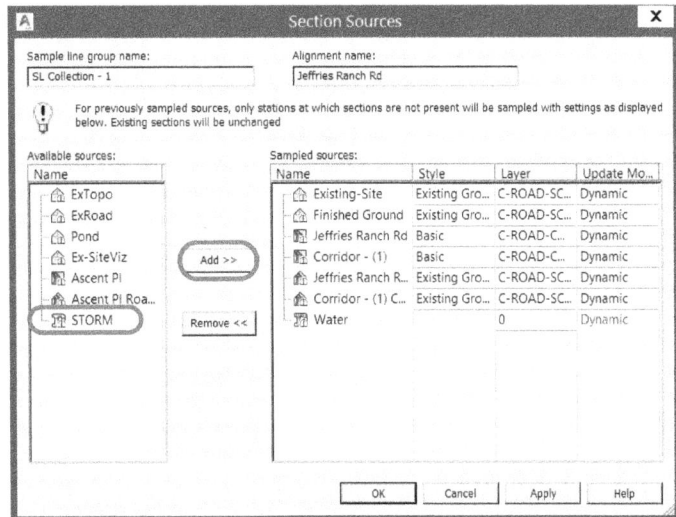

Figure 11–12

6. The *Sample Lines* tab enables you to change the swath widths of individual sections numerically. Click **OK** to exit.

7. Save the drawing.

11.2 Section Volume Calculations

Two types of quantity takeoffs can be calculated based on sections: earthwork volumes and material volumes. Earthwork volumes represent the amount of cut (existing material above the vertical design) or fill (the vertical design above the existing material). Material volumes are the amount of materials required to build the road. Materials include asphalt pavement, concrete curbing, sub-base materials, and other materials.

Earthwork Volumes

Earthwork volumes represent an amount of displaced surface materials. The displacement represents the excavation of high areas or filling of low areas in the existing ground surface, relative to the vertical road design.

One goal road designers strive for is to balance the amount of excavated material (called cut) and the amount of material to be added (called fill). On any site, not all of the excavated material (cut) is reusable. For example, the spoil materials could be from a bog, a type of material that does not compact well, or rock debris. The reuse of cut material can be a percentage of the overall cut value and affects the overall earthwork calculation. An example is shown in Figure 11–13.

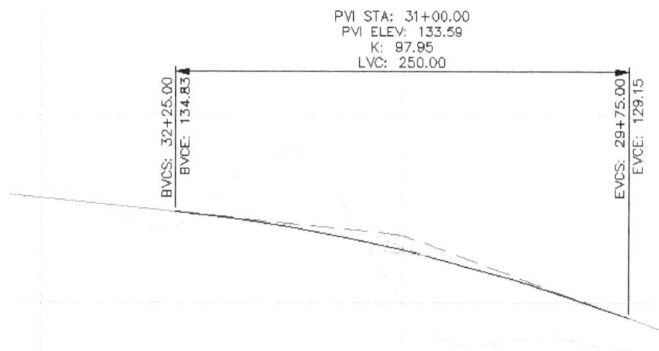

Figure 11–13

The earthworks calculations are applied between the existing ground surface and the datum surface of an assembly. The datum surface represents the roadbed on which the sub-base gravel, asphalt, and concrete materials lie. Earthwork volumes affect the revisions that occur to a roadway design. For example, excessive cut material (material needing excavation) could lead to raising the vertical design or, if possible, moving the horizontal alignment to create less cut.

Mass Haul

A mass haul diagram can be generated and used as a visual representation of the cumulative cut and fill material volumes along a corridor. Contractors use mass haul diagrams as a primary tool in determining and balancing haulage costs when bidding on an earthwork job. Mass haul is the volume of excavated material multiplied by the distance it is required to be moved. When the mass haul line is above the balance line, it indicates how much cut there is going to be at that station. When the mass haul line is below the balance line, it indicates the volume to be filled. To generate a mass haul diagram, you need an alignment, a sample line group, and a materials list. The mass haul diagram calculates and displays the following:

- The distance over which cut and fill volumes balance.

- Free haul and overhaul volumes.

- Volumes offset by borrow pits and dump sites.

Construction costs can be reduced by enabling the designer to compare alternative designs, add dump sites, and borrow pits at key locations in the free haul distance, thus eliminating a portion of the overhaul volume. An example of a mass haul diagram is shown in Figure 11–14.

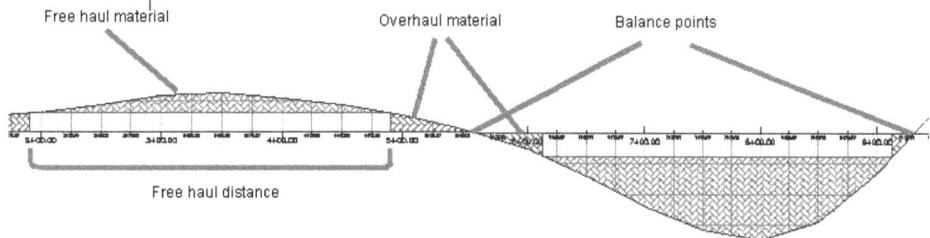

Figure 11–14

Material Volumes

Subassembly shapes represent the materials available for quantity takeoffs. These quantities come from the subassembly shapes (e.g., curb, pave, shoulder, sidewalk, etc.).

Quantity Takeoff Criteria

The Quantity Takeoff Criteria defines the surfaces and materials to be analyzed. Takeoff criteria can identify two surfaces for earthwork calculations and/or a list of shapes for material volumes.

The criteria style entries are generic because they are intended to be used on multiple corridors, which might contain different subassembly components. When computing section calculations, you are prompted to identify which entries correspond to the corridor shapes. The Quantity Takeoff Criteria dialog box is shown in Figure 11–15.

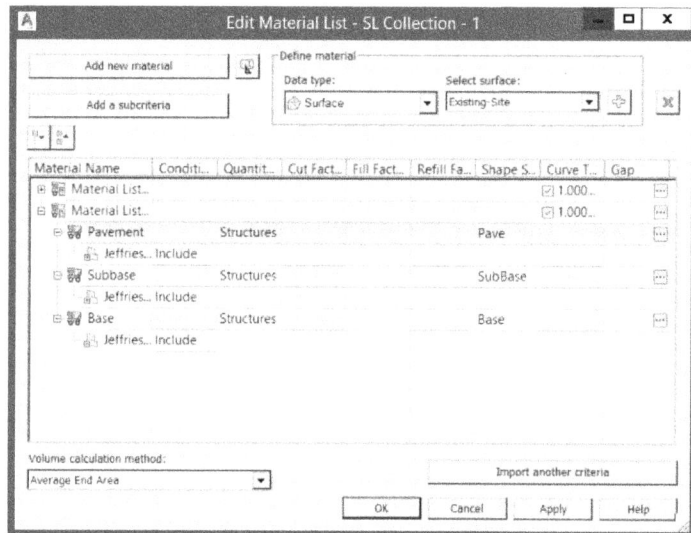

Figure 11–15

Define Materials

After defining the volume criteria, you create data from the criteria settings. In the *Analyze* tab>Volumes and Materials panel, click (Compute Materials) to set the alignment and a sample line group to use for data extraction. The command is shown in Figure 11–16.

Figure 11–16

When the Edit Material List dialog box opens, you can associate surfaces and/or structures (subassembly shapes) to the appropriate entries. Click **OK** to exit. The AutoCAD Civil 3D software then calculates the required report data.

Practice 11b

Quantity Take Off - Part I

Practice Objective

Estimated time for completion: 20 minutes

- List the various types of projects that are going to use alignments and profiles in their designs.

Task 1 - Generate Earthworks Quantities.

In this task you will compute the site cut and fill required to create the datum surface below the corridor. You will then calculate the construction materials that will be placed above the datum (asphalt, gravel, etc.).

1. Open **QTO1-B1-Sections.dwg** from the *C:\Civil 3D Projects\Civil3D-Training\QTO-Sections* folder.

2. In the *Analyze* tab>Volumes and Materials panel, click

   (Compute Materials), as shown in Figure 11–17.

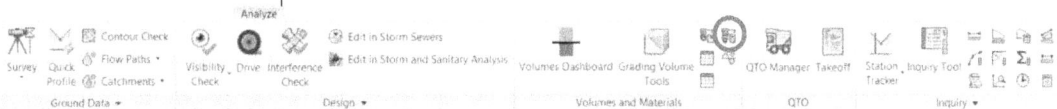

Figure 11–17

3. In the Select Sample Line Group dialog box, accept the default alignment **Jeffries Rand Rd** and sample line group **SL Collection - 1**, as shown in Figure 11–18. Click **OK**.

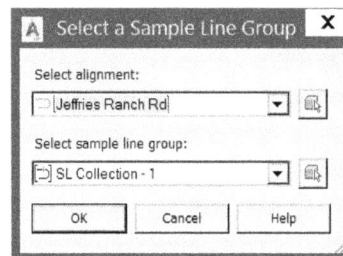

Figure 11–18

4. In the Compute Materials dialog box, select **Existing-Site** for the *EG* and **Finish Ground** for the *DATUM*, as shown in Figure 11–19. Click **OK** when done.

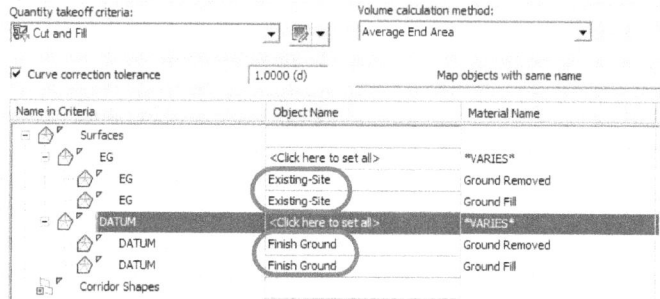

Figure 11–19

5. Generate a volume report. In the *Analyze* tab>Volumes and Materials panel, click ⬚ (Volume Report).

6. In the Report Quantities dialog box, ensure that you select the correct XSL file. Click ⬚ next to the *Select a style sheet* field, as shown on the left in Figure 11–20. Browse to and select **earthwork.xsl**, as shown on the right, and open it. Click **OK** to close the Report Quantities dialog box.

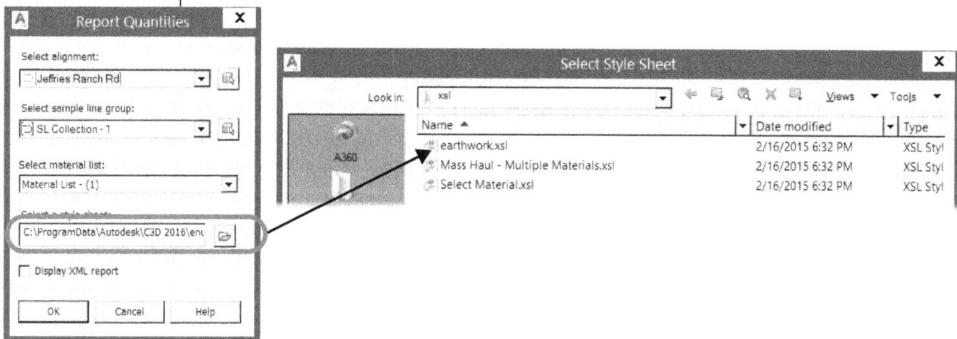

Figure 11–20

7. Internet Explorer will open when the HTML format report is created. Depending on your Internet Explorer security settings, you might be prompted to permit the script to run. Click **Yes** if this prompt displays. Your report will display, as shown in Figure 11–21.

Volume Report

Project: C:\Users\mrasmussen.RATC\appdata\local\temp\QTO1-B2-Sections_1_1_2060.svS
Alignment: Jeffries Ranch Rd
Sample Line Group: SL Collection - 1
Start Sta: 1+50.000
End Sta: 10+00.000

Station	Cut Area (Sq.ft.)	Cut Volume (Cu.yd.)	Reusable Volume (Cu.yd.)	Fill Area (Sq.ft.)	Fill Volume (Cu.yd.)	Cum. Cut Vol. (Cu.yd.)	Cum. Reusable Vol. (Cu.yd.)	Cum. Fill Vol. (Cu.yd.)	Cum. Net Vol. (Cu.yd.)
1+50.000	49.90	0.00	0.00	31.27	0.00	0.00	0.00	0.00	0.00
2+00.000	119.48	156.83	156.83	16.14	43.89	156.83	156.83	43.89	112.94
2+50.000	1188.74	1125.38	1125.38	5.01	18.77	1282.22	1282.22	62.67	1219.55
3+00.000	1334.45	2336.28	2336.28	49.59	50.56	3618.50	3618.50	113.22	3505.28
3+50.000	1262.57	2404.64	2404.64	231.87	260.62	6023.14	6023.14	373.84	5649.30
4+00.000	749.74	1863.25	1863.25	541.58	716.16	7886.40	7886.40	1090.00	6796.40
4+50.000	0.00	694.21	694.21	701.47	1150.97	8580.60	8580.60	2240.96	6339.64
5+00.000	0.00	0.00	0.00	808.42	1398.05	8580.61	8580.61	3639.01	4941.59

Figure 11–21

8. Close the HTML report.

9. Create an AutoCAD table listing earthwork volumes. In the *Analyze* tab>Volumes and Materials panel, select **Total Volume Table**, as shown in Figure 11–22.

Figure 11–22

10. Accept the defaults in the Create Table dialog box, as shown in Figure 11–23, and click **OK**. When prompted, click in empty space to create the table.

Figure 11–23

11. Select a point in Model Space to insert the table, as shown in Figure 11–24. Note that the top left of the table is the reference point.

Station	Fill Area	Cut Area	Fill Volume	Cut Volume	Cumulative Fill Vol	Cumulative Cut Vol
1+50.00	31.27	49.90	0.00	0.00	0.00	0.00
2+00.00	16.14	119.48	43.89	156.83	43.89	156.83
2+50.00	5.01	1188.74	18.77	1125.38	62.67	1282.22
3+00.00	49.59	1334.45	50.56	2336.28	113.22	3618.50

Total Volume Table

Figure 11–24

12. Save the drawing.

Task 2 - Calculate Material Quantities.

Your assemblies include five defined shapes: Pave1 and Pave2 (the top two courses), Base, Sub-base, and Curb. The default Material List only includes one material for Pavement so you will need to adjust it. You will not calculate curb volume at this time.

1. Continue working with the drawing from the previous task or open **QTO1-B2-Sections.dwg**.

2. In the *Analyze* tab>Volumes and Materials panel, click

    (Compute Materials).

3. In the Select Sample Line Group dialog box, accept the default alignment **Jeffries Ranch Rd** and sample line group **SL Collection - 1**, and click **OK**.

4. In the Edit Material List dialog box, click **Import another criteria**.

5. In the Select a Quantity Takeoff Criteria, select **Material List** and click **OK**.

6. In the Compute Materials dialog box, shown in Figure 11–25:
   - For *Pavement Material*, select **Jeffries Ranch Rd Pave1**.
   - For *SubBase Material*, select **Jeffries Ranch Rd SubBase**.
   - For *Base Material*, select **Jeffries Ranch Rd Base**.
   - Click **OK**.

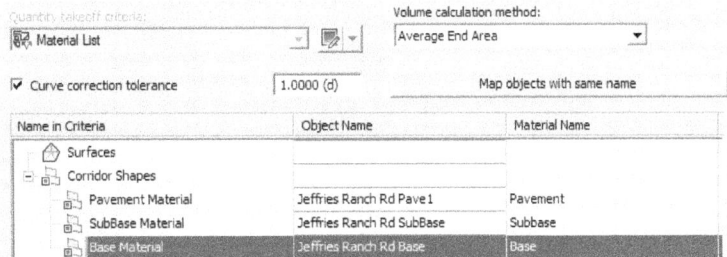

Figure 11–25

7. Click **OK** to close the dialog box and calculate the material.

8. Generate a volume report. In the *Analyze* tab>Volumes and Materials panel, select **Volume Report**.

9. In the Report Quantities dialog box, select **Material List - (2)** and ensure that you select the correct XSL file in the Select a style sheet drop-down list. Click next to the drop-down list. Browse to and select **Select Material.xsl** and open it. Click **OK** to close the Report Quantities dialog box.

10. Internet Explorer will open as the AutoCAD Civil 3D software creates an HTML format report. Depending on your Internet Explorer security settings, you might be prompted to permit the script to run. Click **Yes** if this prompt displays. The report will display with the volume of Pavement 1 from your corridor, as shown in Figure 11–26.

Material Report

Project: **C:\Civil 3D Projects\Civil3D-Training\QTO-Sections\QTO1-C1-Sections.dwg**
Alignment: Jeffries Ranch Rd
Sample Line Group: SL Collection - 1
Start Sta: 1+50.000
End Sta: 10+00.000

	Area Type	Area	Inc.Vol.	Cum.Vol.
		Sq.ft.	Cu.yd.	Cu.yd.
Station: 1+50.000				
	Pavement	2.57	0.00	0.00
	Subbase	37.79	0.00	0.00
	Base	10.32	0.00	0.00
Station: 2+00.000				
	Pavement	2.57	4.76	4.76
	Subbase	37.79	69.98	69.98
	Base	10.32	19.12	19.12

Figure 11–26

11. Close the HTML report.

The road design, specifically the corridor assembly, has a second shape called Pave 2. This is also Pavement, but might be based on a different composition than Pave 1. You can quantify this value as a separate amount, but for demonstration purposes, you will create a total volume for Pavement.

12. In the *Analyze* tab>Volumes and Materials panel, click

   (Compute Materials).

13. In the Select Sample Line Group dialog box, accept the defaults and click **OK**.

14. In the Edit Material List dialog box, shown in Figure 11–27:

- In the *Name* column, select **Pavement**. Click ⊠ (Delete).
- Click **Add new material**.
- Click on the new material name and rename it **Pavement**.
- In the *Quantity Type* column, select **Structures**.
- In the Data type drop-down list, select **Corridor Shape**.
- In the Select corridor shape drop-down list, select **Jeffries Ranch Rd Pave 1**.
- Click ⊕ to add **Jeffries Ranch Rd Pave 1** to the *Pavement* collection.
- In the Select corridor shape drop-down list, select **Jeffries Ranch Rd Pave 2**.
- Click ⊕ to add **Jeffries Ranch Rd Pave 2** to the *Pavement* collection.
- Click **OK** to apply the changes and close the dialog box.

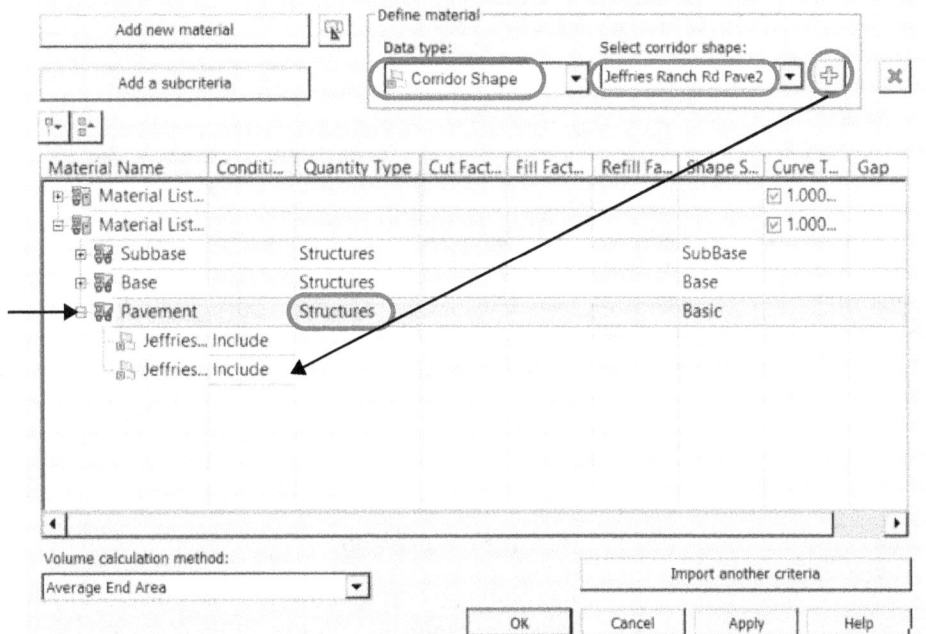

Figure 11–27

15. As in Steps 8 to 10, generate a volume report. In the *Analyze* tab>Volumes and Materials panel, select **Volume Report**.

   • In the Report Quantities dialog box, ensure that you select the correct XSL file in the Select a style sheet drop-down list. Click 📂 next to the drop-down list. Browse to and select **Select Material.xsl** and open it. Click **OK** to close the Report Quantities dialog box.

   • Internet Explorer will open as the AutoCAD Civil 3D software creates an HTML format report. Depending on your Internet Explorer security settings, you might be prompted to permit the script to run. Click **Yes** if this prompt displays. Your report will display, as shown in Figure 11–28.

Material Report

Project: C:\Users\mrasmussen.RATC\appdata\local\temp\QTO1-C1-Sections_1_1_0567.svS
Alignment: Jeffries Ranch Rd
Sample Line Group: SL Collection - 1
Start Sta: 1+50.000
End Sta: 10+00.000

	Area Type	Area	Inc.Vol.	Cum.Vol.
		Sq.ft.	Cu.yd.	Cu.yd.
Station: 1+50.000				
	Pavement	5.15	0.00	0.00
	SubBase	37.79	0.00	0.00
	Base	10.32	0.00	0.00
Station: 2+00.000				
	Pavement	5.15	9.53	9.53
	SubBase	37.79	69.98	69.98
	Base	10.32	19.12	19.12

Figure 11–28

16. Save the drawing.

You can also create drawing tables displaying this information using the **Material Volume Table** command in the Volumes and Materials panel.

11.3 Pay Items

An important element in any design is the cost of the design. The cost of a design can be determined by putting a price on a specific unit of work. To do this in the AutoCAD Civil 3D software you assign a pay item to specific objects. Using the QTO Manager helps to automate this task and to reduce errors and eliminate disputes with contractors. There are three commonly used pay item properties:

- **Item number:** A unique number for each item in a plan.

- **Specification:** Determines how the work is measured and paid for, the material to use, and the method for incorporating the material.

- **Cost estimate:** Ensures that the design falls in the available project budget.

Pay items can be manually assigned to any of the following items once they have been created in the drawing file: AutoCAD lines, polylines, blocks, and AutoCAD Civil 3D entities. You can also assign pay items to AutoCAD Civil 3D code set styles and pipe network and pressure pipe network parts lists so that corridor objects and new pipes/structures are automatically tagged with the correct pay items, as shown in Figure 11–29.

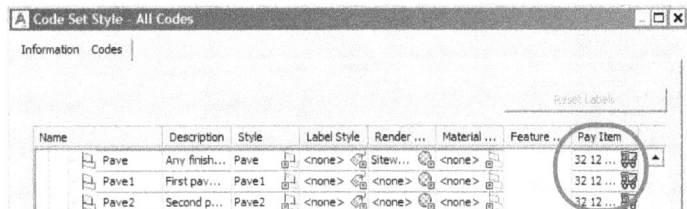

Figure 11–29

How To: Assign a Pay Item

1. In the *Analyze* tab>QTO panel, click (QTO Manager).
2. Open the pay item file required for the project.
3. Assign a pay item to an object.
4. Run a report.

Practice 11c

Quantity Take Off - Part II - Integrated Quantity Takeoff

Practice Objective

Estimated time for completion: 15 minutes

- Calculate the cost of design by assigning pay items to specific objects and then running a report.

Task 1 - Assign pay item ID.

A tool available in the AutoCAD Civil 3D software enables you to automate the process of quantity takeoff. The traditional method involves a manual process of counting pay items individually (e.g., street lights) or performing linear measurements to obtain quantities of items, such as curb and gutter.

1. Open **QTO1-C1-Sections.dwg** from the *C:\Civil 3D Projects\ Civil3D-Training\QTO-Sections* folder.

2. In the *Analyze* tab>QTO panel, click 🐄 (QTO Manager), as shown in Figure 11–30.

Figure 11–30

3. In the Panorama, expand 📂▾ and select **Open pay item file** as shown in Figure 11–31.

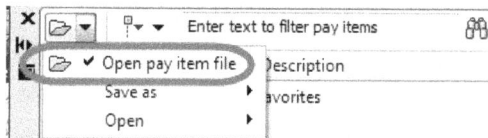

Figure 11–31

4. In the Open Pay Item File dialog box, shown in Figure 11–32:
   - In the Pay item file format drop-down list, select **CSV (Comma delimited)**.
   - Next to the Pay item file drop-down list, click 📂.
   - From the *C:\Civil 3D Projects\Civil3D-Training\ QTO-Sections* folder, select **Payitems-BidItems.csv**.
   - Click **OK** to accept the changes and close the dialog box.

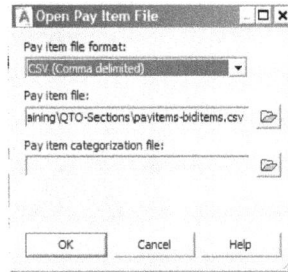

Figure 11–32

5. The *Pay Item ID* list will be populated with pay item numbers from the CSV file. To display only the required pay items, type **shrubs** in the *Filter* field at the top and press <Enter>. Only the shrubs pay items will be listed, as shown in Figure 11–33.

Figure 11–33

6. Assign a Pay Item ID to the object in the drawing. In Model Space, select a shrub, right-click, and select **Select Similar**, as shown in Figure 11–34.

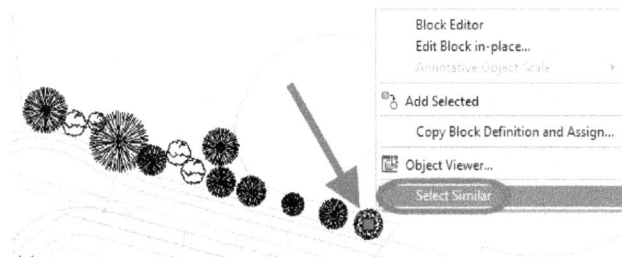

Figure 11–34

At the Command Line, a message prompts you that pay items have been assigned to objects.

7. With all similar objects selected, select pay item **632.02** in the Panorama, right-click, and select **Assign pay item**, as shown in Figure 11–35. Press <Esc> to clear the current selection.

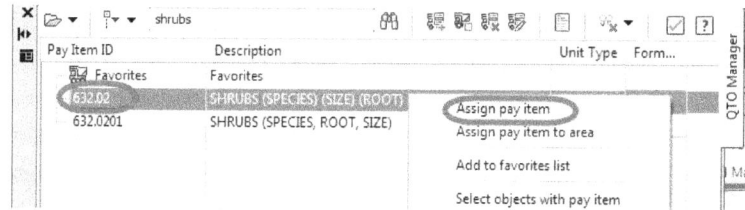

Figure 11–35

8. Next, apply Pay items to street light objects. Type **light** in the *Filter* field at the top and press <Enter>. Only pay items with the word *lighting* will be listed, as shown in Figure 11–36.

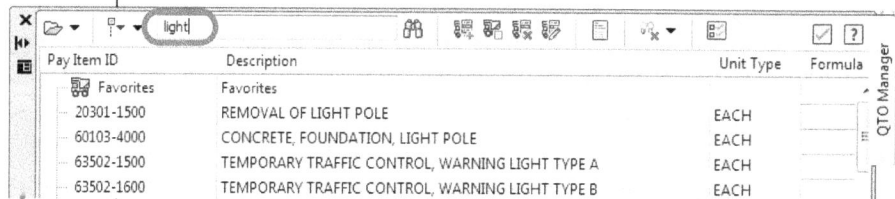

Figure 11–36

9. To assign a Pay Item ID to the object in the drawing, ensure that the previous selection set has been cleared by pressing <Esc>. In Model Space, select a street light, as shown in Figure 11–37, right-click, and select **Select Similar**.

Figure 11–37

10. With all similar objects selected, select pay item **60103-4000 CONCRETE, FOUNDATION, LIGHT POLE** in the Panorama, as shown in Figure 11–38. Right-click and select **Assign pay item**. In the Command Line, a message prompts you that pay items have been assigned to objects. Press <Esc> to clear the current object selection.

Figure 11–38

11. As these objects are now linked to QTO pay items, using the AutoCAD **Copy** command will also copy the reference to the pay item list. Press <Esc> to clear the selection set. Launch the AutoCAD **Copy** command, select any of the street lights, and copy to the far west end of the parking lot, as shown in Figure 11–39.

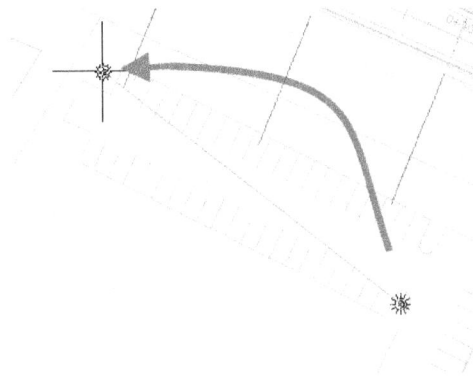

Figure 11–39

Task 2 - Compute Quantity Takeoff.

Once pay items have been assigned to AutoCAD Civil 3D or AutoCAD objects in the model, you will be able to compute quantities and generate a report.

1. Continue working with the drawing from the previous task or open **QTO1-C2-Sections.dwg**.

2. View the objects that have been tagged with Pay Item IDs. In the **Analyze** tab>QTO panel, click 🛒 (QTO Manager).

---

3. Type **light** in the *Filter* field at the top, and press <Enter>. Only the lighting pay items will be listed, as shown in Figure 11–40.

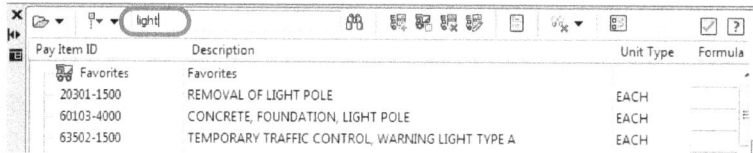

Figure 11–40

4. In the QTO Manager Panorama, select pay item **60103-4000**, right-click, and select **Select objects with pay item**, as shown in Figure 11–41. All tagged pay items in the drawing with the Pay Item ID 659.07 will be highlighted. Review your selection and press <Esc> to clear the current object selection.

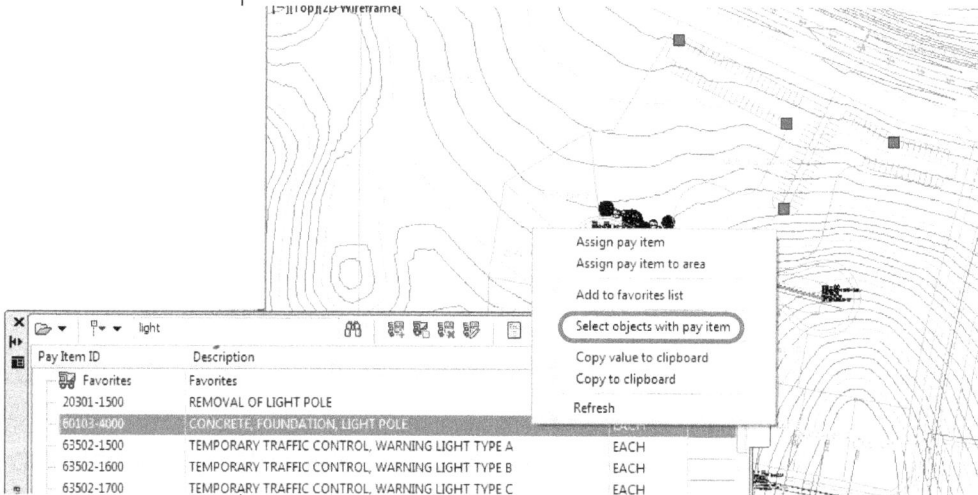

Figure 11–41

5. To generate a Quantity report, in the *Analyze* tab>QTO panel, click (Takeoff), as shown in Figure 11–42.

Figure 11–42

6. In the Compute Quantity Takeoff dialog box, shown in Figure 11–43:

    • In the *Report type* area, select **Summary**.

    • In the Report extents drop-down list, select **Drawing**.

    • Accept all other default values.

    • Click **Compute** to accept the changes and calculate the quantities.

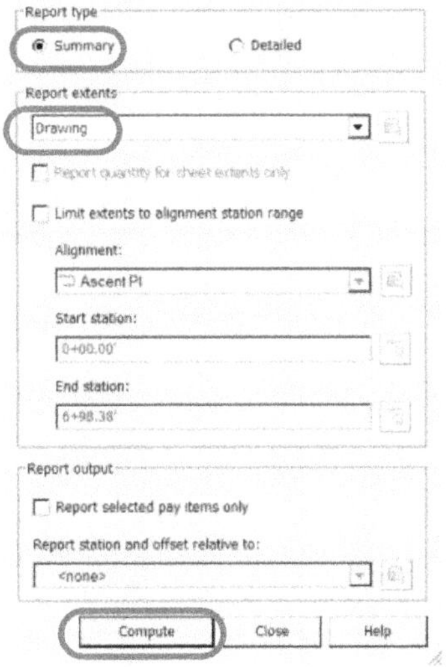

Figure 11–43

7. In the Quantity Takeoff report, select **Summary (HTML).xsl** as the output type, as shown in Figure 11–44.

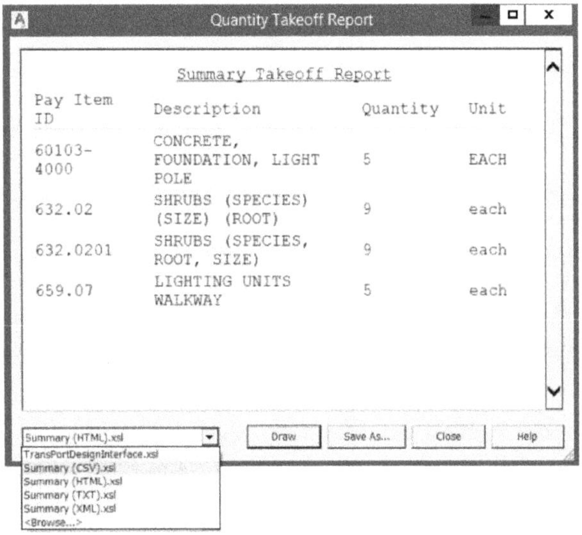

Figure 11–44

8. A number of different output formats will enable you to import the results into other software. You can also tag AutoCAD Civil 3D objects (such as corridor materials with Pay Item ID).

9. You can save this report or draw a table in your CAD drawing. Click **Close** to close the dialog box, and click **Close** again to close the Compute Quantity Takeoff dialog box.

10. Save the drawing.

11.4 Section Views

A section view can display sampled surface sections, corridor assemblies, and any pipes or structures. Similar to profiles, sections use a section view to annotate their elevations and center line offsets. Styles affect the look of a section view.

Section views can annotate an assembly's offsets, elevations, and grades. The All Codes style assigned to the assembly in the sample line group makes all of the points and links available for labeling. The Section Label styles do not interact with the assembly, only with the corridor surfaces.

- As with Profile views, Section views can be moved and retain the correct information.

- Section views can be created individually or in groups.

Section View Wizard

In the *Home* tab, the Profile & Section Views panel enables you to create a single section view, multiple sections organized into columns and rows, and project objects to a section view. The **Single** and **Multiple View** commands open the Section View wizard, which guides you through the process of creating Section views. There are six tasks in the Section View wizard, as shown in Figure 11–45.

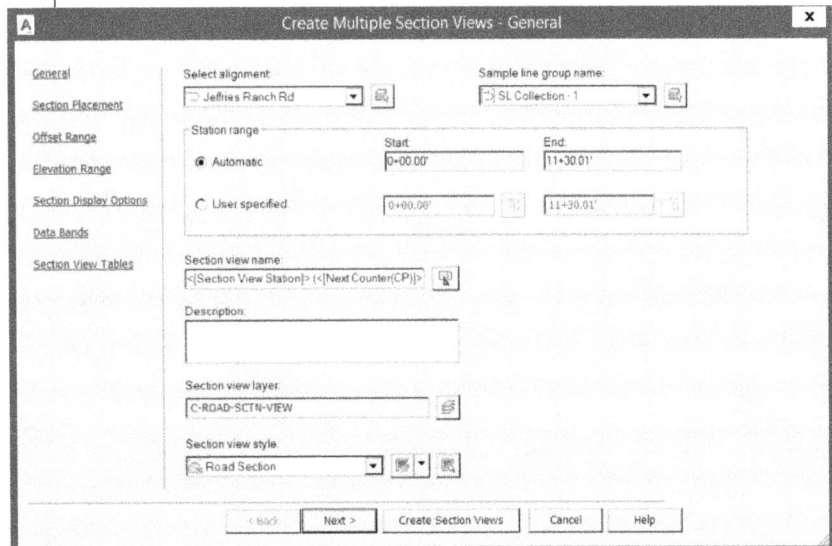

Figure 11–45

- **General:** Specifies basic information about the Section view, including which alignment to use, the sample group and line, and the view template. If creating multiple views, the Group Plot Style method specifies how to create multiple section views (**All** or **Page**). You can define page styles that define sheet sizes and plottable areas (sheet size minus margins and border).

- **Section Placement:** Only displays when you are creating multiple views. It enables you to set the Group Plot Style to use for setting the row and column settings for placing multiple section views.

- **Offset Range:** Enables you to set the width of the view.

- **Elevation Range:** Enables you to set the height of the view.

- **Section Display Options:** Enables you to select what gets drawn in the view and the section style.

- **Data Bands:** Enables you to specify one or more band set styles for the sections and their positions in the view.

- **Section View Tables:** Enables you to add and modify volume tables calculated using the Section view (a material list must be created from the sample line group for this option to be available).

Section View Styles

A Section view style defines the vertical and horizontal grid and its annotation. The horizontal lines represent the elevations and the vertical lines represent the center line offset.

Section View Band Styles

A band style defines the offset and elevation annotation at the bottom of a Section view. The style affects the annotation's format and the information that displays in the band. Using the band styles provided in the sample templates, set your existing ground surface as **Surface 1**, and the proposed surface (such as a Corridor Top surface) as **Surface 2**.

Section Styles and Section Label Styles

A section style assigns a layer and other layer properties to a surface section. The section label styles annotate grade breaks, slopes, and offsets.

Multi-Purpose Styles

In Multi-Purpose styles, the All Codes style assigns object and label styles for corridor assemblies. This is the most important style for section labeling.

The All Codes style defines object styles for points, links, or shapes. It specifies which labels display in a Section view.

- All link styles annotate a grade or slope.

- All point styles annotate an offset and elevation.

Page Styles

A page style defines the plottable area of a sheet size. The plottable area is what remains after removing the non-printing margins and border from the sheet size. The page style also defines a sheet grid. The Plot Group styles use the grid to space sections on a sheet.

Practice 11d | Creating Sections Part II

Practice Objective

- Show what is happening with existing and proposed surface data at predefined intervals along an alignment using section views.

Estimated time for completion:
10 minutes

Task 1 - Create a single Section view.

1. Open **QTO1-D1-Sections.dwg** from the *C:\Civil 3D Projects\ Civil3D-Training\QTO-Sections* folder.

2. In the *Home* tab>Profile & Section Views panel, expand

   Section Views and click 🏠 (Create Section View), as shown in Figure 11–46. The Create Section View wizard opens.

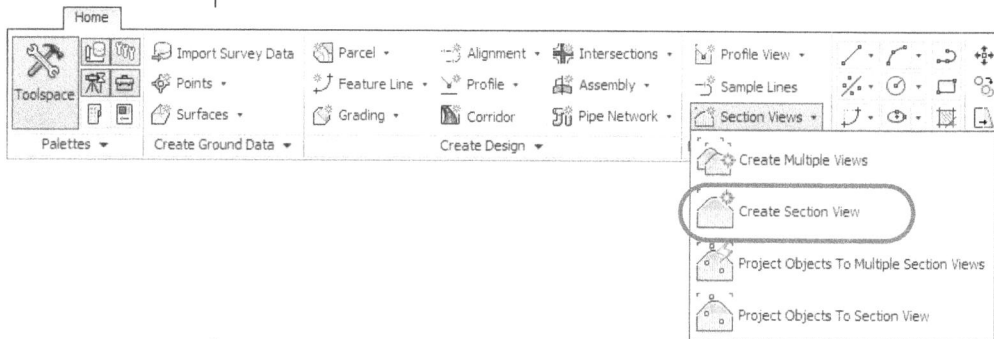

Figure 11–46

3. In the *General* page, in the *Sample Line* field, select **4+50.00** as shown in Figure 11–47. Set the *Section view style* to **Road Section** and click **Next>**.

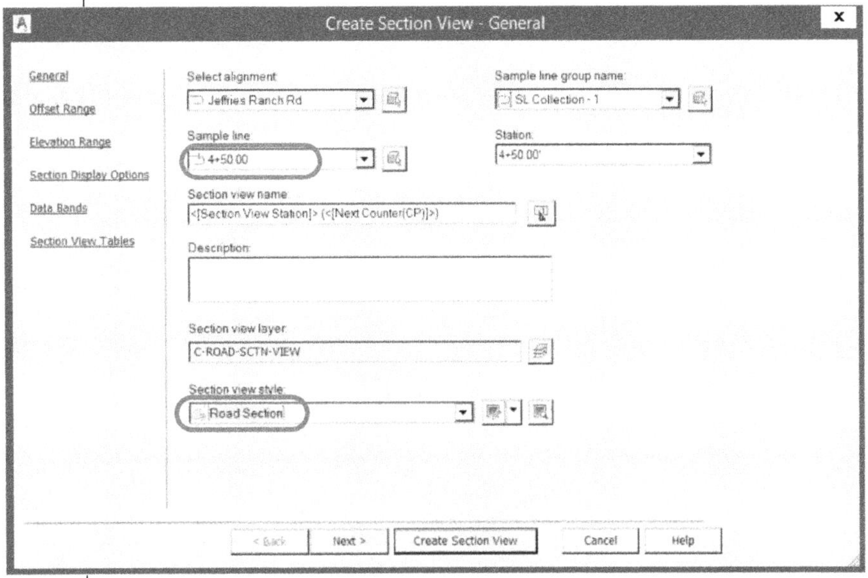

Figure 11–47

4. In the *Offset Range* and *Elevation Range* pages, accept the defaults and click **Next>**.

5. In the *Section Display Options* page, do the following:

- Set the *Style* to **Existing Ground** for Existing-Site.
- **View-Edit with Shading** for the *Jeffries Ranch Rd and Corridor - (1)* sections.
- **Finished Ground** for the *Jeffries Ranch Rd and Corridor - (1) Surfaces*.
- Assign the label options and styles to **_No Labels** for all, as shown in Figure 11–48 and click **Next>**.

Note that the quantity take offs only display if the material quantities are calculated before the section views are created.

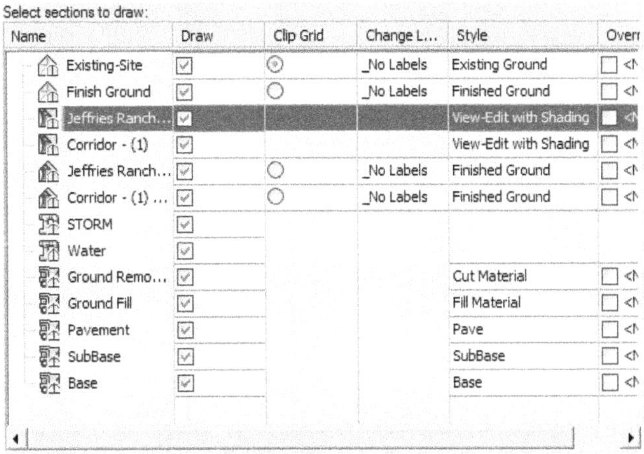

Name	Draw	Clip Grid	Change L...	Style	Over
Existing-Site	☑	⊙	_No Labels	Existing Ground	☐ <N
Finish Ground	☑	○	_No Labels	Finished Ground	☐ <N
Jeffries Ranch...	☑			View-Edit with Shading	☐ <N
Corridor - (1)	☑			View-Edit with Shading	☐ <N
Jeffries Ranch...	☑	○	_No Labels	Finished Ground	☐ <N
Corridor - (1) ...	☑	○	_No Labels	Finished Ground	☐ <N
STORM	☑				
Water	☑				
Ground Remo...	☑			Cut Material	☐ <N
Ground Fill	☑			Fill Material	☐ <N
Pavement	☑			Pave	☐ <N
SubBase	☑			SubBase	☐ <N
Base	☑			Base	☐ <N

Figure 11–48

6. On the left, click **Section View Tables** to skip setting the Data Bands because **No_Labels** was selected in Step 5.

7. In the *X Offset* field, type **0.5** and click **Add>>** to add the Total Volume Table to the list. Then expand the Type drop-down list and select **Material**. Click **Add>>** again to include the material table in the section view, as shown in Figure 11–49.

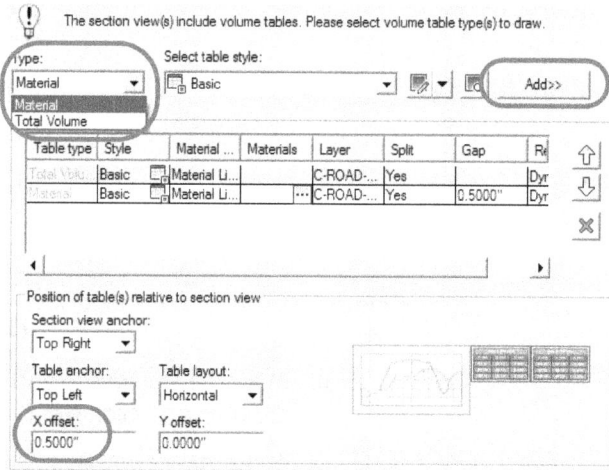

Figure 11–49

8. Click **Create Section View**. At the *Identify section view origin* prompt, click in empty space in Model Space, north of the surface to locate this section in the drawing.

9. Pan and zoom to display the section close-up. The labels are provided by the default AutoCAD Civil 3D template.

10. Adjust the section by dragging or deleting unwanted labels. (Hold <Ctrl> when selecting.) The drawing is shown in Figure 11–50.

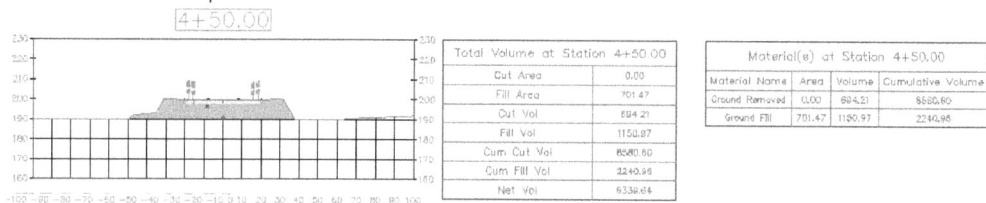

Figure 11–50

Task 2 - Create a Multiple Section view.

1. Continue working with the drawing from the previous task or open **QTO1-D2-Sections.dwg**.

2. In the *Home* tab>Profile & Section Views panel, expand

   Section Views and click ![icon](Create Multiple Section Views).

3. In the Create Multiple Section Views dialog box, click **Create Section View**. Click in empty space in Model Space next to the previous single section view to insert all of the sections, as shown in Figure 11–51.

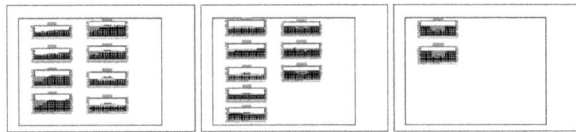

Figure 11–51

4. Save the drawing.

Chapter Review Questions

1. What does a mass haul diagram represent?

    a. The total cut and fill materials for a project site.

    b. The total weight of a corridor mass.

    c. The total weight that can be hauled on a corridor model.

    d. Cumulative cut and fill material volumes along a corridor.

2. What are sample line groups?

    a. Objects that sample corridor elements for cross-sections.

    b. Groups of lines where the surveyor sampled the soil.

    c. Lines connecting corridor points.

    d. Groups of lines that connect corridor shapes.

3. What does the Create Section View dialog box do?

    a. Creates a model space viewport for viewing sections.

    b. Creates grid(s) with a cross-section and labeling of a corridor model inside it at specified stations.

    c. Creates a paper space viewport for viewing sections.

    d. Nothing, there is no such thing.

4. Where do you assign Pay Items?

    a. In the Grading Volume Tools.

    b. In the Volumes Dashboard.

    c. In the QTO Manager.

    d. In the Volume Reports.

5. Which of these tools enable you to compute the volume of a corridor material?

    a.

    b.

    c.

    d.

Command Summary

Button	Command	Location
	Compute Materials	• **Ribbon:** *Analyze* tab>Volumes and Materials panel • **Command Prompt:** ComputeMaterials
	Create Multiple Section Views	• **Ribbon:** *Home* tab>Profile & Section Views panel • **Command Prompt:** MultipleSectionViews
	Create Section View	• **Ribbon:** *Home* tab>Profile & Section Views panel • **Command Prompt:** SectionViews
	QTO Manager	• **Ribbon:** *Analyze* tab>QTO panel • **Command Prompt:** QTOManager
	Sample Lines	• **Ribbon:** *Home* tab>Profile & Section Views panel • **Command Prompt:** CreateSampleLines
	Takeoff	• **Ribbon:** *Analyze* tab>QTO panel • **Command Prompt:** Takeoff
	Total Volume Table	• **Ribbon:** *Analyze* tab>Volumes and Materials panel • **Command Prompt:** GenerateQuantitiesReport
	Volume Report	• **Ribbon:** *Analyze* tab>Volumes and Materials panel • **Command Prompt:** GenerateQuantitiesReport

Plan Production

The final stage of any project is printing plan sets. Plan sets are sent to contractors for bid and construction purposes. In this chapter you create plan and profile sheets for the road design. Then you modify the sheet set properties and title block to make the project information automatically display on every sheet.

Learning Objectives in this Chapter

- List the steps involved in the plan and profile sheets creation workflow.
- Divide the alignment up into printable areas using various commands.
- Edit view frames and match lines to better represent your design in plan and profile sheets.
- Create plan and profile sheets using the Plan Production tools and previously created View Frame objects.
- Edit sheet and sheet set properties to make annotating sheets easier.

12.1 Plan Production Tools

In the digital age, although large amount of resources and time are dedicated to creating digital data, printed sets of plans are still necessary for a number of reasons, including:

- Obtaining approval from a Client

- Review and approval from governing agencies

- Bidding

- Construction layout

- Recording as-built conditions

The AutoCAD® Civil 3D® software includes a Plan Production system that enables the automated generation of plan, profile, or plan and profile sheet sets. The Plan Production tools are found on the *Output* tab and shown in Figure 12–1.

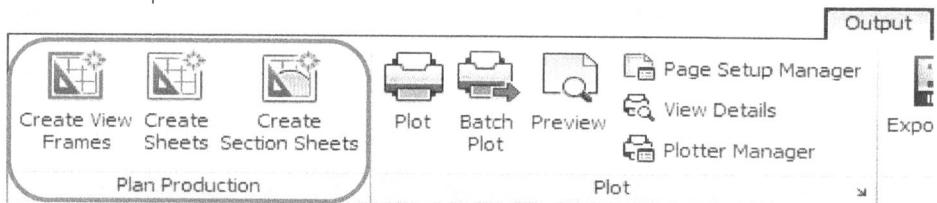

Figure 12–1

Overview

Use the following workflow to create plan and profile sheets:

1. Configure custom title blocks and styles or use those provided in the Autodesk templates.

2. Create View Frames. The **Create View Frames** command organizes these frames into View Frame Groups and creates interactive Match Lines.

3. Adjust View Frames and Match Lines, as required. This adjustment can be done using object properties or by manipulating the objects directly in Model Space.

4. Create sheets. When you are satisfied with the layout of the frames and Match Lines, plotting layouts can be generated in the current drawing or in new ones.

5. Plot and manage. Sheets generated from this system are automatically included in the Sheet Set Manager for ease of plotting and for organizing with other sheets. (Refer to the Help system for more information on AutoCAD Sheet Sets.)

More Information

Describing how to customize a title block and styles can be involved. Due to time limitations, only the fundamentals of this system are covered in this training guide, not its configuration.

12.2 Plan Production Objects

The first step in using the Plan Production tools is to assemble all of the relevant data. This process is the same, whether you use the AutoCAD Civil 3D Plan Production tools or not. Some of the steps you might use in assembling this base plan involve external referencing pertinent data into your drawing to give the plan geographic reference (i.e., ROW lines, contours, survey data, aerial photographs, etc.). AutoCAD Civil 3D design objects are also data-referenced into the base plan.

The AutoCAD Civil 3D software provides a tool to help automate plan and production sheet creation: the Create View Frames wizard. It is the next step in plan production after the base plan has been created. Using this wizard, you can create View Frames, View Frame Groups, and Match Lines, all of which are plan production objects. The wizard is shown in Figure 12–2.

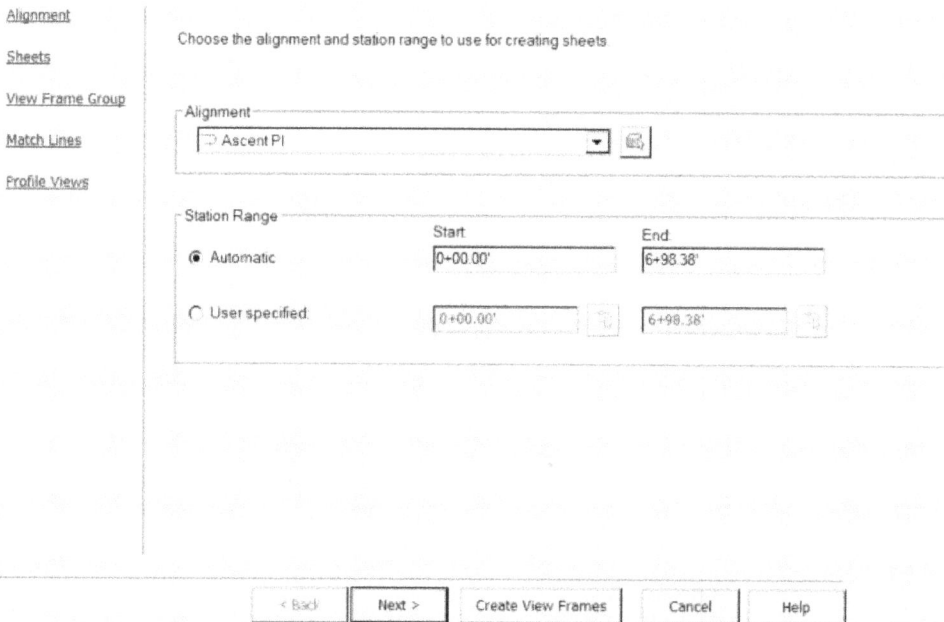

Alignment

Sheets

View Frame Group

Match Lines

Profile Views

Choose the alignment and station range to use for creating sheets

Alignment
Ascent Pl

Station Range

Start 0+00.00'   End 6+98.38'
○ Automatic

○ User specified: 0+00.00'   6+98.38'

< Back   Next >   Create View Frames   Cancel   Help

Figure 12–2

View Frames

View Frames are interactive, rectangular objects that are placed along a selected alignment. These rectangular shapes represent a view for each plan sheet that is created in the AutoCAD Civil 3D software. View Frames divide the alignment into segments. These segments are based on the base drawing scale and the viewport settings on the Layout tab from the drawing template that is used to define the views.

View Frame Groups

View Frame Groups are collections of the View Frames along a single alignment. View Frame Groups enable you to manage a group of views, including properties, such as styles and labeling.

Match Lines

A Match Line is a line that designates a location along an alignment that is used as a common reference point for two adjacent plans. If you create plan and profile or profile only sheets, the **Insert Match Lines** option is automatically selected and you cannot edit it.

Match Lines, as with all other AutoCAD Civil 3D objects, are style-driven. Typically, they have labels that can identify both adjacent plans, one plan, or no plans. You can also have these labels displayed at the top, bottom, or middle of the Match Line.

12.3 Plan Production Object Edits

After using the AutoCAD Civil 3D wizard to create View Frame Groups, View Frames, and Match Lines, you might need to make some minor adjustments to best present your design. You can access three properties: *Name, Description*, and *Object style*. In addition to adjusting the field properties of the object, you might also want to adjust the geometry properties of the object.

Name

The *Name* is a unique identifier that is appropriate to the object. For example, you might name the View Frame with the alignment name and station, or name the View Frame Group with the alignment name and the starting and ending station that the group encompasses.

Description

The *Description* field provides a detailed description of the View Frame or Match Line.

Object style

Adjusting the *Object style* impacts the presentation of the object. One application of this property is to ensure that the object conforms to company preferences or standards. The View Frame Properties dialog box is shown in Figure 12–3.

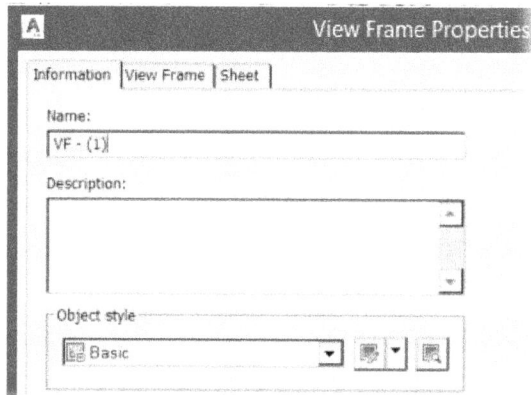

Figure 12–3

View Frame Geometry Properties Edits

You can change the View Frame's location and rotation along the alignment using the object grips, as shown in Figure 12–4.

- The *circle grip* (1) enables you to rotate the View Frame.

- The *diamond grip* (2) enables you to move the View Frame along the alignment.

- The *square grip* (3) enables you to offset the View Frame relative to its original location.

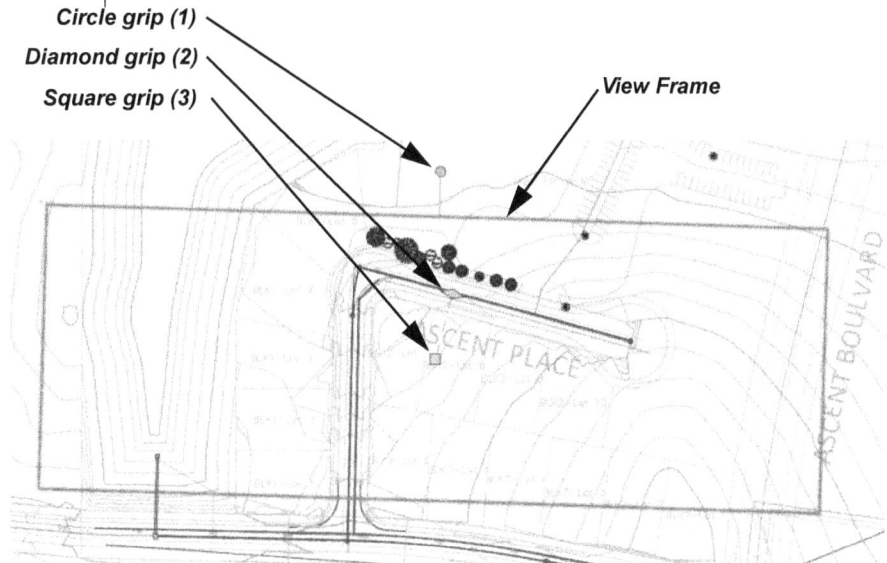

Figure 12–4

Match Line Geometry Properties Edits

Using the object grips, you can change the Match Line`s location, rotation, and length, as shown in Figure 12–5. However, you can only move the Match Line in the View Frame overlap area.

- The *circle grip* (1) enables you to rotate the Match Line.

- The *triangle grips* (2) enables you to extend the length of the Match Line.

- The *diamond grip* (3) enables you to move the Match Line in the overlap area of the two referenced View Frames.

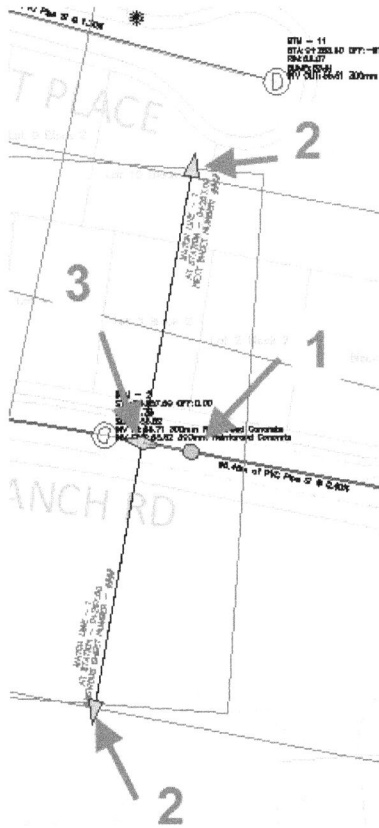

Figure 12–5

Practice 12a	# Plan Production Tools I

Practice Objective

* Create and edit view frames to divide the alignment into printable areas.

Estimated time for completion: 20 minutes

For this practice, two alignments from the project have been combined into one alignment and profile to better demonstrate the full power of the plan production tools in the AutoCAD Civil 3D software when used with longer corridor projects. Combining alignments is not necessary or recommended for real projects.

Task 1 - Create View Frames.

1. Open **PPR1-A1-PlanProduction.dwg** from the *C:\Civil 3D Projects\Civil3D-Training\PlanProduction* folder.

2. You will create the plan - profile sheets at a scale of 1"=20'. The sheets will be created more consistently if the Model Space scale matches the final output scale. If not already done, set the *Annotation Scale* to **1"=20'**, as shown in Figure 12–6.

MODEL ▦ ⬚ ▾ ⌞ ⊙ ▾ ⟍ ▾ ∠ ⬚ ▾ 💢 💢 🔏 (1" = 20' ▾) ⚙ ▾ ✛ ● � 🔳 🔳 ꝗ ⊡ ☰

Figure 12–6

3. In the *Output* tab>Plan Production panel, click ⬚⁺ (Create View Frames).

4. In the wizard, in the *Create View Frames - Alignment* page, set the following, as shown in Figure 12–7:

   * In the Alignment drop-down list, select **Michelle Way**.
   * In the *Station Range* area, select the **Automatic** option.
   * Click **Next>**.

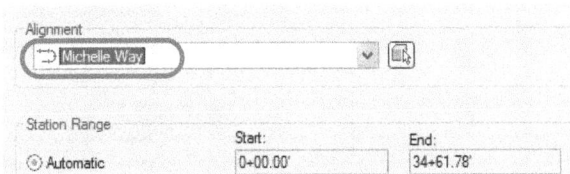

```
┌─Alignment───────────────────────────────────┐
│  ⇨ Michelle Way                     ▾  📇   │
│                                              │
│                                              │
│  Station Range                               │
│                        Start:       End:     │
│  ⦿ Automatic          0+00.00'     34+61.78' │
└──────────────────────────────────────────────┘
```

Figure 12–7

5. In the *Create View Frames - Sheets* page, do the following:

- In the sheet settings, select the **Plan and Profile** option.

- In the *Template for Plan and Profile sheet* area, click ⁝⁝⁝.

- In the *Drawing template file name* field, click ⁝⁝⁝ and browse to **C3D Training Plan and Profile.dwt**. This file is located in *C:\Civil 3D Projects\Civil3D-Training\ PlanProduction*.

- In the *Select a layout to create new sheets* area, expand the drop-down list and select **Arch D Plan and Profile 20 Scale**, as shown in Figure 12–8.

- Click **OK**.

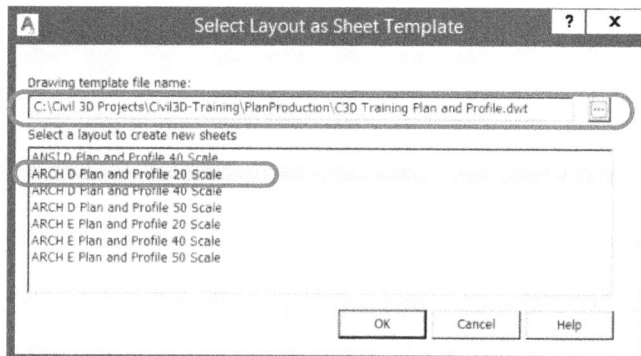

Figure 12–8

- For the *View Frame Placement*, select the **Along alignment** option, as shown in Figure 12–9.

- Click **Next>**.

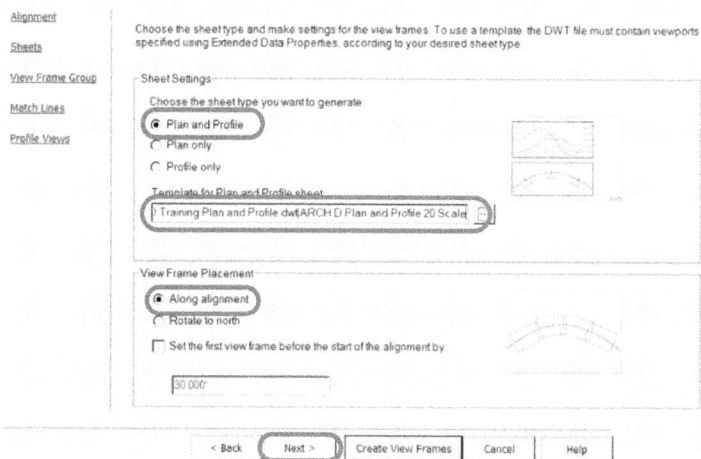

Figure 12–9

This will append the alignment name and a counter to the VFG.

If these settings in the name template are standard, you can save them in the Setting tab in the master DWT file.

6. In the *Create View Frames - View Frame Group* page, accept the default for the *Name*.

7. To name the View Frame with the starting station, click

   ▣ (Edit View Frame Name).

8. In the Name Template dialog box, shown in Figure 12–10:
   - In the *Name* field, type **VF - Sta**.
   - In the Property fields drop-down list, select **View Frame Start Raw Station**.
   - Click **Insert**.
   - Click **OK** to close the dialog box.

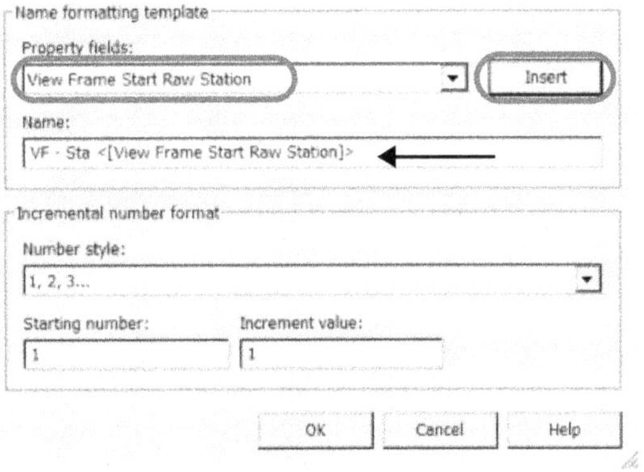

Figure 12–10

9. Accept the default Label and Label style. Accept the Label location of **Top left** (as shown in Figure 12–11), and click **Next>**.

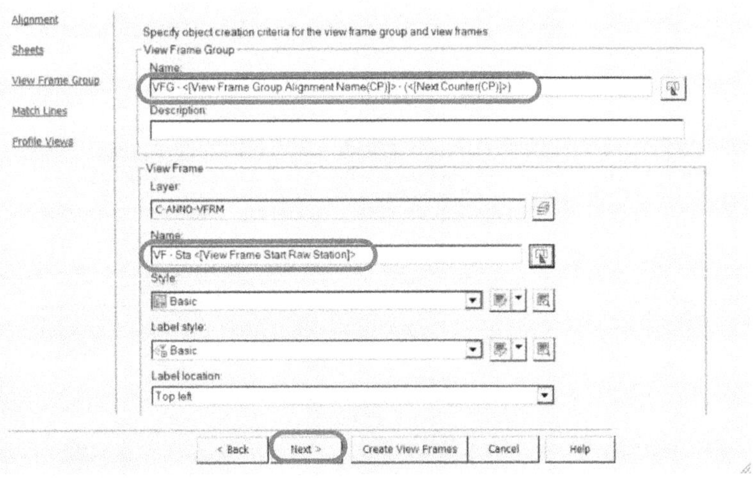

Figure 12–11

The procedure to do this is similar to Step 8.

10. In the *Create View Frames - Match Lines* page, shown in Figure 12–12:

- Select **Allow additional distance for repositioning**.
- Change the *Match Line* name to **ML - <[Match Line Raw Station]>**.
- Accept all other defaults and click **Next>**.

Figure 12–12

11. In the *Create View Frames - Profile Views* page, accept the default values for the *Profile View Style* and the *Band Set*. Click **Create View Frames**, as shown in Figure 12–13.

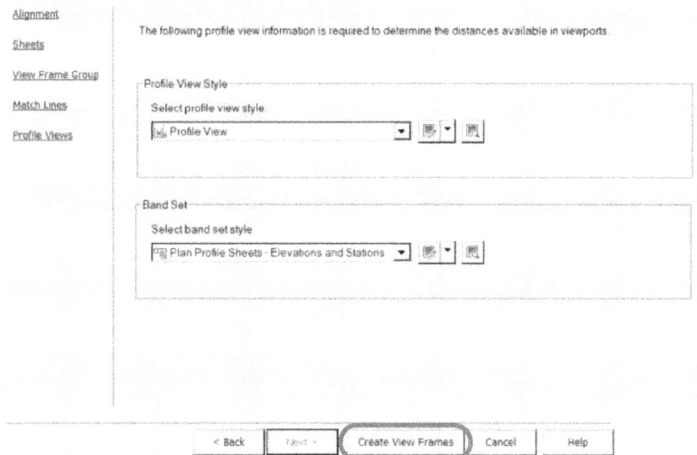

Figure 12–13

12. In the Toolspace, *Prospector* tab, expand the *View Frame Groups* collection, expand the *VFG - Michelle Way View Frame Group*, and then expand the *View Frames* collection and the *Match Lines* collection. Note that the Create View Frame wizard has created three Plan Production objects, two View Frames, and one Match Line, as shown in Figure 12–14.

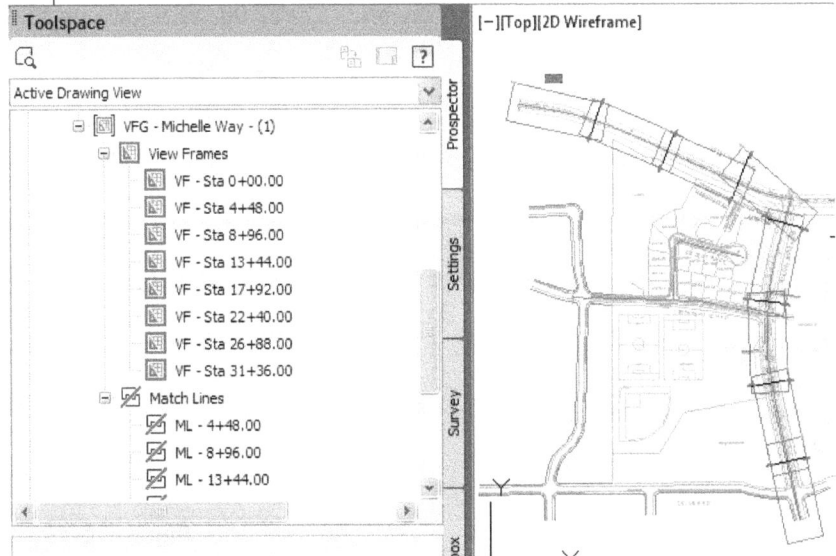

Figure 12–14

13. Save the drawing.

Task 2 - Edit View Frames and Match Lines.

1. Continue working with the drawing from the previous task or open **PPR1-A2-PlanProduction.dwg**.

2. Select the preset view P&P-Edit VF.

3. In Model Space, select the Match Line object for Michelle Way **ML - 17+92.00**, as shown on the right in Figure 12–15.

*Alternatively, you can select the Match Line in the Toolspace, Prospector tab. Expand the View Frame Groups collection, expand the VFG-Michelle Way collection, expand the Match Line collection, select **ML - 17+92.00**, right-click, and select **Select**, as shown on the left in Figure 12–15.*

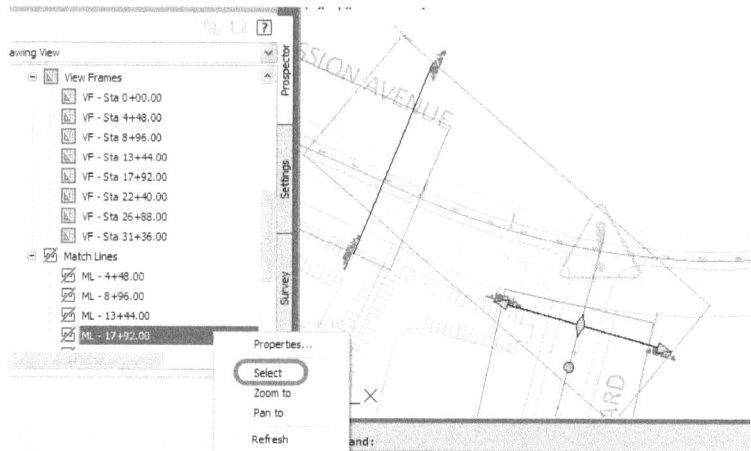

Figure 12–15

If Quick Properties does not display, click

 (Quick Properties) in the Status bar to toggle it on.

4. Select the move grip (the diamond grip), and type **1765**. In the Quick Properties dialog box, also rename it as **ML - 17+65.00**, as shown in Figure 12–16. Press <Esc> to release the Match Line object.

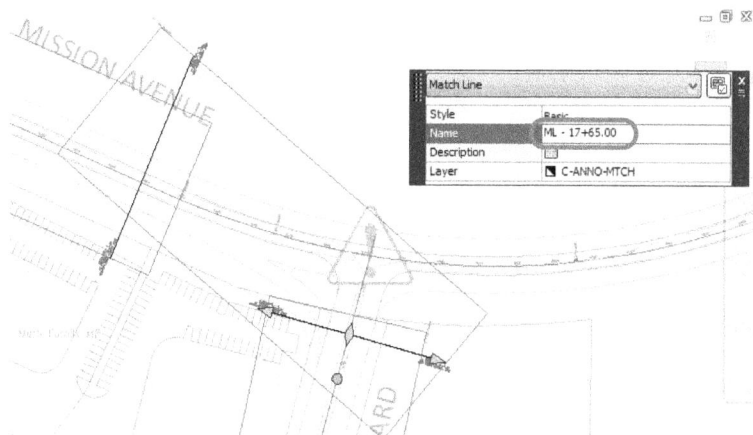

Figure 12–16

5. Now you can adjust the View Frame object corresponding to ML - 17+65.00. Select the View Frame object, select the rotation grip (the circular grip), and graphically rotate the View Frame object so that it is parallel to the Mission Avenue alignment, as shown in Figure 12–17.

Figure 12–17

6. Press <Esc> to exit the View Frame object selection.

7. Save the drawing.

12.4 Creating Sheets

Once the Match Lines, View Frames, and associated View Frame Groups have been established, you can start the next phase of generating sheet sets.

The AutoCAD Civil 3D software includes a wizard that helps you create sheets from the View Frames. The flexibility of this wizard, in addition to the selection of styles, enables you to create sheets automatically that conform to many of your existing standards. The wizard is shown in Figure 12–18.

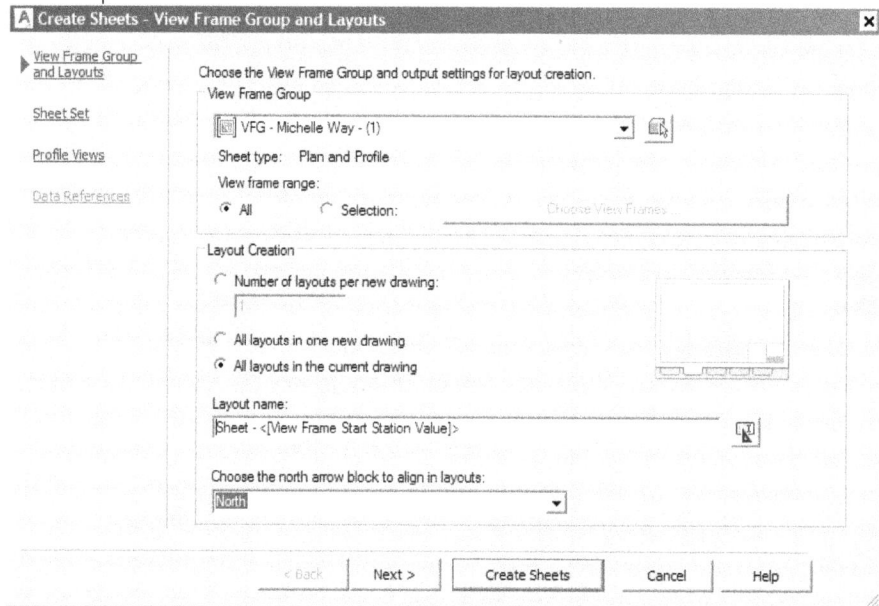

Figure 12–18

Since a dynamic link does not exist between the View Frames and the sheet, it is important that the required View Frames are established before creating the sheets. Changing or editing View Frames after the sheets are created has no effect on the sheets.

- In addition to using the wizard for creating sheets, this workflow also uses the AutoCAD Sheet Set Manager.

Practice 12b

Plan Production Tools II

Practice Objective

- Create plan and profile sheets using the Plan Production tools and previously created View Frame objects.

Estimated time for completion: 10 minutes

Task 1 - Create sheet files and a new Sheet Set Manager file.

1. Open **PPR1-B1-PlanProduction.dwg** from the *C:\Civil 3D Projects\Civil3D-Training\PlanProduction* folder.

2. In the *Output* tab>Plan Production panel, click ▧ (Create Sheets).

3. In the wizard, in the *Create Sheet - View Frame Group and Layouts* page:
   - Ensure that the *View Frame Group* is **VFG - Michelle Way**.
   - Set the *View frame range* to **All**.
   - In the *Layout Creation* area, set the *Layout* creation to **All layouts in the current drawing**.
   - For the *Layout name*, click ▧ (Edit Layout Name).

4. In the Name Template dialog box, shown in Figure 12–19:
   - In the *Name* field, delete the current name.
   - Type **Sheet -**.
   - In the Property fields drop-down list, select **View Frame Start Station Value**
   - Click **Insert**.
   - Click **OK** to close this dialog box.

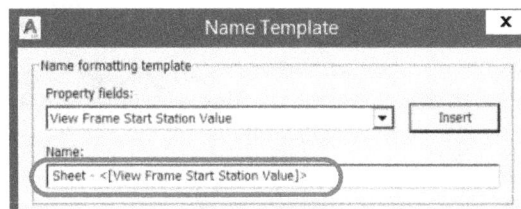

Figure 12–19

5. Expand the Choose the north arrow block to align in layouts drop-down list and select the **North** block, as shown in Figure 12–20. Once this is complete, click **Next>**.

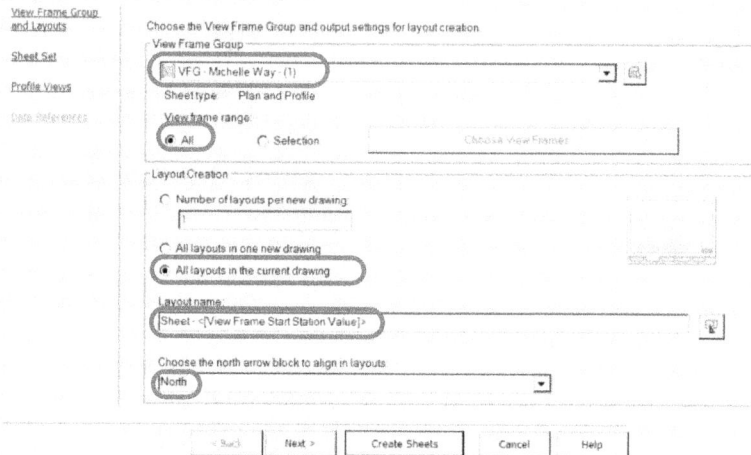

Figure 12–20

6. In the *Create Sheets - Sheet Set* page, set the following:

   • Select the **New sheet set** option, and type **Ascent Phase1** in the *Sheet Set name* field. Leave the *Sheet set file (.DST) storage location* field set to the default, as shown in Figure 12–21. Click **Next>**.

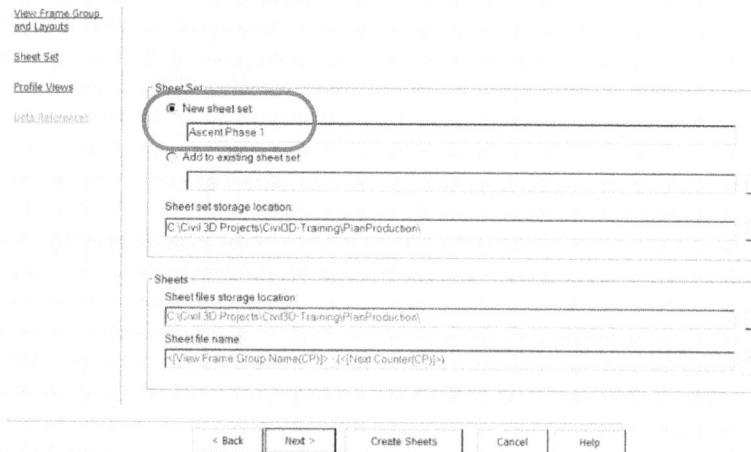

Figure 12–21

7. In the *Create Sheets - Profile Views* page, accept the defaults, as shown in Figure 12–22, and click **Create Sheets**.

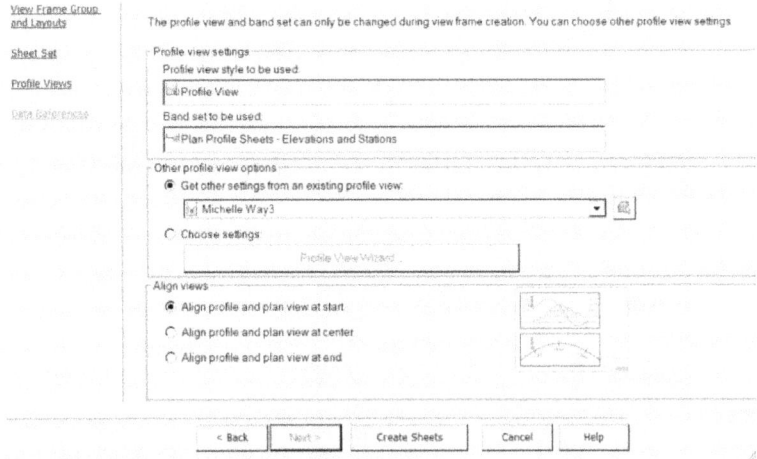

Figure 12–22

8. The wizard prompts you that the drawing will be saved before creating the new sheets. Click **OK** to accept this.

9. When prompted for the location of the profile, select a blank space in your drawing, as shown in Figure 12–23. The AutoCAD Civil 3D software will use this location to insert a profile of your alignment.

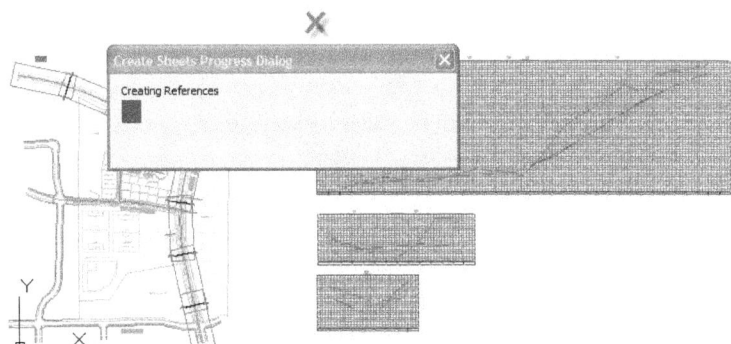

Figure 12–23

10. The AutoCAD Civil 3D software creates the sheets and the Sheet Set Manager files. The Sheet Set Manager opens, as shown in Figure 12–24.

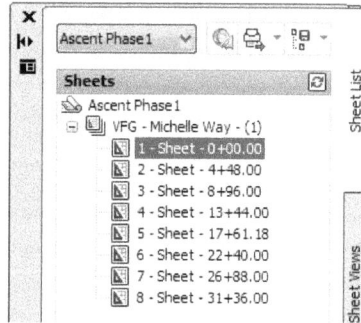

Figure 12–24

11. Hover the cursor over the filename in the Sheet Set Manager to display all of the properties of the sheet, including the name and location of the drawing file, as shown in Figure 12–25.

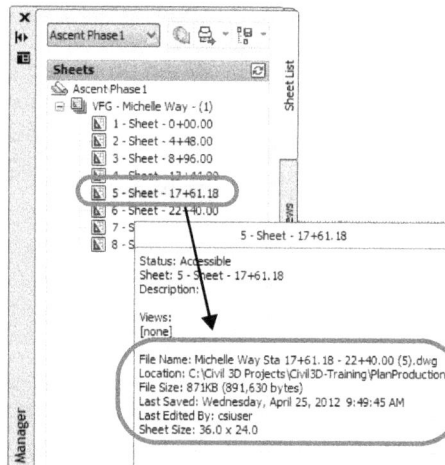

Figure 12–25

12. Save the drawing.

12.5 Sheet Sets

The sheet set is not exclusive to the AutoCAD Civil 3D software, but is used in all AEC products. A sheet set is a collection of sheets that are created from a combination of several different drawings. Sheets listed in the Sheet Set Manger file (DST) refer to layouts in a drawing file. The sheet set can reference any number of layouts from any number of drawings.

For example, you might be working on a commercial site plan or a highway project drawing. Using the Sheet Set Manager, you can create a construction set or tender documents by compiling a sheet set that lists all of the required sheets from the two master plans. Additionally, if the project is a multi-disciplined project that includes structural engineers and architects, you can compile a list of sheets from those sources as well. Figure 12–26 outlines the structure of sheet sets in a project.

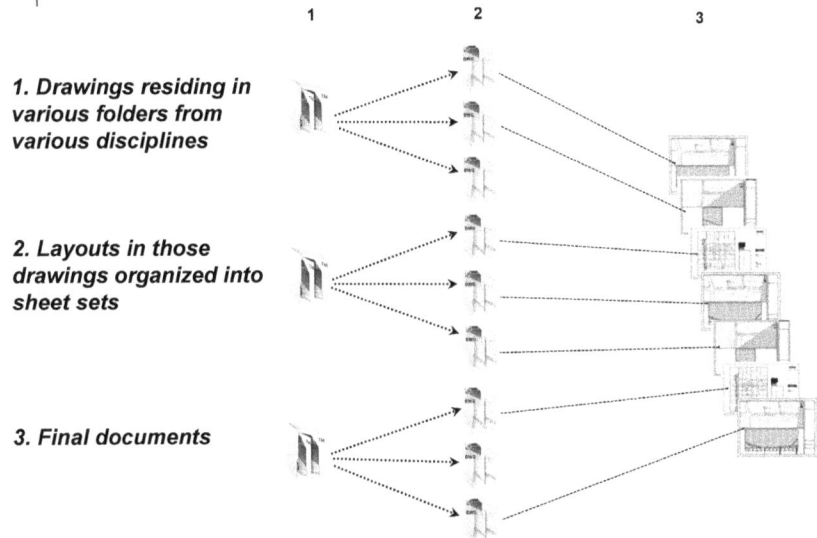

1. Drawings residing in various folders from various disciplines

2. Layouts in those drawings organized into sheet sets

3. Final documents

Figure 12–26

Structuring Sheet Sets

Figure 12–27 displays a typical hierarchical structure of the sheet set elements.

- The *Sheet Set Name* (1) identifies the sheet set (i.e., the DST file). This file can reside anywhere on your server.

- The *Sheet* subset (2) is used to organize sheets in a logical manner (i.e., Plan Profiles, Structural, Electrical, etc.).

- The *Individual Sheets* (3) are layouts from drawings imported into the sheet set.

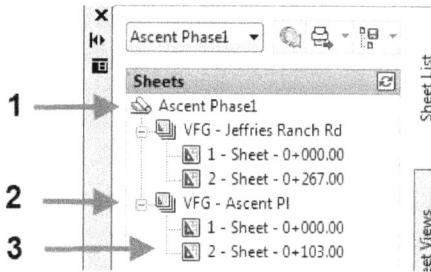

Figure 12–27

Each of the elements represents a core component in a typical sheet set. Corresponding to the other AutoCAD Civil 3D object functionality, right-clicking on any of these elements lists all of the available options for that element.

Editing Sheet Sets

You can modify and re-organize sheet sets in a number of ways. For example, you can reorder the sheets in the set, rename or renumber sheets, create new sheets or subsets, and import new layouts as sheets. To reorder elements in the sheet set, drag the element to a new location. Reordering sheets using this method does not automatically renumber the sheets. The options to edit sheet sets are shown in Figure 12–28.

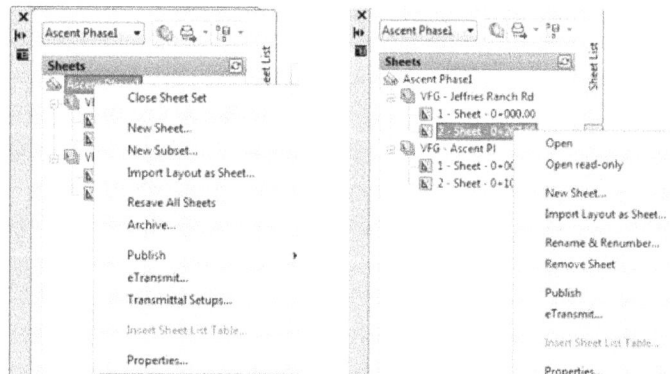

Figure 12–28

To rename and renumber sheets automatically, enter a *Number* and *Sheet title*. To change the associated filename, type a new *File name*. You can also have the associated filename change when you rename the sheet. To enable this feature, select the **Sheet title** option to rename the drawing file to match the sheet title, as shown in Figure 12–29.

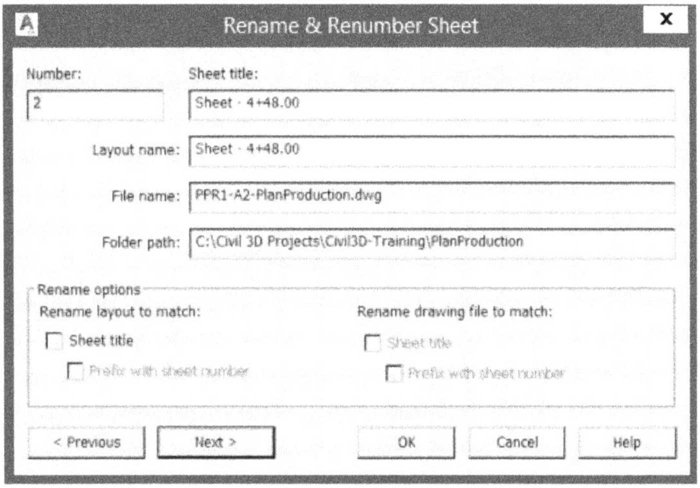

Figure 12–29

Sheet Set Manager Properties

In the Sheet Set Properties dialog box, you can change the name, the path of the drawing files or template associated with the sheet set, and any custom properties associated with the sheet set.

To access the properties, right-click on the Sheet Set Manager name and select Properties. Information specific to the sheet set displays.

The Sheet Set Properties dialog box contains the following, as shown in Figure 12–30:

- Sheet Set properties (1)

- Project Control properties (2)

- Sheet Creation properties (3)

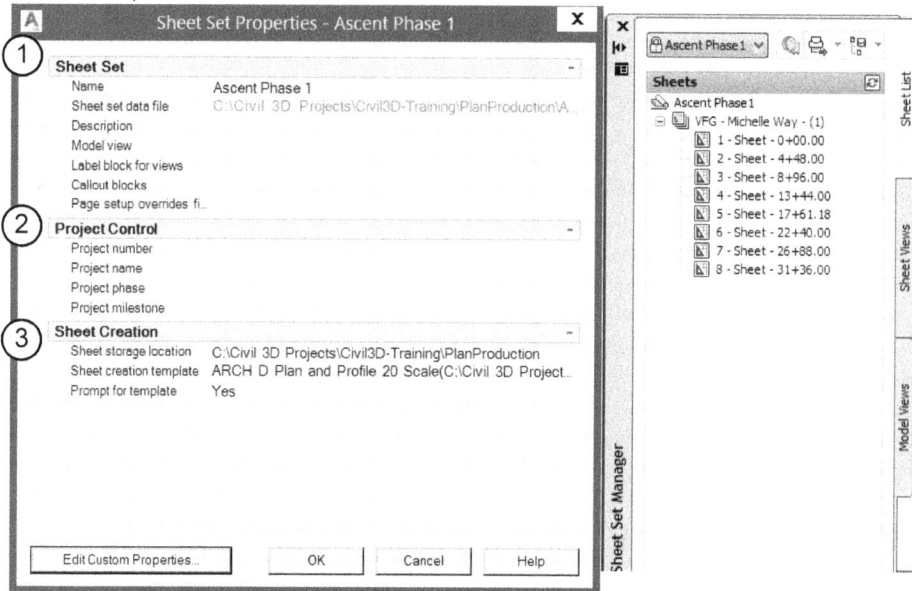

Figure 12–30

1. Sheet Set Properties

The sheet set properties provide access to the following:

- Name of the sheet set.

- Sheet set data file location (read only).

- Description.

- Model view drawing location (the location of the resource drawings).

- Label block for views (the location of the drawing and blocks that contain the block, which can be used for the views).

- Callout blocks (a list of blocks that can be used for callouts).

- Page setup override file (a drawing template that contains the page setup overrides for the sheet set). The page setup override enables you to override existing page setups for individual drawings in the sheet set.

2. Project Control Properties

You can use four preset project properties: *Project Number, Name, Phase,* and *Milestone.* These properties can also be displayed on the individual sheets. In addition to these four properties, you can create custom properties. There are two types of properties:

- *Sheet Set properties* are applied to all of the sheets in the set.

- *Sheet properties* are only applied to a single sheet.

3. Sheet Creation Properties

In the Sheet Creation Properties dialog box, you can access the location of the folder to store your sheets, and the default template that is used when creating a new sheet. The sheet storage location is where the new drawing sheet that is created is stored. The sheet creation template is the template that is used when creating the new sheet.

Practice 12c

Plan Production Tools III

Practice Objective

- Edit sheet and sheet set properties to make annotating sheets easier.

Estimated time for completion: 20 minutes

Task 1 - Define the Sheet Set Manager properties.

1. You can continue working with the files created in the previous practice, noting that the files are located in the root folder *...\PlanProduction* or open **PPR1-C1-PlanProduction.dwg** from the *C:\Civil 3D Projects\Civil3D-Training\PlanProduction* folder.

2. If the Sheet Set Manager is not displayed, open it in the *View* tab>Palettes panel. Expand the panel and click 🖌 (Sheet Set Manager) from the drop-down list, as shown in Figure 12–31.

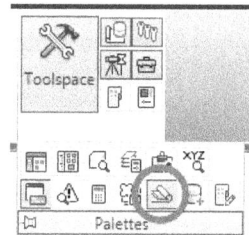

Figure 12–31

3. Expand the Sheet Set drop-down list and select the **Ascent Phase1** sheet set at the top of the Manager palette. If it is not in the list you will have to open and browse to **Ascent Phase1.dst** in the *C:\Civil 3D Projects\Civil3D-Training\ PlanProduction* folder, as shown in Figure 12–32.

Figure 12–32

4. Select **VFG - Michelle Way**, right-click, and select **Rename Subset…**, as shown on the left in Figure 12–33. For the *Subset Name*, type **Plan-Profile - Michelle Way**, as shown on the right. Click **OK** to close the dialog box.

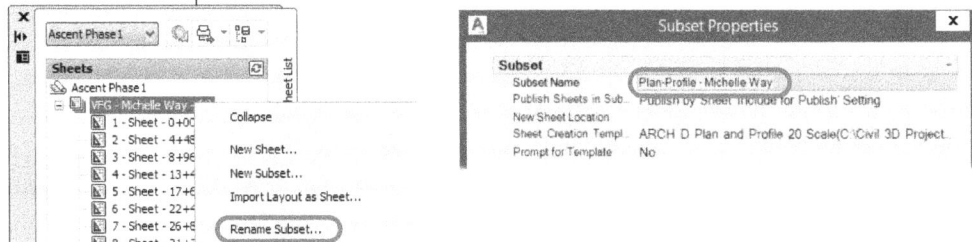

Figure 12–33

5. In the *Plan-Profile - Michelle Way* collection, select **1 - Sheet - 0+000.00**, right-click, and select **Rename & Renumber**, as shown in Figure 12–34.

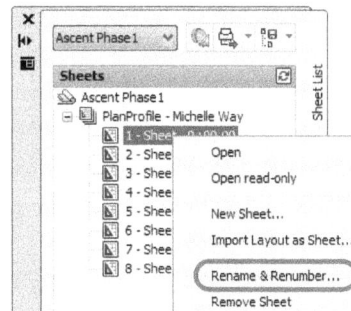

Figure 12–34

6. In the *Rename & Renumber Sheet* dialog box, change the *Number* to **3** to make room to add a title sheet and overall plan sheet later, and select **Sheet title** in the *Rename layout to match* area, as shown in Figure 12–35. Click **Next>**.

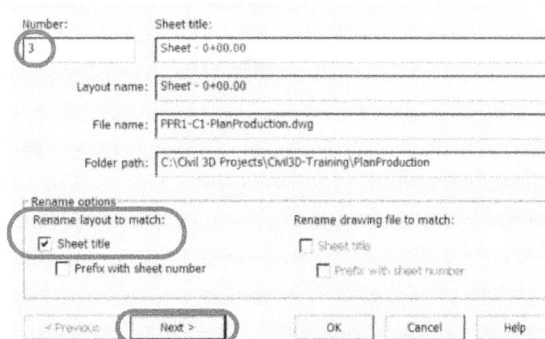

Figure 12–35

7. Change the next sheet number to **4**, and continue to click **Next>** to continue increasing the page number for each sheet until all of the sheets are renumbered, as shown in Figure 12–36. Note the changes to the sheet names. Click **OK** to accept the changes and close the dialog box.

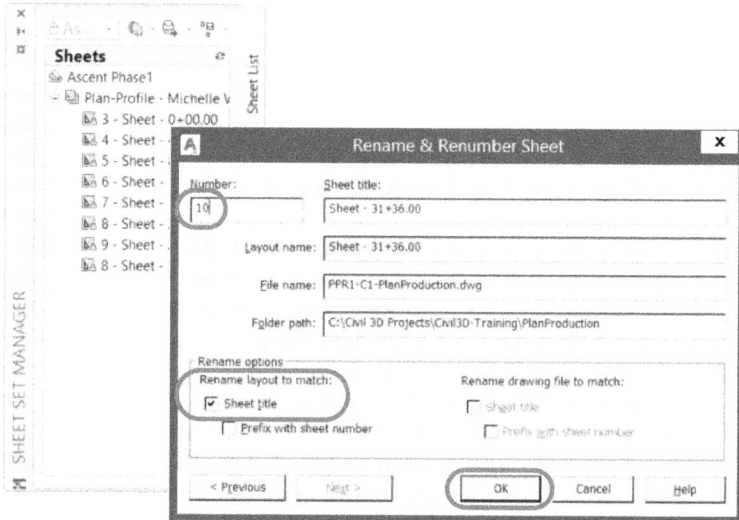

Figure 12–36

8. Save the drawing.

Task 2 - Define the Sheet Set properties.

---

1. Continue working with the drawing from the previous task or open **PPR1-C1-PlanProduction.dwg**.

2. If the Sheet Set Manager is not displayed, open it in the *View* tab>Palettes panel. Expand the panel and select the **Sheet Set Manager**. Expand the Sheet Set drop-down list at the top of the Manager palette and select the **Ascent Phase 1** sheet set. If it is not in the list you will have to open and browse to **Ascent Phase1.dst** in the *C:\Civil 3D Projects\Civil3D-Training\PlanProduction* folder.

3. To navigate to one of the drawings, double-click or right-click on the **3-Sheet - 0+000.00** entry and select **Open**, as shown in Figure 12–37.

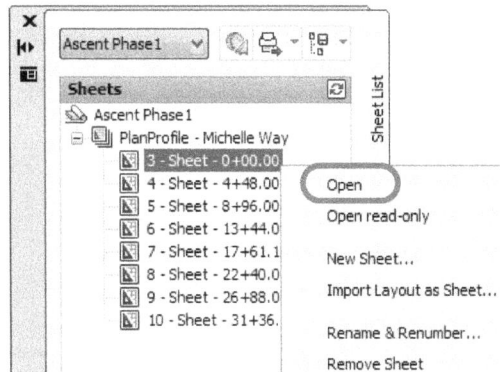

Figure 12–37

4. Once the drawing is open, zoom in to the lower right corner of the drawing, as shown in Figure 12–38. Note the title block. The values for the **Project Name**, and **Project Number** do not display any values.

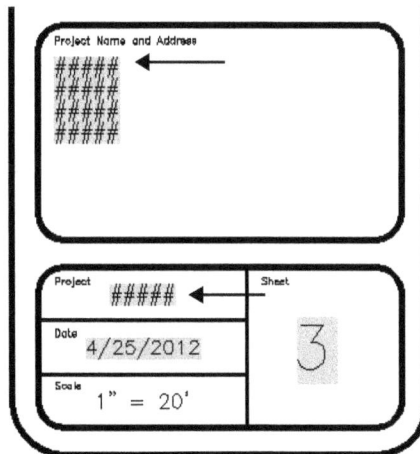

Figure 12–38

5. In the Sheet Set Manager for *Ascent Phase1*, select the sheet set name **Ascent Phase1**, right-click, and select **Properties**, as shown in Figure 12–39.

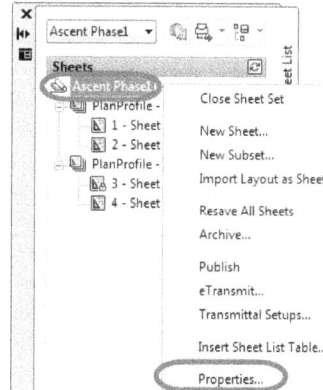

Figure 12–39

6. In the Sheet Set Properties - Ascent Phase1 dialog box, type **30052010** in the *Project Number* field and type **C3D Training** in the *Project Name* field. Click **OK** to complete the procedure. You might need to type **regen** and press <Enter> in the Command Line to display the updated fields. The values in your drawing title sheet should now be displayed, as shown in Figure 12–40.

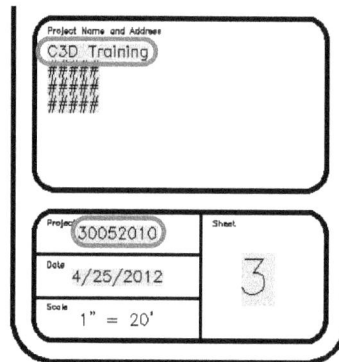

Figure 12–40

7. Save and exit all of the drawings.

Task 3 - Define Sheet Set properties.

1. Open a new drawing session by selecting **File>New**. Then select **_AutoCAD Civil 3D (Imperial) NCS.dwt** from the default template location.

2. If the Sheet Set Manager for *Ascent Phase 1* is not active, you can open the Sheet Set .DST file using one of the following methods:

   - Select the AutoCAD Civil 3D file and click **Open**. Select **Sheet Set** and browse to **Ascent Phase1.dst** from the *C:\Civil 3D Projects\Civil3D-Training\PlanProduction* folder, or select **Open the Sheet Set Manager** and select the **Ascent Phase 1** in the drop-down list.
   - In the *View* tab>Palettes panel, select the **Sheet Set Manager** in the drop-down list.

3. In the Sheet Set Manager dialog box, select the sheet set **Ascent Phase1**, right-click, and select **New Subset**, as shown on the left in Figure 12–41. Type **Base Plans** for the *Subset Name*, as shown on the right. Set the *Prompt for Template* to **No**, so that all new sheets use the preset template. Click **OK** to exit the dialog box.

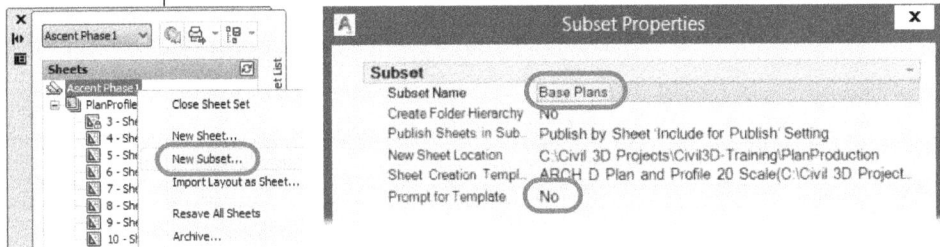

Figure 12–41

4. In the Sheet Set Manager, select the subset **Base Plans** and drag it to the top, as shown in Figure 12–42.

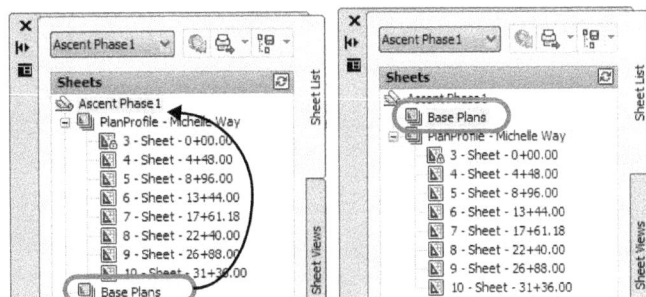

Figure 12–42

5. To create a new sheet, select the subset **Base Plans**, right-click, and select **New Sheet**, as shown in Figure 12–43.

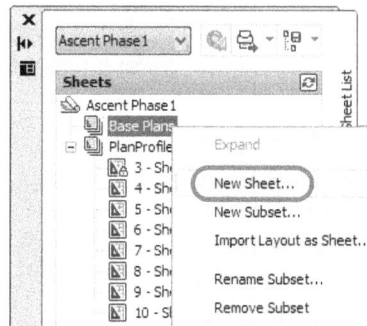

Figure 12–43

6. In the New Sheet dialog box, type **00** in the *Number* field, and type **Index** in the *Sheet title* field, as shown in Figure 12–44. Select the **Open in drawing editor** option to open the drawing when done. The Sheet Set Manager will create a drawing named **00 Index.dwg**.

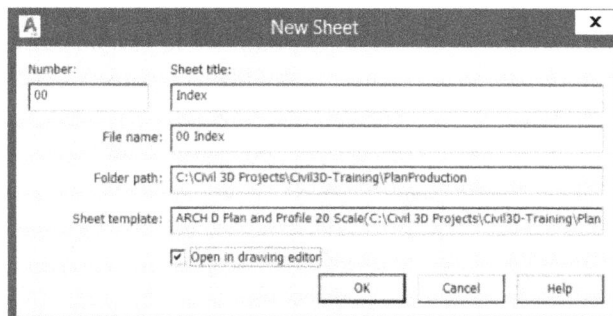

Figure 12–44

7. The Sheet Set Manager has created a new drawing based on the template and the sheet set properties. Select and delete the two viewports, since they are not necessary. Zoom in so to display the entire title block.

8. In the Sheet Set Manager, select the sheet set **Ascent Phase1**, right-click, and select **Insert Sheet List Table**, as shown in Figure 12–45.

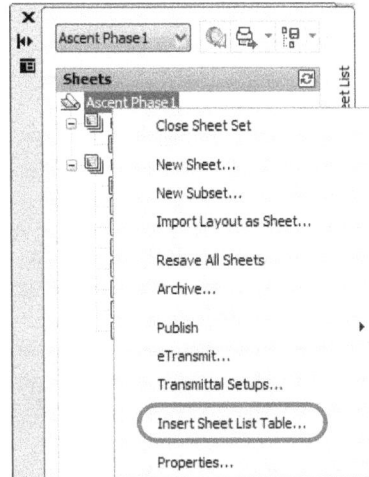

Figure 12–45

9. In the Sheet List Table dialog box, expand the Table Style name drop-down list, and select **Legend**. Select the **Show Subheader** option and click **OK** to close the dialog box, as shown in Figure 12–46.

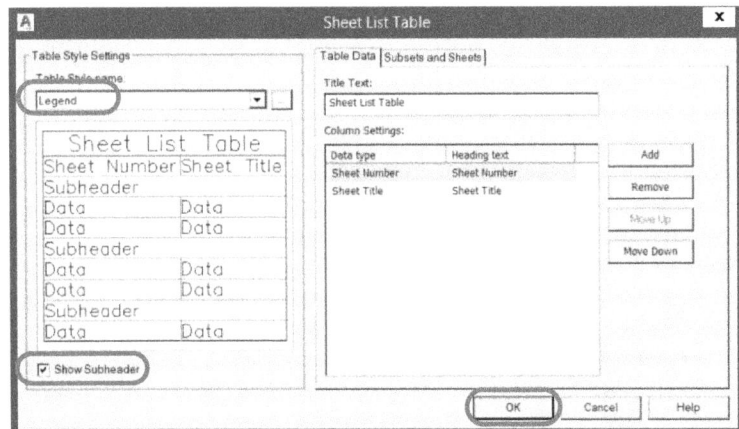

Figure 12–46

10. When prompted for the location of the table, select a point in the middle of the title block, as shown in Figure 12–47. If the table scale is too small, use the AutoCAD **Scale** command to scale the table by a factor of **30.**

Sheet List Table	
Sheet Number	Sheet Title
Base Plans	
00	Index
PlanProfile — Michelle Way	
3	Sheet — 0+00.00
4	Sheet — 4+48.00
5	Sheet — 8+96.00
6	Sheet — 13+44.00
7	Sheet — 17+61.18
8	Sheet — 22+40.00
9	Sheet — 26+88.00
10	Sheet — 31+36.00

Figure 12–47

11. Save the drawing.

Chapter Review Questions

1. What are two of the steps required to create plan and profile sheets using the Plan Production tools?

    a. Create layouts.

    b. Create View Frames.

    c. Create new drawings with references to data.

    d. Generate Sheets.

2. How can you integrate the AutoCAD Civil 3D software's Plan Production system layouts into an existing sheet set?

    a. When generating the sheets, select the option to **Add to existing sheet set** on the Sheet Set page in the Create Sheets wizard.

    b. Open the sheet set and manually import the sheets and views one by one.

    c. It is not possible, you have to have a separate sheet set for each alignment and profile.

    d. When generating the view frames, select the option to **Add to the existing sheet set** in the Sheets page.

3. How is the scale of the plan and profile sheet determined?

    a. Using the **Annotation Scale** tool in the Status Bar.

    b. Using the scale in the *Graph* tab in the Profile View Style dialog box.

    c. Using the template and layout selected during the View Frame creation process.

    d. Select the Toolspace, *Setting* tab. Right-click on the current drawing, select **Edit Drawing Settings**, and then in the Drawing Settings dialog box, select the *Units and Zones* tab.

4. How do you ensure that the project name and number display on every sheet automatically?

   a. This cannot be automated.

   b. Set up the sheet template with project name and number fields, and then set the project name and number in the **Sheet Set Manager>Sheet Set Properties**.

   c. Set up the sheet template with project name and number fields, and then set the project name and number during the View Frame Creation process.

   d. When generating the sheets, select the option to add the project name and number to the sheets.

5. After creating the plan and profile sheets you can easily create additional sheets using the Sheet Set Manager.

   a. True

   b. False

Command Summary

Button	Command	Location
	Create Section Sheets	• **Ribbon:** *Output* tab>Plan Production panel • **Command Prompt:** CreateSectionSheets
	Create Sheets	• **Ribbon:** *Output* tab>Plan Production panel • **Command Prompt:** CreateSheets
	Create View Frames	• **Ribbon:** *Output* tab>Plan Production panel • **Command Prompt:** CreateViewFrames

Appendix A

Additional Information

It is important to remember how to open an existing survey database and take advantage of the points and figures within it. Here, you learn how to open a survey database for editing and review purposes. Additional design requirements are also listed for the project. Use this information to create additional practices for learning and reinforcing commands taught in this training guide.

Learning Objectives in this Appendix

- Open a survey database for editing, or as read only.
- Review the design requirements for the project.

A.1 Opening a Survey Database

1. To set the working folder for the Survey Database, in the Toolspace, *Survey* tab, select **Survey Databases**, right-click, and select **Set working folder...**, as shown in Figure A–1. Browse and select the *C:\Civil 3D Projects\Civil3D-Training/ Survey/Survey Databases* folder, as shown on the right. When done, click **OK** to close the dialog box.

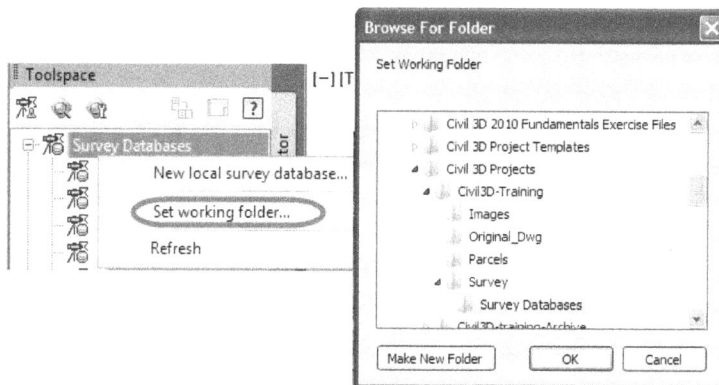

Figure A–1

2. To open a survey database, expand the survey database branch, select the survey database that you want to open, right-click and select **Open for edit** or **Open for read-only**, depending your requirements, as shown in Figure A–2.

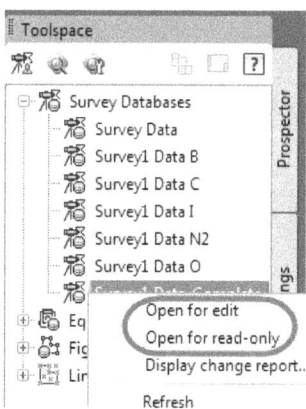

Figure A–2

A.2 Design Data

Parcel Size

The following data, shown in Figure A–3, describes the parcel size used in the training dataset:

- Minimum Area: **10225 Sq. Ft.**

- Minimum Frontage: **65'**

- Frontage Offset: **20'**

- Minimum Width: **65'**

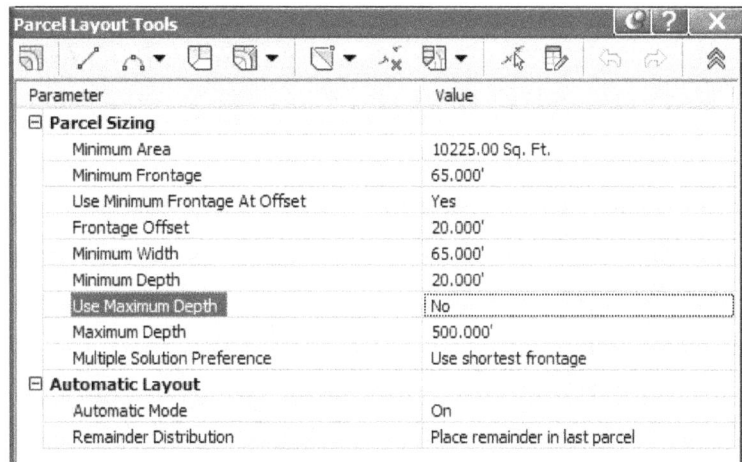

Parcel Layout Tools	
Parameter	Value
Parcel Sizing	
Minimum Area	10225.00 Sq. Ft.
Minimum Frontage	65.000'
Use Minimum Frontage At Offset	Yes
Frontage Offset	20.000'
Minimum Width	65.000'
Minimum Depth	20.000'
Use Maximum Depth	No
Maximum Depth	500.000'
Multiple Solution Preference	Use shortest frontage
Automatic Layout	
Automatic Mode	On
Remainder Distribution	Place remainder in last parcel

Figure A–3

Pipe Size Conversion

The following table contains a listing of pipe size conversions between metric and imperial.

Metric Size (mm)	Imperial Size (inches)	Metric Size (mm)	Imperial Size (inches)
-	-	1050	42
150	6	1200	48
200	8	1350	54
250	10	1500	60
300	12	1650	66
375	15	1800	72
450	18	1950	78

525	21	2100	84
600	24	2250	90
675	27	2400	96
750	30	2700	108
825	33	3000	120
900	36		

Road Design Criteria

Figure A–4, Figure A–5, Figure A–6, Figure A–7 and the corresponding tables specify the design criteria for the expressway design on Mission Avenue, the grand boulevard on Ascent Blvd., the collector streets at Jeffries Ranch Rd., and the residential street design for Ascent Place.

Expressway: Mission Avenue

Figure A–4

Daily Traffic Volume (vehicles/day)	# of Lanes	Right-of-way Requirement	Minimum Intersection Spacing
30,000 - 90,000	4, 6, or 8	195' (min.)	2600'

Function
- To permit relatively unimpeded flow for through traffic between major elements.
- To function as part of the Truck Route System.

Access Conditions
- Intersections are grade separated where warranted.
- Divided roadways with full control of access.
- Direct access to abutting property is prohibited.
- Only roadways of Major category or higher can intersection with Expressways.
- Intersections should be half a mile apart but in special circumstances can be a minimum of a quarter of a mile apart.
- At-grade intersections should be signalized.

Traffic Features			
Posted Speed (mph)	40-50	On-street Bikeway	No
Parking	None	Bus Route	No
Sidewalk	None	Truck Route	Yes
Traffic Signals	For interim condition only	Sound Attenuation	Yes
Pedestrian Crossing	Grade-separated, at-grade for interim condition		

Note
- Interchange spacing is generally similar to that of Freeways. However, closer spacing may be considered under special circumstances.
- Expressways are designed in accordance with TAC standards and for capacity conditions based on Level of Service D'.
- Pedestrian crosswalks are permitted at intersections. However, grade separated walkways are used where warranted.
- The right-of-way varies from a minimum of 195' depending on the number of lanes, sloping requirements, road grades, and noise attenuation requirements.
- A noise attenuation study is required at the Outline Plan application stage for residential lots adjacent to interchange areas, including the Transportation Utility Corridors (TUG) areas, to determine noise attenuation and right-of-way requirements.

Typical Cross Section	See TAC Standards	
Classification	**Design Speed**	**Intersection Design**
Urban Arterial Divided (UAD) 50 Urban Arterial Divided (UAD) 60 Urban Arterial Divided (UAD) 70	30-45 mph	See Appendix II-A Sheets/ -9

Horizontal Alignment

Minimum Stopping Sight Distance	Minimum Radius of Curvature
Major UAD 50 = 30' Major UAD 60 = 40' Major UAD 70 = 45'	Major UAD 50 = 295', 425' - 20,000' (desirable) Major UAD 60 = 395', 850' - 20,000' (desirable) Major UAD 50 = 560', 1300' - 20,000' (desirable)

Median and Left Turn Bay
- The minimum median width on a Major street is 20' for a parallel left turn lane and 30' for parallel dual left turn lanes.
- The introduced median is used to transit an undivided road to a divided road with a left turn median.
- Slot left turn bays are required as an interim design on wide medians, such as those reserved for future LRT or future widening in the median.
- No left turn bays are permitted on curves with a center line radius of less than 1300' nor in 195' of the end of a center line transition curve (spiral) if the radius is less than 1300'.
- Standard left turn bays shall be provided on Major streets at all intersections. For left turn bay designs.
- The minimum storage length for a left turn bay is 195' with a 12' wide left turn lane.
- Dual left turn bays and slot turn bays are to be designed to TAC standards.

Note
- Major streets are classified as Urban Arterial Divided (UAD) roadways and are designed for speeds of 30, 40, and 45 miles per hour. Most Major streets fall in the 40 mph category. However, developers must be informed by the approving authority of Land Use and Mobility of the applicable design speed.
- A standard curb with a 1.5' gutter is to be used on the median and on the outside edges.
- A reverse gutter is used where necessary.
- Street light poles, power poles, and traffic signal poles are to be located a minimum of 12' from the lip of gutter.

Vertical Alignment

Minimum and Maximum Grades
- Maximum grade:
  - Major UAD 50 = 7.0%
  - Major UAD 60 = 6.0%
  - Major UAD 70 = 5.0%
- Minimum grade:0.6%

The maximum and minimum grades also apply to the development of superelevation.

Grade at Intersections
- The grade line of the approaching street (maximum approach grade of 4%) shall tie to the lane line of the Major street with a vertical curve of a minimum length of 100'. i.e., the crossfall of the Major street shall be extended and intersects the grade of the approaching street. The resulting vertical curve ends at the lane line of the Major street.
- The maximum profile grade on a Major street at an intersection shall be 4% for a minimum distance of 330' measured from the Vertical Point of Intersection (VPI) to the center line of the intersecting street on both sides of the intersection.

Vertical Curves and Superelevation
- The length of a vertical curve is calculated based on the stopping sight distance.
- For Major streets, crest vertical curves are to be designed using the "K" values for 14 mph higher than the design speed.
- Superelevation shall be developed through the transition spiral by using the following superelevation tables:
- Major UAD 50 emax = 0.06
- Major UAD 60 emax = 0.08
- Major UAD 70 emax = 0.08
- The superelevation through all Major street intersections shall not exceed 4%.
- A right turn ramp on a Major street shall have a minimum of 4% crossfall within the length of the island.

Grand Boulevard: Ascent Boulevard

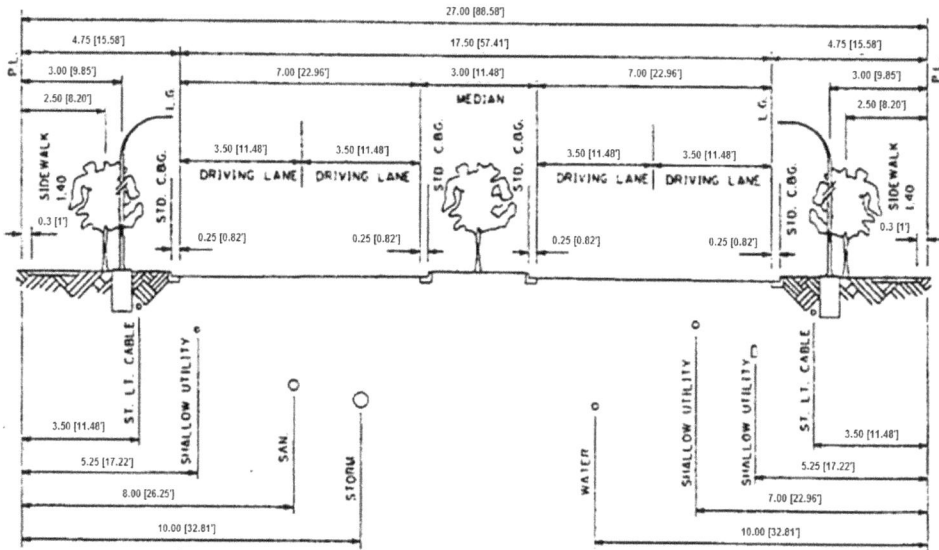

Figure A–5

Daily Traffic Volume (vehicles/day)	# of Lanes	Right-of-way Requirement	Minimum Intersection Spacing
5,000 - 10,000	2	85.3' (min.)	393.7/196.85'

Function
- Functions are similar to Primary Collector and Collector streets.
- To serve as secondary traffic generators.
- To serve as a main route in the community to accommodate substantial traffic volumes.
- Might be used as bus routes and are designed to accommodate Frequent Transit Service.

Access Conditions
- A minimum intersection spacing of 393.7' shall be provided between a Major Street and the first intersection on the Grand Boulevard from the Major Street.
- Intersection spacing for those subsequent to the above condition shall be a minimum 196.85' spacing.
- No access to abutting commercial properties.
- Access to abutting multi-family residential properties is permitted and is generally restricted to right turns in and out.
- Residential frontage of single and multi-family development is permitted.
- Single family, semi-detached, and duplex style homes must access from a rear alley.

Traffic Features				
Posted Speed (mph)	30	On-street Bikeway	Signed Bicycle Route
Parking	Yes	Bus Route	Yes
Sidewalk	4.59' separate walk on both sides	Truck Route	Yes
Traffic Signals	As warranted	Sound Attenuation	Yes
Pedestrian Crossing	At Grade		

Note
- Undivided roadway with intersections controlled by signage.
- Parking is permitted on both sides but might be restricted under special circumstances.
- Sidewalk is normally only required on one side, but is preferable on both sides. Refer to Section E - Sidewalks and Walkways for more details.

Typical Cross Section	

Collector Streets: Jeffries Ranch Road

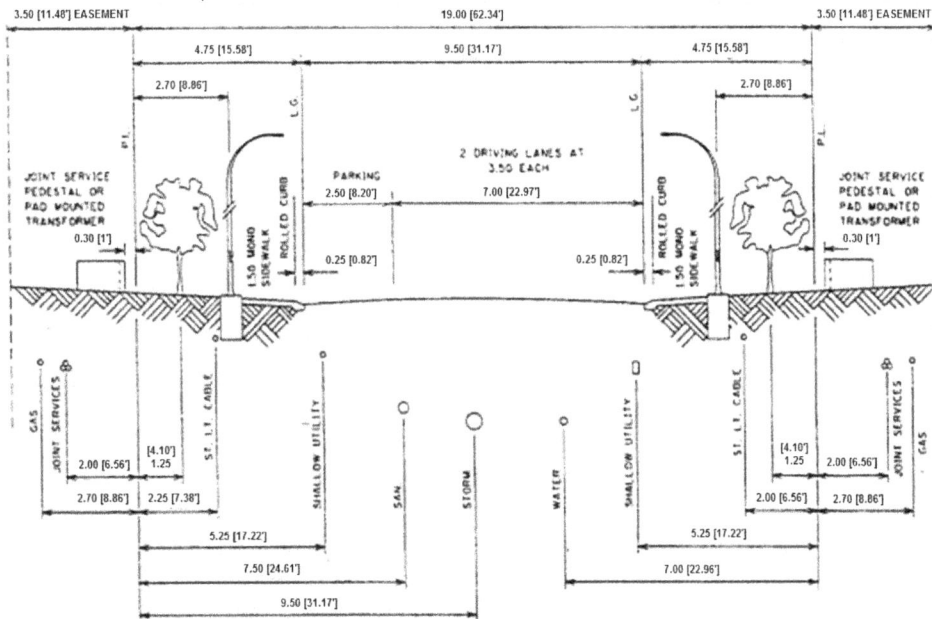

Figure A–6

Daily Traffic Volume (vehicles/day)	# of Lanes	Right-of-way Requirement	Minimum Intersection Spacing
1,000 - 5,000	2	59.06' and 68.90'	19.69'

Function
- To be used where the Daily Traffic Volumes exceed the volumes for a Residential Road but are less than 5,000 vehicles/day.
- To collect and distribute traffic from Major streets to lesser standard streets.
- To serve as secondary traffic generators, such as neighborhood commercial centers, parks, and golf courses, and from neighborhood to neighborhood.
- All Collector streets designated as bus routes must use the 68.90' right-of-way cross-section.
- Might be used as bus routes.

Access Conditions
- Direct access is permitted to abutting properties.
- Minimum intersection spacing is 19.69'. Wherever possible, a desirable intersection spacing of 262.5' should be used.
- Collector streets might intersect with Residential streets, Residential Entrance streets, other Collector streets, Primary Collector streets, Local Major streets, and Major streets.

Traffic Features			
Posted Speed (mph)	30	On-street Bikeway	Signed Bicycle Route
Parking	Except at bus zones	Bus Route	Yes
Sidewalk	4.59' separate walk or 4.92' mono walk on both sides	Truck Route	No
Traffic Signals	As warranted	Sound Attenuation	No
Pedestrian Crossing	At grade		

Note
- Collector Streets are undivided roadways.
- There are two types of Collector Streets:
  - 68.89' R.O.W.: 2 driving lane of 11.48' wide and 2 parking lane of 7.38' wide.
  - 62.34' R.O.W.*: 2 driving lanes of 11.48' wide and 1 parking lane of 8.20' wide.
- This standard can only be used where residential and/or commercial frontage occurs on one side of the road and where no bus route is planned.

Typical Cross Section	

Classification	Design Speed	Intersection Design
Urban Collector Undivided (UCU) 50	30 mph	

Horizontal Alignment

Minimum Stopping Sight Distance	Minimum Radius of Curvature
Collect UCU 50 = 213'	Collector UCU 50 = 295'

Median and Left Turn Bay
- Medians, left turn bays, and intersection channelization are not normally required.
- A tear-drop median is required on a Collector street when the Collector street is designated as a bus route and intersecting with a Major street.

Note
- The cumulative length of Collector streets before feeding onto Major streets shall not be excessive. The maximum number of dwelling units serviced shall not exceed 500.
- Low profile rolled curb with 0.82' gutter is to be used except in areas identified as bus zones and adjacent to parcels which that do not contain residential development (e.g., commercial sites, parks, school reserves, etc.) where a standard curb is to be used.
- Standard curb is to be used on Collector streets if the grade is greater than 6%.
- Reverse gutter is used where necessary.

Vertical Alignment

Minimum and Maximum Grades
- Maximum grade: 8.0%
- Minimum grade: 0.6%

Grade at Intersections
- The grade line of the approaching street (maximum approach grade of 4%) shall tie to the Collector street in the following manner:
  - Tie to the property line grade if the approaching street is undivided.
  - Tie to the lane line of the Collector street with a vertical curve of a minimum length of 98.43' if the approaching street is divided. I.e., the crossfall (or 2% if the road is crowned) of the Collector street shall be extended and intersects the grade of the approaching street and the resulting vertical curve ends at the lane line of the Collector street.
- It is desirable to ensure that the grade on the Collector streets is less than the permitted maximum of 8% at intersections to improve operational aspects, such as stopping and starting in winter conditions.

Vertical Curves and Superelevation
- The length of vertical curve is calculated based on the stopping sight distance.
- The maximum superelevation rate for a Collector street shall not exceed emax=4%.

Residential Street: Ascent Place

Figure A–7

Daily Traffic Volume (vehicles/day)	# of Lanes	Right-of-way Requirement	Minimum Intersection Spacing
<1,000	2	49.21' (min.)	196.85'

Function
- To provide direct access to properties.
- To collect and distribute traffic from residential properties to Collector and Residential streets.

Access Conditions
- Direct access is permitted to abutting residential properties.
- Access is not permitted to commercial properties.
- Residential streets might intersect with other Residential streets, Residential Entrance streets, Collector streets, and Primary Collector streets.

Traffic Features			
Posted Speed (mph)	30	On-street Bikeway	Signed Bicycle Route
Parking	Yes	Bus Route	No
Sidewalk	1.1 mono walk on at least one side, preferable on both sides	Truck Route	Yes
Traffic Signals	No	Sound Attenuation	Yes
Pedestrian Crossing	At Grade		

Note
- Undivided roadway with intersections controlled by signage.
- Parking is permitted on both sides but might be restricted under special circumstances.
- Sidewalk is normally only required on one side but is preferable on both sides. Refer to Section E - Sidewalks and Walkways for more details.

Typical Cross Section	

Classification	Design Speed	Intersection Design
Urban Local Divided (ULD) 50	30 mph	

Horizontal Alignment

Minimum Stopping Sight Distance	Minimum Radius of Curvature
Residential ULD 50 = 213.25'	Residential ULD 50 = 262.47'

Median and Left Turn Bay
- Minimum median width is 11.48'.
- Left turn bays and intersection channelization are not required.

Note
- Same requirements as Residential streets.
- Standard curb with 0.82' gutter is to be used on the median and low profile curb with 0.82' gutter on the outside edges, except in areas adjacent to parcels which do not contain residential developments where standard curb is to be used.

Vertical Alignment

Minimum and Maximum Grades
- Maximum grade: 8.0%
- Minimum grade: 0.6%

Grade at Intersections
- The grade line of the intersecting street (maximum approach grade of 4%) shall tie to the property line grade of a Residential Entrance street.

Vertical Curves and Superelevation
- The length of vertical curve is calculated based on the stopping sight distance.
- Superelevation is not required.

Traffic Circle Design Criteria

The following specifies the design criteria for the traffic circle at Jeffries Ranch Road and Accent Boulevard, as shown in Figure A–8.

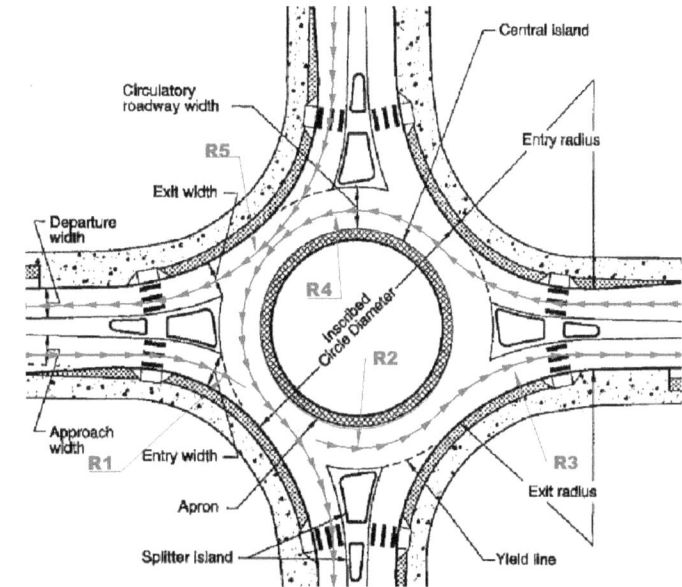

Inscribe Circle Diameter	Approximate R_4 Value		Maximum R_1 Value	
	Radius ft	Speed mph	Radius ft	Speed mph
Single-Lane Roundabout				
98.43'	31.1'	13	177.16'	25
114.83'	42.65'	14	200.13'	27
131.23	52.49'	15	226.38'	28
147.64'	62.34'	16	239.50'	29

Figure A–8

Five critical path radii must be checked for each approach:

- **R1 (entry path radius):** The minimum radius on the fastest through path before the yield line.

- **R2 (circulating path radius):** The minimum radius on the fastest through path around the central island.

- **R3 (exit path radius):** The minimum radius on the fastest through path into the exit.

- **R4 (left-turn path radius):** The minimum radius on the path of the conflicting left-turn movement.

- **R5 (right-turn path radius):** The minimum radius on the fastest path of a right-turning vehicle.

It is important to note that these vehicular path radii are not the same as the curb radii. First the basic curb geometry is laid out, and then the vehicle paths are drawn.

Intersection Design

The following specifies the design criteria for the intersection design at Mission Avenue and Accent Boulevard, as shown in Figure A–9.

Figure A–9

Appendix B

AutoCAD Civil 3D
Certification Exam Objectives

The following table will help you to locate the exam objectives within the chapters of the *AutoCAD® Civil 3D® 2018: Fundamentals* and *AutoCAD® Civil 3D® 2018 for Surveyors* student guides to help you prepare for the AutoCAD Civil 3D Certified Professional exam.

Exam Topic	Exam Objective	Student Guide	Chapter & Section(s)
Styles	Create and use object styles	• AutoCAD Civil 3D Fundamentals	• 1.6 • 4.3
		• AutoCAD Civil 3D For Surveyors	• 1.6
	Create and use label styles	• AutoCAD Civil 3D Fundamentals	• 1.6 • 4.2 & 4.3
		• AutoCAD Civil 3D For Surveyors	• 1.6
Lines and Curves	Use the Line and Curve commands	• AutoCAD Civil 3D Fundamentals	• 3.1
		• AutoCAD Civil 3D For Surveyors	• 3.6
	Use the Transparent commands	• AutoCAD Civil 3D Fundamentals	• 3.1 • 6.3 • 7.6
		• AutoCAD Civil 3D For Surveyors	• 3.6 • 4.5

Exam Topic	Exam Objective	Student Guide	Chapter & Section(s)
Points	Create points using the Point Creation commands	• AutoCAD Civil 3D Fundamentals	• 4.5
		• AutoCAD Civil 3D For Surveyors	• 4.4
	Create points by importing point data	• AutoCAD Civil 3D Fundamentals	• 4.7
		• AutoCAD Civil 3D For Surveyors	• 4.7
	Use point groups to control the display of points	• AutoCAD Civil 3D Fundamentals	• 4.8
		• AutoCAD Civil 3D For Surveyors	• 4.8
Surfaces	Identify key characteristics of surfaces	• AutoCAD Civil 3D Fundamentals	• 5.2
		• AutoCAD Civil 3D For Surveyors	• 7.2
	Create and edit surfaces	• AutoCAD Civil 3D Fundamentals	• 5.3 to 5.6
		• AutoCAD Civil 3D For Surveyors	• 2.4 • 7.3 to 7.6
	Use styles and settings to display surface information	• AutoCAD Civil 3D Fundamentals	• 5.2
		• AutoCAD Civil 3D For Surveyors	• 7.2
	Create a surface by assembling fundamental data	• AutoCAD Civil 3D Fundamentals	• 5.1
		• AutoCAD Civil 3D For Surveyors	• 7.1
	Use styles to analyze surface display results	• AutoCAD Civil 3D Fundamentals	• 5.10
		• AutoCAD Civil 3D For Surveyors	• 7.10
	Annotate surfaces	• AutoCAD Civil 3D Fundamentals	• 5.8
		• AutoCAD Civil 3D For Surveyors	• 7.8
Parcels	Design a parcel layout	• AutoCAD Civil 3D Fundamentals	• 3.3 & 3.4
	Select parcel styles to change the display of parcels	• AutoCAD Civil 3D Fundamentals	• 3.2
	Select styles to annotate parcels	• AutoCAD Civil 3D Fundamentals	• 3.2, 3.5, 3.7, & 3.8
Alignments	Design a geometric layout	• AutoCAD Civil 3D Fundamentals	• 6.3 & 6.4
	Create alignments	• AutoCAD Civil 3D Fundamentals	• 6.3 & 6.4

Exam Topic	Exam Objective	Student Guide	Chapter & Section(s)
Profiles and Profile Views	Create a surface profile	• AutoCAD Civil 3D Fundamentals	• 7.3
	Design a profile	• AutoCAD Civil 3D Fundamentals	• 7.5 & 7.6
	Create a profile view style	• AutoCAD Civil 3D Fundamentals	• 7.2
	Create a profile view	• AutoCAD Civil 3D Fundamentals	• 7.4
Corridors	Design and create a corridor	• AutoCAD Civil 3D Fundamentals	• 8.1 to 8.3
	Derive information and data from a corridor	• AutoCAD Civil 3D Fundamentals	• 8.6 & 8.7
	Design and create an intersection	• AutoCAD Civil 3D Fundamentals	• 8.5
Sections and Section Views	Create and analyze sections and section views	• AutoCAD Civil 3D Fundamentals	• 8.7 • 11.1, 11.2, & 11.4
Pipe Networks	Design and create a pipe network	• AutoCAD Civil 3D Fundamentals	• 10.3, 10.4, & 10.7
Grading	Design and create a grading model	• AutoCAD Civil 3D Fundamentals	• 9.1 & 9.3
	Create a grading model feature line	• AutoCAD Civil 3D Fundamentals	• 9.2
Managing and Sharing Data	Create a data sharing setup	• AutoCAD Civil 3D Fundamentals	• 2.3
Plan Production	Create a sheet set	• AutoCAD Civil 3D Fundamentals	• 12.5
	Use view frames	• AutoCAD Civil 3D Fundamentals	• 12.2 & 12.4
Survey	Identify key characteristics of survey data	• AutoCAD Civil 3D Fundamentals	• 4.2
		• AutoCAD Civil 3D For Surveyors	• 3.2
	Use description keys to control the display of points created from survey data	• AutoCAD Civil 3D Fundamentals	• 4.6
		• AutoCAD Civil 3D For Surveyors	• 4.6
	Create a boundary drawing from field data	• AutoCAD Civil 3D Fundamentals	• 4.7
		• AutoCAD Civil 3D For Surveyors	• Ch. 5 (all) • Ch. 6 (all)

Index

A

Alignments
    By Layout **6-16**
    Criteria-Based Design **6-5**
    Edit **6-15**, **6-18**
    From Objects **6-9**
    Introduction **6-4**
    Labels **6-23**, **6-25**, **6-28**
    Layout Tools **6-14**
    Overview **6-2**
    Properties **6-21**, **6-27**
    Table **6-26**
    Types **6-6**
        Segment **6-6**
Assembly
    Attach Subassemblies **8-6**
    Create **8-11**
    Detach Subassemblies **8-8**
    Mirror **8-9**
    Share **8-10**
    Types **8-2**
Attach command **5-74**

C

Corridors
    Create **8-21**, **8-31**
    Feature Lines **8-27**
    Intersection **8-34**, **8-37**
        Corridor Regions **8-36**
        Geometry Details **8-35**
    Slope Patterns **8-27**
    Surfaces **8-44**, **8-48**
        Surface Boundaries **8-45**
    Visualizing **8-50**

D

Data Shortcuts **2-5**
    Create Data Shortcuts **2-14**
    Create new Shortcuts folders **2-11**
    Data-reference **2-16**
    eTransmit **2-7**
    Promote **2-7**
    Set the Working folder **2-10**
    Synchronize **2-6**
    Update Notification **2-6**
    Workflow **2-8**
Drawing Settings **1-30**
    Abbreviations **1-34**
    Ambient Settings **1-35**
    Object Layers **1-33**
    Parcels **3-9**
    Transformation **1-32**
    Units and Zone **1-31**

F

Feature Line **9-4**
    Elevation Editor **9-4**
    From Objects **9-6**
    Labels **9-18**

G

Grading **9-2**
    Create **9-12**
    Creation Tools Toolbar **9-11**
    Criteria **9-18**
        Set **9-19**
    Infill **9-15**
    Modify **9-21**
    Styles **9-18**
    Volume **9-22**
        Tools **9-20**

L

Lines and Curves **3-2**

O

Object Viewer **5-44**

P

Panorama **1-21**
Parcel
    Analysis **3-12**
    By Layout **3-20**, **3-23**
    Display Order **3-10**
    Free Form Create **3-25**

From a Legal Description **3-5**
From Objects **3-13**
Frontage **3-25**
Labels **3-37**, **3-42**
Labels and Styles **3-12**
Pick Sub-Entity **3-21**
Properties **3-11**
Renumber **3-30**
Report **3-46**
Right of Way **3-13**
ROW **3-9**
Sizing **3-21**
Slide Line **3-20**, **3-25**, **3-26**
Swing Line **3-25**, **3-33**
Table **3-43**
Pipes **10-2**
Annotate **10-40**
Catalog **10-4**
Connect to Structures **10-23**
Connect/Disconnect From Part **10-31**
Create Network from Object **10-19**, **10-20**
Draw in Profile View **10-28**
Edit **10-30**, **10-32**
In Sections **10-38**
Network Layout Tools **10-22**, **10-24**
Network Parts Lists **10-5**
Pipe (and Structure) Properties **10-30**
Pipe and Structure Rules **10-10**
Pipe Network Labels **10-37**
Pressure Network parts **10-8**
Pressure Pipe Networks **10-45**
Appurtenances **10-47**
Create **10-48**
Fittings **10-46**
Reapply Pipe Rules **10-12**
Reports **10-39**
Structure Catalog **10-5**
Swap Part **10-31**, **10-47**
Table **10-39**, **10-41**
Plan and Profile Sheets
Create **12-17**
Create View Frames **12-9**
Edit Sheet Sets **12-22**
Match Line **12-5**
Geometry Edits **12-8**
Sheet Set **12-21**
Manager Properties **12-23**, **12-26**
View Frame **12-5**
Geometry Edits **12-7**
Groups **12-5**
Point Cloud **5-74**
Attach **5-74**
Create Surface from Point Cloud **5-80**, **5-85**
Crop **5-78**
External References **5-74**
Object Snap **5-74**

Transparency **5-76**
UCS **5-74**
Points
Create **4-27**
Description Key Sets **4-30**, **4-33**
Edit **4-58**, **4-60**
Overview **4-6**
Point Groups **4-49**, **4-55**
Reports **4-62**, **4-64**
Profile
Band Elevations **7-23**
From Surface **7-10**, **7-16**
Labels **7-24**
Layout Tools **7-21**
Overview **7-2**
Segment Types **7-24**
View
Reposition **7-3**
Wizard **7-12**
Profile View **7-18**
Projects
Create Drawings **2-4**
Multiple Drawings **2-2**, **2-3**
Share Data **2-4**, **2-5**, **2-8**
Single-Design Drawing **2-2**

Q
QTO
Define Materials **11-12**
Earthwork Volumes **11-10**, **11-13**
Mass Haul **11-11**
Material Volumes **11-11**, **11-16**
Pay Items **11-21**
Assign **11-21**, **11-22**
Compute **11-25**
Quantity Takeoff Criteria **11-12**

S
Sample Lines
Create **11-6**
Create Sample Line Group **11-2**
Modify **11-5**
Sample Line Tools toolbar **11-3**
Sample More Sources **11-9**
Section Views **11-29**
Wizard **11-29**
Settings **1-19**
Command **1-39**
Feature **1-38**
LandXML **1-37**
Overrides **1-40**
Pipe Network **10-3**
Point **4-25**
Sites **6-3**
Create a New Site **3-16**
Parcels **3-8**

Styles **1-41**
    Apply Style to Points **4-23**
    Figure **4-3**
    Import **1-49**, **1-55**
    Label **1-36**, **1-45**, **1-53**
    Multi-Purpose **11-31**
    Object **1-43**, **1-52**
    Page **11-31**
    Pipe and Structure **10-9**
    Plan and Profile Sheet Objects **12-6**
    Point Label **4-11**, **4-20**
    Point Marker **4-7**, **4-18**
    Profile
        View **7-4**
    Purge **1-50**, **1-55**
    Reference **1-51**
    Section **11-31**
        View **11-30**
        View Band **11-30**
    Surface Contour **5-21**
Subassemblies
    Attach **8-6**
    Detach **8-8**
    Select Similar **8-9**
Surface
    3D Solid Surface **5-61**, **5-72**
    Analysis **5-44**, **5-63**
    Boundary **5-27**
    Breaklines **5-24**, **5-29**, **5-32**
        Survey Figures **5-26**
    Contour Data **5-17**
    Create **5-16**
    DEM Files **5-14**
    Drawing Objects **5-14**
    Edit **5-37**, **5-46**
        Copy Surface **5-42**
        Line Edits **5-38**
        Point Edits **5-39**
        Raise/Lower **5-43**
        Simplify **5-39**
        Smooth Contours **5-40**
        Smooth Surface **5-41**
        Surface Paste **5-42**
    Labels **5-57**
    Point Files **5-14**
    Point Groups **5-15**, **5-20**
    Process **5-2**
    Properties **5-7**, **5-43**
    Quick Profile **5-45**
    Rebuild **5-9**
    Volume Calculations **5-59**
Survey
    Database **4-42**
    Figure **4-3**
    Figure Prefix Database **4-4**, **4-5**
    Figures **5-32**

    Import **4-42**, **4-46**
    Open a Survey Database **4-45**
    Workflow **4-2**

T
Template **1-30**, **1-48**
Toolspace
    Prospector tab **1-16**, **1-23**
    Settings tab **1-18**, **1-24**
    Survey tab **1-19**, **4-41**
    Toolbox tab **1-19**
Transparent Commands **3-3**
    Bearing and Distance **3-3**
    Point Number **3-3**
    Profile Grade and Elevation **3-4**
    Profile Grade Elevation **7-23**
    Profile Grade Length **7-23**
    Profile Station and Elevation **3-4**, **7-22**
        From COGO Point **7-22**
        From Plan **7-22**
    Profile Station at Grade **3-4**, **7-23**
    Profile Station from Plan **7-22**
    Station and Offset **3-4**
    Zoom to Point **3-3**

U
User Interface **1-7**
    Application Menu **1-8**
    Command Line **1-11**
    InfoCenter **1-9**
    Quick Access Toolbar **1-8**
    Ribbon **1-9**
    Status Bar **1-11**

W
Workspaces **1-5**
    2D Drafting & Annotation **1-6**
    3D Modeling **1-6**
    Civil 3D **1-6**
    Planning and Analysis **1-6**

www.ingramcontent.com/pod-product-compliance
Lightning Source LLC
Chambersburg PA
CBHW060938210326
41598CB00031B/4660